CONTENTS

INTRODUCTION

The aim of the **Pocket Scots Dictionary** is to provide information on the Scots language in as clear and accessible a form as possible for readers of all ages. It continues the Scottish National Dictionary Association's policy, begun with the **Concise Scots Dictionary** (published in one volume in 1985), of bringing the vast resources of the 10-volume **Scottish National Dictionary** to a wider public. In compiling the present dictionary, the editors have re-examined the definitions of the two larger dictionaries and many of these have been re-drafted to make them as straightforward and easily understood as possible.

The Dictionary concentrates on the Scots language of the present day but it also includes all the more important words current in the last two centuries, giving special attention to the classics of Scottish literature, including the ballads. Some of the more abstruse contents of the larger dictionaries have been omitted—etymologies, most obsolete and specialized words and usages, the less common spelling variants, and some of the historical and geographical detail given in the larger dictionaries. As a result the *Pocket Scots Dictionary* not only offers more information on the Scots language since the time of Burns than any other work of comparable scale and price, but does so in a form easily used by anyone.

Up-to-date information

The Dictionary includes new information which has been added to our files since the completion of the larger dictionaries: see for example the entries on **gallus** and on **children's hearing** (under **child**).

Information on grammar

Parts of speech are labelled only when the entry contains more than one of these, *eg*

   laib *verb*..........*noun*

Many entries include distinctively Scottish past tense forms of verbs and plural forms of nouns, *eg*

   brak, brek, break *verb*, *past tense also* **brak**........
   coo .....*plural* **kye** ...
   child......*plural also* **childer**......

The pocket SCOTS dictionary

Edited by

ISEABAIL MACLEOD

RUTH MARTIN

PAULINE CAIRNS

ABERDEEN
UNIVERSITY
PRESS

© *The Scottish National Dictionary Association Ltd 1988*
First Published 1988

Aberdeen University Press, Aberdeen, Scotland
A Member of the Pergamon Group
Distributors Pergamon Press plc
Headington Hill Hall, Oxford OX3 0BW

British Library Cataloguing in Publication Data

Pocket Scots dictionary.
  1. English language. Scottish dialect—
Scots and English dictionaries
I. Macleod, Iseabail II. Martin, Ruth
III. Cairns, Pauline
427'9411'03

ISBN 0 08 036581 7

Computer Typeset by AUP Typesetters (Glasgow) Ltd
Printed and bound in Great Britain by
Aberdeen University Press

Time and place

Words which are believed to be obsolete are marked with a †. If you come across any words so marked which you know to be still used in some part of the country, please let the Scottish National Dictionary Association know at 27 George Square, Edinburgh, EH8 9LD.

Where words are used only in a limited area or areas, this is shown by giving the areas according to the list given below and map on p vi. For information on the precise regional distribution of more widely distributed words, the larger dictionaries should be consulted.

On the whole we have used only the main dialect areas (listed in the left-hand column below) but occasionally it was found necessary to introduce smaller areas. Most of them are based on the pre-1975 counties, and the boundaries can be compared with their modern equivalents in the maps on pp vii and viii.

List of dialect areas:
  Shetland
  Orkney
  N (North)
                      includes Caithness
  NE (North-East)
                      includes Aberdeen (the city)
  ECoast mainly fishing terms, found along the eastern seaboard
  ECentral (East Central)
                      includes Angus
                                    Perth
                                    Fife
                                    Lothian
                                    Edinburgh
  WCentral (West Central)
                      includes Glasgow
                                    Argyll
                                    Ayr
  SW (South-West)
  S (South)
  Ulster (for information on Ulster Scots see p xvi).

Scots is spoken much less in the Gaelic-speaking (or recently Gaelic-speaking) parts of Scotland but a few words, mostly of Gaelic origin, from these areas have been included, labelled *Highland* and/or *Hebrides*.

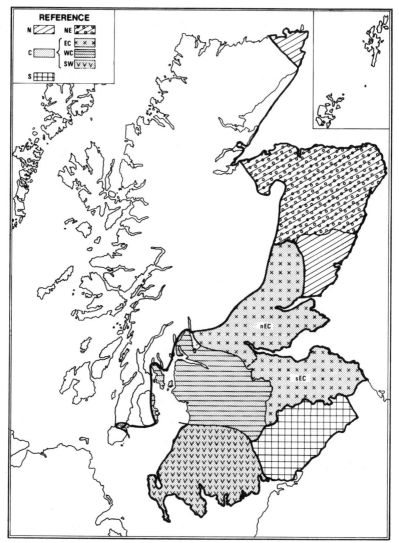

Map 1 Scotland: the main dialect divisions of Scots

Map 2 Scotland: pre-1975 counties

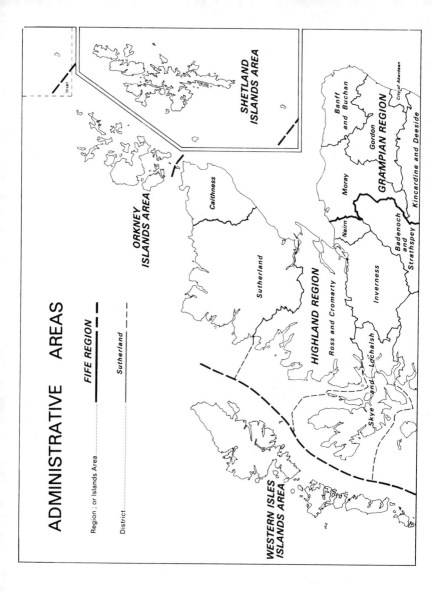

ADMINISTRATIVE AREAS

Region : or Islands Area.............. **FIFE REGION**

District .... Sutherland

SHETLAND ISLANDS AREA

ORKNEY ISLANDS AREA

Caithness

Sutherland

HIGHLAND REGION

Ross and Cromarty

Skye and Lochalsh

Inverness

Nairn

Moray

Banff and Buchan

Gordon

City of Aberdeen

GRAMPIAN REGION

Badenoch and Strathspey

Kincardine and Deeside

WESTERN ISLES ISLANDS AREA

Inset

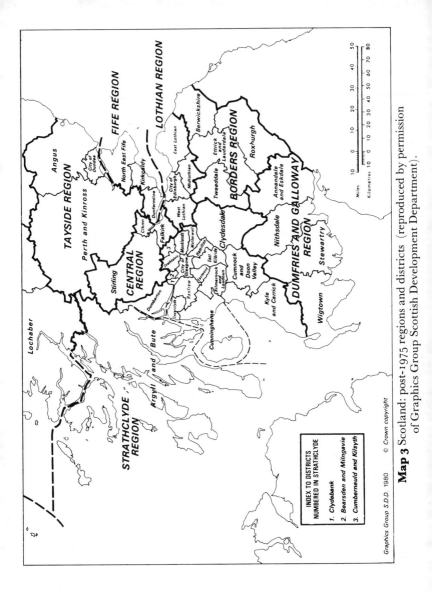

Map 3 Scotland: post-1975 regions and districts (reproduced by permission of Graphics Group Scottish Development Department).

Organisation of entries

Longer entries may be divided into parts of speech and/or meaning categories (introduced by numbers in bold type), *eg*

   cair 1 ...... **2** ......

The main part of the entry may be folowed by:

   (1) derivatives of the headword, *eg* **darger** under **darg**

   (2) compounds, *eg* **kailyaird** under **kail**

   (3) phrases, *eg* **gie's yer crack** under **crack.**

Quotations are sometimes added to clarify definitions, *eg* *"Dinna fash yersel"* under **fash.**

Etymology

Although, because of lack of space, etymologies are not normally included, the dictionary does contain some information on the origins of words. For example the grouping together in one entry of words such as **heeze** and **heyzer** is an indication of their common origin.

Cross-references

These are printed in bold type, *eg*

loon see **loun.**

When a word is printed in bold within a definition, this usually indicates that it will be found as an entry in its own alphabetical place, *eg* **dunny** an underground cellar or passage in an old **tenement** building . . .

SPELLING

The spellings of Scots display very wide variation, so much so that even the much larger *Concise Scots Dictionary* and *Scottish National Dictionary* do not give all variants. In this dictionary we have tried to include the most common variants and those most likely to cause confusion. If you fail to find the word you want under a particular spelling, try skimming the same and the nearby pages for a slightly different spelling under which it may be entered. The following suggestions will give an idea of many of the more common ways in which the spellings may vary and which are worth trying if you do not find the word at once:

Omit a final-e	For lik see **like**
Add a final -e	For tit see **tite**

Try single instead of double consonants or double instead of single consonant

For tittlin see **titlin**
For smedum see **smeddum**

Try double instead of single vowel

For beke see **beek**

A selection of other common ways in which the spellings may vary are these:

Vowels	*Examples*
For a or a..e try **ai**	For skale see **skail**
Failing that, try **au**	For dar see **dare**, then **dair**, then **daur**.
For ai try **a** or **a..e**	For maik see **mak** or **make**.
For al try **au** or **aw**	For malkin see **maukin**, for halkit see **haukit**, then **hawkit**.
For ea try **a..e** or **ai** or **ae**	For leam see **lame**, for lear see **lair**, for brea see **brae**.
For ee try **ea**	For beel see **beal**.
For ei try **e..e** or **ee**	For reid see **rede**, for leit see **lete** or **leet**.
For i try **y**	For clipe see **clype**.
For oa try **o..e** and conversely	For toam see **tome**; for gloming see **gloamin**.
For oo try **u..e** or **ui** or **ou**	For loom see **lume**, for coot see **cute** then **cuit**, for loon see **loun**.
For ou try **ow** and conversely	For louden see **lowden**; for mow see **mou**.
For ou or ow try **oo** or **o** or **u**	For slouch see **slooch**, for how see **hoo**, for dowg see **dog**, for scoug see **scug**.
For ul try **ou**	For sculk see **scouk**.
For y try **i**	For hyves see **hives**.
Consonants	*Examples*
(1) *At the beginning of the word*	
For c- try **qu-**	For coit see **quoit**
For f- try **wh-**	For fang see **whang**

For k- try **c-**   For kow see **cow**
For ph- try **f-**   For pheesant see **feesant**
For qu- try **c-**   For queet see **cuit**
For quh- try **wh-**   For quha see **wha**
For sc- try **sk-**   For scale see **skail,**
     for screik see **skreek;**
and conversely
For sl- try **scl-** or **skl-**   for skull see **scull**
     For sly see **scly,**
     for slent see **sklent;**
and conversely
For wh- try **f-** or **w-**   for sclype see **slype**
     For whumart see **foumart,**
     for whaun see **wand**
For w- try **wh-**   For weesht see **whisht**

(2) *Not at the beginning of the word*

For c try **s**   For mence see **mense**
For ch try **sh**   For glumch see **glumsh**
For ck try **k**   For mack see **mak**
For d try **th**   For swidder see **swither**
For dg try **g**   For swadge see **swage**
For f try **v**   For halfer see **halver**
For g try **dg**   For fage see **fadge**
For gh try **ch**   For sough see **souch**
For k(k) try **ck**   For biker see **bicker**

On ly, lz and ny, nz, see Note below.

For sh try **ch**   For hansh see **hanch**
For th try **d**   For shouther see **shouder**
For v try **f**   For shave see **shaif**

Note: In a number of Scottish words, –lie, –lyie and –lzie interchange as spellings, *eg* in **scailie** and **scailyie** and **tulyie** and **tuilzie.** Similarly with –nie, –ng(y)ie, –nyie, –nzie, *eg* in **skainie, skainyie** and **skainzie,** and in **spaingie, spangyie** and **spainyie.** This should not as a rule present too difficult a problem in finding the desired entry, since the spelling which has been chosen as the Dictionary's entry-word is likely to be alphabetically quite close to the variant you tried first. See **z, 3** on p 357.

Word beginnings and endings The spellings of these also vary widely in Scots. Look out for these alternatives:

en- and **in-**   **-er, -ar, -ir, -or, -our** and **-ur**
on- and **un-**   **-in, -ing, -an** and **-en**
ower-, over- and **our-**   **-le** and **-il(l)**
-ed and **-it**

PRONUNCIATION

Pronunciations are shown in the following ways:
(Note that when English words are used as examples, the sounds indicated are as in the Standard English of Scottish speakers.)

1. When the spelling(s) of the headword(s) already clearly indicate(s) the word's pronunciation(s), these spellings are left to speak for themselves. But note that:

(1) **ng** in Scots, *eg* in **hunger, ingle, ingan,** is almost always pronounced as in English *sing*, not as in English *single*.

(2) In Scots, **ch** occurring in the middle or at the end of a word is most often sounded as in *loch* or *dreich* or in the place-names *Buchan* or *Brechin*. Exceptions to this will be pointed out in a pronunciation note to the word in question (see 2. below), when this seems necessary (*eg* for **fleech**, pronounced [fleetch]).
At the beginning of a word, **ch** has its usual English sound, as in *cheese*.

(3) **gh,** which normally occurs only in the middle or at the end of a word, has the same sound as **ch** (see (2) above).

(4) **th** in Scots has the same two pronunciations as in English, one as in *the*, *that*, brea*the*, the other as in *thank*, *thin*, *three*, tee*th*.

(5) **wh** is pronounced *hw-*, not *w-* as in southern English, *eg* **wheet**, pronounced [hweet].

(6) In some dialects north of the Tay, the **k** in initial **kn-** in *eg* **knife** is pronounced either as *k* or, near the Tay, as *t*, so that *knife* in these dialects is pronounced either *k(e)nife* or *t(e)nife*; similarly with the **g** in **gn-** as in **gnash** in some of the same dialects; elsewhere **kn-** and **gn-** are pronounced simply as *n-* as in English.

(7) **ui** varies with the dialect:

in some conservative dialects (*eg* Shetland, Orkney, Angus, South Scots) the pronunciation is similar to the vowel of French *peu* or German *schön*;

in North and East Fife, the pronunciation is like *a* in *late* or *blade* or *ai* in *pair* or *ay* in *day*;

in many other dialects the pronunciation in some words is like *ai*, so that **puir** is pronounced like *pair*, but in other words like *i* in *bit*, so that **buit** is pronounced like *bit*.

(8) **oo** is as in *groove* or *moon*.

(9) **ey** as in **gey** (very), is the same as the vowel in the Scots (and Scottish Standard English) pronunciation of *mine* or *tile*.

(10) *Stress* In Scots, in words of more than one syllable, stress most often falls on the same syllable as it would in English, *eg* words such as **hoolet** have stress on the first syllable, but prefixes such as **dis-** in **disjaskit** or **un-** in **unbraw** are usually unstressed. Exceptions to this will be pointed out in a pronunciation note to the word in question (see 2. (3) (d) below).

2. Where the headword spellings do not clearly indicate the pronunciation, or do not make clear which of two or more possible pronunciations is correct, this is clarified in one of the following ways:

(1) By giving a rhyme-word, either Standard English or a well-known Scots word: eg:

fleech [rhymes with 'teach']

douce [rhymes with 'goose']

ay [rhymes with 'buy']

aye [rhymes with 'gey']

2) By giving a better-known word, either Scots or Standard English, which contains the sound in question:

aicher [-ch- as in 'dreich']

sauch, saugh [-ch, -gh as -ch in 'loch']

rowan [-ow- as in 'cow']

guse [-u- as -ui- in 'guid']

(3) By re-spelling the whole word, using the following respellings:

(a) *Consonants*
[ch] for the sound of *ch* in *loch* or *dreich* or of *gh* in *laigh*, *eg* **dreich** [dreech].
[tch] for the sound of *ch* in *beech* or *tch* in *catch*, *eg* **fleech** [fleetch], **reach** [reetch].
[j] for the sound of *dge* in *lodge* or *g* in *magic*.

Other consonants, including [g],[k], [m], [n], [ng], [sh], and [ch], [j], [y] at the beginning of words, have their usual sounds, but see the notes on [ng], [th], [wh] and [kn] and [gn] in 1. (1), (4), (5) and (6) above.

(b) *Vowels*
[a] as in *cat, man*.
[au] or [aw] as in *caught, saw*.
[ai] or [ay] as in *faith* or *pay* (the same vowel as in *gate* or *gave*).
[e] as in *get, hen*.
[ee] as in *meet, see* (the same vowel as in *breathe, heat* or *be*).
[i] as in *bit, pin, fix*.
[o] as in *cot* (the same vowel as in *broad*).

[oa] as in *coat, coal* (the same vowel as in *close* (adjective) or *close* (verb)).
[oo] as in *groove* or *moon* (the same vowel as in *would* or *shoe*).
[u] as in *cut, bus*.
[ui] as in Scots *guid, puir* (see the note on this vowel in 1.(7) above)

(c)*Diphthongs*
[iy] as in *I, buy, five*.
[ey] as in *bite, mine, tile*, Scots *gey*.
[oi] or [oy] as in *Boyd, noise, boil*.
[ow] as in *cow*, Scots *ower* (over), *pow* (head) (the same sound as in English *out, house, hour*).
[ee**oo**] the same sound as in English *feud, duty, few*, Scots (in some dialects) *teuch* (tough), *heuk* (hook).
[ee**u**] [ee] followed quickly by [u], found in some Scots dialects in *teuch* (tough), *heuk* (hook).

(d) *Stress*
In words of more than one syllable, stress is shown by printing the stressed syllable in bold type in the re-spelling,
eg **curroo** [ku**roo**]
lagamachie[laga**machie**]

(4) By respelling the part of the word most likely to cause difficulty, using the same respellings as in (3) above, thus:
room, roum [–oo–]
pown [–ow– as in 'cow']
multiplepoinding[–**pin**ding]

(5) Examples
scour, scoor, scowr [rhymes with 'poor']
routh, rowth [–ou–, –ow– as –ow– in 'cow']
May[mey]
cuiter, couther [k(ee)**oo**ter], **koo**ther]
retour[re**toor**]

THE SCOTS LANGUAGE
by A. J. Aitken

1. Introduction

For some three centuries Scotland has had English as its language of official dealings, of education and of the daily speech of many Scots, but alongside English, the two ancient native languages of Scotland—Gaelic and Scots today continue in a great many ways to influence the conversation and the life of millions of Scots people. Gaelic is still spoken as a mother tongue by some 80,000 Scots. And the influence of Scots pervades the speech of four and a half million of locally educated Scotsmen and Scotswomen in a range of speech-styles, from the full Doric of, say, the fisher-folk and farming people of the North-East, through various 'mixtures of Scots and English', to a form of English spoken in a Scottish accent and including an occasional Scottish word or turn of phrase. Much of the best of Scotland's great national literature is in Scots. A dialect of Scots is also spoken over much of the north and east of Northern Ireland and in neighbouring east Donegal in Ireland itself. This Ulster Scots results from large-scale settlements from Scotland, especially south-western Scotland, in the seventeenth century 'Plantation of Ulster'.

2. The history of Scots

Both Scots and English are descended from the Anglo-Saxon family of dialects. Early in the seventh century A.D. a northern offshoot of the Anglian people of the Anglo-Saxon kingdom of Bernicia or northern Northumbria began occupying what is now southern and south-eastern Scotland, where their presence is shown by such ancient Anglian place-names as Tyninghame, Haddington, Hawick, Jedburgh, Selkirk, Yetholm, Newbattle and Morebattle. This people's name for their Anglian or early northern English tongue was *Englisc*, which medieval Scottish writers wrote as *Inglis*, that is 'English': it was not till much later that it received its alternative name *Scots*. The remainder of what is now Scotland was then occupied by peoples speaking for the most part various Celtic languages, including the ancestor of modern Gaelic. This had been brought from Ireland to Argyll some centuries earlier by a people known as Scots.

By the early eleventh century the Kings of the Scots had come to rule most of the mainland of Scotland, and the Gaelic tongue was in use everywhere as far south as the present Border and was well on its way to becoming the chief language of Scotland. But as a result of the peaceful 'Norman conquest' of Scotland brought about by the kings of medieval Scotland, notably King

David I (1124-53), what happened was quite the opposite of this. Northern English now spread west and north from its original base in the south-east, until in the fourteenth century it was spoken throughout most of Scotland east and south of the Highlands. For example, it was from the outset the leading language of the dozens of new royal and baronial burghs founded at this time throughout southern, central and eastern Scotland as far north as Dingwall and Cromarty. And Gaelic began its long retreat which continues today; by the late Middle Ages it had withdrawn beyond the Highland Line.

The character of the northern English of medieval Scotland was much modified from the *Englisc* of earlier times into something much closer to modern Scots, so that we may now reasonably begin to call it early Scots. First, it had begun taking in many new words from the French spoken by the Norman aristocracy and clergy of medieval Scotland. Along with the new Norman aristocracy, many incomers of lower rank had also been arriving in Scotland, chiefly from the northern and midland shires of England, the former Danelaw, with its many Viking settlers from Scandinavia. From these new arrivals early Scots received many formerly Scandinavian speech-habits and words.

In the fourteenth century, the Scottish nobility gave up their French speech for what was now the majority speech of the Lowlands, Scots. About this time also, Scots was beginning to be spoken in Caithness, Orkney and Shetland, where it was eventually to replace the old Norse or Norn tongue spoken under the former Norse earls of these provinces.

Apart from some traces in earlier Latin documents, the history of Scots as a written language begins in 1376 with John Barbour's great poem *Brus*, on the exploits of King Robert Bruce and Sir James Douglas. More and more writings follow, in verse and in official and literary prose, till by the late fifteenth century Scots was the chief language of written communication of the Scottish nation, in place of Latin which had earlier occupied this position. In the Lowland half of Scotland, too, Scots was the spoken tongue of all ranks, from king to cottar. About this time Lowland Scottish writers began calling their national language *Scots*, after the name of the nation, as an alternative to the older name *Inglis*. There were now two national and official languages in use in Britain, English in Tudor England, Scots in Stewart Scotland. Since both of these were of Anglo-Saxon origin, they were linguistically similar but far from identical, with Scandinavian elements, for example, more numerous and prominent in Scots.

This was the high point in the fortunes of Scots, during the reigns of James IV, James V and Mary (1488-1567). But even before the close of this period, there had begun the process of 'anglicisation' of Scots which led to the replacement of Scots by English as the official and the chief literary language of Scotland and as its formal or 'public' spoken language. The process began in the language of poetry but soon spread also to prose. To begin with, it took the form of an occasional use of southern English spellings in place of the normal Scots ones, say southern English *one, go, any* instead of Scots *ane, ga, ony*. From about 1560 all Scots writing was in a mixed dialect in which pairs of alternative forms like these existed side by side, often in the same text, with the English alternatives gradually becoming more popular.

Among the most important · conditions favouring this trend were the Scottish Reformers' heavy dependence on England for support and for propaganda material before and after the Reformation in 1560, and the fact that, being themselves inclined to anglicisation, they never felt the need to produce a version of the Bible in Scots but were content to use existing English ones, especially the Geneva Bible of 1560. Following the Union of the Crowns in 1603, which removed the Scottish court to London, Scottish publishers ceased printing prose in Scots and after 1610 virtually all published work by Scottish prose writers is in English pure and simple. In handwritten texts anglicisation continued more gradually, but by about 1700 here too most prose had become fully English in language.

Scots verse, on the other hand, never died out completely, and had a major revival in the eighteenth century led by Allan Ramsay (1686-1758), followed by Robert Fergusson, Robert Burns and others, opening a new modern era of literature in Scots.

During the seventeenth century we meet various indications, notably in informal writings such as private letters, that the spoken language of some members of the Scottish aristocracy was beginning to be anglicised in roughly the same way as had already happened to the written language. Among several influences behind this, an important one was the greatly increased contacts between the Scottish and English gentry that followed the Union of the Crowns. By the next century, as communication between Scotland and England increased still further following the Union of the Parliaments of 1707, nearly all Scots of the 'educated' or middle classes seem to have had as their 'polite' or more or less formal spoken language something approaching that of their English compeers in London. It is true that this Scottish version of spoken English was interspersed with occasional Scots words and turns of phrase which were known as Scotticisms, and that it was rendered in a noticeable Scottish accent. Both of these peculiarities were now generally regarded as 'provincial' or 'vulgar', and unsuitable for persons who wished to be thought of as 'polite'. Indeed, strenuous efforts were made by many of the eighteenth-century Scottish gentry to 'cure' themselves of their Scotticisms and their Scottish accent, for example by attending lectures on elocution given in Edinburgh from 1748 onwards by English, Irish and Scottish experts on 'correct' English. That these efforts were largely unsuccessful is clear from the persistence of many of the offending Scotticisms and of some form of Scottish accent in the speech of nearly all locally educated Scotsmen and Scotswomen today.

Early in the nineteenth century the craze to get rid of the linguistic traces of one's own nation petered out. It now became fashionable to value the rural dialect for its expressiveness and richness and to express regret that it was—so it was believed—dying out. Whereas in the late eighteenth century most members of the educated classes regarded any form of contemporary spoken Scots as a 'very corrupt dialect' of English, in the nineteenth century this kind of disapproval was reserved for the allegedly 'debased' and 'slovenly' speech of the working classes of the poorer areas of the cities. It is only in the past two or three decades that linguists and others have begun to protest against this disparagement of the speech of the majority of present-day Scots and to claim that all of the several kinds of Scottish speech are of equal worth, even though they occupy differing roles or places in society. Unfortunately the older view still widely persists that some kinds of Scots are 'inferior' to others or even that any kind of Scots is inferior to English, and this continues to cause injustice, especially in education and employment.

3. What is Scots like?

(1) How is it pronounced?

The differences between Scots and English pronunciation, some of which can be seen in the Note on pp xiii–xv, have grown up gradually since Anglo-Saxon times. For example, pairs of words like Scots *stane* and English *stone* or Scots *gae* and English *go* originally had the same pronunciations, *stān* and *gān*. In the twelfth century, however, English speakers in the south gradually modified their way of pronouncing this $\bar{a}$-sound to $\bar{o}$, while the northern English and Scots continued to pronounce it $\bar{a}$. Similarly Scots *loch* and *thocht* keep the original *ch* pronunciation, which southern English lost after the sixteenth century. Quite often, as in these cases, it is the northern speakers who have kept an older pronunciation, but one exception is the Scots *buit, muin, puir* beside the English *boot, moon, poor*. Very many other changes have taken place, indeed are still taking place: for example, the tendency to pronounce a glottal stop in place of -*t*- seems to be spreading much faster throughout Scotland than in England.

(2) How is it spelled?

'Fixed' spelling systems in which each word has one and only one spelling are a fairly modern phenomenon; it is well known, for example, that William Shakespeare varied between several different ways of spelling his name. In the fifteenth and sixteenth centuries Scots had one of the most variable spelling systems of any European language, though there were of course strict limits to the numbers of alternative spellings allowed: most vowels could be spelled in any one of three, four or five ways. At that time Scots and English differed quite a lot in the spellings they used, not only when the pronunciations in the two languages were different, as in the word for 'load', Scots *lade, laid* or *layd* with an *ai* sound, English *lode* or *load* with an *oa* sound, but also sometimes for the same sound. So the word 'wheel' was pronounced much the same in the two languages, but in Scots was mostly spelled *quhele* or *quheill* or *quheyll* but in English *whele* or *wheel*. One effect of the anglicisation process mentioned in pp xvii–xix above was to replace some Scots spellings, such as *quh-*, with the corresponding English spellings, in this case *wh-*. Another effect was the new practice of marking with an apostrophe a sound which had been lost in the pronunciation of Scots but kept in English, in *e.g.* *ha'e* for 'have' or *fu'* for 'full'. A few of the older Scottish spellings did, however, survive into modern Scots, including *ch* in *loch* and *thocht* and *ai* as in *laid* or in *hail* 'whole', *ei* as in *deid* 'dead', and *ui* as in *guid* 'good'. Nor did Scots ever catch up with English in regularising its spellings into a 'fixed' system, so that, despite some recent efforts at regularisation, modern Scots spelling continues quite variable (see p x above), though much less so than that of sixteenth century Scots.

(3) What is its grammar?

Scots shares many of its linguistic characteristics with the neighbouring northern dialects of English in England but far less with the more southern or with Standard English. Nowhere is this more obvious than in the grammar, in, for example, the plurals *een* 'eyes', *shune* 'shoes', *kye* 'cows', *hors* 'horses', *caur* 'calves', *thir* (plural of this), *thae* (plural of *that*), all still current in Scots and only recently given up by northern English. Still current in both Scots and northern English are: past tenses of such verbs as *greet* 'to weep', past tense *grat*, past participle *grutten*, and examples of this sort for many other verbs are to be found in the dictionary; the ancient northern rule for *-s* endings of present tense verbs, as in *them that says he's owre auld* (Standard English *those who say he's too old*); and the distinction between *ae man* and *that ane* (Standard English *one man* and *that one*). Perhaps more specially Scots are the negative constructions of the verbs *be, will* and *can*, in which Scots prefers to say *He'll no come* rather than *He winna come* for English *He won't come*, and *Is he no comin? Will he no come?* are almost always preferred to *Isna he comin? Winna he come?* for *Isn't he coming? Won't he come?* (Scottish Standard English behaves very much like Scots, but with *not* in place of *no*).

(4) Where does it get its words from?

As a result of the events mentioned on p xvi, Scots also shares with the northern dialects of England a large collection of words of Scandinavian origin, such as *bairn, brae, graith* ('equipment'), *kirk, lass, big* ('to build'), *flit* ('to move house'), *hing* ('to hang'), *dreich* ('dreary'), *lowse* ('loose'). Words in Scots from other sources are more often special to Scots only: French words, some dating from the Franco-Scottish Alliance (1296-1560), such as *deval* ('to stop'), *disjune* ('breakfast'), *fash* ('to bother'), and *vennel*, and *gardyloo* and *Hogmanay*; Dutch or Flemish words from early Flemish incomers, including Flemish craftsmen in medieval Scottish burghs, or from Scots traders in Flanders or Holland in the later Middle Ages and after, such as *callan* ('a lad'), *cuit* ('the ankle'), *mutch, pinkie* ('the little finger'), *golf* and *scone*; words taken over from Gaelic at various dates, like *cairn, glen, loch, strath, capercailzie, ptarmigan, ingle* ('a household fire'), *oe* ('grandchild'), *sonse* ('plenty, prosperity'), *tocher* ('a dowry'), and *gillie, sporran, whisky,* and, quite recently, *ceilidh;* Latin, prominent in Scots law, with, for example, *homologate, hypothec, sederunt,* and among school words, with *dominie, dux, fugie, janitor, pandie, vaig* and *vacance*; Anglo-Saxon, naturally, which supplied several words special to Scots, like *bannock, but and ben, gloamin, haugh, heuch, wee* and *weird;* and newly invented words, both those devised in medieval times, such as *boorach, gumption* and *slaister,* and more modern ones, like (housing-)*scheme, henner* ('a gymnastic trick') and *fantoosh.*

(5) How do the dialects differ?

Scots is generally reckoned to have four main dialects, Insular (i.e. of Shetland and Orkney), Northern (including North-Eastern), Central and Southern, with further sub-divisions, as shown on the map on p vi. Dialect differences, like differences between related languages, grow up over time, when speech-habits change in some places but continue as before in others. Some of the very large number of differences in pronunciation between Scots dialects had already grown up by the fifteenth century, especially some of those separating the Northern from the other dialects: Northern *f-* for other dialects' *wh-* as in *fa* (who), *fite* (white), and Northern *ee* for other dialects' *ui* as in Northern *beet* (boot) and *gweed* or *geed* (good), elsewhere *buit* and *guid.* Another ancient pronunciation difference is that between Southern and South-Eastern *twae, whae, whare* and Western and Northern *twaw, whaw* (or Northern *fa*), *whaur* (or Northern *faur*) ('two', 'who', 'where'), and similarly in some other words. Only the dialects of the far north and the extreme south keep up the old grammatical distinction, lost in all other dialects, between such pairs as *he wis aye gutteran aboot* with the ending *-an*, and *he's fond o gutterin* *aboot* with the ending *-in* or *-een*. The dialects also differ in their stocks of words. To take only one example out of hundreds, the following are the words for 'mud' in different parts of the country: *dubs, gutters, glabber, clabber* and *glaur*. For many of these differences there are at present no obvious explanations.

3. The English of Scotland

The description of the Standard English of Scottish speakers as 'English with a Scottish accent' is apt. When in the eighteenth century and later numbers of middle-class Scots learned to speak English as an alternative to, or replacement of, their native Scots, they did so with underlying habits of pronunciation carried over from Scots. Hence it is that Scottish Standard English has much the same individual consonant and vowel sounds as Scots itself. For example, both Scottish Standard English and Scots speakers pronounce *wh-* as 'hw' rather than 'w', and both have simple vowel pronunciations rather than the diphthongs used by many speakers from England in the 'ai' sound in, say, *late* or the 'oa' sound in *coat*. For the same reason, most Scottish Standard English speakers have only one 'oo' sound in pairs like *pool* and *pull*, whereas southern English speakers have two quite distinct sounds. Conversely, however, Scottish Standard English speakers have two separate sounds in, say, *tied* and *tide*, whereas most speakers in England have only one. And so on: there are many other shared Scottish Standard English and Scots pronunciation habits, as well as specially Scottish shared pronunciations of the words *length* and *strength* (with 'n' rather than 'ng'), of *lodge* as 'ludge' rather than 'lodge', of *fifth* and *sixth* as 'fift' and 'sixt', the Scottish pronunciations of *Wednesday, raspberry, tortoise* and other words, and of *loch, patriarch* and *technical* with 'ch' rather than 'k'.

Scottish Standard English also shares some grammatical habits with Scots (see p xx above). And its speakers make constant use of the Scotticisms which were such an object of horror to their eighteenth century ancestors, not only deliberately, to achieve a 'couthy' effect, as with 'keep a calm souch' or 'like a hen on a het girdle', or in the use of words like 'dreich' or 'kenspeckle' or 'peelie-wallie', but also in some cases without being aware that the word or phrase is in fact specially Scottish, such as 'pinkie', or 'to miss yourself', or 'Is that you away, then?' or 'I put her gas at a peep'.

4. Why Scots matters

The Scots tongue continues to play a part in the awareness of many Scots of their separate national identity, and despite the inferior place it now occupies as compared with English in modern Scotland, most Scots think and talk of it as the nation's language. As we have just seen, elements of it are present in the daily speech of all classes of native-educated Scots, and everywhere in Scotland there can be found some speakers at least with a more or less large amount of conversational Scots at their command, in some places more than others, of course. For several historical reasons, the special resources of Scots are much richer than those of any of the dialects of England. One witness to this is the present dictionary, with its great array of Scots words and expressions, mostly still current, in a list which no English dialect can match.

But most of all Scots matters because much of the best of Scotland's unique national literature is written in it, either in the 'mainstream' dialect of Robert Burns, Walter Scott, Hugh MacDiarmid and W.L. Lorimer, whose splendid translation of the New Testament appeared in 1983, or in one of several local dialects, such as the poetry and prose composed by able writers since the eighteenth century in north-east Scotland, since the nineteenth century in Shetland, and more recently some superb work by many able writers in the dialects of present-day Clydeside. Important new work of all these kinds and others continues to appear.

In compiling this dictionary we hope we have helped towards knowledge of, and pride in, the Scots language, and so made some contribution towards the Scottish people's confidence in itself as a nation.

Acknowledgements

The editors would like to thank the many people who have contributed to this book in numerous different ways. In particular we would like to express our gratitude to the following:

Professor A J Aitken and Mairi Robinson, who have been editorial consultants to the project from the beginning. As well as writing the essay on the Scots language (on p xvi), Professor Aitken has given specially helpful advice on the spelling of Scots and on the pronunciation scheme.

Professor Robert Black whose unstinting help on legal terminology has enabled us to increase our coverage of this important area.

Elizabeth Glass, whose very efficient keyboarding has greatly aided the progress of the Dictionary.

Caroline Macafee for general comments on the Dictionary.

The following have given us helpful advice from an educational standpoint: Alasdair Anderson, Sheila Douglas, Gregor Lamb, Irene MacFarlane, Dorothy Matthew, Alan MacGillivray (and other members of the Schools Committee of the Association for Scottish Literary Studies). Last but not least, Mairi Macleod has provided useful comments from the point of view of a school pupil.

Over and above the practical help we have received recently, we are always mindful of the debt we owe to our predecessors in Scottish lexicography, especially to David Murison, the second and main editor of the *Scottish National Dictionary*. Without their years of tireless effort the compilation of the present small volume would have been impossible.

We would like to thank Colin MacLean and other members of the staff of AUP for all their help and encouragement, and Ruari McLean for his expert help with the design.

Funding of dictionaries is always a problem and we would like to express our gratitude to the many people and organisations who have recently helped us to continue, in particular the Scottish Arts Council, The Binks Trust, The James Wood Trust , The Orcome Trust and the TSB Foundation Scotland.

A

a', all, aw, aa, aal 1 all. **2** every.

  a' body everybody. **a' body's body** a general favourite. **a' gait** everywhere. **a'kin kind** every kind (of).

A *see* **I**

aal *see* **auld**

aback 1 back; away, off, aloof. **2** behind, in the rear.

abeen *see* **abune**

abeich, abeigh [rhymes with 'dreich'] aside, away, apart from others.

ablach 1 †a mangled carcass. **2** a (small) insignificant or contemptible person.

able, yable *now S,* **yibble** *S* **1** able. **2** physically fit, strong. **3** having an appetite for.

ablins *see* **aiblens**

ablow under, below.

a'body *see* **a'**

aboon *see* **abune**

aboot, about 1 about. **2** on the move, going about (especially after an illness).

  aboot it about the same.

†abuilyiements garments; equipment, arms.

abune, aboon, abeen *N* **1** above. **2** in good cheer, in or into better condition.

academy *now mainly in names* a secondary school: *"Largs Academy".*

accountant the chief clerk in a bank branch, the deputy of the (assistant) manager.

ach, auch exclamation of impatience, disappointment, contempt etc.

acherspyre *of grain* sprout during malting.

acker: in acker in fragments, in bits *Shetland NE.*

acquant, acquent acquaint(ed).

adae, ado, adee *NE* **1** to do: *"I hae naething ado".* **2** going on, being done: *"what's adee?"* **3** the matter with: *"fat's adee wi ye?"*

adder, adderstane *see* **ether**

addle, †adle foul, dirty liquid, especially from dung.

adee, ado *see* **adae**

adoun, adoon, †adown [rhymes with 'soon'] down.

advocate *law* **1** a professional pleader in a court of justice, a barrister; *see also* **Lord Advocate** (*under* **lord**). **2** *law* a solicitor *Aberdeen.*

  advocate-depute an **advocate** appointed by the **Lord Advocate** (*see* **lord**) to prosecute under his directions.

ae, yae *now WCentral, S* **1** one. **2** the same: *"a' ae kind."* **3** only: *"oor ae wean."* **4 the ae** the very ..: *"the ae warst woman".* **5** a certain: *"ae day".* See also **ane.**

aefauld, afald 1 single. **2** simple, sincere; honest, faithful; single-minded.

aff, off, of *adverb* of, off.

  preposition **1** off. **2** away from (a place). **affcome** the way something turns out, outcome, result; (good *or* bad) reception; escape. **affgo** start, outset. **aff-loof** offhand. **aff-pit 1** excuse, evasion, reason for delay. **2** a delay. **3** a person who or thing which delays. **affset 1** an ornament. **2** a delay, an excuse. **3** an outset, a start. **afftak 1** a mocking remark. **2** a person who ridicules others, a mimic.

  aff an on 1 undecided, changeable, unsettled. **2** *of health* sometimes better, sometimes worse. **aff o(f)** off, from, away from.

affeir, effeir belong, be appropriate to, be fitting or proper for.

afore *adverb* **1** *of time* before, previously. **2** *of place* before, in front; in advance. **3** *of a clock* fast.

  preposition **1** *of time* before, earlier

than. **2** *of place* before, in front of; in advance of; into the presence of. **3** *of what is to come* confronting, in store for. **4** *of rank etc* above, before; in preference to.

conjunction **1** *of time* before. **2** rather than.

aft oft.

aften often.

after *see* **efter**

again [rhymes with 'lane'] *adverb* back.

preposition **1** against. **2** in preparation for (a particular time etc). **3** *of time* towards, by.

conjunction in preparation for a particular time etc when; until.

agait, agate 1 on the road, going about. **2** away.

a' gait *see* **a'**

age: be ages with be of the same age as.

agee *see* **ajee**

agley, aglee [rhymes with 'gey' or 'me'] off the straight, oblique(ly); wrong, awry.

ahin(t), ahent *adverb* **1** behind, remaining, at the back, following. **2** in one's past life, in time past. **3** at a later time, late, too late. **4** *of a clock* slow.

preposition behind; later than, after; too late for; in view of.

†**aiblins, ablins** perhaps, possibly.

aicher [-ch- as in 'dreich'] *Orkney Caithness,* †**icker** *SW* an ear of corn.

aicht *see* **aucht**[3]

aifter *see* **after**

aik, ake oak.

ail: what ails ye at what objection have you to?: *"What ails ye at my Dad?"*

ain (one's) own.

  my *etc* **ainsel** myself etc.

aince, ance, anes, wance, yince once.

  aince errand for the express purpose, as a special errand.

aipple an apple.

air ere, early, soon.

airm, erm an arm.

airn *see* **iron**

airn mail *see* **mail**[2]

airt[1] art, skill.

airt[2] *noun* **1** a point of the compass, a quarter. **2** a direction, way, manner.

verb **1** direct, guide to a place; set facing or moving in a certain direction; incite, urge forward. **2** direct one's way (to); make (for).

ais *see* **ass**

aishan *see* **etion**

aislar ashlar, square-hewn stone.

ait, yit *ECentral, S* oat.

ait *see* **eat**

aither, ether, edder *Shetland NE* either.

aither *see* **ither**

aiven *see* **even**[2]

aiver, aver a workhorse, carthorse; an old or worthless horse.

aiverie, yivvery anxious for, wanting very much; hungry.

aizle, eizel *NE,* **izal 1** an ember; a spark. **2** †a burnt-out cinder.

ajee, agee 1 to one side, aside, off the straight. **2** *of a door etc* ajar, partly open. **3** off the straight; in a disturbed state.

ake *see* **aik**

a'kin *see* **a'**

Alan an arctic skua *Shetland Orkney.*

  Allan-hawk name given to several sea birds, *eg* an arctic skua, a great northern diver.

alane, aleen alone.

alang along.

ald *see* **auld**

ale, eel *Shetland Orkney,* **ile** *N,* **yill 1** ale. **2** lemonade, ginger beer etc *NE.*

aleen *see* **alane**

alicreesh liquorice.

all *see* **a'**

Allan-hawk *see* **Alan**

alow[1] [rhymes with 'so'] below.

alow[2] [rhymes with 'cow'] on fire, ablaze.

alreadies *see* **a'ready**

alshin *see* **elshin**

amaist almost.

amang, among, amo 1 among. **2** in(to) the midst of, amid.

amends: amends o advantage of, upper hand of.

amna *see* **be**

amo, among *see* **amang**

amry *see* **aumry**

an *see* **and, than**

an a', ana *see* **and**

ance *see* **aince**

ancient, auncient, anshent 1 ancient. **2** *of children* precocious, behaving like an adult.

and, an and.

    an a', ana' 1 and everything or everyone else. **2** besides, as well: *"I want a piece ana'."* **3** *"big an strong an a' as she is"*: although she is so big and strong.

ane[1], **yin** *not N,* **een** *N* one.

ane[2] a, an.

aneath, aneth under, below, beneath.

    aneath the breath in a whisper.

anent 1 over against, opposite, in front of, before. **2** in a line with; on a level with, alongside of. **3** concerning, about. **4** in the sight, opinion or presence of.

anes *see* **aince**

aneth *see* **aneath**

aneuch *see* **eneuch**

angleberry, ingleberry a fleshy growth on horses, cattle or sheep.

anither, anidder *Shetland NE* another.

anshent *see* **ancient**

anter †venture, chance.

    antrin, antron occasional, chance, single, odd; peculiar, strange.

†**Antiburgher** a member of that section of the **Secession Church** (*see* **secede**) which separated in 1747 from the rest of the membership over the question of taking the **burgess oath.**

apen *see* **open**

apo, apon *see* **upon**

approbate and reprobate *law* assent to part of a deed and object to the rest (a course disallowed by law).

April Gowk *see* **gowk**[1]

aquavitae [akwaveetay] spirits, whisky.

arbiter *law* a person chosen or appointed to decide in a dispute between parties, an arbitrator.

a'ready, alreadies, areddies already.

argh *see* **ergh**

argie [g- as in 'get'] *verb* argue, especially contentiously.

    noun an assertion.

    argie-bargie *noun* a quarrel, haggling.

    verb dispute, haggle.

ark a chest, especially a large one for storing grain etc.

arles, erles earnest (money), a preliminary or token payment.

arnit, arnut an edible plant root, earthnut.

†**arselins** backwards.

art and part *law* indicating participation in a crime.

ase *see* **ass**

asheer *see* **asseer**

ashet 1 an oval serving plate, especially for a joint. **2** a pie-dish *WCentral*.

ashypet a scullery-maid.

aside *adverb* close by.

    preposition beside; close to, in comparison with.

ask, esk a newt, eft. =

asklent aslant; aside, astray; askew.

†**aspar** apart, with legs apart.

ass, ais, ase, ess ash, ashes.

asseer, asheer assure *NE*.

asteep: set one's brain(s) asteep make a mental effort, think hard.

astragal a glazing bar in a window.

astrict bind legally.

at[1]**: be at someone** to bother or hurt someone. **be at someone about something** talk to a person about a thing; keep finding fault with, tease someone.

    what are ye at? what do you mean?

at[2]**, it** *now NE, relative pronoun, conjunction* that.

at *see* **that**

aten *see* **eat**

Athole brose honey and oatmeal mixed with whisky (and water), sometimes with cream added.

athoot *preposition, also* **ithoot** without.

    adverb outside.

    conjunction unless.

athort 1 across; from one side of (a place or thing) to the other. **2** across in various directions; all over.

atour, attower [rhymes with 'tower'] across; (down) over; out of; above; beyond *now law*.

attercap, ettercap 1 a spider. **2** a spiteful or nasty person.

attery, attry 1 containing infected matter, pus. **2** grim, angry, forbidding; stormy.

attower *see* **atour**

atweel certainly, indeed.

atween between.

  atween hands at intervals; in the meantime.

atweesh betwixt, between.

auch *see* **ach**

aucht[1], **aught, echt, eicht, eight 1** eight. **2** eighth.

  eightsome a group of eight persons or things, often of a dance, especially a reel; the reel itself: **eightsome reel.**

aucht[2], **aught** property.

aucht[3], **aught, aicht** *Orkney NE,* **yaucht** *NE* **1** owe, be owing. **2** *also* **ought** own, possess.

aucht *see* **awe**[2]

aught *see* **aucht**[1], **aucht**[2], **aucht**[3]

auld, ald, aul, aal, old, owld 1 old. **2** the same, usual: *"Pate will still be the auld man".* **3** *indicating family relationships:* great-: *"auld uncle";* grand-: *"auld mither";* oldest: *"auld brither".* **4** *of bread* stale.

  the auld enemy the English. **auld-farran(t) 1** old-fashioned, quaint. **2** *of children* having the ways or shrewdness of older people; precocious. **3** wise, witty, ingenious. **auld-fashioned 1** old-fashioned. **2** *of children or young people* = **auld-farrant** 2. **the Old Firm** Rangers and Celtic football teams considered together. **Auld hornie** *see* **horn. auld licht** *see* **licht**[1]. **Auld Man** *see* **man. Auld Reekie** nickname for Edinburgh. **Auld Year** the previous year; the year that is about to end; the last few days of the year. **Auld Yule** *see* **Yule**

auld lang syne *see* **lang**[1].

aumose *see* **awmous**

aumry, amry a cupboard, pantry, usually a separate piece of furniture.

auncient *see* **ancient**

Auntie Beenie a rather old-fashioned looking woman.

austern austere.

ava, awa 1 at all. **2** †of all.

avald *see* **awald**[1], **awald**[2]

ave *see* **awe**[1]

aver *see* **aiver**

Averil April.

averin a cloudberry *NE.*

avizandum *law* further consideration.

aw oh!

aw *see* **a**[1]

Aw *see* **I**

awa, away *adverb* **1** away. **2** on, along: *"come awa to your bed".* **3** dead; wasted, made very thin: *"he's awa to skin and bane".*
  exclamation expressing surprise, disbelief etc: *"awa wi ye!".*
  awa frae past, unable to *Shetland N: "he wis awa fae speakin".* **awa wi't** done for; out of one's senses; lost; dead.

awa *see* **ava**

awald[1], **avald, yaval** *NE* [awald, avald, yaval] *especially of sheep or drunk people* lying on one's back and unable to rise.

awald[2], **avald, yaval** *Orkney NE* [awald, avald, yaval] *of grain* grown for the second year on the same land.

away *see* **awa**

awe[1], **ave** a float-board on a water-wheel.

awe[2], **owe, yaw** *NE* **1** owe. **2** own, possess.
  wha is aucht who owns ..?

awee a small amount, especially of time: *"bide awee".*

aweel *used to introduce a remark* well: *"Aweel, Jamie, what think ye?".*

awfu, awfy, yafu *adjective* **1** awful. **2** shocking; ugly; remarkable; difficult; very great.
  adverb very, extremely; very much.
  an awfu .. a great many ...

awmous, aumos 1 alms. **2** †a good deed.

awn *see* **own**

ay[1] [rhymes with 'day'] *exclamation expressing surprise or wonder* ah!, oh!

ay[2]**, aye** [rhymes with 'eye'] **1** yes. **2** *as a greeting, sometimes sarcastic* hello, well there you are: *"Ay ay Souter!"*. **3**

ay ay just so, that's it.

aye, ay, ey [rhymes with 'gey'] **1** always, continually; at all times. **2** still; all the same.

aynd, end [rhymes with 'pained'] breath *now Shetland.*

ayont *see* **beyont.**

B

ba[1], **baa**, **baw**, **ball 1** a ball. **2** football; **the Ba** the annual game of football formerly played in some areas on Shrove Tuesday. **3 the Ba** a game of handball played on certain annual holidays in the Borders and in Orkney.

ba[2], **baa**, **baw** hush (a child) to sleep.
baw baw(s), **beddie ba(s)** child's word for bed or going to sleep.

baa speak in a bellowing or bleating way, like a cow, sheep etc.

baa *see* **ba**[1], **ba**[2]

bab at the bowster, **babbity bowster**, **bob-at-the-bowster 1** an old country dance, finishing off a ball etc. **2** a children's game differing according to district.

baby's piece *see* **piece**

bachle *see* **bauchle**

back address (a letter).
backie a carry on the back; a piggyback. **backlin(g)s** backwards.
back-cast an unexpected blow. **back-door trot(t)** diarrhoea. **back end** of harvest, late autumn. **back-gaein** *adjective* not thriving. *noun, also* **back-gangin** a relapse. **backland** the back of a piece of ground; the building on it; a house behind another. **backset** something which keeps one back, slows down progress, causes a relapse in an illness. **backsey** name for various parts of a loin of beef etc. **backside 1** the back part of a building; the outside space next to it. **2 backsides** the parts of a town off the main streets.
at the back of not long after: *"at the back of six"*. **back and fore** backwards and forwards. **come up one's back** come into one's mind, fit in with what one intends to do. **on the back of** = **at the back of**. **with one's back to the wall** hard-pressed, facing desperate danger or difficulty.

backet 1 †a shallow wooden container for lime, salt etc. **2** a wooden box for fuel, ashes etc; a dustbin.

backgreen *see* **green**[1]

backie, **bauky**, **bawkie** a bat (the animal).

backside-foremaist *see* **foremaist**

bad unwell, in pain, physically ill.
badly ill, not very well.
bad man *see* **man**
the bad place hell. **no bad** pretty well; pretty good.

badder *see* **bather**

badderlocks a kind of edible seaweed.

badrans *see* **baudrons**

baest *see* **beast**

baff[1] a blow (with something soft).

baff[2], **baffie** a slipper.

bag *noun* the stomach; the paunch.
verb stuff, cause to swell like a bag.
baggie (mennen) a kind of large minnow.
bag raip the thick double straw rope round the eaves of a thatched stack.

baggie a swede.

bagnet, **bagonet**, **baignet** a bayonet.

bahookie *see* **behouchie**

baikie[1], **bakie** a square wooden container for ashes, coal, rubbish etc.

baikie[2] **1** a peg to which a tether was fastened *NE*. **2** the stake to which a cow etc was tied in the stall.

baik *see* **beck**

bailie, **bylie 1** a town magistrate next in rank to the **provost**, since 1975 used only as a courtesy title by certain local authorities. **2** the person in charge of the cows on a farm.

bair *see* **bear**

baird *see* **beard**

bairge[1], **barge** *SW, Ulster* speak loudly and angrily.

bairge[2] *verb* move clumsily, violently and noisily.

bairn 1 a child; a baby; someone's child.
2 the Bairns nickname for Falkirk football team.
  bairnlie childish; childlike.
baised confused, bewildered.
baist *see* **beast**
bait *see* **boat**
baith, both both.
  baith the two (of them) both (of them).
  the baith *see* **the**
bajan *see* **bejan**
bak *see* **bauk**
bake, byaak *NE verb, past tense also* **beuk**
  1 bake. **2** †knead (dough).
  noun a thick or soft biscuit.
  bake-board, bakebreid a baking board.
bakie *see* **baikie**[1]
balderry any of several types of wild orchid.
bale(-fire) a large fire; a bonfire or beacon-fire.
bale *see* **beal**
ball *see* **ba**[1]
ballant a ballad.
balloch *see* **bealach**
Balmoral a kind of bonnet with a **toorie** (*see* **tour**[1]) on the crown and a band, worn to one side.
baloo [baloo] word used to hush a child to sleep; a lullaby.
bambor *see* **baombe**
ban *see* **band**[1], **band**[2]
band[1], **ban, baun(d) 1** a band, something which binds. **2** a hinge, fastening for a door. **3** a rope, straw-twist *etc* used to bind corn *etc*. **4** a marriage bond. **5 bands** the two short white linen strips hanging from a minister's collar.
  bandster the member of a party of harvesters who binds the sheaves.
band[2], **ban, baun(d) 1** a band, a company, group. **2** a (church) choir.
  bandwin the band of three to eight reapers who work together along with one **bandster** (*see* **band**[1]).
band *see* **bind**
bane, been bone.
bang be better than, beat, thrash.

bangster a violent person; a bully.
bang up jump, rise hastily.
bank: the Bankies nickname for Clydebank football team.
bannet *see* **bonnet**
bannock, bonnock, bannie, banno *Orkney* a round flat cake, often of oat-, barley- or pease-meal, baked on a **girdle**.
banshee a female spirit, often connected with a family, whose wail was thought to forecast death or disaster.
banstickle a stickleback.
banyel a bundle; a heap; a crowd.
baombe *sheep counting,* **bambor** *children's rhymes* five.
bap *noun* a bread roll, varying locally in shape, size and texture.
  verb walk in a plodding, flat-footed way.
bar-the-door the game of **leave-o**.
bar, bawr, baur a joke, humorous situation, practical joke.
bard 1 a poet; a strolling singer or player; a person who uses coarse insulting language. **2** a noisy, scolding woman.
barefit, berfit, barfit *N* barefoot(ed). **barefit broth** broth made with a little butter but no meat *NE*.
barge *see* **bairge**
barken clot, harden or plaster over, blacken.
barley *mainly in children's games* a truce, pause.
  barley play a cry for truce in games.
  cry (a) barley call for a truce.
barley-bree malt liquor, whisky.
baron a baron; one who holds land directly of the Crown, in Scotland until a later date than in England including commoners.
  baronial, Scottish baronial of an ornate style of architecture with numerous turrets, crow-step gables etc. **barony** the lands held by a **baron**.
  †**baron bailie** a **baron**'s deputy with both civil and criminal jurisdiction in the **Baron Court**. †**Baron court** a court held by a **baron** or his deputy in his **barony**.

barra, borra a (hand-)barrow.

†**barrace, barras** *noun* **1** a barrace, a barrier in front of a castle etc. **2** an enclosure for combats, tournaments etc.

barrie[1] a baby's coat; a cloth wrapped round a baby.

barrie[2] *originally Gipsy from Yetholm, Roxburghshire, now used more widely* fine, excellent, very good; big; smart in appearance.

bash *verb* beat, smash.

noun a heavy blow (which will smash something).

on the bash having a drinking bout.

bass 1 a mat of bast, coarse straw, rushes etc, especially a doormat. **2** a workman's tool-basket or bag; a fish-basket.

bassie, bawsey an old horse.

bassie *see* **bossie**

baste *see* **beast**

bate *verb* beat.

noun something which is much better than something else.

bather, budder *Shetland N,* **badder** *Shetland N* bother.

batie *see* **bawtie**

batter *verb* paste (to a wall, together), stiffen as with paste.

noun **1** a paste or glue. **2** a medicinal plaster. **3 batters** the covers of a book.

battle *see* **bottle**

bauch, baugh [-ch, -gh as -ch in 'loch'] **1** poor, weak, not very good. **2** *of a knife etc* blunt. **3** *of ice* thawed, not slippery. **4** backward, timid, foolish.

bauchle, bachle *verb* walk clumsily, wear (shoes) out of shape; spoil.

noun **1** an old shoe, especially one worn down at the heel; a loose slipper. **2** an old, useless, worn-out person or thing. **3** an untidy or clumsy person.

baud *see* **bawd**

baudrons, †badrans 1 affectionate name for a cat. **2** a hare.

baugh *see* **bauch**

bauk, bawk, bak 1 a balk, an unploughed ridge; a wooden beam. **2** a ridge still seen in a field after the **bauks** were tilled. **3** a crossbeam, rafter. **4** the beam of a pair of scales etc. **5** a hen roost. **6 bauks** a church gallery. **7** a seat in a (fishing) boat.

bauky *see* **backie**

baul(d) 1 bold. **2** †*of things, eg fire* strong, fierce.

bauldy bald: *"bauldy-heidit."*

baun(d) *see* **band**[1], **ban(d)**[2]

baur *see* **bar**

bauson *see* **bawsant**

baw *see* **ba**[1], **ba**[2]

baw baw(s) *see* **ba**[2]

bawbee 1 a coin, originally valued at six pennies **Scots,** equivalent to a halfpenny sterling (see p 358). **2** a halfpenny. **3 bawbees** money.

bawd, baud a hare.

bawk *see* **bauk**

bawkie *see* **backie**

bawr *see* **bar**

bawsant, bauson *of an animal* having a white mark or streak on the face.

bawsey *see* **bassie**

bawtie, batie (name for) **1** a dog. **2** a hare; a rabbit.

†**baxter** a baker.

be, bey *S* [rhymes with 'gey'] *verb, past tense also* (**I, he, she, it**) **wes, wis** *now Orkney NE,* **wus, wur;** (**we, you, they**), **war** *now NE,* **ware, wur.**

amna am not. **sae beins** that being so *NE.* **binna 1** be not, are not: *"God send they binna mony."* **2** unless. **immen** am not. **twar** it were *now NE.* **wasna, wiznan** *NE* was not, were not.

be *see* **by**

bead, bede 1 a bead. **2** a glass or quantity of spirits: *"he had a good bead in him yesterday".*

beadle *noun* a **church officer.**

beak *see* **beek**

beal, beel, bale 1 fester. **2** (be) fill(ed) with pain, rage etc.

bealin a festering sore, boil, pimple etc.

bealach *especially mountaineering,* **balloch** [*Gaelic* beealach] *especially in* *place names* a narrow mountain pass.

beam, been steep (a barrel, tub etc) to make it tight *N*.

beamfill't, beamfoo filled to overflowing; having everything one wants.

bear, bere, bair a hardier and coarser kind of barley.

beard, baird a beard.

beardie 1 *also* **chinney beardie** the rubbing of a man's rough chin against another person's chin or cheek, the squeezing of another's chin with the hand. **2** a kind of stickleback. **3** *also* **beardie lotchie** a loach.

bease *see* **beast, boose**¹

beast, baste, baist, baest *noun, also* **beastie,** *plural also* **beas, bease 1** a beast. **2** a cow, bull, calf, ox. **3** a creature of any sort, a bird, fish, insect etc, a (body- and head-)louse etc.
verb beat, get the better of, do better than.

beck, baik bow, curtsy.

bed: beds the spaces chalked on the ground for playing **peever**¹; the game itself.

bedrall, bedal, a bedridden person. **bedfast** bedridden.

beddie ba(s) *see* **ba**²

bede *see* **bead**

bedellus [bedellus] the chief porter and macebearer in the Universities of St Andrews, Glasgow and Edinburgh.

bedrall *see* **bed**

bee-baw-babbety a (kissing) game or dance.

beef any butcher's meat.

beek, beak 1 warm (oneself). **2** *of the sun* shine brightly.

beel *see* **beal**

been *see* **bane, beam**

beenge, binge bow (humbly); cringe, fawn.

beerial burial *NE*.

beest, beist the first milk of a cow after calving.

beet 1 †relieve, lessen; help; mend. **2** supply something missing to (something)

eg replace hooks on (a fishing line).
†**beet a mister** fulfil a need, make good a deficiency.

beet *see* **buit**¹, **buit**²

beetle *see* **bittle**

beezer *informal* a thing or person bigger or better than usual.

begeck, begeik *verb* deceive, disappoint. *noun* a trick, disappointment.

behad *see* **behaud**

behangt exclamation of impatience.

behaud, behad 1 behold **2** hold back, wait. **3** watch (a person) carefully, keep an eye on.

behouchie, bahookie *often to children* the behind, backside.

beig *see* **big(g)**¹

beil, beild *see* **bield**

bein *see* **bien**

beins *see* **be**

beis *see* **by**

beist *see* **beest**

bejan(t), †**bajan** a first-year student at a Scottish university *now only St Andrews*.

belang 1 belong. **2** own, possess. **3** belong to (a place) be a native of: *"he belangs Glesca."*

belch, belge, bilch *noun* **1** *often contemptuous* a stout, usually short person. **2** contemptuous term for a person, especially a child.

beld, bell bald.

belfert *see* **bilf**

belge *see* **belch**

bell a bubble.

bell *see* **beld, heather**

bellies *noun, also as double plural* **bellises** bellows.

belloch bellow, roar.

bellum noise, din; a blow; force.

belted Galloway *see* **Galloway**

belly¹: **belly-blind** blind man's buff; the blindfolded person in it. **belly flaucht** flat on one's face or stomach; headlong. †**belly-timber** food, provisions.

belly², **bully** *N*, **billy** *SW* bellow.

belt 1 the belt the **tawse** (*see* **taw**¹). **2** a blow, a hit.

belted plaid(y) *see* **plaid.**

Beltane 1 1 or 3 May; an old Scottish quarter-day. **2** a pagan fire festival on these days (and sometimes also on 21 June); identified by the church as the feast of the Invention of the Cross (3 May).

belyve quickly, at once; soon.

ben¹ *adverb* **1** in or towards the inner part of a house etc; in or to the best room or another room; inside. **2** *mining* inwards, towards the workings.

preposition through (a house) towards the inner part; in or to the best room or another room: *"ben the hoose".*

noun **1** the inner room, the best room. **2** *mining* a miner's right to enter the pit: *"claim one's ben."* **3** one's place in a queue: *"stand one's ben".*

benner inner. **benmost** furthest in, in the second, inner room.

ben² a mountain, hill, one of the higher Scottish mountains.

bend 1 †spring, leap. **2** *also* **bend the bicker** drink hard.

†**bender** a hard drinker.

benk *see* **bink**

bennel any long reedy grass.

benorth on or to the north of; in the north.

bense walk or move with great energy; bounce.

bensell vigorous action; force; violence (of a storm, fire etc).

bent 1 bent, a kind of coarse grass. **2 bents** sandy hillocks covered with bent.

†**take to the bent** flee (from danger or from one's creditors).

bere *see* **bear**

berfit *see* **barefit**

berry thresh (corn); thrash (a child).

besom, bisom, bizzom [**bizz**om]**, bussom 1** a besom; any broom. **2** a term of contempt for a person, especially a woman: *"ye wee besom ye".*

besouth, besooth on or to the south of; in the south.

bessie a bad-mannered, boisterous, bad-tempered woman or girl *NE.*

best maid a bridesmaid.

bestial domestic animals, livestock.

betak 1 hand over; deliver (goods, a blow). **2** †overtake. **3** recover *NE.*

better completely recovered from an illness.

†**beuch, beugh** [bee**ooch**] *noun* **1** a bough, a branch of a tree. **2** the shoulder or limb of an animal or person. **3** the bow of a ship.

beuk *see* **bake, buik**

bew *see* **blue**

†**bewast** on or to the west of.

bey *see* **be**

beyont, ayont, beyond 1 beyond. **2** *of time, number, degree* above, more than etc.

Bhoys *see* **boy**

bibble *see* **bubble**

bick¹ a bitch, a female dog.

bick², **bick burr** imitation of the call of the grouse.

bicker¹ *verb* **1** †attack or fight (with arrows, stones etc). **2** *of water in general* move quickly and noisily; *of rain* pelt, patter; *of boiling water* bubble quickly. **3** *of living creatures* move quickly and noisily, rush. **4** †gleam, flicker, sparkle. **5** laugh heartily *NE.*

noun **1** a (street- or school-)fight; a quarrel. **2** a quick, noisy movement.

bicker² a beaker, a (wooden) drinking cup; a (porridge) bowl.

bid invite (to a wedding etc).

bidding 1 a command. **2** an invitation.

bide *verb* **1** remain, stay (especially temporarily), dwell, reside. **2** await, stay for. **3** put up with, stand.

noun pain now *NE.*

bidie-in a person who lives with another of the opposite sex without marriage *NE.*

†**bield, beild, beil** *noun* protection, relief; shelter.

verb help; protect; cover over; shelter.

bien, bein 1 in good condition. **2** comfortable(-looking), pleasant, cosy. **3** well-to-do, well-off. **4** *of a house etc* well stocked.

big(g)¹, beig 1 big. **2** conceited, swollen-headed.

big house the main house of the **laird** on an estate. **big miss** a great loss by death, or by the departure of a friend. **big sma faimily** a large family of young children.

big(g)² *verb* **1** build, construct. **2** *of birds* build nests. **3** stack (hay, corn etc).

biggin(g) 1 (the act of) building. **2** a building. **bigly** pleasant to live in; handsomely made.

bilch *see* **belch**

bile¹ boil.

boiling a boiled sweet.

bile² a boil, an infected swelling.

bilf, bulf a sturdy young man *NE*.

bilfert, belfert a bigger than usual thing or person *NE*.

bill *see* **bull**

billet a bullet.

billy 1 a lover. **2** a (close) friend. **3** a brother. **4** a fellow, lad. **5 grand billies** on very friendly terms.

billy *see* **belly²**

Billy *slang* a Protestant, Orangeman *Glasgow*.

bind, bin [rhymes with 'tin(ned)'] *verb, past tense also* **band**; *past participle also* **bun(d) 1** bind. **2** tether.

noun **1** measure, size, capacity. **2 bin** humour, mood *NE*.

be neither to haud nor bind be beyond control.

bine *see* **boyne**

bing 1 a heap or pile. **2** a slag-heap.

binge *see* **beenge**

bink, benk *now Shetland* **1** a bench. **2** a wall rack or shelf for dishes etc; a kitchen dresser. **3** a bank, *eg* a **peat bank. 4** a hob on a fireplace; a shelf, ledge etc at the side of such.

binna *see* **be**

binner move noisily; run, gallop.

bird, burd 1 a bird. **2** a young bird. **3** the young of an animal. **4** a lady, woman; a girl. **5** term of endearment, especially to children.

burd-alane quite alone.

birk¹ 1 a birch. **2 birks** a small wood consisting mainly of birches.

birk² move energetically or restlessly.

birkie *noun* **1** a smart (usually young) fellow. **2** a conceited person. **3** a sharp-tongued, quick-tempered person, usually a woman.

adjective **1** lively, spirited. **2** sharp-tongued, huffy.

birl¹, burl *verb* **1** revolve quickly, whirl round, dance; make a rattling or whirring sound. **2** move quickly, hurry along. **3** toss a coin.

noun **1** a turn, twist, revolving movement. **2** a whistle; the sound made by a whistle.

birl² pour out, serve (wine etc).

†birlieman one of the group of persons elected or appointed to act as judges or **arbiters** in local disputes.

birn *see* **burden, burn²**

birny *see* **burn²**

birr¹ 1 force, energy, bustling activity. **2** enthusiasm. **3** a whirring sound.

birr²: in a birr *of hair etc* standing up on end, tousled; brushed so as to stand out from the head.

birse 1 bristles, (a) bristle. **2** anger, temper: *"his birse is up"*.

birsie 1 bristly; hairy. **2** hot-tempered, passionate.

birse *see* **brizz**

birse tea a last cup of tea with whisky instead of milk.

birsle, bristle 1 scorch. **2** toast; warm thoroughly.

(weel-)birsled well-cooked, fried until crisp.

birst, burst, brust burst.

noun **1** an injury caused by over-exertion. **2** a bout of drunkenness. **3** a big feed, *often* **a hunger or a burst** scarcity or plenty.

birze *see* **brizz**

bisom see **besom**

bit 1 a bit. **2** a small piece of ground; a spot, place. **3** one's job.

    bittie, bittock a small piece; a short distance or time. **a bittie** somewhat, rather.

    I can't get out of the bit I can't make any progress, I'm stuck. **come to the bit** come to the point of decision.

bittle, beetle *noun* **1** a beetle, a mallet. **2** a kitchen utensil for bruising barley, mashing potatoes etc.

    verb **1** beat (linen, clothes etc). **2** thrash.

bizz *verb* **1** buzz. **2** *of liquids* hiss, fizz.

    noun a state of commotion, bustle.

bizzom see **besom**

bla see **blae**

blab drink messily; drink (alcohol) too much *NE*.

blab see **blob**

blabber babble.

black *noun* **blacks** mourning clothes.

    adverb **1** completely, utterly. **2** intensely, extremely.

    blackie a blackbird.

    blackberry the blackcurrant. **black bun** a very rich spiced fruit cake, baked in a pastry crust and eaten at **Hogmanay. black cock** a male black grouse. **blackman 1** *in threats to children* the bogyman, the Devil. **2** a kind of toffee; or other dark-coloured sweet. **3** an ice-cream with a plain wafer on one side and a marshmallow-filled wafer with chocolate edges on the other. **4** a piece of black matter in the nose. **black-strippit ba** a striped boiled sweet, a bull's eye. **black sugar** liquorice (juice). **black traicle** see **traicle**

blad see **blaud**[1], **blaud**[2]

bladdoch, bledoch, blatho *now Orkney* buttermilk.

blade, bled *noun* **1** a blade. **2** a leaf of cabbage, turnip, tobacco etc; a tea-leaf.

    verb strip the leaves from (a plant).

bladry, blathrie foolishness, showing off, harm.

blae, †bla *adjective* **1** blue; bluish; dark bluish grey. **2** livid or bluish from cold, bloodlessness etc.

    blaes a bluish-grey hardened clay, soft slate or shale.

    blaeberry a bilberry.

blaffart see **bluffert**

blaf(l)um a deception; a hoax, illusion; nonsense, idle talk.

blaiken make pale.

blain a scar from a sore or wound; a weal.

blame fault: *"it's not my blame"*.

blan see **blin**[1]

bland mix, mingle.

blare see **blear**

blased, bleezed *of milk* slightly soured.

blash 1 a splash of liquid etc. **2** a heavy shower of rain etc. **3** a weak mixture of drink, soup etc. **4** a semi-liquid or soft slimy mass, a dirty mess. **5** a large drink (of alcohol). **6** a torrent of words.

    blashy 1 rainy, wet, gusty. **2** *of food or drink* weak.

blast *noun* **1** a smoke, a puff of a pipe. **2** a stroke, a sudden attack of illness.

    verb **1** shout loudly, violently. **2** smoke (tobacco). **3** pant, breathe hard.

    bleester *of wind* blow in blasts. **blastie** a dwarf; a bad-tempered, unmanageable child or animal.

blate 1 timid, modest, shy: *"ye needna be sae blate."* **2** dull, stupid, easily deceived. **3** *of crops* backward in growth.

blather see **blether**[1]

blatho see **bladdoch**

blathrie see **bladry**

blatter *verb* **1** talk a lot, noisily and fast; babble. **2** *of rain, hail etc* rattle, beat with violence. **3** run noisily with short steps

    noun **1** a loud rattling or rustling noise. **2** a storm of rain, hail etc. **3** a blow; a heavy fall; a gunshot. **4** a meaningless flow of words.

blaud[1], **blad 1** damage, by harsh or careless treatment, injure. **2** *of storms, etc* buffet, beat *now Angus*. **3** make a viol-

ent, thrusting movement; slap, strike.
noun **1** an injury; a blow. **2 blauds** a disease causing pimples. **3** a blast of wind, a downpour of rain.

blaud², blad *noun* a piece, lump; strip of cloth.

blaw¹, blow, byauve *NE* [bee**auve**], **blyave** *NE* [blee**auve**] *verb* **1** blow. **2** brag, boast; exaggerate. **3** smoke (a pipe). **4** *draughts* take a piece from (one's opponent).
noun **1** a blowing (of a horn etc). **2** a blow, a blast, gust. **3** a puff (of a pipe). **4** boasting, a boast; a boaster.
blawdoon a backdraught in a chimney or fireplace.
blaw in someone's lug flatter a person.
blaw up flatter, make (a person) believe what is untrue.

blaw² a blow, a stroke.

blaw³ blossom.

blaze *see* **bleeze¹**

blea bleat, as a lamb or kid.

bleach, bleech [bleetch] strike; beat.

blear, bleer, blare 1 blear; **blear someone's ee** deceive someone. **2** shine dimly.
bleared 1 debauched-looking. **2** *of writing* blotted. **blearie** *adjective* **1** watery-eyed. **2** †*of liquid food* (too) thin. *noun* liquid food, gruel.

bleck¹ 1 baffle; puzzle. **2** beat, be better than.

bleck² *noun* **1** blacking (for leather). **2** (a small piece of) soot or smut. **3** a black person. **4** a scoundrel, rascal.
verb **1** make black, blacken, dirty. **2** blacken with ink, write on (paper). **3** blacken in character etc.

bled *see* **blade**

bledder *see* **blether¹**

bledoch *see* **bladdoch**

bleech *see* **bleach**

bleed *see* **blude**

bleem *see* **blume**

bleer *see* **blear**

bleester *see* **blast**

bleeter *see* **bluiter**

bleeze¹, blaze *noun* **1** a blaze. **2** a blazing

brand, a torch, *eg* as used when spearing fish. **3** a beacon fire, a bonfire.
verb **1** blaze. **2** light up (water) to attract fish.
bleezed, bleezin (fou) very drunk.

bleeze² **1** blaze, proclaim. **2** boast, brag.

bleezed *see* **blased**

bleib *see* **blob**

blellum an idle, ignorant, talkative man.

blenk *see* **blink**

blent *see* **blink**

blether¹, bledder, blather *verb* **1** talk foolishly, or too much (about nothing or about something untrue). **2** †stammer, speak indistinctly.
noun **1 blethers** foolish talk, nonsense; long-winded (boasting) talk. **2** a person who talks foolishly or too much. **3 blethers** nonsense!, rubbish! **bletheration, bletherie** foolish talk. **blether(an)skate, blether(um)skite 1** a silly, foolish person (who talks too much). **2** a boaster.

blether², bledder, blather a bladder.
blether and leather a football.

blib a weak watery helping of tea, soup etc.

blichan [-ch- as in 'dreich'] contemptuous term for a person or animal.

blid *see* **blude**

blide *see* **blithe**

bliffert *see* **bluffert**

blin¹ *verb, past tense also* **blan** *mainly in poetry* stop; come to an end.

blin², blind *adjective* **1** blind. **2** *of mist etc* dense *now NE*. **3** *especially of a cow's teat* having no opening.
verb **1** blind. **2** close (the eyes) as in sleep *now NE*.
blin bargain a bargain made without care or full knowledge, a pig in a poke.
blind coal a kind of anthracite. **blin drift** drifting snow. **blind fair** *often of albinos* extremely fair. **blind Harrie** blindman's buff. **blin hooie** exchange. **blin lump** a boil which does not come to a head.

blink, blenk, blent *verb* **1** blink. **2** †glance kindly, look fondly (at); ogle. **3** glance at with the evil eye; bewitch; turn (milk etc) sour. **4** gleam, shine. **5** give a spark to or of; light (a lamp). **6** be drunk.

noun **1** a blink. **2** a (pleasant) glance, brief look. **3** a brief or bright gleam; a (short) period of shining, now especially of sunshine between clouds. **4** a short time, moment. **5** a wink of sleep.

blinker 1 the eye. **2** a star; the moon. **3 blinkers** eyelashes. **4** †a cheat, a spy. **5** a person who is nearly blind or blind in one eye. **6** a lively, attractive girl. **blinkin eed** weak-eyed.

blinter *noun* a gusty wind.
verb **1** strike. **2** glimmer, flicker. **3** squint; blink.

blirt *verb* cry, weep, burst into tears.
noun **1** an outburst (of weeping). **2** a gust of wind with rain.

bliss bless.

blithe, blide 1 blithe. **2** cheerful, glad, in good spirits. **3 blithe o** happy because of, glad of.
blithemeat a thanksgiving feast after the birth of a child; food given to people in a house at the time of a birth.

blob, blab, bleib now *NE* **1** a drop of moisture, a bubble. **2** a pimple; a blister.

block a bargain, agreement.

block, hammer, and nail a children's game.

blood *see* **blude**

blotch blot (writing).

blotsheet blotting paper.

bloust, blowst [rhymes with 'oust'], **bluist** *noun* boast; boasting.
verb brag, boast.

blouster [-ou- as in 'shout'], **bluister 1** a violent squally wind. **2** a boaster.

blout, blowt [rhymes with 'shout'] a sudden burst, especially of wind, rain etc.
blouter a blast of wind.

blow *see* **blaw**[1]

blowder [rhymes with 'louder'] a sudden gust of wind.

blowst *see* **bloust**

blowt *see* **blout**

blud *see* **blude**

bludder *see* **bluther**

blude, blood, blid, blud now *Shetland*, **bluid, bleed** *N noun* **1** blood. **2 not a blude** not a single person or thing.
verb (cause to) bleed.
blude run bloodshot.

bluder *see* **buller**

blue, bew, blyew [bleeoo] blue.
bluebell 1 a harebell (*see* **hare**). **2** an English bluebell. **blue bonnet** †a man's flat-topped round cap without a peak; the wearer of such a cap. **blue clue** a ball of the blue wool used in telling the future at **Halloween. blue do** a poor performance, a failure, a black outlook. **blue ee** a black eye.

bluffert, bliffert 1 a squall (of wind and rain). **2** *also* **blaffart** a blow, slap *NE*.

bluid *see* **blude**

bluist *see* **bloust**

bluister *see* **blouster**

bluiter, bleeter *NE noun* **1** a big, clumsy, useless person; a foolish talker. **2** a rumbling noise.
verb **1** make a rumbling noise. **2** talk foolishly; blurt out.

blume, bleem *N* **1** bloom. **2** a potato top.

blunk, blunkart *noun, now NE* **1** a small block of wood or stone. **2** a dull, lifeless person.

blush (raise a) blister.

bluther, bludder 1 be dirtied with something wet. **2** dirty (the face, eyes, mouth) with tears etc.

blyave *see* **blaw**[1]

blybe *NE, noun* a large quantity of liquid, especially of spirits.
verb drink heavily.

blyew *see* **blue**

†blype a layer of skin as it peels or is rubbed off.

boak *see* **boke**

boakie, bockie a piece of hard matter in the nose.

boal *see* **bole**

boannie *see* **bonny**

boast, bost 1 boast. **2** threaten; scold.

boat, bait 1 a boat. **2** a ferry.

bob[1] a dance.

Bobbin John a kind of hand-sower.

bob[2] a mark, butt.

bob-at-the-bowster *see* **bab-at-the-bowster**

bock *see* **boke**

bockie, bokie a hobgoblin; a scarecrow.

bockie *see* **boakie**

bodach [**bod**dach] **1** an old man. **2** a small and unimportant person. **3** a spectre, bugbear.

boddam, botham *Shetland Orkney NE* bottom.

boddle *see* **bodle**

bode *noun* **1** an offer, a bid (especially at an auction). **2** the price asked by a seller; the offer of goods at a certain rate. **3** an invitation, especially to a wedding.
verb now NE **1** expect, desire, aim at. **2** offer with insistence, press (something) on (someone).

boden provided; prepared; equipped.

bodle, boddle 1 †a small copper coin. **2 not worth a bodle** not worth anything.

bodsy a little, neat person.

bodword a message; an invitation.

body, buddy a person, a human being: **1** (*referring to someone else or yourself*): "*could you no leave a body in peace*". **2** a little person.

bog work in wet, dirty surroundings; work slowly.
bog-bleater a bittern. **bog-cotton** cotton-grass. **bog-hay** hay gathered from uncultivated or marshy ground.

boggar *see* **bouger**

boggle *see* **bogle**

bogie: the game's a bogie a call to cancel a game and start again when there has been a fault.

bogle, boggle 1 an ugly or terrifying ghost; a bugbear. **2** a scarecrow.

boiling *see* **bile**[1]

boke, boak, bock, bowk, byock *NE verb* belch; retch, vomit.
noun **1** a belch. a retch. **2** a feeling of sickness or disgust.
gie (someone) the (dry) bock(s) cause to fell sick, retch or vomit; disgust.

bokie *see* **bockie**

boldin *see* **bowden**

bole, boal 1 a recess in a wall, later one used as a cupboard; a small opening in a wall. **2** a pay-desk window.

boll, bow [rhymes with 'pole' or 'cow'] *noun* a dry measure of weight or capacity (see p 359).

bolt *see* **bowt**

bo-man a bogyman.

bombaze *see* **bumbazed**

bonallay [bon**all**ay] a drink with or toast to a departing friend; a farewell greeting.

bondage, bonnage 1 bondage. **2** service due from a tenant to his **superior** or from a farm-worker to a farmer.

bonnet, bannet, bunnet 1 a soft flat brimless cap worn by men and boys, often one with a peak. **2** a bonnet, a woman's (brimmed) head-dress.
bonnetie a boys' game played with bonnets.

bonnock *see* **bannock**

bonny, boannie, bony 1 beautiful, pretty. **2** *of boys or men* handsome, attractive. **3** good, excellent, fine. **4** great, considerable.
bonny penny a high price.

bonspiel a match or contest, now a curling match.

bony *see* **bonny**

boo, bow 1 bow, (as a sign of respect etc). **2** bend, curve; become bent or crooked. **3** cause to bend.
boo-backit hump-backed.

boodie a ghost, hobgoblin *NE*.

boof *see* **buff**[1]

booger *see* **bougar**

book *see* **buik**

book *see* **bouk**[1], **bouk**[2], **bouk**[3]

bool[1], **boull** [-oo-] **1** a bowl, the ball used in bowls; **bools** the game itself. **2** a ball or rounded object, *eg* a round stone, a round sweet. **3** a marble.

have a **bool in one's mou** speak in an affected way.

bool², **boull** [-oo-] a curved or semi-circular band, forming the handle of a pot, bucket etc.

boolie, bowlie [-ow- as in 'cow'] *adjective* crooked, bent. *noun* a bowlegged person. **bowlie-backit** hump-backed; round-shouldered. **bowly-legged** bow-legged.

boon¹ above. **boonmost** highest, uppermost.

boon² a band of reapers, shearers etc.

boon *see* **boun¹**, **boun²**

boorach, boorock *noun* 1 †a mound, small hill. 2 a heap or mass. 3 a crowd, group, cluster. 4 a small, humble house. 5 a muddle, mess, state of confusion; a fuss.
verb 1 heap up. 2 crowd together. 3 mess or grub about.

boord *see* **buird¹**

boor(d)ly *see* **buirdly**

boorock *see* **boorach**

boortree *see* **bourtree**

boose, bease a stall for a horse or cow.

boost, boust drive off, shoo away.

boot *see* **bout²**, **bout³**, **buit¹**

bootch, boutch a botch, bungle, muddle.

booyangs = **nickie-tams**.

boozy *see* **bowsie**

bord an edging, border, hem on a garment, hat etc.

bordelhouse a brothel.

borders: the Borders the area lying between the Scottish-English border and Lothian. **Borders (Region)** a **Region** formed from the former counties of Peebles, Berwick, Roxburgh and Selkirk and part of the former county of Midlothian.

bore *noun* a hole, crevice, *eg* a shelter or hiding-place; an opening.
verb press (against etc).

borestone, borestane 1 a stone bored to hold a flagstaff. 2 a boundary stone.

bore at, in *etc*, study deeply or intently.

borow *see* **burgh**

borra *see* **barra**

borrow a surety, pledge.

boss 1 hollow; empty. 2 without money or brains.

bossie, bassie a wooden basin or bowl for carrying meal to the baking board or in which meal is mixed and kneaded.

bost *see* **boast**

both *see* **baith**

botham *see* **boddam**

bothy *noun* 1 a rough hut used as temporary accommodation *eg* by shepherds, salmon-fishers, mountaineers. 2 permanent living quarters for workmen, especially a separate building on a farm used to house unmarried male farm-workers.
verb live in a **bothy.**

bottle, battle, buttle *noun* a bottle, a bundle (of hay or straw); a sheaf.
verb bundle up (hay or straw) for fodder.

bouch [-ow-], **bowch** [-ch- as in 'loch'] 1 bark. 2 cough.

boucht¹, **bought** [bucht] a bend, fold; a knot; a coil of rope.

boucht², **bought, bucht** [bucht, bowcht, bocht] a sheepfold.

boucht *see* **bought**

bouet, bowat [booet] a (hand) lantern.

bouff¹, **bowf** *verb* 1 *especially of a large dog* bark; make a loud dull sound. 2 cough loudly.
noun 1 a bark; a loud, dull sound. 2 a dog.
boufin smelly.

bouff², **bowf** contemptuous term for a big person *NE*.

bouff *see* **buff¹**

bougar [-oo-], **booger, buggar, boggar** a cross-beam in a roof; a rafter.

bought, boucht [bucht] 1 the bend of the arm (or leg). 2 a branch, twig; a fork of a tree.

bought *see* **boucht¹**, **boucht²**

bouk¹, **book, bowk** steep (dirty linen etc) in stale urine etc before bleaching.

bouk² [-oo-], **book, buik** 1 the carcass of

a slaughtered animal. **2** the body of a person (living or dead).

bouk³ [-oo-], **book** *noun* bulk, size, quantity.

verb **1** bulk. **2** *of a rope* increase on a capstan as its coils are wound round.

boukit -sized, in size: *"little-boukit, muckle-boukit"*.

boull *see* **bool**¹, **bool**²

bouman *see* **bow**¹

boun¹ [-oo-], **boon** prepared, ready.

verb get ready, prepare.

boun², **bound** [-oo-], **boon 1** a bound, boundary, limit. **2 boons** a district or stretch of land within certain boundaries. **3** extent, width.

bountree *see* **bourtree**

bourd [boord] a jest, joke; a funny story etc.

bourtree, **boortree**, **bountree** [-oo-] an elder tree.

boust *see* **boost**

bouster *see* **bowster**

bousterous, **bowsterous** [-ow-] boisterous, fierce; rowdy.

bout¹, **bowt** [-ow-] a hank or skein of thread or cloth.

bout², **bowt**, **boot 1** a bout. **2** the extent of ground covered as a plough etc moves across a field.

bout³, **boot** [-oo-] bolt, sift (flour etc).

bout *see* **bowt**

boutch *see* **bootch**

boutgate [boot-] **1** a roundabout way; an underhand means. **2** the doing of a round of work, *eg in ploughing* two furrows, outwards and back.

†**bow**¹ [boo] a stock or herd of cattle, especially of cows.

bouman the man who had charge of the cattle on a farm; a tenant with a **bow**¹.

bow² [rhymes with 'cow'] **1** a bow (the weapon). **2** an arch, especially of a bridge, an arched gateway *in place-names, eg* **Netherbow**. **3** the curve of a street, furrow etc. **4** an ox-bow. **5** the semi-circular handle of a pail, pot etc.

bowdy (-leggit) bandy-legged.

bow-backit hump-backed. **bowbrig** an arched bridge. **bowbutts** ground for archery practice. **bow-houghed** bandy-legged.

not bow an ee not close one's eyes, not sleep.

bow³ [rhymes with 'cow'] a buoy.

bow *see* **boll**, **boo**

bowat *see* **bouet**

bowch *see* **bouch**

bowden [-ow- as in 'cow'], †**boldin** swell (up).

bowel hive(s) enteritis etc in children.

bowf *see* **bouff**¹, **bouff**²

bowie [-ow- as in 'cow'] **1** a broad, shallow dish, bowl or small tub. **2** a barrel for water or ale. **3** a bucket.

bowk *see* **boke**, **bouk**¹

bow-kail [-ow- as in 'cow'] cabbage.

bowl [-ow- as in 'cow'] *in Scots used also where English prefers* basin: *"pudding bowl"*.

bowlie *see* **bool**²

bowlt [-ow- as in 'cow'] crooked, distorted.

bowly *see* **bool**²

bowse *NE* [-ow- as in 'cow'] **1** swing out (*eg* a boat). **2** bounce.

bowsie [-ow- as in 'cow'], **boozy** big, fat, puffed up.

bowsie-(man) [**bow**zy-, **boozy**] a bogeyman.

bowster, **bouster** [-ow-] a bolster.

bowsterous *see* **bousterous**

bowstock [-ow- as in 'cow'] a cabbage with a properly-developed heart *NE*.

bowt, **bolt**, **bout** [rhymes with 'out'] bolt. **bowtfoot** a club-foot.

bowt *see* **bout**¹, **bout**²

box *informal* a melodeon or accordion.

boxin wainscotting, wooden panelling. **box-bed** a bed enclosed in wooden panelling, the front having either sliding panels, hinged doors, or curtains.

on the box receiving weekly assistance from a poor fund, more recently from National Health Insurance benefit.

boy 1 a man of any age; a bachelor of any age still living with his parents. **2** an apprentice. **3 the boy** term of praise: *"ye're the boy, said his father"*. **4 the Bhoys** nickname for Celtic football team.

boyne, bine 1 a shallow tub; a wash-tub. **2** a broad shallow container especially for skimming milk.

bra *see* **braw**

†braboner, brebnar a weaver.

brace a fireplace; a mantelpiece.

brachan, breckan, brechan bracken.

†brade, braid make a sudden movement; start, spring.

brade *see* **braid**

brae 1 the (steep or sloping) bank of a river or lake or shore of the sea. **2** a bank or stretch of ground rising fairly steeply; a hillside; a road with a steep gradient. **3** the brow of a hill. **4** an upland, mountainous district: **the Braes o Balquhidder.**
   go down the brae go to ruin; *of an old person* become physically weaker.

brag, braig 1 brag. **2** challenge, defy. **3** reproach, scold.

braicham *see* **brecham**

braid, brade, broad broad.
   braid out unrestrainedly, indiscreetly.
   braid Scots the Scots language (*see* **Scots**).
   braid Scotland in the whole (breadth) of Scotland.

braid *see* **brade, breed**[1]

braig *see* **brag**

brain[1] *NE noun* a loud noise.
   verb roar, bellow.

brain[2] hurt, especially by a blow to the head, wound, beat severely.

brainge *see* **breenge**

braird *see* **breard**

braith *see* **breath**

brak, brek, break *verb, past tense also* **brak 1** break. **2** cause a change in (the weather).
   noun **1** a break. **2** ground broken up for cultivation; a division of land under

the old system of rotation of crops. **3** the breaking up of a storm, frost, ice etc; a market.

broken 1 †outlawed; ruined and living irregularly or lawlessly: *"broken men"*. **2** ruined, bankrupt. **3** *of milk* curdled, especially of cream in the churn.

brakwast breakfast.

brak a bottle open a new bottle. **brak wi a fu han:** bankrupt, fraudulent.

bramble, brammle, brummle a blackberry; its bush.

brammel, bramlin a striped worm found in old dunghills and leaf-heaps, used as bait for freshwater fish.

brammle *see* **bramble**

bran, brawn 1 brawn (as food). **2** a fleshy part of the body; the calf. **3 brawn** a boar *SW, S.*

brander, †brandreth 1 a gridiron. **2** a framework used in construction work; a trestle. **3** the iron grating over an entrance to a drain etc.

brandit, brannet of a reddish-brown colour with darker stripes or markings, brindled.

brandreth *see* **brander**

brangle *verb* **1** shake. **2** fight, squabble, quarrel.
   †*noun* 1 a lively dance. **2** a state of confusion; a tangle.

brank 1 hold oneself proudly, prance, strut. **2** dress up in finery.

branks[1] **1** a kind of bridle or halter, originally with wooden side-pieces. **2** †an instrument of public punishment, an iron bridle and gag.
   put the branks on restrain, cut (a person) down to size.

branks[2] the mumps.

brannet *see* **brandit**

brash *noun* **1** an attack. **2** an extra effort. **3** a short bout of illness. **4** a sudden gust of wind or burst of rain.
   verb **1** †break through or down; bash, batter. **2** bring up liquid into the mouth by belching.

brat 1 a (poor or ragged) garment. **2** a bib,

pinafore; a (worker's) coarse apron. **3** the thick(er) surface on a liquid, *eg* skin on porridge.

brattle *noun* **1** a loud clatter, a rattle, *eg* of horses' hooves. **2** a peal of thunder. **3** †a sharp attack; a fight, struggle. **4** a short rush; a sudden bound. **5** a sudden blast of wind and rain, a spell of bad weather.

verb clatter, clash, rattle.

brave splendid, excellent, fine.

braw, bra, brow *NE adjective* **1** fine, handsome, good-looking; well-dressed. **2** very good, excellent, fine. **3** *of sums of money etc* considerable: *"it cost a braw penny"*.

adverb **1** well, finely. **2** very.

brawly 1 very well, excellently. **2** well, in good health. **braws 1** good clothes, one's best clothes. **2** beautiful or good things.

Braw Lad, Braw Lass the young man and girl chosen annually by the people of Galashiels to represent the **burgh** at the **Braw Lads' Gathering** on 29 June.

brawlins the berries of the cowberry or cranberry.

brawn *see* **bran**

braxy a usually fatal intestinal disease of sheep.

bread *see* **breid**

break *see* **brak**

breard, breird, breid, breer, braird 1 †the top surface; the brim. **2** the first shoots of grain etc.

breast *see* **breist**

breath, braith 1 breath. **2** an opinion, a line of thought.

brebnar *see* **braboner**

brecham, braicham a collar for a draught-horse or ox.

brechan a **plaid; tartan**.

brechan, breckan *see* **brachan**

bred *see* **brod**²

bree¹ **1** liquid in which something has been steeped or boiled, stock; soup, gravy. **2** whisky. **3** juice. **4** liquid or moisture of any kind.

bree² **1** †an eyebrow. **2** the brow, the forehead.

breers 1 the eyelashes. **2** the eyebrows.

breechin *see* **britchin**

breed¹, **breid**, †**braid** breadth.

breed²: **breed of** resemble, especially in manners.

breed *see* **breid, brod**³

breeds the innards of an animal (as food).

breek, breik *noun* **breeks 1** trousers; underpants, knickers. **2** a forked stick such as is used for a catapult.

verb **1** put into trousers. **2** tuck up (a dress etc) especially for farm work.

breeklums affectionate term for a small child. **breekums 1** (very) short trousers; knee-breeches. **2** a small person; affectionate term for a little boy *NE*.

pull up one's breeks pull up one's socks.

breel move quickly and noisily.

breem¹, **brim** *especially of a sow* be in heat.

breem² broom (the plant) *NE*.

breenge, breinge, brainge *verb* **1** rush forward recklessly or carelessly; plunge; make a violent effort. **2** drive with a rush; batter, bang *now NE*.

noun a violent or clumsy rush, a dash, a plunge.

breengin pushing, sharp-tongued; bustling.

breer brier.

breer *see* **breard**

breeshle hurry.

breest *see* **breist**

breet *NE* **1** a brute. **2** a (poor etc) fellow, creature.

breether *see* **brither**

breeze *see* **broose**

breid, breed, bread 1 a loaf or roll of bread. **2** an oatcake *N*.

breid-berry small pieces of bread with hot milk poured over.

bread-and-cheese 1 = **cheese-an-breid** (*see* **cheese**¹). **2** the inside of a thistle head.

breid *see* **breed**¹, **breard**

breik *see* **breek**

breinge *see* **breenge**

breird see **breard**

breist, breest, breast noun 1 a breast. 2 straight cut downwards into peat. 3 the front part, eg of a cart.
verb spring up or forward; climb.
breist-seat the front seat in the gallery of a church NE.
in a breist abreast.

brek see **brak**

brenn see **burn²**

brent¹ spring forward.

brent² 1 of the brow smooth, unwrinkled. 2 steep, precipitous.

bress brass.

brewster see **browst**

bricht bright.

bridder see **brither**

bridie: Forfar bridie a kind of pie made of a circle of pastry folded over, with a filling of meat, onions etc.

brief, brieve law 1 an official document; a summons, legal writ. 2 †a warrant from **chancery** authorizing an inquest or inquiry by a jury.

brig a bridge.

brim see **breem**

brindle slang money, cash.

brinkie-brow, brinkie-broo used to children the forehead now NE.

brisket the breast of a person.

bristle see **birsle**

britchin, breechin a breeching, a strap round the hindquarters of a shaft horse to let it push backwards.

brither, brother, bruther, breether NE, **bridder** Shetland noun a brother.
verb admit or initiate into a trade, corporation or society.
brither-dochter a niece on one's brother's side. **brither-son** a nephew on one's brother's side.

brittle difficult, **kittle¹**.

brizz, birse, birze verb 1 bruise, crush. 2 push, press.
noun 1 a bruise. 2 pressure; struggle.

broach, brotch, brutch 1 a broach. 2 †a brooch.

broad see **braid, brod²**

broch, bruch, brugh [-ch, -gh as -ch in 'loch'] 1 a **burgh; the Broch** used as a proper name for the nearest town, now only Fraserburgh, Aberdeenshire or Burghead, Banffshire. 2 a late prehistoric structure, consisting of a large round tower with hollow stone-built walls; (not, as once supposed, built by the **Picts** (see **pecht**)). 3 a halo round the sun or the moon, the latter indicating bad weather. 4 curling a circle round the tee now NE.

brochan thick or thin gruel (with butter, honey etc); sometimes porridge.

brock¹ 1 a badger. 2 contemptuous term for a person.

brock² 1 broken or small pieces; rubbish. 2 scraps of bread, meat etc; leftovers; kitchen refuse used for feeding pigs. 3 the rakings of straw from a harvested field now NE. 4 small potatoes.

brockit, brucket having black and white stripes or spots: 1 of an animal having a white streak down its face. 2 of oats black and white growing together. 3 of persons streaked with dirt; filthy. 4 of things marked eg with soot or mud, streaky, lined.

brocky name for a cow with a **brockit** face NE.

brod¹ noun 1 something with a point, a goad, a spur. 2 a prod or prick with a goad etc. 3 a stimulus, strong influence.
verb goad, prick, pierce, jab.

brod², broad, bred 1 a board. 2 a table spread for a meal. 3 a games board, now especially a draughtboard. 4 a committee etc. 5 a (church) collection plate.

brod³, breed a brood.
brudy prolific; able or apt to breed.

broden see **browden**

brog noun a boring instrument, a goad.
verb prick, pierce.

brogue, brog originally a Highlander's shoe of untanned hide stitched with leather thongs; now a heavy shoe, especially one decorated with a distinctive pierced pattern along the seams.

broken *see* **brak**

brolach a mess; rubbish *N*.

broo¹ **1** liquid, especially that in which something has been boiled. **2** liquid or moisture of any kind.

broo² a brow.

broo³, **brow: nae broo** an unfavourable opinion: *"I've nae broo o him'*.

broo *see* **buroo**

brook¹, **bruik** *verb* make black or dirty. *noun* soot on pots, kettle etc.

brook² a kind of boil, ulcer or sore.

broon, broun brown.

broonie, brownie a good fairy, supposed to carry out household tasks in the night; *also* a goblin.

broose, brouse [-oo-], **breeze** *NE* a race at a country wedding from the church or the bride's home to the bridegroom's home.

broostle, brussel *verb* be in a great hurry, bustle. *noun* bustling *S*.

broozle bruise, crush, smash.

brose 1 a dish of oat- or pease-meal mixed with boiling water or milk, with salt and butter etc added. **2** a meal of which **brose** was the chief ingredient; one's living, livelihood.

brosie 1 covered or fed with **brose**. **2** stout (with too much food or drink). **3** coarse, clumsy.

broth¹ a thick soup made from mutton, barley and vegetables, Scotch broth.

broth² sweat profusely.

brotch *see* **broach**

brother *see* **brither**

broun *see* **broon**

brouse *see* **broose**

brow *see* **braw, broo**³

browden [-ow- as in 'cow'], **broden** *adjective:* **browden on** extremely fond of; intent on. *verb* **browden (on) (over)** fond (of), be intent (on).

brownie *see* **broon**

browst [-ow- as in 'cow'] a brewing.

browster [-ow- as in 'cow'], **brewster** a brewer.

bruch *see* **broch**

brucket *see* **brockit**

bruckle 1 easily broken, brittle; crumbling. **2** morally weak; yielding to temptation. **3** unstable, uncertain; hazardous.

brudy *see* **brod**³

brugh *see* **broch**

bruik *see* **brook**¹

brulzie [**brool**yie] turmoil, commotion, quarrel.

brummle *see* **bramble**

brussel *see* **broostle**

brust *see* **birst**

brutch *see* **broach**

bruther *see* **brither**

bubble, bibble *noun* **1** a bubble. **2** mucus from the nose. *verb* **1** bubble. **2** weep in a loud snivelling way.

bub(b)ly 1 snotty, dirty with nasal mucus. **2** tearful, snivelling. **3** *usually* **bubbly jock** a turkey cock.

sair hauden doun by the bubbly jock overwhelmed with too much to do.

buccar, bucker a fast-sailing boat used in smuggling.

Buchan *see* **hummel**

bucht *see* **boucht**²

buck¹ pour or gush out; make a gurgling noise *now NE*.

buck² **1** push, butt; fight. **2** walk to and fro.

bucker fuss, move or work aimlessly, awkwardly, yet fussily *NE*.

bucker *see* **buccar**

bucket 1 a quantity of drink: *"he can take a good bucket"*. **2** a dustbin; a wastepaper basket.

buckie¹ **1** a mollusc, usually a whelk; its shell. **2** a snail-shell. **3** something of little value: *"it's not worth a buckie"*.

buckie² a hip, the fruit of the wild rose.

buckie³ a bad-tempered obstinate person: *"Deil's buckie"*.

buckle 1 join or be joined in marriage. **2** dress.

budder *see* **bather**

buddy *see* **body**

buff[1], **bouff**, **boof** [rhymes with 'roof'] *noun* a blow (making a dull sound).
verb **1** strike, beat. **2 buff** thresh (grain) without untying the sheaf. **3 buff** *of a storm* beat down, flatten (grain) *NE*.
play buff strike (on something) making a dull sound.

buff[2] silly talk.
neither buff nor stye neither one thing nor the other; nothing at all.

buffie fat, chubby.

bugdalin [**bug**dalin] anything used to line the hold of a ship before putting the cargo in; any loose material, especially for packing, filling in.

buggar *see* **bougar**

buik, book, beuk, byeuk [bee**ook**] *noun* **1** a book. **2** a record book or register. **3** the Bible; the reading of the Bible, family worship.
verb **1** book. **2** record the names of (an engaged couple) in the register of the **session clerk** (*see* **session**) before marriage *NE*.
buik-lare learning, education.
at one's buik reading, studying. **be i the gudeman's buiks** be in favour.

buik *see* **beuk, bouk**[3]

buird, boord, byoord [bee**oord**] *NE* **1** a board. **2** a table, often one spread for a meal *now NE*. **3** a board for laying out a corpse; a bier *now NE*.

buirdly, burly, boor(d)ly 1 burly. **2** rough *now NE*.

buist[1] **1** a box or chest. **2** a small box for ointment, spices, sweets etc; a small box for documents, money etc.

buist[2] [-oo- or -ui- as in 'guid'] an identification mark on sheep.

buit[1] **boot, beet** *N* **1** a boot. **2** †**buits** an instrument of torture.

buit[2], **beet** *N*: †**na buit** no alternative or choice.
to the buit in addition, into the bargain, to boot.

bulder *see* **buller**

bulf *see* **bilf**

bull, bill a bull.
bullie a bullfinch.

bullax an axe, hatchet *N*.

buller, bulder *Shetland Orkney Caithness noun* **1** a bubble; a whirlpool; a bubbling or boiling up of water: **the Bullers of Buchan. 2** a roar, bellow *now NE*. **3** nonsense, foolish talk.
verb **1** *of water* boil or bubble up; rush noisily *now NE*. **2** roar, bellow like a bull.

bullie *see* **bull**

bullox *verb* spoil, make a mess of.
noun a mess.

bully *see* **belly**[2]

bum[1] *verb* **1** make a humming or buzzing noise. **2** make a droning sound. **3** cry, weep. **4** brag, boast. **5** go on vigorously *NE*.
noun **1** a humming or droning sound. **2** a person who reads, sings or plays badly. **3** a musical note *NE*.
bummer 1 an insect that makes a humming noise, especially a bumblebee or bluebottle. **2** a humming top. **3** a factory siren. **4** a thing or person (or animal) which is very large or wonderful of its kind. **bummin** very good, worth boasting about *NE*.
bumbee a bumblebee. **bum-clock** a humming beetle.

bum[2] **1** strike, knock. **2** throw away carelessly or noisily; send away without ceremony.

bumbazed, bombazed perplexed, confused.

bumfle, bumphle *verb* **1** puff out, bulge. **2** roll up untidily; rumple up.
noun an untidy bundle; a pucker, untidy fold, especially in cloth.
bumflie bundled up, rumpled; untidily put on.

bumfy *of a person* lumpy in shape.

bummle *verb* **1** *of a bee* hum. **2** read, play or sing badly; stutter, stammer; speak carelessly. **3** bustle about (without doing very much); blunder about.

noun **1** a wild bee. **2** a person who reads, sings or plays badly. **3** a bungle, mess.

bumps 1 *usually* **give someone his or her bumps** mark a child's birthday by thumping him or her on the back, a thump for each year of age; *compare* **dumps**. **2** very fast turns of a skipping rope.

bumphle *see* **bumfle**

bun[1] **1** a bun; in Scots now usually less sweet than in Standard English. **2** = **black bun** (*see* **black**).

bun[2] **1** †the buttocks. **2** the tail of a hare or rabbit.

bun(d) *see* **bind**

bundling a form of courtship in which the partners lie in bed together with their clothes on *Shetland Hebrides*.

bung[1] *verb* throw violently, hurl.

noun **1** the act of throwing forcibly. **2** a violent rush *NE*.

bungy huffy.

in a bung in a temper, in the sulks *NE*.

bung[2] an old worn-out horse.

bung-fu 1 completely full. **2** very drunk.

bunker, bunkart 1 a chest or box, often one used also as a seat. **2** a rough outdoor seat. **3** a large heap, *eg* of stones *NE*. **4** a small sandpit, now especially on a golf-course. **5** a storage receptacle for household coal.

bunnet *see* **bonnet**

bur the tongue or top edge of the upper of a shoe *Shetland N*.

burble a tangle; something in disorder.

burd *see* **bird**

burden, burthen, birn 1 a burden. **2** a load, an amount used as a measure. **3** **burden** *law* a restriction affecting property.

burgess oath the oath required of anyone wishing to become a burgess in the major **royal burghs** (*see* **royal**); there was bitter dispute in the 18th century between the **Burgher's** (*see* **burgh**) and **Antiburghers** as to whether or not it required the swearer to uphold the

Established Church, and thus whether or not it could be sworn with good conscience.

†**burgh, burrow, borow-** a borough, a town with special privileges conferred by charter and having a municipal corporation.

Burgher a member of that section of the **Secession Church** (*see* **secede**) which upheld the lawfulness of the **burgess oath.**

burl *see* **birl**

burly *see* **buirdly**

burn[1] **1** a brook, stream. **2** water drawn for domestic use, especially from a well or fountain; the water used in brewing.

burn[2], **birn, brenn** *verb* **1** burn. **2** be burnt suffer; be cheated or swindled in a bargain. **3** light up (water) when fishing at night to attract and spear fish.

noun a burn.

birny rough. **burny** *child's word* hot.

burn nits burn nuts at **Halloween** to foretell the marriages of the younger members of the party. **burn-the-wind** a blacksmith. **skin and birn** lock, stock and barrel.

Burns: Burns Night 25 January, the anniversary of the birth of the poet Robert Burns. **Burns Supper** a celebration meal, held annually to commemorate the birth of Robert Burns, accompanied by songs and recitations and various speeches including the **Immortal Memory** (*see* **immortal).**

buroo, broo the Labour Exchange, now the Unemployment Benefit Office; unemployment benefit received from it.

on the broo on the dole.

burie push roughly, jostle.

burrow *see* **burgh**

burr-thistle a spear thistle.

bursar a holder of a **bursary.**

bursary a scholarship or endowment given to a student in a school, university etc. **bursary competition** a competitive examination for university

bursaries held by each of the four older Scottish universities, now only Aberdeen, Dundee and Glasgow.

burst *see* **birst**

burthen *see* **burden**

bush *see* **buss**

busk *verb* **1** prepare, make ready, equip. **2** dress; deck, dress up.

buss, busk, bush 1 a bush. **2** a thicket; a clump of trees; a wood. **3** a clump of some low-growing plant, *eg* heather, rushes, fern, grass. **4** a mass of seaweed on sunken rocks.

bussom *see* **besom**

but, butt *preposition* **1** without, lacking; free from. **2** out or away from the speaker or spectator; over; across, through (a house etc).
adverb in or towards the outer part of a house etc; into the kitchen or outer room; out.
adjective **1** outer, outside; of the **but. 2** of the parlour or best room *NE*.
noun the kitchen or outer room, especially of a **but and ben.**
but and ben *adverb* **1** in (or to) both the outer and inner parts, backwards and forwards, to and fro; everywhere. **2** at opposite ends (of the same house, passage or landing). *noun* a two-roomed cottage. **but the hoose 1** the kitchen or outer end of a **but and ben. 2** the best room *NE*.

butch [-u- as in 'but'] butcher, slaughter (an animal) for meat.

butchermeat butcher's meat.

butt[1] a ridge or strip of ploughed land; an irregularly shaped ridge; a small piece of ground cut off in some way from adjacent land.

butt[2] **1** ground for archery practice. **2** *games* a line drawn on the ground to indicate the starting point. **3** *grouse-shooting* a wall or bank of earth erected to hide the guns.

butt *see* **but**

butter: buttered made with butter as an ingredient: *"buttered bannocks"*. **but-**

terie a butter biscuit; a breadroll made of a high-fat, croissant-like dough.

butter-brods, butter-clappers a pair of wooden boards for shaping butter. **butter-kit** a container for butter.

buttle *see* **bottle**

buttons, buttony a boys' game rather like marbles, but played with buttons with different names and values.

by, bye, be *preposition* **1** by. **2** in comparison with, as distinct from: *"Archie was auld by me"*. **3** except, besides: *"There's mony folk by him."* **4** *of age, quality etc* past: *"by their best"*. **5** concerning, about: *"I ken nothing worse by him"*.
adverb **1** by. **2** nearby; present: *"with everybody by"*.
conjunction **1** by the time that, as soon as: *"I was drookit be I made the school"*. **2** compared with (what); than: *"he's caulder by he was"*.

byous *adjective* wonderful, extraordinary, exceptional. *adverb* very.

by's, beis *preposition* **1** except; instead of. **2** compared with.

by-bite a snack between meals. **by-common** out of the ordinary, unusual. **bygane 1** *of (a period of) time* past; ago: *"these seven years bygane"*. **2** *of actions, things* belonging to past time; done etc in the past. **bygane** things of the past or done in the past, especially past offences or injuries. **bygaun, bygoing** passing by. **in the bygaun** in the passing, incidentally. **by-hand** finished, over and done with. **by-ordinar** *adjective* extraordinary, unusual. *adverb* extraordinarily, unusually.

by oneself out of one's mind, beside oneself. **by wi** over and done with, finished.

byaak *see* **bake**

byauve *see* **blaw**[1]

bye *see* **by**

byeuk *see* **buik**

byke[1] *noun* **1** a bees', wasps' or ants' nest; a beehive. **2** a dwelling. **3** a swarm,

especially of people.
verb, of bees swarm *now NE.*
byke² a nose.
byke³ weep, whine, sob.
bylie *see* **bailie**
byock *see* **boke**

byoord *see* **buird**[1]
byous *see* **by**
byre a cowshed.
    byreman a cattleman. **byre-woman** a woman who looks after cows.

C

ca[1], **call, caw** *verb* **1** call. **2** order (a drink). **3** call (a person) names. **4** urge on (by calling), drive (animals). **5** drive (a vehicle etc). **6** bring home (turnips etc) from the fields. **7 ca awa** be driven; drive, proceed; keep going, plod on. **8** hammer in or on. **9** knock, push. **10** set or keep in motion (*eg* a skipping rope). **11** ransack, search *NE*.

noun **1** a call. **2** a hurry *NE*. **3** a knock, blow. **4** a search. **5** the motion of the waves. **6** a turn, *eg* of a skipping rope. **be called to a church** be invited formally by a congregation to be its **minister. ca canny** go warily, act with care. **ca for someone** call on, visit. **ca someone for .. 1** abuse as being .., *mainly* **ca someone for everything** heap abuse on someone. **2** name after. **ca the girr** proceed, carry on. **ca oot** dislocate. **ca through** *verb* **1** work with a will. **2** pull through (an illness). *noun* **ca-through 1** drive, energy. **2** a disturbance. **3** *of clothes* a slight or preliminary wash. **4** a search.

ca[2] a cart road, a **loaning** (*see* **loan**[1]).

ca[3] a calf.

cab steal, pilfer *now NE*.

cabal, cabble *now NE* **1** a group met together for gossip or drinking. **2** a violent dispute.

cabbrach *adjective* lean, scraggy.

noun a big, bad-tempered, uncouth person.

cabby-labby, kebby-lebby a quarrel, wrangle; hubbub, uproar.

caber, †kebar 1 a heavy pole or spar, a long slender tree-trunk. **2** a rafter, beam. **3** a large stick or staff.

toss the caber throw the heavy pole, as in **Highland Games** (*see* **game**).

cack, kach human faeces.

cadden nail a large nail or iron pin *now NE*.

caddie[1], **cadie 1** †a military cadet. **2** †a messenger or errand-boy. **3** a ragamuffin, a rough fellow. **4** *golf* an attendant who carries a player's clubs.

caddie[2] a pet-lamb *Shetland Orkney*.

caddis 1 (cotton- or wool-)fluff, ends of thread. **2** shreds of material, rags *NE*.

cadge[1] shake, knock *NE*.

cadge[2] **1** peddle wares. **2** carry loads, parcels etc.

cadger 1 a travelling dealer, especially in fish; a carrier, a carter. **2** a bad-tempered person *NE*.

cadger's news stale news.

cadgy, kidgie *mainly NE* cheerful; friendly, hospitable.

cadie a cap.

cadie *see* **caddie**

caff, cauf, kaff, †calf chaff, often used for stuffing mattresses etc.

cag, †kag 1 a keg. **2** the stomach, belly.

cahoochy, cahoutchie rubber.

cahow [rhymes with 'moo'] a call in the game of hide-and-seek announcing the beginning of the search *NE*.

caibie a hen's crop or gizzard *NE*.

caif tame *S*.

cailleach [**kail**yach, **kall**yach] **1** an old woman. **2** the last sheaf of corn cut at harvest. **3** the harvest festival.

caip, cape a coping.

caip stane a coping-stone.

caip *see* **kep**[1]

cair 1 stir *N*. **2** scrape or rake up *N, S*. **3** prepare (threshed corn) for winnowing *N*. **4** mix together *Shetland NE*.

cair *see* **caur**

caird[1], **kyaard, †kard 1** a tinker; a tramp; rough person. **2** a person who scolds *N*.

caird[2], **card, kyard** *NE* [kee**ard**], **†kard** a card, the instrument for carding wool etc *now Sh N*.

caird³: caird through ither mix together.

caird *see* **card**

cairl *see* **carle**

cairn 1 a pyramid of loose stones, as a boundary-marker or other landmark, often now on the tops of mountains or as a memorial; a heap of stones in general. **2** a heap or quantity of something. **3 Cairn (terrier)** a type of small West Highland terrier, now a separate breed.

cairngorm a yellowish semi-precious stone.

cairry, carry *verb* **1** carry. **2** †conduct, escort, lead.

noun **1** (heavy) weight, burden. **2** a lift in a vehicle. **3** the motion of the clouds; the clouds in motion.

carried 1 carried away, elated. **2** conceited. **3** delirious.

cairry-out (a portion of) food or drink bought in a restaurant or pub to be eaten elsewhere.

cairt¹, cart cart.

kill the cairter a very strong variety of whisky. **cairtle** a cart-load *mainly NE*.

cairt², cart a playing card. **the cairts** a game of cards.

cake, kyaak *NE* [keeak] **1** a cake, often an oatcake. **2** cake, fruit loaf etc given to children or callers at New Year.

cake of breid an oatcake.

calamy calomel.

cald *see* **caul(d)**

cale *see* **kail**

calf *see* **caff, cauf¹**

call *see* **ca¹**

callan(t), calland, cullan *WCentral* **1** an associate; a youth, fellow. **2** affectionate or familiar term for an older man *NE*.

caller, cauler 1 *of fish, vegetables etc* fresh, just caught or gathered. **2** *of air, water etc* cool, fresh, refreshing. **3** healthy, vigorous.

caller oo *see* **oo³**.

callivan *see* **keelivine**

calm *see* **cam¹**

calshes boys' trousers with jacket or vest attached.

calshie surly, bad-tempered *now NE*.

calumny *see* **oath**

cam¹, calm, caum 1 †limestone. **2** pipeclay. **3** a slate pencil.

cam² the tilt or angle given to a furrow as it falls over from the ploughshare, adjusted by the setting of the coulter.

cam *see* **come**

caman the club or stick used in the game of **shinty.**

camceil, camsile a sloping ceiling or roof *WCentral*.

came *see* **kame**

cameral a haddock after spawning *NE*.

cammock a crooked staff or stick *now NE*.

camovine camomile *now NE*.

camshachle, camshauchle distorted, bent, twisted, disordered.

camsheugh [-shooch, -shuch] *now NE* **1** †crooked, distorted, deformed. **2** surly, bad-tempered, perverse.

camsile *see* **camceil**

camstairy, camsteery perverse, unruly, quarrelsome.

can¹ a chimney-pot, *often* **chimley can, lum can.**

can²: canna cannot. **cudna** could not.

noun **1** skill, knowledge, ability *mainly N*. **2** †supernatural power, witchcraft.

canally, kinallie *NE*, **canailly** [kanally, kanaylly] the canaille, the rabble; a mob, unruly crowd.

Candlemas, Canlemas 2 Feb, a Scottish quarter-day.

Candlemas ba a football match played on 2 Feb. **Candlemas bleeze** a gift made by pupils to a schoolmaster at **Candlemas** *SW, S.* †**Candlemas term** the second or spring term in the Universities of St Andrews and Glasgow.

candy: candibrod sugarcandy. **candyman** a hawker, ragman, because he gave candy in exchange for rags etc. **candy rock** candy in blocks or sticks.

cangle wrangle, dispute.

canker *noun* bad temper.

   verb **1** fret; become bad-tempered *now NE*. **2** *of plants* become infected with blight.

   canker(i)t 1 cross, ill-natured. **2** *of weather* threatening, stormy *now NE*.

Canlemas *see* **Candlemas**

canna *see* **can**²

canna(ch) cotton-grass.

cannas *now NE* **1** canvas. **2** a canvas sheet for catching grain etc.

cannel the sloping edge of an axe, chisel or plane after sharpening.

cannle a candle.

canny 1 cautious, careful, prudent, astute. **2** skilful. **3** favourable, lucky. **4** frugal, sparing. **5** gentle, quiet, steady. **6** pleasant; good, kind. **7** comfortable, easy.

   canny moment the moment of childbirth. **canny nanny** a yellow stingless bumblebee. **canny wife** a midwife.

   no canny unnatural, supernatural.

cantle¹ *now NE* **1** a corner, projection, ledge. **2** (the crown of) the head.

cantle² **1** stand or set on high. **2** stimulate, strengthen.

   cantle up 1 brighten. **2** recover one's health or spirits. **3** bristle with anger.

cantrip 1 a spell, charm; magic, *mainly* **cast cantrips**. **2** a trick, antic, piece of mischief.

canty 1 lively, cheerful; pleasant. **2** small and neat. **3** comfortable.

cap¹, **caup**, †**cop(e)** a (wooden) cup or bowl.

   drink out o a toom cappie be in want.

   kiss cap(s) drink out of the same cup or glass, usually as a sign of friendship.

cap² bend, twist, warp.

cap *see* **kep**¹

cape *see* **caip**

capercailzie, capercaillie [cap**per**kaylie] a wood-grouse.

capernoitie, capernoited [cap**per**-] capricious, crazy; drunk, giddy; irritable.

†**cappel** a horse, especially a cart- or work-horse.

cappit ill-humoured, bad-tempered.

car¹ a kind of sledge for carrying peats or hay.

car², **ker**, **caur** left (hand or side), left-handed.

   carry, corrie-fisted, carry-handed, car-handit left-handed; awkward.

car *see* **caur**

carb wrangle, quarrel.

carcage a carcase.

card, caird 1 a chart, map. **2** a photograph.

card *see* **caird**²

†**cardow** work at a trade illegally without being a freeman of the town.

†**carecake** a small cake eaten on Shrove Tuesday.

carfuffle, curfuffle *verb* put into confusion or disorder.

   noun **1** a disorder, mess. **2** a disagreement, quarrel. **3** a fuss.

car-handit *see* **car**²

cark care, anxiety *now NE*.

carl-doddie ribwort; greater plantain.

carle, kerle, cairl 1 a man, fellow; a man of the common people, a peasant or labourer. **2** male; strong, large.

   the auld carle the Devil.

carline, kerlying a (usually old) woman.

   carline spurs furze *N*.

carnaptious irritable, quarrelsome.

carrant 1 an expedition, a sudden journey. **2** a social gathering, wild party; an uproar.

carried *see* **cairry**

carritch *Presbyterian Churches* the catechism.

carry *see* **cairry, car**²

carry-handed *see* **car**²

carsackie, kerseckie [karsackie, ker**seck**ie] an overall, pinafore; a labourer's smock.

carse, kers(e) land along the banks of a river.

cart a crab-louse; **carts** the skin-disease it causes *NE*.

cart *see* **cairt**¹, **cairt**²

carvie 1 caraway. **2** a sweet containing caraway seed.

cas-chrom [*Gaelic* kas **chrowm**] a kind of foot-plough *Hebrides Highland*.

case: in a case in a state of excitement *NE*.

cassie, casey, kaisie a straw-basket or pannier *now Shetland Orkney Caithness NE*.

cassie *see* **causey**

cast, kest, kiest *NE verb, past tense also* **kiest, cuist.** *past participle also* **casten, cassin, cuisten 1** cast. **2** vomit (up) *now Fife*. **3** dig, cut (peats etc); dig, clear out (a ditch etc). **4** *of animals* give birth to. **5** *of bees* swarm. **6** *of a horse* throw (its rider). **7** toss (the head). **8** throw (off) clothes *etc.* **9** sow (seed).
noun **1** a cast. **2** a turn or twist. **3** one's lot, fortune, fate. **4** an opportunity, chance *now NE*. **5** a friendly turn; help, assistance. **6** appearance, a look.
casten *of colours* faded.
cast aboot manage, arrange, look after *now NE*. **cast something at someone** reproach someone with something. **cast the colours** perform the flag-waving ceremony at Selkirk **Common Riding** (*see* **common**). **cast oot** disagree, quarrel. **cast something up to someone** reproach someone with something.

castock a stalk of **kail** or cabbage.

casual accidental; liable to occur *now NE*.

casualty *law* an incidental item of income or revenue; that due from a tenant or **vassal** in certain contingencies.

cat^1: cattie 1 the game of tip-cat. **2** a catapult.
cat's een germander speedwell. **cat's face** a round of six scones. **cat heather** a kind of heath *NE*. **cat's lick** a hasty superficial wash. **cat('s) tail(s)** cottongrass. **cat-wittit 1** hare-brained, unbalanced. **2** spiteful; short-tempered.
cat and bat, cat and dog the game of tip-cat.

cat^2: cat and clay, claut and clay a handful of straw mixed with soft clay used in building or repairing walls.

catch *verb, past also* **catchit, caucht, cotch** catch.
noun **1** a hold, grasp. **2** a sharp pain, a stitch.
catchers a game played with a ball, or a bat and ball.
catch the salmond a boy's game *NE*. **catch-the-ten** a card game.

catechesse catechize.

catechis, cattiches 1 the catechism. **2** a catechizing; *latterly also* cross-questioning *now NE*.

†**cateran, catherane, ketharan** a Highland robber or irregular fighter; a band of these.

catterbatter a quarrel, disagreement *Fife S*.

cattiches *see* **catechis**

cattie *see* **cat^1**

cattle *noun* **1** lice etc. **2** birds and beasts in general, *now NE*. **3** term of contempt for people.
cattle beas(ts) livestock. **cattle bucht, cattle court, cattle reed** a cattle yard. **cattle creep** *see* **creep.**

caucht *see* **catch**

cauf^1, calf a calf.
cauf grund, calf kintra the place of one's birth and early life.

cauf^2 the calf (of the leg).

cauf *see* **caff**

cauk^1, cawk, kalk *NE, Perth* chalk, lime.

cauk^2 calk (a horse), fix a guard on or sharpen (a horseshoe) to prevent slipping *NE*.

cauker^1, cawker a glass of whisky.

cauker^2, cawker a stroke on the palm of the hand from a strap.

caul(d)^1 a weir or dam *mainly SW*.

caul(d)^2, cald, cowld, cold cold. **caulded** suffering from a cold. **cauldrif(e) 1** cold, causing or susceptible to cold. **2** cold in manner; indifferent *now NE Fife*.
cauld iron fishermen's word to keep away possible bad luck when one of the prohibited words has been uttered.

cauld kail het again re-heated **broth** or other food; a stale story etc. **cauld steer** sour milk or water and oatmeal stirred together *now NE*.

cauler *see* **caller**

caum *see* **cam**[1]

caup *see* **cap**[1]

caur, car, †**cair** calves *mainly NE*.

caur *see* **car**[2]

causey, cawsay, cassie 1 a paved area, a roadway, street, pavement, *latterly* mainly cobblestones. **2** the paved area around a farmhouse. **3 cassie** the cobbled part of a **byre** or stable *NE*.

causey saint a person who is well-behaved and pleasant when away from home. **causey stane** a paving- or cobblestone.

crown of the causey the middle of the road; a conspicuous, creditable, respectable or dominant position.

cavel, kavil, kevil 1 a lot cast. **2** †one's fate; chance.

cavie[1], **keavie** a hen-coop.

cavie[2] the game of prisoners' base *now Fife*.

caw *see* **ca**[1]

cawk *see* **cauk**[1]

cawker *see* **cauker**[1], **cauker**[2]

cawsay *see* **causey**

ceilidh, kailie *mainly Ulster* [kaili] *noun* **1** originally an informal social gathering among neighbours, with or without singing, playing instruments, story-telling etc, spontaneously performed by some or all of those present; a visit, chat, gossip *Highland*. **2** an organized evening entertainment (in a hall, hotel etc) of Scottish music etc, with some at least of the performers engaged in advance.

verb visit, chat.

Central Region a **region** formed from the former county of Clackmannan and parts of the former counties of Perth, Stirling and West Lothian.

certie, certis, (by) my certie to be sure.

cess a tax, especially a local tax.

chack[1], **check** *noun* **1** a check. **2** a groove or notch, a rabet. **3 check** a door-key. *verb* **1** check. **2** make a **chack 2** on (a board etc). **3 check** scold, reprove.

chack[2] *verb* **1** snap shut; bite. **2** make a clicking noise; *of the teeth* chatter *now NE*. **3** *also* **check** catch (*eg* fingers in a door), hack, chop.

noun **1** *also* **check** a cut or hack; a bruise, nip. **2** a snack.

chackart 1 a stonechat; a whinchat; a ring-ouzel. **2** term of endearment or affectionate reproof *NE*. **chackie mill** a death-watch beetle *NE*.

chack[3] check, checked fabric.

chackie a striped cotton bag used by farm servants for carrying their clothes.

chacks *see* **chuck**[2]

chaff chafe, rub, wear *NE Fife*.

chaffie a chaffinch.

chaft, *mainly* **chafts 1** jaws. **2** cheeks.

chaft blade 1 the jaw-bone. **2** the cheek-bone.

chain(y) tig *see* **tig**

chairge, charge 1 charge. **2** an expense, a cost. **3 charge** *law* an order to obey a **decree** of court.

†**chalder** a large dry measure of capacity varying for different goods, times and districts; see p 359.

challenge find fault with, reprove.

chalmer, chamer *see* **chaumer**

champ trample; crush, pound, mash.

champers, champies, champit tatties mashed potatoes.

chance: chances tips, perquisites.

not chancy 1 unfortunate, unlucky. **2** not to be relied on, dangerous.

chancellor the foreman of a jury.

change, cheenge, chynge *noun* **1** a change. **2** exchange, trade; custom, business, patronage *now NE*. **3** † = **change-house**.

verb **1** change. **2** exchange. **3** *of food* go bad, deteriorate *N*.

change-house an inn.

change one's breath have a drink.

change one's feet put on dry shoes and stockings. **change oneself** change one's clothes.

channel 1 a gutter. **2** *also* **channer** shingle, gravel.

channel stane a curling-stone.

channer *now SW,* **chunner** grumble.

channer *see* **channel**

chanter 1 the double-reeded pipe on which a bagpipe melody is played. **2** a separate pipe with a weaker reed used for learning and practising bagpipe fingering.

chanty a chamber-pot.

chap¹ a lover.

chappie a little boy.

chap², **shap** *now Shetland N noun* **1** a knock, blow. **2** a stroke of a clock or bell.

verb **1** knock, strike. **2** *dominoes or card games* tap on the table as a sign that one cannot play at one's turn. **3** tap at a door or window. **4** mash (vegetables). **5** chop. **6** choose; pick sides. **7** strike a bargain with; agree to or ratify (a bargain).

chapper 1 a beetle, a tool for pounding *NE.* **2** a door knocker.

chapper-up a person whose job is to wake people by banging on their doors. **chappit tatties** mashed potatoes. **chap hands** shake hands.

chape cheap.

be chape o get off lightly with (something).

chapper *see* **chap²**

chappie *see* **chap**¹

cha(p)pin *see* **chopin**

chappit *see* **chap²**

chaps, chips *NE* **1** pick out, choose. **2** choose (sides for a game). **chaps me** I claim, I prefer.

charge *see* **chairge**

chark *see* **chirk**

charlie a chamber-pot.

chase hurry.

chasie 1 a kind of marbles game. **2** a game of tig.

chassal *see* **cheswell**

chat¹ impudence, impertinent talk.

chat² a snack; a morsel.

chat³ a call to a pig *NE.*

chat⁴ **1** a small haddock. **2** a small potato.

chate *see* **cheat**

chattered nibbled; frayed, tattered.

chattering-bite = chitterin bit (*see* **chitter**).

chatters, shatters iron staples in a rudder-post into which the rudder is fixed.

chattit chafed, frayed *NE.*

chatty-puss a call to a cat.

chaumer, chawmer, chalmer, chamer 1 a chamber. **2** a private room, originally a bedroom, latterly also the parlour. **3** a sleeping place for farm workers.

chauve *see* **tyauve**

chaw¹ *verb* **1** *also* **chow** chew. **2** provoke, vex; make jealous.

noun **1** *also* **chow** chew. **2** a disappointment, snub; a cutting reply.

chaw² a jaw, a talk, gossip, lecture *N.*

chaw *see* **haw**¹

chawmer *see* **chaumer**

cheat, chate *NE* **1** cheat. **2 I'm cheated, it cheats me** I'm very much mistaken: *"he's a hamely chiel yon, or I'm cheated".*

cheatry cheating, deceit, fraud.

check *see* **chack**¹, **chack**²

cheek the side of anything, *eg* of a door, fireplace.

cheen, chine *now NE* chain.

cheenge *see* **change**

cheeny china.

cheep *verb* **1** whisper; make a pitiful sound. **2** squeak, creak.

noun **1 not a cheep** not a whisper, hint, word. **2** *also* **cheeper** a light kiss.

cheepin shoppie a shebeen, an illegal drinking place *ECentral.*

cheer, chyre a chair.

cheese¹ the receptacle of a thistle.

cheese-an-breid the first green shoots *eg* on hawthorn hedges.

cheese²: not say cheese not mention, keep quiet about something.

cheese *see* **chuse**

cheet, cheetie-pussy a cat; a call to a cat.

cherk *see* **chirk**

chess a window-sash, window-frame.

chessart, chesser, chisser a vat in which cheese is pressed.

cheswell, chassal, chisell = **chessart.**

cheuch *see* **teuch**

Cheviot a breed of sheep.

chice *see* **chuse**

chickenweed, chickenwort chickweed.

chief *noun* the head of a **clan** or feudal community.

adjective friendly, on close terms.

chieftain a **clan** chief; compare **chief.**

chiel(d) 1 a child. 2 *also* **child** a lad, (young) man, fellow. 3 a young woman *now Fife*.

child, chile *noun, plural* **childer** a child.

children's hearing a system set up in Scotland in 1971 to deal with children in difficulties, for example because of lack of parental care, truancy, criminal behaviour. A hearing takes place before a panel of three specially-trained lay volunteers, drawn from the **children's panel** for the area. At the hearing the panel members discuss with the child and his/her parents what the difficulties are in order to make the best decisions about the child's future.

child *see* **chiel(d)**

chile *see* **child**

chimley, chimbley, chumley 1 a chimney. 2 a grate, hearth, fireplace *now NE*.

chincough [rhymes with 'loch'] whooping cough.

chine *see* **cheen**

chingle, jingle shingle.

chinney beardie *see* **beard**

chips *see* **chaps**

chirk, chark, cherk make a harsh unpleasant noise.

chirl, churl chirp, warble, murmur.

chirle the jowls, a double chin *now Orkney*.

chirls, churls 1 kindling wood. 2 small coal.

chirm *noun* a bird's call, chirp.

verb 1 warble, murmur. 2 fret, complain.

chirple twitter *N*.

chirt squeeze, press, squirt.

chisell *see* **cheswell**

chisser *see* **chessart**

chitter 1 chatter, shiver (with cold etc). 2 *in poetry* flicker, flutter. 3 *of birds* twitter.

chitterin bit a snack eaten after swimming.

chittle nibble, gnaw *SW*.

chock choke.

choice *see* **chuse**

choke *see* **chowk¹**

chollers 1 the jowls, a double chin. 2 the gills of a fish. 3 the wattles of a cock *SW, S*.

chook *see* **chowk¹**

chookie *see* **chuck¹**

choop, jupe a hip of the wild rose *SW, S*.

chop *see* **shop**

chopin, chap(p)in *liquid measure* a **Scots** half-pint (approx = 0.85 litre) (see p 359).

chore [*cho*ray, chore] steal *ECentral, S*.

chouk *see* **chowk¹**

choup [chowp]: **not a choup** not a single word *NE*.

chow [rhymes with 'cow'] **shinty.**

chow *see* **chaw¹**

chowk¹, chouk, chook, choke: chowks the cheeks, jaws.

chowk² [-ow- as in 'cow'] choke *SW, S*.

chowl¹ [-ow- as in 'cow'] jowl.

chowl² [-ow- as in 'cow']: **chowl one's (chanler-)chafts** make a face.

chows [-ow- as in 'cow'] small coal.

chree *see* **three**

christen *see* **kirsten**

christening bit, christening piece *see* **piece**

Christmas a Christmas present, Christmas box: *"there's yer Christmas"*.

chuck¹, chuckie, chookie a chick, a chicken.

chuck², juck 1 a pebble (or occasionally a marble). 2 chucks, *also* **chacks** a game involving throwing and catching pebbles.

chuckie (stane) a small stone, a pebble.

chuck³ food.

chucken a chicken.

chuckie *see* **chuck¹**, **chuck²**

†chuffie fat(-faced), chubby, stout.

chug, chuggle *see* **tug**

chum accompany as a friend: *"I'll chum you to the shops"*.

chumley *see* **chimley**

chun a sprout, *eg* of a potato.

chunner *see* **channer**

church: church officer a paid official employed by the **kirk session** (*see* **kirk**) to carry out duties, including looking after the church and the **minister**.
Church of Scotland title of the established reformed church in Scotland, for most of its history presbyterian.

churl *see* **chirl**

churls *see* **chirls**

chuse, choice *verb, also* **cheese, chyse** *NE* choose.
noun, also **chice** a choice.

chynge *see* **change**

chyre *see* **cheer**

chyse *see* **chuse**

cimmer *see* **cummer²**

cinner, shinner *now NE*, **shunner** a cinder.

City Chambers the municipal offices of Edinburgh, Glasgow, Dundee and formerly Perth.

clabber, glabber mud, clay, mire.

clabbydhu [-doo] a kind of large mussel.

clachan a (small) village.

clack 1 a sharp sound. **2** *also* **cleck** gossip, chatter, insolence.

clackan †1 a shuttlecock. **2** a wooden bat or racquet.

claddach the gravelly bed or edge of a river.

cladding cladding boarding; lining with such.

claes, clathes, clothes clothes.
claes beetle a mallet for beating clothes when washing them. **claes pole 1** a clothes-prop. **2** a fixed pole to which the clothes-line is attached. **claes rope** a clothes-line. **claes screen** a clothes-horse.

clag, cleg *verb* smear (with mud, clay etc).
noun **1** a lump or mass of clay, mud, snow etc. **2** a quantity of any kind of soft (sticky) food.
claggum treacle toffee. **claggy** sticky; *of weather* producing heavy sticky soil.

claik¹ *noun* **1** a shrill, raucous bird-cry. **2** (a) gossip.
verb **1** *of birds* cry. **2** *of children* cry continuously and impatiently. **3** gossip, chatter.

claik² smear, dirty (with something sticky) *NE*.

claik³ 1 a barnacle. **2** †a barnacle-goose.

clair, clare 1 clear. **2** prepared, ready.

claisp *see* **clesp**

claith, cloth 1 cloth. **2** clothing.

claiver *see* **claver¹**

clam¹, clam shell a scallop (shell).

clam² sticky, damp, clammy.

clam *see* **clim**

clamant urgent, calling for redress.

clamb *see* **clim**

clamihewit 1 a blow, a thrashing. **2** an uproar, a hubbub.

clamjamfry, clanjamfrey 1 a crowd of people; rabble, riff-raff. **2** rubbish, junk.

clamp¹ patch.

clamp², clamper, clumper walk noisily or heavily, clump.

clamp³ a piece of spiked iron worn on the shoe by **curlers** (*see* **curl**) to prevent slipping.

clams, glaums a clamp; pincers; a vice.

clan a local or family group, especially in the Highlands or Borders, having a common name and united under a **chief**.

clang clung.

clanjamfray *see* **clamjamfray**

†clank a resounding blow.

clap *noun* **1** a heavy blow. **2** an affectionate pat. **3** †a clapper *eg* of a mill.
verb **1** pat affectionately. **2** press down,

flatten. **3** flop, crouch (down).

clappit having the flesh clinging to the bones; shrunken.

clap o the hass the uvula. **in a clap** in a moment.

clapperdin a gossip *NE*.

clapshot a dish of boiled potatoes and turnips mashed together *Orkney Caithness.*

clare *see* **clair**

clarsach a Highland or Irish harp.

clart, claurt, clort, klurt noun **1** mud. **2** a lump of something unpleasant. **3** a big, dirty, untidy person.
verb **1** smear, dirty. **2** act in a slovenly, dirty way; work with dirty or sticky substances.
clarty dirty, muddy; sticky.

clash noun **1** a blow, collision. **2** a mass of something soft or moist; a downpour. **3** chatter, talk, gossip. **4** a tale, story.
verb **1** strike, slap. **2** slam (a door). **3** throw forcefully or noisily (especially anything wet or liquid). **4** *often of rain* fall with a crash or splash. **5** tell tales, gossip, chatter.
adverb with a crash, bump.
clash-pyot a tell-tale.

clash-ma-clavers gossip, idle tales.

clat a lump, clot, especially of something soft.

clat *see* **claut**

clatch, clotch noun **1** a splashing sound. **2** a wet mass, clot. **3** a dirty, untidy person, a slut; a clumsy woman.
verb move with a splashing or squelching sound.

clathes *see* **claes**

clatter noun, *often* **clatters** gossip, scandal; rumours.
verb **1** gossip, talk scandal. **2** *of birds* chatter, call.

claught, claucht 1 a clutch, grasp, grab. **2** a handful.

claught *see* **cleek**

claurt *see* **clart**

claut, clat, clawt 1 a claw. **2** a clutch, hold.

3 a hoe; an implement for scraping dung, dirt etc. **4** a handful; a lump.

claut and clay *see* **cat**²

claver¹, **claiver** gossip.

claver², **clivver** clover.

claw¹, **clow** [-ow as in 'cow'] *WCentral*, noun **1** a claw. **2** a scratching, (often of the head as a sign of mild astonishment).
verb **1** claw. **2** scratch gently; scratch (the head) as a sign of astonishment etc. **3** scrape; clean out, empty. **4** beat, strike.
claw aff do (something speedily or eagerly). **not claw an auld man's heid** fail to live to a ripe old age. **claw someone's back** flatter someone, get into someone's good books. **claw someone's hide** punish, beat. **gar (ane) claw whaur it's no yeuky, gar (ane) claw without a youk** give (someone) a thrashing.

claw²: **in a claw** in a state.

clawt *see* **claut**

claymore 1 a Highlanders' large two-edged sword. **2** a basket-hilted single-edged broadsword.

clean pure, absolute, complete.
clean toun *see* **toun.**

clear: Clearances a series of mass removals of their tenants by Highland landlords in the 19th century especially in order to bring in sheep or to enlarge and improve the farms.
the clear (stuff) whisky *now NE*. **luik wi clear een** look long and earnestly *NE*.

cleathin the mould-board of a plough *NE*.

cleck 1 hatch. **2** give birth to. **3** invent; conceive.
cleckin 1 the act of hatching or giving birth. **2** a brood, litter: of animals; *contemptuously* of human beings.

cleck *see* **clack**

cleed, clethe verb, past also **cled, cleed 1** clothe. **2** cover thickly; fill.

cleek, cleik, click noun **1** a hook. **2** a salmon gaff. **3** a latch, a catch. **4** the hooked piece of iron used by children for guiding a **gird**[1] 4. **5** *mining* a hook attaching the **hutches** to the pulley, usually **stop the cleek** interrupt the output of coal.

verb, past tense also **claucht, claught** **1** seize, snatch, take for oneself. **2** lay hold of, clutch. **3** hook, catch or fasten with a hook. **4** link arms, walk arm in arm with. **5** *dancing* link arms and whirl round. **6** hook (a man).

cleekit 1 *of horses* having spring-halt. **2** crocheted.

cleek in wi associate, be intimate with.

cleesh whip *S*.

cleester, klister *verb* smear, plaster.
noun a sticky mass.

cleg, gleg a gadfly, horsefly.

cleg *see* **clag**

cleik *see* **cleek**

clem[1] *schoolboy's word* **1** mean, unprincipled. **2** curious, queer.

clem[2] stop (up) (a hole) *N*.

†**clench** *see* **clinch**

clep, clip 1 a clip. **2** *fishing* a gaff. **3** an adjustable iron handle for suspending a pot over the fire.

Clerk of Session a clerk of court in the **Court of Session** (*see* **session**).

clesh *see* **clish**

clesp, claisp clasp.

clethe *see* **cleed**

cleugh, cleuch [kleeooch] **1** a gorge, ravine. **2** a cliff, crag.

cleuk, clook [kleeook, klook], **1** a claw. **2** a hand. **3** *mainly* **cleuks** clutches.

clever, cliver, cluvver 1 clever. **2** swift, quick. **3** handsome, well-made. **4** *of persons or things* good, nice.

click *see* **cleek**

clift[1] a cliff.

clift[2] **1** a plank, board. **2** a cleft, fissure; a cave.

clim *verb, past also* **clam, clamb, climmed,** †**clum,** climb.

clinch, †**clench** limp.

cling *verb, past participle* **clung** shrink, contract; shrivel.

clink[1] *noun* **1** money, cash. **2** a blow.

verb **1** strike, slap, beat. **2** move quickly, hurry.

clink doun 1 flop, sit or fall suddenly. **2** dump, deposit. **in a clink** in a flash.

clink[2] clench, rivet.

clinkit thin, shrunken.

clint a cliff, crag, precipice.

clip 1 a colt. **2** a cheeky or mischievous child, usually a girl.

clip *see* **clep**

clipe *see* **clype**[1]

clipshear an earwig.

clish, clesh repeat gossip.

clish-clash idle talk, gossip. **clish-maclaver 1** idle talk, gossip; endless talk. **2** a talkative busybody.

clitter *see* **cloiter**

clitter-clatter 1 a rattling, clattering noise, a continuous crackle. **2** noisy, lively talk, senseless chatter.

cliv *see* **cluif**

cliver *see* **clever**

clivver *see* **claver**[2]

cloak *see* **clock**[1]

clocher, clougher [-ch-, -gh- as -ch in 'loch'] **1** bronchial mucus. **2** a rough or wheezing cough.

clock[1]**, cloak** *noun* the clucking sound made by a broody hen.
verb **1** †cluck. **2** brood, sit on, hatch (eggs). **3** sit idly for a long time.

clocker a broody hen. **clockin** the desire to brood; the desire to marry. **clocking hen 1** a broody hen. **2** a woman past the age of childbearing. **3** a woman during the time of having and rearing a family. **4** a sum of money earning interest.

clock[2]**, cloke** a beetle.

clo(c)ker a (large) beetle; a cockroach.

clock[3] cloak.

clod *noun* **1** a sod. **2** a peat. **3** a (usually wheaten) loaf.
verb **1** pelt with missiles. **2** throw. **3** free (land) from clods or stones.

clog a log or block of wood.

cloit[1]**, clyte** *noun* a sudden heavy fall.
verb **1** fall heavily or suddenly.

2 sit down suddenly.

cloit², clyte, gloit a dull, heavy person.

cloiter, clyter, clitter 1 do dirty, wet work. **2** work in a dirty, disgusting way, especially in liquids.

cloke *see* **clock²**

cloker *see* **clock²**

clomph walk heavily.

clood *see* **clud**

cloof *see* **cluif**

clook *see* **cleuk**

cloor *see* **clour**

cloose, clouss, cluse a sluice.

cloot¹, clout [-oo-] *noun* **1** a patch. **2** a piece of cloth, a rag, often a dishcloth, duster. **3** a baby's nappy. **4** *mainly* **cloots,** *often contemptuous* clothes. **5** *Royal Company of Archers* (*see* **royal**) (a hit on) a target.
verb patch, mend (clothes); repair (pans, footwear etc) with a metal plate.
clootie made of cloths or rags: *"clooty rug"*. **clootie dumpling** a **dumpling** wrapped in a cloth and boiled.
a tongue that wad clip cloots a sharp tongue.

cloot², clout *noun* a blow.
verb strike, slap.

cloot³, clute, cluit *noun* **1** one of the divisions in the hoof of cloven-footed animals; the whole hoof. **2 auld Cloot(s),** **(auld) Clootie** the Devil.

clorach *NE* **1** work in a slovenly way. **2** clear the throat noisily. **3** sit lazily by the fire as if ill.

clort *see* **clart**

close¹ *of work etc* constant, relentless.
verb be stuffed up, have difficulty breathing because of asthma, bronchitis etc.
close bed an enclosed bed, a **box-bed** (*see* **box**).

close², closse 1 an enclosure, courtyard. **2** a farmyard. **3** an **entry,** passageway, alley. **4** the **entry** to a **tenement,** the passageway giving access to the **common stair** (*see* **common**).

close mou the entrance to a **close²** 3 and 4.
it's a' up a closie (*wi*) it is a hopeless position, it is a poor outlook (for). **in the wrang close** in a really tight spot, badly mistaken.

closhach, clossach *NE* **1** the carcass of a fowl. **2** a mass of something, especially semi-liquid. **3** a hoard of money.

closse *see* **close²**

clotch *see* **clatch**

cloth *see* **claith**

clothes *see* **claes**

clotterd clotted, congealed, caked.

clougher *see* **clocher**

clour [-oo-], **cloor** *noun* **1** a blow. **2** a lump, swelling caused by a blow. **3** a hollow, dent, especially in metal.
verb **1** batter, thump; damage, disfigure. **2** dent. **3** dress or chisel (stone).

clouss *see* **cloose**

clout *see* **cloot¹, cloot²**

clow [rhymes with 'cow'] **1** a clove, the spice. **2** †*also* **clow gillie flower** a clove pink.

clow *see* **claw¹**

clud, clood cloud.

cludder *see* **cluther**

cludgie *slang* a lavatory.

cluif, cloof, cliv *Shetland Orkney Caithness* a hoof, originally cloven.

cluit *see* **cloot³**

clum *see* **clim**

clumper *see* **clamp²**

clung *see* **cling**

clunk, glunk *Orkney Caithness* **1** a hollow, gurgling sound made by liquid in motion. **2** a plopping or popping sound.

clunkart a very large piece or lump of something.

cluse *see* **cloose**

clute *see* **cloot³**

cluther, cludder a close group; a disordered crowd.

cluvver *see* **clever**

clyack *NE* **1** the last sheaf of corn of the harvest dressed as a girl or decorated with ribbons. **2** the end of harvest. **3** the harvest-home supper.

Clyde: I didna come up the Clyde on a banana boat I'm no fool.

clype[1], **clipe** *verb* **1** be talkative, gossip. **2** *also* **clype on** tell tales, inform against someone. **3** report, tell.
noun **1** a (piece of) gossip, a lie. **2** a tell-tale.

clype[2] **1** a large messy mass. **2** a big, awkward or ugly person.

clype[3] a heavy, noisy fall; a blow.

clyre 1 a source of grievance. **2 clyres** a disease in cattle.

clytach incomprehensible talk, originally in a foreign language, especially Gaelic, senseless chatter.

clyte strike, rap (one's knuckles) against a hard object.

clyte *see* **cloit**[1], **cloit**[2]

clyter *see* **cloiter**

co *see* **quo**

coachbell, scodgebell, switchbell an earwig.

coag *see* **cog**[1]

coal, coll coal.
coalie-back, colly buckie a pickaback ride.
coal coom coal dust. †**coal hood** any of several species of black-headed birds.

coarse *see* **coorse**[1]

coarum *see* **quorum**

coat, cot, cwite *NE*, **quite** *NE* **1** a coat. **2** *mainly* **coats** a petticoat; a skirt.
on ane's ain coat tail(s) forced to make or pay one's own way; independent(ly). **gae coats kilted** be pregnant.

cob beat, strike.

cobble *see* **coble**[2], **coble**[3]

coble[1], **cowble** rock.

coble[2], **cobble, cowble** a short flat-bottomed rowing-boat, used especially in salmon-fishing.

coble[3], **cobble** a pond, a watering place *NE*.

cock[1]: **cockie leekie, cock-a-leekie** chicken and leek soup.
cock's eggs the small yolkless eggs laid by a hen about to stop laying. **cock laft** the gallery in a church. **cock laird** a small landowner who farms his own estate *now NE*. **cock paddle** a lumpfish. **cocks and hens** name for the buds, stems or seeds of various plants, and of games played with them.

cock[2] raise (a fist) threateningly.
cockit bonnet a boat-shaped cap of thick cloth, with the points at the front and back. **cock one's wee finger** drink, tipple.

cocker rock, totter, walk unsteadily.

†**cockernony 1** a women's hairstyle in which the hair is gathered up on top of the head. **2** a woman's cap with starched crown.

cockie leekie *see* **cock**[1]

cockieleerie 1 the crowing of a cock. **2** the cock itself.

cockle totter, be unsteady.

cod[1] a cushion, pillow.

cod[2] a pod or husk (of peas, beans).

coff buy.

coffee: gie (someone) his coffee scold, thrash.

coft bought, purchased.

cog[1], **cogue, coag** a wooden container made of staves, a pail or bowl.

cog[2] a wedge or support.

coggle, cogle, kugl [-u- as in 'but'] rock, totter, shake.
coggly unsteady, easily overturned.

cognition *law* authoritative or judicial knowledge or the acquisition of this by inquiry or investigation, cognizance; a process to ascertain certain facts, *eg* to prove a person insane.

cogue *see* **cog**[1]

coil *see* **quile**

coin *see* **quine**

coit *see* **quoit**

cold *see* **caul(d)**[2]

cole, coll a haycock.

cole *see* **coll**

colf fill in, stop up.

coll, cole cut; taper; shape; trim.

coll *see* **coal, cole**

collate *law* pool (inheritances) as in next.

collation *law* the pooling of inheritances with a view to their equitable distribution amongst their heirs.

colleague [col**league**] associate, be friendly with (for purposes of crime or mischief), plot.

college: the college a university: *"she's at the college now"*.

College of Justice name for the body of judges (**Lords of Council and Session** (*see* **lord**)) and others composing the **Court of Session** (*see* **session**).

collie a sheepdog, usually black (and white).

collieshangie, killieshangie, cullieshangie **1** a noisy quarrel, uproar. **2** a dog-fight.

collogue [col**logue**] *noun* **1** a whispered conversation, private interview. **2** a discussion; a conference.
verb **1** talk together, chat. **2** be in league, have an understanding with, scheme.

collop a (thin) slice of meat.

colly buckie *see* **coal**

comb *see* **kame**

come, cum *verb, past also* **cam** come.
come away **1** *of seeds, plants* germinate, grow rapidly. **2** *usually in commands* come along. **come back on a person** *of food* repeat. **come hame** be born *NE*. **come in** collapse. **come in by** come in, draw near. **come o** become of (one), happen to. **come on** **1** *usually command* come along. **2** *exclamation* I don't believe a word of it! **3** be about (to do something). **come ower** **1** *usually of misfortune* happen to (a person). **2** repeat, make mention of. **come tae** **1** calm down. **2** become reconciled; comply. **3** come near *NE*. **come the time** *eg* **five years come the time** five years old on one's next birthday; five years on the anniversary (of an event). **come to the door** *of a knock* sound on the door. **come through** recover from an illness.

come your ways come along. **a week** *etc* **come Monday** a week etc on Monday.

commissary clerk the **sheriff clerk** (*see* **sheriff**) when acting in relation to confirmation of executors.

commissioner a member of the **General Assembly** of any of the Scottish Presbyterian Churches. *See also* **Lord High Commissioner** (*under* **lord**).

Commissioner *see* **teind**

common: common debtor when A owes money to B which B recovers by taking from C a sum owed by C to A, A is known as the common debtor.

Common Riding name for the **Riding of the Marches** (*see* **ride**) in certain towns, *eg* Selkirk, Hawick. **common stair** *in a* tenement the communal staircase giving access to the flats etc.

compear appear before a court or other authority.

compleen, complain **1** complain. **2** be ailing, unwell.

complainer *law* a plaintiff, *latterly* a victim of a crime who has reported it to the authorities.

compluther, complouter, complowther, comploiter **1** agree, fit in (with). **2** mix with.

conceit, consait, concait *NE* **1** conceit. **2** an idea, opinion, notion. **3** a good opinion of (oneself etc): *"hae a guid conceit o yersel"*. **4** interest, concern. **5** a fancy article, a quaint or dainty object or person.

conceity **1** conceited, vain. **2** witty, apt. **3** neat, dainty.

condescend: condescend on enter into particulars about; specify, detail.

condescendence a specification, statement of particulars, often of legal statements of fact.

condie *see* **cundy**

confeesed confused.

confirmation *law* a process whereby executors are judicially recognized or confirmed in their office and receive a title to the property of a deceased person.

confusion *law* a mixture of liquids; a way of extinguishing a debt, right or claim where either party acquires the title of the other by inheritance or otherwise.

conjoin *law* order a joint trial of (two processes involving the same subject and the same parties).

conjunct *law* possessed or shared in jointly.

†**conjunctly and severally** *law* where each of the persons named is singly liable etc for the whole of the obligation, jointly and severally.

conjunct and confident persons *law* persons related by blood and connected by interest, *eg* in a bankruptcy case where recent transfer of property is challengeable.

connach waste; spoil; consume.

consait *see* **conceit**

consistorial *law* of actions between spouses involving status (*eg* for divorce, separation).

consumpt consumption, amount consumed.

conteen contain.

conteena, continue 1 continue. **2** *law* adjourn, put off (a case etc).

content [content] a drink of hot water, milk and sugar.

conter *preposition* against.
adjective opposite.
verb oppose, contradict, thwart.

contermacious, contramashious perverse, self-willed, obstinate.

continue *see* **conteena**

contrair *adjective, adverb, noun* contrary.
verb go contrary to, oppose, contradict.

convener 1 a person who convenes a meeting. **2** the chairman of a committee, *eg* a local council.

convention: †**Convention of Royal Burghs** a body formed by a meeting of representatives of the **Royal Burghs** (*see* **royal**), dealing mainly with taxation and trade. **Convention of Scottish Local**

Authorities (COSLA) *since 1975* a body formed from representatives of Regional and District Councils (*see* **region** and **district**).

conversation (sweet), conversation (lozenge) a flat sweet of varying shape with a motto on it.

convoy [convoy] *verb* **1** convey. **2** escort, accompany, conduct. **3** carry, transport (goods etc).
noun the escorting or accompanying of a person on his way; company; *see also* **Scotch Convoy** (*under* **Scots**).

a Scots convoy accompanying a person on his journey home some of the way, or all the way and being accompanied in return some of the way back.

coo, cow *noun, plural* **kye, coos** a cow.

coo *see* **cow**[1]

cooard, coord coward.
cooard(l)y cowardly. **cooardy lick** a blow given as a challenge to fight.

cood[1]**, quid** *NE,* **cweed** *NE* cud.

cood[2]**, quid** *NE,* **cweed** *NE* **1** a shallow tub, a wooden dish or basin, especially for milk. **2** a large tub for washing, storage, carrying.

coof, cuif 1 a fool. **2** a useless person. **3** a lout. **4** a coward.

cook, koog disappear suddenly from view; dart in and out of sight.

cook *see* **cuik**

cookie 1 a plain bun. **2** a prostitute.
cookie shine a tea party.

cool, cowl a (usually woollen) close-fitting cap.

coom[1] *noun* soot; coal-dust; **dross**; peat-dust; fine turf mould.
verb dirty, blacken, stain.

coom[2] the sloping part of an attic ceiling.
coomed vaulted, arched; *of a ceiling* sloping.
coomceil, coomsyle *verb* lath and plaster (a ceiling). *noun* a sloping ceiling or roof. **coomceiled** having a sloping ceiling.

coonjer *see* **counger**

coont, count *verb* **1** count. **2** do arithmetic.

3 settle accounts with.

noun **1** a count. **2 coonts** arithmetic, sums.

coont kin wi compare one's pedigree with that of, claim relationship with.

coonter-lowper a shop-assistant.

coop a small heap.

coop *see* **coup**[1]

coop-cairt *see* **coup-cairt**

coor, curr 1 cower. **2** bend, lower, fold.

coorie 1 stoop, bend, crouch down; cringe. **2** snuggle, nestle.

coord *see* **cooard**

coorgy a blow or push given as a challenge to fight.

coorse[1]**, coarse 1** coarse. **2** *of weather* foul, stormy. **3** *of persons* wicked, bad, naughty; rough, awkward, over-direct in manner(s). **4** hard, trying; disagreeable *NE*.

coorse[2]**, course** a course.

in coorse 1 of course. **2** in due course.

coort *see* **court**

coos *see* **coo**

cooser, cuisser a stallion.

cooshie-doo *see* **cushat**

coot, queet a guillemot *NE*.

coot *see* **cuit**

cooter, couter 1 a coulter. **2** a nose.

cooter *see* **cuiter**

coothie *see* **couthie**

cootie *of fowls* having feathered legs.

cop(e) *see* **cap**[1]

copy a copy-book.

corbie 1 a raven. **2** a rook. **3** a carrion crow; a hooded crow.

corbie messenger a slow or unfaithful messenger. **corbie stanes = crawsteps** (*see* **craw**[1]).

be a gone corbie be a goner, be done for.

cord one of the ropes (held by close relatives and friends of the deceased) by which a coffin is lowered into a grave.

cordiner a shoemaker.

core 1 a team of **curlers** (*see* **curl**). **2** a (convivial) party or company.

cork an overseer, master, employer; a person in authority.

corky a feather-brained person.

corn 1 oats. **2** a single grain.

verb **1** feed (a horse or poultry) with oats or grain. **2** *of people or poultry,* take food etc *NE*.

corned exhilarated with drink. **cornin time** meal-time.

corn kist a storage-bin for corn. **corn kister** a type of song sung at farmworkers' gatherings. **corn yaird** a stackyard.

coronach, †cronach a funeral lament; a dirge.

corp 1 a corpse. **2** the deceased.

corp candle a will-o'-the-wisp.

corrie a hollow on the side of a mountain or between mountains.

corrie-fisted *see* **car**[2]

corrieneuchin [-ch- as in 'dreich'] conversing intimately.

corruption temper, anger.

cors *see* **cross**[1]

cose, coss exchange; barter *now Shetland Orkney*.

cosh snug, comfortable; friendly, intimate.

cosie 1 *of people* warm and comfortable, well wrapped-up. **2** *of places* sheltered, providing comfort and protection.

COSLA *see* **convention**

coss *see* **cose**

cost payment in kind for rent, dues or wages.

cot: cottar a tenant occupying a cottage with or without land attached to it; a married farmworker who has a cottage as part of his contract.

cot-folk those who live in farm cottages. **cot house** a (farmworker's) cottage.

cot *see* **coat**

cotch *see* **catch**

couk *see* **cowk**

counger [-oo-], **coonjer, cunjer 1** keep in order, scold. **2** overawe, threaten.

count *see* **coont**

countra, kintra, country, cwintry *N,* **quin-**

tra N **1** country. **2** a district; its inhabitants; the territory of a **clan.**

country clash the gossip of the district.

countra Jock a farmworker.

coup¹, cowp, coop *Shetland Orkney noun* **1** an upset, overturning; a fall. **2** a rubbish tip.

verb **1** upset, overturn; lay low, ruin. **2** tilt up; empty by upturning. **3** swallow, drink (quickly). **4** over-balance, fall over, capsize; go bankrupt. **5** bend, heel over.

coupy a sheep that has turned over on its back and is unable to get up *S*.

coup the creels 1 turn a somersault, fall head over heels. **2** upset the plans or get the better of *NE*. **coup the laidle** play seesaw.

coup², cowp buy, trade (goods, horses); barter, exchange.

couper 1 a trader, dealer. **2** a horse-dealer.

coup-cairt, cowp-cairt, coop-cairt 1 a closed cart. **2** a tipping cart.

couple, cupple, kipple 1 a couple. **2** a pair of rafters, forming a V-shaped roof support; one of these, a principal rafter.

cour *see* **cower**

course *see* **coorse²**

court, coort 1 a court. **2** a (covered) enclosure for cattle.

Court of Session *see* **session.**

cout *see* **cowt**

couter *see* **cooter**

couter *see* **cuiter**

couther *see* **cuiter**

couthie, coothie *adjective* **1** agreeable, sociable, friendly, sympathetic. **2** *of places or things* comfortable, snug, neat; agreeable.

covenant: the Covenant the National Covenant (1638) or the Solemn League and Covenant (1643).

Covenanter a supporter of either of these.

cover, kiver 1 cover. **2** the maximum livestock a farm will carry.

cow¹, kow, coo 1 a twig or branch; a tufted stem of heather. **2** a broom, especially one used in curling.

cow², kow *verb* **1** poll, crop; cut (hair). **2** cut, cut short. **3** do better than, outdo. *noun* a haircut.

cow a', cow a'thing, cow the cuddy *etc* be better than everything.

cow³, kow a hobgoblin; a frightening creature.

cow⁴ scold, criticise.

cow *see* **coo**

cowan 1 a builder of **dry-stane dykes** (*see* **dry**); a builder, especially an untrained one. **2** an unskilled or uninitiated person; an amateur.

cowble *see* **coble¹, coble²**

cowda *see* **cuddoch**

cower, cour recover, get well from.

cowk, couk [-ow- as in 'cow'] retch.

cowl *see* **cool**

cowld *see* **caul(d)**

cowlie [-ow- as in 'cow'] **1** contemptuous term for a man. **2** a boy *Edinburgh*.

cowp *see* **coup¹, coup²**

cowp-cairt *see* **coup-cairt**

cowshus [-ow- as in 'cow'] cautious.

cowsy [-ow- as in 'cow'] *mining* a self-acting slope on which full descending **hutches** pull up empties.

cowt, cout [rhymes with 'lout'] **1** a colt. **2** a rough, awkward person. **3** an adolescent.

cra *see* **craw¹, craw²**

crabbit in a bad temper, cross; bad-tempered.

crack *verb* **1** boast, brag. **2** talk, gossip.

noun **1** *mainly* **cracks** loud boasts or brags. **2** a talk, gossip, conversation; a story, tale. **3** an entertaining talker, a gossip. **4** a moment, a short space of time, *eg* **in a crack. 5** a 'go', a **shot** in a game etc.

cracker 1 a boaster. **2** a talker, gossip. **3 crackers** pieces of bone or wood used as castanets. **4** the lash of a whip.

crack like a (pen-)gun *etc* talk in a lively way, chatter loudly. **gie's yer crack(s)**

give us your news.

crackins, cracklings 1 the residue from a melting process, *eg* fat. **2** a dish of fried oatmeal.

craft *see* **croft**

craig[1], **crag 1** a crag, rock; cliff. **2** a projecting spur of rock.

craig[2], **crag 1** the neck. **2** the throat, gullet.

   craiged, craigit -necked, *eg:* **(lang-) craiged heron** a heron *NE*.

craighle, creachle, crechle [-ch-, -gh- as -ch in 'dreich'] cough drily or huskily; wheeze.

craik *verb* **1** *of birds* utter a harsh cry, croak. **2** *of things* creak. **3** ask persistently, clamour. **4** grumble, complain.

   noun **1** the harsh cry of a bird, especially a corncrake. **2** a corncrake.

craise *see* **craze**

craive *see* **cruive**

cramasie crimson.

crame, creame a merchant's booth, stall.

crampet 1 a roof-gutter bracket, a support *NE*. **2** *especially curling* a spike fixed to the shoe; the iron foot-board from which a player throws his stone.

cran[1], **crane 1** a crane (the bird). **2** a heron. **3** a swift.

cran[2] a crane (the machine).

†**cran**[3] *measure of fresh, uncleaned herrings* one barrel, latterly fixed at 37.5 gallons (170.48 litres).

cran[4] a tap.

cranachan a dish made by mixing toasted oatmeal into whipped cream, sometimes adding fruit or other flavouring.

crane a cranberry.

crane *see* **cran**[1]

crank[1] a harsh noise.

crank[2] difficult.

   crankie unsteady, insecure, unreliable.

crannie the little finger *N*.

crannog an ancient lake dwelling.

cranreuch [**kran**rooch] hoar-frost.

crap *see* **creep, crop**

crappit *see* **crop**

crasie, crazy a sunbonnet.

crave 1 *law* ask for as of right; demand or claim as properly or legally one's due. **2** press for payment of a debt.

craw[1], **cra, crow** a crow, the bird; a rook.

   crawberry a crowberry; a cranberry. **craw bogle** a scarecrow. **crawcrooks 1** †crowberries. **2** cranberries. **crawstep** step-like projections up the sloping edge of a gable. **craw-taes 1** crow's feet, wrinkles at the corner of the eye. **2** creeping crowfoot; bird's-foot trefoil; the English bluebell, wild hyacinth. **craw's weddin** *etc* a large assembly of crows.

   sit like craws in the mist sit in the dark.

craw[2], **cra** a crow, a crowing of a cock etc.

cray *see* **crue**

craze, craise weaken, *eg* by injury.

crazy *see* **crasie**

creachle *see* **craighle**

cream of the well the first water drawn from a well on New Year's morning.

creame *see* **crame**

crechle *see* **craighle**

creek: creek o day break of day, dawn *now NE*.

creel 1 a deep basket for carrying peats, fish etc. **2** a fish-trap, lobster-pot.

   in a creel in confusion or perplexity; mad.

creen *see* **croon**[2]

creep *verb, past tense also* **creepit, crap,** *past participle also* **cruppin** creep.

   creepie *noun* a low stool; a footstool. **cruppen doun** shrunk or bent with age. **cattle creep** a passage for animals under a railway. **cauld creep(s)** gooseflesh, the creeps. **creep afore ye gang** *proverb* walk before you run. **creep in 1** *of daylight hours* shorten. **2** grow smaller, shrink. **creep out** *of hours of darkness* lengthen. **creep ower** swarm, be infested (with vermin). **creep thegither** shrink, huddle up with cold or age.

creesh, creish *noun* fat, grease, tallow.

verb **1** grease; oil; lubricate. **2** beat, thrash.

creeshie greasy; fat; dirty.

creesh someone's loof pay, tip, bribe someone.

creest, creist *noun* **1** †a crest. **2** a self-important or officious person.
verb brag, boast; put on airs.

creish *see* **creesh**

crib[1] a hen-coop.

crib[2] a curb, kerb.

criffins, crivvens *exclamation of astonishment* goodness!

crile, cryll, croyll a dwarf, a small or deformed creature.

crine shrink, shrivel.

cripple *adjective* lame.
verb walk lamely, hobble.

crit *see* **croot**

crive *see* **cruive**

crivvens *see* **criffins**

crochle *NE verb* limp.
noun **crochles** a cattle disease causing lameness.

crochle *see* **croichle**

crock[1] an old ewe.

crock[2] an earthenware container for foodstuffs, *eg* milk, salt, butter.
crockanition smithereens.

croft, craft *now mainly NE noun* a croft; a smallholding.
crofter a person who occupies a smallholding.

croichle, crochle a cough.

crommack *see* **crummock**

crommie, crummie a cow with crooked horns, often used as name for a pet cow.

cronach *see* **coronach**

croo *see* **crue**

crood, croud, croodle †*of doves etc* coo.
croodlin doo 1 a wood-pigeon *now NE.* **2** term of endearment.

crood *see* **crud**

croodle, crowdle *Fife verb* cower; nestle.

croodle *see* **crood**

crook *see* **cruik**

croon[1]**, croun** a crown.

Crown Agent *law* the chief Crown solicitor in criminal matters.

croon[2]**, crune, creen** *NE verb* **1** bellow, roar. **2** lament, mourn; wail. **3** sing in a low tone; mutter, hum.
noun **1** †a bellow. **2** a wail, lament, mournful song.
crooner a gurnard.

croop *see* **croup**

croose *see* **crouse**

croot, crute, crit a small puny child or young animal.

croove *see* **cruive**

croozie *see* **cruisie**

crop, crap 1 a crop. **2** the top of a tree or plant. **3** the stomach.
crappit heids stuffed haddocks' heads. **crop and root** completely, root and branch *NE.* **crap o the wa** the space between the top of a wall and the roof of a building. **craw in someone's crap** irritate, annoy; henpeck; give cause for regret. **have a crop for all corn** be greedy; have a capacity for absolutely anything.

cross[1]**, cors 1** a cross. **2** a market cross; a market-place.
cross-fit a starfish.

cross[2] across.

crottle, crotal a dye-producing lichen.

croud *see* **crood**

croun *see* **croon**[1]

croup, croop, crowp 1 *of birds, especially crows* croak, caw. **2** speak hoarsely. **3** grumble.

crouse [-oo-]**, croose 1** bold, courageous, spirited. **2** confident, self-satisfied; cheerful. **3** conceited, arrogant, proud. **4** cosy, comfortable.
craw crouse boast, talk loudly and confidently.

crow *see* **craw**[1]

crowdie[1] oatmeal and water mixed and eaten raw.
cream crowdie = cranachan.

crowdie[2] a kind of soft cheese.

crowdle *see* **croodle**

crowl[1] crawl.

crowl² contemptuous term for a dwarf, a very small person.

crowp *see* **croup**

croy *see* **crue**

croyll *see* **crile**

crub curb.

crud, crood *noun, mainly* **cruds** curds. **crudle** curdle.

crue, croy, croo, cray, kro *Shetland Orkney* an animal pen or fold, *eg a* pigsty.

cruels scrofula, the king's evil.

cruik, cruke, crook 1 a crook. **2** a hook. **cruikit 1** crooked. **2** lame.

as black as a cruik very black, dirty. **cruik one's elbow** drink (alcohol), especially rather freely. **cruik one's mou** move the mouth so as to speak or whistle. **a cruik in the lot** a misfortune, difficulty. **not to cruik a finger** not to make the least effort.

cruisie, croozie an open, boat-shaped lamp with a rush wick; a candleholder.

cruive, croove, crive, craive 1 a fish-trap in a river or estuary. **2** a pen, fold, *eg* a pigsty, a hen-coop.

cruke *see* **cruik**

crulge cower, crouch.

crum, crumb 1 a crumb. **2** a very small piece of something.

crummie *see* **crommie**

crummock, crommack a stick with a crooked head, a shepherd's crook.

crump *verb* **1** crunch, munch. **2** crackle. *adjective, also* **crumpie, crumshy** *NE, especially of ice* crisp, brittle.

crune *see* **croon²**

crunkle, grunkle *NE* crinkle, wrinkle, crackle.

crunt a heavy blow *SW*.

cruppen, cruppin *see* **creep**

crute *see* **croot**

cry *verb* **1** call on (a person) for help etc. **2** summon. **3** call, give a name to. **4 be cried** have one's marriage banns proclaimed. **5** be in labour. *noun* **1** a call, summons. **2 cries** the proclamation of banns: *"pit in the cries"*. **3** the distance a call can carry. **4** a short visit (in passing), *usually* **gie** (someone) **a cry** (**in**). **crying** labour; a confinement, birth *now NE*. **like a cried fair** in a state of bustle. **cry** (**a**) **barley** *see* **barley. cry at the cross** make public. **cry in** (**by**) call in, visit. **cry names** call (someone) names. **cry upon, cry up to** call in upon, visit.

cryll *see* **crile**

CSYS *see* **Scots**

cuddie *see* **cuddy¹, cuddy²**

cuddin *see* **cuddy²**

cuddle 1 squat, sit close. **2 cuddle up tae** approach so as to coax or wheedle. **3** throw or place a marble close to the target.

cuddoch, cowda a young cow.

cuddy¹, cuddie 1 a donkey. **2** a horse. **3** a joiner's trestle. **4** a gymnasium horse. **5** *mining* a loaded bogie used to counterbalance the **hutch** on a **cuddy-brae**. **cuddy-brae** an inclined roadway with a **cuddy 5** on it. **cuddy heel** an iron heel on a boot or shoe. **cuddy-lowp(-the-dyke)** the game of leapfrog.

cuddy², cuddie, cuddin a young coalfish.

cude, cuid hare-brained *S*.

cudna *see* **can²**

cuff¹: cuff o the neck the nape or scruff of the neck.

cuff² 1 winnow for the first time. **2** remove a layer of soil with a rake from (a piece of ground) before sowing, replacing it afterwards.

cuid *see* **cude**

cuif *see* **coof**

cuik, kyeuk [keeook], **cook 1** cook. **2** cook coax.

cuil, cule, queel *NE* cool.

cuisser *see* **cooser**

cuist, cuisten *see* **cast**

cuit, cute, queet *NE,* †**coot** an ankle.

cuiter, couter, cooter, couther 1 nurse, pamper, look after carefully.

2 coax, wheedle.

cuithe, queeth *NE* a young coalfish.

cuittle, †cuttle 1 †whisper. **2** coax, flatter. **3** †cuddle, caress *SW*.

cuittle *see* **kittle**[1]

cule *see* **cuil**

cullan *see* **callan**

Cullen skink a smoked-fish soup.

cullie *see* **culyie**

cullieshangie *see* **collieshangie**

culpable homicide *law* a killing caused by fault which falls short of murder, corresponding to English manslaughter.

culyie, cullie 1 fondle. **2** cherish. **3** coax, entice.

cum *see* **come**

†cummer[1]**, cumber** trouble, distress; difficulty; a hindrance or encumbrance.

cummer[2]**, cimmer, kimmer 1** a godmother. **2** *also* **gimmer** a female friend; a gossip. **3** a midwife. **4** a girl, lass.

cundy, condie 1 a covered drain, the entrance to a drain. **2** a tunnel, passage.

†cuningar a rabbit-warren.

cunjer *see* **counger**

cunning, kinnen, kjunning *Shetland* [kee**unn**ing] a rabbit.

cunyie, cunzie, quin(z)ie [**kun**yie] a coin; *building* a quoin.

Cupar: he that will to Cupar maun to Cupar a stubborn person will have his way.

cupple *see* **couple**

curator [**cur**ator] *law* a person either entitled by law or appointed by the Court or by an individual to manage the affairs of a legally incapable person, *eg* a **minor.**

curch a kerchief, a woman's cap.

curchie curtsy.

curcuddie [cur**cud**die]: **dance curcuddie** perform a crouching dance.

curcuddoch [cur**cud**doch] sitting close together or side by side.

curdie a very small coin.

curdoo, curdow coo (as a pigeon); make love.

curfuffle *see* **carfuffle**

curl play at **curling.**

curler a person who plays at **curling.** **curling** a game played by sliding heavy stones on ice. **curling-stone** the smooth rounded stone, now usually of polished granite, used in **curling.**

curl-doddy name for various plants with a rounded flower-head, *eg* devilsbit scabious, ribwort plantain, clover.

curly green(s), curly kail curly colewort.

curmur [kur**mur**] make a low rumbling or murmuring sound; purr.

curn[1] **1** †a single grain of corn. **2** a grain or particle. **3** a (small) number or quantity; a few.

curn[2] a currant.

curr *see* **coor**

curpin 1 a horse's crupper, the strap. **2** the behind or rump.

curple a crupper *SW*.

†currach, curragh a coracle.

curran a currant.
 curran bun = **black bun** (*see* **black**).

currie a small stool.

currieboram, curriebuction a confused, noisy or frightened crowd *NE*.

currie-wurrie a violent dispute.

cushat, cushie, cushie-doo, cooshie-doo term of endearment.

cusing *see* **kizzen**

cut *verb, past tense also* **cuttit** cut.
 noun **1** a measure of linen or woollen yarn (see p 360). **2** temper, (bad) humour: *"he's in bad cut"*. **3** a group of sheep divided from the rest.
 cutting *piping* (the playing of) a single very brief grace-note. **cutting loaf** bread old enough to be easily cut. **cuttit 1** cut. **2** curt, abrupt. **cutty** *adjective* short, stumpy. *noun* **1** a short, dumpy girl. **2** affectionate name for a child. **3** a mischievous or disobedient girl. **4** contemptuous term for a woman. **5** = **cutty-pipe. 6** a hare. **cutty clay, cutty pipe** a short, stumpy (clay) pipe. **cutty quine** contemptuous term for a woman *now NE*. **†cutty sark 1** a short chemise

or undergarment *SW*. **2** name of a witch in Burns' 'Tam o' Shanter'. **cutty spoon** a short-handled spoon, usually of horn. **cutty stool 1** a low, usually three-legged, stool. **2** †the **stool of repentance** (*see* **repent**), the place in a church where those guilty of misconduct were obliged to sit. **cutty wran** a wren.

cut before the point to anticipate.

cutchack a small, blazing, coal or peat fire *NE*.

cute *see* **cuit, quoit**

cuttance 1 an account, description; news *NE*. **2 no cuttance** no encouragement.

cutter a hip-flask.
   rin the cutter carry out liquor from a public house or brewery unobserved.

†**cuttle** *see* **cuittle**

cweed *see* **cood**[1], **cood**[2]

cwintry *see* **countra**

cwite *see* **coat**

D

da *see* **the**

dab[1] *verb* **1** peck. **2** pierce slightly, stab. **3** aim (a marble etc) at. **4** push, shove. *noun* **1** a blow, slap. **2** melted fat, gravy etc in which potatoes are dipped.

dabbie a game played with marbles or tops. **dabbity 1** a (small) ornament. **2** a game played with small cut-out pictures.

not let dab not to give information (that ..).

dab[2]: **common dab, plain dab** a plain, ordinary or unpretentious person or thing *NE, Perth*.

daberlacks *mainly NE* **1** = **badderlocks**, a kind of seaweed. **2** wet, dirty scraps of cloth etc. **3** hair in lank, tangled, separate locks. **4** a tall unattractive person.

dacent decent.

dacker[1], **daiker 1** bargain. **2** walk slowly, aimlessly or weakly. **3** be doing undemanding work.

dacker[2] search (a house, person) for stolen goods etc (by official warrant) *NE*.

dackle hesitate, dawdle, go slowly *NE*.

dad, daud, dod *verb* **1** strike heavily, beat; jolt. **2** dash, bump about, thud. **3** pelt; bespatter *now Shetland*. **4** *of wind, rain etc* blow in gusts, drive. **5** bang, slam (a door). *noun* **1** a heavy blow, thud. **2** a large piece, lump, quantity (knocked off).

dae, do, dee do.

disna does not. **dinna** do not. **didna** did not. **doer** a person who acts for another; a **factor**, agent. **be daein 1** be content, satisfied. **2 I can't be doing with it** I can't put up with it.

daff act playfully or foolishly.

daffin 1 fun; foolish behaviour. **2** †wild behaviour; dirty language.

daft 1 foolish, stupid, lacking intelligence. **2** crazy, insane; lacking commonsense. **3** frivolous, thoughtless. **4 daft aboot** extremely fond of, crazy about.

daftie an imbecile; a mentally handicapped person; a fool.

daft days 1 a time of merrymaking and fun; one's youth. **2** the period of festivity at Christmas and New Year.

dag[1] *mainly NE* **1** thin drizzling rain. **2** a heavy shower (of rain).

dag[2], **dag on(t), dog on it** damn it!

daich *see* **daigh**

daidle[1], *also* **daidlie 1** a (child's) pinafore or bib. **2** an apron.

daidle[2] **1** idle, waste time; potter about. **2** waddle; stagger.

daidle[3] dirty, wet (one's clothes etc) *NE*.

daidle[4] dandle, fondle (a child).

daigh, daich [-gh, -ch as -ch in 'dreich'] **1** dough. **2** a mixture of meal and hot water for chicken food.

daighie 1 doughy. **2** *of persons* inactive, lacking in spirit.

daigie a kind of marbles game.

daik *mainly NE* **1** deck, adorn. **2** smooth down (the hair etc).

daiker *see* **dacker**[1]

daimen rare, occasional.

dainner *see* **denner**

dainshach particular; fussy about food *now Caithness*.

dainty 1 pleasant, agreeable. **2** large, fair-sized; *of time* considerable.

daise 1 daze. **2** become rotten, spoiled by age, damp etc.

daith, deith death.

dale[1], **deal 1** a deal. **2** a part, portion, share.

dale[2] **1** a deal, a plank. **2** a shelf. **3** a diving-board at a swimming pool *WCentral*.

dale³ a goal, stopping place or base in a game.

dam¹ urine.

dam²: the dams the game of draughts.
dambrod a draughtboard; the game of draughts *now NE.*

dame 1 a (farmer's) wife, housewife. **2** a young (unmarried) woman *now NE.* **3** †a mother.

Dan, Dannie *boy* nickname for a Roman Catholic *WCentral.*

dance: the (Merry) Dancers the Northern Lights, Aurora Borealis *N.*

dander, dauner stroll, saunter.

danders the cinders from a smith's fire.

dandie hanlin a type of fishing line *now NE.*

†dandilly petted, pampered; over-ornamented.

dang damn.

dang *see* **ding**

Dannie *boy see* **Dan**

†daover, dover *sheep-counting and children's rhymes* nine.

darg, dark *noun* **1** a day's work. **2** work: *"the day's darg"*. **3** the product of a day's work.
verb work, toil.
darger a casual unskilled labourer.

Dark Blues nickname for Dundee football team.

darn: *in cattle* **dry darn** constipation; **soft darn** diarrhoea.

darn *see* **dern**

dass 1 a ledge on a hillside. **2** a layer in a pile of hay etc.

dat *see* **that**

dative appointed by a court: **executor dative;** *see also* **tutor dative** *(under* **tutor)** *and compare* **nominate.**

daud *see* **dad**

dauner *see* **dander**

daugh [-gh as -ch in 'loch'] soft coaly fireclay.

daumer stun, confuse.

daunton subdue, suppress, overcome; challenge, defy.

daur dare.

daut pet, fondle, make much of.
dautie a pet, darling.

†davach a measure of land varying from area to area *mainly N.*

daver 1 wander aimlessly or dazedly. **2** stun, stupefy; chill.

daw¹ dawn.

daw² a lazy person; a slut.

dawkie drizzly.

day-nettle 1 hemp-nettle. **2** dead-nettle.

de *see* **the, there**

deacon¹ 1 the chief official of a craft or trade; the president of one of the **Incorporated Trades** of a town. **2** a master of a craft; an expert.

deacon² *Presbyterian Churches* one of the laymen or laywomen elected and ordained to manage the temporal affairs of a congregation.

dead *see* **deid**

deaf, deef *of soil etc* poor, unproductive.
deafening sound-proofing (of a building) by pugging. **deafie** *of sound* dull; *of a ball etc* without bounce.
deaf nut a nut without a kernel; an unimportant person or thing.

deal *see* **dale¹**

dean: dean of the Faculty 1 the head of a faculty in a Scottish university. **2** *law* the elected leader of the Bar. **†Dean of Guild** the head of the Guild of a **royal burgh** *(see* **royal)**; a member of the town council, who presided over the **Dean of Guild Court** (a court with jurisdiction over the buildings of a burgh).

deas 1 a dais. **2** a desk or pew in a church. **3** a wooden seat also used as a table or bed. **4** a stone- or turf-seat outside a cottage.

deasil the custom of walking sunwise round a person or thing to bring good fortune.

deave 1 deafen. **2** annoy with noise or talk; bore.

decern *law* pronounce judicially; decide judicially or formally; decree.

declaration *law* the statement made before his committal and in the presence of the **sheriff** by a person whom it is intended to try on **indictment.**

declarator *law, also* **action of declarator** an action brought by an interested party to have some legal right or status declared, but without claim on any person called as **defender** to do anything.

declinature *law* the refusal by a judge to exercise jurisdiction, appropriate in a case in which, because of relationship to a party or other interest, his decision might be thought affected; refusal to accept some office, appointment or benefit, *eg* as a trustee nominated by the truster.

decree [deecree] *law* a final judgment.

dee die.

dee *see* **dae, dey**[1]**, thou, thy**

Dee nickname for Dundee football team.

deed indeed.

deedle *see* **diddle**[2]

deef *see* **deaf**

deek catch sight of, see *mainly S*.

deem *mainly NE* 1 a dame. 2 an elderly woman. 3 a young woman; an unmarried woman. 4 a kitchenmaid on a farm.

deemis extremely, very.

deep plate a soup plate or similarly-shaped smaller dish.

deevil *see* **deil**

defait, defeat 1 defeated. 2 exhausted, worn out *now NE*.

defamation *law* Scots law term covering both libel and slander in English law.

defeat *see* **defait**

defences *law* the pleading of a **defender** in a civil action.

defender *law* a defendant, latterly only in a civil case.

de fideli [day fidayliy] *law* an oath taken by people appointed to perform certain public or other duties that they will faithfully carry them out (a breach of which does not amount to perjury).

deforce impede, prevent by force (an officer of the law or body of officials)

from the discharge of duty.

deforcement the crime of **deforcing.**

deg strike (a sharp-pointed object) quickly into something *now NE*.

deid, dead *adjective* dead.

noun death; the cause of (someone's) death.

  deid-bell 1 a passing bell. 2 a sudden deafness and ringing in the ears, thought to foretell death *now Shetland*. **deid-claes** a shroud. **deid-deal** the board on which a corpse is laid *now Fife*. **deid-ill** a fatal illness. **deid-kist** a coffin. **deid-licht** a strange light, thought to foretell death *now NE*. **deid man's bells** the foxglove. **deid thraw** death throe. **in the deid thraw** *now NE* 1 between hot and cold. 2 between one state and another; undecided.

deil, deevil, divil, devil a devil.

  deevilock a little devil, imp *NE*.

  deil's dizzen thirteen.

  deil a .. not a .., never a ... **deil ane** not one; no one at all. **deil kens** goodness knows. **deil (may) care** no matter; for all that.

deith *see* **daith**

dek *sheep-counting,* **dick, dock** *children's rhymes* ten.

delf a place dug out; a hole or pit.

delict *law* a wrong, now only a civil, but formerly also a criminal one.

deliverance 1 a formal decision or judgment, later a judicial decision; now used of the orders of the court in **sequestrations** (*see* **sequestrate**), including any order, warrant, judgment, decision, **interlocutor** or **decree**. 2 the findings or decision of the **General Assembly** or other Church court on a report from a committee or special commission.

dell delve, dig *Shetland Orkney N*.

delt pet, spoil *NE*.

dem dam *now NE*.

dem *see* **them**

demain, demean treat badly, injure *now NE*.

den[1] a narrow valley, especially one with trees.

den[2] **1** *games* a base, place of safety. **2** the forecastle of a herring boat.

denner, dainner *NE noun* dinner.
verb dine, have dinner; give dinner to.

dentylion dandelion.

denumb stupefy, confound *NE*.

deochandorus [d(ee)ochandorus] a drink taken when leaving.

depone declare on oath.

deposit, deposition *law* a contract under which a **moveable** is entrusted by one (the depositor) to another (the depository or depositary) to be kept either for payment or without reward.

depute [**de**pute] *adjective, following the noun* appointed or acting as a deputy: *"advocate depute"*.
noun a deputy.

der *see* **their, there**

†**deray** disturbance, noise.

dere *see* **there**

derf 1 bold, daring, hardy. **2** unbending, taciturn. **3** *of things* hard, rough, violent.

derk dark *S*.

dern, darn *adjective* **1** secret, hidden. **2** †dark, dreary.
verb hide; go into hiding.

dert dart.

desert *law* drop, cease to go on with (a **summons**, action etc).

deserter *see* **grave**

design set forth a person's occupation and address.

destination *law* a direction as to the persons who are to succeed to property, mainly in a will etc affecting **heritable** property.

destrick *see* **district**

deuk, jeuk, duck 1 a duck. **2** †*only* **duck** a small stone used in a children's game; the game itself.

devil *see* **deil**

deval [de**val**] *verb* stop, leave off.
noun **1** a slope, *eg* that required for drainage. **2** stop *now NE*.

devel a severe and stunning blow.

devolution *law* the referring of a decision to an **oversman** (*see* **owersman**) by **arbiters** who differ in opinion.

dewgs, juggins small pieces, shreds.

dey[1] [rhymes with 'my' or 'gey'], †**dee** a dairymaid *now Caithness*.

dey[2] [rhymes with 'gay' or (*NE*) with 'gey'], **tae 1** child's word for father. **2** a grandfather.

dey *see* **there**

deyd [-ey- as in 'gey'] a grandfather; a grandmother *NE*.

diacle a small dial or compass *now Shetland Orkney*.

dib a puddle; *humorously* the ocean.

diced having a chequered pattern.
diced up trim and neat.

dichens *S*, **dichels** [-ch- as in 'dreich'] a scolding, beating.

dicht, dight [rhymes with 'licht', or (*Orkney S*) with 'light'] *verb* **1** †arrange, dress, prepare, make fit for use. **2** wipe or rub clean or dry. **3** clean (up) by sweeping, removing dust etc, make tidy. **4** sift or winnow. **5** scold, thrash.
noun **1** a wipe, a quick wash; a rub. **2** a blow, smack; a heavy defeat *now NE*.

dick *see* **dek**

diddle[1] **1** dance with a jigging movement. **2** move (the elbow) to and fro in fiddling; fiddle. **3** dandle (a child).

diddle[2], **deedle** sing without words.

diddle[3] busy oneself without getting much done.

dick *see* **dek**

didna *see* **dae**

diet 1 a church service: *"diet of worship"*. **2** a day or date fixed for a meeting (*eg* of a court), or for a market.

differ *verb* quarrel, dispute.
noun **1** a difference of opinion; a disagreement. **2** a difference.

dight *see* **dicht**

dike *see* **dyke**

diled *see* **doilt**

dilgit, dulget a lump; an untidy heap

or bundle *NE*.

diligence *law* application of legal means against a person, especially for the enforcing of a payment or recovery of a debt; a warrant issued by a court to enforce the attendance of witnesses, or the production of writings.

dill soothe, quieten down, die away.

dilp a slovenly woman.

dilse dulse, a kind of edible seaweed.

din¹ **1** loud talk or discussion; a fuss, disturbance. **2** a report, rumour; a scandal.

din² **1** dun, mousy. **2** dark-complexioned, sallow.

dine dinner; dinnertime.

ding *verb, past tense* **dang, dung** **1** knock, beat or strike (with heavy blows); defeat, overcome (with blows); beat, get the better of. **2** *of rain, wind etc* beat or fall heavily and violently. **3** drive (with violence). **4** strike, force, drive from *etc*.
noun a knock or blow, a smart push.
go one's dinger go at something very vigorously or boisterously.

ding dang speedily, in rapid succession; in confusion.

dinge dent, bruise.

dingle tingle.

dingle-dousie [-**doo**zie] a lighted stick etc waved rapidly by a child to make patterns of light.

dink **1** neat, trim, finely dressed, dainty. **2** prim, precise; haughty.

dinmont a wether, a castrated ram between one and a half and two and a half years old.

dinna *see* **dae**

dinnle 1 shake, vibrate. **2** *of bells, thunder etc* peal, roll, drone. **3** tingle with cold or pain; twinge.

dint affection, liking.

dip melted fat in which potatoes are dipped.

dir *see* **there**

dird *noun* a hard blow, knock; a sharp or stunning fall, a bump; a bounce, romp

now NE.
verb push violently, bump; bounce, jolt *now NE*.

dirdum 1 a loud noise, quarrelling, uproar. **2** a quandary, problem. **3** a heavy stroke or blow. **4** blame; punishment, a scolding. **5** bad temper; violent excitement. **6** *usually ironic* a great deed.S

†**dirgie, dredgie** [-g- as in 'ginger'] a funeral feast, especially of drink.

†**dirk**¹ *adjective* dark.
verb slink, go surreptitiously.

dirk², **durk 1** a short dagger worn in the belt by Highlanders, now as part of Highland dress. **2** a stab, a prod *now Shetland Orkney*.
verb stab with a dirk.

dirl *verb* **1** pierce or (cause to) tingle with emotion or pain. **2** cause to vibrate, shake. **3** vibrate, rattle, reverberate; ring when struck; whirl.
noun **1** a knock causing such; a shock, jar, clatter. **2** the pain caused by such a blow; a tingling sensation. **3** a vibrating motion and noise, a clatter or rattle. **4** a gust (of wind) *Shetland N*. **5** a hurry, bustle *Shetland N*.
dirl aff recite, sing, play continuously.
dirl up strike up, (a song, tune), play vigorously.

dirt *verb* defecate on.
dirten *now NE* **1** dirtied, filthy, soiled with excrement. **2** mean, contemptible; conceited.

dis *see* **this**

†**discomfish** overcome, defeat.

disconvenient inconvenient.

discreet polite, well-behaved.

dishealth ill-health, illness.

dishilago *see* **tushilago**

disjaskit 1 dejected, downcast, depressed. **2** dilapidated, neglected, untidy. **3** exhausted, worn out; weary-looking.

disna *see* **dae**

displenish strip (a farm) of furnishings or stock, sell off the contents of.

dispone *law* make over, convey (land).

disposition *law* a deed of conveyance, an assignation of property.

Disruption the split which took place in the Established Church of Scotland in 1843 when 450 of its 1200 ministers formed themselves into the **Free Church** (*see* **free**).

dist *see* **dust**

district, destrick 1 a district. **2** *only* **district** a division of a **region**: *"District Council"*.

dit shut, close; obstruct, block.

dittay *law* a statement of the charge(s) against an accused person; an **indictment**.

divert an entertainment, amusement; an amusing person or thing.

divil *see* **deil**

divot [**div**vot] **1** a turf, sod, peat. **2** a thick clumsy piece of bread etc.

dixie a sharp scolding *now Orkney NE*.

dizzen a dozen.

do *see* **dae**

dob prick.

dobbie a dull, stupid clumsy person.

dochter, dother a daughter.

dock *noun* **1** the buttocks. **2** the rear or butt-end of something.
    verb dock, shorten (clothes).
    dockit *of speech or temper* clipped, short.

dock *see* **dek**

docken 1 a dock plant. **2** something of no value or significance: *"it disna maitter a doaken"*.

doctor a kind of minnow.

dod *mild exclamation* God!

dod *see* **dad**

doddie a hornless bull, cow or sheep.

doddle 1 something attractive. **2** something which is easy to do.

dods *noun* a fit of the sulks.
    tak the dods sulk.

doer *see* **dae**

dog, dowg, dug a dog.
    dog('s) flourish one of various umbelliferous plants. **dog('s) hip** the fruit of the dog-rose, the rosehip.

dog *see* **dag**[2]

doh *see* **heich**

doilt, diled 1 dazed, confused stupid. **2** wearied, grief-stricken.

doist, dyst *noun* a heavy blow; a thud, bump, crash.
    verb fall, sit or throw (down) with a thud, bump.

doit[1] **1** †a small copper coin. **2** something of little value: *"not worth a doit"*.

doit[2], **dyte** *verb* **1** act foolishly, be crazed or confused in mind. **2** walk with a stumbling or short step *now NE*.
    noun a stupid person, a fool.
    doitered witless, especially in old age.
    doitit not in sound mind, foolish, silly.

dole *law* the corrupt, malicious, or evil intention which is an essential constituent of a criminal act.

dolder something large of its kind.

doll a portion, large piece especially of dung.

dom, domsie = **dominie** *mainly NE*.

dominie a schoolmaster.

donk *see* **dunk**

donnert dull, stupid, witless, especially in old age.

donsie *adjective* **1** unfortunate, luckless. **2** †glum, sickly, feeble, delicate. **3** †badly behaved, ill-tempered. **4** †neat, tidy.

doo, dow 1 a dove, pigeon. **2** term of endearment: *"ma wee doo"*.
    doocot a dovecote.

dooble, double double.
    doubling *piping* in **pibroch** the form in which a variation may be repeated, usually with more complete or perfect development; a kind of trill before a note.

doodle dandle, lull (a child).

doodle *see* **doudle**

dook[1], **douk** [-oo-] *verb* **1** duck. **2** bathe. **3** baptize as a Baptist.
    noun **1** a duck (into water). **2** a bathe. **3** a drenching, a soaking. **4** liquid into which something is dipped.
    dook for apples *Halloween game* try to get hold of apples floating in a tub etc

with the teeth, by dipping one's head in the water and without using the hands.

dook[2] *noun* **1** a wooden peg etc driven into a wall to hold a nail. **2** a plug, a bung of a cask, boat etc.

verb insert such wooden pegs etc in (a wall).

dool[1], **dule** grief, distress.

dool[2], **dult** **1** a boundary mark *now Orkney*. **2** *games* the goal or place of safety *now WCentral*.

doolie **1** a hobgoblin, a spectre, ghost. **2** a stupid, dithering, nervous person.

dooms extremely, very.

doon[1], **doun** **1** down. **2** doon of below. **3** *of a river* in flood.

doonie a member of the **hand-ball** (*see* **hand**) team playing towards the downward goal, the **doonies** usually coming from the lower part of the town *Orkney S; see also* **uppie**.

doon-by down there, in the neighbourhood. **doon-haud** a handicap, something that prevents one rising in the world. **doonhamers** nickname for the inhabitants of Dumfries, and for Queen of the South football team. **doon-lyin** (giving) birth. **doon mouth** a sad expression. **doonset(ting)** **1** a (good etc) settlement, *eg* on marriage. **2** a scolding. **3** a laying-low (*eg* from a heavy blow, misfortune). **4** *of food etc* a (grand etc) spread. **doon-sitting** the action of settling in a place *NE*. **doon-tak** a humiliation.

doon the watter down the river (of pleasure trips or resorts on the Clyde). **gae doon the brae** go downhill in health, fortune etc.

doon[2] down, soft feathers.

doop *see* **doup**[2]

door: **door-cheek** a door-post; a door, doorway. **door-stane** a flagstone in front of the door; the threshold.

he hasn't been over the door he hasn't been outside or out of the house. **tak the door wi ye** go out and shut the door as you go.

doose strike, knock, thrash.

doosht a dull, heavy blow, a push; a thud.

doot, dout, doubt **1** doubt. **2** fear, be afraid, suspect. **3** expect, rather think. **I hae my doots** I am doubtful.

dooth *see* **douth**

doozie a light, a flame (of a candle, lamp etc).

dorb a peck; a prod *NE*.

dorbie a stonemason.

dorlach [-ch as in 'loch'] **1** a large piece of something solid *NE*. **2** †a quiver (for arrows); a bundle used to carry one's belongings.

dort: **tak the dorts** sulk, go into a huff. **dorty** **1** bad-tempered, sulky; cheeky; haughty. **2** difficult to please. **3** feeble, delicate, sickly.

dose a large quantity or number. **a dose of the cold** a cold.

dosened *see* **dozened**

doss[1] spruce, neat, tidy.

doss[2] a knot or bow (of ribbon, flowers etc) *N*.

doss[3] toss or pay down (money) *mainly NE*.

dot *noun* a small person.

verb walk with short quick steps.

dother *see* **dochter**

dotter walk unsteadily, stagger.

dottered stupid, feeble-minded (from old age).

dotterel an old idiot.

dottle[1] **1** something small, a very small piece. **2** the plug of tobacco in a pipe after smoking. **3** a cigarette end. **4** the core of a boil etc.

dottle[2] be in or fall into a state of dotage, become or make crazy.

double *see* **dooble**

doubt *see* **doot**

douce, douse [rhymes with 'goose'] **1** sweet, pleasant, lovable. **2** sedate, sober, respectable. **3** neat, tidy, comfortable.

doudle, doodle *noun* a musical instrument made from a reed *S*.

verb play (a wind instrument,

especially a **doudle** or the bagpipes).

douk *see* **dook**[1]

doun *see* **doon**[1]

doup[1] [dowp, (*Shetland Orkney*) doop] **1** the bottom of an eggshell. **2** the buttocks. **3** the seat of a pair of trousers. **4** the bottom or end of something.

doup[2] [-oo-], **doop** stoop, bend, duck.

doup o day the close of day.

dour [rhymes with 'moor'] **1** dull, humourless, sullen. **2** hard, stern, severe, determined. **3** slow, sluggish, reluctant. **4** *of weather* bleak, gloomy. **5** *of land* hard, barren.

douse *see* **douce**

dout *see* **doot**

douth, dooth, dowth *mainly S* **1** depressed. **2** gloomy, dreary, dark.

dove [rhymes with 'cove'] become drowsy, doze.

dovie stupid.

dover 1 doze off. **2** wander hesitatingly, walk unsteadily.

dover *see* **daover**

dow[1] **1** be able, have the strength or ability (to do something). **2** be willing, have the strength of mind or courage, dare. **3** †thrive, prosper.

dowless feeble, lacking in strength or energy.

dow[2] fade away, wither, become musty.

dow *see* **doo**

dowf, duff *adjective* **1** dull, spiritless; stupid; weary. **2** sad, melancholy. **3** *of a sound* dull, hollow. **4** *of a part of the body* numb, insensitive *now Shetland*.

noun **1** a stupid or gloomy person. **2** a dull blow with something soft.

dowfart dull, spiritless; stupid.

dowg *see* **dog**

dowie 1 sad, dismal; dull. **2** weak, delicate, ailing.

dowt a cigarette-end.

dowth *see* **douth**

doze 1 stupefy, stun. **2** spin (a top) so fast that it appears not to move.

dozened, †dosened 1 stupefied, dazed,

physically (weakened through age drink etc). **2** numb, stiff with cold.

drabble, draible *verb* **1** dirty (one's clothes, boots etc). **2** spill. **3** *of rain* drizzle *NE*.

noun **1** a spot of dirt. **2** a small quantity of liquid food. **3** rubbish, especially something too small for use.

draffie out of condition, unable to walk or run easily.

draft *see* **draucht**

drag 1 a large heavy harrow. **2** *also* **draig** the motion of the tide.

draggle *see* **draigle**

draible *see* **drabble**

draigle, draggle *verb* **1** bedraggle, dirty, muddy. **2** mix (flour, meal etc) with water *NE*. **3** move slowly or wearily.

noun a dirty, untidy person.

draigelt soaked through, drenched.

draigon 1 a dragon. **2** a paper kite.

draik drench, soak.

drackie damp, wet, misty.

dram a drink of spirits; in Scotland, a drink of any size, usually whisky.

dram *see* **drum**[1]

drammock, drummock a mixture of raw oatmeal and cold water.

drap, drop *noun* **1** a drop. **2** the dripping of water or the line down which it drops from the eaves of a house. **3 draps** small shot, pellets.

verb **1** drop. **2** stop (work); stop (raining). **3** rain slightly, drizzle.

drop(ped) scone a small, round, flat cake, made by allowing thick batter to drop onto a **girdle**, frying pan etc, smaller and thicker than an English pancake and usually eaten cold with butter, jam etc, a **pancake** (*see* **pan**).

a drappie a drink. **drapping** dripping; *of weather* showery.

no a drap's blude not a blood-relation.

draucht, draft *noun* **1** draught. **2** a load. **3** the guts of an animal. **4** a sheep etc withdrawn from the flock.

verb **1** break in, harness (a horse) *NE*. **2** line off (land) with the plough by straight furrows.

draunt drawl, whine, drone.

drave 1 a drove. **2** the annual herring fishing. **3** a shoal of fish; a catch.

draw 1 aim (a blow); raise (one's hand, foot etc) in attack. **2 draw to** head for; come to like (someone). **3** *of tea* infuse, become infused.

noun a puff at a pipe, a smoke.

draw straes afore someone's een make fun of someone; deceive someone.

draw up become friendly with.

dredgie *see* **dirgie**

dree¹ **1** endure, suffer (pain, misfortune etc). **2** †spend (time) miserably. **3** last, continue.

dree one's (ain) weird endure one's fate, suffer the consequences.

dree² suspect; fear.

dreel 1 drill, exercise; bore. **2** move rapidly. **3** work quickly and smoothly. **4** scold.

dreep 1 drip. **2** drain, strain (*eg* potatoes after boiling). **3** come off (a wall etc) by letting oneself down to the full stretch of the arms and dropping.

dreeping roast, dripping roast a constant source of income.

Sammy dreep a 'drip', a spiritless, ineffective person.

dreetle *see* **driddle**

dreg¹ **1** *distilling* the refuse of malt from the still. **2** a small quantity, a drop of spirits.

dreg² dredge (shellfish etc).

dreg³ drag.

dreich 1 dreary, dull, bleak; long, boring, uninteresting. **2** slow; backward; slow to pay debts. **3** depressed.

dreich a drawin(g) slow to move, slow in deciding.

dreid 1 dread. **2** suspect, fear.

dress 1 iron (cloth). **2** neuter (a cat).

drib¹ *noun* **1** a drop, a small quantity of liquid. **2 dribs** dregs.

verb extract the last drops of milk from (a cow).

drib² beat, thrash; scold *NE*.

dribble 1 tipple, drink. **2** drizzle.

driddle, dreetle 1 walk slowly or uncertainly; dawdle, saunter. **2** potter, idle, waste time. **3** spill, dribble. **4** play the fiddle, strum.

driffle 1 drizzle, rain or snow lightly. **2** scold.

drift 1 falling snow driven by the wind. **2** †a drove, flock, herd.

dring¹ loiter, delay.

dring² a poor or miserly person.

dripping roast *see* **dreep**

drite *verb* defecate.

noun dirt, excrement.

drizzen make a low, mournful sound.

drocht *see* **droucht**

drod a short, thickset person.

droddum the buttocks.

drog a drug.

droich [-ch as in 'dreich'] a dwarf, a stunted person.

drochle a small (dumpy) person or animal.

drook *see* **drouk**

droon, droun drown.

droon the miller put too much water in alcohol.

drooth *see* **drouth**

drop *see* **drap**

dross small coal, coal-dust.

droucht [-oo-], **drocht** drought; drying breezy weather.

drouchtit parched. **drouchty** dry *NE*.

drouk [-oo-], **drook** a drenching, soaking.

droukin dripping with moisture. **droukit** drenched, soaked; steeped. **droukit stour** mud.

droun *see* **droon**

drouth, drooth *noun* **1** drought; drying breezy weather. **2** thirst. **3** a drunk, a habitual drinker.

drouthy 1 *of the weather* dry. **2** thirsty, addicted to drinking.

drove road a road or track used for driving cattle or sheep to markets.

drow¹ [rhymes with 'cow'] a cold, wet mist, a drizzle.

drow² [rhymes with 'cow'] an attack of

illness, a fainting fit; a spasm of anxiety.

drucken drunken.

drug pull forcibly, drag.

drum[1], **dram** sad, dejected, sulky.

drum[2] the cylindrical part of a threshing machine.

drum major a domineering woman.

drumb(l)e *see* **drunnel**

drumlin a long whaleback mound of glacial deposit.

drumlie 1 *of streams or water* troubled, clouded, muddy; *of alcohol* full of sediment. **2** *of the weather* cloudy, gloomy. **3** troubled, muddled, confused.

drummock *see* **drammock**

drunnel, drumb(l)e make or be muddy or disturbed.

drunts the sulks, a fit of ill-humour.

drush powdery waste, *eg* of peat *now NE*.

dry: drying green *see* **green. dry dyke** = **dry-stane dyke. †dry lodging** lodging without board. **dry shave** the rubbing of another's cheek with an unshaven chin or with the fingers. **dry-stane dyke** a stone wall built without mortar. **dry-stane dyker** a person who builds such walls.

du *see* **thou**

dub 1 a pool, especially of muddy or stagnant water; a pond. **2** a small pool, especially of rain water, a puddle. **3** *humorous* the ocean. **4** a sea pool. **5 dubs** mud.

dub-skelper a person who moves about a lot (regardless of the state of the roads).

duck *see* **deuk**

dud 1 duds ragged clothes, rags, tatters. **2** a coarse cloth for domestic purposes, *eg* a dish-cloth.

duddie ragged, tattered.

duff a soft spongy substance *now Shetland*.

duff *see* **dowf**

duffie a lavatory *mainly S*.

dug *see* **dog**

duist *see* **juist**

dule *see* **dool**[1]

dulget *see* **dilgit**

dult 1 a dolt. **2** the pupil at the bottom of the class.

dult *see* **dool**[2]

Dumfries and Galloway (Region) a **region** formed from the former counties of Dumfries, Kirkcudbright and Wigtown.

dump *verb* **1** beat, thump, kick. **2** walk with short, heavy steps, stump about. *noun* a blow, a thump, a thud.

get one's dumps get thumps on the back as a birthday ritual; *compare* **bumps**.

dumpling a kind of rich, boiled or steamed fruit pudding.

dunch, dunsh *verb* **1** punch, thump, bump. **2** *of animals* butt. *noun* **1** a blow, a bump, a nudge. **2** a butt from an animal.

dunder *see* **dunner**

dung *see* **ding**

dungeon a person of great knowledge.

†duniwassal a Highlander of rank below the chief; a gentleman of secondary rank.

dunk, donk dank, damp, moist.

dunkle dent, make a slight depression in.

dunner, dunder 1 make a noise like thunder, rumble, bang. **2** move quickly and noisily.

dunny an underground cellar or passage in an old **tenement** building; a basement *WCentral*.

dunsh *see* **dunch**

dunt *noun* **1** a heavy, dull-sounding blow or stroke, knock. **2** the wound caused by such. **3** a dent. **4** a heavy fall, thud, bump; the sound of such. **5** a throb or quickened beat of the heart. **6** a blow, a shock, disappointment. **7** an insult. **8** a chance, opportunity, occasion *now Shetland*. **9** a lump, a large piece. *verb* **1** beat, stamp, thump, bump, knock, (with a dull sound). **2** *of the heart* throb, beat rapidly or violently; *of a sore* throb. **3** stamp down (herrings) in a barrel. **4** shake together the contents of (*eg* a sack) by knocking on the ground. **5** crush or dent by striking.

durk a large clumsy thing or person.

durk *see* **dirk**

dush push or strike with force, butt.

dust, dist *Orkney NE.* **1** dust. **2** particles of meal and husk.

dux the best pupil in a school, class or subject.

dwaible, dwabble, dweeble 1 flexible, flabby, soft. **2** weak, feeble, shaky.
dwaibly shaky, wobbly, weak.

dwall dwell.

dwam *noun* **1** a swoon, a fainting fit; a sudden attack of illness. **2** a stupor; a daydream.
verb **1** faint. **2** decline in health. **3** fall asleep, take a nap.

dwamie sickly, faint; dreamy. **dwamle** a sick or faint turn.

dwang *noun* **1** a wooden strut or bar; an iron lever. **2** toil.
verb **1** worry, harass, subject to pressure. **2** toil, work hard.

dweeble *see* **dwaible**

dwine pine, waste away, fail in health; fade, wither.

dy *see* **thy**

dyang *see* **gang**

dyke, dike 1 a wall of stones, turf etc. **2** a hedge *SW.*
verb surround with a **dyke.**
dyker a builder of **dykes.**

dyte *see* **dowt**[2]

dyvour [dyiver] **1** a debtor, a bankrupt. **2** a rogue, a good-for-nothing.

E

e *see* **he**

ears *see* **hear**

'ear *see* **year**

earl, yerl *now S* an earl.

Earl o Hell the Devil.

earn, ern, yirn an eagle; a white-tailed or sea-eagle *now Orkney*, a golden eagle *now Shetland Caithness*.

earn *see* **yirn**[1]

earock a young hen.

easel *see* **east**

easement 1 personal comfort; relief from physical discomfort. **2** †**easements** accommodation, buildings.

easin(s) 1 the eaves of a building. **2** the corresponding part of a haystack. **3** the angular space between the top of the side wall and the roof inside a house.

east 1 east. **2** in an easterly direction along. **3** in one of two possible directions: *"move that ashet a bittie east"*.

easter 1 eastern, lying towards the east, the more easterly of two places. **2** the east wind. **eastle, eas(t)el** *S* **1** towards the east, eastwards. **2** to the east of *S*. **eas(t)lins** eastward *NE*.

East Neuk *see* **neuk**

easy-osy *of people* easy-going, inclined to be lazy; *of things* involving the minimum of effort.

eat, et(t), ait *verb past also* **ett, eet, eated**, *past participle also* **etten, aten** *SW* **1** eat. **2** allow (grass etc) to be eaten by grazing animals: *"he eats the herbage with his sheep"*.

eath *see* **eith**

ebb *noun* the foreshore.

adjective shallow, lacking in depth, scant.

echt *see* **aucht**[1]

edder, ether a straw-rope used in thatching a haystack *NE*.

edder *see* **aither, ether, udder**

Edinburgh rock a stick-shaped sweet made of sugar, cream of tartar, water and various flavourings, originally made in Edinburgh.

ee, eye *noun, plural also* **een 1** an eye. **2** an opening, *eg* an opening through which water passes, the hole in the centre of a millstone. **3** regard, liking, craving.

eehole an eyesocket.

put out a person's ee get an advantage over, supplant.

ee *see* **the**

eechie [-ch- as in 'dreich'] **(n)or ochie** [-ch- as in 'loch']: **neither eechie nor ochie** neither one thing nor another; absolutely nothing.

eediot, eedyit, eejit an idiot.

eek *see* **eik**[1], **eik**[2]

eeksie-peeksie, icksy-picksy *NE* much alike, six and half-a-dozen.

eel *see* **ale, yeld, Yule**

eeld *see* **eild**

eelie *see* **ely, oil**

eel-stab a V-shaped cut in the ear of an animal as a mark of ownership.

†**eem 1** an uncle. **2** any near male relative; a close friend.

eemage, image 1 an image. **2** a ghost of one's former self, a pitiful figure.

eemir *see* **humour**

eemis *see* **immis**

eemock, emot an emmet, an ant.

eemost *see* **umost**

een *see* **ane**[1], **ee, even**[1]

e'en *see* **even**[2]

eendy, eenty *words used in children's rhymes* one.

eenin(g) evening.

eenoo, evenoo, enow 1 just now, at the present time, a moment ago. **2** in a short time, soon, at once.

eenty *see* **eendy**

eer¹ an iron stain on linen *NE*.

eer² your.

eer *see* **ure³**

eerant, errand 1 an errand. **2 errands** purchases, parcels, shopping.

eerie 1 afraid, especially affected by fear of the supernatural. **2** ghostly, strange. **3** gloomy, dismal, melancholy.

eer(ie)oy *see* **ieroe**

eesage, eese, ees(e)less, eest *see* **use**

eeswal *see* **usual**

eet *see* **eat**

eetle ottle words used in counting-out rhymes: *"eetle ottle black bottle, eetle ottle out"*.

eezie ozie *see* **heeze**

effeir *see* **affeir**

eft 1 aft. **2** towards the rear of something.

efter, after, aifter 1 after. **2** *in telling time* past: *"half an hour after ten"*.
  afterin(g)s 1 the last drops of milk taken while milking. **2** final results, consequences; remainder.
  aftercome an effect, consequence. **efterhin, afterhend** after(wards). **efternuin, efterneen** *N* **1** afternoon. **2** a meal taken during the afternoon.

egg: aff (o) one's eggs 1 mistaken. **2** nervous.

ei *see* **he**

eicht *see* **aucht¹**

eident [ei- rhymes with 'gey'] **1** diligent, busy. **2** *of rain* continuous, persistent. **3** conscientious, careful, attentive.

eight, eightsome *see* **aucht¹**

eik¹, eek *noun SW, S* **1** the natural grease in sheep's wool. **2** human perspiration.

eik², eek *noun* an addition, extension, increase; an additional part or piece.
  verb increase, add (to), supplement.

eild, eeld 1 †the age of a person. **2** old age. **3** antiquity, long ago.

eild *see* **yeld**

†eith, eath easy.

eizel *see* **aizle**

elbuck an elbow.

elder 1 aɪ. elder. **2** *Presbyterian Churches* a person appointed to take part in church government.

eldin(g) fuel.

eldritch 1 of or like elves etc. **2** weird, ghostly, strange, unearthly.

eleeven eleven.

†elfshot *noun* **1** a sickness (usually of cattle) thought to be caused by fairies. **2** a flint arrowhead, thought to be used by fairies.
  adjective shot by an **elf-shot**.

Elfin 1 fairyland, the land of the elves. **2** Hell.

†ell 1 an ell, the measure of length, the Scots **ell** = approximately four fifths of the English. **2** a square **ell** (see p 360).

ellwan(d), elvan 1 a measuring rod, one **ell** long; *latterly* a yardstick. **2** the group of stars known as the Belt of Orion.

else 1 else. **2** otherwise. **3** already, previously.

†elshin, alshin an awl.

ely, eelie disappear, vanish gradually.

Embro Edinburgh.

emmerteen an ant.

emot *see* **eemock**

en, end *noun* **1** an end. **2** a room; one room of a two-roomed cottage. **3** †*shoemaking* the thread used in sewing leather. **4** *weaving* a warp thread of yarn or silk.
  verb **1** end. **2** stand on end. **3** kill; die.
  endless obstinately long-winded. **en(d)-rig** the land at the end of the furrow on which the plough is turned. **endways** forward, straight ahead; successfully.

end *see* **aynd**

endlang, enlang *adverb* **1** right along, straight on. **2** lengthwise, at full length.
  †*preposition* along, by the side of, from end to end.

enemy *see* **auld**

eneuch, aneuch [an(y)ooch, an(y)uch] enough.

enew sufficient in number or quantity.

Englified anglicized (in speech or manner).

English Episcopal, Episcopalian.

English blanket a blanket with a thick nap. **English pint** the Imperial pint, $\frac{1}{3}$ Scots pint (see p 359).

English and Scots a children's game imitating the old Border Raids.

enlang *see* **endlang**

enow *see* **eenoo**

enquire *see* **inquire**

entry 1 an alley or covered passage, usually in or between houses. **2** the front doorway of a house; an entrance-lobby or porch, especially in a block of flats. **3** the entrance to an avenue leading to a house; the avenue itself.

equal-aqual equally balanced, alike, similar, quits.

erchin *see* **hurcheon**

erd earth.

ere *adverb* early, soon.
conjunction before, until *Shetland NE*.

erethestreen the night before last.

ergh, argh [-ch,-gh as -ch in 'loch'] *adjective* **1** timorous. **2** hesitant, reluctant. **3** scanty, insufficient; exhausted.
verb be timid, hesitate.

erle *see* **herle**

erles *see* **arles**

erm *see* **airm**

ern *see* **earn**

errand *see* **eerant**

erse *noun* **1** the arse. **2** the hinterland, the interior.

†**Erse 1** Irish; Highland, Gaelic. **2** used by Lowlanders to describe Highlanders, their language, customs etc.

escheat *law* the forfeiture of a person's property, on his conviction for certain crimes.

esh ash(-tree or -wood).

esk *see* **ask, yesk**

esp an aspen tree.

ess *see* **ass**

estreen *see* **yestreen**

et *see* **eat**

ether, edder, adder an adder.
adderstane a small prehistoric bead, used as a charm.

ether *see* **edder, aither, udder**

†**etin** [**ea**ten] a giant.

etion, aishan [rhymes with 'nation'] stock, kindred, breed.

etnach juniper.

et(t) *see* **eat**

etten *see* **eat**

etter *noun* pus; venom, poison
verb fester.

ettercap *see* **attercap**

ettle *verb* **1** plan or intend to do; intend, plan (something). **2** aim; take aim at, try to reach. **3** attempt, try. **4** guide. **5** make for. **6** try to express, get at. **7** desire very much, be eager for. **8 ettle to do** be about to. **9** expect, anticipate, guess.
noun **1** one's aim, object. **2** an effort, attempt.

euther *see* **yowder**

even¹, een evening.
at een in the evening.

even², e'en, aiven *adjective, adverb* **1** even. **2** just, simply.
verb **1** even. **2** estimate, compare with, liken to. **3** bring to the same level or condition. **4** make (someone) out to be. **5** †talk of (someone) as a possible marriage match for (someone).
evenly smooth, even, level.
evendoon 1 *of rain* straight, perpendicular. **2** sheer, absolute, downright. **3** honest, frank, sincere. **even on** continuously, without stopping, straight on.

evenoo *see* **eenoo**

ever, iver ever.
everly constantly, perpetually.

evite avoid, escape.

ewder *see* **yowder**

ewe *see* **yowe**

ewe gowan *see* **gowan**

ewest close, next to.

excaise, exkeese *NE* excuse.

excamb *law* exchange (land).

excambion *law* exchange of land or property.

executry *law* the whole **moveable** property of a deceased person.

†**exeem 1** free, exempt. **2** set free, deliver.

exerceese, exercise 1 an exercise. **2** family worship, prayers. **3** a sermon, delivered to a **presbytery** by one of its members, or by a divinity student before ordination.

exkeese *see* **excaise**

expensive extravagant.

export a better-quality stronger beer, slightly darker in colour than **heavy.**

extract *law* an official certified copy of a judgment of a court or of any other publicly-recorded document.

ey *see* **aye**

eye *see* **ee**

eyrisland *see* **ure**[4]

F

fa¹, **fall,** [fa, faw] *verb* **1** fall. **2** happen to *mainly in blessing or curses: "Fair fa' your honest, sonsie face."* **3** †get, obtain. **4** †lay claim to, hope to get: *"he mauna fa that".* **5** have a right to, deserve. **6** be able to get, keep or afford. **7** fall (to one) as a duty or turn *now Shetland.* **8** have to be, do etc *now Shetland.* **9** crumble, fall to pieces.

noun **1** a fall. **2** *in measures* the distance over which a measuring rod falls (see p 360). **3** †one's fate, fortune; a share, portion.

fa awa 1 waste away, decline in health. **2** faint *Shetland NE.* **fa by** take to one's bed, through illness or childbirth *NE.* **fa ower** fall asleep. **fa-tae 1** a lean-to building. **2** a quarrel, row *now Shetland Orkney.* **fa wi bairn** become pregnant.

fa², **fall** [fa, faw] a falling mouse- or rat-trap.

fa *see* **wha**

faa *noun* the guts of an animal, used for sausages etc *Shetland Orkney.*

faal *see* **whaal**

faap *see* **whaup**

fabric an ugly or clumsy thing, animal or person.

face: facie bold; impudent, cheeky.
   face caird a court card.
   the face of clay any man alive *NE.* **put a face in** put in an appearance.

facile *law* easily influenced by others; weak-minded.

fack a fact.

factor a person appointed to manage property for its proprietor.

faculty *law* a power given to do something at will.
   the Faculty of Advocates the members of the Scottish bar.

faddom fathom.

fader *see* **faither**

fadge 1 a flat round thick loaf or bannock formerly of barley meal. **2** a kind of potato scone.

fae¹ a foe.

fae², **frae, thrae, fra** *S preposition* from.
   conjunction **1** from the time that, as soon as. **2** †since, because, seeing that.
   look frae one have a fixed or vacant look, stare stupidly *now S.*

faem foam.

faggot term of abuse for a woman or child, often a messy, clumsy or irritating one.

faik *noun* **1** a fold of a garment *now NE.* **2** a **plaid**, wrap, shawl. **3** a strand of rope *N.*
   verb **1** fold, tuck (cloth or a garment) around. **2** coil (a rope or line) *now Shetland Fife.*

faiks *see* **fegs**

fail¹, **feal** *now Shetland Orkney Caithness* turf as a material for building or roofing; a piece of turf, a sod.

fail² *of people* give way under strain, collapse.

fain 1 loving, affectionate, amorous. **2** fond of *now Shetland Orkney.*

faiple a loose drooping underlip.

fair¹ *adjective* complete, absolute, utter: *"ye're a fair disgrace".*
   adverb completely, simply; directly.
   verb, of weather clear (up).
   the Fair City Perth. **fair-spoken** frank, friendly.
   a fair strae death death from natural causes.

fair²: **the Fair** the annual summer holiday, especially **the Glasgow Fair.**
   fairin(g) a present, often food from a fair or at a festive season. **gie someone his fairins** punish someone.

fairly *see* **ferlie**

fairnytickle *see* **ferntickle**

faisible, feasible 1 *of things* neat, tidily made; satisfactory. **2** *of people* neat, tidy; respectable, decent.

faither, father, fader *now Shetland NE noun* a father.
verb **1** father. **2** show who one's father is by resemblance etc.

faizart, *now Shetland* **1** a hermaphrodite fowl. **2** a puny effeminate man, a weakling.

faize[1] *verb* **1** unravel, fray. **2** make (metal or wood) rough, splintered or jagged *now NE.*

faize[2] *verb* **1** annoy, ruffle *now NE.* **2** make an impression on.

fall *see* **fa**[1], **fa**[2]

fallow[1], **follow, fella, fallie** a fellow.

fallow[2] follow.

false *see* **fause**

fan *see* **whan**

fang *noun* booty, plunder, stolen goods *now NE.*
verb **1** seize, capture; get, catch. **2** prime a pump.
aff the fang 1 *of a pump* having lost its suction. **2** *of people* without one's usual spirit or skill.

fang *see* **whang**

fangle *see* **fankle**

fank[1] *noun* a coil of rope, noose, tangle.
verb **1** tangle, twist. **2** †catch in a noose, snare.

fank[2] a sheepfold.

fankle, fangle *now NE verb* **1** trap, ensnare. **2** tangle, mix up.
noun a tangle, muddle.

fanners a winnowing machine, grainsifter.

fantoosh flashy, ultra-fashionable.

far, fer, faur far.
far ben 1 friendly, intimate, in great favour. **2** *of the eyes* dreamy, far away. **3** having deep or specialized knowledge. **far oot 1** on bad terms, not friendly. **2** distant in relationship. **far seen** far-sighted; deeply-skilled. **far throu 1** *of clothes etc* finished, worn out. **2** very ill, at death's door.

far *see* **whar**

farce a funny story, a joke.

fardel[1] **1** †a fourth part, a quarter. **2** a three-cornered cake, especially an oatcake, usually the fourth part of a round. **3** a large slice or piece of food *now NE.*

fardel[2] the third stomach of a ruminant.

farden a farthing.

fargis *see* **farkage**

farin food, fare.

farkage, fargis *Orkney* an untidy heap or bundle *now Orkney.*

farl a three-cornered piece of oatcake, scone etc.

farlan a long box for herrings awaiting gutting.

farm *see* **ferm**

farrant *see* **auld**

farrow, forrow *adjective, of a cow* not in calf.

fash *verb* trouble, annoy, anger, inconvenience: *"Dinna fash yersel".*
noun **1** trouble, pains, annoyance; bother. **2** a troublesome person.
fashious 1 troublesome, annoying. **2** fractious, bad-tempered.

fashions manners, behaviour.

fast: fast day *Presbyterian Churches* a day preceding the celebration of halfyearly Communion, treated as a holiday with a service of preparation *now mainly Highland.*

fast *see* **fest**

fastern's een Shrove Tuesday.

fat[1] a vat *now Shetland*

fat[2], **fattie, fatum** *marbles* applied to marbles in a ring game which are disqualified if they come to rest inside the ring.

fat *see* **what**

fate a feat.

faten *see* **whatten**

father *see* **faither**

fatten *see* **whatten**

†fatterals ribbon ends; anything loose and trailing.

fattie, fatum *see* **fat**[2]

fatuous †*law* in a state of imbecility and therefore incapable of managing one's own affairs.

fauch *noun* **1** a fallow field. **2** the breaking up of such land.
verb **1** plough or harrow (fallow ground). **2** scratch, rub, scrub hard *NE*.

fauchie *N* **1** pale (brown). **2** pasty-faced, sickly looking.

fauchle *verb* **1** work lazily, listlessly or ineffectually. **2** walk with difficulty, trudge, plod *now Caithness*.
noun a slow inept worker *now SW*.

faucht a fight, struggle, exertion *now WCentral SW*.

fauld¹ *noun* **1** a fold (of cloth etc). **2** a strand (of rope).
verb **1** fold. **2** shut, close. **3** *of the legs etc* double up, bend under one.

fauld² a fold, a pen.

fault *see* **faut**

faup *see* **whaup**

faur *see* **far**

fause, false false.
false face a faceshaped mask. **fause-hoose** a conical structure inside a corn stack to aid drying.

faut, fault *noun* **1** a fault. **2** a want, lack. **3** harm, injury *Shetland NE*.
verb find fault with, blame.
fauter a wrongdoer, especially against Church discipline.

favour: for any favour for goodness' sake.

†**feal** loyal, faithful.

feal *see* **fail**

fear *noun* a fright, a scare.
verb frighten, scare.
feared, feart, frightened. **feardie** a coward.

feasible *see* **faisible**

feat **1** neat, trim. **2** †fitting; clever.

feather, fedder *now Shetland Orkney N* **1** a feather. **2** the projecting wing on the sock of a plough, which cuts out the furrow.

featherfooly feverfew *now NE*.

fecht *verb, past* **focht** **1** fight. **2** wrestle,

kick or fling the limbs about *now NE*.
a bonnie fechter a good or fearless fighter, especially for a cause.

feck **1** †effect, force, value. **2** the majority, the greater part. **3** a (great etc) quantity, number, amount.
feckfu **1** effective, capable. **2** sturdy, forceful, powerful *now Fife*. **feckly** mostly, almost *now NE*.

fecket a woollen garment with sleeves and buttoned front.

fedder *see* **feather**

†**fee** **1** *also* **fees** a servant's wages, especially those paid half-yearly or for specific services. **2** an engagement as a servant.
verb **1** engage, hire as a servant. **2** accept an engagement as a servant.
feein(g) market one where farmers engaged servants.

feech, feuch [-ch as in 'dreich'] expression of disgust, pain or impatience.
feechie foul, dirty, disgusting.

feel¹ *verb* perceive by smell or taste.

feel² cosy, neat; comfortable; soft smooth to the touch.

feel *see* **fuil**

feem **1** fume. **2** a state of sudden heat, a sweat. **3** a state of agitation or rage.

feenish finish.

feer *ploughing* make the first guiding furrow on (the land).

feerd *see* **fuird**

feerich [-ch as in 'dreich'] *now NE* **1** ability, activity. **2** a state of agitation, excitement, rage or panic.

feerious *see* **furious**

Feersday *see* **Fuirsday**

feery-farry a bustle, a state of excitement or confusion.

fees *see* **fee**

feesant a pheasant.

feeze **1** twist, screw, cause to revolve. **2** wriggle (the body), wag (the tail). **3** work hard. **4** get oneself into another's favour.

fegs, faiks, *also* **by (my) fegs, guid fegs** *exclamation* indeed!, goodness!.

†**feid** hostility, enmity; a feud.

feignie, fenyie, †**fenzy** [fen(y)ie] **1** feign *now NE*. **2** act deceptively.

feik *see* **fyke**

fell¹ a (steep, rocky) hill; a stretch of hill-moor.

fell² **1** slaughter, kill. **2** injure; thrash.

fell³ **1** fierce, cruel, ruthless. **2** severe, acute. **3** extremely strong, big, loud etc. **4** energetic and capable, sturdy. **5** clever, shrewd. **6** †*of cheese* strong-tasting; *of drink* powerful, potent.
adverb **1** extremely, greatly, very. **2** vigorously, energetically; sternly.

fella *see* **fallow**¹

feltie(flier) [**fel**tie **flee**er] a fieldfare.

fence *law* open the proceedings of (a court) by uttering a formula forbidding interruption.

fend 1 defend, protect, shelter. **2** provide with food, sustenance. **3** support oneself.
noun **1** a defence, resistance. **2** an effort, attempt. **3** provisions, food.
fendie 1 able to look after oneself, thrifty. **2** active, lively, healthy.

fent¹ a slit or opening in a garment.

fent² faint.

fenyie, fenzy *see* **feignie**

fer *see* **far**

ferd *see* **fourt**

ferdy strong, active *now Shetland*.

†**fere**¹ healthy, sturdy; sound.

fere² a companion, comrade.

ferlie, fairly *noun* **1** a strange sight, a marvel, a curiosity, wonder. **2** a piece of (surprising) news; an object of gossip.
verb wonder, marvel, be surprised (at).

ferm, farm 1 farm. **2** a fixed yearly amount, as rent for land.
ferm toun the homestead of a farm.

fern bracken.

ferntickle, fairnytickle a freckle.

fernyear last year; the preceding year.

ferrier 1 a farrier. **2** a veterinary surgeon.

ferry farrow, produce young.

ferry-louper an inhabitant of Orkney who has come from the mainland.

fesh, fess 1 fetch. **2 fesh up** bring up, rear *now NE*. **3 fesh on** bring forward, advance *now NE*. **4** breathe with difficulty, pant *now Shetland*.

fest, fast 1 fast. **2** busy, occupied *now NE*.

fettle *noun* strength, vigour, condition.
verb **1** put to rights, repair; settle. **2** attend to the needs of, feed and clothe. **3** attack, 'go for' (a person). **4 fettle to, fettle wi** tackle (a job) with vigour.
adjective neat, trim; exactly suited *now SW*.

feu *law* **1** a feudal tenure of land, *latterly* giving exclusive possession and use in return for payment of a **feu duty** to a **superior. 2** a piece of land held by this tenure. **3** = **feu duty.**
feu duty the fixed annual payment for a **feu** (now being phased out).

feuch¹ [-ch as in 'dreich'] puff (at a pipe), smoke *NE*.

feuch² [-ch as in 'dreich'] a resounding blow *NE*.

feuch *see* **feech**

feugle *see* **fuggle**

few: a good few a good many, a considerable number of.

fey [rhymes with 'gey'] **1** *of people* fated to die, doomed, especially as portended by peculiar, usually elated behaviour; *more vaguely* otherworldly. **2** behaving in an excited or irresponsible way.

fey *see* **whey**

†**fiars** [**fee**ers] the prices of grain for the year, used to determine **ministers' stipends,** *latterly* fixed in spring by the local **sheriff** in the **Fiars Court.**

ficher [-ch- as in 'dreich'] **1** fumble, fiddle nervously with the fingers *Shetland NE*. **2** work in a bungling way *now NE*.
ficher wi handle (a woman) indecently, grope, 'touch up'.

fickle *adjective* difficult, tricky.
verb puzzle, perplex.

fidder *see* **futher**

fiddle a hand-machine for sowing grain.
fiddler's biddin a last minute invitation.

fiddler's news stale news.

fiddle face a long face; a sad face.

fidge fidget; move restlessly from excitement; twitch, itch.

fient 1 a fiend. **2** *as exclamation* the devil: **fient nor** would to the devil that.., **fient (a), the fient (a)** devil a, never a.

fiery *see* **fire**

Fife (Region) a **region** formed from the former county of Fife.

figmaleerie *see* **whigmaleerie**

file *see* **while**

files *see* **whiles**

filk *see* **whilk**

fill pour out.

filler a funnel for pouring liquids through.

fillebeg *literary* a kilt.

fillie a felloe, a rim of a wheel.

filsh a big, disagreeable person.

find *verb, past tense, past participle* **fun(d) 1** feel, be conscious of. **2** feel with the fingers, grope. **3** be aware of (a smell or taste).

fine *adjective* **1** comfortable, contented; in good health. **2** pleasant-mannered, likeable.

adverb very well, very much: *"I like it fine"*.

fine an(d).. very, properly, really..: *"it's fine and tight"*.

fineer 1 veneer. **2** ornament fancifully.

fine-gabbit *see* **gab**[1]

fingering a kind of fine wool.

finicky fussy, fiddling.

Finnan (haddock), **Finnan (haddie)** a haddock cured with the smoke of green wood, peat or turf.

finnock a young sea-trout or salmon.

fir: fir tap, fir yowe *now NE* a fir-cone.

fir *see* **for**

fire *noun* **1** fuel. **2** a foreign body in the eye.

verb **1** bake (oatcakes, scones, etc) by browning in an oven or over a flame. **2** inflame (a part of the body) by chafing. **3** heat (a house): *"keep the house fired"*.

fiery cross a wooden cross burnt at one end and dipped in blood at the other, carried from place to place by a succession of runners to call the fighting men of the district to arms. **firies** *skipping* very fast turns of the rope *Angus*. **fire-flaucht** (flashes of) lightning. **fire master** the chief officer of a firebrigade. **fire-raising** *law* arson. **fireside tartan** *see* **tartan**.

firlot a measure of capacity, the fourth part of a **boll** (see p 358).

firm *see* **furm**

first: first fit *noun* **1** the first person (or animal) met on a journey, especially by a wedding or christening party on the way to church. **2** the first person to enter a house on New Year's morning, considered to bring good (or bad) luck for the year. *verb* be the first to visit (a person) in the New Year; go on a round of such visits. **first floor** the ground floor of a building.

Monday *etc* **first** next Monday etc, Monday etc immediately following; *compare* **next**.

firth a wide inlet of the sea; an estuary.

firtig *see* **fortig**

fiscal = **procurator fiscal** (*see* **procurator**).

fish, fush 1 a salmon. **2** white fish, as opposed to herring.

fissle, fussle *verb* **1** make a rustling, scuffling noise. **2** †fidget, bustle.

fit, foot 1 a foot. **2** a foothold, step: *"lose one's fit"*.

fitter patter, move restlessly. **a left fitter** name (used by Protestants) for a Roman Catholic. **fittock 1** the foot of an old stocking worn as a shoe or as an extra sock or drawn over a boot. **2** a peat cut from the bottom of a peatbank when the upper layers have been removed.

fit folk pedestrians, especially those going to church, market etc on foot. **fit road** a footpath. **fit spar** a bar of wood across the floor of a boat for pressing the feet against when rowing. **feet-**

washin the ceremony of washing the feet of a bridegroom or bride, performed by friends on the eve of the wedding.
change one's feet change one's footwear. **gie (someone) up his fit** scold. **mak one's feet one's friend** go off quickly, take to one's heels *NE*. **tak (one's) fit in (one's) hand** start off, leave.

fit *see* **what**[1]

fitch move slightly or restlessly, edge along *now Shetland Orkney Caithness*.

fite *see* **white**[1], **white**[2]

fither *see* **whether**

fitin a whiting *NE*.

fitter *see* **fit**

fittit pleased, satisfied.

fittock *see* **fit**

five-stanes the game of **chucks** (*see* **chuck**[2]) played with five stones or pebbles.

fivver fever, often scarlet fever.

fizz make a fuss, bustle; be in great rage.

flae 1 a fly. **2** a flea.
flae-luggit harum-scarum, hare-brained.

flaff 1 flap, flutter. **2** *of the wind* blow in gusts.
flaffer flutter, flap.

flag a large snowflake *N*.

flagarie, †**fleegarie** [flagairie] **1** †an ornament, something excessively fancy. **2** a whim.

flaip a dull heavy fall.

flair flatter; boast.

flair *see* **fluir**

flake 1 a framework used as a fence, gate etc. **2 flakes** a temporary pen for sheep or cattle *NE, SW*.

flan, flam 1 a gust of wind (blowing smoke down a chimney) *now Shetland Orkney N*. **2** a sudden squall of wind.

flannen flannel.

flap fall down flat suddenly.

flash a tab of cloth on the garter of a kilt stocking.

flaucht 1 a burst of flame, a flash of lightning. **2** a flake (of snow) *now Shetland*.

flaucht *see* **flocht**

flauchter pare (turf) from the ground.

flauntie capricious, flighty.

flaw[1] **1** a kind of nail; the point of a horse-shoe nail. **2** a lie.

flaw[2] a gust or squall of wind.

flech [-ch as in 'dreich'] *noun* **1** a flea. **2** a restless, active person *NE Perth*.
verb rid of fleas.

flee[1]: **fleein** very drunk.
flee intae scold severely. **flee-up(-i-the air)** a frivolous or pretentious person.

flee[2] a fly, the insect.
let that flee stick to the wa drop a particular (embarrassing) subject. **not worth a flee** not worth anything at all.

fleece *see* **fleesh**

fleech [fleetch] coax, flatter, beg.

fleed *see* **flude**

fleegarie *see* **flagarie**

fleein *see* **flee**[1]

fleem, fleume *now Shetland Orkney* phlegm.

fleep a lazy lout, an oaf *Orkney Caithness NE*.

fleer *see* **fluir**

fleesh, fleece 1 a fleece. **2** a large number, a lot.

fleet *verb* float.
noun a set of nets or lines carried by a single boat.

fleg[1] *verb* frighten, scare. **2** drive away. **3** take fright, be scared.
noun a fright, a scare.

fleg[2] *noun* a severe blow.
verb fly or rush from place to place.

flenders *see* **flinders**

flesh butcher's meat.
flesher a butcher.

†**flether** flatter, cajole.

fleuk a flounder.

fleume *see* **fleem**

†**flewit** a blow, a slap.

fley [rhymes with 'gey'] frighten, scare; drive off by frightening.

flicht[1] **1** flight, the act of flying.

flicht[2] flight, the act of fleeing.

flicht[3] a flake, a small speck of soot, dust, snow etc.

flichter *verb* 1 *of birds* flutter, fly awkwardly; *of persons* rush about excitedly. 2 *of the heart* flutter, quiver, palpitate. 3 *of light* flicker. 4 startle, frighten.
noun 1 a fluttering; a state of excitement. 2 a small speck or flake of snow, soot etc. 3 a flicker, a glimmer.

flinders, flenders fragments, splinters, pieces.

fling *verb* 1 kick. 2 dance especially a Scottish dance. 3 jerk sideways as a sign of displeasure. 4 jilt.
noun 1 the act of kicking, a kick. 2 a dance. *see also* **Highland Fling** (*under* **Hieland**).
flingin tree the part of a flail which strikes the grain.

flird *verb* flutter; move restlessly.
noun 1 something thin, flimsy or tawdry. 2 a vain, dressy or fickle person.

flisk 1 dart from place to place, caper, frisk. 2 whisk. **fliskie** 1 restless, flighty, skittish. 2 *of a horse* apt to kick.

fliskmahaigo, fliskmahoy a flighty or frivolous woman.

flist *verb* 1 whizz; explode with a sharp hiss or puff. 2 fly into a rage *now NE*. 3 boast, brag; exaggerate *N*.

flit remove, transport from one place to another, *eg* to another house; move (tethered animals) to fresh grazing.
flitting 1 the act of moving from one house to another. 2 goods, especially household goods when being moved.
moonlight flitting removal of one's household at night to avoid paying debts.

floan *NE* 1 show affection, especially sloppily. 2 lounge, loaf.

float[1] grease, scum, especially on a boiling pot of soup, jam etc.

float[2] a flat spring cart without sides.

flocht, flaucht *noun* a flutter, a state of excitement; a bustle, a flurry, a great hurry.
flochter 1 flutter, flap; spread open, sprawl. 2 fluster.

flooer *see* **flour**

†florie vain, showy.

flosh *see* **flush**

flour, flooer, flower *noun* 1 a flower. 2 a bunch of flowers, a bouquet. 3 †the first water drawn from the well in the New Year. 4 wheaten flour.

flourish *verb* blossom, be in flower.
noun blossom, especially on fruit or hawthorn trees.

flow 1 a wet peat bog, a morass. 2 a very small quantity (of a powdery substance, *eg* meal, dust) *now NE*.

flower *see* **flour**

flude, fleed flood.

fluff *verb* 1 puff, blow. 2 flutter, move lightly in a breeze *now Shetland*.

fluffer flutter, flap.

fluir, flair, fleer *NE* floor.

flush, †flosh a piece of boggy ground, a pool of water.

fluther[1] flutter.

fluther[2] a boggy piece of ground.

flype[1] 1 fold back; turn wholly or partially inside out. 2 tear off (the skin) in strips, peel. 3 *of the tongue, lip, etc* curl.

flype[2] fall heavily.

flyte *verb* scold, rail at; quarrel violently.
noun a scolding (match).
flyting 1 scolding, quarrelling using abusive language. 2 †a contest between poets in mutual abuse.

fob pant with heat or exertion *NE*.

focht *see* **fecht**

fodge a fat, clumsy person *ECentral S*.

fodgel plump, buxom.

fog *noun* 1 fog, grass left in the field in winter. 2 moss, lichen.
verb 1 gather moss *now NE*. 2 save money *now NE*.
foggie bee a kind of wild bee.

fole a small, soft, thick oatcake *mainly Orkney*.

fole *see* **fuil**

folk *see* **fowk**

follow *see* **fallow**

follower the young of an animal,

especially one still dependent on its mother.

folp *see* **whample**

fommle *see* **whummle**

fond 1 foolishly keen, infatuated. **2** eager, glad (to do etc).

fond *see* **found**

foo, fow [foo] **1** how. **2** why, for what reason.

fool, foul a fowl, bird.

fool *see* **foul, fuil**

foon *see* **found**

fooner *see* **founder**

foos the houseleek *now NE.*

foost, foust [-oo-], **foosht** *verb* become or smell mouldy.

noun a mouldy condition or smell.

foot *see* **fit**

footer *see* **fouter**

footh *see* **fouth**

footie *see* **foutie**

for, fir, fur 1 for. **2** because of, as a result of, through. **3** *with infinitive*: *"She went out for to buy some".* **4 be for** wanting (to have): *"are ye for pudding".* **5** for fear of, to prevent: *"He winna wait for missing the bus".*

forad *see* **forrit**

foraneen *see* **forenuin**

forby *adverb* **1** besides, in addition, as well. **2** near, beside *now Ulster.* **3** extraordinarily *now Ulster*: *"he was forby kind".*

preposition **1** in addition to. **2** except. **3** compared with, relative to. **4** beside, beyond.

fordel a store, a reserve *NE.*

forder, further *verb* **1** further. **2** make progress, succeed.

adjective **1** further. **2** †*of limbs, teeth* front, fore.

fore: to the fore 1 on hand, in reserve. **2** alive, still in existence. **3** in advance, ahead.

forebreist the front part of something, *eg* of the gallery in a church.

foredoor 1 the front door of a building. **2** the front part of a box cart, with a seat on top for the driver.

fore-end the first or front part or portion (of something); the beginning or earlier part (of a period of time).

forefit the front part of the foot.

forefolk ancestors, forefathers.

foregain *now Orkney NE* opposite to, over against, in front of.

foregang an image of a person or some other supernaturual sign, thought to foretell a death; any premonition of misfortune.

forehaimmer, forehammer a sledge-hammer.

forehand 1 *of payments, now only of rents* made in advance. **2** first, foremost, leading.

forehandit 1 paid in advance. **2** farseeing, having thought for the future.

foremaist, foremost foremost.

backside foremaist back to front.

forenent 1 opposite to, in front of. **2** in return for, in exchange or payment for.

forenicht the evening; *latterly especially* the winter evening as a time for entertainment.

forenuin, forenoon, for(a)neen forenoon, morning.

foreroom the front part of a boat *now Shetland Fife.*

foreshot *distilling* the whisky that comes over first.

foreside the front or front part of something.

foresman a foreman, the head workman.

forest *law* a large area of ground, not necessarily still wooded, originally reserved for deer-hunting and belonging to the Crown.

free forest a forest in which the hunting rights were granted to the proprietor by the Crown under charter. **free forester** a person who was granted or claimed the rights of **free forest**; latterly a person who poached on deer forests.

foresta a manger, a feed trough in a **byre** *NE.*

forestair an outside staircase.

foresupper the period between the end of work and supper-time.

foresye a cut of beef from the shoulder.

forethaft the seat next to the bow in a rowing boat.

forewal(l) the front wall of a building.

Forfar bridie *see* **bridie**

forfauchlet worn out, exhausted.

forflutten severely scolded, excessively abused.

forfochtin, forfoughen [-ch-, -gh- as -ch in 'loch'] exhausted: *"sair forfoghten"*.

forgaither, forgather 1 assemble, gather together, congregate. **2** meet, fall in with, often by chance. **3** associate, keep company with. **4** get married *NE*.

forget, foryet *now Shetland verb* forget.
noun (an instance of) forgetfulness, absent-mindedness.
forgettle forgetful.

forgie [forgie] forgive.

forhoo *mainly of a bird* leave, abandon (a nest).

forisfamiliate *adjective, law, of a minor* living independently of his or her parents because of being married, having a separate estate etc.
verb provide separately for (a son or daughter).

forjeskit exhausted, worn out.

fork *noun* **1** a forkful. **2** a thorough search.
verb **1** *mainly* **fork for** search, hunt for (money, work etc). **2** fend for oneself.
forker, forkie, forkietail an earwig. **forkin 1** the crotch. **2** the point where a river divides.

forky-golach *see* **golach**

forlaithie *noun* a surfeit, an excess (of something): a feeling of revulsion *now NE*.
verb disgust through excess, sicken *NE*.

forleet neglect, leave behind, abandon.

†**fornyawd** tired, fatigued, worn out.

forpet a **lippie 1** mainly used for the sale of root vegetables and oatmeal *NE*.

forrit, furrit, forward, for(r)ad *adverb* **1** forward. **2** available for sale,

on the market.
adjective **1** forward. **2** *of a clock etc* fast. **3** present, at hand. **4** appearing in public for sale or a contest.
forritsome forward, impudent, bold.
forrit owre bent forward, stooped.
come forrit come forward in church to take communion.

forrow *see* **farrow**

Forsday *see* **Fuirsday**

forspoken put under a spell, bewitched, latterly especially by excessive praise.

forsta understand *Shetland Orkney NE*.

fortak hit, deal a blow at *NE*.

forth *see* **furth**

forthink *now NE* **1** think of with regret, regret that, repent of. **2** have second thoughts, reconsider.

forthy *see* **furth**

†**fortig** *now Shetland NE*, †**firtig** fatigue.

forwandert *literary* weary with wandering, bewildered, lost.

forward *see* **forrit**

foryet *see* **forget**

foster *verb* **1** promote, encourage (something). **2** feed, nourish.
noun **1** †a foster-child. **2** an adopted child *now Caithness*.

fosy *see* **fozie**

fot a footless stocking used as a gaiter *S*.
fottie a baby's bootee *S*.

fotch shift, turn, change the position of.

fother fodder.

fou [-oo-], **full** *adjective* **1** full. **2** full of food, well-fed. **3 fou** drunk: *"fou as a puggie"*; *roarin fou."*. **4 fou** comfortably well-off, well-provided for. **5** proud, pompous, conceited. **6** *of herrings* full of milt or roe, sexually mature.
adverb fully, very, exceedingly.
noun **1** a fill, one's fill, a full load. **2** †a **firlot. 3** a herring full of milt or roe *E*.
verb fill; load.
fuller a **filler** (*see* **fill**) *NE*. **fou-hand(it)** having the hands full, having enough.
ower fou hauden too well provided, too well off *S*.

foul, fule, fool [fool] *adjective* **1** foul. **2** dirty; unwashed.

the foul thief the Devil *now Shetland*.

foul *see* **fool**

foumart, thoumart [foomart, thoomart) **1** a polecat; latterly mainly a ferret or weasel. **2** term of abuse *mainly NE*.

found, foon [foon(d)] *verb* **1** found. **2** base one's opinions or conduct (up)on. **3** be based or established on.
noun **1** a foundation, base. **2** *also* **fond** a fund of money *now NE*.

founder, fooner [foon(d)er] *verb* **1** founder. **2** collapse, break down because of drink, exhaustion, illness etc. **3** fell, strike down (a person, animal etc).
noun **1** a collapse, breakdown in health. **2** a severe chill.
founderit exhausted, worn out, collapsed (especially due to cold or chill).

four *see* **fower**

fourt, fort, (*S*) **fowert,** †**ferd** fourth.

fousome [foosome] *adjective* **1** filthy, nasty, horrible. *now NE*. **2** *of food* filling, over-rich *now Shetland NE*.

foust *see* **foost**

foustie [foostie, fowstie] a kind of large thick bread roll, now white and floury but originally containing oatmeal *Angus Perth*.

fouter [-oo-], **footer** *noun* **1** †a horrible, nasty person. **2** an annoying person *mainly N*. **3** a slacker, a muddling, aimless person. **4** a chap, fellow. **5** a troublesome, fiddling job.
verb **1** potter, trifle, work in a fiddling, unskilled way. **2** thwart, inconvenience.
fouterie *of a person* fussy, inept; *of a task* trivial; fiddling, time-wasting.

fouth, footh plenty, abundance, an ample supply.

foutie [-oo-], **footie 1** mean, despicable, underhand. **2** obscene, indecent.

fow [rhymes with 'cow'] *noun* a pitchfork.
verb **1** lift or toss straw, hay etc with a fork. **2** kick about restlessly,

especially in bed *NE*.

fow *see* **foo**

fower, four four.
fowersie a game in which a set or group of four stones etc have to be picked up while another is thrown in the air.
fowersome 1 a group of four persons or things. **2** *also* **foursome reel** a reel danced by four people.
†**fower hours** a light meal or refreshment taken around this time.

fowk, folk *noun* **1** folk. **2** people, persons, mankind. **3** the inhabitants of a place. **4** the members of one's family, community etc. **5** servants, employees. **6** individual persons: *"here's twae folks fae Glasgow"*. **7** human beings as opposed to animals or supernatural beings.

foy a farewell feast; a party to celebrate a marriage, special occasion etc.

foze *see* **wheeze**

fozie, fosy *adjective* **1** *often of overgrown or rotten vegetables* soft, spongy. **2** *of rope etc* ragged, frayed *NE*. **3** fat, flabby, out of condition. **4** unintelligent, dull, stupid.

fozle *see* **wheeze**

F.P. *see* **free**

fra *see* **fae**²

fraca 1 a fracas. **2** a fuss, a bother. **3** a warm, close friendship or affection.

frack *see* **freck**

frae *see* **fae**²

fraik *noun* **1** †a freak, a whim, an odd notion. **2** flattery; affectionate fussing. **3** a flatterer, a wheedler. **4** a slight illness about which too much fuss is made *Orkney Angus*.
verb **1** flatter, make a fuss of, pamper. **2** pretend to be ill, make a fuss about a minor illness.

Frainche *see* **French**

frainesy, †**frenesy** frenzy.

fraise *see* **phrase**

frame 1 a square or hoop of wood hung from the shoulders on which to carry pails. **2** a painfully thin person or animal.

frank willing, eager, ready *now Angus*.

frase *see* **phrase**

fratch quarrel, argue, disagree *S*.

fraucht 1 the hire of a boat; the fare or freight charge for transport by water. **2** a load, a burden; as much as can be carried or transported at one time by one person. **3** †an amount, quantity, number. **4** a large amount, a generous supply.

frawart contrary, perverse; adverse, unfavourable.

Frayday *see* **Friday**

freath *see* **freith**

†freck, frack 1 bold, active, eager, forward. **2** able-bodied, vigorous.

Fredday *see* **Friday**

free, frei *now S adjective* **1** free. **2** single, unmarried. **3** ready, willing. **4** *of pastry etc* brittle, crumbly.

verb **1** free. **2** clear (someone of a suspicion etc). **3** *games, mainly hide-and-seek etc* put out of the game by reaching 'home' first.

noun **1 the Free** = **Free Church** (*see below*) or **United Free Church** (*see* **United**). **2** a member of these churches. **freedom** permission. **freely** entirely, completely, quite.

Free Church (of Scotland), Free Kirk *originally* the church which broke away from the Church of Scotland in 1843; *now* the minority of it who refused to unite with the United Presbyterian Church in 1900, often known colloquially as the **Wee Frees. free forest** *see* **forest. free-living** self-indulgent. **Free Presbyterian, F.P.** *(especially West Highland)* a member of the body which left the Free Church of Scotland in 1892. **†free trade** smuggling.

freen(d) *see* **friend**

freenge fringe.

freest frost *NE*.

freet[1] **1** rub, chafe, injure *now Fife*. **2** †fret, be vexed.

freet[2] **1** fruit *Caithness NE*. **2** milk

produce *Caithness*.

freet *see* **freit**

frei *see* **free**

freit, freet 1 freets superstitious beliefs, observances or acts. **2** a superstitious saying. **3** an omen. **4** a whimsical notion.

freith, freath 1 froth, foam, lather. **2** a hasty wash given to clothes.

fremd, fremmit 1 strange, unfamiliar, foreign; unrelated. **2** strange, unusual, uncommon. **3** strange in manner, distant, aloof.

the fremd strangers, the world at large.

fremmit *see* **fremd**

French, Frainche French.

French cake a kind of small sponge cake, iced and decorated. **French loaf** a kind of sweetened loaf giving a heart-shaped slice.

French and English a boys' game.

frenesy *see* **frainesy**

frequent associate, keep company with.

fresh *adjective* **1** *mainly of a habitual drunkard* sober. **2** *of weather* not frosty, thawing. **3** *of animals* thriving, fattening.

noun (the setting of) a thaw, a period of open weather.

verb **1** thaw *now NE*. **2** pack (herring) in ice ungutted, to be eaten fresh.

freuch [fr(ee)**ooch**] dry and brittle, liable to break *now NE*.

Freuchie [froochie, fru**chie**]: **gae tae Freuchie (and fry mice)!** go to blazes!

fricht *noun* fright.

verb frighten, terrify.

Friday, †Fredday *NE*, **†Frayday** Friday.

Friday('s) penny the penny etc given to children as pocket-money *NE*.

friend, freen(d) 1 a friend. **2** a relative.

be friends to be related to *now NE*.

frizz *of cloth etc* fray, wear out.

frizzel 1 the steel used for striking fire from a flint. **2** †the hammer of a flint-lock pistol or gun.

fro, froh froth, foam.

froh milk a mixture of cream and whey

beaten up and sprinkled with oatmeal *NE*.

frock 1 a sailor's or fisherman's knitted jersey. **2** a short oilskin coat or cape.

frog a young male horse from one to three years old *NE*.

froh *see* **fro**

front the front garden.

in front of *of time* before; prior to.

froon, froun frown.

frost *noun* ice.

verb protect (a horse) from slipping on ice by spiking its shoes.

frothy *see* **furth**

froun *see* **froon**

frow [rhymes with 'cow'] a big buxom woman *mainly NE*.

frugal frank, kindly, hospitable *Shetland Caithness NE*.

frull frill.

frush 1 crumbly. **2** *of wood, cloth etc* brittle, decayed, rotten. **3** frank, bold, rash. **4** tender, easily hurt or destroyed, frail.

fry 1 a small number of fish for frying especially when presented as a gift. **2** a state of worry or distraction, a disturbance.

fryne grumble, whine.

fud *noun* **1** the buttocks. **2** the tail of an animal. **3** the female genitals.

verb frisk about; walk briskly or with a short, quick step.

fud *see* **whud**

fudder *see* **futher, whidder**

fuddle get drunk on, drink the proceeds of.

fude, †fuid [rhymes with 'guid'] food.

fuff *verb* **1** puff (smoke or vapour) hiss. **2** go off in a huff or rage.

exclamation indicating an explosive noise, or expressing contempt, fsst!, bah!

fuffle *verb* dishevel, ruffle, disarrange clothes etc).

noun fuss, violent exertion.

fuggle, feugle *NE* **1** a small bundle of hay, rags etc, especially one used to stop up

a hole. **2** an unburnt plug of tobacco in a pipe.

fugie [f(ee)oojie] **1** a runaway, a fugitive; a coward. **2** a runaway cock from a cock-fight. **3** a challenge to fight given by one schoolboy to another. **4** a truant from school.

verb, mainly **fugie the schule** play truant *now NE*.

fuid *see* **fude**

fuil, feel, fool, †fole *noun* a fool.

adjective foolish, silly.

fuile *see* **fulyie**

fu(i)lzie *see* **fulyie**

fuird, feerd, *NE* a ford.

fuirdays 1 †late in the day. **2** †broad daylight. **3** the earlier part of the day, the morning *now SW*.

Fuirsday, Forsday, Feersday Thursday.

fule *see* **foul**

full *see* **fou**

†fulyie, fuile, fu(i)lzie [fool(y)ie] filth, dirt, garbage; dung, excrement.

fum a wet spongy peat or turf *now SW*.

fummle fumble.

fummle *see* **whummle**

fumper *see* **whumper**

fun *see* **whun**[1], **whun**[2]

fun(d) *see* **find**

†fundlin a foundling.

†fundy, funnie suffer a chill, become stiff with cold.

fung, funk 1 *especially of a restive horse* kick. **2** throw violently and abruptly, toss, fling. **3** strike with the hands or feet *now NE*. **4** fly up or along at high speed and with a buzzing noise, whizz. **5** fly into a temper or rage, sulk *NE*.

fungibles *law* consumable goods; perishable goods which may be estimated by weight, number or measure.

funk *see* **fung**

funnie *see* **fundy**

funny a game, usually of marbles, played for fun, where no score is kept and all winnings are restored to the loser.

fup *see* **whup**

fupperty jig a trick, dodge *mainly NE*.

fur *see* **for, fur(r)**

furious, feerious *NE* **1** furious. **2** †*law* mad, insane, especially violently. **3** extraordinarily good, excellent *NE*.

furl *see* **whurl**

furm, firm form.

fur(r) *noun* **1** a furrow made by the plough; the strip of earth turned over in the process. **2** the deep furrow or trench separating one **rig**[1] from another *now Shetland*. **3** a deep furrow etc cut by the plough to act as a drain. **4** the act of furrowing, a ploughing; a turn-over with a spade *now Orkney NE*.

verb **1** plough, make furrows in. **2** make drills in or for, draw soil around (plants), earth up.

furrit *see* **forrit**

furrow the earth turned over in a furrow by the plough.

furth, forth, furt *Shetland adverb* **1** forth. **2** outside, out of doors, in(to) the open air *now Shetland NE*.

preposition out of, from, outside.

noun the open air *now NE*.

furthie, forthy, frothy *NE* **1** forward, bold; go-ahead, energetic; impulsive *now NE*. **2** †frank, friendly, affable. **3** generous, hospitable.

furth the gait candid(ly), honest(ly), straightforward(ly) *now NE*. **furth of 1** out of, outside, away from, beyond the confines or limits of: *"furth of Scotland."* **2** †out of the revenues of, at the expense of.

the furth out of doors, in the open, away from home *now NE*.

further *see* **forder**

fush *see* **fish**

fushion, fusion [fooshen] **1** the nourishing or sustaining element in food or drink. **2** physical strength, energy; bodily sensation, power of feeling *now NE*. **3** mental or spiritual force or energy; strength of character, power *now NE*.

fushionless 1 *of plants* without sap or pith, dried, withered. **2** *of food* lacking

in nourishment, tasteless, insipid. **3** *of actions, speech etc* without substance, dull, uninspired. **4** *of people* physically weak, without energy; numb, without feeling *NE*. **5** *of things* without strength or durability; weak from decay. **6** spiritless, faint-hearted, lacking vigour or ability.

fushnach *see* **fussoch**

fusion *see* **fushion**

fusker a whisker, moustache *NE*.

fuskie *see* **whisky**

fussle *see* **fissle, whistle**

fussoch, fushnach *SW* **1** waste straw, grass etc *now SW*. **2** a loose bundle of something *now NE*.

fussy affected in dress or manner, dressy.

†futher, fudder, fidder 1 a cart-load. **2** a large number of people, a company.

futher *see* **whidder**

futley *see* **whittle**[2]

futrat *see* **whitrat**

futtle *see* **whittle**[1]

fuzzie effervescent, hissing, fizzing *now NE*.

fy *exclamation* †hurry!

fy ay, fy na yes, indeed! certainly (not)! *NE*.

fy *see* **whey**

fyke, feik, fyk *now Shetland verb* **1** move about restlessly, fidget. **2** fret, be anxious or troubled. **3** †bother, trouble, vex. **4** exert oneself, take trouble or pains (with). **5** bustle about, fiddle, make a fuss about nothing.

noun **1** a restless movement a twitch; **fykes** the itch, the fidgets, (a fit of) restlessness. **2** a fuss, bustle, excitement. **3** trouble, bother, worry; **fykes** petty cares. **4** an intricate and usually trivial piece of work, a trifle. **5** a whim, a fussy fad. **6** a fussy, fastidious person.

fykie 1 *of people* restless, fidgety, finicky. **2** *of a task etc* tricky, troublesome, intricate and difficult to manage. **make a fyke** make a fuss (about).

fyle 1 make dirty, soil. **2** soil with excrement. **3** defecate. **4** †pollute; infect. **5**

defile morally, debauch, desecrate. **6** †convict, blame.

fyle one's fingers wi have to do with, meddle with (something debasing).

fyle the stamach upset the stomach, make one sick.

fyllies *see* **whiles**

G

ga, gaw gall, bile etc.

gab[1] *noun* **1** speech, conversation, way of speaking. **2** entertaining talk, chat, cheek. **3** a chatterbox, gossip.
verb talk, chatter.
gabbie chatty; fluent. **gabbit** talkative.

gab[2] **1** a **gob**[1], a mouth, beak. **2** †the palate, taste.
-gabbit -mouthed; *eg* **fine-gabbit** fussy about food.
haud one's gab, steek one's gab hold one's tongue, shut up. **set up one's gab** speak out boldly or rudely. **thraw one's gab** make a face *now NE*.

gab[3]: **the gab o May** stormy weather at the beginning of May.

gabbart a barge, a small cargo ship, mainly on the Clyde.

gabbie, gabbit *see* **gab**[1]

gabbit *see* **gab**[1], **gab**[2]

†gaberlunzie a beggar, a tramp.

gaberts scaffolding.

gad exclamation of disgust.

gad *see* **gaud**

gadder *see* **gaither**

gadge *see* **gauge**

gadgie a man, fellow *originally S, now also Edinburgh*.

gae, go *verb, past tense also* **gaed, geed** *Orkney N,* **gied.** *past participle also* **gane, geen** *Shetland N. present participle also* **gaun 1** go. **2** cover on foot, walk. **3** *of animals* graze *now NE*.
noun **go** a fuss, bother; a state: *"in a go"*.
gane 1 past, ago: *"Sunday gane a week"*. **2 nae farrar gane (than)** as recently (as). **3** over, more than (a certain age): *"he's eighteen gane", "she's gane forty-twa"*. **4** mad, crazy. **gaun** *of a child* at the walking stage. **gaun (-aboot) bodie** a tramp. **gaun gear 1** the machinery of a mill. **2** people in failing health, especially those about to die *NE, SW*. **3** money or property that is being wasted *NE, SW*. **gaunie, gennay** going to. **gaein aboot** *of a disease or complaint* a lot of it about.
gae about the bush speak about in a roundabout or tactful way. **gae awa 1** die. **2** faint. **3** command expressing impatience, disbelief etc: *"g'wa wi ye"*. **gae back** get worse, run down, fall off. **gae by someone's door** pass someone's house without calling in, shun. **gae done** be used up or worn out, come to an end. **gae in** shrink. **gae in twa** break in two, snap *now NE*. **gae in wi** agree with. **gae into** open and search (a bag etc). **gae lie** go to bed *SW*. **gae ower** be beyond a person's power or control; get the better of (someone). **gae tae** shut, close. **gae thegither 1** come together, close. **2** *of lovers* court. **gae through 1** waste, *especially* **gae through't** become bankrupt, penniless. **2** bungle, muddle (speech) *mainly N*. **gae through the fluir** be overcome with shame, embarrassment, astonishment. **gae through ither** make a mess of things. **gae wi 1** keep company with, court (a lover). **2** go pleasantly or smoothly for *now NE, Perth*. **upon go** *of persons, things* restlessly active; much in use *now Shetland NE*.

gae *see* **gie**

gaebie *see* **gebbie**

gaed, gaein *see* **gae**

Gael a Highlander, a Gaelic-speaker.

Gaelic [galick, gaylick] **1** the Celtic language of the Highlands and Islands. **2** (Irish or Manx) Gaelic.

gaff *noun* a guffaw, a hearty laugh.
verb **1** guffaw, laugh heartily. **2** babble, chatter.

gaffaw *noun* a guffaw, a hearty laugh.

verb laugh loudly and heartily or coarsely, guffaw.

gage *see* **gauge**

gaig 1 a crack, chink. **2** a chap in the hands.

gaikit *see* **geck**

gaillie, gellie 1 a galley, a kind of ship. **2** a garret, especially in a **bothy**; a **bothy** *NE*.

gaily *see* **gey**

gainder, gainer *see* **ganner**

gaing *see* **gang**

gair¹ 1 a gore, a triangular piece of cloth in a garment. **2** †*in ballads* a triangular opening in a garment. **3** a strip or patch of green grass, usually on a hillside *mainly SW, S*. **4** a patch of marshy ground in heather *often* **green gair** *Orkney S*. **5** a dirty streak or stain on clothes.

gairy bee the black and yellow striped wild bee *now S*.

†gair² 1 greedy. **2** mean; thrifty, careful.

gaird guard.

gairden a garden.

gairdener's ga(i)rtens ribbon-grass.

gairten *see* **garten**

†gairy a crag *SW*.

gaishon a thin, starved-looking person, a 'skeleton' *SW, S*.

gaisling a gosling.

gait¹, goat a goat.

gait hair, goat('s) hair cirrus cloud.

gait², gyte *NE* a single sheaf of grain tied near the top and set up to dry.

gaither, gadder *now Shetland*, **gether, gedder** *NE*, **gather 1** gather. **2** save. **3** make a collection (of money contributions), collect (money) in subscriptions. **4** *harvesting* bring together enough corn to form a sheaf when cut *now NE*. **5** plough so as to throw the soil in (a central ridge). **6** collect one's wits, pull oneself together, get better, improve in health. **7** *of butter* form, collect in the churn. **8** prepare (a fire) for the night or a long time without attention, place a **gathering-coal** on the raked embers.

gaithered, weel-gaithered rich, well-to-do. **gaitherin(g) 1** gathering. **2** gathering a signal on drum or bagpipe to (fighting) men to assemble; a tune used for this purpose; one of the types of **pibroch. 3 Highland Gathering** = **Highland Games** (*see* **game** 2). **gatherin(g) coal, gatherin(g) peat** a large piece of coal or peat laid on the embers to keep a fire alive for a long time without attention. **gathering psalm** the psalm sung at the beginning of a church service.

gaither-up a mixed collection.

gaive move clumsily, aimlessly or restlessly *S*.

galash a galosh.

Galatian, Galoshan [galashan, galoshan] **1** †a play performed by boy **guisers** (*see* **guise**) at **Hogmanay. 2** the name of the hero in such a play. **3** an actor in such a play.

gale *see* **gavel, gell³**

gall gale, bog-myrtle.

gall *see* **gaw**

gallant *adjective* **1** gallant. **2** large, ample.
noun gallant.
verb gad about, gallivant; flirt.

gallon †a gallon Scots = (approx) 3 Imperial gallons (see p 359).

Gallovidian of Galloway; a native of Galloway.

Galloway 1 a Galloway, a small sturdy type of horse. **2** a breed of (black,) hornless cattle.

belted Galloway a breed of **Galloway** cattle with a broad white band round a black body.

gallows, gallus *noun* gallows.
adjective **1** wicked *mainly WCentral*. **2** **gallus** wild, unmanageable, bold; mischievous, cheeky.

galluses 1 trouser braces. **2** †a yoke for carrying pails.

Galoshan *see* **Galatian**

galraivitch *see* **gilravage**

galshach, *mainly* **galshachs** *NE* **1** sweets, titbits. **2** trashy (especially sweet) food.

3 luxuries, treats.

galt *see* **gaut**

gamf *see* **gumph**

gams 1 (large) teeth *now NE.* **2** the jaws.

game, gemm 1 a game. **2 games,** *often* **Highland Games** a meeting consisting of athletics, piping and dancing, held originally in the Highland area.
gamie, gemmie a gamekeeper.
game-watcher a gamekeeper *NE.*
make game joke.

gamf *see* **gumph**

gamp 1 gape *S.* **2** eat or drink greedily *S.*

gamphrell *see* **gumph**

gan go.
gan on aboot make a fuss about.

gandiegow a squall of wind and rain; a noisy quarrel *mainly Shetland Orkney Caithness.*

gandy, gannie boast, talk cheekily.

gane *see* **gae, gin**[1]

gang, ging *NE,* **gaing** *Shetland,* **geng, gyang** *NE* [geeang], **dyang** *NE* [deeang] *verb* go.
noun **1** a journey, trip (especially when carrying goods). **2** a load, the quantity that can be carried at one time, especially of water. **3** (a stretch of) pasture. **4** a passage, thoroughfare. **5** way of walking, gait. **6** a row, in knitting plaiting or weaving *now Shetland Orkney Caithness.* **7** a layer, especially of corn-sheaves in a cart or stack.
gangrel(l) 1 a tramp. **2** a toddler *N.*
gang awa faint. **gang done** be used up or worn out, come to an end *now NE.* **(gang) a gray gate** *see* **gray**[1]. **gang lie** go to bed *SW.* **gang one's ways** go away, leave. **gang oot amang folk** work as a charwoman, washerwoman etc in private houses. **gang ower** overcome, beat *now Orkney NE.* **gang throw** waste. **gang together** get married *Shetland NE.*

gange *NE* chatter; boast; exaggerate.

gangrel(l) *see* **gang**

ganner, gainer, gainder *noun* a gander.
verb wander about aimlessly or foolishly.

gannie *see* **gandy**

gansel 1 †garlic sauce served with goose. **2** a disagreeable or rude comment, a scolding.

gansey, genzie a guernsey, a jersey, especially one worn by fishermen.

gansh 1 *of a dog,* snatch (at), snap, snarl. **2** stammer.

gant, gaunt yawn.

gantree, gantry 1 *also* **gantrees, gantrice** a gantry. **2** a bottle stand in a bar.

gapus *see* **gaup**

gar[1] **1** filth, slime. **2** any soft doughy mixture *Shetland.*

gar[2]**, ger 1** give instructions, take steps (to do or make something): *"the Captain garr'd set up a gallows".* **2** make (a person or thing do something): *"to gar him come".*

gardevine a (large) wine or spirits bottle.

gardy 1 the arm, *now NE.* **2 gardies** hands or fists (raised to fight).

†**gardyloo** a warning call that waste, dirty water etc was about to be poured into the street from an upper storey *mainly Edinburgh.*

garibaldi a kind of bun or scone.

garnel *see* **girnel**

garron[1] **1** a small sturdy type of horse, used especially for rough hill work. **2** an old, worn-out horse. **3** a strong, thickset man or sturdy boy *NE.*

garron[2] a wooden beam *now Orkney Caithness.*
garron nail a large nail or spike, especially the kind used in fixing the body of a cart to its axle.

garten, gairten, gerten *now Shetland Orkney,* **garter 1** a garter. **2** a leaf of ribbon-grass.
get the green garter said about an older sister or brother when a younger one marries first.

garth 1 an enclosure, yard, garden *now only as a place-name especially of farms.* **2** a shallow part of a river or stretch of shingle used as a ford *NE.*

garvie a sprat.

gash¹ *literary* pale, grim.

gash² †a chin that juts out.

 gash-gabbit 1 with a lower jaw that juts out. **2** *also* **gash-mou'd** with a sagging, badly-shaped mouth.

gash³ *noun* chat, talk, impudent language. *adjective* talkative.

 gash-gabbit talkative, glib.

gash⁴ **1** shrewd, wise. **2** well or neatly dressed, respectable.

†**gast** a fright.

gate, get 1 a way, road, path. **2** a street *now mainly in street-names*. **3** way, direction. **4** -where, *eg* **nae gate** nowhere, **some gate** somewhere. **5** length of a way, distance. **6** a journey, trip *now Fife WCentral*. **7** way, means, method of doing something; a knack. **8** -how, rate, *eg* (**at**) **ony gate** at any rate, **nae gate** in no way. **9** a way of behaving, manner *now NE*.

 gate en(d) a neighbourhood.

 gang one's gate go on one's way. **gang one's ain gate** follow one's own opinions etc. **in the gate** on the way, along the road *now NE*. **out o the gate** out of the way. **out the gate** on one's way, along the road, up the road. **tak the gate** set off.

gate-slap an opening, gateway *NE, SW*.

gather *see* **gaither**

gaud, gad 1 †a rod or bar of iron or steel. **2** a goad. **3** a wooden slat used to direct the corn to the scythe or binder *NE*. **4** a fishing-rod *S*.

gauge, gage, †**gadge** *noun* **1** a gauge, a standard measure. **2** *net-making* a template used in netmaking.

 †*verb* check the contents of a cask; perform the duties of an exciseman.

 gauger an exciseman.

gaun, gaunie *see* **gae**

gaunt *see* **gant**

gaup, gowp [-ow- as in 'cow'] *verb* **1** gawp, stare open-mouthed. **2** eat greedily, devour.

 noun **1 gaup, gaupie** a fool, a person who gapes. **2** †a large mouthful, a gulp.

3 gowp a stare *NE*.

 gaupit stupid silly. **gawpus, gapus** a fool, a clumsy stupid lout.

gaut *now Shetland Orkney N*, **galt** a pig, usually a boar or hog.

gavel, gale *NE* **1** a gable. **2** one of the side ropes of a herring-net *Orkney NE, Fife*.

 like the gavel (end) of a hoose very big and stout.

gavelock, gellock *SW* **1** a crowbar, lever. **2** an earwig or other similar insect.

gaw, gall *noun* **1** a gall, a sore etc. **2 gaw** a defect, mark *eg* a gap in woven cloth. **3** a drainage channel *now Fife*.

 verb **1** †gall, make sore. **2** gall, irritate.

gaw *see* **ga**

gawk *noun, also* **gawkie** an awkward, clumsy person, a fool.

 verb **1** *also* **gawkie** play the fool, flirt *now Angus*. **2** wander aimlessly, idle. **3** stare idly or vacantly *now SW*.

 gawkit stupid, clumsy.

gawpus *see* **gaup**

gawsie 1 *of people or their appearance* plump, fresh-complexioned, cheery, handsome, imposing. **2** *of animals* handsome, in good condition. **3** *of things* large; handsome, showy.

gay *see* **gey**

gazen *see* **gizzen**

geak *see* **geck**

geal *see* **jeel**

gean a wild cherry.

gear 1 possessions, goods, money, *often* **goods and gear**. **2** livestock, cattle. **3** stuff, material. **4** worthless things, rubbish *now N*. **5** food, drink.

 gear gatherer a hoarder, a person who makes money.

 guid gear gangs in sma buik applied to a small but capable person. **naither gear nor guid** nothing at all.

gebbie, gaebie 1 the crop of a bird *ECentral*. **2** a person's stomach. **3** a person's mouth, a bird's beak *ECentral*. **4** a horn spoon *Shetland Orkney NE*.

geck, geak [g- as in 'get'] *noun* **1** †a scornful gesture or remark, a trick. **2** †a

scornful or disdainful manner *SW*.
verb **1** mock at, scoff at. **2** toss the head scornfully, raise the head proudly. **3** stare rudely. **4** turn the head in a flirty or foolish way *now NE*.

gaikit silly *Shetland NE*. **geckin** lively, playful.

geck-neck(it) (having) a twisted neck *NE*.

ged a pike.

gedder *see* **gaither**

gee [g- as in 'get'] a fit of temper, a mood, fancy.

tak the gee take offence, sulk.

geebald [jeebawld] a type of long-handled sickle *S*.

geeble *see* **jibble**

geed *see* **gae**

geelum [g- as in 'get'] a rabbet-plane.

geem *see* **gum**[1]

geen *see* **gae**

geenyoch [g- as in 'get'] ravenous; greedy.

geese *see* **guse, gussie**

geesen *see* **gizzen**

geesie *see* **gussie**

geeskin *see* **joskin**

geg[1] [g- as in 'get'] a gig, a poacher's hook for catching fish.

geg[2] [g- as in 'get'] gag, trick *mainly Glasgow*.

geg[3] [g- as in 'get'] the thing (*eg* a penknife, a piece of wood) used in the game of **smuggle the geg** a boys' game, the aim of the two teams respectively being to protect or capture the **geg**[3].

geggie [g- as in 'get'] a travelling theatrical show.

geil *see* **gell**[1]

geill *see* **jeel**

geing, ging [g- as in 'get'] human excrement; filth.

geisen *see* **gizzen**

gell[1], **geil** [g- as in 'get'] *Shetland Caithness* tingle, smart, ache with pain or cold *now Shetland Caithness*.

gell[2] [g- as in 'get'] a crack (in wood).

gelled *of unseasoned wood* split or cracked in drying.

gell[3], **gale** [g- as in 'get'] **1** a gale. **2** *only* **gale** inspiration, spiritual uplift: *"he prayed with a great gale of the spirit"*. **3 in a gale** in a state of excitement from anger, joy etc. **4** *mainly* **gell** a brawl, row, squabble. **5** †*only* **gell** a romp, a drinking-bout, *often* **on the gell**.

†**gell**[4] [g- as in 'get'] sharp, keen, brisk.

gell[5], **gellie** [g- as in 'get'] a leech.

gellie *see* **gaillie**

gellock *see* **gavelock**

gemm(ie) *see* **game**

gener 1 gender. **2 puddock's gener** frog-spawn *Fife*.

general: General Assembly *Presbyterian Churches* the highest church court made up of representative **ministers** and **elders** assembled annually in Edinburgh. **general merchant** *see* **merchant**.

geng *see* **gang**

gennay *see* **gae**

gennick *see* **jonick**

gent [g- as in 'get'] a tall, thin person *Shetland SW, S*.

genteelity, gentility 1 gentility. **2** gentry, people of good birth.

gentie [jentie] *now NE, Fife* **1** neat, dainty, graceful. **2** genteel; courteous, well-bred.

gentle †well-born.

the gentle persuasion the Episcopalian denomination *NE*.

gentrice [jentris] **1** †the character or behaviour of a person of good birth or high rank. **2** good birth or breeding. **3** people of good birth or breeding, gentry.

gentry 1 = **gentrice** 1 *now NE*. **2** good birth, rank of a gentleman *now Angus*.

genzie *see* **gansey**

geordie 1 a guinea coin, *mainly* **yellow geordie**. **2** a country person.

ger *see* **gar**[2]

gerrock [g- as in 'get'] a coal-fish in its first year *NE*.

gers *see* **girse**

'Gers nickname for Rangers football team.

gerten *see* **garten**

gester 1 a gesture. **2** strut, swagger *now WCentral*.

get, git *verb* **1** get. **2** find, get by looking: *"ye'll get it in ma pooch"*. **3** marry: *"who did Tibbie get?"* **4** be called, be addressed as: *"Mackenzie's ma name but I aye get Jock fae her"*. **5** be able, be allowed, manage (to do something): *"I couldna get sleeping"*; *"they cannot get met on a week day"*; *"can I get downstairs?"* **6** be struck, get a hit *NE*: *"I gat i the lug wi a steen"*.

noun, also **gyte 1** a child, young of animals etc. **2** a brat; a bastard. **3** a coalfish in its second stage *now NE, Fife*.

getling *often abusive* a young child, infant.

get awa(y) die. **get by 1** avoid, do without *now Shetland NE*. **2** get past, succeed in passing. **get (one's) hands on** catch (someone). **get into** succeed in opening (something). **get on to be, get on for** get a job as, be promoted to. **get on to** scold, attack in words. **get out** give full vent to, finish up. **get out wi** let out (a roar). **get ower 1** last out, subsist *now NE*. **2** get the upper hand of. **get (it) ower the fingers** be told off. **get roon** master, get the hang of, manage to do. **get through** escape, recover from. **get up in(to) years** grow old. **get well up** rise in position, succeed.

get *see* **gate**

gether *see* **gaither**

getling *see* **get**

gey, gay, gie [g- as in 'get'] *adjective* **1** excellent, splendid. **2** wild, wicked. **3** *of quantity or amount* fairly large, considerable, good(-sized), great: *"a gey few"*.

adverb considerably, very; rather: *"gey far"*.

gaily, geylies 1 pretty, rather; very. **2** fairly well, pretty well, pretty nearly. **3** *of health* well enough, fairly well.

gey and rather, very: *"gey and handy"*.

gey kind o rather badly.

geyze [gey- as in 'gey'] become leaky, warp.

ghaist 1 a ghost. **2** contemptuous term for a nasty (looking) person or for a sickly or undersized person. **3** *also* **guest** (a piece of) shaly coal burnt to its ashy state, a white slaty cinder.

ghillie *see* **gillie**

gib, gibbie a cat; a tom-cat, especially a neutered male.

gibbery[1] gingerbread *N*.

gibbery[2] a kind of marbles game *N*.

gibbie *see* **gib**

gibble-gabble [g- as in 'get'] chatter.

gibbles tools, things.

gibblet [g- as in 'get'] a tool, utensil.

giblet-check a groove to allow a door to fit flush with the wall *now NE*.

gid gad, gid gow [g- as in 'get'] exclamation of disgust.

gie [g- as in 'get'], **give, gae 1** give. **2** strike: *"give him across the head with the butt of your rod"*.

gies give us, give me. **gimme** give me. **given 1** *usually implying exasperation* 'blasted': *"A had tae sit twa given hours"*. **2 given name** first name, Christian name.

gie ower give up, abandon *now Shetland NE*.

gie *see* **gey**

gied *see* **gae**

gif [g- as in 'get'] if *now literary*.

giff-gaff [g- as in get] *noun* **1** helping each other, give and take, fair exchange. **2** exchange of talk *now ECentral SW*.

verb exchange (especially words).

gig [g- as in 'get'] *mining* a winding engine.

gig *see* **jeeg**

gigot [jiggot] a leg (of lamb, pork etc).

gilgal [g- as in 'get'] a commotion, uproar *now Shetland*.

gill [g- as in 'get'] a ravine, gully.

gillie, ghillie [g- as in 'get'] *noun* **1** a sportsman's attendant, usually in deerstalking or angling in the Highlands. **2** †a male servant, especially an attendant on a Highland chief; a Highlander. **3** †a young lad.

verb act as a sportsman's attendant.

gillie callum the **sword-dance** (*see* **swurd**); the name of the tune to which it is danced.

gillieperous [g- as in 'get'] a fool *NE*.

gilly-gawpus [g- as in 'get'] a stupid person, a fool *now NE*.

gilp *see* **jilp**

gilpie [g- as in 'get'] **1** †a lively, mischievous youth. **2** a lively young girl, a tomboy.

gilpin [g- as in 'get'] a big, stout or wellgrown young person; a lout.

gilravage, galraivitch, gulravage *now Shetland,* **gulravish** [g- as in 'get'] *verb* **1** eat and drink greedily, indulge in high living. **2** make merry, enjoy oneself noisily, create a disturbance. **3** rove about, especially to plunder.

noun **1** merry-making, horseplay, commotion. **2** a state of confusion, a disturbance. **3** a noisy disorderly crowd, a mob *SW*.

gilse *see* **grilse**

gilt¹ [g- as in 'get'] **1** gild. **2** become yellow.

gilt² [g- as in 'get'] a young sow.

gim neat, spruce *now NE*.

gimme *see* **gie**

gimmer [g- as in 'get'] a year-old ewe; a ewe between its first and second shearing.

gimmer *see* **cummer**²

gin¹, **gane** [g- as in 'get'] **1** if, whether: *"gin you please sir".* **2** oh that, if only: *"Oh gin they were awa!"*

gin² [g- as in 'get'] *preposition* **1** by, before: *"gin ten o'clock".* **2** in readiness for *NE*: *"gin Yeel".* **3** than *NE*.

conjunction by the time that, when, before, until: *"gin we get there it's time to milk the ky".*

ging *see* **gang, geing**

ginge ginger.

gingebreid gingerbread.

ginger lemonade, aerated water of any flavour *WCentral*.

gink, ginkum [g- as in 'get'] **1** a trick, notion *NE*. **2** a habit.

ginnle [g- as in 'get'] *mainly WCentral noun* **ginnles 1** the gills (of a fish). **2** the cheeks.

verb catch (a fish) by the gills.

gip [g- as in 'get'] the jaw of a fish *now NE, Fife*.

gipe *see* **jupe**

gird¹, **gir(r)** [g- as in 'get'] **1** a saddle girth. **2** a band or hoop for a barrel. **3** a child's hoop. **4** †a hoop for a skirt or petticoat.

gird² [g- as in 'get'] *noun* **1** a knock, blow. **2** †a moment.

verb **1** rush (at), do vigorously. **2** †strike, deliver a blow, *often* **let gird**. **3** push, force.

gird³ [g- as in 'get'] **1** †fasten with a band. **2** fit (a barrel etc) with hoops.

girding 1 fitting a barrel with hoops. **2** a saddle-girth *now Shetland*.

girdle [g- as in 'get'] an iron plate used for baking, traditionally circular with a hooped handle for hanging over a fire.

girdle scone a scone baked on a girdle, frying pan or hotplate.

like a hen on a het girdle restless(ly), anxious(ly), impatient(ly).

girl [g- as in 'get'] *S* **1** shudder with fear or dread. **2** *of the teeth* be set on edge.

girn¹ [g- as in 'get'] *verb* **1** snarl, grimace. **2** screw up (the face) or gnash (the teeth) in rage or disapproval. **3** complain, whine, grumble. **4** grin, sneer. **5** *of clothes* gape *now Lothian*. **6** *of soil* crack.

noun **1** a snarl. **2** a whine, whimper; whining; grumbling. **3** a grin, gimace *now Shetland Caithness*. **4** a gaping furrow.

girnie *adjective* ill-tempered. *noun* a fretful, bad-tempered person. **girnie-gib** [g- as in 'get'], **girnigo gabbie** = **girnie.**

girn² [g- as in 'get'] a snare.

girnel, garnel [g- as in 'get'] **1** a storage

chest for meal. **2** †a granary, storehouse.

girr *see* **gird**[1]

girran [g- as in 'get'] a small boil *Highland*.

girse, gers, gress, grass *noun* **1** grass. **2** **girse** a stalk or blade of grass *now NE*.
verb **1** pasture (animals). **2** grass.
girsie grassy.
girse-beef beef from grass-fed cattle. **girse-gawed** *of toes* having cuts or cracks between them. **grass-ill, grass sickness 1** a disease of young lambs. **2** a disease of horses.

girsle 1 gristle. **2** †a quill pen, especially its shaft or stump. **3** a small piece of crisp or caked porridge etc; anything charred.

girst grist, corn for grinding *now Ulster*.

†**girth**[1] security; sanctuary.
girth cross a cross marking the limits of a place of sanctuary.

girth[2] a hoop.
gurthie very fat; heavy.

girzie [g-as in 'get'] a maid-servant.

gissie *see* **gussie**

git *see* **get**

gitter *see* **gutter**

give, given *see* **gie**

gizen *see* **gizzern**

†**gizz 1** a wig. **2** the face.

gizzen, geesen, geisen, gazen [g- as in 'get'] **1** *of wood etc* shrink, warp, leak. **2** *also* **kizen** *WCentral* dry up, wither, shrivel *now Shetland Orkney NE*. **3** be parched with thirst.
adjective **1** *of wooden containers* cracked, leaky. **2** dry, parched, shrivelled.

gizzent [g- as in 'get'] (over)full; soaked *NE*.

gizzern, giz(z)en *now Angus,* **guzzern** [g- as in 'get'] **1** the gizzard of a fowl *Shetland Caithness*. **2** *humorous* the human throat *now Angus*.

glabber *see* **clabber**

glack, glak 1 a hollow between hills, a ravine. **2** an open area in woodland *NE, Perth*. **3** a handful, morsel *NE*. **4** an angle or fork *eg* the fork of a tree *now NE*.
glack someone's mitten put money in someone's hand, tip someone *NE*.

glaff *see* **gliff**

glag, glagger *NE noun* a gurgling or choking noise.
verb make such a noise.
glagger long (for).

glaiber talk on and on, babble.

glaik, gleck 1 †**glaiks** tricks, pranks. **2** a silly, thoughtless person. **3** a flash or gleam of reflected light.
verb trifle or flirt (with).
glaikie thoughtless, foolish *now N*.
glaikit 1 foolish, stupid; thoughtless. **2** *especially of a child* over-fond, clinging *now Fife*. **3** †playful; flirtatious.
gie someone the glaiks, †**fling the glaiks in someone's een** deceive someone.

glaiks 1 a lever attached to the churnstaff to make churning easier *mainly Ulster*. **2** an instrument for twisting ropes from straw etc *SW, Ulster*.

glaim, gleam [g- as in 'get'] **1** gleam. **2** a flame *now Angus*.

glairy-flairy showy.

glaise a warm at a fire.

glaister a thin covering of snow or ice.

glaizie 1 glazy, glittering, shiny. **2** *of sunshine* bright but watery, indicating more rain.

glak *see* **glack**

glam, glammach, glammer *see* **glaum**

glamour *noun, also* **glamourie 1** glamour. **2** magic, enchantment, witchcraft.
verb **1** bewitch; dazzle. **2** deceive.

glamp *see* **glaum**

glamse *mainly Shetland Orkney Caithness noun* a snap.
verb snap (at); make a snapping, smacking noise.

glance 1 glance. **2 glance (up)on** occur to *now Lothian*: *"it glanced on me a' at yince"*.

Glasgow *see* **fair**[2], **Glesca**

glashan a coal-fish in its second or third

year *now Argyll*.

glass, gless glass.

glessack a small glass marble *now Caithness*. **glessie 1** a home-made sweet, a kind of toffee. **2** *also* **glesser** a glass marble.

casting the glass(es) a method of fortune-telling using egg-white *now Orkney Caithness*. **talk gless haunles** speak (over) politely in an affected accent.

Glaswegian (of) a native or inhabitant of Glasgow.

glaum, glam, glammach *NE verb* **1** snatch, grab (at). **2** seize or snatch at with the jaws; devour. **3** *also* **glammer, glamp** grope.

noun, also **glamp** a clutch or grab, usually unsuccessful.

glaums *see* **clams**

glaur *noun* **1** soft, sticky mud; ooze, slime. **2** contemptuous term for a person or thing.

verb make muddy, dirty; make slimy or slippery.

glaurie muddy, dirty. **glaursel** completely covered with mud *S*.

gleam *see* **glaim**

glebe, glibe 1 glebe a piece of land given to a parish minister for his use, in addition to his **stipend**. **2** a lump, piece *now Shetland*. **3** the soil; land; cultivated land, a plot, a field *now Shetland S*.

gleck *see* **glaik**

gled[1] glad.

gled[2] **1** a kite, the bird. **2** applied to other birds of prey, mainly the buzzard. **3** a greedy person.

gledge *verb* squint, look sidelong.

noun **1** a squint, a sidelong look. **2** a glimpse.

glee *see* **gley**

gleed 1 a live coal or peat, an ember. **2** a spark, glimmer of fire or light. **3** a glowing fire.

gleed *see* **gley**

gleek 1 †jeer. **2** look, peep.

gleem-glam *see* **glim-glam**

gleesh a large bright fire or flame *NE*.

gleet *mainly verse* glitter, shine.

gleg 1 quick, sharp, keen: *"gleg o ee; gleg i the hearing"*. **2** quick of movement; nimble. **3** keen, smart, alert, quick-witted: *"gleg in the uptak"*. **4** lively; merry. **5** *of cutting implements* sharp-pointed, keen-edged. **6** *of mechanisms* smooth-working, quick-acting.

adverb keenly, sharply.

glegly 1 †*of sight or hearing* sharply, keenly, quickly, attentively. **2** briskly, quickly *now Shetland*.

glegness sharpness, keenness, cleverness.

gleg-eared with ears cocked *now WCentral*. **gleg-eed** sharp-eyed. **gleg-gabbit** smooth-tongued, talkative, glib *now WCentral*.

as gleg as a gled as keen or eager as a hawk; very hungry.

gleg *see* **cleg**

gleid *see* **gley**

glen a (narrow) valley usually a river valley.

Glengarry a kind of flat-sided cap pointed at the front and back (with two ribbons hanging behind), now usually worn with Highland dress.

glent, glint *verb* **1** gleam, glint, shine, sparkle. **2** move quickly, flash past *now Shetland*. **3** glance, peep. **4** glint cause (a light) to shine, flash on *now Orkney NE*.

noun **1** a gleam, flash of light, a faint glitter. **2** a look, glance. **3** a glimpse. **4** glint a slight suspicion, a flash of intuition. **5** glent a glancing blow, a slap. **6** glint a scrap, bit.

glintin dawn, daybreak.

in a glent in a flash, in a moment *now Shetland*.

Glesca, Glasgow: Glasgow bailie, Glasgow magistrate a salt herring of fine quality; occasionally a red herring. **Glesca keelie 1** contemptuous term for a (rough and tough) Glaswegian. **2** nickname for a member of the Highland Light Infantry. **Glesca screwdriver** a hammer.

gless, glessack, glesser, glessie *see* **glass**

glet *see* **glit**

gley [rhymes with 'gey'], **glee, gly** *now Shetland verb* **1** squint; cast a sideways glance. **2** look with one eye, take aim *now NE*.

noun **1** a squint; a sideways or sly look, a glance; a squint in the eye. **2** being off the straight, irregularity; error *NE*. **3** aim, the act of aiming *NE*.

adjective squint-eyed.

adverb off the straight *often* **gae gley**.

gley(e)d, gleid 1 squint-eyed, having a squint or cast in the eye. **2** one-eyed, blind in one eye. **3** off the straight, slanting, crooked. **4** mistaken, misguided *now Lothian*. **gleytness 1** having a squint, being squint-eyed *now Shetland NE*. **2** obliqueness *now NE*. **gleed e(y)ed = gleyed** 1. **gae gleyed** go astray, especially morally.

be aff the gley be wide of the mark, be wrong *NE, Lothian*.

glib 1 smooth, slippery. **2** smart, cunning. **3** talkative, fluent (without being insincere).

adverb smoothly, easily, readily.

glib-gabbit, glib-moued *(now NE)* talkative, fluent; gossipy; smooth-tongued.

glibe *see* **glebe**

glid moving smoothly; slippery.

gliff, glaff, gloff, gluff *verb* **1** frighten, startle. **2** gasp (with surprise, cold etc) *now Orkney*. **3** gliff glance (at), look at hurriedly.

noun **1** a hurried or startled glance; a glimpse. **2** a moment, a short while; a short snatch. **3** a very slight resemblance. **4** a flash, glint. **5** a slight attack, touch (of an illness): *"a gliff o the cauld"*. **6** a whiff, puff, breath of air; a gust, blast of hot or cold air. **7** a very brief or sudden sensation *now S*. **8** a sudden fright, a scare, a shock.

glim 1 a gleam, glimmer *now Shetland*

Caithness Ulster. **2** a glimpse, glance *now Shetland*.

glime *verb* take a sidelong glance, squint. *noun* a sidelong look, sly glance.

glim-glam, gleem-glam the game of blindman's buff *NE*.

glimmer *of the eyes* be dazzled; blink, wink, look unsteadily.

glimmerin *of the eyes* half-closed, peering *now NE*.

glimp a glimpse *now Fife*.

glink glance, look sidelong (at).

glint, glintin *see* **glent**

glipe contemptuous term for a person.

glisk *verb* **1** glance (at) *now WCentral*. **2** gleam, glimmer *Shetland*.

noun **1** a glance, peep, glimpse. **2** a gleam, sparkle, flash. **3** a moment, twinkling. **4** a momentary sensation or reaction; a short spell; a whiff, trace. **5** a resemblance, a slight similarity.

a glisk of cauld a slight cold.

glister glisten, glitter.

glit, glut, glet 1 filth; slimy, greasy or sticky material. **2** mucus, discharge from a wound etc. **3** slimy vegetation found in ponds etc. **4** slime on fish or decomposing meat.

glittie 1 slimy, greasy, oily, mucous. **2** smooth, slippery *SW, S*.

gloam *verb* become dusk, darken *now NE, WCentral*.

noun twilight, a faint light *now NE*.

gloamin 1 dusk. **2** dawn *now SW, Ulster*.

gloamin fa, gloamin hour dusk. †**gloamin shot** a twilight interval before the lighting of lights, a short time of relaxation in the evening.

gloan excitement *NE*.

glob a blob *now Angus S*.

glock, gluck *of liquid* gurgle.

gloe *see* **gluive**

gloff, *see* **gliff**

glog *verb* **1** swallow, gulp down *now NE*. **2** gurgle *NE Argyll*.

noun **1** a gulp *NE*. **2** a gurgling noise *now NE*.

gloid do something in a messy or

awkward way *Angus*.

gloit *see* **cloit**²

gloom *verb, of a horse* show signs of temper or viciousness *now Argyll*.
noun **1** a frown, scowl. **2 glooms** a state of depression *now NE*.

glore glory.

glorgie *of weather* sultry, close.

gloss 1 *of a fire* a bright glow *now S*. **2** a doze *now NE*.
verb doze *now NE*.
glossy *of a fire* glowing, clear *now Fife*.

glotten thaw partially.

glowe glow.

glower *verb* **1** stare, gaze intently. **2** †*literary, of the moon, stars etc* gleam, shine brightly. **3** be drunk to the point of being glassy-eyed. **4** scowl.
noun **1** a wide-eyed stare, an intent look. **2** a scowl, a fierce look.

gloy straw, especially as used for thatching etc *now Shetland Orkney Caithness*.

gloze blaze *now Angus Perth*.

gluck *see* **glock**

gluff *see* **gliff**

glugger gurgle *now N*.

gluive, gloe a glove.

glum look sullen *now Angus*.

glump *now Angus*, **glumph** *verb* be glum, sulk, look gloomy.
noun **glumph** a sulky or gloomy person.

glumsh *verb* be or look sulky or gloomy, grumble, whine.
noun a sulky, sullen, surly mood, look or reaction.
adjective **1** sulky, cross-looking *now NE*. **2** sad *now Perth*.

glundie a fool.

glunk *see* **clunk**¹

†**Glunimie** contemptuous term for a Highlander.

glunsh¹ *verb* look cross, scowl; grumble, snap at.
noun a cross look, scowl.
adjective sulky, cross, bad-tempered.

glunsh² gobble, gulp food.

glush, glushie *of snow* soft, slushy *now Fife*.

glut gulp.
glutter *noun* a gurgling noise in the throat. *verb* **1** gurgle, splutter. **2** swallow noisily, disgustingly or greedily.

glut *see* **glit**

gly *see* **gley**

glyde †a worn-out horse or person.

gnaff *see* **nyaff**

gnap *verb* **1** bite, gnaw *now NE*. **2** speak affectedly: *"gnap at English for that's genteel."*
noun a bite of food *now NE*.
gnap-(at)-the-win thin oatcakes, light bread or other food *NE*.

gnash biting, bitter talk *now S*.

gneck a notch *NE*.

gnib quick in action or speech.

gnipper and gnapper bit by bit, every bit *NE*.

gnyauve [(g)nee**awve**] gnaw *N*.

go exclamation of surprise or admiration: *"gweed go!"*.

go *see* **gae**

goam pay attention to, notice; recognize, greet.
goamless stupid.

goat *see* **gait**¹

gob¹, **gub** the mouth; a bird's beak.
gob-stopper a large, round, hard sweet.

gob² *noun* a mass or lump, usually of something soft.
verb spit *now WCentral*.

goblet, goglet *now NE* an iron pot or pan with a straight handle.

gock *see* **gowk**¹

god: god('s)-send a wreck or other profitable flotsam etc.

gog *games* the tee or mark in curling, marbles etc.

goggie *child's word* **1** an egg. **2** a baby bird.

goggles blinkers for horses *now NE*.

goglet *see* **goblet**

goke *see* **gowk**¹

golach, golack, goulock 1 an insect *eg* a kind of beetle, an earwig. **2** contemptuous term for a person *now N*.
forky golach *NE*, **hornie golach, horned**

golach an earwig.

golaich [go**laich**] a breed of short-legged hen.

gold *see* **gowd**

goldie, goldilocks *see* **gowd**

golf *see* **gowf**[1]

gollan name for various wild flowers, *eg* a daisy, a corn marigold *now Orkney Caithness*.

goller, guller, gulder *verb* **1** roar, shout, bawl. **2** gurgle.
noun **1** a shout, roar. **2** an outburst (of oaths). **3** a loud laugh. **4** a gurgle.

gollie 1 roar, shout, bawl. **2** scold *WCentral*. **3** weep noisily.
noun a shout, roar *now NE*.

gollop gulp.

gomerel a fool, stupid person.

goniel a fool *now S*.

gonterns exclamation of surprise or delight.

goo[1]**, gou 1** a strong, lasting, often nasty taste. **2** a nasty smell. **3** a liking, taste for.
gooly tasty, having a distinctive flavour.

goo[2]**, gow** [-ow as in 'cow'] a gull *N*.

goo[3] *of a baby* coo.

good *see* **guid**

goods and gear *see* **gear**

goon *see* **goun**

goog *noun* something soft, moist or messy *now NE*.

goold, gooldie *see* **gowd**

gooly *see* **goo**[1]

goor, gor(e) *noun* **1** mucus, waxy matter, especially in the eye. **2** mud, dirt; muddy, stagnant water. **3** slush in running water *now Shetland NE*.
verb, of streams in thaw become choked with snow and ice *NE*.
gorroch *verb* **1** mix, stir, (something soft and messy) *now SW*. **2** make a mess of, spoil *now SW*. *noun* a trampled muddy spot. **goory** *noun, also* **goories** fish refuse *Shetland Orkney NE*. *adjective* muddy, slimy.

goose *see* **guse**

goosy *see* **gussie**

gor, *also* **my gor, by gor** exclamations of surprise or disbelief.

gor *see* **goor**

gorb *noun, also* **gorbel, gorbet 1** *also* **gorblin** *NE* a baby bird. **2** an infant. **3** a greedy person.
verb eat greedily *SW, Ulster*.
gorbie = **gorb** *noun* 1,2.
God's gorbie a clergyman.

gorble gobble up, eat ravenously *now SW*.

gor-cock *literary* the male of a red grouse.

gore a deep furrow *now NE*.
gie a ploo gurr cut a furrow deeper than usual and at a slant *NE*.

gor(e) *see* **goor**

gorge, gurge *now S*, **grudge** *now S* **1** choke up (a channel) with mud, snow etc *now Shetland*. **2 gurge** swell *now S*.

gorlin 1 a baby bird. **2** a very young person, especially a boy *now SW*.

gorroch *see* **goor**

gorsk *see* **gosk**

goshens plenty, a good catch (of fish).

gosk, gorsk strong, coarse, grass produced by cattle droppings in a pasture *now NE*.

gospel greedy fond of church-going.

gote, gott, gut, gyte, gwite *NE* **1** a ditch, drain etc. **2** a narrow rocky inlet of the sea, a channel.

goth *exclamation* God!

gotherlisch slovenly; confused *mainly NE*.

gott *see* **gote**

gou *see* **goo**[1]

goudie, gowdie Gouda (cheese).

gouff *see* **guff**[1]**, guff**[2]

goug *see* **guga**

gould *see* **gowd**

goulock *see* **golach**

goun, gown, goon 1 a gown. **2** a nightgown, nightshirt, especially a child's one *often* **gounie**.

Gourock: it's all to one side like Gourock it is lop-sided.

gouster, gowster [-ou-, -ow- as -ow- in

'cow'] *verb* boast.

noun **1** a wild, violent boasting or swaggering person. **2** a violent outburst.

goust(e)ous 1 hearty, vigorous. **2** *of weather* dark and stormy. **goustery** wet and windy.

govanenty [govanenty] exclamation of surprise *now Caithness*.

gove 1 stare, gaze; stare stupidly. **2** wander aimlessly about. **3** *of animals* start (with fright), toss the head. **govie** an awkward or silly person *now Ulster*.

govie, govie dick, govie ding exclamations of surprise.

govie *see* **gove**

gow[1] [rhymes with 'cow'] a fool *now SW*.

gow[2] [rhymes with 'cow'] *now literary* a blacksmith.

gow[3] [rhymes with 'cow' or 'goo'] *usually* **gow ower** talk a person into something, persuade.

gow *see* **goo**[2]

gowan [-ow- as in 'cow'] **1** *also* **ewe gowan, May gowan** *now Angus* a daisy. **2** *also* **(large) white gowan** an ox-eye daisy or marguerite.

horse gowan name for various wildflowers, especially a daisy, a dandelion. **lapper gowan** a globe-flower *now S*. **yellow gowan** name for various yellow wild flowers *eg* a buttercup, marigold.

gowd [-ow- as in 'cow'], **goold, gould, gold** gold.

gowden golden. **gowden gowpens** *see* **gowpen**. **gowdie 1** *also* **goldie, gooldie** a goldfinch. **2** one of various fishes, *eg* a gurnard. **3** **gowdie (duck)** a golden-eye duck *now Shetland*. **goldilocks** wood crowfoot *now S*. **gowd spink** a goldfinch.

gowdie *see* **goudie**

gowf[1] [-ow- as in 'cow'], **golf** golf.

golf links a golf course by the seashore. **gowf stick** a golf club.

gowf[2] [-ow- as in 'cow'] hit, strike, slap.

gowf *see* **guff**[2]

gowk[1] [-ow- as in 'cow'], **goke, gock** *noun* **1** *also* **gowkoo** the cuckoo. **2** a fool. **3**

a joke, trick, especially an April Fools' Day joke.

verb **1** fool, deceive often in connection with April fooling. **2** wander about aimlessly, knock about *now Angus*.

gowkie stupid. **gowkit** foolish.

April Gowk an April fool. **gowk aits** oats sown after the arrival of the cuckoo. **gowk('s) day** April Fools' Day. **gowk('s) errand** a fool's errand. **gowk's meat** wood sorrel. **gowk('s)-spit(tle(s))** cuckoo-spit. **gowk('s) storm** a brief storm; a spring storm coinciding with the arrival of the cuckoo. **gowk's-thimles** a harebell.

(the) gowk and (the) titlin(g) two unlikely companions, *eg* a tall and a short person seen together.

gowk[2] [-ow- as in 'cow'] stare *now Angus Perth*.

gowl [-ow- as in 'cow'] *verb* **1** howl, yell, roar, weep noisily. **2** scold angrily. **3** a scowl. **4** *of the wind* howl, gust noisily. *noun* **1** a yell, howl, bellow, growl. **2** a howling gust of wind *now Shetland*.

gown *see* **goun**

gowp[1] [-ow- as in 'cow'] *verb* **1** *of the heart or pulse* beat strongly or wildly. **2** *of sores or pains* throb, ache violently. *noun* a throb of pain.

gowp[2] [-ow- as in 'cow'] gulp.

gowp[3] [-ow- as in 'cow'] scoop up (*eg* water), wash with the hands, hollow out.

gowp *see* **gaup**

gowpen [-ow- as in 'cow'] *noun, also* **gowpenfu 1** as much as can be held in the two hands held together. **2** cupped hands.

verb scoop up or ladle out with the hands held cupped together.

gowd in gowpen, gowden gowpens untold wealth.

gowst *verb* boast.

noun a gust.

gowster *see* **gouster**

gowstie [-ow- as in 'cow'] **1** *of places* vast, dreary, desolate; eerie. **2** *of buildings* large, bare, cheerless *now S*. **3** *of people, now NE* painfully thin; ghastly, pale; breathless from being overweight, fat and flabby. **4** *of wind, weather, the sea* wild, stormy; eerie.

grab 1 a thing grabbed, plunder. **2** a good bargain, an advantage, often one got dishonestly *now NE*. **3** a mean or greedy person.

grabbie greedy. **grabble** grab, grope.

grace: gracie devout, virtuous, well-behaved. †**gracious 1** happy, prosperous. **2** friendly.

†**grace drink** the drink taken at the end of a meal after grace has been said.

†**graddan** a kind of very coarsely-ground oatmeal.

graduand a person about to graduate.

graff, graife a grave.

graft a grave.

graife *see* **graff**

graig make a noise in the throat, *eg* in clearing it *NE*.

grain¹ **1** a branch, offshoot *eg* of a tree; of a stream, river; of a valley. **2** a prong (of a fork, salmon spear etc).

grain² **1** groan. **2** complain, grumble; be unwell.

graip¹ *noun* a large fork used in farming and gardening.

verb fork up.

graip², **growp** [-ow- as in 'cow'] grope.

graisle fizzle, crackle, crumple *now SW*.

graith *verb* **1** prepare, make ready (*eg* a horse for riding or work). **2** †equip, dress (a person), especially in armour.

noun **1** materials or equipment; tools, machinery; accessory equipment of a mechanism, *eg* a mill, plough, loom. **2** the rigging or tackle of a ship. **3** furnishings, belongings. **4** clothing; accessories. **5** armour, weapons, etc, now only as used by the Royal Company of Archers. **6** the trappings, harness etc for a horse. **7** goods; supplies. **8** possessions, wealth, money. **9** *fishing* the attachment by which the hook is hung from the line *now NE*. **10** stale urine used in washing and dyeing; urine (*now Shetland*). **11** a soapy lather; dirty, used soapsuds. **12** contemptuous term for people, riffraff.

graithing equipment, trappings; harness, dress.

gralloch *noun* **1** a deer's entrails. **2** the disembowelling of a deer.

verb disembowel (a deer).

gramarie *literary* magic, enchantment, witchcraft.

gramashes, gramashins *WCentral* leggings, gaiters.

Grampian (Region) a **region** formed from the former counties of the city of Aberdeen, Aberdeen, Kincardine, Banff and part of the former county of Moray.

granich [-ch as in 'dreich'] sicken, disgust *NE*.

grannie *noun* **1** the last sheaf cut at harvest-time *Ulster*. **2** a hairy caterpillar, the larva of the tiger moth *now SW*. **3** a chimney-cowl. **4** used in contemptuous exclamations: *"We might have improvised a sledge." "Improvised yer grannie!"*

verb, in a game defeat heavily, often without the loser scoring.

grannie('s) bairn a grandchild, especially one reared by its grandmother and spoilt. **grannie('s) mutch(es) 1** columbine. **2** snapdragon. **grannie mutch(ie)** nickname for an old woman. **grannie's sooker** a peppermint sweet, a **pan drop** (*see* **pan**¹). **granny's tartan** *see* **tartan**. **granny's tuith, grannie's teeth** *carpentry* a router plane. **grannie at** address as 'granny'.

grapple 1 drag (water) for a corpse. **2** grope *now Angus*.

grappling a method of catching salmon by means of a special arrangement of hooks.

grapus the Devil, a hobgoblin *now NE*.

grass *see* **girse**

grassum *law* a sum paid by a tenant at the grant or renewal of a lease or feu-right.

grat *see* **greet**

gravat [grav̱at, grauv̱at] **1** a (woollen) scarf. **2** *often* **hempen gravat** a hangman's noose.

grave 1 bury (a corpse). **2** dig *Shetland*.
graveyaird deserter a sickly looking person *now NE*. **graveyaird hoast** a churchyard cough *now WCentral*.

grawl *see* **grilse**

gray[1] *verb* **1** dawn *Shetland Orkney NE*. **2** cover with a thin sprinkling of snow *SW*.
grayback 1 a hooded crow. **2** a flounder *NE*. **3** a salmon or salmon trout in the autumn run *SW, S*. **4** an immature herring gull or lesser black-backed gull. **gray cheeper** a meadow pipit. **gray dark** dusk. **gray face** a crossbred sheep, black-face crossed with Leicester. **gray fish** a coalfish, especially in its second or third year *now Shetland*. **gray hen** a female black grouse. **gray horse** a louse *now Angus Fife*. **gray lord** a fully-grown coalfish. **gray meal** the refuse and sweepings of a meal-mill. **gray paper** brown paper *Shetland Orkney N*. **gray plover** a golden plover in its summer plumage *now SW*. **gray stane** a grey volcanic rock, *eg* a boulder used as a landmark or boundary stone.
(gang) a gray gate suffer disaster, (come to) a bad end *now SW*. **the gray o the morning** dawn. **the gray o the evening** twilight.

gray[2] a light wind *now ECentral*.

great, gret, grit, gryte 1 great. **2** coarse. **3** thick, bulky, roomy *now Angus*. **4** big, stout *now Shetland NE*. **5** *of a river etc* in flood, high *now Orkney*. **6** †*of the heart* full with emotion, especially grief. **7** friendly, close.
great ewe a ewe big with young. **great folk** people of rank or position. **great-hearted** filled with emotion, ready to cry, sorrowful *now NE, Fife*.

gree[1] **1** make peace between (people); settle (something). **2** come to terms, make an agreement. **3** be or live in harmony, be friends; be of one mind. **4** correspond, fit.
greeable peaceable, kindly, agreeable.
greement agreement, harmony.

gree[2] first place, victory; the prize, *often* **bear the gree** win the prize *now literary*.

greeance agreement *now NE*.

†**greek** daybreak.

greement *see* **gree**[1]

green[1] *adjective* **1** covered with grass, grassy *now Shetland Orkney Caithness*. **2** young, youthful, full of life. **3** *of milk* new, fresh, especially milk from a newly calved cow. **4** *of a cow* recently calved. **5** *of manure* fresh, unrotted. **6** *of cloth, especially linen* unbleached. **7** *of a fire* newly kindled and smouldering.
noun **1** grassy ground; the grassy ground forming part of the grounds of a building *eg* **kirk green, backgreen, drying green. 2 greens** green vegetables, especially **kail.**
green-berry a green gooseberry. **green brees** green, stagnant water, especially oozing from a dunghill or cesspool *now NE*. **green garter** *see* **garten. green grass** a children's rhyme; the game in which it occurs *now NE*. **green kail** a non-curly variety of **kail;** a soup made from this. **green-kailworm** a caterpillar of the cabbage butterfly. **green lady 1** a ghost (believed to be a sign of death). **2** a Health Visitor (in certain towns). **green lintie** the greenfinch. **green wood** growing trees or branches, living wood.
that dings a' green thing that beats everything *now NE*.

green[2] **1** long for. **2** *of a pregnant woman* have a craving (for particular foods).

greep *see* **gruip**

greeshach shivery; chilly *N*.

greeshoch a glowing fire of red-hot embers; the embers themselves, especially of a peat fire.

greet *verb, past tense* **grat, gret** weep, cry, lament; complain; grumble.

noun a sob; a fit of weeping.

greetie *adjective* **1** weepy, given to tears. **2** inclined to rain, showery. *noun* a child's whimper. **greeting ee** a watering eye. **greetin face** a person who usually looks miserable or tearful. **greetin fou** at the tearful stage of drunkenness. **greetin meetin** a farewell meeting, especially the last meeting of a council before an election. **greetin Teenie** a cry-baby; a person who is always complaining.

the greet in one's craig a sob in one's throat *now Shetland NE*. **get one's greet out** relieve one's feelings by weeping.

gress *see* **girse**

gret *see* **great, greet**

grew *noun* **1** *also* **grew hound** a greyhound. **2 the grews** greyhound racing.

grice, gryse a pig, especially a young pig.

grieve 1 the overseer or head-workman on a farm; a farm-bailiff. **2** †a manager or overseer of a mine-works etc.

grilse, gilse, grawl *SW* a young salmon on its first return to fresh water.

grime, grim *verb* sprinkle, fleck, cover thinly especially with snow *now SW, S*.

adjective, only **grim** grey, roan, mottled black and white; grimy.

grip, grup *verb* **1** grip. **2** catch, seize. **3** seize, take possession of (lands or belongings) violently or illegally. **4** get the better of, outsmart *NE*.

noun **1** grip. **2** a handclasp; sometimes one used between members of a secret society, *eg* the Freemasons. **3 grips** someone's embrace or clutches. **4** *usually* **grips** sharp pains, especially colic, gripes. **5 the grip** *building industry* a system of sub-contracting work to casual labour, the 'lump'.

gripper the person who catches and holds a sheep to be sheared *now SW*. **grippie** mean, miserly, greedy, likely to cheat. **grippit** hard-up, short of money *now NE*. **gruppit** sprained.

grip in pinch, make narrow or tighter *Shetland NE*. **grip to** grab, hold on to; stick close to *now Shetland NE*. **hae a guid grip o (the) gear 1** be well off. **2** be mean. **hae a guid grip of Scotland** have large (flat) feet. **haud the grip** keep a firm hold; hold to one's faith or purpose; last. **be in grips** wrestle, struggle. **slip the grip** die *now NE*.

grip *see* **gruip**

grist 1 the size or thickness of yarn. **2** size *now Orkney*.

grit *see* **great**

groatie, groatie-buckie a kind of cowrie shell *Shetland Orkney Caithness NE*.

groff, grofe coarse *now Shetland Orkney N*.

groff guess a rough guess, a pretty good idea *now Shetland*.

gromish crush, bruise *Caithness NE*.

groof, grufe: grooflins flat on one's face *now Shetland*, **on one's groofs** lying face downwards.

groosie *see* **gruse**

groozle, gruzzle 1 breathe heavily, grunt. **2** *of a child* gurgle *now S*.

groser *now NE, ECentral*, **groset, gros(s)art**, †**grosell** a gooseberry.

grouff [-ou- as -ow- in 'cow'] a short, disturbed sleep; a snooze.

ground *see* **grun(d)**

grounge *see* **grunch**

grow [rhymes with 'cow']: **growth** weeds, rank vegetation. **growthie 1** *of weather* warm and moist, encouraging growth. **2** *of plants* growing fast and thick; weedy. **3** *of persons or animals* well-grown, thriving. **grown-up** overgrown, choked with weeds etc.

grow-grey made of natural, undyed wool.

growk *especially of a child or dog* look longingly at food etc *now NE, Perth*.

grown *see* **grow**

growp *see* **graip**[2]

browse *see* **gruse**

growth(ie) *see* **grow**

groze squeeze.

grub grasp at (money).

grubber an iron harrow, especially for weeding in drills.

grudge complain, be unhappy, discontented or unwilling.

grudge *see* **gorge**

grue[1] *verb* **1** feel horror or terror, shudder, shrink in horror or fear. **2** *of the flesh, heart, blood etc* creep, quake, run cold with horror or fear. **3** shiver from cold. **4** make a face.
noun a shudder, shiver, feeling of horror or disgust.
adjective **1** ugly, horrible. **2** shuddering with fear, dread or loathing, afraid *now Caithness.*

grushion *often of food* a nasty or sticky mess *NE.*

it gars me grue it makes my blood run cold. **tak the grue (at)** become disgusted or fed up (with).

grue[2] melting snow and ice found on rivers in early spring.

gruel 1 porridge, especially thin porridge *now Shetland Orkney.* **2** food made of oatmeal; any food.

grufe *see* **groof**

gruggle rumple, crease *NE.*

grugous grim, ugly, sulky.

gruip, grup, grip, greep *noun* **1** the gutter in a **byre. 2** a field drainage ditch *now Orkney NE.*
verb, carpentry cut a groove in (a board) for fitting into a corresponding 'tongue'.

grulsh a dumpy person or animal *now Ulster.*

grummel, gummle *noun* rubbish, rubble; mud, sediment.
verb make muddy.
grumlie, gumlie muddy, full of dregs or gravel; confused, gloomy.

grummle *verb* grumble.
noun **1** grumble. **2** a grudge, complaint, quarrel.
grummlie 1 bad-tempered, grumbling. **2** *of weather* unsettled, blustery *now NE.*

grumph *noun* **1** a grunt. **2** name for a pig.

3 a grumbler, complainer.
verb grunt; grumble.

grumphie *noun* (name for) a pig. *verb* grunt like a pig *now Angus.*

grunch, grounge [grunje] *now S verb* **1** grumble; object, refuse *now S.* **2** growl, grunt *now Orkney.*
noun a grumble, grunt, growl *now S.*

grun(d), ground 1 ground. **2** the bottom or lowest part of anything. **3** the bottom of the sea. **4** the bottom, root (of a matter), text (of a sermon). **5** the pit of the stomach. **6** farm-land, a farm, an estate. **7** ground reserved for the burial of a person or family. **8** *piping* the main theme in **pibroch.**
grund blackie a blackbird that nests on the ground. **grund ebb 1** the ebb-tide at its lowest, low water *Shetland NE.* **2** the lowest part of the foreshore *Caithness NE.* **ground officer** the manager of an estate. **grund-stane** a foundation stone *now Shetland.*

grundiswallow groundsel *now NE.*

grunkle *see* **crunkle**

gruntie *humorous* a pig.

gruntle *noun* **1** the snout, usually of a pig *now S.* **2** *contemptuous, of a person* the nose and mouth, the face or head. **3** a grunt.
verb grunt, groan *now S.*

grunyie, grunzie [grunyie] the snout of an animal or (*contemptuous*) of a person.

grup *see* **grip, gruip**

gruppit *see* **grip**

gruse, growze, = grue[1], shiver, shudder. **groosie** shivery.

grush grit, fine gravel.

grushie 1 *of a child* thriving. **2** *of plants* thick, abundant.

grushion *see* **grue**[1]

gruzzle *see* **groozle**

gry a horse.

gryse *see* **grice**

gryte *see* **great**

gub *see* **gob**[1]

guddle *verb* **1** catch (fish) with the hands by groping under the stones or banks of a stream. **2** do dirty, messy work *now NE*. **3** do things in a careless, messy way, mess about, make a mess. **4** *of children* play messily.

noun **1** a crowbar. **2** a pointed iron bar for making holes for fenceposts. **3** hard, dirty or messy work. **4** a mess, muddle, confusion. **5** a person who does things in a messy way.

gude *see* **guid**

gudge *noun* **1** a gouge *now Shetland Orkney NE*. **2** anything short and thick, especially a short, strong, thick-set person *now Caithness NE*.
verb **1** gouge *now Shetland Angus*. **2** raise or separate by driving in wedges *NE*.
gudgie short and thickset, squat.

guess a riddle, puzzle.

guest an object thought to foretell the arrival of a stranger *now Shetland Orkney*.

guest *see* **ghaist**

guff[1], **gouff** [guff, gowf] a fool *now ECentral S*.
guffie stupid *now S*.

guff[2], **gouff, gowf** *now Fife* [-ou-, -ow- as -ow- in 'cow'] *noun* **1** a (usually unpleasant) smell or whiff. **2** a taste, after-taste. **3** a puff, whiff, current of air etc.
verb give off a smell, steam, smoke etc.
guffie fat, flabby or fluffy about the cheeks *now S*.

guff[3] *noun* **1** a grunting, snuffling sound (of a pig); a low bark *now Shetland*. **2** a suppressed laugh, a snort *now Caithness*.
verb **1** snort, snuffle *now Shetland Orkney*. **2** cackle with laughter; babble, talk foolishly. **3** belch.
guffie name for a pig.

guffie *see* **guff**[1], **guff**[2]

guga, goug [goog(a)] a young gannet *Hebrides*.

guid, gude, good, gweed *NE adjective* **1** good. **2** *of people* respectable, distinguished in rank or social standing.

3 *of clothes* best; *of rooms* the best, used on formal occasions. **4** -in-law, *eg* **guid brither** brother-in-law.
noun **1** good. **2** God: *"he feared the Gude", "Gude forgie me!"*
gooding manure. **guidly 1** goodly. **2** godly, pious *now NE*.
a guid bit a long time. **(the) Guid Book** the Bible. **guideen** *greeting* good evening. **the guid folks** the fairies, brownies etc. **guid gaun** going well, active, flourishing. **guid gear** *see* **gear**. **guid grip** *see* **grip**. **a guid mair** a good many more *now NE*. **guid man 1 the guid man** *mainly child's word* God. **2** term of address used between equals who do not know each other well. **3** the head of the household. **4** a husband. **5** the owner or tenant of a small estate or farm, ranking below a **laird**. **6** the Devil. **the guidman's craft** a plot of land left uncultivated to please the Devil so that he would not harm the rest of the land. **the guid place** Heaven *now Shetland*. **guidsire, gutcher** a grandfather. **guid wife 1** *as a polite term of address* the mistress of a house, a wife. **2** the mistress of (a particular place, especially a farm). **3** the landlady of an inn. **4** a wife. **guid willed** keen *now Shetland*. **guidwillie** willing, ready; generous, hearty. **guid words** children's prayers etc.
as guid (as) *of price, value, measure* as much (as), practically: *"as good as five"*. **(be)come guid for** guarantee, be surety for. **dae guid** get good results, thrive, prosper. **get the guid o** get what advantage or benefit is to be had from (a thing). **guid and weel** well and good, so be it. **hae guid on one, had guid in one's mind** *asking for money etc* likely to be generous. **haena guid doing something** find something difficult to do *now Shetland Angus*. **ken the guid o** realize or enjoy the benefits of. **tak the guid o 1 = get the guid o. 2** damage, spoil.

guideen *see* **guid**

guide *verb* **1** run (an organization etc); direct, manage, control (something). **2** manage, use (money etc, well, sparingly etc) **3** treat, use, handle, care for (people (*especially* children) or animals). **4** behave (oneself): *"young fowk winna guide themselves."*
noun a manager, controller, usually of money or property *now Shetland NE*.
guider 1 a manager, administrator *now Shetland*. **2** a home-made children's cart steered by a rope *ECentral*.

guil, guld a corn marigold *now NE, SW*.

Guild *see* **dean**

guild an association formed within a **burgh,** enjoying exclusive rights of trading in it and taking an important part in its government, a merchant guild.

guilt: tak guilt til ane(sel) feel or show guilt, be conscience-stricken.

guis *see* **guiss**

guise *noun, also* **gy** *now Orkney* a masquerade; a piece of fun.
verb **1** disguise. **2 guising** going about as a **guiser** 1.
guiser, guisard *noun* **1** masquerader, now especially one of a party of children who go in disguise from door to door offering entertainment in return for gifts or money, especially at **Halloween** (*see* **Hallow**). **2** an odd-looking person *now NE. verb* go about as a guiser.
hae a guise (wi) have (a bit of) fun (with) *now Shetland NE*.

guiss, guis guess.

guld *see* **guil**

gulder *see* **goller**

gull a thin cold mist and a chilly breeze *NE*.

guller *see* **goller**

gullet 1 a narrow, deep channel or rocky inlet. **2** a gully, ravine.

gullie *noun, also* **gully knife** a large knife. **gullie gaw** wound, cut gash *N.* **guide the gully** *of God* control things. **haud the gullie ower the dyke (to)** stand up

for oneself (against) *now Angus*.

gullion 1 a marsh, swamp, bog. **2** a pool of mud or of semi-liquid manure and decayed vegetable matter *Ulster*.

gulravage, gulravish *see* **gilravage**

gulsoch, gulsa *now Shetland* **1** jaundice. **2** over-eating; feeling of sickness caused by this *now NE*.

gum¹, **geem** *NE* [g- as in 'get'] *noun* the gum (in the mouth).
gumstick a stick etc used by a teething child.

gum² gum, glue.
gumflour an artificial flower.

gum³ *noun* **1** mist, haze, condensation, *eg* on glass *now Caithness NE*. **2** *also* **yella gum** jaundice, especially in the newborn. **3** a disagreement, ill-will.
verb become misted over *NE*.

gum⁴ coal-dust.

gumlie, gummle *see* **grummel**

gump, gumph search, grope for; especially **guddle** (fish).

gumph, gump 1 *also* **gamf, gumphie** *now S,* **gumpus** *now NE* a fool. **2 gumphs** the sulks, *often* **tak the gumps.**
gamphrell a foolish person.

gumsh munch *NE*.

gumstick *see* **gum**¹

gun *noun* a tobacco pipe, a briar-pipe.
verb gossip, talk fast or brightly.
gunner a person who shoots game for sport *now Orkney WCentral*.
be great guns (wi) be close friends (with) *Shetland NE*.

gunch [gunsh] **1** a thick piece, a hunk. **2** a short, thickset person *Caithness*.

gundie, gunnie a father-lasher *now NE*.

gundy toffee.

gunk a bitter disappointment, *often* **do a gunk (on someone), gie (someone) the gunk** cause (someone) pain, unhappiness, disappoint; jilt.
verb disappoint, shame; jilt *now Ulster*.

gunner *see* **gun**

gunnie *see* **gundie**

gunplucker a father-lasher *NE*.

gurge *see* **gorge**

gurk a stout, heavily-built person *Caithness NE*.

gurl *verb* **1** *of the wind* roar, howl. **2** growl. **3** *of water* gurgle.
adjective **1** *of weather, wind etc* cold, stormy, wild. **2** *of people* bad-tempered, surly.
noun **1** a gale, a squall. **2** a growl, a snarl. **3** a gurgle.
gurlie 1 *of weather etc* stormy, threatening, bitter. **2** *of people* bad-tempered, surly. **3** *of dogs* growling, snarling *now NE*. **4** gurgling.

gurr[1] growl, snarl.
gurry 1 a dogfight, brawl *now SW*. **2** a hurry, a bustle, a state of confusion. **gurry-wurry 1** = **gurr**[1] *now Angus*. **2** = **gurry** 1.

gurr[2] drive, spirit *now NE*.

gurr *see* **gore**

gurthie *see* **girth**[2]

guse, geese *Shetland Orkney N,* **goose 1** a goose. **2 goose,** *piping* a bagpipe with a **chanter** but no drones.
guse-grass 1 goose-grass, cleavers. **2** brome grass.

gus-gus *see* **gussie**

gushet 1 a gusset. **2** a breast-pocket of a jacket or coat. **3** *also* **gushet-neuk** *NE* a triangular piece of land, especially between neighbouring properties; an odd corner of land; a nook. **4** a triangular patch left in ploughing or reaping an irregularly-shaped field. **5** the corner of a building, a corner in a building.
gushet house a house standing at a corner or forming the angle between two roads.

gussie, gissie, goosy, gees(i)e 1 a pig, especially a young pig or sow. **2** *also* **gus-gus** a call to pigs. **3** a fat person. **4** a segment of an orange *Angus*.

gust *noun* taste; relish.
verb **1** taste (food drink etc). **2** *often* **gust the gab** whet the appetite, fill the mouth with tasty food or drink *now NE, Fife*. **3** smell (strongly, bad) *now Angus*.

gustie tasty, savoury.

gut: guts eat greedily or gluttonously.
gutser 1 a very greedy person *NE*. **2** a belly-flop. **gutsie 1** greedy. **2** *of a building* roomy. **gutter** a woman employed in gutting fish. **guttie** *adjective* **1** thick; very fat; pot-bellied. **2** fond of good eating, greedy. *noun* **1** a pot-bellied person *now SW, S*. **2** a minnow.
gut-scraper a fiddle-player.

gutcher *see* **guid**

gut *see* **gote**

gutta *see* **guttie**

gutter, gitter *noun* **1 gutters** mud, muddy puddles. **2** the doing of something in an unskilful or dirty way. **3** a muddle, mess. **4** a stupid, awkward or messy worker.
verb **1** do something in a dirty, messy or unskilful way. **2** potter, tinker, fritter away time. **3** talk nonsense, gabble, gibber *now WCentral*.
gutterie muddy, messy.
gutter-bluid 1 a low-class person. **2** a native of a particular town; a person whose ancestors have been born in the same town for generations, especially Peebles. **gutter-gaw** a sore on the foot. **gutter-hole** a drain or drainage-hole for kitchen refuse.

gutter *see* **gut**

guttie, gutta anything made of rubber: **1** *also* **guttie ba** a golf-ball; **2 guttie** a catapult; **3 gutties** gymshoes, plimsolls *WCentral*.
gutty-perky guttapercha, rubber *mainly* **gutty-perky-ba** a golf ball.

guttie *see* **gut**

guy *verb* guide, steer *now NE*.
noun **guys** the handlebars of a bicycle.

guzzern *see* **gizzern**

guzzle *noun* a bout of excessive eating and drinking.
verb take by the throat, throttle.

gweed *see* **guid**

gweeshtens, gweeshtie gosh!, goodness! *NE*.

gwite *see* **gote**

gy *see* **guise**

gyang *see* **gang**

gyang *see* **gang**

gymp *see* **jimp**

gype [g- as in 'get'] *verb* **1** stare foolishly or open-mouthed. **2** play the fool; make a fool of *now Shetland Angus*.
noun a foolish awkward person, a silly ass, a lout *now Shetland NE*.

gyper *NE verb* talk nonsense. *noun* nonsense; fun. **gypit** silly, foolish.

gyre carlin(g) [g-as in 'get'] a supernatural being, usually female, an ogress, witch *now Shetland*.

gyte [g- as in 'get'] *adjective* **1** mad, insane; mad with rage, pain etc: *"gang gyte"*. **2** mad with longing, love-sick, eager. **3** *of things* nonsensical, crazy; **gae gyte** go to pot, go awry.

gyter *NE noun* **1** nonsense, foolish talk. **2** a stupid, talkative person. *verb* talk a great deal in a silly way.

gyte *see* **gait**[2], **gote**, **get**

H

ha, hall 1 a hall. **2** *also* **ha house** a farmhouse as opposed to the farm cottages. **3** †the main room of an ordinary house.

  ha-bible a large family bible.

ha *see* **hae, haw**²

haar¹, **haur 1** a cold easterly wind. **2** a cold mist or fog, especially an east-coast sea fog.

  haary 1 *of wind* cold, piercing. **2** misty, foggy.

haar² speak with a burr *now Angus*.

  haar-frost hoar-frost.

haavin *see* **half**²

habber, hubber 1 stammer, stutter *Shetland N*. **2** snarl; (make) a gobbling noise *N*.

habbie an inhabitant of Kilbarchan.

  Standard Habbie name applied by Ramsay to the stanza form aaabab used in the mock elegy *The Piper of Kilbarchan* (*Habbie Simpson*), later much used by Burns and others.

  habbie-horse a hobby-horse.

habble *verb* **1** hobble *now Angus*. **2** perplex, confuse; hamper *mainly S*. **3** tangle (thread etc).

  noun **1** = **hobble** *noun* **2, 3. 2** †a coarse or slovenly person.

  habble jock a turkey cock *Angus*.

habit: †be in good habits be on good terms.

habit and repute *mainly law* held to be or regarded as (a thief, witch, married person etc).

hack, hawk *noun* **1** a pronged tool for breaking up or raking soil etc. **2** a joiner's adze; a miner's pick-ended hammer. **3** a crack or chap in the skin. **4** *curling* a cut in the ice to steady the player's foot; *now* a metal footplate. **5** a notch on a graded scale; a certain amount (of time, distance) *NE: "Wil-*

lie's late! Aye he's aye a hack ahint!"

  verb **1** hack. **2** chop up (meat, firewood etc). **3** *of the skin* crack, chap, roughen.

  hacking stock a chopping block.

  ca a hack i the crook celebrate an event.

  tak doon a hack take (someone) down a peg *Shetland NE*.

hackberry *see* **hagberry**

hackit *see* **hawkit**

hackle *see* **heckle**¹

hacky duck, hucky-duck a children's game in which two teams take it in turn to leap on the lined-up backs of their opponents *ECentral*.

had *see* **haud**

hade *see* **heid**

haddie, haddo a haddock.

hae, have, ha, hiv *verb, past tense also* **haid** *now Shetland*, **hid**, *past participle* **haen** *now N* **1** have. **2** put, bring, take, send: *"Mrs. B has her compliments to you".*

  noun †property, possessions.

  be well had be well off.

  haet: deil haet not a grain or particle. **deil a haet, (the) fient a haet** devil a bit! **no a haet** not the smallest amount. **haiveless 1** shiftless, incapable, careless, extravagant *N*. **2** senseless, meaningless. **haver** the holder of documents, especially those required as evidence in a court. **havings** behaviour, manners. **hinna** has not, have not.

  hae easy daein be able to do easily.

hae *see* **hum**²

haen, haet *see* **hae**

hafer *see* **half**¹

haff *see* **half**¹

haffet 1 the cheek, the temple. **2** a side-lock of hair. **3** the wooden side of a **box-bed** (*see* **box**), chair etc.

haft *see* **heft**¹, **heft**³

hag *verb* hack, cut, chop wood.

  noun **1** a notch, hack. **2** †a portion of a

wood marked for felling. **3** brushwood; felled wood used for fuel. **4** a hollow of marshy ground, *eg* where channels have been made or peats cut. **5** a hillock of firmer ground in a bog. **6** a ledge of turf overhanging a stream *SW, S*.

hagger *verb* cut clumsily, hack *NE*. *noun* a deep jagged cut *NE*. **haggle 1** cut unevenly, hack. **2** stumble forward, struggle on *mainly S*. **3** carry (something cumbersome) with difficulty *now S*.

strike a hag in the post celebrate an event.

hagberry, hackberry a bird cherry.

haggard a stackyard *mainly SW, Ulster*.

hagger *see* **hag**

haggis a traditional Scottish dish of sheep's offal, oatmeal etc.

haggle *see* **hag**

haid *see* **hae**

haigs *see* **hegs**

haik *verb* **1** trudge; wander aimlessly. **2** carry or drag with difficulty. **3** treat roughly, drive hard.
noun a person or animal given to roaming about, usually on the scrounge.
be on the haik for be on the lookout for.

haik *see* **heck**

haikit *see* **hawkit**

hail^1, **hale**, **whole** *adjective* **1** sound, in a healthy state; wholesome; robust, vigorous. **2** uninjured, undamaged in body or mind. **3** *of things* whole, complete, undamaged. **4** *now especially law* the whole of, the full number of: *"the whole Heritors or their agents"*.
adverb wholly, completely, fully.
noun the whole, the full number or amount.
hail-heartit undaunted, stalwart. **hailheidit** unhurt; *of things* complete, entire *N*. **gang hail-heidit for** give one's entire energy to *N*. **hailscart** unscathed, scotfree. **hail-skinnt** having an unblemished skin. **hail-tear** at full speed. **hail watter** a downpour. **hail wheel** full tilt

now Angus.
get hail o recover from. **hail and fere** in full health and vigour; unharmed. **hail at the heart** in good spirits.

hail^2 small shot, pellets.

hail^3 *verb* heal.

hail^4, **hale 1** the winning of a goal; a goal. **2** the shout when a goal is scored. **3** the goal area.
hail the dool(s) score a goal; be the winner; celebrate.

hail *see* **hale**

hailscart *see* **hail**^{1}

haimmer 1 a hammer. **2** †a clumsy noisy person.

haims, hames, hems hames, part of the collar of a draught horse.
pit the hems on curb, keep in order.

hain 1 enclose by a hedge or fence; keep unused. **2** keep from harm, protect. **3** *also* **hain in** save (up), be thrifty, hoard.
haining an enclosed piece of ground.

hain *see* **hine**

hainch, hench, hinch [-nsh] *noun* **1** a haunch. **2** an underhand throw. **3** a halt or limp. **4** a 'leg-up'; a help up with a heavy object.
verb **1** throw a stone etc by jerking the arm against the thigh. **2** walk jerkily or with a limp.

haingle *verb* move about feebly; loiter, hang about.
adjective slovenly, careless; lazy, not inclined to work.

haip *see* **heap**

hair^1: **hairy** *adjective, especially of work* untidy, rough, slovenly. *noun* a woman slum-dweller; *now* a woman of loose morals, a prostitute; *contemptuous* a young woman: *"a wee hairy"*. **hairy grannie** a large hairy caterpillar. **hairy moggans** footless stockings. **hairymouldit** covered with mould, mouldy. **hairy oobit** *see* **oobit**. **hairy tatties** a dish made of mashed potatoes and flaked dried salt fish *NE*. **hairy worm** = **hairy oobit** (*see* **oobit**) *Fife NE*.
hair-tether *mainly witchcraft* a tether

made of hair.

a hair in someone's neck a shortcoming etc which gives another a hold over one. **a hair to make a tether** a fuss about nothing. **hair and hoof** every particle.

hair^2 hoar.

hair moul(d) the mould on cheese, bread, jam etc exposed to damp. **hairstane, harestone** a large, grey, moss-covered stone, especially one conspicuously fixed as a boundary mark *now NE*.

hairbour *see* **herbour**

hairm, herm harm.

hairp *see* **harp**

hairse hoarse.

hairshach *see* **hareshard**

hairst, harvest, hervest, harst 1 harvest. **2 hairst, harst** a harvest job. **3** the autumn *now Shetland NE*.

hairst plait a loop of twisted straw used as a decoration at harvest time.

hae a day in hairst wi someone have a score to settle with someone; owe someone a favour *now NE*.

hairt *see* **hert**

hairy *see* **hair**^{1}

haister 1 cook too hastily, scorch. **2** perplex, pester *now SW*.

haith, heth a mild oath or exclamation of surprise.

haithen *adjective* **1** heathen. **2** outlandish, incomprehensible *now Shetland Ulster*. *noun* **1** a heathen. **2** a difficult or intractable person or thing *now Shetland*.

haivel, have-eel a conger-eel.

haiveless *see* **hae**

haiver, haver *verb* **1** talk in a foolish or trivial way, speak nonsense. **2** make a fuss about nothing, pretend to be busy. **3** dawdle, potter about; lounge.

noun **1 haivers** nonsense, gossip, chatter. **2** a piece of nonsense, a foolish notion. **3** a gossip, a chat. **4** a person who talks nonsense. **5** a state of fussy indecision; a person in this state, an idler.

haiverel *noun* **1** a foolishly chattering

person, a fool. **2** a lounger, a lazy person *now Shetland*. *adjective* **1** garrulous, speaking foolishly *now SW*. **2** foolish, stupid. **havering** *adjective* nonsensical, gossiping, babbling. *noun* a chatter, gossip, nonsense.

haizer, hazer dry (partially), air in the open, bleach (newly-washed clothes etc).

hake *see* **heck**

hale, hail 1 haul, drag, pull (up) *now Shetland NE*. **2** flow copiously, run down, pour.

hald *see* **haud**

hale *see* **hail**^{1}, **hail**^{4}

half^1**, haff, hauf** *noun* **1** a half. **2** a part; one of two unequal parts; one of three or more divisions or portions. **3** a half-measure of a specified amount, especially of whisky = a half-gill; **a wee hauf** a quarter gill, a small whisky. **4** *of time: with the preceding hour, eg* **half-five** = half past five; *(now rarely) with the following hour, eg* **half five** = half past four.

adjective, adverb half.

verb **1** divide into two equal parts, halve; go halves with. **2** divide into more than two equal shares *NE, Lothian*.

halver, halfer, haufer, haf(f)er *noun, usually* **halvers 1** a half-portion, a share. **2** *also* **halfies** exclamation used especially by children when claiming a half share in a find. *verb* halve, divide equally. **go halvers** share equally. **halfie 1** = **half**^{1}. **2** a half-holiday. **3 halfies** *see* **halver** 2. **halflin(g) 1** a half-grown boy, especially a farmworker. **2** a half-witted person *now Caithness*. **3** a half-mature herring *ECentral*. **halflins 1** half, partly, almost. **2** half-way, midway. **halflin plane** a large-size plane used by carpenters.

half-bred *of sheep* crossed from a Border Leicester ram and a Cheviot ewe. **half-cousin** the child of one's parent's cousin, a second cousin. **half-deal man**

a half share fisherman. **half gaits** half way. **half gone** about the middle period of pregnancy. **half house** a semi-detached house *NE*. **halflang** *often of a young farmworker* adolescent, half-grown. **half loaf** a loaf of **plain bread** (*see* **plain**), half the size of a standard quartern loaf. **half-marrow** a marriage-partner, mate *now Angus*. †**half note** a ten-shilling note. **half-road(s)** half-way. **half ways** half-way; partly.

a.. and a half something which is large or extraordinary of its kind: *"a letter and a half"*. **a half and a half** a small whisky with a half pint of beer as a chaser. **half an atween** neither one nor the other, not quite.

half² *SW noun, also* **halve-net** a bag-shaped net to hold fish as the tide ebbs. **halver** a person who fishes with such a net. **go haavin** fish with such a net; go salmon fishing.

halflang, halflins *see* **half¹**

haliday *see* **haly**

hali(e)hoo *see* **hoo³**

halk a hawk.

hall *see* **ha**

hallaby [**hall**abie] nonsense word, only in children's counting rhyme.

hallach *see* **hallock**

hallan 1 †an inner wall, partition, or door-screen erected between the door and the fireplace. **2** a similar partition in a **byre** or stable, or between the living-room and the **byre**. **3** †a cottage, house.

    hallanshaker a beggar, a vagabond, tramp *now literary*.

hallicat *see* **hallock**

hali(e)hoo *see* **hoo³**

hallion a slovenly-looking or clumsy person, a rascal, a clown.

hallirackit *see* **hallock**

hallock, hallach *noun* a thoughtless giddy young woman or girl or occasionally young man.

    adjective **1** crazy, hare-brained *NE*. **2** uncouth, noisy *NE*.

verb behave in a crazy wild or irres-ponsible way.

    hallockit, hellicat, hallicat, hallirackit *especially of a girl or young woman* = *adjective*.

hallow¹ hollow.

hallow² All Saints.

    hallowday All Saints' Day. **Halloween, **†**hallow eve(n)** 31 October, the eve of All Saints' Day, the last day of the year in the old Celtic calendar, associated with witches and the powers of dark-ness, and celebrated with bonfires, tell-ing the future etc; *now* a children's fes-tival when they go around as **guisers** (*see* **guise**) often with turnip lanterns (*see also* **dook for apples** (*see* **dook¹**)). **hallow fair** a market held on 1 November in various places, especially Edinburgh. **hallowma(s), hallowmes** All Saints' Day.

halve-net *see* **half²**

halver *see* **half¹, half²**

haly, holy, holy.

    †**haliday** a holiday. **haly man** the Devil.

ham *see* **hum¹**

ham-a-haddie 1 a confused or unlikely story or situation. **2** a mix-up, a fuss.

hame, home, hem *noun* home.

    adverb **1** home. **2** at home. **3 bring hame** bring into the world; give birth to. **come hame** come into the world, be born. **4** into service: *"I was new come hame to the dressmaking"*.

    hamely 1 homely. **2** friendly, kind(ly), courteous. **hameward, hamewart, hamewirth** *now NE,* **hameart** *adverb* homeward. *adjective* belonging to or made at home, native, homely, *com-pare* **hameart. hamewith** homeward(s). **hamecoming 1** a coming or return home. **2** the festivities that take place on the arrival of a bride at her new home. **3** a birth. **hame-drauchtit** *NE* **1** selfish, keen to help oneself or one's home. **2** homesick; fond of, or drawn to home. **hamefare** the journey of a bride to her new home; the festivities

on that occasion *now Shetland Orkney*.
hame-farin staying at home *Shetland WCentral*. **hame-gaun 1** a return (journey), the act of going home. **2** death; the burial of the dead. **hame-made** *noun* a home-made article. *adjective* homely, countrified, unrefined. **hameower** *adverb* homewards. *adjective* **1** *of speech* homely, simple, in the (Scots) vernacular. **2** plain, simple.
gae hame die.

hameart, hamel, †**hamelt 1** belonging to home, domestic, internal. **2** †vernacular; in the native (Scots) tongue. **3** homely, familiar, plain, simple.

hameart *see* **hame**

hames *see* **haims**

hamesucken *law* (the crime of committing) an assault on a person in his own house or dwelling-place.

hamill *see* **hummel**

hamit 1 home-produced, homegrown. **2** home-loving, homely, familiar; rough-and-ready, untidy.

hammel *see* **hemmel**

hamp stutter, stammer; read with difficulty *now S*.

han *see* **hand**

hanch, hansh, hum(p)sh 1 snap (at), show the teeth, snatch. **2** eat greedily and noisily, munch.

†**hanchman** the personal attendant of a Highland Chief.

hand, han, haun 1 a hand. **2** direction, quarter, neighbourhood: *"near hand"*; *"from about Auchneel hand"*. **3** a handle. **4 hands** a pair of bats for shaping butter-pats. **5** the horse that walks on the left-hand side of a plough-team. **handie 1** a hand. **2** a small wooden tub, especially a milk-pail with one of the staves sticking up to form a handle. **handless** awkward, clumsy, incompetent, slow. **handy 1** ready with the hands. **2** *of an animal* quiet to handle. **3 nae handy** not easy to do or put up with; awful(ly), excessive(ly): *"at a rate nae handy"*.

handba(ll) 1 hand-ball. **2** a team game played in the Borders. **handban(d)** the wristband or cuff of a shirt. **hand barrow** a wooden frame with shafts which can be carried by two people. **handbreed** a hand's breadth. **handclap** a clap of the hands; an instant. **hand-cloot** a towel. †**handfast 1** betroth (two persons or one with another) by joining of hands. **2** become engaged to marry, especially agree to a probationary period of living with (someone) before marriage. **hand-idle** having nothing to occupy one's hands, with idle hands. **handlawhile** a short space of time. **handlin** a handline. **hand-plane** a carpenter's smoothing plane. **handsho** a mitten, a fingerless glove *now Orkney*. **hand-waled** handpicked, carefully selected, choice. **handwrite** handwriting, penmanship.

aboot hand(s) at hand, in the vicinity. **aff one's hand** on one's authority, on one's initiative. **amang (one's) hands 1** at spare moments, at intervals. **2** in one's possession. **behind the hand** after the event. **between hands** in the interval. **for one's own hands** for one's own part, for one's own interest. **fra hand** out of hand; at once. **hae through hand(s)** deal with, dispose of, discuss or investigate thoroughly; take to task, cross-examine. **hand for nieve** hand in hand, side by side; hand in glove. **hand o(f) writ(e)** handwriting, style of writing. **hand(s) owre head(s)** indiscriminately. **hand-roun-tea** a tea at which people are served individually and not seated at table. **in hand** *of a sum of money* in cash. **in hands with** occupied with, busy with. **keep in hand** keep in suspense; delay. **put hand to anesel** commit suicide. **put oot one's hand** help oneself at table. **put tae one's hand 1** lend a hand, buckle to. **2** = **put oot one's hand. Scotch hand** = **hand 4. there's my hand** I assure you.

handle, hanle, haunle handle.

handling 1 a commercial transaction. **2**

a (difficult) task. **3** a share in some affair, a hand in something. **4** a rounding up and penning of sheep for dipping, shearing etc. **5** an entertainment, meeting, party, social gathering.

handsel, hansel *noun* **1** a gift intended to bring good luck to something new or to a new beginning, *eg* the New Year, a new house. **2** the money received by a trader for his first sale, thought to bring good luck. **3** a piece of bread or other light snack given to farmworkers before beginning work.

verb **1** give or offer a **handsel** at the beginning of a year or day, or to mark some special occasion; present (someone) with earnest-money at the beginning of an engagement. **2** inaugurate with some ceremony or gift to bring good luck. **3** celebrate the first use of (something) with a **handsel**; use for the first time; be the first to try, test or taste (something).

Handsel Monday the first Monday of the New Year, formerly a holiday.

hang *see* **hing**

hangrell a stick, arm etc on which something is hung, *eg* the gallows, a treebranch for holding bridles etc in a stable.

hank[1] **1** a hank, a loop, coil. **2** a skein, *eg* of yarn (see p 360). **3** hold, influence, control. **4** a hesitancy in speech; hesitation, delay *now S*.

verb **1** entangle, catch as by a loop. **2** fasten, secure, link, especially by a loop. **3** tie tightly, constrict. **4** gather into coils or hanks, loop.

hank[2]: *usually* **hanks** the places on each side of a boat where the sideboards come together at stem (**fore hanks**) or stern (**aft hanks**).

hanker loiter, linger expectantly; hesitate.

hanle *see* **handle**

hansel *see* **handsel**

hansh *see* **hanch**

hantle, hankle a considerable quantity (of things), a large number (of people), a great deal.

hanty convenient, handy.

hap[1] *verb* **1** cover, surround, so as to shelter or hide. **2** cover over *eg* with earth, straw etc as a protection against cold or wet; pile (earth) on; thatch; bury. **3** wrap a garment round (a person), wrap (a person) up in clothes; tuck up (in bed). **4** clothe, dress. **5** make up (a fire) so as to keep it burning for a considerable time.

noun **1** a covering, especially a protection against the weather. **2** a wrap, shawl, or **plaid**; a warm outer garment; a bed-quilt or blanket.

hapwarm a warm wrap or thick outer garment.

hap[2], **hop** *verb* **1** hop, jump. **2** walk with a limp. **3** †**hap** *of tears etc* trickle down.

hoppin beds, hap-the-beds hopscotch.

hap step and lowp hop, step and jump.

hap[3], **haup** *usually of animals in harness* turn towards the right.

hap[4], **haup** a hip, the fruit of the wild rose.

hap-the-beds *see* **hap**[2]

happen happen to, befall.

happenin(g) casual, occasional, chance.

happer 1 a hopper (in a mill). **2** a basket or container, especially one for seed.

happy lucky, fortunate, auspicious.

hapshackle, hopshackle *verb* hobble (a horse etc), tie up (an animal) to prevent it from straying.

noun a hobble for tethering a horse etc, a fetter, shackle.

hapwarm *see* **hap**[1]

hard, herd *adjective* **1** hard. **2** *of alcoholic drink* strong, undiluted, raw. **3** closefisted, stingy.

noun **1** difficulty, hardship; **if hard comes to hard** if the worst comes to the worst. **2** **gae through the hard** experience hardship or misfortune. **3** spirits, especially whisky.

adverb **1** hard. **2** tightly, firmly, securely.

harden (up) *of weather* clear up, become

settled after rain. **hardie 1** a kind of white bread roll with a hard surface *Angus*. **2** a hard sort of butter biscuit (*NE*); a variety made in Cupar and popular as ship's biscuits (*Fife*). **hardlies, hardlins, harly** hardly, scarcely.

hard breid 1 a kind of thin oatcake. **2** stale bread, especially for making into breadcrumbs. **hard fish** dried or salt fish. **hard heid 1** a sea scorpion or father-lasher. **2** name for various plants, *eg* black knapweed; ribwort. **hard neck** brass neck. **hard-sutten** *of eggs* almost ready to hatch after long incubation. **hard-set** wilful, obstinate *now Lothian*. **the hard stuff, hard tackle** whisky. **hard up 1** *of persons* in poor health, unwell. **2** *of things* in bad condition, in a state of disrepair.

hard *see* **hear**

harden, harn a very coarse cloth made from **hards.**

hardlies, hardlins *see* **hard**

hards coarse refuse of flax or hemp, oakum, tow.

hardy 1 bold. **2** in good health. **3** frosty.

hare 1 a hare. **2** the last sheaf or handful of grain cut in the harvest-field.
harebell a single-bell-shaped blue flower, the bluebell of Scotland. **hare('s) lug** a kind of angling fly.

hareshard *NE*, **hareshaw, hairshach** *now Fife* a hare-lip.

harestone *see* **hair²**

harigals the guts, especially of an animal or fowl.

hark, herk *verb* **1** listen (to), hearken. **2** whisper; mutter *Shetland Orkney N*.
noun a whisper.

harl¹, haurle *verb* **1** drag (violently or roughly), pull, haul. **2** drag oneself, trail; move slowly, with dragging feet *now Shetland Orkney Angus*. **3** troll for fish with a fly or minnow for bait. **4** gather by trailing or dragging, scrape (together).
noun **1** what has been gathered as by dragging or scraping; an amount of

anything, large or small. **2** a rake or scraper used, *eg* for scraping up soft mud etc. **3** the act of dragging, a tug. **4** a slattern, a dirty, untidy or coarse person.

harl² *verb* roughcast with lime and small stones.
noun a mixture of sand and lime used for roughcasting.

harle, herald (duck) a kind of duck, the red-breasted merganser.

harly *see* **hard**

harn¹: harns brains, the brain; the intelligence.
harnless stupid. **harnpan** the skull.

harn² roast on embers, toast, make crisp, bake or fire.

harn *see* **harden**

harnish, herness, harness 1 harness. **2** *weaving* the mounting of a loom.
harness plaid, harness shawl a **plaid** (especially one made in Paisley) or shawl of fine quality or intricate pattern.

haroosh *see* **hurroo**

harp, hairp, herp 1 a harp. **2** a sieve, riddle. **3** a shovel with spars used *eg* for digging up potatoes etc.

harr a hinge of a door or gate *now Shetland*.

harra *see* **harrow**

Harris tweed *see* **tweed**

harro a cry of distress, alarm or encouragement, latterly of rejoicing.

harrow, harra a harrow.
die in the harrows die in harness.

harry *see* **herrie**

harst *see* **hairst**

harvest *see* **hairst**

hash *verb* **1** slash, hack, mangle. **2** slice, cut up, chop; munch, chew. **3** spoil, destroy, deface. **4** overwork, harass. **5** be pressed, harassed. **6** talk volubly, emptily or illogically. **7** move or work in a muddling, flurried way.
noun **1** contemptuous term for a person. **2** a heap, a large quantity; a crowd. **3** a row, uproar, brawl. **4** ribald

talk, nonsense. **5** a rush or excessive pressure of work; work done hastily, carelessly. **6** a strong wind, especially along with rain. **7** grain dried in a kiln and then chopped.

hasher 1 an implement used to slice up turnips for fodder. **2** a careless, hustling person. **hashie 1** *of persons* slapdash, careless or slovenly in dress, work or habits. **2** *of weather* wet, wet and windy, stormy. **hashie-bashie** a marbles game in which smaller marbles are knocked out of holes by striking them with a larger one. **hashter** work done in a slovenly way, or badly arranged.

hashie a hash, a mixture of chopped meat etc.

hashter see **hash**

hask give a short dry cough.

haslock see **hause**

hasp see **hesp**[1], **hesp**[2]

haspal an untidy, carelessly-dressed person.

hass see **hause**

hassock 1 a large round tuft of peat used as a seat. **2** a shock of bushy hair.

haste see **heest**

hastie hasten, hurry.

hasty see **heest**

hat 1 a hat. **2** a layer of froth etc forming on the surface of a liquid.
  like a hatter with maximum energy or vigour. **hattie** name of various games involving a hat or cap. **hattit kit** a preparation of milk with a top layer of cream. **†horse and hattock** a call, originally by witches, to put on a hat and ride.
  gie someone a hat greet someone in passing by raising one's hat.

hat see **hit**

hate see **heat**, **het**[1]

hather see **heather**

hatter *verb* **1** batter, bruise; treat roughly *now Shetland*. **2** harass, vex, overtire. **3** collect in crowds, swarm. **4** move confusedly or laboriously; work in a careless way *now S*.
  noun **1** a mixed collection, a confused heap; a state of disorder. **2** a difficulty; a struggle, fluster *S*. **3** a skin rash.

hauch, haugh [-ch, -gh as -ch in 'loch'] *verb* cough, especially in order to clear the throat.
  noun **1** a forcible breath, a gasp, especially the act of breathing hard on a surface before polishing *NE*. **2** a soft loose cough; a clearing of the throat.

hauch see **haugh**

hauchle see **hochle**

haud, had, hald, hold, howld *verb* NB *This verb is often used where English has* keep: **1** hold. **2** keep, go on: *"we'll haud content"*. **3** continue, keep (in health) *now Angus*: *"hoo are ye haudin yoursel?"*. **4** keep, cause to continue to be or to do something. **5** go on one's way, go in a certain direction; continue on or along (one's way etc). **6** *of a market, fair etc* be observed, celebrated. **7** wager, bet. **8 hauds ye** I accept your wager *NE*. **9** stop; restrain oneself: *"haud you there!"* **10** restrain, keep back: *"wha could haud their temper?"* **11** burden, afflict, *often* **hauden doun**: *"a young woman sair hauden doon wi a sma family"*. **12** keep, maintain (people or animals); keep (provisions etc) in store. **13** preserve (cattle etc) for stock. **14** round up, pen (sheep) *S*. **15** *of seeds etc* strike root *now NE*. **16** *mainly* **haul(d)**, *of fish* hide, lurk under stones.
  noun, also **haul 1** a hold. **2** property, a habitation; **house and haud** house and home. **3** a support, prop. **4** a refuge, shelter *now Shetland*. **5** a den of an animal, *eg* a rabbit-hole. **6** the overhanging bank of a stream, or a stone, beneath which a fish lurks. **7** a dispute, a tiff.

hauder-on *in a shipyard* a riveter's assistant *Lothian WCentral*. **haudin(g) 1** a holding; a small farm or house held on lease. **2** possession, means of support. **3** furniture, equipment; the stock of a farm *now S*.

gang by (the) haud(s) support oneself in walking by holding onto chairs etc.

haud(a)back *call to animals* turn left or away. **haud aff (o) anesel** look after oneself, defend oneself or one's own interests *NE*. **haud aff (ye)** *call to animals* turn to the right. **haud again** hold back; resist. **haud-again** opposition, hindrance *now NE*. **haud at 1** keep at (something). **2** urge on by criticism etc, nag. **haud awa 1** keep away, keep out or off. **2** continue on one's way, go away. **haud awa frae** with the exception of. **haud by 1** pass by, keep away from. **2** have (little etc) respect for. **haud-doon** a handicap, burden. **haud-fast** a staple etc used for fixing. **haud one's feet** keep (on) one's feet. **haud for** aim at, make for. **haud forrit** continue to improve (in health). **haud in** *noun* a stinting, a lack. *verb* **1** hold in. **2** *of a container* hold in the contents, not leak or spill. **3** *also* **haud in about** bring or come closer; save, economize, be miserly. **haud in aboot** keep in order, keep a check on *now Angus*. **haud in wi** keep in with. **haud one's mooth** be silent. **haud on 1** carry on, keep up. **2** supply, keep adding or putting on: *"Haud the peats on the fire"*. **haud out 1** keep out. **2** keep maintaining. **3** live, reside. **haud sae** stop doing something. **haud till** keep saying. **haud to 1** *especially of a door* (keep) shut. **2** keep hard at work. **haud up 1** hold up. **2** present (a child) for baptism *now NE*. **3** *call to animals* stand still. **haud up to** court, make up to. **haud up wi** keep pace with. **haud a wee** wait a little, stop for a moment. **haud wi** own up to. **in a haud** in difficulties, in trouble. **see's a haud o** give, hand over. **neither to haud nor to bind** ungovernable, beyond control.

hauf *see* **half**[1]

haugh, hauch [-gh, -ch, as -ch in 'loch'], †**haw** a piece of level ground, on the banks of a river, river-meadow land.

haugh *see* **hauch, hoch**[1]

haul a very large quantity.

haul(d) *see* **haud**

haun *see* **hand**

haunle *see* **handle**

haunt a custom, habit, practice.

haup *see* **hap**[3], **hap**[4]

haur *see* **haar**[1]

haurd *see* **hear**

haurle *see* **harl**[1]

hause, hawse, hass *noun* **1** the neck. **2** the throat, gullet. **3** a narrow place: a neck of land; a narrow stretch of water (*now Orkney*); a defile, the head of a pass (*SW, S*). **4** a narrow neck-like part, *eg* of an axle.

†*verb* embrace, take in one's arms.

hausebane the collarbone. **hauselock, haslock** the wool on a sheep's neck, often regarded as the finest part. **hause-pipe** the throat, windpipe.

gae doun (into) the wrang hause *of food etc* go down the wrong way.

haut limp, hop.

have *see* **hae, heave**

have-eel *see* **haivel**

haver oats, the oat.

haver *see* **hae**[1], **haiver**

haw[1], **chaw** a haw, hawthorn(-berry).

haw-spitter a peashooter *SW*.

haw[2], **hyaave** *NE* [heeaave] *of a pale*, wan colouring, tinged with blue or green *now NE*.

ha(w) clay a kind of clay formerly used for whitening doorsteps etc *now S*.

haw *see* **haugh**

Hawick ba 1 †a game played at Shrovetide with a football in the River Teviot. **2** a round, brown, mint-flavoured boiled sweet made in Hawick.

hawk *see* **hack**

hawkie a cow with a white face; any cow; pet name for a favourite cow.

hawkit, haikit, hackit 1 *of animals* spotted or streaked with white; white-faced *now NE*. **2** *of people* foolish, stupid, harum-scarum.

hawse *see* **hause**

hay *see* **hey**[1]

hazel beat or thrash, as with a hazel stick.
  hazel oil a caning, a sound beating (with a hazel stick).

hazer *see* **haizer**

hazy weak in intellect, mentally unbalanced.

he, e, ei *S personal pronoun* **1** he, it. **2** used by a wife of her husband or a servant of his master.
  noun a man, a male person *now NE*.

head, headicks and pinticks *see* **heid**

heal[1] health, physical well-being.

heal[2]**, hele 1** hide, conceal; keep secret. **2** *in freemasonry* protect, *often* **heal and conceal.**

healy *see* **heelie**

heap, haip 1 a heap. **2** a great deal, a lot: *"a heap better"*. **3** a slovenly woman; a coarse rough person.
  be heid of the heap be in the forefront, take first place.

hear, *verb, past also* heer(e)d, hard, haurd hear.
  hearer one who listens to the preaching of a certain **minister**, a churchgoer.
  hearing 1 a scolding. **2** *see* **children's hearing** (*see* **child**).
  hear one's ears hear oneself speak. **hear till him!** *etc* just listen to him!

hearing *see* **herrin(g)**

hearken *verb* **1** *also* **hearken tae** eavesdrop, play the eavesdropper. **2** listen to, hear with attention. **3** **hearken someone his lessons** *etc* hear someone repeat lessons etc. **4** whisper (something). **5** *of the wind* blow gently.

heart *see* **hert**

heat, hate heat.
  heater a wedge-shaped glazed sugared bun *NE*.
  get a heat make (oneself) warm. **heat the house** hold a housewarming *now Lothian; see also* **house.**

heathen a lump of gneiss etc, a glacial boulder *NE*.

heather, hedder, hather heather.
  heathery 1 heather-covered; of or like heather. **2** rough, dishevelled; mountain-bred. **heathery head** (a person with) a tousled or shaggy head of hair. **heather ale** a drink brewed from heather, hops, barm, syrup, ginger and water *now Orkney NE*. **heather ask** a lizard. **heather bell** the flower of the heather. **heather-birn(s)** the stalks and roots of burnt heather. **heather blackie** a ring ouzel. **heather-bleater, heather-bluitter** a snipe. **heather-claw** a dog's dew-claw. **heather-cock** a black or red grouse. **heather-cow** a tuft or twig of heather; a broom made of heather-twigs. **heather lintie 1** a twite or mountain linnet. **2** a linnet. **heather-lowper** a hill-dweller, countryman *NE*.
  bell heather a kind of heath with bell-shaped flowerlets; *loosely, also* cross-leaved heath. **set the heather on fire** cause a great furore or sensation.

heather-range, heather-reenge a hydrangea *now NE, ECentral*.

heave, have *Orkney NE* [rhymes with 'shave'] **1** heave. **2** throw, pitch, toss (without implying effort or strain as in English). **3** rise up above the surface, come into view.
  hoven *of grazing animals* blown up with having eaten too much fresh green fodder.
  gie someone the heave 1 push, shove. **2** sack or dismiss from a job.

heavy 1 *also* **heavy-footed** pregnant. **2** *of a river* swollen. **3** *of a drink, mainly of spirits* large. **4** *of beer, corresponding to English* bitter.
  be heavy on, be a heavy neighbour on be hard on (clothes), consume a great deal of (food or drink).

hech, hegh [-ch, -gh as -ch in 'dreich'] exclamation of sorrow, fatigue, pain, surprise or contempt: *"hech me"; "hech sirs"*.
  verb **1** †make such a sound. **2** pant, breathe hard or uneasily *now S*.
  hech how exclamation of weariness or regret. **(the) auld hech how** the old

routine.

hech-how [-ch as in 'dreich'] name for various types of hemlock *Argyll SW*.

hechle [-ch as in 'dreich'] **1** pant, breathe quickly. **2** walk or move with difficulty. **3** †foretell, prophesy.

hecht, †**hicht** promise, vow, pledge, undertake.

hecht *see* **heicht**

heck, haik, hake 1 a rack, a slatted wooden or iron framework, *eg* for fodder in a stable etc, or placed in or across a stream. **2** †a part of a spinning wheel or weaving machine to guide the thread onto the bobbin. **3** a framework attached to the sides of a cart to let it take a higher load *now NE*.

hecker a glutton, hearty eater *ECentral, S*. **live at heck and manger** live extravagantly, be in clover.

heckham-peckham *see* **heckum peckum**

heckle[1] *noun* **1** *also* **hackle** a hackle, heckle, flax-comb; the long neck-feathers of a cock etc. **2** a severe beating, sharp criticism; a person who gives this. **3** *also* **hackle** a cockade of hackle-feathers dyed in various colours and worn in the bonnets of certain Scottish regiments.

verb **1** dress (flax etc) with a **heckle**[1]. **2** speak sharply (to), scold severely.

heckle(d) biscuit a type of hard biscuit made in Angus with a pinhole surface. **be (kept) on heckle-pins** be (kept) in suspense or on tenterhooks.

heckle[2] a network of straw ropes which covers the apex of a cornrick, or a thatched roof *NE*.

Hecklebirnie, Heckiebirnie Hell *now NE*.

heckum-peckum, heckham-peckham a type of artificial fly used for trout-fishing.

hecturi *sheep-counting,* **heeturi** *children's rhymes* six.

hedder *see* **heather**

heech [-ch as in 'dreich'] exclamation of exhilaration by dancers in a **reel**.

heech *see* **heich**

heed: never heed never mind, don't bother.

heed *see* **heid, huid**

heek *see* **hick**[2]

heel the rind or last portion of a cheese; each end of a loaf of bread, especially when cut off the loaf.

heel-cap patch, mend or reinforce the heels of (shoes or stockings). **heel-ring** a circular piece of metal to reduce wear on the heel of a boot. **heel-shod** a piece of iron to protect the heel of a heavy boot or shoe.

coup by the heels lay low. **give heels to** cause to hurry; *curling* make the progress of (a stone) more rapid by sweeping the ice in front of it. **heels ower gowdie, heelster gowdie, heelster heid(s)** head-over-heels, topsy-turvy, upside-down. **take one's heels** take to one's heels, run away.

heelan *see* **hieland**

heeld lean to one side; overturn, upset *now Shetland Orkney*.

†**heelie, healy** *adjective* proud, haughty, arrogant.

verb offend, affront, hurt; be offended, take offence.

noun an affront, a slight; a feeling of pique.

heelie *see* **huilie**

heeliegoleerie, †**hilliegeleerie** topsy-turvy, in a state of confusion *now ECentral*.

heelster *see* **heel**

heer(e)d *see* **hear**

heest, haste, hist haste.

hasty brose a kind of quickly-made **brose** *NE*.

haste ye back 'come back again soon', an invitation to visit again.

heeturi *see* **hecturi**

heeze, heise, hize *now NE verb* **1** hoist, lift, raise (up). **2** raise, exalt, extol. **3** carry, convey (a person) to a place; hurry, or hustle (a person) off. **4** hasten, hurry. **5** dance in a lively way; make merry *now NE*. **6** swarm, abound with.

noun **1** a heave, a hitch up. **2** an aid,

encouragement, a helping hand. **3** a romp; a practical joke, a teasing *NE*.

heezie 1 a heave, a hitch up. **2** †a drubbing, rough handling. **heezie-hozie, eezie-ozie** a game in which two players stand back to back, interlink arms, and, stooping alternately, raise each other from the ground *now S*. **heyzer** [rhymes with 'miser'] a clothes-prop *NE*.

heezel *see* **hissel**

heff *see* **heft**³

heffer laugh heartily, guffaw *ECentral, S*.

heft¹, **haft** haft.

hae heft an blade in one's hand have complete control, have the whip hand *NE*.

heft² *verb* **1** †lift up; remove by lifting. **2** lift in order to estimate the weight.

heft³, **heff**, †**haft** *verb* **1** accustom (sheep or cattle) to a new pasture by constant herding to prevent them from straying. **2** *of animals* become accustomed to a new pasture; *of people* become settled or established (in a place, occupation etc).

noun **1** a pasture which animals have become familiar with; attachment to a particular pasture. **2** the number of sheep that graze on such a pasture.

heft⁴ hold back (milk) in a cow's udder so that it becomes hard and swollen; leave (a cow) unmilked.

heftit 1 *of an udder* hard and dry, through not being milked. **2** *of milk* accumulated in the udder. **3** *of a cow* having a large quantity of milk in the udder. **4** full of liquid to bursting point. **5** swollen with wind, flatulent. **6** full to repletion.

hegh *see* **hech**

hegs, haigs *exclamation* (yes) indeed!

heich, heech, heigh [rhymes with 'dreich'], **high** *adjective* **1** high. **2** tall. **3** (*compare* **laich**) occupying the higher situation, situated above another of its kind; situated in the upper part or on the upper floor of a building. **4** arrogant, proud,

condescending. **5** in high spirits, lively, excitable. **6** out of one's mind, raving in delirium *NE*. **7** north *SW*.

adverb **1** high. **2** loudly, in a loud voice. **3** proudly, haughtily, disdainfully.

noun a hill, height, an eminence, upland.

Higher *secondary education* at a more advanced or difficult level, of both a State examination and the certificate awarded to successful candidates: *"Higher English"*; one of these examinations or certificates: *"I got two highers"*.

high-bendit dignified in appearance, haughty, ambitious. **High Court = High Court of Justiciary** (*see* **justiciary**); NB in England, this refers to the supreme civil court. **high English** the awkward, affected form of English used by Scots trying to imitate 'correct' English. **heich-heidit = heich** *adjective* 4. **High kirk** the principal church in a town or region, *eg* St Giles in Edinburgh. **High School** name for the principal school in many Scottish towns; a **senior-secondary school**; a comprehensive school. **high tea = tea** *noun* 2. **high tig** *see* **tig**.

be heich upon ae shouther have one shoulder higher than the other *Shetland N*. **be very heich in the bend** very condescending. **carry a heich heid** behave haughtily. **up to high doh** in a state of extremely agitated excitement.

heichen, highen, hichten heighten.

heicht, hecht, hicht, height *noun* **1** height. **2** a high place, a hilltop. **3** *of behaviour, emotion etc* a high pitch.

verb raise higher, heighten, lift.

heid, hade, heed, head *noun* **1** the head. **2** an item; the chief or essential point *Orkney NE*. **3** *bowls and curling* that part of the game in which all the stones or bowls on both sides are played to one end of the rink. **4** a measure of yarn, formerly of length, but now weight (see p 358, 360).

verb **1** †behead, decapitate. **2** head, lead, top. **3** put the finishing touches to (a rick or stack) and secure its top. **headicks and pinticks** a game played with pins. **heidie** *adjective* **1** headstrong, passionate, impetuous, violent; proud, haughty. **2** clever. **3** apt to make one giddy or dizzy. *noun* **1** a headmaster. **2** *in ball-games* a header. **heidie knite** a clever person *NE*. **heidmaist** topmost, highest up.

heid-band 1 a headband. **2** the waistband of a garment, especially of trousers. **3** a halter. **heid-banger** an idiot, a very stupid person. **heid-bauk 1** the float-rope with corks attached, from which the older type of herring-net was suspended in the water *Shetland NE*. **2** the vertical edge of a fishing-net *now Shetland*. **heid bummer** *often sarcastic* a manager, a prominent or important person. **heid-dyke** the outer wall of a field or holding; a wall separating arable from uncultivated land, the boundary wall. **heid-heich** with the head high, proudly, confidently, with dignity. **heidsman** a chief, commander; a leader, superior; a foreman. **heid-mark** an individual characteristic which distinguishes one from another, as opposed to any artificial means of differentiation. †**know by heid-mark** have a personal acquaintance with. **heid rig(g)** the ridge of land at the end of a field on which horse and plough etc are turned. **heid room 1** †the higher or outer part of a **croft**; the marginal or boundary land. **2** scope for action, authority. **heidsheaf 1** the last sheaf of grain placed on the top of a **stook** or rick. **2** the finishing touch; the last straw *now NE*. **heid tow** a headrope. **heid washing** the washing of the head as a ceremony of initiation *eg* when a new apprentice enters his trade *now SW*. **heid yin, high heid yin** a leader, a person in authority.

aff at the heid, awa in the heid off one's head. **be at heid an aix wi** be involved with *now NE*. **get one's heid in one's hands** *usually in threats* get a severe scolding or punishment. **get one's heid oot** launch out on one's own, get one's freedom of action. **go oot o heid** be forgotten. **heids and heels** completely, wholly. **heids an(d) thraws** *of articles arranged in a row* with alternating head and feet or top and bottom; in disorder or confusion, higgledy-piggledy. **in the heid o(f)** busied or occupied with, deeply involved in. **on the heid o(f) 1** immediately after, on top of *Shetland NE*. **2** = **in the heid o(f)**. **on the heids o** in confirmation of; on the strength or security of; over, concerning. **ower the heid(s) o(f)** because of, on account of, concerning. **tak one's heid** go to one's head, make drunk. **wi one's heid under one's oxter** looking downcast or dejected, sorry for oneself.

heid, heidie craw *see* **huid**

heidiepeer of equal height or age.

heifer [heef*er*] a young cow, the precise meaning varying considerably as to whether or not the animal has calved, or how often she has calved.

heifle *see* **hypal**

heigh *see* **heich**

height *see* **heicht**

heir: heir portioner one of several female heirs who succeed to equal portions of a **heritage,** failing a male heir; the successor of such a joint heiress. †**heir-at-law, heir of line** one who succeeded by law to the **heritable** property of a deceased person. **heir of provision** one who succeeds in virtue of express provisions, as in a (marriage-)settlement.

heise *see* **heeze**

heist, hyste [rhymes with 'diced'] hoist.

hele *see* **heal**[2]

hellicat *see* **hallock**

helm 1 a helmet. **2** a crowd, noisy gathering *now NE*.

help: helper, helpender *now NE* **1** a helper.

2 a **minister's** or teacher's assistant.
helplie helpful; willing to help.

help ma bob exclamation of astonishment or exasperation *Central*.

helter-shank the rope of a halter.

hem the outer part of a millstone.

hem *see* **hame**

hemmel, hammel a shed and enclosure for housing cattle.

hempen gravat *see* **gravat**

hempie *noun* 1 †a rogue, a person deserving to be hanged. 2 a mischievous or unruly young person, now especially a girl. 3 †a hedge-sparrow.
adjective wild, roguish.

hems *see* **haims**

hen *noun* 1 a hen, *often used where English uses* chicken. 2 term of address for a girl or woman. 3 a dare, a challenge.
verb 1 withdraw through cowardice, chicken out. 2 challenge, dare.
henner *Lothian* 1 an acrobatic or gymnastic feat. 2 = **hen** *noun* 3. **hennie** timid, cowardly.
hen-bauk a tie-beam on the roof of a country cottage. **hen-cavie, hencrae** a hencoop. **hen's eeran** a fool's errand. **hen('s) flesh** goose-flesh *now Shetland S*. **hen's gerse** as much grass etc as would produce food for a hen; something of very little value *now Shetland*. **hen-hertit** chicken-hearted. **hen-laft** a hen roost; the roof-joists of a house and the space above them. **hen-pen** the droppings of fowls, used as manure *now NE, Central*. **hen picks** *NE*, **hen plooks** *S* = **hen's flesh**. **hen-ree** a hen run. **hen-taed, hen toed** pigeon toed. **hen taes** crowfoot. **hen's taes** *of bad handwriting* scrawls. **hen-wife** 1 a woman who has charge of or deals in poultry. 2 a man who concerns himself about matters usually left to women.
have a memory like a hen have a bad memory. **see (somebody) by the hens' dish** see (somebody) part of the way home. **sell one's hen(s) on a rainy day** make a bad bargain.

hench *see* **hainch**

hender *see* **hinder**[2]

henk walk or move unsteadily, walk with a limp, hop on one leg *now Shetland*.

henner, hennie *see* **hen**

henshelstane the stone shelf or slab in front of a baker's oven-door.

†**hent, hint** take hold of, grasp, seize; raise (up etc).

hent *see* **hint**[1]

her *see* **hir**

herald (duck) *see* **harle**

herbour, hairbour harbour.

herd, hird *noun* 1 a person who tends or watches over sheep or cattle, a shepherd. 2 a spiritual guide, a pastor. 3 †*curling* a stone played so as to guard the winning shot.
verb 1 watch over (sheep or cattle). 2 watch over, attend to *now SW*. 3 keep (someone) away from. 4 keep (land) clear of animals.
herding 1†the tending and confining to their own grazing of sheep and cattle. 2 a grazing allotted to a particular herd. 3 the post of herdsman.
herd craws prevent rooks from interfering with crops.

herd *see* **hard**

here exclamation expressing surprise.
hereanent *now mainly law* concerning this matter; in regard to what has just been said. †**thereattour, hereawa 1** in this neighbourhood, hereabouts. 2 hither.

herial, herrial *noun* 1 †the best living animal, due by feudal custom to the landlord on the death of tenant; a money payment instead; the right to claim such payment. 2 something which causes great loss or expense *NE*.

heritable *adjective* 1 capable of being inherited, subject to inheritance; *law* applied to that form of property (houses, lands, and rights pertaining to these) which went by inheritance to the **heir-at-law** (*see* **heir**), as opposed to **moveable** property. 2 *law* pertaining to or connected with houses, lands etc. **3** *of people* holding property etc, by hereditary right.

heritable bond *law* a personal obligation for a money loan, fortified by a conveyance or **heritage** as security.

†**heritable jurisdictions** collective term for various ancient rights formerly enjoyed by feudal proprietors of land or by holders of certain offices, entitling them to administer justice in local courts; abolished in 1747. **heritable security** *law* security for a loan consisting of the right of **heritable** property conveyed by the debtor to the creditor.

heritage 1 heritage, inheritance. **2** †property, which descended to the **heir-at-law** (*see* **heir**) on the decease of the proprietor, **heritable** estate. **3** †such property inherited by a person as rightful heir; an inheritance, birthright. **4** *law* the technical term for property in the form of land and houses. **5** *in reference to a* **feu** the possession of lands by **heritable** right.

heritor 1 a heritor, an heir or heiress. **2** †the proprietor of **heritable** property. **3** †a property-owner, a landowner, a landed proprietor; *in parochial law* a proprietor of land or houses formerly liable to payment of public **burdens** connected with the parish, including administration of the poor, schools, and upkeep of church property.

herk *see* **hark**

herle, erle a heron *ECentral*.

herling, hirling an immature sea-trout.

herm *see* **hairm**

hern, huron a heron *S*.

herness *see* **harnish**

heronshew a heron.

herp *see* **harp**

herrial *see* **herial**

herrie, harry *verb* **1** harry, rob, plunder. **2** rob (a nest) of eggs or young, or (a beehive) of its honey. **3** take all the fish from (a stretch of water etc). **4** ruin,

make poor. **5** exhaust land.

herrie out dispossess, expel *now NE*.

herrie-watter *Caithness*, †**herrie-water-net 1** †a kind of fishing net. **2** a very selfish person *Caithness*.

herrin(g), hearing *NE* a herring.

herrin hake a hake. **herrin sile** a young herring.

hersel(f) 1 herself. **2** †*literary, supposedly of a Highlander's speech* myself, I. **3** name for the female head of any institution, *eg* the mistress of the house, a female boss.

†**thership** plunder; violent robbery; ruin.

he(r)skit *see* **hert**

hert, heart, hairt *noun* **1** the heart. **2** the stomach *Shetland Orkney Caithness NE*. **3** the central core of sheaves in a corn-rick. **4** (the) **Hearts** = **Heart of Midlothian.**

verb build up the inner sheaves of a cart-load or stack of corn.

hert(e)nin encouragement; strengthening. **hertie 1** hearty, cordial. **2** drunk, tipsy *now Shetland Caithness*. **3** fond of fun and good company, cheerful. **4** generous. **5** having a good appetite *now NE*. **6** suffering from a weak heart. **hertless 1** disheartened, dejected. **2** cheerless, dismal, discouraging.

hert-alane absolutely alone, lonely, desolate. **hert's care** anxiety *now Shetland Orkney*. **hert-dry** thoroughly dry *NE*. **hert-fever** an illness causing a feeling of exhaustion. **hert-glad** very glad, delighted. **hert-hale 1** *of the body* organically sound. **2** heart-whole. †**hert-heezin** encouraging, heartwarming. **hert-hunger 1** a ravenous desire for food *NE*. **2** a longing for affection *Shetland NE*. **hert-lazy** exceptionally lazy, naturally indolent. **hert-likin** affection, love *now Shetland NE*. **hert-peety** deep compassion *Shetland, NE*. **hert-rug** a strain on the emotions *now Shetland Orkney*. **hert-sab** a sob from the heart. **hert-sair** *noun* pain or grief of heart; a great vexation, constant grief. *adjective* heartsore. **hert scad, hert scald, hert scaud, he(r)skit** *Shetland Orkney* 1 heartburn. 2 a feeling of disgust or repulsion *now WCentral, Ulster*. 3 a source of bitter grief, trouble, disappointment or aversion *NE*. **hertsome** 1 encouraging, animating; cheering, attractive, pleasant. 2 *of a meal* substantial, hearty *now SW*. 3 merry, lively. **hert sorry** deeply grieved. **hert-stoun(d)** a pain at the heart. **hert-warm** deeply affectionate, cordial *now Shetland*.

gae wi one's hert be appetising, to one's liking. **gang against one's hert** be disliked *NE*. **gar someone's hert rise** make someone sick. **hae one's hert an one's ee in** be extremely interested in, be eager to possess. **the hert o corn** one of the best, a good fellow. **Heart of Midlothian** 1 name for the old **Tolbooth** of Edinburgh (demolished 1817), now the site of the this marked by a heart-shaped arrangement of cobbles in the roadway. 2 name of one of the Edinburgh football teams. **hert of the yearth** the plant self-heal *S*. **taste someone's hert** be to someone's liking.

hervest *see* **hairst**

heskit *see* **hert**

hesp¹, **hasp** *noun* a hasp, a catch or clasp. *verb* fasten with a hasp, fix.

buckled wi ae hasp tarred with the same brush, birds of feather.

hesp², †**hasp** a length of yarn, or skein of wool etc (see p 360).

a ravelled hesp a confused state of affairs, a difficult situation.

het¹, **hate, hot** 1 hot. 2 warm, comfortable. 3 †*of peas and oats* quickly growing, early maturing. 4 *of grain or root crops* fermenting, decayed.

hot-furr a newly-turned strip of earth, used especially for sowing early peas. **het girdle** *see* **girdle**. **het heart** a heart suffering from bitter disappointment; the disappointment itself. **het pint** a drink made from hot spiced ale served

at wedding festivities etc. **het-skinned** fiery, irascible. **het beans and butter** a children's game like hunt-the-thimble. **gie (someone) a het skin** give (someone) a sound thrashing. **gie (someone) it het (an reekin)** scold or beat (someone) severely. **keep the puddin het** keep the pace up. **(ower) het a-hame** applied to someone who appears to have left the comforts of home for no apparent reason.

het² it, the person who chases etc in children's games.

het *see* **hit, hoot**

heth *see* **haith**

hettle fishermen's name for the rough stony sea-bottom some distance from the shore, beyond the area covered with seaweed *now Caithness*.

heuch, heugh [heeooch, heeuch] *noun, plural also* †**hews** 1 a precipice, cliff, a steep bank. 2 a **glen** or ravine with steep, overhanging sides. 3 a pit, mineshaft, quarry(-face). *verb* earth up (plants) in drills.

heuk [heeook, heeuk], **hook** 1 a hook. 2 †a reaper. 3 contemptuous term for an old woman *NE*.

hooky hook-shaped, crooked; crafty, grasping *now ECentral S*.

heukbane [heook-], †**hook bone** the hipbone; a cut of beef from that part of the animal (corresponding to Eng rump steak).

hews *see* **heuch**

Hexham: to Hexham to Hell, to blazes *S*.

hey¹, **hay** [rhymes with 'gey'] 1 hay. 2 the hay harvest.

hey-bog marshy ground whose grass was formerly used for winter fodder. **hey-bogie** a low hay-truck. **hey-broo** a drink made by boiling hay *N*. **hey-fog** the second growth of grass in a hayfield. **hey-folk** haymakers. **hey-neuk** a corner of a **byre** or stable in which hay is stored for immediate use.

hey² [rhymes with 'gey'] a halfpenny

Angus.

hey³ [rhymes with 'gey'] *exclamation* hey, a call to attract attention etc.

verb exclaim **hey**³; summon with a shout.

like hey-ma-nanny vigorously, quickly. **give hey-ma-nanny** scold or punish vigorously.

heyser *see* **heeze**

hi a call to a horse, mainly a command to turn left.

Hibs, Hi-bees nicknames for the Edinburgh football team Hibernian.

hicht *see* **heicht, hecht**

hichten *see* **heichen**

hick¹ *noun* a hiccup, hiccuping *now NE.*
verb 1 hiccup. 2 catch the breath before bursting into tears; sob noisily *S.*

hick², **heek** 1 delay, hesitate; waver, haggle in bargaining *now SW, S.* 2 hesitate in speaking *now NE.*

hickertie-pickertie higgledy-piggledy.

hid *see* **hae**

hidder *see* **hither**

hiddin *see* **huid**

hiddle 1 hide, conceal. 2 nestle closely, take shelter *NE.*
hiddlie hidden, sheltered, remote *now Angus.* **hidlin** hidden, secret; secretive. **hidlin wise** secretly, by stealth *now SW.*

hide¹, **hod**, **howd** hide.
hidie, hoddy *Angus adjective* carefully hidden; very suitable for hiding anything or anyone in. *noun* the game of hide-and-seek; the call given by a player to indicate that he is ready to be looked for *now Perth.* **hidie-hole** a hiding place.

hide² 1 a hide, the skin of an animal; *now humorously or contemptuously* human skin. 2 †a female domestic animal; a woman.
hide bind a disease of horses and cattle.

hidie *see* **hide**¹

hidlin *see* **hiddle**

hidlins *adverb* secretly, stealthily.
noun plural 1 hiding places, refuge. 2 concealment, secrecy *now SW.*

adjective secret, clandestine, underhand.

hieland, highland, heelan *noun* 1 high land, high ground. 2 *now usually* **the Highlands** the mountainous district of Scotland lying north and west of the **Highland line.** 3 **the Highland** = **Highland Show.**

adjective of or like the Highlands or Highlanders *eg* 1 *of sports, dancing etc* originally native to the **Highlands.** 2 *of the language of the Highlands* Gaelic, in **Gaelic, Gaelic**-speaking. 3 of the character (supposed to be) typical of Highlanders: (1) warmly hospitable; (2) having an exaggerated sense of birth and descent; (3) uncouth, unskilled, inelegant, *often* **no sae hieland** not too bad(ly); (4) not quite truthful or honest, evasive *now NE;* (5) naive, impractical, 'green', *often* **no sae hieland.** 4 of breeds of animals native to the Highlands.

Highlander 1 a native or inhabitant of the Highlands. 2 a soldier in one of the **Highland** regiments. 3 one of the Highland breed of cattle.

Highland dance a dance, based on traditional figures, performed as a spectacle, usually solo. **Hielan Donald** nickname for a **Highlander** 1 *now N.* **Highland dress** the **tartan** outfit worn by Highlanders and others, *ie* the **kilt**¹ or **trews** and **plaid**, and any of the accessories, *eg* bonnet, belt, **dirk**², **sporran** and long socks. **Highland fling** a solo **Highland dance. Highland Games** *see* **game** *noun* 2. **Highland Gathering** = **Highland Games. Highland line** name for the imaginary boundary between the **Highlands** *noun* 2 and **Lowlands** (*see* **lawland**) of Scotland, a line drawn approximately from Dumbarton to Ballater and thence to Nairn. **Highlandman's garters** ribbon grass *now Shetland NE.* **Highland pony** one of a breed of ponies originating in the Highlands. **hieland pyot** a missel thrush

NE. **Highland reel** a reel as performed in the Highlands; a tune for such; a **Highland dance** performed by two people. **Highland regiment** one of the regiments in the British Army originally raised in and recruited from the **Highlands** *noun* 2, whose members are entitled to wear **Highland dress. Highland (Region)** the northernmost **region** of Scotland. **Hielan sheltie** = **Highland pony. Highland Show, Royal Highland Show** a large agricultural show held annually by *The Royal Highland and Agricultural Society,* since 1960 at a permanent site at Ingliston near Edinburgh.

high *see* **heich**

high tea *see* **tea**

highen *see* **heichen**

Higher *see* **heich**

highland *see* **hieland**

Hi Hi nickname for Third Lanark football team.

hilch, hilsh *verb* **1** limp, hobble, lurch. **2 hilch up** move with a jerk; hitch up (a load on one's back).

noun a limp; an uneven way of walking.

hill[1], **hull** *now NE, WCentral* **1** a hill. **2** an (artificial) mound. **3** a moor where rough grazing rights are shared by the community. **4** any piece of rough grazing on a farm. **5** a **peat moss** (*see* **peat**). **6** a peat-stack, *now N.* **7** *mining* the dump of hewn coal at the pithead; the pithead, the surface.

hiller a little hill, a heap, a small mound *Caithness.* **hillock 1** a fat sluggish person. **2** a large quantity.

hill berry a crowberry *now Caithness.* **hill cart** *mining* a small low cart. **hill-clap** a rumbling noise in the air over hills *mainly Shetland.* **hill dyke** the wall dividing a **hill** 3 from the lower arable land. **hill lintie** a twite *now N.* **hill-run 1** *especially of wild moorland* hilly, upland. **2** *of people* uncultured, rough. **hill woman** *mining* a female worker at the pithead.

gather the hill gather together flocks pastured on a hillside. **to the hill** in an upward direction.

hill[2]: **hill on** *etc* go at a fair pace, hurry *NE.*

hilliegeleerie *see* **heeliegoleerie**

hilsh *see* **hilch**

hilt[1] a plough-handle.

hilt[2]: **ilka hilt an(d) hair** every bit *now SW.* **(neither) hilt (n)or hair** nothing at all, not a trace.

hilt[3] walk with a limp.

hilter-skilter, †**hilty-skilty** *adverb* helter-skelter.

adjective heedless.

†**drink helter-skelter** drink heavily, mixing one's drinks.

himberry *see* **hindberry**

hime a hymn.

himsel(f) 1 = himself. **2** name for the head or chief male person in any body or institution, a male boss.

hin *see* **hint**[1]

hinch *see* **hainch**

hind, hyne 1 a farm-servant, now a ploughman. **2** a married skilled farm-worker who occupies a farm-cottage, and has certain perquisites in addition to wages *chf S.* **3** †a youth, a stripling. **hinds' raw** a row of cottages occupied by farm-workers.

hind *see* **hint**[1], **hyne**

hindberry, himberry a wild raspberry.

hinder[1], **hinner 1** *of time* last, (recently) past *now SW.* **2** *of place* coming from or situated behind, in the rear etc. **hinders** the buttocks; the hindquarters of an animal *now Shetland.*

hinder[2], **hender,** †**hin(n)er** *verb* **1** hinder, detain, prevent, delay. **2** linger, dawdle *Shetland NE.* **3** waste (time) *Shetland NE.*

noun a hindrance, obstruction.

hinderend 1 the later or final part, the back portion of anything. **2** the end, *especially of life or time* the concluding part. **3** *of people* the behind, the backside. **4** the remains of anything, refuse;

the worst of anything. **the hinderend o a'** the last straw *NE*. **at the hinderend** in the long run, finally; on the Day of Judgment. **lauch one's hinderend** die laughing *NE*. **hinderment** hindrance, delay *now Shetland NE*. **hindersome** obstructive, troublesome, detrimental. **you'll no hinder me to do ..** nothing could (have) prevent(ed) me from doing.

hindmaist, hinmaist, hindmost 1 last, furthest behind, in the rear. **2** last, final. *noun* the last, the farthest back; *of time* the close, the end.

hindmaist day the Day of Judgment.

hine, hain a haven, a (natural) harbour *now ECentral*.

hiner *see* **hinder**[2]

hing, hang *verb* **1** hang. **2** have the notice of one's intention to marry displayed on a registrar's notice board. **3** lean (out of a window) in order to watch events in the street. **4** delay, hover indecisively; shirk. **5** be in a poor state of health.
noun **1** hang. **2** the act of leaning out of a window as in *verb* 3.

hinger 1 a device by which something is hung. **2 hingers** hanging drapery, curtains, a tapestry. **hinger-in** a person who perseveres, a conscientious, hard-working person. †**hangie** the hangman. **hinging 1** *of coal* lying at a steep angle; undercut and ready to fall. **2** *of a golf ball or its position* lying on a downward slope. **3** *of sky etc* threatening rain. **hanging burn** a sheep-mark *now S*. **hinging gate** a bar or grating hung across a stream. **hingin-like** ill-looking. **hinging lock** a padlock. **hinging-luggit** dejected, depressed, abashed. **hinging mince** a non-existent thing, an absurdity. **hinging-mou'd** dejected, sulky *NE*. **hinging post** one of the wooden posts supporting a roof *now Perth*. **hanging scaffold** *mining* a movable platform in a shaft. **hinging stair** steps built into a wall at one end, and cantilevered. **han-**git judicially hanged. †**hangit-faced** villainous, wicked. **hangman** a cheese made by hanging the curds up to dry in a cloth exposed to the sun *NE*. **hing net** a vertical stake-net.

hing the cat work slowly or to rule; lounge about, hold things up *ECentral*. **hing by one's ain head** be self-reliant. **hing in 1** carry out a task with energy, persevere; hurry. **2** persist in courting someone; curry favour *NE*. **hing one's lugs** look dejected or abashed. **hing on 1** linger expectantly, wait. **2** delay or hinder (someone) in doing something, keep (someone) waiting *NE*. **hing-on** (a source or period of) delay, tedium or weariness; a hindrance. **hing on a (lang) face** look glum or doleful. **hing tae** join in, attach oneself (to someone or something). **hing-tee** a mistress, girlfriend *N*. **hing-the-gither** clannish. **ill-hung-thegither** clumsily built; dressed without care or taste. **hing up** *of weather* keep dry. **on the hing** in the balance.

hinkum sneev(l)ie a silly stupid person; an underhand person, a tell-tale *NE*.

hinmaist *see* **hindmaist**

hinna *see* **hae**

hinner *see* **hinder**[1], **hinder**[2]

hinnie, honey *noun* **1** honey. **2** term of endearment.
adjective sweet as honey.

hinnie-pear a sweet pear. †**hinnie-pots** a children's game.

a' hinnie and jo(e) all affability, all smiles.

hint[1], **hind, hin, hent** *adjective* belonging to or at the back, rear.
noun **1** the back, rear; *of time* the end; the period immediately following. **2** *ploughing* the furrow left between two **rigs**[1], the **mould furrow** (*see* **muild**[1]).
adverb, preposition behind.

hintin(g) the **mould furrow** (*see* **muild**[1]). **hintbacks** surreptitious, behind the back *now Shetland Orkney*. **hint-end** the back part; the last part of; the hindquarters. **hint-hairst** the period of the year after harvest and before winter.

hint-han(d) 1 *curling, of the last stone played in a rink, or the player(s) of such a stone* (the) last, hindmost. **2** slow, careless, late. **hint-side** the rear. **hint-side foremost** back to front, backwards.

hint the han stored for future use *NE*.

hint² a moment, instant.

hint³: neither hint nor hair nothing at all *NE*.

hint *see* **hent**

hip¹ a projecting piece of land.

hippin a baby's nappy. **hippit 1** hipped. **2** *also* **hip-grippit** having a feeling of stiffness or overstrain in the lower back, hips, or thighs. **hipsie-dipsie** a thorough thrashing.

hiplocks the coarse wool on the hips of sheep.

hip² *verb* **1** miss, skip, pass over, not take into account. **2** hop, skip *now S*.

noun the act of hopping, a hop *S*.

hippertie-skippertie light, frivolous *now NE*. **hippity** with a limp, lamely; lame, crippled.

hippans hips, the fruit of the wild rose *NE*.

hipple go lame, limp, hobble.

hipsie *see* **hip¹**

hir, her, hur **1** her. **2** *supposedly Highland speech* my, his. *See also* **she.**

hirdum-dirdum uproar, noisy revelry *now Fife.*

hirdy-girdy *noun* uproar, confusion *now ECentral.*

adverb in disorder or confusion.

hire *verb* **1** engage oneself as an employee, take service. **2** season (food), make it more palatable by the addition of rich ingredients *now NE*.

noun a titbit given as a bribe; a reward.

hiring fair, hiring market a fair or market held for the purpose of engaging farm-workers.

hire house a farm **bothy**; farm labour or service *NE*.

hirling *see* **herling**

hirple limp, hobble.

hirs(al)ly *see* **hirst**

hirsel¹ 1 a herd or flock, now only a flock of sheep. **2** an area of pasturage to be grazed by a flock of sheep under the care of one shepherd. **3** a large number or quantity, a crowd.

hirsel², hurschle *verb* **1** move with a rustling or grating noise *now NE*. **2** move along awkwardly or without getting up, slither, cause to slide along or down; shuffle. **3** hurry, bustle *now Angus Perth*. **4** wheeze, breathe noisily.

noun **1** the act of moving the body sideways in a sitting position, a slithering, hitching motion. **2** the sliding motion of something slipping or being shifted with difficulty; the noise or result of such motion, a confused fall *now NE*. **3** a wheeze.

hirsel aff (the stage) die peacefully. **hirsel yont** move further up or along to make room for others, move over or away.

hirst 1 a barren piece of ground. **2** *also* **hist** a great number (of people), a great quantity (of things), a heap (of objects) *NE*. **3** a threshold.

hirstie, histie, hirs(al)ly *of soil* dry and stony, barren.

hirtch *NE verb* **1** move jerkily, edge forward. **2** sidle.

noun a slight sideways push or jerky motion, a hitch; a shrug of the shoulders.

his *see* **us**

hish¹, hiss 1 make a hissing sound in order to drive (an animal) away etc. **2** incite (*eg* a dog) to attack.

hish² 1 be quiet! **2** a soothing sound, especially for rocking a child to sleep.

hish-hash a muddle, confusion.

hishie, hushie a very quite sound, a whisper.

verb lull to sleep, sing a lullaby.

neither hishie (n)or w(h)ishie not the slightest sound.

Hi-Spy (the call used in) the children's

game of hide-and-seek.

hiss see **hish**[1]

hissel, hizzle *NE,* **heezel** *S* **1** hazel. **2** a hazel stick used as a cudgel; a stout stick of any wood *now Caithness.*

hist see **heest**

histie see **hirst**

hit *verb, past tense also* **hat** *now Shetland Caithness NE,* **het, hut;** *past participle also* **hitten, hutten, hut** hit.

hit see **it**

hitch *verb* hobble, limp; hop.
noun the little hop made in playing hopscotch.

hitchie-koo a ball game *NE.*

hither, hidder *now Shetland* hither.
hither an yon(t) *adverb* this way and that. *adjective* untidy; careless; muddled, separated.

hitten see **hit**

hiv see **hae, huif**

hives 1 a skin rash; any childish ailment without distinctive symptoms. **2** inflammation of the bowels in children.

hiz see **us**

hize see **heeze**

hizzie, hussy 1 †a housewife; the mistress of a household etc. **2** a woman, especially a frivolous woman; a servant girl. **3** a woman of bad character. **4** **hussy** a pocket-case for needles, thread etc *now Orkney Caithness.*
hizzie-skep housekeeping, household management.

hizzle see **hissel**

ho: nae (ither) ho but no (other) choice, no hope but *NE.*

hoast, host 1 cough. **2** something of little value or which causes no difficulty.
hoast up get something off one's chest.

hobble *verb* **1** rock, bob up and down. **2** *also* **hubble** shake with laughter *NE.* **3** swarm with living creatures. **4** *also* **hubble** bother *Caithness Ulster.*
noun **1** a shaking. **2** a difficulty, predicament. **3** *also* **hubble** a scuffle.
hobble bog a quagmire *NE.*

hobby a person dressed in coarse country clothing; a stupid slovenly fellow.

hoch[1]**, houch, haugh** [rhymes with 'loch'] *noun* **1** the hough, hock, the hind-leg of an animal. **2** *now usually* **hough** a hind-leg joint of meat, the shin. **3** *usually of people* the hollow behind the knee-joint, the (back of the) thigh.
verb hamstring; put a stop to; overthrow, defeat.
hoch band a hobble, a strap tied to an animal's leg to restrict its movement.

hoch[2] [rhymes with 'loch'] exclamation expressing weariness, regret or disapproval.
hoch aye expression of assent.

hochle, houghel, hauchle [-ch-, -gh- as -ch in 'loch'] walk slowly, awkwardly, hobble, totter.
noun **1** an awkward shifting of position. **2** a clumsy, awkward, messy person.

hochmagandy, houghmagandie [-ch-, -gh-as -ch in 'loch'] illicit sexual intercourse.

hock see **howk**[1]

hocker, hucker crouch, bend down; walk bent double.

hod see **hide**[1]

hodden *noun* **1** coarse homespun, an undyed greyish woollen cloth . **2** rustic, homely.
hodden gray 1 homespun wool or woollen cloth of the natural undyed colour. **2** a person dressed in a simple rustic fashion; a homely, unaffected individual.

hoddle waddle; hobble; walk quickly.

hoddock a haddock *NE.*

hoddy see **hide**[1]

hodge *verb* **1** move awkwardly, hobble along. **2** fidget *now NE.* **3** shake, especially with laughing *now NE.* **4** hitch up, tug, heave *now Shetland.*
noun a shove, push *now Shetland NE.*

hodgel a dumpling, usually one made of oatmeal, fat and seasoning *S.*

hog(g) 1 *also* **hogget** a young sheep. **2**

curling a stone which does not pass over the **hogg-score.**

hogged stuck, at a standstill.

hogg-score *curling* either of the two distance lines drawn across the rink over which every scoring shot must pass.

†**hogg-shouther** push with the shoulder, shove about.

hogger, hugger *noun* **1** a coarse stocking without a foot, worn as a gaiter. **2** an old sock-foot worn as a slipper, or over a shoe (to stop slipping on icy roads); a kind of slipper worn by factory-workers *Angus*. **3** an old stocking-leg used as a purse; any pouch used to keep money in; a hoard.

hogget a hogshead, a large cask; a measure.

hogget *see* **hog(g)**

Hogmanay 1 31 December, New Year's Eve. **2** a New Year's gift; any form of hospitality, especially a drink given to a guest to celebrate the New Year, or money given to tradesmen and employees on that day: *"Give them their Hogmanay".*

hoise raise, heave up.

†**hoit** move awkwardly or clumsily.

hold *see* **haud**

hole *noun* **1 holes, holie** a kind of marbles game. **2** a small bay. **3** a shallow pool, a puddle.

verb **1** dig (up), loosen (*eg* potatoes) from the ground. **2** *frequently* **hole on, hole about** linger, linger too long in one place or at one task. **3** wear into holes.

holiepied full of holes especially of open-work embroidery *NE*.

hole i(n) the wa 1 a small house etc often between two larger buildings. **2** a **box-bed** (*see* **box**), a bed in a recess.

holf *see* **howf**

hollin holly, a holly-tree *now NE*.

holm *see* **howm**

holograph *law* (a document) entirely in the handwriting of one person and, in the case of a will, signed by him or her.

holy *see* **haly**

home *see* **hame**

hommill *see* **hummel**

homologate confirm, approve, *especially law* ratify.

honest of good character and standing, worthy.

honesty decency, a mark of respectability; *of clothes etc* best.

the Honest Lad, the Honest Lass the leading participants in the annual festival in Musselburgh. **the Honest Men** nickname for Ayr United football team.

honey *see* **hinnie**

Honours of Scotland the regalia of the Kingdom of Scotland, *ie* the Crown, Sceptre, and Sword of State.

hoo¹, how 1 how. **2** why.

hoo an a' be however, nevertheless. **hoo's a' wi ye** how are you? **hoo that** in what way, how.

hoo² 1 scare (birds or straying animals) away from growing crops; scare (people etc) away *now NE*. **2** shout to attract attention. **3** *of an owl* hoot; hoot like an owl.

hoo³, how a cap.

hal(l)i(e)hoo, seelyhoo the caul sometimes found on the head of a newborn child, regarded as a good omen.

hooch [-ch as in 'dreich'] exclamation expressing excitement shouted by dancers during a **reel**.

verb **1** cry **hooch**, shout. **2** whoop with mirth. **3** breathe hard on an object before polishing it *now NE*.

hood *see* **huid**

hooie exchange, barter.

hooie *see* **heuk**

hook-bone *see* **heukbane**

hooker a glass of whisky, a dram.

hooker-doon a cloth cap with a peak.

hookie: by the hookie a mild oath.

hoolachan a reel, the Reel of Tulloch (*see* **reel**).

hool(e) *see* **huil**

hoolet, houlet, †howlat [hoolit] *noun* **1** an owl. **2** *insulting* a person showing real or imagined characteristics of an owl (*eg* stupidity).

verb **1** henpeck. **2** go about with a miserable expression; be solitary.

hoolie *see* **huilie**

hoomet a woman's hood or hat (of unusual shape) *NE*.

hoon(d) *see* **houn(d)**

hoop *see* **howp**[1]

hoops exclamation encouraging someone to raise himself or lift something heavy.

hoor *see* **hure**

hoose *see* **house**

hooster *see* **houster**

hoot, hout, het, hoots exclamation expressing disagreement, impatience etc.

hoozle *see* **hose**[1]

hop *see* **hap**[2]

hope[1] *mainly S* **1** a small valley or hollow in the hills. **2** a hill.

hope[2], **howp** a small bay or haven *now in place-names*.

hope *see* **howp**[1]

hoppin beds *see* **hap**[2]

hopshackle *see* **hapshackle**

hork *see* **hurk**

horl **1** a whorl, a small wheel. **2** the metal tag or point of a bootlace *now WCentral*.

horn **1** a horn or something resembling a horn, *eg* a handle; a spout. **2** †*mainly law* the trumpet used to proclaim an outlaw, mainly a debtor: **put to the horn** proclaimed as an outlaw or bankrupt. **3 horns** the metal tags or tips on laces or thongs *now Orkney*.

horned golach *see* **golach**. **horner** an earwig *NE*. **hornie** **1** *mainly* **Auld Hornie** nickname for the Devil. **2** a policeman. **3** a cow (of a horned breed). **4** a form of the game of tig. **5 fair hornie** fair play. **hornie golach** *see* **golach**. **hornie (h)oolet, hornie owl** the long-eared owl *NE*.

horn daft quite mad. **horn-dry** *of clothes etc* thoroughly dry. **horn-en(d)** the best

room in a **but and ben** (*see* **but**) *NE*. **horn-hard** as hard as horn, extremely hard *now Shetland*. **horn-idle** having nothing to do, completely unemployed.

auld in the horn advanced in years and experience, wise, shrewd. **get out one's horns** begin to behave more freely or boldly. **have one's horn in somebody's hip** criticize severely, oppose. **lang in the horn = auld in the horn.**

horoyally a ceilidh, a singsong, an uproarious party *Highland*.

horse a trestle, a support, as used by masons to support scaffolding.

be sic mannie, sic horsie be all of one kind, be birds of a feather.

horse-beast a horse. **horse-buckie** a large whelk. **horse-couper** a horsedealer. **horse gowan** *see* **gowan**. **horseman** **1** a man who tends horses, especially a farm servant who looked after and worked a pair of horses, on larger farms ranked according to seniority as **first, second** etc **horseman. 2** one of a fraternity of **horsemen** with initiation ceremonies, passwords etc, usually regarded as a relic of Devilworship. **horse-mussel** a large freshwater mussel.

hort *see* **hurt**

hose[1] **1** the socket for the handle on any metal implement, *eg* a rake. **2** the sheath enclosing an ear of corn.

hozle, hoozle the socket into which the handle or shaft of a hammer, fork, golf club etc is fitted.

hose-fish a cuttlefish. †**hose-net 1** a small stocking-shaped net fixed to a pole, used for fishing in small streams. **2** a trap.

hose[2] swallow greedily *now NE*.

hoshen, hushion 1 a footless stocking used to cover legs or arms in cold weather. **2** a stocking used as a container, *eg* a purse.

host *see* **hoast**

hostie the host, consecrated bread.

hot, hut(t) *noun, now only* **hut**(t) **1** a basket, especially one used for carrying manure etc *now SW*. **2** a small heap. **3** a small stack of corn etc built to protect the crop temporarily from the weather before its removal to the stackyard.
verb **1** heap up, heap together. **2** put up (sheaves) in small stacks as a protective measure against weather etc.

hot *see* **het**[1]

hotch *verb* **1** jerk up and down, bob; jog. **2** fidget, hitch about with impatience or discomfort. **3** heave with laughter. **4** cause to move jerkily, shrug, hitch up; shift along in a sitting position to make　room for others.
noun **1** a jerk, jolt, bounce, hitch, shrug; a twitch. **2** a big fat clumsy woman; a slut.
hotchin 1 seething, overrun with, infested. **2** restless with impatience, extremely eager.

hotter *verb* **1** jerk, jolt about. **2** walk unsteadily, totter. **3** bubble, boil steadily. **4** shudder, shiver with cold or fear, shake with laughter or excitement. **5** crowd together, swarm.
noun **1** a shaking or jolting, a rattling sound. **2** the bubbling made by boiling liquid. **3** a shiver; a start; a quiver(ing) *NE*. **4** †a seething mass, a crowd; a swarm; the noise or motion of such a crowd. **5** a confused heap.
hotterel a mass of festering sores or chaps *NE*.

houch *see* **hoch**[1]

houf *see* **howf**

hough *see* **hoch**[1]

houghel *see* **hochle**

houghmagandie *see* **hochmagandy**

houlet *see* **hoolet**

houn(d), **hoon**(d), **hun**(n) *noun* a dog; a hunting dog.
verb **1** hound. **2** *of a male dog* run about from place to place after females.

houp [howp] hops, as used in brewing *NE*.

houp *see* **howp**[1], **howp**[2]

house, hoose *noun* **1** a house. **2** a flat. **3** *curling and carpet-bowls* the circle round the **tee**[1] within which the stones etc must lie to be counted in the score.
verb **1** house. **2** take, put, or drive (mainly animals) into a house; shelter. **3** store (goods, etc) *now NE*. **housing scheme** *see* **scheme**.

house ba *game* rounders. **house devil** a person who behaves badly at home. **house-en**(d) **1** the end or gable of a house. **2** a stout or heavily-built woman. **house-fast** housebound. **house-gear** household furnishings or equipment. **house-heat**(ing) a house-warming. **house-heid** the roof of a house. **house-side** a big clumsy person. **house-tied** = **housefast**.

one's house at hame one's home.

houster, hooster, howster *verb* gather together in a confused way *now Fife*.
noun a badly-dressed, untidy person.

hout *see* **hoot**

hove, huve *now Shetland* **1** raise. **2** throw, fling, cast away. **3** rise. **4** swell; expand.
hovie *of bread etc* well-risen

hoven *see* **heave**

hover pause, wait a little.
hover a blink wait a little. **in** (**a**) **hover** in a state of hesitation, uncertainty or indecision *now Shetland*.

how, hyow [heeow] *noun* a hoe.
verb **1** hoe. **2** †uproot (broom or whins).

how *see* **hoo**[1], **hoo**[3]

howd *now NE* **1** sway, rock, bump up and down. **2** *of a boat or ship* pitch, bob up and down.
noun a lurching rocking movement from side to side.

howder, howther *verb* **1** rock, jolt, bump *now NE*. **2** †*of a large number of people etc* swarm, mill around, bustle about.
noun **1** *of a boat* a rocking, jolting, sideways motion *NE*. **2** †a rough-and-tumble. **3** a blast of wind, a blustering wind *NE*. **howdle** move with a rocking or bumping motion, limp.

howd *see* **hide**[1]

howdie, howdie wife a midwife; formerly an untrained sick-nurse; a woman who laid out the dead.

   howdieing 1 a confinement, birth. **2** midwifery.

howdle see **howd**

howe[1] *noun* **1** a hollow, depression, a low-lying piece of ground. **2** a wide plain surrounded by hills. **3** a hollow, depression, a hollow space, a cavity. **4** *curling, also* **howe ice** the smooth stretch of ice down the centre of the rink *now SW*.

   adjective **1** hollow, lying in a hollow, deep-set, sunken. **2** hungry, famished *now Orkney*. **3** *of the voice etc* hollow, deep, echoing, guttural *now Orkney*.

   howe backit 1 †*of a horse* saddle-backed. **2** *of people* round-shouldered; hollow-backed. †**howe-dumb-dead** the depth, the darkest point (of winter, night etc).

   be in the howes be depressed. **howe o (the) winter** midwinter.

howe[2] **1** the hull of a ship. **2** a boat with neither sails nor mast up.

howf, houf [howf] *noun* **1** a burial ground, latterly often a private one. **2** *also* **holf** an enclosed open space, a yard (for storing timber). **3** a favourite haunt, a meeting place, often a public house, sometimes a rough one. **4** a rough shelter or refuge; a natural or improvised shelter used by mountaineers.

   verb **1** live, dwell; go to or visit often. **2** take shelter or refuge *now Angus*.

howffin a clumsy, shy and rather stupid person *now NE*.

howk[1]**, hock** *Shetland verb* **1** dig (ground), dig (a trench etc), uproot. **2** investigate. **3** unearth, extricate. **4** hollow out, scrape or scoop out the inside of (something). **5** mine (coal), quarry (stone). **6** *mainly of pigs* root, burrow in the earth. **7** often **howk about** loiter, stand around or pass the time idly.

   noun the act of digging or burrowing *now Shetland Orkney*.

howk[2]**: the howk** a (stomach) disease affecting the eyes of cattle *mainly NE*.

howlat see **hoolet**

howld a hold (of a ship).

howld see **haud**

howm, †**holm** a stretch of low-lying land beside a river.

howp[1]**, houp, hope, hoop** *now Shetland Orkney* hope.

   I hope would you believe it! *"I hope he'd forgotten the key".*

   na howp bit no alternative but.

howp[2]**, houp** [howp] a mouthful or gulp of liquid, a dram *NE*.

howp see **hope**[2]

howster see **houster**

howther see **howd**

howtowdie [-ow- as in 'cow'] a large (young) chicken for the pot, a young hen which has not begun to lay.

hoy[1] **1** drive, urge on with cries of 'hoy'. **2** hail, summon. **3** shout 'hoy'.

hoy[2] heave up (a heavy object), toss up.

hoy[3] walk with a quick brisk step, hurry.

hozle see **hose**[1]

hree see **three**

hubber see **habber**

hubble see **hobble**

hubbleshew, hubbleshue 1 an uproar, tumult *now Shetland*. **2** †a mob, rabble.

hucker see **hocker**

hucky-duck see **hacky-duck**

hud *mainly S* **1** the back of an open fireplace, consisting of a seat-like block. **2** a shelf in a fireplace used as a hob.

hud see **huid**

hudd a hod, a receptacle for carrying mortar *now SW*.

hudder, huther *verb* **1** †act in a confused or hasty way; work or walk clumsily or hastily. **2** heap together in disorder; throw on (clothes) hastily or untidily *now Angus*.

   noun **1** an untidy worker or person. **2** a confused crowd or heap *now SW*.

hudderie, hutherie 1 *also* **hudderie-dud-derie** dirty or untidy in appearance or habits. **2** *mainly of hair* shaggy, unkempt, dishevelled. **hudd(e)rin** *adjective* **1** *mainly of a woman* slovenly, slatternly *now SW, Ulster*. **2** awkward, clumsy.

hudd(e)ron a slovenly person.

hudge *noun* a large quantity, a vast amount (of money etc).
verb mass, heap up *now NE*.

hudge-mudge *now NE* secrecy; furtive whispering.
hudg(e)mudgan whispering (especially behind someone's back).

hue 1 appearance, aspect. **2** a very small amount *now WCentral*.

huff swell, puff up *Angus*.

hugger *mainly NE verb* **1** shudder, shiver, hug oneself (to keep warm). **2** crowd or huddle together as a protection against cold. **3** *of clothes* slip down or hang untidily.
huggert, huggering 1 round-shouldered. **2** huddled up or shrunk with cold, pinched-looking.

hugger *see* **hogger**

huggery-muggery furtive; disorderly, untidy.

hugmahush a slovenly person; a lout *NE*.

huid, hood, hud, heed *NE*, **heid** *NE noun* **1** a hood. **2** *also* †**hood sheaf** one of a pair of sheaves of corn placed on the top of a **stook** or corn stack as a protection against the weather *now S*.
verb **1** hood. **2** top (a **stook**) with two protective sheaves.
huidie 1 = **huidie craw** 1 and 2. **2** a sunbonnet worn by field-workers. **huidie craw, heidie craw** *Shetland N* **1** a hooded crow. **2** a carrion crow. **3** the black-headed gull *now Shetland*. **4** a sinister-looking person. **hoodin(g)** = **huid** *noun* 2 *now Ulster*. **huidin** *now Shetland Orkney*, **hiddin** *mainly NE* a joint, fastening *eg* of a flail, of a fishing line. **huidit 1** hooded. **2** *of birds* having hood-like head-colouring *eg* **huidit craw** = **huidie craw** 1, 2 and 3 *now Orkney*. †**huidock 1** = **huidie craw** 1. **2** a greedy, grasping person.

huif, hiv *now Caithness NE* a hoof.

huil, hool(e), hull *noun* **1** a hull, pod, shell etc. **2** the pericardium, the covering of the heart, *often* **leap (oot o) the huil** *of the heart* burst. **3** the skin of a person or animal.
verb shell (peas etc), husk.

huilie, hoolie, heelie *NE adjective* moderate, slow, cautious, careful.
adverb **1** moderately, slowly, gently. **2** *exclamation* be careful!, go slow!, have patience!
verb pause, halt, hesitate.
ca one's hogs til a huilie market make a bad bargain *NE*. **come huilie tae** not do very well. **huilie and fair(ly)** slowly and gently but steadily.

huird hoard.

huive *originally of people on horseback* remain stationary, stay, wait.

huizlin(g) a severe drubbing *S*.

hule [like 'guid'] **1** a mischievous, perverse or objectionable person or animal *now SW*. **2** = devil *now S*: "what the hule's come on ye".

hulk *noun* a big unwieldy mass, a hump.
verb hang idly about (a place), skulk about.

hull *see* **hill**¹, **huil**

hullie *ECentral adjective* hollow.
noun a container for live crabs and lobsters, originally holes in the rocks below the high-water mark, now baskets or boxes anchored in the harbour.

hulster 1 hoist a load onto one's back; struggle along under a heavy burden. **2** walk heavily as if laden *now NE*. **3** have on too many clothes, be cluttered up with too many clothes *NE, S*.

hum¹, ham *verb* **1** *also* **hummle** chew partially, especially chew (food) till soft before transferring it to an infant's mouth. **2** eat greedily, crunch *NE*.
noun a piece of food chewed and given to a child.

hum²: hum an hae, humph an hae hesitate.

humanity *Scottish Universities* the formal name for the study of the classical languages and literature, especially (and now only) Latin; the chair or class of Latin.

humble *see* **hummel**

humbug a nuisance, an imposition *NE*.

hum-drum *adjective* in low spirits; sullen. *noun* an apathetic, lazy-minded person.

humdudgeon 1 a fuss. **2 humdudgeons** sulks.

humel *see* **hummel**

humf *see* **humph**[2]

humfie, humfy *see* **humph**[1]

humler *see* **hummel**

humlie *see* **hummel**

humlock 1 common hemlock or other umbelliferous plants such as cow parsnip. **2** a dried hemlock stalk used as a peashooter.

hummel, hommill, hamill, humble *adjective* **1** *of cattle etc* having no horns, naturally or by polling. **2** *of corn etc* awnless, not bearded. **3** without projections, flat, level, smooth; unarmed; *of a boat* without a mast or sail; lying with mast and sail lowered *N*. *noun* an animal that has no horns or has been polled. *verb* **1** remove the awns from (barley etc). **2** break up (stones or driftwood) into smaller pieces and shape for use *now Shetland*.

hummeller, humler a machine for removing the awns from barley; the part of a threshing mill that does this.

hum(m)lie *noun* **1** = **hummel** *noun*. **2** a country person; a Highlander; a native of Buchan. **Buchan humlie** one of the hornless Aberdeen Angus type of cattle.

hum(m)el doddie *NE adjective* hornless. *noun* a woollen mitten.

hummer murmur, mumble, grumble; mutter to oneself.

hummie, †hummock a pinch (of salt etc), as much as can be taken up between the thumb and four fingers.

hummle *see* **hum**[1]

hummlie *see* **hummel**

hummock *see* **hummie**

humour, eemir *NE noun* **1** humour. **2** matter or pus from a wound or sore. **3** a skin eruption *NE, S.* **4** a feeling of resentment or bad temper.

humph[1], **hump** *noun* **1** a hump a curvature of the spine, a hump-back. **2** the act of carrying a heavy load. *verb* **1** carry about (a heavy burden), lift up (something heavy). **2** move around laboriously under the weight of a heavy burden.

humphed hunched. **humphie, humfie** *adjective also* **humphie-backit** having a hump, hunchbacked. *noun also* **humfy-back** a hunchbacked person.

come up one's humph come into one's head, occur to one to do something. **set up one's humph** become angry and antagonistic.

humph[2], **humf** *noun* **1** a bad smell of something going bad; a stench. **2** a high flavour, a taste of foodstuff going bad. **humphed** stinking, putrid. **humphy** having a bad smell or a high taste.

humple[1], **humplock** *now WCentral* a small heap or mound, a hillock.

humple[2] walk unevenly or haltingly; hobble.

hum(p)sh *see* **hanch**

hun *see* **houn(d)**

hunch [hunsh] heave or shove with the shoulder. **hunchie** a hunchback.

hunch-cuddy-hunch a boys' team game.

hunder, hundred, hunner *noun* **1** a hundred. **2** †*weaving* a unit of measurement denoting the fineness of a web. **3** a definite number (of livestock, goods etc) which is greater than 100, usually 120, but varying according to time and place *now Orkney*. *adjective* **1** hundred. **2 hunert** *now Shetland NE* = hundredth *now NE*. **the Old Hundredth** the long-metre version of the 100th Psalm, its tune. **get**

a hundred pound get a piece of good fortune, often a birth in the family.

hunert *see* **hunner**

hunger starve.

hungered, hungert starved(-looking).

hungry mean, miserly; greedy.

a hunger or a burst scarcity or plenty.

hunker *verb* **hunker doon 1** squat; crouch. **2** huddle, sit or settle oneself in a crouching or cramped position. **3** submit, resign oneself.

noun **on one's hunkers 1** in(to) a squatting position. **2** in a quandary; on one's last legs.

hunker-bane the thigh bone. **hunker-slide 1** slide on ice in a crouched position. **2** get out of a duty or a promise. **hunker-slider** a slippery customer. **hunker-sliding** *noun* dishonourable or shifty conduct, evasive behaviour. *adjective* evasive, dishonourable.

hunn *see* **houn(d)**

hunner *see* **hunder**

Huns insulting nickname for Rangers football team, especially by Celtic fans.

hunt: hunt (th)e gowk go on a fool's errand, be made a fool of, especially an April fool. **huntegowk 1** the game of April fool, a fool's errand especially on April Fool's Day. **2** April Fool's Day. **3** an April fool, a person sent on a fool's errand.

hunt the staigie a children's game in which one player has to catch the others *NE*. **(neither) hunt nor hare** nothing at all, not a vestige.

hup *noun* a call to an animal in harness to turn to the right or to go faster.

verb **1** *of a horse in harness* go to the right. **2** *of the driver* call to a horse to go to the right or to go forward at a quicker pace *NE*.

hup aff go to the right! **hup back** come back, bearing right.

neither to hup nor wynd move neither to the right or left on command; prove unmanageable; be obstinate. **wo hup** slow down and bear right.

hurb a puny or good-for-nothing creature; *humorously of a child* a rascal.

hurcheon, erchin *noun* **1** a hedgehog. **2** an unkempt, uncouth person.

hurdies the buttocks, hips, haunches of human beings or animals.

ower the hurdies in difficulties, deep (in debt).

hure, hoor a whore.

hurk, hork *verb* **1** crouch on one's haunches, especially over a fire *S*. **2** laze idly about *now SW*. **3** grub (in the dirt) like a pig; poke about, rummage *now SW, S*.

hurkle 1 crouch. **2** walk with the body in a crouching position; stumble along, stagger *now NE*. **3** yield, give in *now NE*.

hurkle-backit hunchbacked, misshapen *now SW*. **hurkle-bane** the hipbone.

hurl[1] *verb* **1** dash, hurtle, fall from a height *now Shetland ECentral*. **2** convey in a wheeled vehicle, drive, push or pull along on wheels. **3** move on wheels, trundle along, ride in a wheeled vehicle.

noun **1** a violent rush forwards or downwards, *eg* of falling stones or wind. **2** a ride or drive in a wheeled vehicle, a lift along the road.

hurlie 1 *also* **hurl-barrow** a wheelbarrow; a handcart. **2** *also* **hurlie bed** a bed on wheels. **3** *also* **hurlie-cart** a child's homemade cart. †**hurlie-hacket** a sledging game.

hurl[2] *verb* **1** make a deep rumbling hollow sound, as of rushing water. **2** wheeze *Shetland Orkney NE*.

noun **1** a rumbling or grating noise; thunder. **2** the sound of laboured breathing; the death rattle.

hurlie congested with phlegm *N*.

hurlie a call to a cow to come to be milked *SW*.

hurlie *see* **hurl**[1], **hurl**[2]

hurly, hurly hinmaist the last *NE*.

huron *see* **hern**

hurr *verb* make a whirring sound; purr *Shetland Orkney Caithness.*

exclamation a purring, murmuring sound expressing pleasure or contentment *now Shetland.*

hurroo, haroosh *noun* an excited, high-spirited, disorderly gathering, an uproar.

verb urge on with shouts *Shetland Ulster.*

hurry 1 a disturbance, riot, quarrel. **2** a scolding *now Fife NE.* **3** a rush of work, an exceptionally busy time.

hurried harassed, hard pressed.

hurry-burry, hurry gurry a tumult, confusion.

in a couple of hurries without delay. **in a hurry** suddenly, unexpectedly. **take yer hurry (in yer han)** take your time.

hurschle *see* **hirsel**²

hurt, hort *now Caithness* hurt.

hurtsome hurtful, injurious.

huschou *see* **hush**²

hush¹ *noun* **1** a rushing, gushing sound *now Shetland Orkney.* **2** a whisper, a slight sound; a rumour *now NE.* **3** a rush of people *now Shetland.* **4** a large quantity or abundance (of something) *now Shetland.* **5** a fat, clumsy, dirty person *now NE.*

verb **1** *of water* rush forth, gush out *now Shetland Ulster.* **2** fling together, bundle hurriedly or carelessly.

hush², **huschou** *NE* a cry to frighten off birds etc.

hushie *see* **hishie**

hushie-ba an expression for lulling a child to sleep, a lullaby.

hushion *see* **hoshen**

hushle¹, **hussle** *verb* **1** fidget or move about awkwardly or restlessly *NE.* **2** shrug the shoulders, as if to rid oneself of an irritation *S.* **3** work or dress in a careless or slovenly way *now Shetland.*

noun **1** a heap, an untidy bunch or mass *now Shetland Caithness.* **2** an untidy, carelessly-dressed person. **3** a rustling sound *NE.*

hushle² a strong, drying, gusty wind *Shetland Orkney SW.*

hushoch, hushloch a confused heap, a tangled mass, a loose quantity of something.

husk cough violently.

hussle *see* **hushle**

hussy *see* **hizzie**

husta exclamation expressing surprise, objection or alarm *NE.*

hut *see* **hit, hot, it**

hutch *noun* **1** *mining* the box-like container in which coal is carried from the coal face. **2** a small rick or temporary stack of corn. **3** an embankment built up to check erosion caused by running water *S.*

verb set (sheaves of corn) in small temporary ricks to dry.

huther *see* **hudder**

hutt *see* **hot**

hutten *see* **hit**

huve *see* **hove**

huz *see* **us**

huzle *see* **wheeze**

hyke *verb* **1** move with a jerk *now Ulster.* **2** sway, rock, swing.

hyne, hind 1 *of place* hence, away, far (off), at a distance. **2** far on, late *NE.*

hindie(s) *mainly child's word* = **hyne** *NE.*

hyne *see* **hind**

hyow *see* **how**

hypal, heifle *NE* an uncouth, unkempt, broken-down or good-for-nothing person or animal.

hype a big unattractive person *N.*

hypothec *law* the right of a creditor to hold the effects of a debtor as security for a claim without taking possession of them.

the hale hypothec the whole of anything, the whole business etc, everything.

hypothecate *law* give, take or pledge as security, mortgage.

hyste *see* **heist**

hyte¹ **1** mad, highly excited, enraged. **2**

excessively or madly keen.

gae hyte go mad with rage or passion, fly into a hysterical state.

hyte² a call to a horse.

hyter *NE verb* walk unsteadily, lurch; stumble, trip.

noun **1** a lurch, a stumble *NE*. **2** a stupid person.

adverb with weak or uncertain stumbling step; in a state of ruin.

hythe a harbour, a landing place, an inlet among rocks *NE*.

I

I, A, Aw I, me.

i *see* **in**

ice shoggle an icicle.

icker *see* **aicher**

icksy-picksy *see* **eeksie-peeksie**

idder *see* **ither**

idleset, idlesee *Shetland NE* **1** idleness, laziness. **2** lack of work, unemployment.

ieroe [eero], **eer(ie)oy** *Shetland Orkney Caithness* a great-grandchild.

ignorant ill-mannered, forward, presumptuous.

ile *see* **ale, eel, oil**

ilk[1] *adjective* the same thing or person, the same place, estate or name, especially in names of landowners, distinguishing the head of a landed family: *"Grant of that ilk"*.
noun family, race; quality, kind.

ilk[2] *adjective* each, every, of two or more. *pronoun* each one, every one.
ilk ane each one of two or more, everybody, all and sundry.

ilka, ilkie *N* each, every, of two or more.
ilka ane each one, everyone. **ilkaday** *noun* a weekday *now NE*. *adjective* ordinary, everyday as opposed to Sunday or festive.

ill *adjective, adverb* **1** *of people* evil, wicked. **2** *of behaviour, language* bad, malevolent. **3** unwholesome, harmful. **4** harsh, severe, cruel. **5** difficult, troublesome. **6** awkward, inexpert, having difficulty in. **7** *often in curses* unlucky; unfriendly, hostile. **8** poor in quality, scanty. **9** *of weather* stormy. **10** *of coinage* counterfeit *now Shetland NE*. **11** bad, unsatisfactory, ineffective.
noun **1** harm, injury, mischief from natural or supernatural causes. **2** illness, disease. **3** badness, malice.
ill-aff 1 badly off, poor. **2** miserable, ill used. **3** perplexed, at a loss. **ill-coloured** having a bad or unhealthy colour. **ill-daer 1** an evildoer, a wicked person. **2** an animal that does not thrive. **ill-daein** badly-behaved, dissolute; not thriving. **ill-deedie** mischievous, wicked. **ill-ee 1** the evil eye. **2** a longing, yearning *NE*. **ill-faured 1** ugly, not good-looking, unbecoming. **2** ill-mannered, bad-tempered, coarse. **3** hateful, obnoxious, unpleasant. **4** poor in quality, unattractive, scruffy, *Shetland Orkney NE*. **ill-gab** insolent, impudent language. **ill-gate 1** a bad habit. **2** ill-gates immoral behaviour, mischievousness. **ill-gien** wicked, nasty, malevolent. **ill-guide** ill-use, treat cruelly. **ill-hertit** malevolent; greedy, mean. **ill-hung-thegither** *see* **hing. ill-less** harmless, innocent. **ill-natured** bad-tempered, irritable. **the ill place** Hell *now Shetland*. **ill-scrapit** *of the tongue* slanderous, rude, bitter. **ill-set 1** malevolent, nasty, wicked. **2** harsh, cruel. **3** surly, out of humour. **4** ungenerous. **ill-thochted** *see* **thocht. ill-thriven** *see* **thrive. ill-tongue** a malevolent or abusive tongue; bad language, slander. **ill-trickit** apt to play tricks, mischievous. **ill-willie 1** *of animals* bad-tempered. **2** grudging, disobliging, mean. **3** unfriendly, hostile.
ill aboot keen on, fond of. **ill for** inclined to (some bad habit etc). **ill tae dae wi** difficult to please or humour.

image *see* **eemage**

immen *see* **be**

immis, eemis 1 *of the weather* uncertain, gloomy, likely to rain etc. **2** *of an object* insecurely balanced, unsteady.

immortal: The Immortal Memory name for the speech made in praise of Robert Burns at **Burns Suppers** (*see* **Burns**).

implement *law* the fulfilment or execution of a contractual obligation.

imsh *see* **nimsh**

in, i *preposition* **1** in. **2** into. **3** on, upon, along. **4** with: *"provided in a living"*. **5** as: *"in a gift"*.
adverb **1** *leaving out certain verbs:* *"the dog wants in"*. **2** *of a gathering, meeting etc* assembled, in session: *"the schule's in"*. **3** under one's breath, in a whisper: *"said in to herself"*. **4** alert, attentive. **5** *of a debtor* in debt (to someone).
verb bring (the harvest) in from the fields.
noun, children's games (one of) the side which is in possession of the goal or home, or whose turn it is to play.
in o in, into, inside.

inbring bring into or to a place, import.

inby, in by 1 from outside to inside, further in. **2** inside, in the inner part (of a house etc), at someone's house. **3** in the farmland nearest the farm-buildings.

inch 1 a small island. **2** a piece of rising ground in the middle of a plain. **3** a stretch of low-lying land near a river or other water, sometimes cut off at high tide.

income 1 an entrance, arrival. **2** an illness etc with no obvious external cause; a swelling, abscess, festering sore; a sharp attack of pain.

Incorporated Trades the trade associations in a **burgh.**

India Pale Ale *see* **pale ale**

indictment *law* the form of process by which the accused is brought to trial at the instance of the **Lord Advocate** (*see* **lord**).

indie india-rubber.

induct *Presbyterian Churches* install (an ordained **minister**) in a charge.

infeft invested with legal possession of (**heritable** property).
infeftment the investing of a new owner with a real right in, or legal possession of land or **heritage**; the document which conveys this right.

†**infield** the field or land lying nearest to the farm or homestead, especially the better part of a farm, kept continuously under crop before crop-rotation; *compare* **outfield.**

ingaen *see* **ingaun**

ingaither 1 collect (money, dues etc). **2** gather in, harvest (crops).

ingan [-ing as in 'sing'] an onion.

ingang [**in**gang] **1** a lack, shortage. **2** an entrance, entry.

ingaun, ingaen 1 an entrance, way in. **2** the assembling in a building, especially for a church service. **3** entry to a new tenancy.

ingine 1 an engine. **2** natural cleverness, wit, genius, ingenuity.

ingle a fire on a hearth; an open hearth, the fireside, a chimney corner.
ingle-neuk the fireside, chimney corner.

ingleberry *see* **angleberry**

†**Inglis** English.

inhibition *law* a **writ** prohibiting a debtor from parting with or committing his **heritable** property to the prejudice of a creditor.

ink-fish a squid.

inkling 1 a small amount. **2** an inclination, a slight desire *Shetland Orkney N.*

in-kneed knock-kneed.

inlaik, inlake, inleak a deficiency, lack, shortage, reduction.

inlat, inlet 1 an inlet. **2** an entrance, avenue. **3** an encouragement, opportunity, welcome.

Inner House the first and second divisions of judges of the Court of Session (*see* **session**).

inower 1 in, inside, within. **2** over (a fence or boundary) into the area within.

inpit, input *verb* put in.
noun a share, contribution.

inquire, enquire 1 inquire at inquire of, ask for information from. **2 inquire for** ask about the health of (a person).

institute *law* the person first named in a **testament** or **destination** of property.

intae, into 1 into. **2** in, within.
    be intae 1 find fault with, scold. **2** hook (a fish).
    speak intae anesel speak under one's breath.

intaed, intoed with turned-in toes, pigeon-toed.

intak(e) *verb* take in.
    noun **1** the place where water, *eg* for a mill, is diverted from a river etc by a channel. **2** a piece of land reclaimed and enclosed on a farm. **3** a narrowing, *eg* the number of stitches decreased in knitting. **4** the act of taking in *eg* food, harvest. **5** a fraud, deception.

interdict *noun, law* a court order prohibiting some action complained of as illegal or wrongful, until the question of right is tried in the proper court.
    verb prohibit or restrain from an action by an **interdict.**
    interim interdict a provisional **interdict** (which can be granted without the participation of the **defender**).

interlocutor [interlocutor] *law, strictly* an order or judgment given in the course of a suit by the **Court of Session** (*see* **session**) or a **Lord Ordinary** (*see* **lord**) before final judgment is pronounced; any court order.

intil 1 into. **2** in, inside, forming a part or ingredient of.

intimmers 1 the inner timbers of a ship. **2** the mechanism, the works. **3** *humorous* the stomach, bowels etc.

into *see* **intae**

intoed *see* **intaed**

intromit *law* handle or deal with (funds or property, especially those of another person living or dead), with or without legal authority.
    intromission 1 the assuming of the possession or management of another's property with or without authority. **2 intromissions** the transactions of an agent or subordinate.

Irish of or from Ireland or (formerly) the Highlands.

irne mail *see* **mail**[2]

iron, airn iron.
    iron-eer rust.

irregular marriage a marriage contracted without a religious ceremony or formal civil procedure.

irritancy *law* the nullification of a deed resulting from neglect or contravention of the law or of an agreement.

is *see* **this**

ish the termination of a legal term, term of office or service, or any period of time; the expiry (date) of a lease etc.

isk *see* **yesk**

Islands Council name for the local government council set up in 1975 in each of Shetland, Orkney and the Western Isles (*see* **isle**): **Shetland Islands' Council; Orkney Islands' Council.**

isle: the Northern Isles the Orkney and Shetland Islands. **the Western Isles** the (Outer) Hebrides. **Western Isles Council** the local government body set up in 1975 to administer the area of the Western Isles (Lewis, Harris, North Uist, Benbecula, South Uist and Barra). *compare* **Islands Council** (see **Island**) and **region.**

iss *see* **this**

it, hit, hut it.
    awa wi't, by wi't ruined in health or fortune.

it *see* **at**[2]

itchy-coo anything causing a tickling, *eg* the prickly seeds of the dog-rose put by children down each other's backs.

ither, other, aither, idder *Shetland NE* **1** other. **2** further, additional, more: "*ither twa*".

ithoot *see* **athoot**

iver *see* **ever**

ivery every.

iz *see* **us**

izal *see* **aizle**

J

ja *see* **jaw**

jabb tire out, exhaust *NE*.

jabble *verb* **1** splash. **2** *of the sea* become choppy.
noun **1** a liquid and sediment stirred up together, especially a weak mixture as of tea or soup. **2** a choppy area of water. **3** confusion, agitation.

jack, jeck, jaik, jake *noun* **1** = **Jock** *noun* 1 *now NE*. **2** a jack. **3 jacks** small stones, bones or metal objects used in the game of **chucks** (*see* **chuck**²) or knuckle-bones; the game itself. **4** *also* **jackie** a jackdaw.
jack easy indifferent; easy-going, offhand.

jad *see* **jaud**

jag¹ *verb, also* **jog** prick, pierce.
noun **1** *also* **jog** a prick; a sharp blow, prod; an injection, inoculation. **2** a prickle, a thorn; something causing a sting, *eg* on a nettle.
jaggie prickly, piercing; *of nettles* stinging.
the Jags nickname for a football team with *thistle* in its name, *mainly* Partick Thistle.

jag² *noun* a sharp violent shake or jolt *now Shetland Caithness*.
verb shake violently, jolt, jerk, bump.

jaik *see* **jack**

jail *see* **jile**

jairg *see* **jirg**²

jake *see* **jack**

jalouse [jalooze] suspect, be suspicious.

jam 1 mend, patch *now Shetland Orkney*. **2** put in a quandary, cause to be at a loss. **3** inconvenience. **4** occupy one's time to the exclusion of all else, preoccupy oneself exclusively.

jam(b) 1 a projecting wing or addition to a building *now NE*. **2** an overlarge, rambling house.

jandies jaundice.

Janet Jo a children's singing game.

janitor, *also (informal)* **jannie** a doorkeeper; a caretaker of a public building, especially a school.

janker a long pole on wheels used to transport timber.

janner *see* **jaunner**

jap *see* **jaup**

jarg *see* **jirg**²

jarie *see* **jaurie**

jaud, jad term of abuse for a horse or other animal; a woman; an old or useless article.

jaudie 1 the stomach of a pig or sheep, used in making haggis etc. **2** an oatmeal **pudding**; a haggis.

jauk 1 idle, dawdle, slack. **2** *of footwear* be loose-fitting *NE*.

jaunner, janner *noun* **1** idle, foolish talk. **2** a chatterbox.

jaup, jawp, jap *verb* **1** *of water etc* dash, splash, spill. **2** splash, spatter with water, mud etc.
noun **1** the splashing of the sea, a breaker, the surf, a choppy sea. **2** a splash (of water, mud etc). **3** contemptuous term for a small quantity, a drop (of drink, alcohol) *now NE*.
jaupit exhausted, wearied.

jaurie, jarie an earthenware marble.

jaw, ja *verb* pour, splash; dash, splash, surge.
noun **1** a wave, breaker *now NE*. **2** a rush, outpouring, splash; liquid splashed or thrown. **3** a drink.
jaw-box a sink; a drain. **jaw-hole 1** a primitive drain; *originally* a hole in the wall of a house for pouring away slops etc. **2** the mouth of a cesspool, a sewer.
jaw-lock lockjaw.

jawp *see* **jaup**

jeck¹ **1** *mainly* **jeck up** give up, discard,

abandon. **2** dislocate (a joint).

jeck² move smoothly; fit in (with) *NE*.

jeck *see* **jack**

Jeddart *see* **Jethart**

†**jedge and warrant** an order from a **Dean of Guild** (*see* **dean**).

jee, gee *verb* move, budge; move to one side or another, swerve; raise.
noun a move, a sideways turn.
jeed off the straight.
(not) jee one's ginger (not) bother one's head.

jeedge *see* **judge**

jeeg, jig *noun* **1** a jig. **2 jeegs** carryings-on, capers *now NE*. **3 jig** an instrument for catching fish.
verb **1** jig. **2** creak, make a creaking noise. **3** *also* **gig** move briskly. **4 jig** catch fish with a **jig**.
jeeger an odd or eccentric person. **the jiggin** dancing; a dance. **jeegle** jiggle. **jeegly** unsteady, shaky.

jeel, geill, geal *noun* **1** jelly. **2** extreme coldness. **3** a chill.
verb freeze, congeal; *of jelly etc* set.

jeelie, jelly 1 jelly. **2** jam.
jeelie-can, jeelie-jaur, jeelie-mug *NE,* **jeelie-pig** a jam-pot. **jeelie neb, jeelie nose** a bloody nose. **jeelie pan** a very large pan for making jam or jelly. **jeelie piece, piece and jeelie** bread and jam.

Jeen June *NE*.

jeep *see* **jupe**

jeest¹ joist.

jeest² jest, joke.

jeet jet, the mineral.

jeet *see* **jute**

†**jellie 1** jolly. **2** pleasant, attractive, agreeable. **3** upright, honest, worthy, excellent.

jelly *see* **jeelie**

†**Jenkin's hen: die the death of Jenkin's hen** die an old maid.

Jenny, Jinny 1 a woman, especially a country girl. **2** a man who occupies himself with what are regarded as female concerns; an effeminate man. **3 jennies** callipers.

Jenny a'thing(s) a female owner of a small general store; her shop. **Jenny's blue een** speedwell. **Jenny-hun(d)er-feet** a centipede. **Jenny-lang-legs** a cranefly, daddy-long-legs. **Jenny-mony feet = Jenny-hunder-feet. Jenny muck** a working woman; a female farmworker *Caithness NE*. **Jenny-nettle(s) 1 = Jenny-lang-legs. 2** a stinging nettle. **Jenny spinner = Jenny-lang-legs.**

jerk *see* **jirk**

Jerusalem traveller a louse.

Jessie contemptuous term for an effeminate man or boy: *"a big Jessie"*.

Jethart, Jeddart Jedburgh.
Jethart justice quick or arbitrary justice, condemnation without a hearing. **Jethart snails** a kind of toffee from Jedburgh.

jeuk *see* **deuk, jouk**

jib milk (a cow) to the last drop.

jibber silly talk, idle chatter.

jibble, geeble *verb* spill (a liquid) by shaking its container.
noun **1** a splash, the splashing or lapping of a liquid. **2** a small quantity of a liquid etc.

jick dodge, evade; try to avoid.
jicker move, walk, ride etc quickly.

jig, jiggin *see* **jeeg**

jiggin *see* **jeeg**

jile, jyle, jail jail.
get the jile be sent to prison.

jillet a flighty girl, a flirt.

jilp, jilt, gilp *verb* splash, spill.
noun **1** a small quantity of liquid splashed or spilt. **2** a small quantity of liquid, especially a thin or insipid drink *now NE*.

jilt contemptuous term for a girl or young woman.

jilt *see* **jilp**

Jimmie 1 very familiar form of address to a man, usually a stranger. **2 jimmie** a **white pudding** (*see* **white¹**) or oatmeal **pudding**, *often* **mealie Jimmie**.

jimp, gymp *adjective* **1** slender, small, graceful, neat, dainty. **2** *of clothes* close-fitting. **3** scanty, barely adequate, sparing.

verb give short or scant measure.

jimpit 1 on the short side, stunted. **2** scanty.

jimp *see* **jump**

jine *see* **join**

jing: (by) jing(s) a mild exclamation.

jing-bang a considerable number, usually **the hail jing-bang** the whole lot.

jingle *see* **chingle**

jingo-ring a children's singing game.

jink¹ *verb* **1** turn quickly, move or dodge nimbly. **2** move along in quick, sudden or jerky movements, dart, zigzag. **3** †move jerkily to and fro as when spinning or playing the violin; play the violin briskly. **4** frolic, flirt. **5** dodge; cheat, trick. **6** dodge (school etc), play truant.

noun **1** a quick or sudden twisting movement, a jerk. **2** a coil, twist, kink *now NE*. **3** the act of dodging or eluding someone; a dodge, trick *now NE*. **4** *mainly* **jinks** playful tricks or frolics. **5** **jinks** *or* **jinkie** a chasing game.

jink² a chink, a crack.

Jinny *see* **Jenny**

jint [rhymes with 'pint'] joint.

jirble 1 splash. **2** pour out unsteadily in small quantities.

jirg¹, **jerk** *NE* make a squelching or splashing sound, gurgle.

jirg², **jarg**, **jairg 1** creak, grate, jar. **2** grate, grind (the teeth).

jise *see* **joice**

jist *see* **juist**

jizzen childbirth.

jo, joe 1 joy. **2** *term of endearment* sweetheart, dear. **3** a sweetheart, lover, usually male.

joater *see* **jotter**

job¹ **1** job. **2** †*mainly* **jobbing** illicit sexual intercourse.

job² *verb* pierce, prick.

noun a prick; a prickle.

jobbie prickly.

Jock 1 a man, a fellow, especially a countryman, a farmworker. **2** (nickname for) a soldier in one of the Scottish regiments. **3** a bull *SW*.

Jockie 1 = **Jock** 1, 2. **2** a vagrant, tramp, gipsy. **Jockie blindie, Jockie blind-man** blindman's buff. **Jockie coat** a greatcoat, a heavy overcoat.

Jock brit contemptuous term for a miner.

the deil's gane ower Jock Wabster *proverb* things have got out of hand; the fat's in the fire. **play Jock needle Jock preen** play fast and loose, act in a shifty way *NE*. **Jock Tamson's bairns** the human race, common humanity; a group of people united by a common interest: *"We're a Jock Tamson's bairns"*.

jockteleg, jocteleg a clasp-knife.

joco [jo**co**] jovial, merry, pleased with oneself.

joe *see* **jo**

jog *see* **jag**¹

John: Johnnie a'thing(s) an owner of a small general store; his shop.

John Barleycorn personification of barley as the grain from which malt liquor is made; ale or whisky. **John o Gro(a)t's buckie** the cowrie shell. †**John Thomson's man** *proverb* a hen-pecked husband.

joice, jise [rhymes with 'choice' or 'price'] juice.u

join, jine *verb* **1** join. **2** become a communicant of (a particular religious denomination), especially **a joined member. 3** begin (work).

noun the clubbing together of several people to buy drink; a social gathering or outing *now NE*.

joiner a woodworker, carpenter.

joint adventure *law* a partnership undertaken for a specific limited purpose.

joiter *see* **jotter**

joke make a joke against, tease.

jokie jocular, fond of a joke.

†**joke-fellow-like** familiar, (in a) friendly (way).

jonick, gennick genuine, honest, fair, just.

joodge *see* judge

joog *see* jouk

joogle[1], jougle *verb* joggle, shake, wrestle. *noun* a joggle, a shaking.

joogle[2] juggle.

jook *see* jouk

joost *see* juist

joot *see* jute

jooter saunter, totter.

jorg make a squelching or grating sound.

joskin, geeskin a country bumpkin, farm-worker.

jossle shake, totter.

jot *noun* jots small pieces of work, odd jobs *now NE.*
verb do light work, potter (about) *NE.*

jotter, joater, joiter *noun* 1 a rough note-book, now especially a school exercise book. 2 an odd-job-man; a ne'er-do-well, a dawdler.
verb do odd jobs or light menial work; work in a dilatory fashion.

joug, joog, jug 1 a jug. 2 a mug or drinking vessel. 3 †name for the various standard measures of the pint in Scotland (see p 359).

jougle *see* joogle

jougs [jowgs], juggs an instrument of public punishment consisting of a hinged iron collar attached by a chain to a wall or post and locked round the offender's neck.

jouk, jook, juke, jeuk [rhymes with 'hook'] *verb* 1 duck, dodge a blow *etc.* 2 duck out of sight, hide, skulk. 3 bow; behave (too) humbly. 4 cower, crouch. 5 evade, avoid (someone or something). 6 play truant. 7 shirk, flinch. 8 appear and disappear quickly, dodge in and out, dart, flicker. 9 dodge by trickery, cheat, deceive.
noun 1 a quick ducking or dodging movement. 2 a bow etc. 3 shelter, a sheltered spot. 4 a trick.
joukery-pawk(e)ry trickery, deceit, roguery.
jouk an let the jaw gae by *proverb* give

way prudently in the face of over-whelming force, submit to the force of circumstance.

jow [rhymes with 'cow'] *noun* 1 a single peal or stroke of a bell; the ringing or tolling of a bell. 2 the surge or swell of water or waves. 3 a swing, swinging.
verb 1 ring, toll. 2 rock, swing, jostle, jog. 3 spill (a liquid) from a container.

jowel *now NE,* jewel a jewel.
jewel-coal a high-grade coal.

†jowler [-ow- as in 'cow'] a heavy-jawed hunting dog.

jubish [joobish] dubious, suspicious.

juck *see* chuck[2]

judge, joodge, jeedge *NE, noun* a judge.
verb 1 judge. 2 jeedge swear, curse *NE.*
judgement reason, senses, wits, sanity.
judgement-like appearing to threaten divine retribution, awful.

judicatory a court of judicature in church or state, a tribunal having judicial authority.

judicatum solvi [joodikaytum solviy] *law, of a security* pledged for the payment or satisfaction of a judgment.

judicial of or pertaining to judgment or the judicature: *"judicial declaration".*
judical factor a person appointed by the Court of Session (*see* session) or sheriff court (*see* sheriff) to administer *eg* the property of a person unable to administer it for himself.

juffle shuffle.

jug *see* joug

juggs *see* jougs

juist, just, duist, joost, jist, jeest *NE* 1 just. 2 really, simply, no less than; truly: *"ye didna go! I did just."*
verb check the accuracy of (a weight or measure), correct to the standard *now Shetland Orkney.*
juist that quite so, precisely.

juke *see* jouk

jummle 1 jumble, mix up, get mixed up with, confuse. 2 agitate, shake, churn. 3 make a churning or confused noise.
jummlie turbid, muddy.

jump, jimp now *Shetland* jump.

   jumpin-jack a child's toy made from the wishbone of a fowl *now NE*. **jumpin-rope** a skipping rope.

jundie, junny push (with the elbow), jog, shove.

†**junior secondary (school)** a state secondary school providing less academic courses than the **senior secondary school**, attended by pupils who were not successful in the **qualifying examination** (*see* **qualify**).

junny *see* **jundie**

junt 1 a large lump of something *now NE*. **2** a squat, clumsy person *NE*.

jupe, jeep *NE*, †**jup 1** a jacket, short coat or loose tunic worn by men. **2** a child's smock. **3** *also* **gipe** a woman's loose jacket or bodice.

jupe *see* **choop**

jus quaesitum tertio [juss kwayseetum tershio] *law* a contractual right of one party, arising out of a contract between two others, to which the first is not a party.

jus relictae, jus relicti [juss relictay, juss relictiy] *law* the share of a deceased spouse's **moveable** goods to which the surviving wife (**relictae**) or husband (**relicti**) is entitled; one-third if there are surviving children, one-half if there are none.

just *see* **juist**

justice: Lord Justice Clerk *now* one of the principal judges and vice-president of both the **High Court of Justiciary** (*see* **justiciary**) and of the **Court of Session** (*see* **session**). **Lord Justice General** now the president of the **High Court of Justiciary** (*see* **justiciary**).

justiciary: High Court of Justiciary the supreme criminal court of Scotland; *informally also* **High Court** (*see* **heich**)

jute, joot, jeet *NE, noun* **1** weak or sour ale; bad whisky. **2** any insipid drink, dregs, weak tea etc. **3** a tippler, boozer, drunkard *now NE*.

jyle *see* **jile**

K

kae, kyaw [keeaw] *NE, SW* **1** a jackdaw. **2** its call. **3** †contemptuous term for a person.

kach *see* **cack**

kaff *see* **caff**

kag *see* **cag**

kaid *see* **ked**

kail, kale, cale 1 a green vegetable, cole, brassica, especially the curly variety (often served boiled and mashed); cabbage. **2** soup with this vegetable as a main ingredient; soup of other ingredients (with or without meat), with the name of the main ingredient added, *eg* **pea kail, mealie kail, salmon kail. 3** a main meal, dinner.

kail-bell the dinner-bell; a call to dinner. **kail gullie** a blade fixed at right angles to the handle, for cutting kail stems *now Orkney N.* **kail ladle** a tadpole. **kail time** dinner-time. **kail worm** a caterpillar. **kail yaird 1** a cabbage garden, a kitchen-garden. **2** a type of sentimental fiction popular in the late 19th and early 20th centuries dealing with rural domestic life. **lang kail** great or Scotch kail, a less curly, purplish variety; a dish made this.

mak saut to his kail make a living. **get one's kail through the reek, get one's kail het** get a severe scolding. **scaud one's lips in ither folk's kail** interfere, meddle.

kailie *see* **ceilidh**

kalk *see* **cauk**¹

kame, came, comb *noun* **1** a comb. **2** a combing. **3** a long narrow ridge.
verb **1** comb. **2** rake (loose hay or straw from a stack to trim it). **3** scold.

get an ill kame for one's head bring mischief upon oneself.

kain *see* **kane**

kaisie *see* **cassie**

kane, kain 1 a payment in kind, a portion of the produce of a tenancy payable as rent. **2** a quantity of cheese (latterly about 3 tons (3.048 tonnes)).

†**pay (the) kain** pay the reckoning or the penalty.

kard *see* **caird**¹, **caird**²

Katie contemptuous term for a woman.

Katie beardie 1 a woman with a beard or moustache. **2** a loach.

kauch, kiaugh [keeawch] care, worry, bustle *SW*.

kavil *see* **cavel**

keavie *see* **cavie**¹

keb *mainly SW, S, of a ewe* give birth prematurely or to a dead lamb; lose a lamb by early death.

keb *see* **ked**

kebar *see* **caber**

kebbuck a cheese, a whole cheese, latterly especially home-made.

kebby-lebby *see* **cabby-labby**

kecher *see* **kicher**¹

keck the sharp cackling sound made by a bird.

keckle 1 *of hens etc* cackle. **2** laugh noisily; giggle. **3** laugh with joy or excitement *now Shetland NE.*

ked, †kaid, keb a sheep-tick.

keech *see* **kich**

keechle [-ch- as in 'dreich'] giggle, titter.

keeg *see* **keek**²

keeger, quigger mix up messily, mess about, work in a slovenly or ineffective way *NE.*

keehoy [keehoy] the game of hide-and-seek.

keek¹ peep, glance.

keeker 1 a peeping Tom. **2** an eye. **3** *also* **blue keeker** a black eye. **keeking glass** a mirror.

keek-bo *noun* the game of peep-bo. *exclamation, also* **keekie-bo 1** used in the game when the player in hiding has been seen. **2** used in similar play with a young child. **keek hole** a chink or peep-hole.

keek o day sunrise, peep of day. **keek and hide = keek-bo.**

keek[2], **keeg** *NE* **1** a cunning or malicious person. **2** contemptuous term for a young woman.

keek *see* **kick**

keel[1] **1** ruddle, red-ochre, especially as used for marking sheep. **2** the owner's mark made with this. **3** *weaving* the mark made with ruddle by the warper at each end of his warp to ensure that the weaver returns the correct amount of woven yarn. **4** a coloured crayon or pencil.

keel[2] **1** the back, the small or middle of the back *Shetland Orkney Caithness*. **2** the backside.

keel-up a heavy fall on one's back.

keelick, keelup a blow, stroke, a thud.

keelie[1] a kestrel.

keelie[2] a rough male city-dweller, a tough, now especially from the Glasgow area.

keelin, killing a cod.

keelivine, killavyne, callivan a (lead) pencil.

keelup *see* **keelick**

keen 1 lively, brisk; eager. **2** *curling, of ice* crisp, smooth. **3** greedy, miserly. **4** *of prices* highly competitive.

be keen of be eager for, be fond of.

keep *verb* **1** tend, take care of. **2** fare (as regards health). **3** keep going (talk, noise etc) *NE*.

noun **keeps** a game of marbles in which the winnings are kept *SW*.

keepie-in a pupil kept in after school as a punishment. **keepie-up** a game of keeping a ball in the air by means of the feet, knees or head.

keep-up upkeep.

keep aff o anesel stand up for oneself.

keep in aboot restrain, keep in order.

keep in one's hand 1 restrain oneself,

stop oneself striking. **2** be stingy. **keep me** may God keep me. **keep someone's pooch** provide someone with pocket money. **keep up 1** stay awake. **2** *of weather* stay fine.

keeper *see* **record**

keer cure *NE*.

keeriosity curiosity *now NE*.

keeroch contemptuous term for any strange or messy mixture *NE*.

keething *see* **kythe**

keevee: on the keevee on the alert; in high spirits; worked up.

keiching *see* **kitchen**

keind *see* **kind**

kell 1 a caul, a woman's ornamental hair-net or cap. **2** scurf or dirt on the head or face.

kelp 1 a mischievous young person *S*. **2** a big raw-boned youth *NE*.

kelpie a (horse-shaped) water demon, found in rivers and fords.

Kelso Laddie the leading male participant in the Kelso **Riding of the Marches** (*see* **ride**).

kelt[1] a salmon or sea-trout on its way back to the sea after spawning.

†**kelt**[2] a kind of homespun black or grey cloth.

kelter 1 wriggle, struggle. **2** †overturn, upset.

†**keltie: give someone keltie** force a large alcoholic drink on a person who has tried to avoid drinking; give someone a double dose of punishment.

Kelvinside accent a very affected, over-refined pronunciation of Scottish English.

kemp struggle, contend, strive; compete.

kempie a bold or pugnacious person; a lively child.

kemple, kimple 1 a bundle or load of straw or hay. **2** a lump or piece (of food) *NE*.

ken *verb* know.

noun knowledge, acquaintance, comprehension, insight.

kenable obvious, easily recognizable.

kenning 1 recognition, acquaintance; teaching, understanding. **2** a very little of anything.

kenmark a distinguishing mark, a mark of ownership on an animal.

kennawhat a something-or-other *now Shetland Orkney NE*. **(guid) kens what etc** goodness knows what etc.

kench *see* **kinch**[1]

kendle *see* **kennle**

kennel a channel, a street gutter *now Ayr*.

kennle, kendle, kinnle kindle.

kenspeckle, kenspreckle *NE* easily recognizable, conspicuous, familiar.

kent a long pole for leaping ditches etc.

kep[1]**, caip, cap** *noun* a cap.

verb, only **cap** confer a degree on (a **graduand**) by touching his or her head with a cap.

kep[2] *verb* **1** catch (a falling object or liquid). **2** stop, head off; ward off (a blow). **3** meet; *of a train, bus, etc* connect with (another). **4** keep, contain, restrain, guard. **5** hold (the hair) up with a band, comb etc.

noun **1** the act of catching, a catch, especially with the hands. **2** the heading off or intercepting of animals. **3** a contrivance for checking, stopping or holding especially doors or windows. **4** a chance, opportunity *WCentral S*.

kepper 1 a person who is good at catching. **2** a thing which is easy to catch. **3 keppers, keppies** = **catchers** (*see* **catch**).

kep again check, intercept, turn back.

ker *see* **car**[2]

kerious, kwerious curious.

kerle *see* **carle**

kerlying *see* **carline**

kers(e) *see* **carse**

kerseckie *see* **carsackiet**

kest *see* **cast, kist**

ket[1] carrion, the flesh of an animal, a sheep that has died of accident or disease *S*.

ket[2] **1** a matted fleece of wool. **2** couch-grass *S*. **3** a spongy kind of peat *SW*.

ketch *see* **keytch**

ketharan *see* **cateran**

kethie, kethock an angler fish.

kettle 1 a large cooking pot *now Shetland*. **2** a riverside picnic, especially on the Tweed, at which newly-caught salmon are cooked on the spot. **3** *also* **kettlie** the game of hopscotch.

kevil *see* **cavel**

key 1 mood, humour. **2 keys** *in children's games* a state of or call for truce.

keytch [-ey- as in 'keytch'], **kytch, ketch** pitch, toss aside or to and fro; hitch up.

kiaugh *see* **kauch**

kibble sturdy, well-built, active, agile *NE*.

kich, keech [-ch as in 'dreich'] *noun* **1** excrement, filth or dirt of any kind. **2** exclamation of disgust, a warning, often to a child, not to touch something dirty.

verb defecate.

keechie filthy, dirty, nasty.

kicher[1]**, kecher** [-ch- as in 'dreich'] have a short, persistent, tickling cough.

kicher[2] [-ch- as in 'dreich'] titter, giggle *now Shetland NE*.

kick, keek *Shetland Orkney verb* **1** kick. **2** show off, walk haughtily *N*.

noun **1** a kick. **2** something newfangled. **3** a trick, caper. **4** a habit, whim *NE*. **5 kicks** airs, manners *NE*.

kicker a tedder, a machine for spreading hay. **kicky** showy, especially in dress.

kick ba (a) football.

kick the can(nie) *etc* a game in which a player hunts for others while preventing any of them creeping out to kick a can etc. **kick bonnety (kick)** a game played by kicking a cap or bonnet until the owner can substitute another which is in turn kicked.

kicker: stand the kickers (o) resist, refuse to budge (for) or be disturbed (by) *NE*.

kickmaleerie a flimsy trifling thing.

kidgie *see* **cadgy**

kiest *see* **cast**

kilch push, shove, jerk, ram *SW, S*.

kill[1], **kiln 1** a kiln. **2** a wooden tripod round which a stack of hay etc is built.
kill-crack a small crack in the glazing of pottery.
fire the kill start trouble, raise a commotion.

kill[2] **1** thrash, beat; hurt badly. **2** overcome from weariness.

killavyne *see* **keelivine**

Killie nickname for Kilmarnock football team.

killieshangie *see* **collieshangie**

killing *see* **keelin**

killogie [kiloagie], **kiln-logie** a kiln or one of its parts, *eg* the lower part, the fire-(place), the covered space in front of the fire.

killyvie [killivee] a fuss, disturbance *WCentral*.

killywimple a trill or affectation in singing.

Kilmarnock: 1 Kilmarnock bonnet a broad flat woollen bonnet of blue, black or red. **2** †*also* **Kilmarnock hood** a knitted woollen cap worn as a nightcap or by indoor workers such as weavers.

Kilmaurs kail a hardy variety of **kail** mainly used for feeding cattle *WCentral*.

kiln *see* **kill**[1]

kiln-logie *see* **killogie**

kilt[1] *verb* **1** tuck (up) (one's clothes). **2** lift (up), suspend (a thing); hang (a person).
noun a part of modern male Highland dress, a kind of skirt, usually of tartan cloth, reaching to the knee and thickly pleated at the back.
kilted dressed in a kilt. **high-kiltit** having the skirts well tucked up; immodest, indecent. **kiltie** a wearer of the **kilt**; a soldier in a Highland regiment.

kilt[2] overturn, upset.

kilter good spirits.

kim spirited, lively *now NE*.

kimmer *see* **cummer**[2]

kimple *see* **kemple**

kin *noun* a kinsman, relation.

adjective related, akin.
redd oot kin trace one's family history.

kinallie *see* **canally**

kinch[1], **kench** *noun* **1** a twist or doubling in a rope, a kink; a loop, noose, running knot. **2** a tight corner, a difficult problem. **3** a sudden twist in wrestling.
verb **1** twist a loop in (a rope) with a stick to tighten it. **2** tie up.

kinch[2] an (unexpected) advantage or opportunity.

kind, keind *noun* **1** kind. **2** †character or nature. **3** inherited character *now S*.
verb **1** **kind to** be like, resemble, take after *S*. **2** sort, arrange in kinds.
adverb somewhat, rather: *"an odd kind chiel"*.
kindly 1 natural; normal; characteristic, congenial *now Orkney*. **2** †native, true-born, rightful. **3** *of a tenant* having a right to the tenancy because of its long continued occupation by oneself or one's ancestors: *"kindly tenant"*.
(a) kind of, kinna somewhat, rather. **in a kind** after a fashion *now NE, Fife*.
yon kind not quite normal or proper; not worth much; in indifferent health.

king †a person or animal who played the most important role, *eg* the leader in a game, the winner in a cock-fight.
king's chair a seat formed by two children grasping each other's wrists.
king's hood 1 the second stomach of a ruminant. **2** †the human stomach.
be a king tae be superior to.

kink[1] *verb, of wood* warp.
noun a crease, fold.

kink[2] *verb* gasp or choke convulsively; suffer an attack of coughing, especially whooping-cough; choke with laughter.
noun a catching of the breath as in whooping-cough; a fit of coughing; a violent and irrepressible fit of laughter.
kinkcough, kinkhost whooping-cough.

kin-kind kind, sort, description *now NE*.

kinna *see* **kind**

kinnen *see* **cunning**

kinnle *see* **kennle**

†**kinrick** a kingdom.

kintra *see* **countra**

kip[1] **1** a jutting or projecting point on a hill; a peak *mainly S*. **2** a turned-up nose *now Ulster*.

kippit *of a nose, a cow's horn* turned or tilted up.

kip[2] play truant from school.

kip[3] a (small) bundle *now Orkney*.

kip[4] a state of hurry or great excitement.

kippage 1 disorder, confusion, fuss. **2** (good etc) spirits.

kippie left-handed *mainly Perth Fife*.

kippit *see* **kip**[1]

kipple *see* **couple**

kir *see* **kirr**

kirk church, now as **the Kirk** often used to refer in all but the most formal contexts to the Church of Scotland.

verb: **be kirked** go to or be received in church, especially for the first time after a wedding, birth, family funeral, or (*of a council*) after appointment.

kirkie enthusiastically devoted to church affairs.

do something at the kirk door do something openly or in public. **kirk greedy** zealous in attendance at church. **kirk road** a road or path used by parishioners going to the parish church, and constituting a right of way. **kirk session** *Presbyterian Churches* the lowest court, consisting of the **minister** and the **elders** of a congregation. **kirk toun** the town or village in which the parish church is situated. **kirkyaird deserter** a sickly-looking person, one who looks as if he should be in his grave *now NE*. **kirkyaird hoast** a churchyard cough.

come into the body of the kirk *of a person sitting etc apart* come forward and join the main company. **kirk and market** in all the public affairs of life. **mak a kirk and a mill o** do whatever one wishes with, make or mar.

kirk green *see* **green**

kirn[1] *noun* **1** a churn. **2** a natural feature resembling a churn in noise, motion or shape. **3** milk in the process of being churned; buttermilk. **4** a churning motion, a confused stirring. **5** a sloppy (muddy) mess. **6** a muddle, jumble, confusion; a stir. **7** a pottering,° a rummage *NE*.

verb **1** churn. **2** stir, mix up with a churning motion *now Shetland NE*. **3** cause to turn or rotate; bore with a drill or circular chisel. **4** search, hunt or poke about; work with one's hands in a sloppy, purposeless or disgusting way. **5** *of a crowd* swarm, mill about. **6** fuss over, be affectionate towards, 'pet' *NE*.

kirning footling, inefficient *NE*.

kirn milk (curds made from) buttermilk.

kirn[2] **1** a celebration marking the end of the harvest, a harvest-home. **2** the last sheaf or handful of corn of the harvest. **kirn baby, kirn dollie** the decorated female effigy made from the last sheaf or handful of corn to be cut, a corndolly. **kirn supper** the celebration held when the corn is cut.

kirnel 1 a kernel *now SW*. **2** a lump under the skin; a swollen gland. **3 kirnels** animal glands used as food *now SW*.

kirr, kir *adjective SW* **1** cheerful; self-satisfied. **2** †amorous, wanton.

kirsten, kirsen, christen christen.

christening bit, christening piece = baby's piece (*see* **piece**).

kiss-my-luif a fawner, toady, an effeminate person.

kist, †**kest** *noun* **1** a chest, a large box. **2** the chest, the part of the body. **3** a coffin.

verb **1** put in a coffin. **2** place in a box or chest, store.

kist neuk a corner of a chest for money or valuables.

kist o whistles 1 a church organ. **2** a wheezy chest.

kit, kitt 1 a small tub. **2** a fair amount *now S*.

kitchen, keiching [**kee**tchin] *noun, also* **kitchie 1** a kitchen. **2** anything served in addition to a plain food such as bread or potatoes.

verb **1** give flavour to, season. **2** make (something) go far, use sparingly.

kitchen fee tallow; dripping.

kith 1 a person's acquaintances, neighbours and kinsfolk. **2** one's native country or district.

kithing *see* **kythe**

kitt *see* **kit**

kittie[1] **1** familiar or contemptuous term for a woman or girl. **2** the jack in the game of bowls. **3** a kittiwake.

kittie cat the piece of wood etc hit by the sticks in **shinty** *S*.

kittie[2] prison, the village lock-up *S, Ulster*.

kittle[1], **cuittle, kyittle** [**kee**ittle] *Shetland Orkney, verb* **1** tickle. **2** please; make excited. **3** stir (a fire). **4** annoy, tease. **5** scold, reprove. **6** *of the wind* freshen, blow more strongly and gustily *now NE*. **7** *of persons* become angry, moved or annoyed. **8** *of a horse* become restive. **9** *of circumstances, health etc* improve *NE*. **10** set (the strings of a musical instrument) in motion, tune (up), strike up (a tune). **11** puzzle, perplex.

noun **1** a tickle. **2** an irritation (of the throat). **3** a pleasurable excitement. **4** a stir, a poke (of a fire). **5** a difficult feat. **6** a polish, shine *NE*.

adjective **1** ticklish, tickly. **2** touchy, easily upset or offended, difficult to deal with. **3** hard to deal with, tricky, puzzling, difficult. **4** †*of writers, their words* difficult (to understand or pronounce). **5** cunning, adept, skilful *now Angus*. **6** liable, inclined to *SW*.

kittlie 1 tickly, causing a tickling sensation; itchy, ticklish. **2** troublesome, difficult, ticklish; puzzling.

kittle cattle persons (or animals) who are unmanageable, capricious, difficult.

kittle[2] give birth, produce young.

kittlin 1 a kitten. **2** the young of other small animals.

kiver *see* **cover**

kizen *see* **gizzen**

kizzen, †**cusing** a cousin.

kjunning *see* **cunning**

kley [rhymes with 'gey'] clay.

klister *see* **cleester**

klondyke: klondyking the exporting to the Continent of fresh fish (originally herring, now mackerel) originally by fast ship, now direct to factory ships for processing on board. **klondyker** a person or ship that does this.

klurt *see* **clart**

knab, nabb a person of importance or prestige, a snob.

knabery gentry. **nabbie** a type of herring-fishing boat.

knab *see* **knap**[2], **nabb**

knack, nack *verb* **1** make a sharp crackling noise; snap (the fingers); break or snap with a sharp sound. **2** strike or slash sharply. **3** make fun of; deride. **4** chatter (away) *NE, Ulster*.

noun a sharp noise; a sharp blow, a crack *now Orkney NE*.

knackie, nacky 1 deft, ingenious, skilful. **2** nimble, smart; trim, neatly-built, spruce. **3** witty, pleasant, facetious, funny.

knag[1], **nag 1** a knot or spur projecting from a tree. **2** a peg etc for hanging things on.

at the knag an the widdie at loggerheads *NE*.

knag[2], **knog** a keg.

knap[1], **knop, nap 1** a rounded knob, a lump or bump *now Orkney NE*. **2** a tassel, *eg* on a bonnet or nightcap. **3** the point of the elbow; the kneecap. **4** a shin of beef. **5** a hillock, knoll.

knapdarloch 1 a knot of hardened dirt and dung hanging from the coat or tail of an animal. **2** contemptuous term for an undersized, dirty, cheeky person *NE*. **knappie 1** lumpy, bumpy *now NE*.

2 crisp, brittle *now Ulster*.

knap², knab, †nab *verb* **1** knock, strike sharply, rap. **2** break sharply, snag; break (stones) for building, road-making. **3** break or snap with the teeth, munch, eat greedily. **4** *especially of a Scot imitating English* speak in an affected, clipped way *now Shetland NE*. *noun* **1** a sharp knock or blow. **2** a snap, bite, a morsel of food, a bite.

    knapper 1 a stone-breaker. **2** a small hammer used by stone-breakers.

knap³ a sturdy lad; a chap *now NE*.

knap *see* **nap**¹

knapparts tuberous vetch, heath pea *N*.

knaw know.

kned knead.

knee bend so as to form a knee-shaped angle.

kneef *mainly N* **1** mentally or physically alert, agile. **2** fit, in sound health and spirits.

kneep a lump *NE*.

kneevle a bit, lump.

kneggum a pungent, disagreeable taste or flavour.

knevell *see* **nevel**

knibloch, kniblack a small rounded stone, a hard clod of earth; a lump.

knick, nick 1 make a cracking, clicking or ticking sound. **2** break, snap. **3** *marbles* propel smartly with thumb and fore-finger.

knidge rub, squeeze, press, especially with the knee *now Shetland N*.

knidge *see* **knitch**

knifie a boys' game in which each player tries to stick an open knife into the ground by sliding or tossing it from different parts of the body.

knip¹ a little, mischievous boy or girl *N*.

knip² pull to pieces, break off, snap.

knitch, knidge 1 a bundle, truss. **2** a (short) sturdy person.

knock¹ beat or pound (flax, cloth or grain).

knock², nock a clock.

knock³ a hillock.

knog *see* **knag²**

knoit¹, knyte *NE* **1** a large piece, a lump *NE*. **2** a knob, a bump; a bunion.

knoit², noit *noun* a sharp blow, a knock. *verb* **1** knock, beat. **2** hobble, walk stiffly and jerkily.

knool *see* **knule**

knoose *see* **knuse**

knoost, noost a large lump, a hunk.

knop *see* **knap**¹

knot *noun* **1** a lump, a broken-off chunk; a lump in porridge. **2** a sturdy, thickset person or animal. **3** a joint in the stem of a plant. **4** a flowerbed, a formal garden. **5** *also* **knotberry** a cloudberry. *verb* form or grow into lumps.

    knotless futile, aimless, ineffective. **a knotless threid** a thread that has no knot and tends to slip; an aimless, use-less, futile person or thing. **knotty-tammies** a dish of hot milk or water and oatmeal formed into partially cooked lumps. **knot grass** name for various grasses with knotty stems.

know [rhymes with 'cow'] a knoll.

    know head a hilltop.

knuckle, nickle 1 a knuckle. **2** *measure* the length of the second finger from tip to knuckle. **3** *marbles* the flick given to the striking marble; the marble so played *NE*.

knule, knool a lump, knob; *of cattle* a small loose horn.

knur 1 a lump, a weal. **2** a decrepit or dwarfish person.

    knurl 1 a lump, bump. **2** a deformed person, a dwarf.

knuse, knoose, noose, noozle squeeze, press down, bruise; cuddle; pummel, drub, hit hard.

knype *mainly NE* **1** knock, strike sharply. **2** jog (on) steadily, keep going, work away.

knyte *see* **knoit**¹

koog *see* **cook**

kow *see* **cow**¹, **cow**², **cow**³

kro *see* **crue**

kugl *see* **coggle**

kwerious *see* **kerious**

kyaak *see* **cake**

kyaard *see* **caird**[1]

kyard *see* **caird**[2]

kyauve *Shetland N* [kee**auve**] *verb* **1** toil, wrestle laboriously, struggle with. **2** move or toss restlessly, tumble about, wrestle in fun *Shetland NE*. **3** knead *NE*.

noun a struggle, exertion, a turmoil.

kyaw *see* **kae**

kye *see* **coo**

kyeuk *see* **cuik**

kyittle *see* **kittle**

kyle[1] a narrow strait or arm of the sea or narrow part of a river.

kyle[2] **1** a ninepin or skittle; **(the) kyles** the game itself. **2** a chance, opportunity.

kyle *see* **quile**

kyloe one of a breed of small Highland cattle.

kype *N* **1** a small scooped-out hollow in the ground, used in the game of marbles. **2** a game played with marbles aimed at a hole in the ground.

kytch *see* **keytch**

kyte the stomach, belly.

kytie corpulent.

kythe show, display, reveal; perform (a miracle).

kithing, keething *NE* appearance.

kythe to, kythe wi take after, accord with; be attracted to.

L

lab *noun* **1** a lump; a bit; a shred. **2** a blow, stroke. **3** a kind of marbles game.
verb **1** beat, strike. **2** pitch, throw.

lab *see* **laib**

labour, lawbour *noun* **1** labour. **2** farm work, tilling the ground.
verb **1** labour. **2** till, cultivate.

labrod a lapboard, a board laid across the knees for working on.

lab-sided lop-sided.

labster *see* **lapster**

lacer a lace, especially a boot-lace.

lach *see* **lauch**

lachter¹, lauchter 1 the eggs laid by a fowl in a season; a single clutch of eggs. **2** a hatch or brood of chickens.

lachter², louchter [**loch**ter], **luchter** *SW, Ulster noun* **1** †a lock of hair; a tuft of grass. **2** the amount of corn grasped and cut in one stroke; the last sheaf cut in harvest; a handful of hay *Caithness*.

lad, lawd 1 a lad. **2** a youth. **3** a male child, a son. **4** a bachelor *now Caithness*. **5** a male sweetheart, a boyfriend. **6** the young bachelor chosen as the leading male participant in various annual local festivals. **7** an (extreme) example of its kind: *"ye're a lad"*.
lad bairn a son.
lad and lass a pair of sweethearts. **lad o pairts** a promising boy, a talented youth.

lade, lead a channel bringing water to a mill; a mill-race.

lade *see* **laid**

lady, leddy, lethy *Orkney* **1** a lady. **2** estate title given to a female landowner or wife of a landowner: *"Lady Leithhall"*.
ladies' gairtens, ladies' garters striped ribbon-grass. **lady lander(s)** a ladybird. **lady provost** courtesy title for the wife of a **lord provost** (*see* **lord**). **lady's thimbles 1** a **harebell** *now Ulster*.

2 a foxglove.

lae *see* **lea**

laen *see* **len**

lafe *see* **laif**

laft, loft *noun* **1** a loft. **2** the upper storey of a two-storey building. **3** a gallery in a church.
verb **1** provide (a building) with a loft by flooring joists. **2** (cause to) rise off the ground.

lag lingering, slow.

lagamachie, legammachie [laga**machie**] a long rigmarole *NE*.

lagger, laiger *verb* **1** make wet or muddy. **2** sink in soft ground.
noun mud.

laggin, laigen, leggin 1 the projection of the staves beyond the bottom of a barrel. **2** the angle inside a dish etc where sides and bottom meet. **3** the edge, rim, *eg* of a hill or shoe.

laib, leb, lab *N verb* lick up, lap, gobble.
noun **1** a mouthful, especially of liquid. **2** an untidy piece of clothing *NE*. **3** a rigmarole *NE*.
laibach *NE verb* babble. *noun* = *noun* **1**, **3** *NE*. **laiber** dirty (clothes etc) with food.

laich, laigh [-ch, -gh as -ch in 'dreich'], **law, low** *adjective* **1** low. **2** in the lower part of a building.
noun **1** a stretch of low-lying ground *often in place-names*. **2** the low side or lowest part of anything.
laich country the Lowlands of Scotland. **laich house 1** a room or rooms in the lower part of a building, *eg* a cellar. **2** a one-storey building. **laich road** the lower of two roads; the road below the earth along which the dead were supposed to travel.

laid, lade, load 1 a load. **2** a measure of quantity varying according to district and commodity. **3** a heavy attack (of cold).

laidron, laithron a rascal, loafer; a slattern.

laif, lafe, loaf 1 a loaf. **2** bread, especially wheat-flour bread.

loaf bread wheat-flour bread (as opposed to oatcakes).

laif *see* **leaf**

laig, lyaag [leeagg] chatter, gossip *NE*.

laig *see* **leg**

laigen *see* **laggin**

laiger *see* **lagger**

laigh *see* **laich**

laiglin *see* **leglin**

laik, lake a small marble used as a stake in a game *mainly NE*.

laimeter *see* **lameter**

lainch *see* **lench**

laip, lape, lep *now Shetland Orkney verb* lap.

noun **1** the act of lapping. **2** a mouthful or small amount (of liquid). **3** a quick wash, a swill.

lair[1] **1** a person's bed. **2** a place where animals lie down, a fold. **3** a burial place or grave; a burial space reserved by a person or family in a graveyard or church. **4** a place where something lies or is laid down. **5** a patch of ground on which cut peats are laid to dry *NE*.

lair[2] *noun* **1** mud. **2** a muddy, wet place *now NE*.

verb (cause to) sink in mud etc.

lair[3], **lear** learning, knowledge, education.

laird 1 †a prince, chief, lord. **2** Christ; now used as a mild oath. **3** the landlord of landed property or an estate. **4** an owner of property, especially a householder.

auld laird the present laird, where there is a male heir. **young laird** the male heir of a **laird.**

lairge, large 1 large. **2** generous; lavish *now NE*; plentiful *now NE*.

lairick *see* **larick**

laith *adjective* loath.

noun ill-will, loathing, scorn *now Orkney*.

verb loathe.

laithron *see* **laidron**

lake *see* **laik, leck**

laland *see* **lallan**

laldie [-a- as in 'cat']: **gie someone laldie** give someone a thrashing. **gie it laldie** do something vigorously or enthusiastically.

lallan, laland (*compare* **lawland**) *noun* **1** †**Lallans** the Lowlands of Scotland. **2** **Lallans** the Scots language; *now* the literary variety used by writers of the Scottish Renaissance movement.

adjective **1** Lowland. **2** Scots in speech (as opposed to Gaelic- or English-speaking).

lamb, lam 1 a lamb. **2** *often* **lambie, my wee lamb** affectionate term of address, *now* especially to a child.

lammie-meh pet name for a lamb.

lamb's ears, lamb's lugs 1 hoary plantain. **2** a woolly-leaved plant.

lame, leam *now Orkney noun* **1** †loam, earth. **2** earthenware, china. **3** a piece of broken crockery, especially one used as a toy.

lame tig *see* **tig**

lament an elegy, a dirge; the tune to which such a song is sung or played, especially on bagpipes.

lameter, laimeter a lame or crippled person or animal.

Lammas 1 August, a Scottish quarter day.

lammer, laumer amber.

lamp 1 stride along, take long springing steps. **2** limp, hobble.

lampit *see* **lempit**

lance a surgeon's lancet, a scalpel.

land[1], **lan, laun(d) 1** land. **2** †the country as opposed to the town. **3** the fields as opposed to buildings of a farm. **4** the soil still to be turned over by the plough; the width of the cut made by the plough. **5** a holding of land, a building site; a building on this, a tenement.

lander 1 = **land beast. 2** a fall on the ground, *eg* when skating. **landing** the journey of a plough from one side of a field to another and back again.

land beast *in a plough-team* the left-hand horse, which walks on the unturned earth. **Land Court** = **Scottish Land Court** (*see* **Scots**). **landlady** the mistress of a house where one is staying, one's hostess. **landlord** the head of the family where one is a guest, one's host. **land mouse** a field vole. **land side** the left-hand side of the plough. †**the land of cakes** Scotland (from the importance of oatcakes in the Scottish diet). **the land of the leal** the land of the faithful, Heaven.

land² saddle (someone) with (something unwelcome).

landimer *see* **lanimer**

landward, landwart, landart 1 in, toward or in the direction of the country as opposed to the town. **2** rural, in or of the country as opposed to (a particular) town, in or of a rural part of a parish or district. **3** awkward, uncouth, countryfied.

lane¹ a marshy meadow; a slow-moving, winding stream *SW*.

lane², lone 1 lone. **2** on one's own, alone: *"he went his lane".*

lang, long 1 long. **2** tall. **3** *of prices etc* high *now NE.*

lang ale a soft drink *NE.* **lang back** long ago. **lang cairt** a two-wheeled cart with a long body used especially for carrying grain. **lang-chafted** long-jawed *now NE.* **lang heid** shrewdness; a shrewd or wise person. **lang kail** *see* **kail. lang kent** familiar. **lang leeks** a variety of the game of leap-frog. **lang lugs 1** a person with long ears. **2** a donkey. **3** a hare. **lang-luggit 1** long-eared. **2** shrewd. **lang-nebbit 1** having a long **neb**, snout etc. **2** *of things* long, tapering or pointed. **3** *of people* gnome-like *now Orkney.* **4** sharp, having an eye

to one's own advantage. **5** inquisitive, critical. **6** *of words* long, over-learned. **lang settle** a long wooden bench, with a back (and sides) often with a chest below the seat, and sometimes also convertible into a bed. **langsome 1** lengthy, boringly long. **2** *of people* slow, dilatory. **3** lonely, bored. **lang syne** *adverb* long ago, long since. *noun* old times, memories of the past, old friendship. **auld lang syne 1** = **lang syne. 2** the song or the tune of this name, now especially Burns' song and its tune, played and sung at the close of social gatherings and at midnight on **Hogmanay. lang drink (o water)** a tall lanky person. **lang may yer lum reek** said to wish someone luck and prosperity. **mak a lang airm** stretch out and help oneself.

langer *see* **langour**

langle, langal *noun* a hobble, tether for an animal.

verb **1** hobble (an animal). **2** hinder, frustrate.

langour, langer boredom, low spirits.

lanimer [lannimer], †**landimer** a boundary, especially of **burgh** lands. **Lanimer Day** the day etc of celebrations accompanying the annual **Riding of the Marches** (*see* **ride**) in Lanark.

lap patch.

lap *see* **leap**

lape *see* **laip, leap**

lapper¹ *verb* **1** lopper clot, curdle. **2** *of water* freeze. **3** cover with or become covered with blood etc.

noun **1** a clot or clots, especially of milk or blood. **2** milk soured and thickened for butter-making. **3** melting, slushy snow *SW, S.*

lapper² lap, ripple.

lapper gowan *see* **gowan**

lapster, labster, lobster a lobster. **lapster creel** a lobster trap.

larach a site or foundation of a building, the remains of an old building.

large *see* **lairge**

larick, lairick [**lar**rick, **ler**rick] a larch tree.

larick *see* **laverock**

larkie the game of hide-and-seek.

larrie a lorry.

lash a large amount.

lashangallaivie [-**gall**aivie] abundance *S*.

laskit elastic.

lass *also* **lassie, lassock, lassickie 1** a girl. **2** *familiar* a woman. **3** an unmarried woman. **4** a daughter. **5** a female servant. **6** a sweetheart, girlfriend. **7** the leading female participant in various local festivals.

lass(ie) bairn, lass wean a daughter. **lass(ie) boy** an effeminate boy.

lat, let, *verb, past tense also* **lat, loot, luit, leet** *NE, past participle also* **latten, letten, luitten** let.

lat aff break wind. **lat at** hit out at. **lat bat = lat on. lat be** leave alone. **lat doun 1** lower the price of. **2** *of a cow* give (milk). **3** swallow. **4** *knitting* drop (a stitch). **lat (it) licht** give information privately or casually *NE*. **lat on 1** not **lat on** not show that one knows (about something). **2** pretend. **lat ower** swallow. **lat see** pass, hand over. **lat someone wi something** agree to someone's desires or opinions in something *N*.

latch[1] a wet muddy place, patch of bog.

latch[2] delay; lag.

latchet a small loop of string, thread, wire etc.

latten *see* **lat**

lauch, lach, *verb, past tense also* **leuch, l(e)ucht, laucht,** *past participle also* **leuchen, lauchen** *now NE*, **laucht, leucht** laugh.

lauch *see* **law**[1]

lauchter *see* **lachter**[1]

laumer *see* **lammer**

laun(d) *see* **land**[1]

lave[1] the rest, the remainder.

lave[2] bale, remove (water) with a bucket.

lave *see* **lea**

laverock, larick, liverock *NE*, **laveroo** *Orkney* [**laiv**rock, **lai**rick, **liv**rock, **lai**vroo] a skylark.

law[1], †**lauch** law.

lawer, lawvyer a lawyer.

law- agent a solicitor. **law burrows** *law* legal security required from or given by a person that he will not injure another. **law lord** one of the judges of the **Court of Session** (*see* **session**), to whom the courtesy title of **lord** is given.

law[2] a rounded hill, often in an isolated position.

law *see* **laich**

lawbour *see* **labour**

lawd *see* **lad**

lawin a bill in a public house; a person's share of this.

lawland, lowland [*compare* **lallan**] *noun* the **Lowlands** any part or all of Scotland east and south of the **Highland Line** (*see* **hieland**) (sometimes excluding the Borders).

adjective belonging to the **Lowlands** of Scotland.

lawlander a person from the **Lowlands**.

lawvyer *see* **law**[1]

lay *verb* **1** *used where English has* put, place, set etc. **2** flatten (crops) by wind or rain. **3** re-steel (a plough-iron etc). *noun* the re-steeling of the cutting edge of a tool.

be laid aside be out of action because of illness. **lay at** strike at, beat. **lay awa** *of a fowl* lay eggs away from the usual nest. **lay by 1** lay aside, discard. **2** set aside, reserve. **3** (cause to) stop or rest. **4 be laid by** be out of action through illness. **lay in 1** set to work energetically. **2** fold (something) down or over on itself; turn up (a hem). **lay into** eat greedily. **lay off** talk at length and confidently (about). **lay on 1** *of rain or snow* fall heavily. **2** eat heartily. **lay till, lay tae 1** start to eat. **2** beat. **3** close (a door) *Shetland Orkney N*. **4** set to, work vigorously.

laylock lilac.

lazy-bed a method of planting (usually potatoes) on undug strips of soil, using manure and sods from the next strip as covering.

lea, lave, lae leave.

lead 1 carry in a cart. **2** *law* call, produce (evidence, witnesses etc): *"lead proof"*.
leader a tendon, sinew. **led farm** a smaller or outlying farm managed through an employee.

lead *see* **lade**

lead *see* **leid**

leaf, laif *noun* **1** a leaf. **2** one of the segments of an orange.

leaf *see* **lief**

leak *see* **leck**

leal 1 loyal, faithful; constant. **2** honest, law-abiding; *see also* **land.**

leam, leme *noun* (a gleam of) light.
verb shine, glitter, flash.

leam *see* **lame**

lean lie down, rest, take a seat.

leap, lape *verb, past tense also* **lap, lape, lep** *Shetland Orkney, past participle also* **luppen 1** leap. **2** split, burst open, especially of potatoes being boiled in their skins.

lear 1 †teach. **2** learn.

lear *see* **lair**³

lea rig *now only in poetry* a strip of grass left untilled in a ploughed field.

learn teach.

lease, leeze 1 separate out (the yarn for the warp threads) before weaving. **2** disentangle; tidy up.

leash, leesh *noun* **1** a leash. **2** a long piece of string, thread etc; anything long of its kind. **3** a stroke of a lash.
verb **1** lash, flog *now Shetland*. **2** move or work quickly or energetically *Shetland N*.

leasing, leesing [-s- as in 'please'] lying, slandering.
leasing-making *law* the spreading of slander against the Crown likely to cause rebellion etc.

leat *see* **leet**¹

leather, ledder *now Shetland Orkney NE*

noun **1** leather. **2** the skin, hide. **3** a heavy blow.
verb **1** beat, thrash. **2** do something fast and energetically.

leave *verb* permit, allow.
noun **1** permission to a pupil to leave the classroom during a school lesson; the playtime interval in school. **2** dismissal.

leaven a mixture of oatmeal and water as a dough for oatcakes or as food for poultry.

leave-o a children's game in which one side hunts out and captures the members of the other.

leb *see* **laib**

leck, leak, lake 1 leak. **2** *of rain* fall in showers.

lecturi, leetera 1 *lecturi sheep-counting* seven. **2** *leetera in children's rhymes* six.

led farm *see* **lead**

ledder, lether a ladder

ledder *see* **leather**

leddy *see* **lady**

ledgit the top of the lower sash of a window *NE*.

lee, lie *verb* **1** lie, tell lies. **2** say something wrong without meaning to.
leesome incredible; shocking *now SW, S*.
lee on tell a lie about, slander.

lee *see* **luif**

leebel *see* **libel**

leeberal liberal.

leebrary a library.

leed, leid 1 a language. **2** a long rambling story; something told over and over again.

leed *see* **leid**

leef *see* **luif**

leefu, leeful *see* **lief**

leek *see* **lyke**

lee lang *see* **lief**

leem *see* **lume**

leemit limit.

leep 1 heat or cook partially. **2** sit lazily by a fire.
leepit 1 warmed up. **2** fond of warmth

and comfort, soft, not hardy.

leepie *see* **lippie**

leerie-la *noun* the call of the cock; a cock. *verb* crow, cry like a cock.

leerup a sharp blow or smack, a lash.

leesh *see* **leash**

leeshence *see* **licence**

leesing *see* **leasing**

leesome¹ **1** pleasant, lovable. **2** *of weather* fine, mild and bright.

    one's leesome lane absolutely alone, on one's own.

leesome² morally or legally permissible; right, just.

leesome *see* **lee**

leet¹, **leat 1** a stack of peats or coal, the size, varying locally and from time to time. **2** a section of an oblong stack of grain or beans.

leet² **1** a list of selected candidates for a post. **2** the prize-winning animals at an agricultural show *SW*.

    long leet a first list of selected candidates to be further selected into a **short leet** the final list of candidates for a post.

leet³ **1** give a sign that one knows or is taking notice; pay attention. **2** make mention, pass on information.

leet *see* **lat**

leetany a long rigmarole *Shetland NE*.

leetera *see* **lecturi**

leeterary literary.

leeve, leve, live live.

    leevin 1 a person, anyone. **2** food. **livin-like** lively, in good health.

    leeve aff live on.

leeze *see* **lease, lief**

left: left fitter *insulting* a Roman Catholic.

    left-hand man one of the two chief supporters of the **standard-bearer** in various **Riding of the Marches** (*see* **ride**) festivals.

leg, laig, leig *now NE noun* a leg. *verb* walk at a quick pace, run.

    tak leg bail run away.

    leg aff set off, leave. **leg on** walk or work energetically or quickly. **lift (a)**

leg 1 move, run, gallop. **2** have unlawful sex. **on (the) leg**, on the move, gadding about. **put legs and arms to** add to or embellish a story. **tak leg(s)** run off, clear out.

legammachie *see* **lagamachie**

leggin *see* **laggin**

leggums leggings *ECentral, S*.

legitim [**ledg**itim] the portion (normally one third or one half) of a deceased parent's (free) **moveable** estate that his or her children are entitled to claim.

leglin, laiglin a wooden bucket used *eg* as a milk pail.

leid, leed, lead [leed, laid] **1** lead, the metal. **2** one of the lead-weights of a pendulum-clock.

    leidie a handmade lead marble or counter for the game of **buttons**.

leid *see* **leed**

leig *see* **leg**

leish, liesh [leesh] active, athletic, supple *SW, S*.

leister [**lees**ter] a pronged spear used (now illegally) for salmon fishing.

lek *see* **like**¹

leme *see* **leam**

lempit, †lampit, lemped, lempeck a limpet.

len, lend, laen *verb* **1** lend. **2** give (a blow). *noun* a loan.

lench, lensh, lainch launch *now Orkney N*.

lenth, length 1 distance; amount: *"this lenth"* as far as this. **2** a person's height.

    at lang lenth, at lenth an lang at last, in the end. **breadth an lenth** one's full length, prone. **gae one's lenth** let oneself go, follow one's feelings as far as on can or dare. **one's lang lenth = breadth and lenth.**

lep *see* **laip, leap**

lerb a lick, a mouthful of liquid *NE*.

less¹: **frae less to mair** from one thing to another.

less² a lease, tenancy.

lest *verb* last. *noun* ability to last. **lestie** lasting.

let *see* **lat**

lether *see* **ledder**

lethy *see* **lady**

letten *see* **lat**

letter: letters *law* a writ or warrant in missive form, latterly mainly one issued by the **High Court of Justiciary** (*see* **justiciary**) or by the **Court of Session** (*see* **session**) under the **signet**.

letters of arrestment *law* a writ to attach property for debt. **letters of inhibition** *law* a warrant prohibiting a debtor from burdening or alienating his **heritage** to the prejudice of his creditor.

lettergae the **precentor** in a church.

leuch, leuchen, leucht *see* **lauch**

leuk, luke, luik, luck, look *verb* 1 look. 2 look at, examine.

noun 1 a look. 2 a look or visit to see or examine something, *often* **a leuk o** *or* **a leuk to.**

leuk the gate o take an interest in; visit. **leuk o(w)er** 1 look after, take care of. 2 pass over, forgive. **leuk ower the door** go outside, especially after an illness. **leuk ower the window** lean out of the window and look out. **not look the road someone is on** take no interest in, ignore. **leuk to** look at. **leuk up** be alive.

leve *see* **leeve**

lew, loo *adjective* lukewarm.

noun a warmth, especially inside a (corn or hay) stack.

lewder, louder, louther, [looder, loother, *NE* **lowder, leeowder]** 1 a wooden lever, a crowbar. 2 a strong, rough stick. 3 a heavy blow.

lewer [like 'lure', or rhymes with 'power'] a lever *SW, S*.

lib[1] 1 castrate (especially farm animals). 2 cut short, damage. 3 remove (growing potatoes) without disturbing the tops.

libel *noun, also* **leebel** *now Orkney* 1 libel; but for Scots legal usage see **defamation**. 2 any piece of writing. 3 *law* a formal statement of the grounds on which a suit or prosecution is brought. 4 *church law* a charge against a person in a church court.

verb, law 1 specify in an indictment; state as grounds for a suit or prosecution. 2 *church law* make a formal charge against.

licence, leeshence 1 licence. 2 permission from a **presbytery** to a divinity student to preach and become a **probationer** (*see* **probation**).

licht[1]**, light** 1 light. 2 *also* **lichtie** the will-o'-the-wisp, (regarded as an omen of death) *NE*. 3 *law* **light** a **servitude** binding one owner of property not to build or plant on it so as to obstruct the light of his neighbour.

†**auld licht, new licht** *church* the moderate or more liberal element (**new licht**) as opposed to the stricter section (**auld licht**) of the **Church of Scotland** (*see* **church**) or (later) of other churches. **between (the) lichts** twilight. **canna see the licht o day to** be blind to the faults of (a person).

licht[2]**, light** *adjective* 1 light, not heavy. 2 dizzy, light-headed. 3 **licht on** not taking too much of. 4 applied to a kind of less alcoholic beer.

noun 1 the light parts of corn seed separated out by winnowing and sifting. 2 **lichts, lights** the lungs (human or animal).

verb 1 light, lighten. 2 make light, lighten, ease. 3 **licht on** set upon, attack; scold.

lichtlie *adverb* lightly. *verb, also* **lichtlifie** make light of, insult.

lichtfit, licht set light-footed, nimble.

lichtsome 1 carefree, cheerful. 2 cheering, pleasant. 3 light on one's feet.

lat licht admit; make known.

lick *noun* 1 a very small amount. 2 a hard blow, **licks** a thrashing. 3 a smart pace, a burst of speed.

adverb with a heavy thud.

lick-penny a greedy or swindling person.

lickery, liquorie liquorice.

lickery stick liquorice root chewed by children as a **sweetie** *WCentral*.

lid 1 one of the halves of a double door,

eg of a **box bed** (*see* **box**). **2** one of the boards of a large book.

lidder *see* **lither**

lie *verb, past participle also* **lien** *now NE* [liyen] **1** be ill in bed. **2** *of the tongue or speech* be still, silent.

noun **1** the act of lying, especially in bed. **2** the place where one lies.

lyin money ready cash. **lying storm** a fall of snow which lies long before melting. **lying time** a period of time worked by an employee either at the beginning of a new job for which he is not immediately paid, or between the closing of the books for the week's work and the payment of wages, payment being kept until the person leaves the job.

lie aff *of a sheepdog* keep at a distance from the sheep. **lie doun** take to one's bed with illness.

lie *see* **lee**

lief, leaf *comparative also* **lour** [loor]: **had (as) lief, had lieffer** would or had rather: *"I'd as lief trust masel".*

loor *taken as verb, with past* **lourd** [loord]: *"I rather lourd it had been mysel."*

lee lang day the whole (long) day. **leefu** kind-hearted, considerate. **(one's) leeful(l) lane** all by one's self.

leeze me (on) I am very fond or pleased with.

lien *see* **lie**

liesh *see* **leish**

life: lifie full of life, lively. **living and life-like** hale and hearty. **liferent** *law* a right to receive till death (or some other specified contingency) the revenue of a property, without the right to dispose of the capital, *corresponding to civil law* usufruct.

lift[1] the sky, the heavens.

lift[2] *verb* **1** *knitting* pick up (stitches). **2** serve (a dish at table). **3** take up or out of the ground (*eg* a crop of corn, potatoes). **4** gather (scythed corn into a sheaf for binding). **5** carry (a corpse) out for burial; start a funeral

procession. **6** mention (especially a person's name). **7** take (a lady) up to dance, lead to the floor. **8** raise (the spirits). **9** get up, stand up and move off *NE*. **10** *of the chest* heave, as when there is difficulty in breathing. **11** collect and carry away (goods or persons), drive (animals) to market. **12** *of a sheepdog* round up (sheep) and move them forward. **13** collect (money, rents etc). **14** collect or gather. **15** take up or cash (money etc), withdraw (money from a bank). **16** †steal (cattle), take by a raid. **17** *of the police* arrest, take into custody.

noun **1** the act of lifting, *eg* in carrying a corpse for a funeral. **2** help, encouragement. **3** the amount of fish, that can be lifted aboard by hand in the net. **4** a rising swell in the sea. **5** a load, burden; a large amount. **6** a collection, a whip-round. **7** a theft; what is stolen. **8** the rounding-up of sheep by a sheepdog before penning.

gie a lift to, lend a lift to give a helping hand to, encourage. **lift and lay** pick things up and lay them down again. **lift one's hand (to)** hit, strike. **lift one's lines** *in the Presbyterian churches* leave a certain congregation.

lig[1] lie, rest.

lig[2] chatter, talk, gossip.

liggat a self-closing (farm) gate *SW*.

light *see* **licht**[1], **licht**[2]

like[1], **lik, lek** *Shetland Caithness adjective, comparative* **liker, mair liker 1** like. **2 liker** more apt, more appropriate: *"a worset goon's the liker you".* **3** likely, probable: *"it's like I'll lay my banes here".* **4** likely to, apparently on the point of: *"they are like to quarrel".*

adverb **1** like. **2** so to speak, as it were: *"juist for the day like".* **3** likely, probably: *"we'll ken very like in the course of a week".* **4** as if about (to do something): *"greeting like to break her heart".*

noun **1** like. **2 the like** that very thing,

indeed; **no the like** nothing of the sort, not at all: *"ye're sleepin - I'm no the like."*

verb **be liken to** be likely or about to, look like doing or being: *"I was lyken to dee".*

likely, likly *now NE adjective* **1** likely. **2** good-looking, handsome. **3** capable or competent in manner; suitable. *adverb* probably. *noun* likelihood, probability, chance. **liken with, liken to** associate (a person) with (another person or thing) by repute, think of in connection with. **not to leave a body in the likeness o a dog** call someone everything that is bad.

be like one's meat look well-fed. **be like onesel 1** be unchanged in appearance. **2** act up to one's reputation.

like² love, have a strong affection for (especially a person of the opposite sex).

like *see* **lyke**

lilt *verb* **1** sing in a low clear voice, sweetly, cheerfully; sing a tune without the words. **2** move in a sprightly way, skip, dance.
noun **1** a lively, sweet or rhythmical song; the tune. **2** a rhythm (in music or speech).

lily a narcissus, especially the common daffodil or pheasant's eye varieties, often **white lily, yellow lily.**

lime mortar, cement: **stone and lime** masonry.

limmer 1 *often of Border robbers* a rascal, scoundrel. **2** *of a mischievous child* a rascal. **3** a loose woman; a man's mistress; a whore. **4** general term of contempt for a woman, a female animal or thing.

lin pause, rest, stop *now Shetland Orkney*.

lin *see* **linn¹, linn²**

line¹ 1 *marbles* a straight line scored on the ground. **2** a line of a psalm read or sung by the **precentor** before being sung by the congregation. **3** a line of writing; any piece of written autho-

rization: **doctor's line** one stating that one is unfit for work. **4 lines** a certificate of church-membership; *see* **lift².** **5** an account with a shop; a bill: *"pit it on the line".* **6** a prescription. **7** a note requesting or explaining a child's absence from school etc. **8** a shopping list. **9** a betting slip.

liner a line-fishing boat. **liney** *marbles* a game played with a **line** (1).

line² beat, thrash *N*.

line someone's luif grease someone's palm, bribe.

linens 1 linen clothes, one's shirts or undergarments *now Shetland*. **2** a shroud.

ling 1 ling, heather. **2** harestail cottongrass; deer-grass.

lingel¹, lingan the waxed thread used by shoemakers.

lingel-backit having a long weak limp back. **lingel-en(d)** the tip of the **lingel¹.**

lingel² 1 a length of rope or cord, *eg* for hobbling an animal. **2** any strap, thong or looped cord. **3** anything long, long-drawn-out and flabby; a rigmarole; a tall lanky person *N*.

linget the seed of flax, linseed.

lingie [linggie] a long rambling story, rigmarole.

lingit thin, lean.

link¹ *noun* **1** a link in the chain from which the pot-hook hung in the fireplace. **2** a joint of the body, especially in the backbone. **3** a lock of hair, a curl. **4 links** a string of sausages or black puddings. **5 links** loops of a winding stream or river, the land enclosed by such: *"Links of Forth".*
verb **1** go arm in arm; give one's arm to. **2** place (a pot) on or take (it) off the pot-hook on the **links.**

link² 1 move fast or easily, trip along *now NE, Perth*. **2** skip, dance *NE*. **3** work vigorously.

linkie a deceitful person; a rogue.

links 1 a stretch of open rolling ground covered with grass or gorse, usually near the seashore. **2** a golf-course (originally on seaside **links**) as at St Andrews.

linn¹, lin 1 a waterfall. **2** a deep and narrow gorge *SW, S*.

linn², lin the pool below a waterfall.

lint 1 a flax plant. **2** flax being prepared for spinning. **3** linen thread, especially that used by shoemakers.

lint-white *of hair* white as flax, flaxen-blond.

lintel 1 a mantelpiece. **2** the threshold of a door.

lintie 1 a linnet. **2** a lively merry girl.

lintwhite a linnet.

lip *noun* the edge of a stream, pool etc.
verb **1** touch with the lips, taste. **2** break, notch or chip (a blade).

lippin-fou, lip-fou full to the brim, overflowing.

lippen 1 trust, depend on. **2** expect confidently, count on.

lipper¹ *of water* ripple, be ruffled. **2** be full almost to overflowing.

lipper², lyper *Orkney Caithness NE* a large festering sore or mass of sores, a scab *now Caithness*.

lippie, leepie *NE* **1** a dry measure varying in weight according to district and commodity, *latterly* $1\frac{3}{4}$ lbs for goods sold by weight and used especially for oats, barley, and potatoes (see p 358). **2** a (wooden, box-shaped) measure of this size *now N*.

liquorie *see* **lickery**

lire, lyre a slice of meat from the shoulder.

lirk¹, lurk 1 a crease, rumple or fold; a wrinkle. **2** a fold of the body, a joint. **3** a fold or hollow in a hill, a ravine. **4** an unusual trait of character, a mental twist *now NE*.

lirk² lurk *NE*.

lisk the groin.

liss *of pain etc* stop, lessen *now Ulster*.

list¹ desire *now Caithness*.

list² enlist (as a soldier).

lit dye, colour, tinge now Shetland Caithness.

lith 1 a joint in a finger or toe, a small

part of the body. **2** one of the divisions of an orange, onion etc. **3** a joint, slice, segment.

lithe, lythe, lyde [liyth, liyd] *adjective* **1** *of a place etc* calm, sheltered, snug. **2** *of persons etc* gentle, kindly *NE*.
noun shelter, protection from the weather; a sheltered spot.
verb **1** shelter from weather *now NE*. **2** thicken (soup, porridge etc) with oatmeal etc *now NE*. **lithocks** [liythocks] a kind of gruel made from fine oatmeal and buttermilk.

lither, †**lidder** lazy, idle; slack *now SW*.

little: littlin, little ane a child.

little-boukit 1 small in body or bulk, shrunken. **2** of little importance, insignificant *NE*. **little folk(s)** the fairies. **little house** a water-closet, lavatory.

liv *see* **luif**

live *see* **leeve**

liver [livver] unload (a ship) *now N, Hebrides*.

liverock *see* **laverock**

lo *see* **luve**

load *see* **laid**

loaf *see* **laif**

loan, lone 1 *also* **loaning** a grassy (cattle-) track through arable land, also used as pasture. **2** the part of farm ground or a roadway which leads to the house.

lobster *see* **lapster**

location *law* the act of hiring out or renting.

loch, †**louch 1** a lake, pond (applied to all natural lakes in Scotland, except the Lake of Menteith, Perthshire); a **sea-loch** (*see* **sea**). **2** a small pool or puddle.

Lochaber axe a kind of long-handled battle-axe; now only ceremonial arms carried by the attendants of Edinburgh's **Lord Provost** (*see* **provost**).

lochan a little **loch.**

Lochgelly a leather strap for punishing school children, manufactured in Lochgelly, Fife.

lock, lowk a (small) quantity, a handful, a bundle, a pinch (of meal, salt etc).

lockfast shut and locked, under lock and key.

lodomy laudanum *now NE.*

loft *see* **laft**

logan a collection *eg* of coins, marbles (scattered for children to scramble for) *NE.*

loit, lyte *verb* defecate; vomit.

noun a (liquid) mass of something filthy or disgusting; a lump of faeces.

London: Lon(d)oners, londies a skipping game with two ropes *Shetland NE.*

London bun a glazed bun with currants and orange peel, sprinkled with crystallized sugar.

lone *see* **lane²**, **loan**

long *see* **lang**

loo *see* **lew**, **luve**

lood *see* **loud**

looder *see* **lowder**

loof *see* **luif**

loog *see* **lug**

look *see* **leuk**

loom *see* **lume**

loon *see* **loun**

loonder *see* **lounder**

loop 1 *knitting* a stitch. **2** any natural bend etc, *eg* the winding of a river.

loopie deceitful, crafty.

loor *see* **lief**

loorach 1 something tattered or trailing. **2** an untidy person.

loory *see* **loury**

loose *see* **lowse**

loose *see* **louse**

loot *see* **lat**, **lout**

loove *see* **luve**

lopper *see* **lapper¹**

lord a judge of the **Court of Session** (*see* **session**).

Lord Advocate the principal law officer of the Crown in Scotland. **Lord Clerk Register** *see* **register**. **Lord High Commissioner** the representative of the sovereign in the **General Assembly** of the **Church of Scotland** (*see* **church**). **Lord Justice Clerk** *see* **justice**. **Lord Lyon (King of Arms)**, *or (not officially*

approved) **Lord Lyon King at Arms** the chief officer of arms of Scotland and head of the **Lyon Court** (*see* **Lyon**). **Lord Ordinary** one of the judges (now 16 in number) of the **Court of Session** (*see* **session**), who sit on cases of first instance in the **Outer House** (*see* **outer**). **Lord President** the president of the **Court of Session** (*see* **session**) and head of the Scottish judiciary. **Lord Provost** courtesy title given to the **provosts** of Edinburgh, Glasgow, Aberdeen, Dundee, Perth. **Lord Rector** = **rector** 1.

Lords of council and session the formal collective designation of the judges of the **Court of Session** (*see* **session**).

†**lorimer** a maker of the metal parts of a horse's harness.

losh *exclamation* Lord!

loss lose.

Lothian, Lowden [-ow- as in 'cow']: **Lothian (Region)** a region formed from the former counties of the City of Edinburgh, East Lothian, Midlothian and West Lothian.

The Lothians name for the (former) counties of East Lothian, Midlothian and West Lothian (with or without the City of Edinburgh).

louch *see* **loch**, **loutch**

louchter *see* **lachter²**

loud, lood loud.

loud out out loud, in a loud voice. **loudspoken** loud-voiced.

louder *see* **lewder**

loun [-oo-], **loon 1** a boy, youth, a fellow, chap, lad. **2** a male child, a son, a baby boy. **3** a young farm-worker; *among workmen* a boy who does the odd jobs. **4** a rogue, rascal. **5** †a sexually immoral person, especially a woman. **6** nickname for a native of Forfar *N.* **7 The Loons** nickname for Forfar Athletic football team.

loun *see* **lown**

lounder, loonder, lunner 1 hit with heavy blows. **2** work with energy and speed at.

loup *see* **lowp**

lour, lourd *see* **lief**

loury, loory *of the sky* dull, overcast, threatening rain.

louse, loose [rhymes with 'goose'] a louse. **lous(e)y arnut** an earth-nut.

lout, loot [rhymes with 'soot'] bend the body, stoop, duck; bow.
lout-shouthered round-shouldered.

loutch, louch [lootch] stoop, slouch.

louther *see* **lewder**

lovage, lovich lavish.

lovanentie dear me!, good gracious!

lovich *see* **lovage**

low [rhymes with 'cow'] *noun* **1** a flame. **2** fire; a fire indoors or out, a blaze. **3** a glow, as of fire etc or of feeling.
verb **1** burn with a bright flame, blaze. **2** gleam, glow, flare. **3** be blazing with love, excitement etc.

low *see* **laich**

lowden [-ow- as in 'cow'] *of sound, the wind etc* lessen, quieten, die down.

Lowden *see* **Lothian**

lowder, lyowder [l(ee)owder], **looder** **1** loiter, idle. **2** walk heavily as if weary, plod; move clumsily or lazily.

lowk *see* **lock**

lowland *see* **lawland**

lowmons *see* **lyomons**

lown, loun [rhymes with 'down'] *adjective* **1** *of the wind* lowered, calm; *of weather* calm, still; *of a place* sheltered, snug. **2** *of places etc* peaceful, undisturbed. **3** *of people* subdued, restrained; *of sounds* quiet, hushed.
noun **1** a peaceful sheltered spot. **2** calm, unclouded weather. **3** peace, quietness.

lowp [-ow- as in 'cow'], **loup, lup** *Shetland Orkney verb* **1** leap, spring. **2** *of water* cascade, roll. **3** spring to one's feet, spring to attention. **4** start or jump with pain, surprise, shock. **5** dance, hop about. **6** walk with a long springing step, bound. **7** *of the heart, blood etc* throb, race. **8** *of things* spring or fly

(in some direction); pop out of. **9** *of frost* thaw, break *N*.
noun **1** a leap, jump, spring. **2** a throb, start. **3** a place where a river is crossed; a shelf in a river-bed over which fish may leap up-river.

lowpin ill a disease of sheep in which they leap in the air.

lowp aff **1** get off a horse. **2** change the subject abruptly. **lowp-(the-)coonter** contemptuous term for a male shop-assistant. **lowp the cuddy** leap-frog. **lowp on** get on (a horse). **lowp up** raise one's price suddenly when making a bargain. **lowp up at** get very angry at.

lowse [-ow- as in 'cow'], **loose** *adjective* **1** loose. **2** immoral; dishonest, lawless. **3** not tied or fastened together. **4** *of clothes* unfastened, loose-fitting. **5** *of the weather* unsettled.
adverb loose.
verb **1** loose. **2** unbind (an animal) from a stall etc, unyoke (a horse from a plough etc); stop ploughing. **3** stop work or other activity. **4** cut or undo the band of a sheaf of corn before feeding it into a threshing mill. **5** become loose or free, become unfastened. **6** let oneself go, explode (in anger at someone). **7** *of frost etc* thaw *now Shetland*.

lowsed **1** freed of the day's work. **2** tired, weary. **lowsen** loosen. **lowsin loft** the loft onto which sheaves are thrown for threshing. **lowsin time** time to stop work, the end of the working day.

lowse-fittit not bound to one place by one's work etc, free to travel.

lozen **1** †a lozenge. **2** a pane of glass (originally a small diamond-shaped one).

lozened *NE* **1** with a diamond pattern, crisscrossed. **2** *of a window* glazed.

lozenger a lozenge, a flavoured sweet.

lubbard a lout.

luce [-u- as -ui- in 'guid'], **luss** scurf, dandruff, loose dead skin.

lucht *see* **lauch**

luchter *see* **lachter**[2]

luck *noun* a piece of luck or good fortune;

a useful or valuable object come upon by chance *now Shetland Orkney*.

verb **1** fare, prosper: *"ill-luckit"*. **2** have good fortune; succeed.

luckie *adjective* full, more than the standard amount. *noun* **1** *familiar, of an elderly woman* old Mrs ..: *"Luckie Broon"*. **2** a midwife. **3** a landlady, hostess of a tavern *now NE*. **4** a grandmother *now NE*. **lucky box** a child's savings-bank. **lucky dad(d)ie** a grandfather *now NE*. **lucky minnie** a grandmother. **lucky pock** a lucky bag, lucky dip.

luck('s) penny a sum of money given for luck.

luck *see* **leuk**

lucken 1 *of the hand or foot* closed tight, clenched. **2** *of cabbages etc* having a firm heart. **3** *of a fish* gutted, but not split right down to the tail.

†**luckenbooth** a booth or covered stall which could be locked up, common in medieval Scottish towns. **luckenbooth brooch** a heart-shaped silver brooch originally used as a love token.

lufe *see* **luve**

lug, loog *Caithness* **1** an ear. **2** a part of something which sticks out, *eg* a flap of a cap or bonnet; a handle of a cup, bowl etc; a flap of a shoe; a spike etc on a tool, *eg* a spade (*now NE*); a corner of a herring-net (*NE*); one of the wings on a wing-chair; one of the hand grips at the top of a full sack; part of the muzzle of a plough. **3** *of a fish* a side fin and surrounding flesh. **4** a chimney corner.

luggie 1 a small wooden (porridge) bowl with one or two handles. **2** a similar but larger container used especially as a milking-pail. **luggit** having a lug or **lugs**: *"lang-luggit"*.

lug-chair a wing-chair. **lug-mark 1** an earmark, especially on a sheep. **2** any recognizable mark.

at one's lug at one's side, close by. **hae the wrang soo by the lug** have hit on the wrong person or thing; have the wrong end of the stick. **lay one's lug** bet (that ..). **lay one's lug in(to)** eat or drink heartily. **(out) ower the lugs** over head and ears, completely absorbed.

luif, loof, liv *now NE*, **leef, lee** *mainly NE* **1** the palm of the hand. **2** the paw, foot or hoof on an animal *now SW*.

luiffie a punishment stroke on the hand.

aff luif offhand. **crack luifs** shake hands in friendship.

luik *see* **leuk**

luit *see* **lat**

luit, luitten *see* **lat**

luke *see* **leuk**

lum 1 a chimney. **2** in old houses, an opening in the roof, for light, air and the escape of smoke. **3** the whole chimney and fireplace, chimney corner and surroundings. **4** the funnel of a steamship or locomotive. **5** a long passage through a cliff; a rock chimney. **6** *also* **lum hat** a tall silk hat, a top-hat.

lume, loom, leem *Caithness NE* **1** an instrument or tool of any kind. **2** an open container, a tub, bowl. **3** a loom, a weaving-loom.

lump a lot, a large amount.

lunk *of weather* close, sultry.

lunkie a hole in a wall, made to allow sheep to pass through, or a stream to flow under.

lunner *see* **lounder**

lunt[1] *noun* **1** a match, a light. **2** a column of fire and smoke, a puff of smoke or steam etc.

verb catch fire, burn, blaze; smoke, give out puffs of smoke, smoke (a pipe).

lunt[2] walk with a springy step, walk briskly.

lup *see* **lowp**

luppen *see* **leap**

lurdan 1 †*of a man* a villain, a rogue, rascal. **2** *of a woman* a slut.

lure the udder of a cow or other animal.

lurk *see* **lirk**[1]

luss *see* **luce**

luve, lufe, †loove, lo, loo love.
  lovie a sweetheart, lover; *child's word* a hug. **loosome** lovable, beautiful.
  love-darg a piece of work or a service done without payment out of friendliness.
lyaag *see* **laig**
lyart [liyart] **1** *of the hair* streaked with white, silver. **2** multi-coloured.
lyde *see* **lithe**
lyin(g) *see* **lie**
lyke, like, leek *Shetland Orkney N* **1** a corpse, an unburied body. **2** a watch kept over a corpse until burial, a wake.
lyowder *see* **lowder**
lyomons [l(ee)oamons), **lowmons** legs *NE*.
Lyon the chief officer of arms of Scotland, the **Lord Lyon King of Arms** (*see* **lord**). **Lyon Court** the Court of Heralds in Scotland. **Lyon Clerk** the Clerk of that Court.
lyper *see* **lipper**[2]
lyre *see* **lire**
lyte *see* **loit**
lythe a pollack.
lythe *see* **lithe**

M

ma *see* my

maa *see* mae², maw¹, maw²

Mac familiar form of address to a man, usually a stranger (not necessarily a Scotsman).

macallum a vanilla ice cream flavoured with raspberry juice.

MacClarty: Mrs MacClarty name for a dirty slovenly housewife.

macer *law* an official serving as usher in a court of law etc, who keeps order, acts as messenger etc.

machair, machar [-ch- as in 'loch'] **1** a stretch of low-lying land next to the sand of the seashore *Hebrides*. **2 the Machairs** the land bordering the Solway Firth or Luce Bay.

machine 1 a horse-drawn passenger vehicle. **2** a motor car.

macht *see* maucht

mack neat, tidy.

Mackay: the real Mackay the genuine article, the true original; a brand of whisky so-named.

mackerel: as clean as a mackerel completely, effectively, entirely.

mad extremely: *"mad keen"*.

mad for extremely eager for.

mad *see* maud

madderam, madrim madness, frantic rage, tantrums; boisterous fun, hilarity *mainly Shetland Orkney*.

made *see* mak

mae¹ [may] more.

be at ane mae wi't be at the end of one's tether; be at the point of death *S*.

mae² [rhymes with 'may' or 'yeah'], **maa** [ma] *of sheep etc* bleat.

sheepie mae child's word for a sheep.

magdum *see* makdom

mager *see* maugre

magg †*verb, of coal carters* pilfer coal for resale.

noun **maggs** a tip, an extra payment for services outside regular duties *ECentral*.

maggie a magpie.

maggie *see* Meg

maggot a whim, fancy, bee in one's bonnet.

maggotive *NE*, **maggoty** perverse, changeable.

magink [-g- as in 'get'] a queer-looking object or creature.

magirkie [majirkie] a kind of cap which also protects the throat.

magistrate title for a **provost** or **bailie** of a **burgh** as having administrative and judicial powers; also applied to stipendiary magistrates (but not to justices of the peace).

magnum bonum a bottle containing two quarts (2.27 litres) of wine or spirits.

magowk make an April fool of.

magowk's day April-fool's day *WCentral SW*.

magre *see* maugre

Mahoun [mahoon] name for the Devil.

maid: auld maid's bairn *proverb* an improbably well-behaved child which a spinster has in mind when criticizing the children of others.

maid *see* maithe

maiden 1 an unmarried heiress; the eldest or only daughter of a landowner or farmer *now NE*. **2** the last handful of corn cut in the harvest-field.

maig, meg *noun* **1** a large clumsy hand, a paw. **2** the flipper of a seal *Shetland Orkney Caithness*.

verb spoil by over-handling *S*.

maik, make a halfpenny.

as daft as a maik watch completely silly.

mail¹, male rent.

mailing a tenant farm; the rent paid for such.

mail², **airn mail**, **irne mail** a reddish stain on cloth, especially that caused by iron oxide.

mail³ a travelling bag, a trunk.

maill *see* **mell²**

main 1 great of its kind *now Orkney Caithness*. **2** thoroughly bad, out and out *Angus Fife: "She was a main deil".* **3** exceedingly, very: *"that was main honest".*

mainly very.

main coal *mining* the principal or best seam of coal. **main door** a door giving access only to a private house, as opposed to a common entrance to a block of flats. **main door flat, main door (house)** a ground-floor flat of a block of flats, which has a door to itself direct from the street.

†**man of main** *in poetry, latterly only in ballads* a mighty man.

mainner, menner *NE* manner.

mains 1 the home farm of an estate. **2** as part of a farm name: *"the Mains of Shaws", "Morton Mains".* **3** name for the farmer of a **mains** *NE*. **4** the outbuildings of a farm.

mair, more 1 more. **2** larger in physical size. **3** *with a comparative: "mair aulder", "mair nearer".*

mair at(t)our besides. **the mair** although, in spite of the fact that. **the mair by token, the mair for token 1** moreover, in addition. **2** especially, in particular. **tae the mair mean taikin** to be more precise, more particularly or especially *NE*. **maister and mair, mistress and mair** a domineering master or mistress, one with the whip hand.

mair *see* **muir**

Mairch, Merch (the month of) March.

mairch *see* **march**

mairriage, marriage, merr(i)age 1 marriage. **2** a large gathering of birds, especially rooks. **3** **mairriage braws** wedding clothes. **mairriage lintel, mairriage stone** the lintel stone of a door bearing the initials and date of marriage of a couple who have set up house there.

mairry, merry marry.

mairt *see* **mart¹**, **mart²**

Mairtimas *see* **Martinmas**

mairtin a (house) martin.

mairtyr, martyr *noun* **1** a martyr. **2** a disgusting mess, a dirty confusion *N.* *verb* **1** martyr. **2** hurt or wound severely *now Shetland*. **3** cover with dirt, spatter with something nasty or sticky *now N.*

maise, mease 1 a large coarse basket slung from a pack-saddle to carry peats etc *Shetland Orkney*. **2** a measure, usually of fish, especially herring, = five hundred, later usually the long hundred of 120 (*see* **hunder** *noun* 3) *mainly SW.*

maisie *see* **Mey**

maisles, mizzles *now NE, ECentral* measles.

maist¹ *adjective* **1** most. **2** *of people* chief, most powerful, greatest. **3** *of things* chief, principal.

adverb **1** most. **2** for the most part, mostly.

maist han almost entirely *Shetland NE.* **maistlins** almost, nearly. **maistly 1** most of all, especially. **2** almost, nearly.

maist² almost.

maister¹, master 1 a master. **2** the landlord of a tenant. **3** a schoolmaster; *latterly especially* **the maister** the only or principal teacher in a small rural community. **4 Master** title for the male heir of some Scottish noble or landed families.

maisterfu(l) powerful, big, strong.

maister², master stale urine, used mainly as a detergent.

mait *see* **meat**

maithe, maid a maggot; an egg or grub of a bluebottle.

maitter, matter matter.

make (a) maitter make a fuss. **there is no (muckle) maitter** it doesn't (much) matter. **to little maitter** to little purpose, with small advantage *now Shetland Angus.*

major-mindit haughty, proud, high-minded *now ECentral S.*

mak, make *verb, past tense also* **meed, mak(k)it 1** make. **2** matter, be important *now N: "it disna mak a fig"*. **3** prepare (ground) for sowing. **4** *of food or drink in the process of cooking* thicken, set, infuse. **5** *of dung* mature. **6** *of the weather* produce or threaten: *"it maks rain"*.
noun make, form, shape.

made distressed, upset *eg* because of overwork or worry *NE.* **made diet** a cooked meal *Shetland NE.* **made lee** a deliberate lie. **made tie** a man's bow-tie sold with the bow ready tied. **sair made** hard put to it, sorely harassed, oppressed *Shetland Orkney N.* **makar** a poet especially literary, referring to one of the 15th and early 16th century Scots poets.

mak a better o improve upon, do better: *"we canna mak a better o't I suppose"*. **mak by 1** overtake, be better than. **2** make money or gain advantage by, profit by *Orkney NE.* **mak ceremony** stand on ceremony, fuss. **mak doon 1** dilute the strength of (spirits). **2** prepare (a bed) by turning down the bedclothes. **3** grind, reduce into smaller fragments. **makdoon** a garment altered to suit a smaller wearer. **mak for 1** prepare for, be on the point of. **2** *of weather* show signs of, 'look like': *"it's makin for snaw"*. **mak into** make or force one's way into. **mak in wi** curry favour or ingratiate oneself with *now Shetland Caithness.* **mak or meddle, mak or mell** interfere, meddle. **mak naething o it** *of an ill person* fail to show signs of improvement. **mak o** fuss over, make much of. **mak on** pretend. **mak-on** a pretence, humbug; an imposter *Shetland NE.* **mak out 1** achieve successfully, accomplish, manage: *"it is terrible steep to climb but we made it out"*. **2** make a living, keep going, succeed. **3** make up (weight). **mak a prayer**

say or recite a prayer. **mak to, mak till** go towards. **mak up 1** make rich, establish successfully in life. **2 mak it up** plan, contrive, arrange: *"we made it up to meet him"*; plan to get married: *"that couple - I doot they're makin't up"*. **3** make (a bed). **mak up for = mak for 2** *Orkney NE.* **mak up on** overtake, catch up with. **mak way** set about, prepare *Shetland Orkney NE.*

makdom, magdum *Shetland Orkney* a person's form, shape or build.

make, mak the equal or peer of a person or thing.

makit *see* **mak**

make *see* **maik**

makkit *see* **mak**

malafooster [malafooster] destroy, ruin.

†**malagrugrous** [malagroogous] grim, gloomy.

malagruize *NE* [malagrooze] **1** disarrange, spoil. **2** injure, hurt, punish with physical violence.

male *see* **mail**[1], **meal**[1], **meal**[2]

†**malison** curse.

malkin *see* **maukin**

mallduck, mallimoke a fulmar *Shetland Orkney.*

malmy *see* **maumie**

malt *see* **maut**

mam child's word for mother.

    mammie 1 mother. **2** †a wet-nurse. **mammie-keekie** a spoilt child *SW, S.*

mamet *see* **moment**

man, maun 1 a man. **2** a husband. **3** used to show surprise, displeasure or irony: *"Maun, Will, I'm dumfounert"*. **4 min, mon** as an emphatic exclamation: *"Hey, mon!, he called to Rab"*.

    mannie 1 a little man. **2** affectionate term for a small boy. **3** contemptuous term for an adult. **4** a skipper *NE.* **5** the one who is 'it' in a game *NE.*

    man-big adult, grown to manhood. **man body** an adult man, a man as opposed to a woman. **man-grown = man-big. man-keeper 1** a newt or water-lizard *mainly SW, Ulster.* **2** a common

lizard *SW, S, Ulster*. **man-length** =
man-big. man-muckle = **man-big**
S.**menfolk** men; the men of a particular
family or the male workers on a farm.
**the Auld Man, the bad man, the black
man** the Devil. **man of business** a
lawyer. **be man of one's meat** have a
healthy appetite and digestion.

manage *see* **manish**

mane, mean *noun* **1** a moan. **2** a voiced
complaint, grievance, grouse. **3** any
mournful sound.
verb **1** mourn, lament. **2** indicate pain
or injury by flinching, or by osten-
tatiously nursing (the affected part).
3 pity or show sympathy towards (a
person or his misfortune). **4** moan,
utter a mournful sound *now ECentral*.
Deil mane ye Devil take you. **mak (a)
mane 1** lament, mourn. **2** complain,
grumble. **mak mane for** show sympathy
towards: *"there's nae mane made for
me, tho' I drap doon"*. **to mane** to be
pitied: *"they're no to mean"*.

man *see* **maun**[1], **maun**[2]

mand *see* **maun**[3]

mang be extremely eager or anxious, long
NE.

manish, manage 1 manage. **2** succeed in
reaching: *"Did you manage Glasgow
despite the snow?"*.

mankit mutilated, maimed.

manse the house provided for the parish
minister.
a son *or* **daughter of the manse** a son *or*
daughter of a Presbyterian **minister**.

mansworn *now literary* forsworn, per-
jured.

mant, maunt (have) a speech impediment,
stammer, stutter.

mantie-maker a dressmaker.

many *see* **monie**

map nibble with twitching of the lips, as
a rabbit does.
mappie, map-map 1 pet name for a rabbit. **2** call to a rabbit. **mappie('s)-mou(s)**
name for various plants especially of
the figwort family, which have blos-

soms in the shape of a rabbit's mouth.

mappit stupid, thick-headed; exhausted,
worn out *NE, ECentral*.

mar, mer 1 mar. **2** obstruct, intercept,
stop. **3** confuse, perplex: *"A'm no
muckle marred"*.

marackle *see* **miracle**

march, merch, mairch *noun* **1 marches**
marches, a boundary or frontier. **2** the
Anglo-Scottish Border. **3** a boundary
(-line): *"march dyke", "march stane"*.
verb **1** have a common boundary
(with): *"this is where my land marches
with his"*. **2** border, form the boundary
of *now NE*: *"the same hedge marched
the two estates."* **3** settle and mark the
boundary of (land etc); fix and mark
(a boundary): *"the lots are distinctly
marched and measured"*.
march bauk a strip of land dividing two
properties.
riding of the marches *see* **ride.**

mardle a large number, a crowd *NE*.

mare *see* **mear**

margh *see* **mergh**

mark, merk *now S noun* **1** a mark. **2** †an
insensitive spot supposedly placed on
the body of a witch by the Devil as a
mark of his possession.
verb **1** mark. **2** note down. **3** take aim.
marked notable, distinguished.
mark stane a stone marking a boundary.

mark *see* **merk, mirk**

market *see* **mercat**

marl 1 a mottle, a mottled or veined pattern. **2 mirls** measles *NE*.
marlie, mirlie mottled or variegated in
pattern.
marled, mirled chequered, variegated,
mottled, streaked.

marmaid a mermaid.
marmaid's purse, marmaiden's purse
the egg-case of a ray *Shetland Orkney
Ulster*.

maroonjous [maroonjes] wild, obstreper-
ous; surly, obstinate *mainly NE*.

Maroons nickname for **Heart of Midlo-**

thian (*see* **hert**) football team.

marriage *see* **mairriage**

marrot a guillemot; a razorbill.

marrow, morrow *noun* 1 a comrade, companion. 2 a marriage-partner, spouse. 3 another of the same kind, *eg* one of a pair: *"a pair o boots that wisnae marrows"*. 4 a match, equal: *"I've never seen his marrow"*.
verb 1 enter into partnership, combine. 2 **marrow wi** marry. 3 match, equal.
marrowless 1 matchless, unequalled now *ECentral*. 2 *of gloves etc* odd, not matching. 3 unmarried now *Angus*.

mart[1], **mairt** 1 a market. 2 a building used for agricultural auctions; the periodical sales themselves.

mart[2], **mairt, mert** 1 an ox or cow fattened for slaughter now *Shetland N*. 2 any other animal or bird which is to be salted or dried for winter meat. 3 a clumsy, inactive person now *NE*.

Martinmas, Mairtimas, Mertimass the feast of St Martin, 11 November; a Scottish quarter day, either 11 or 28 November depending on the context.

martyr *see* **mairtyr**

maschle, meeschle a mixture, muddle, mess *NE*.

masel(l) *see* **mysel**

mash[1] a heavy two-faced hammer.
†**mashie** a golf-club corresponding to the No 5 iron.

mash[2] mesh (of a net).

mashlum mixed grains (and pulses) grown and ground together.

mask[1] *verb* 1 mash (malt); brew (ale etc) now *Orkney*. 2 make or infuse (tea). 3 *of the tea* brew.
noun a brew especially of tea now *Shetland Angus*.
maskin pot a teapot.

mask[2] *noun* mesh of a net *Shetland Orkney N*.
verb catch in a net *Shetland Orkney Caithness*.

mass: massie bumptious, proud. **mawsie** mainly *NE*, *adjective* warm, thick,

comfortable. *noun* a warm woollen jersey etc.

massacker, misacker [masacker] *noun* 1 a massacre. 2 severe injury; destruction mainly *Shetland NE*.
verb 1 massacre. 2 maul, bruise, beat (a person). 3 spoil (something) by rough treatment.

†**massymore** the dungeon of a castle.

mast net (herring).

master *see* **maister**[1], **maister**[2]

mat a thick bedcover.

mat *see* **mote**[3]

match a bout or fit of ..: *"a greetin match"*.

mate *see* **meat**

matfull a sexually mature herring.

matter *see* **maitter**

mattie, matkie a young female herring with the roe not fully developed now *Shetland NE*.

mauch *see* **mauk, moch**[2]

mauchle botch; act or work clumsily now *SW*.

maucht, mought, macht [-ch-, -gh- as -ch in 'loch'] 1 ability, operative power, capacity. 2 physical strength.
mauchtless, mauchless feeble, powerless.

maud, mad a checked **plaid** used as a bedcovering or worn by shepherds mainly *S*.

maugre, magre, mager [mawger, mager] act in despite of; master, spite *NE*.
magerful domineering, wilful mainly *NE*.

mauk, mauch a maggot.
maukie maggoty; filthy. **maukit** 1 *especially of sheep* infested with maggots. 2 filthy *WCentral*. 3 exhausted *S*.
mauk flee a bluebottle.

maukin, malkin 1 a hare. 2 an awkward, half-grown girl; a young servant.

maumie, malmy 1 *of fruit etc* ripe, mellow. 2 *of a liquid* thick and smooth. 3 *of weather* soft, mild. 4 mellow, pleasant.

maun[1], **man** 1 must. 2 *missing out go etc*: *"I maun awa in"*.

maun-be an unavoidable necessity.

maun², **man 1** manage, succeed *now SW*. **2** master, control *now Shetland*.

maun³, **mand 1** a basket made of wicker or wooden slats. **2** a platter for oatcakes, usually made of wooden slats *NE*.

maun *see* **man**

maunt *see* **mant**

maut, **malt 1** malt. **2** †ale, whisky. **3** = **malt whisky**.

   mautman a maltster. **malt whisky** whisky distilled from malted barley in a pot-still, as opposed to a blended whisky (made mainly from grain).

   the maut's abune the meal he's drunk. **meal and maut** food and drink *now NE*.

mavis, **mavie** a song-thrush.

maw¹, **maa** *Shetland Orkney S verb, past tense* **mawit**, **meuw** *SW, S, past participle* **mawn**, cut (hay etc) with a scythe.

maw², **maa** *Shetland Orkney* a seagull, *eg* the common gull, herring gull.

   keep your ain fish guts for your ain sea maws charity begins at home *now NE*.

maw³ child's word for mother.

maw⁴ mew like a cat.

mawn *see* **maw¹**

mawsie *see* **mass**

maxie a serious error in a Latin translation, resulting in the highest deduction of marks *NE*.

may *verb, past tense* **micht**, **mith** *NE* may.

maybe, **mebby**, **mibby** *adverb* **1** perhaps, possibly. **2** *of quantity or measurement* approximately: *"maybe half a mile"*. **3** *to add emphasis* then: *"what do you think you're doing, maybe!"*

   noun a possibility: *"a maybe is not aye a honey bee"*.

   maybe aye and maybe hooch aye perhaps it was or perhaps it wasn't, perhaps yes perhaps no.

May *see* **Mey**

May gowan *see* **gowan**

maze amaze *S*.

meaddie, **meadow** *see* **meedow**

meal¹, **male** *noun* meal, especially oatmeal

as distinct from other kinds, which are called **barley-meal**, **pease-meal** *etc*.

   verb **1** *of grain* yield or turn into meal. **2** add meal to (soup etc) *N*.

mealie-creeshie, **meal-a-crushie** oatmeal fried in fat *WCentral, SW, Ulster*.

mealie dumpling a round **pudding** (*see* **pudding**) of oatmeal and fat with seasoning, boiled or steamed. **mealie pudding** a sausage-shaped **mealie dumpling**, a **white pudding** (*see* **white¹**).

meal ark a chest for storing oatmeal. **meal bowie** a barrel for storing oatmeal. **meal corn**, **meal's corn** grain in general; food. **meal kail: broth** made with oatmeal and **kail**. **meal kist** a chest for storing oatmeal.

meal², **male 1** a meal. **2** a single milking of a cow or cows.

   meal o meat a meal *SW, S*.

meall, **mealock** *see* **muild¹**

mealtit *see* **meltith**

mean 1 possessed jointly or in common, joint-. **2** *of an animal* in poor condition.

mean *see* **mane**

meantime 1 meanwhile. **2** for the time being, at present.

   in the mids of the mean = **meantime**.

mear, **meer**, **mare 1** a mare, a female horse. **2** a wooden frame used as a trestle to support scaffolding *now NE*.

   Tamson's mear Shanks' pony, on foot.

mearing a strip of uncultivated land, usually marking a boundary *N*.

mease *see* **maise**

measlet, **mizzlet** scorched, mottled, blotched *now N*.

measure, **mizzer** *Shetland NE* measure.

meat, **mait**, **mate** *noun* **1** meat. **2** food in general, for people or animals.

   verb **1** provide food for, feed. **2** eat a meal, receive one's meals *now Shetland NE*.

   meat-hail having a healthy appetite. **meat-like and claith-like** well-fed and -dressed *now Shetland Angus*. **meat tea: high tea** (*see* **heich**) *WCentral*.

   ae coo's meat enough land to grow

food for one cow. **like one's meat** plump, well-nourished in appearance.

meath see **meith**

mebby see **maybe**

meddle see **middle**

meechie [-ch- as in 'dreich'] mean, stingy.

meed see **mak, muid**

meedow, meaddie *mainly ECentral,* **meadow** 1 (a) meadow. 2 marshy grassland where the natural coarse grasses are often cut for hay.

meef see **muith**

meel, meelackie see **muild**[1]

meelie see **muild**[2]

meen see **mune**

meenister see **minister**

meenit see **minute**

meer see **mear, muir**

meer see **mearl**

mees see **mess**

meeschle see **maschle**

meeserable, miserable 1 miserable. 2 mean, stingy, miserly.

meesick music.

meeth see **meith, muith**

Meg, maggie, meggie a rather unsophisticated girl, a rough country girl. **Meggie(-lickie)-spinnie** a spider *N.* **Meg(gie) wi the mony feet** a centipede.

meg see **maig**

meggie see **Meg**

megrim a whim, preposterous notion.

megstie me, mexty exclamation of surprise, distress or disapproval.

meichy see **muith**

meid see **meith, muid**

meikle see **muckle**

meill see **mell**[2]

meith, meath, meeth, meid *Shetland* 1 a boundary (marker) *now Shetland S.* 2 a point of reference, indication; a distinguishing feature. 3 a landmark used by sailors to steer by.

melder the quantity of one person's corn ground at one time; such a grinding *now NE.*

meldrop (a drop of) mucus from the nose *S.*

mell[1] 1 mix, mingle, blend. 2 have dealings with *now Shetland Angus.* 3 concern oneself improperly with an affair, a person etc.

milled *of a ewe* mated to a ram of a different breed.

mell[2], **maill, meill** *noun* 1 a maul, a heavy hammer. 2 a heavy blow.
verb strike (as) with a heavy hammer.

melt *noun* 1 *of an animal* the spleen. 2 the milt of a male fish. 3 the tongue.
verb fell (a person or animal) with a blow near the spleen; thrash.

meltith, †mealtit a meal.

†melvie coat (clothes) with a film of meal or flour.

mem ma'am, madam, madame.

memorandum a memento, souvenir.

memorial a document prepared by a solicitor for counsel, indicating the question on which counsel's opinion is sought.

menage, menodge [me**nadge**, me**nodge**] a kind of savings club to which each member contributes a fixed sum weekly for a stated period.

mence see **mense**[1]

mend *verb* 1 reform, improve. 2 restore to health, heal. 3 **mend of** recover from (an illness). 4 *of a wound, disease etc* get better. 5 fatten.

mends *noun, also* **a mends, ane mends** compensation, reparation; atonement.
get mends of get satisfaction from.

mengyie see **menyie**

mennen(t) see **minnon**

menner see **mainner**

menodge see **menage**

mense[1], **mence** *noun* 1 honour, credit *now SW, S.* 2 dignity; moderation; courtesy, hospitality. 3 something which brings credit or honour to one. 4 common sense, intelligence.
verb do honour to; grace, adorn *now SW.*

menseful polite; sensible; seemly, proper. **menseless** 1 unmannerly. 2 greedy, grasping. 3 stupid, foolish. 4 *of* *prices etc* unreasonably high, extortionate.

gie a garment kirk mense wear something for the first time at church on Sunday *SW, S*.

mense² a great amount, large quantity *now Shetland Ulster*.

menyie, mengyie 1 a retinue, group of followers; a body of troops. **2** a crowd, multitude; a rabble. **3** a large or mixed collection of things *N*.

mer *see* **mar**

mercat, market *noun* **1** a market. **2** buying and selling; a commercial transaction *now SW*. **3** the marriage market. **4** a **fairing** (*see* **fair²**) *N*.

mercat-stance the site where a market or fair is held *Shetland Orkney N*.

merch *see* **march**

Merch *see* **Mairch**

merchant 1 *also* **general merchant** a retail shopkeeper, especially of a grocery and general store. **2** a customer, buyer *now NE*.

mercy: the mercies liquor, especially whisky.

mergh, margh [-gh as -ch in 'loch'], **mergie** *Shetland Orkney*, **merky** *Shetland Orkney* marrow.

merk, mark 1 †a mark, a unit of weight. **2** †a unit of currency; a coin of its value. **3** †*mainly* **merkland** a measure of land, originally valued at one **merk** (*see* p 358).

merk *see* **mark, mirk**

merky *see* **mergh**

merl(e) a blackbird.

merr(i)age *see* **mairriage**

merry: merry-begotten *of a child* illegitimate. **merry dancers** the northern lights, aurora borealis. **merry-ma-tanzie** phrase found in the chorus of a children's ring game etc.

merry *see* **mairry**

merse 1 the Merse the district of Berwickshire lying between the Lammermuirs and the Tweed; *also* the whole of the county of Berwickshire. **2** flat alluvial

land by a river or estuary, especially that bordering the Solway *SW*.

mert *see* **mart²**

Mertimas *see* **Martinmas**

†Mes, Mess Master, especially as a title for a clergyman.

Mes John often humorous name for a Presbyterian minister.

mesmerise surprise, astound, dumbfound.

mess, mees measure out (food) *mainly NE*.

Mess *see* **Mes**

message: messages purchases, one's shopping.

message boy an errand-boy.

go a message go an errand. **go the messages** do the shopping.

messan 1 a dog, mongrel. **2** contemptuous term for a person.

messer *see* **misert**

met *see* **mett**

metal 1 *mining, usually* **metals** the strata in which minerals occur. **2** rock broken up and used in road-making.

mett, met 1 measure, measurement; a standard or system of measurement. **2** a unit of measurement of capacity.

mettle spirited, mettlesome.

meuw *see* **maw²**

mextie *see* **megstie**

Mey, May [rhymes with 'gey'] May, the month.

meysie, maisie a wild primrose *Angus*. **Mey bird** a whimbrel *now Ulster*.

as mim as a Mey puddock very demure and staid.

mi *see* **my**

miauve miaow *NE*.

mibby *see* **maybe**

mice *see* **mouse**

mich *Highland*, **much** much.

much aboot it much the same. **not make much of it** show little improvement in an illness.

Michael 1 a rustic. **2** *also* **mickey** a chamber-pot; a privy.

†Michaelday Michaelmas day *NE*.

Michael Fair a fair held in October at Aboyne *NE*.

micht *see* **may**

michty *adjective* **1** mighty. **2** disgraceful, scandalous *mainly NE*.
adverb greatly, thoroughly *Angus*.
noun the Almighty.
michty (me) exclamation of surprise or impatience.

micken common spignel.

mickey *see* **Michael**

mickle *see* **muckle**

mid: mid-couple 1 a leather loop connecting the two parts of a flail. **2** *law* a piece of evidence linking a claimant with the right claimed. **mid house** the small middle room of a **but-and-ben** (*see* **but**) *NE*. **mid-place** = **mid house** *now NE*. **mid-superior** *law* a person who holds an intermediate position of superiority (*see* **superior**) in the occupancy of land between an over-superior and a **vassal** or series of vassals.

midden, midding 1 a dunghill, compost heap, refuse heap. **2** a domestic ashpit. **3** a dustbin. **4** a muddle, mess. **5** a dirty, slovenly person. **6** a gluttonous person or animal *NE*.
midden heid the top of a **midden**; a person's home territory. **midden-stead** the site of a **midden**; a stamping ground.

midder *see* **mither**

middle, meddle 1 meddle. **2** interfere with, bother, harm. **3** have to do with.

middlin 1 of medium size or quality. **2** fair, tolerable.p

midge, mudge *Highland noun* **1** a midge. **2** a small unimportant person or animal.

midge *see* **mudge**

midgie (domestic) rubbish: *"midgie men"*.

mids 1 the middle, centre, midst. **2** *ploughing* the dividing furrow between two ridges *NE*.

mile 1 a mile; *also* a **Scots mile** (*see* p 360). **2** a great distance.
gae one's mile(s) go as far as one dares.

milk, mulk *noun* milk.

verb **1** milk. **2** add milk to (tea). **3** *of a cow etc* give milk.

milk-beal(in) a whitlow *SW, Ulster*.

milk brose oatmeal mixed with boiling milk. **milk broth** a dish made with barley and milk *N*. **milk meat** a dish of milk and meal or bread; **broth** made with skimmed milk *now NE*.

milk and breid oatcakes crumbled in milk.

mill, †miln, mull 1 a mill. **2** a threshing-mill. **3** a snuff-box. **4** a tin box with a lid *mainly NE*.
millart a miller *NE*. **droon the miller** add too much water to tea or whisky. **mill lade, mill-lead** a channel bringing water to a mill. **mill toon** the buildings of a mill; often the farm or village next to it. **mill yins** factory workers.
gang on like a tume mill chatter on without pause. **throo the mill** an ordeal, a searching examination.

milled *see* **mell**¹

millen *see* **muild**¹

mim prim, restrained especially in a prudish or affected way.

mimp 1 speak or act affectedly. **2** eat with the mouth nearly closed.

min *see* **man, mune**

minch, mince *verb* mince.
noun minced meat.
minche(d) collops minced steak cooked with oatmeal, onion, carrot etc. **minschie** a crumb, morsel *NE*.

mind, mine *noun* **1** mind. **2** a memory, recollection *now N*. **3** †one's opinion, judgment.
verb **1** remember, recollect. **2** remember (a person) in a will, give (someone) a small gift. **3** pray for *now Shetland NE*. **4** remind (a person) (of). **5** pass on one person's greetings to another.
minding 1 a small gift (made by way of remembrance), a token of goodwill. **2** a memory, recollection.
be a mind tae intend to *mainly SW, Ulster*. **hae mind (o)** remember, have recollection (of). **keep mind (o)** bear in

mind, take heed (of). **lose mind** forget.

mine, †mind 1 a mine. **2** *mining* a passageway or tunnel running from the surface to a mine-working or connecting one underground working with another.

mineer [mineer] an uproar, a noisy gathering, a fuss *NE*.

mines mine, my one(s).

minent *see* **minute**

ming a smell.

mingin 1 having a bad smell. **2** very drunk.

minister, meenister a clergyman, especially of the **Church of Scotland** (*see* **church**).

†minister's man the manservant of a **minister**, often in country parishes also performing the duties of **church officer** (*see* **church**).

mink, munk 1 a noose, loop. **2** an entanglement, snare; matrimony *NE*. **3** a cow's tether; a horse's halter.

minker a ragamuffin, vagrant; a gallows-bird.

minnie mother.

minnon, mennen(t) *S* a minnow; any small freshwater fish.

minnonette mignonette.

minor *law* a male over 14 or a female over 12 and under 18 or (formerly) 21; *compare* **pupil**.

minschie *see* **minch**

mint *verb* **1** intend, attempt (to do), aim at, to etc. **2** plan, attempt (something) *now NE*. **3** make a threatening movement, feint *now NE*. **4** brandish (a weapon), aim (a blow), threaten (a person) *now NE*. **5** insinuate, suggest, hint (at) *now NE*. **6** mention, speak of.

noun **1** an attempt, effort, intention. **2** a pretended blow, a feint *now NE*. **ill-minted** evil-intentioned *now Shetland Orkney*.

minute, meenit, minent *noun* **1** a minute. **2** an interval or recreation time; a tea-break *NE*. **3** *law* a note of the judgments etc of a court or judge or of the

intentions of a party in a suit regarding matters of procedure. **4** *law, in the Register of Sasines* (*see* **sasine**) *etc* a summary of the contents of a deed presented for registration. **5** *law* a memorandum setting out the heads of an agreement.

in a minute readily.

†minuwae a minuet.

miracle, marakle *now Shetland* [marakle] **1** a miracle. **2** an odd or ridiculous person *Shetland*.

miraculous 1 very drunk. **2** clumsy, loutish *N*.

mird meddle, have dealings with; sport with.

mire a peat-bog *Shetland*.

mire duck a wild duck; a mallard. **mire snipe** a snipe.

mirk, murk, merk, mark *adjective* **1** dark, black, gloomy, obscure. **2** †*of weather etc* dull, murky.

noun darkness, night, twilight.

verb darken.

mirken grow dark *now Shetland*. **mirkness** darkness. **mirky** dark, sombre; dirty.

mirk nicht the dead of night.

mirkie merry, mischievous *now NE*.

mirl, mirled, mirls *see* **murl**

mirligoes vertigo, dizziness.

misacker *see* **massacker**

misbehaden out-of-place, impolite *now Shetland Orkney NE*.

misbelieve disbelieve, doubt.

misca, miscaw, miscall 1 call (a person) bad names, abuse verbally, denounce. **2** slander, disparage. **3** mispronounce.

miscairry, miscarry 1 miscarry. **2** be pregnant when unmarried *now Shetland*.

mischancy 1 unlucky, ill-fated. **2** risky, dangerous.

mischief 1 misfortune, trouble. **2** a physical injury.

mischieve injure, beat (a person), treat cruelly *now Shetland NE*.

miscontentit discontented, dissatisfied *now NE*.

misdoubt, misdoot *verb* **1** distrust, doubt. **2** suspect, be afraid (that).
noun a doubt, suspicion, fear.

miserable *see* **meeserable**

misert *noun, also* †**meeser** a miser.
adjective mean, miserly.
misert pig a child's (earthenware) moneybox *now Shetland*.

misfit offend *NE*.

misfortune illicit sexual intercourse; an illegitimate child.
misfortunat unfortunate, unlucky.

misgae go wrong, fail *now NE*.

misgie, misgive **1** misgive. **2** (cause to) fail, let (a person) down.

misgrown stunted, deformed *now Shetland*.

misguggle, misgrugle handle roughly or clumsily.

misguide **1** treat badly, neglect; bring up badly or cruelly. **2** waste, squander, mismanage *now Shetland NE*.

mishandle mangle, maim, knock about *now Shetland Ulster*.

mishanter [mi**shant**er] **1** a mishap, disaster; misfortune. **2** a physical injury.

misken **1** fail to recognize or identify *now Shetland NE*. **2** have mistaken ideas of one's own importance *now NE*.

mislear hurt, abuse.
misleared **1** misinformed, mistaken. **2** ill-bred, rude. **3** selfish, greedy *now NE*.
†**misliken** speak ill of, undervalue.

mislippen **1** distrust, doubt, suspect. **2** neglect, overlook. **3** deceive, lead astray.

misluck bad luck, misfortune.
misluckit dogged with bad luck, unfortunate *NE*.

mismak **1** prepare or cook (food) badly *now Angus*. **2** disturb (oneself), put (oneself) about, trouble (oneself).

mismarrow mismatch.

mismay trouble, upset.

misred tangled, confused.

misremember forget; remember incorrectly *now SW, Ulster*.

misrestit suffering from loss of sleep.

miss *verb* **1** fail; fail to happen; *of crops* fail to grow; *of a breeding animal* fail to conceive. **2** avoid, escape. **3** escape the notice of. **4** pass over, skip, *eg* in reading. **5** miss something good by being absent: *"you really missed yourself at the party last night."*
noun a loss, want.

†**misset** displease, disconcert; be displeasing to.

missie the eldest unmarried daughter of a farmer.

missionar a travelling evangelical preacher; a member of an Independent church *NE, Ulster*.

missionary a lay preacher *Hebrides Highland*.

missive *law* a letter in which a transaction is agreed upon, which may then be followed by a more formal legal document, and which may or may not be binding subject to certain conditions.

misslie [**miss**lie] alone, lonely because of the absence of a usual companion.

mistak, mistake *verb* **1** mistake. **2** do wrong. **3** make a mistake, go wrong.
noun **1** a mistake. **2** illicit sexual intercourse.
mistaen 1 mistaen with †overcome by, under the influence of (drink). **2** *of a remark* taken amiss, misunderstood.
in a mistak *adjective* mistaken. *adverb* by mistake.

mister need, necessity.
†**beet a mister** supply a need, make good a deficiency.

mistime keep irregular hours, depart from routine *now NE*.

mistress **1** before the name of a married woman, = Mrs. **2** the wife of a person of standing in the community, such as a farmer. **3** one's own or another person's wife.

mistryst **1** fail to meet, break faith (with); seduce. **2** †delude, perplex, dismay.

mite *noun* **1** a small clay marble. **2** the smaller size of button used in the game of **buttons**; **mites** the game itself.

mith *see* **may**

mither, mother, moder *now Shetland,* **midder** *Shetland NE* mother.

  mither's bairn a spoilt child. **mither's pet** the youngest child.

mitten *noun* **1** any kind of glove. **2** a small squat person *NE.*

  verb grab hold of, seize *Shetland NE.*

mittle injure, do bodily harm to, mutilate.

mix 1 mix. **2** *of greying hair* become mixed in colour.

  mixed mentally confused, muddled with drink.

mixtie-maxtie, mixter-maxter, mixie-maxie *noun* a jumble of objects, a mixture, confusion.

  adjective mixed; jumbled; in a state of confusion.

mizzer *see* **measure**

mizzle vanish, melt away *now Angus.*

mizzle *see* **muzzle**

mizzles *see* **maisles**

mizzlet *see* **measlet**

mobbing and rioting *law* the joining together of a number of people to act in a way which is against peace and good order.

moch[1] *noun* a moth.

  verb be infested with moths *NE.*

  moch-eaten moth-eaten; infested with woodworm *mainly NE.*

moch[2], **†mauch, †moich** *noun* a warm moist atmosphere, close misty weather.

  adjective = **mochie** 1.

  verb, of corn, meat, etc become tainted, fusty or rotten *NE.*

  mochie 1 *of weather* humid; misty and oppressive. **2** *of stored articles* spoiled by damp, mouldy *NE.*

mod 1 †*in Celtic areas* a council or parliament. **2 the Mod** the annual national **Gaelic** festival of music and literature.

model an exact likeness *now Shetland.*

moder *see* **mither**

moderate *verb* preside over, act as chairman of (any of the courts of the Presbyterian Churches).

adjective †applied to the less rigorously Calvinist party in the **Church of Scotland** (*see* **church**).

moderator 1 the **minister** who presides over a Presbyterian church court. **2 the Moderator** the **minister** chosen to preside (now for one year) over the **General Assembly** (*see* **general**) of the **Church of Scotland** (*see* **church**) and to perform certain ceremonial duties.

  moderate (in) a call *of a presbytery* preside over the election and induction (*see* **induct**) of a **minister** to a vacant charge.

modewarp, modewurk *see* **mowdiewort**

Moffat measure a liberal measure.

moger, mooger work in a slovenly or messy way.

moggan 1 the leg of a stocking; a coarse footless stocking; a protective covering for the leg, of sacking etc, worn for farm work *N.* **2** a woollen stocking; a stocking foot worn indoors over one's stocking or out of doors over a shoe *Orkney N.* **3** an old stocking leg used as a purse; a hoard of money *NE.* **4** a mitt.

  wet (the sma end o') one's **moggans** be over the ankles in water *NE.*

moich *see* **moch**[2]

moidert confused, dazed, especially as a result of blows, drink, mental strain etc.

moister moisture.

†moistify wet.

†molass a spirit distilled from molasses; whisky adulterated with this.

mole *verb, also* **mollach** loiter, wander idly *NE.*

  molie a mole-catcher. **moleskin** true, reliable.

molligrant, mulligrumph *noun* a complaint; *often* **molligrants** a state of dissatisfaction, a fit of sulks.

  verb complain, grumble.

molligrups a fit of melancholy; stomach-ache.

mollop toss the head disdainfully; give

oneself airs S.

molly-dolly an Aunt Sally at a fair *WCentral*.

moment, mament a moment.

moment hand the second hand of a clock or watch *now ECentral*.

mon among *NE*.

mon *see* **man**

Monanday, Monday Monday.

Monday's haddie a fish that is not fresh.

monie, mony, many 1 many. **2** †many a. **3** big, great, considerable *now Shetland Angus*: "*many company*".

†**monie a monie** very many. **monie ane** †*adjective, following noun* many. *pronoun* many a person *now Shetland NE*. **monie's the ..** many a...

moniefauld the third stomach of a ruminant; **moniefaulds** the guts, intestines *now Angus*.

moniment, monument 1 a monument. **2** an object of ridicule or distaste; a rascal; a silly person.

†**moniplies** [rhymes with 'flies'] **1** the third stomach of a ruminant. **2** a tortuous argument or statement.

monkey *noun* **1** a monkey. **2** a tool with a ratchet for tensing fencing wire.

monkey-chip a kind of marbles game.

month, mont, mounth, mount 1 *usually* the **Mounth** name for the mountains at the eastern end of the Grampians. **2** a stretch of hilly or high ground; a mountain, hill, moor.

monument *see* **moniment**

mony *see* **monie**

moo *see* **mou, mouth**

moog *see* **mug**[1]

mooger *see* **moger**

mool *see* **moul**[1], **moul**[2], **muild**[1]

mooler *see* **muilder**

moolet whimper, whine.

moolock *see* **muild**[1]

moon *see* **mune**

moonlight flitting *see* **flit**

moop *see* **moup**

moor *see* **muir**

moose *see* **mouse**

moost *see* **muist**

moot, mute *verb* **1** say, utter, divulge; hint *Shetland NE*. **2** moot, raise for discussion.

noun a whisper, hint *now Shetland NE*.

moot *see* **mout**

mooth *see* **mouth**

moothlie *see* **muith**

moppie *see* **moup**

mora *law* delay in pressing a claim or obligation which may infer that the action has been abandoned by the **pursuer** (*see* **pursue**).

more *see* **mair**

morn 1 **the morn** tomorrow, (on) the following morning or day. **2** **the morn's morn** tomorrow morning; **the morn's nicht** tomorrow night.

the morn-come-never the end of time. **(the) morn i'e morning** day-break *SW*.

mornin, morning 1 morning. **2** a glass of spirits or a snack taken before breakfast; now usually a mid-morning drink or snack.

morning blink the first glimmer of daylight *now Shetland*. **morning piece** a drink or snack taken during the mid-morning break from work. **morning roll** a soft bread roll.

morrow: the morrow(s) morn(ing) the following morning, tomorrow morning *mainly SW, Ulster*.

morrow *see* **marrow**

mort 1 †a dead body. **2** = **mort lambskin**. **mort cauld** a severe cold *now Shetland*. **mort-cloth** a pall, a cloth covering a coffin. **mort hede 1** *heraldry* a representation of a skull *NE*. **2** a turnip lantern representing a skull *NE*. **mort kist** a coffin *now Shetland*. **mort lambskin** the skin of a sheep or lamb that has died a natural death *S*. †**mort safe** an iron grid placed over a grave or the coffin to deter body-snatchers.

(one's) morth o' cauld = **mort cauld** *now Ulster*.

mortal *adjective* extremely drunk.

adverb very, *especially* **mortal drunk**.

mortal end the end of everything.

†**mortify** *law* assign or bequeath in perpetuity (lands etc) to an ecclesiastical or other institution.

mortis causa *law, of a deed etc* taking effect on the death of the grantor.

mosh *marbles* a hollow scooped in the ground in which the target marble is placed.

moss 1 boggy ground, moorland. **2** a peat bog. **3** peat. **4** moss, the plant. **5** = **mosscrop**.

mosser a person who cuts and dries peats. **mossing** a crop of cotton grass *N.* **mossy** boggy, peaty.

moss aik, moss oak bog oak *SW.* **moss bluiter** a snipe. **moss cheeper** a meadow pipit. **mosscrop** cotton grass, especially harestail. **moss fir** the wood of ancient fir trees sunk into peaty soil, bog fir *now Perth.* **moss flow** a wet peat bog, a swamp. **moss grieve** the estate official in charge of the rights of peat-cutting in a **moss** *NE.* **moss hag, moss hole 1** a hole or pit in an old peat working. **2 moss hags, moss holes** dangerous boggy moorland. †**moss laird** *humorous* a tenant given an area of rough moorland rent-free or at reduced rent in return for making it arable. **moss pot** a water-filled pit in a peat bog *NE.* **moss road** a track to a **peat moss** (*see* **peat**) *now NE.* †**moss trooper** a Border **cattle-reiver** (*see* **reive**).

most¹ a mast *now NE.*

most² must *now Shetland.*

mot *see* **mote**³

mote¹ a mound or hillock; an embankment *now Shetland Ulster.*

mote² **1** a minute speck, a small fragment *now Shetland Orkney.* **2** a flaw, blemish; a drawback *now NE.*

†**mote**³, **mot, mat** may, might, must.

mother *see* **mither**

mou, moo, mow [rhymes with 'do' or 'cow'] **1** a large heap of grain, hay etc; a pile of unthreshed grain stored in a barn. **2** †a pile or stack of peats.

mou *see* **mouth**

†**moud, mowd** [rhymes with 'loud'] a clothes moth.

moud *see* **muild**¹

mouden *see* **mouten**

moudiewort *see* **mowdiewort**

mought *see* **maucht**

moul¹, **mool** [rhymes with 'pool'] †grow mouldy.

moul, mould, moulit mouldy *now NE, Fife.* **moulie, moolie 1** mouldy; little used. **2** mean, stingy.

moul², **mool** [rhymes with 'pool'] a chilblain, especially a broken one on the heel.

moulie, moolie affected with chilblains *now Caithness.*

mould *see* **muild**¹, **muild**²

moulder *see* **muilder**

mounge *see* **munge**

mount *see* **month, munt**¹, **munt**²

mountain, muntain a mountain.

mountain dew whisky.

mounth *see* **month**

moup, mowp, moop *verb* **1** twitch the lips; nibble (at), munch (at), mumble. **2** live with *SW.*

noun, also **moppie, mup-mup** familiar or child's word for a rabbit.

mourn *see* **murn**

mouse, moose 1 a mouse. **2** *also* **mouse end** the lump of flesh or tissue at the end of a leg of mutton. **3** a small lead weight tied to a cord, used by joiners to guide cords into a sash window and by electricians to drop wires.

mouse fa, mouse fall a mousetrap *now Fife.* **mouse moulding** a narrow moulding filling the angle between floor and skirting board or wall. **mouse pea, mouse pease** names for various kinds of vetch. **mouse web** a spider's web, cobweb.

mak mice feet o, mak like mice feet reduce to fragments; destroy *Shetland NE.*

mout, moot [rhymes with 'soot'] **1** moult. **2** fritter away, use up bit by bit *now*

Shetland. **3** crumble away, decay slowly.

moutache [moo**tash**] a moustache.

mouten, mouden *NE* [-ow- as -ow- in 'cow'] *adjective, of fat* clarified.
verb melt, dissolve; clarify (fat).

mouter *see* **multure**

mouth, mooth, mow, mou, moo *noun* **1** a mouth. **2** a threshold or entrance to an enclosed place or stretch of country. **3** *of a peat stack* the end from which one begins to take the peats for fuel. **4** the beginning (of a season, event etc). **5** the open top of a shoe. **6** the blade (of a shovel etc). **7** a speech, utterance *now SW.* **8** a talkative boastful person.
verb tell, utter, mention.
mouthie a mouth-organ.
mouth-ban(d) utter, express, mention.
mouth-bund tongue-tied; unable to pronounce something properly. **mouth cord** the rope linking the inner bit rings of a pair of horses to keep them together *WCentral.*
ask if someone has a mouth invite someone to eat or drink. **doon o mouth** in low spirits. **fin one's mouth** put food in one's mouth. **get roun the mou wi an English dishclout** become affectedly anglicised in speech. **in the mouth o the pock** at the outset, barely started. **mak a puir mouth** complain of one's poverty, exaggerate one's need. **wi mouth and een (baith)** gapingly, staringly *now NE.*

moveable *adjective, law* applied to that form of property which is not **heritable** (personal belongings etc), and which formerly passed to the next of kin instead of to the **heir-at-law** (*see* **heir**).
noun, law **moveables** such property.

mow [rhymes with 'cow'] *of males* have sexual intercourse (with).

mow *see* **mou, mouth**

mowd *see* **moud**

mowdiewort [-ow- as in 'cow'], **moudiewort, modewarp,** †**modewurk** *noun* **1** a mole. **2** a sneaking, underhand person.

3 a recluse; a slow-witted or slovenly person. **4** a mole on the skin, a wart.
verb **mowdy** loiter or prowl furtively about *SW.*
moudie 1 = **mowdiewort. 2** a mole-catcher. **moudieman** a mole-catcher. **moudieskin** the skin of a mole *now SW.* **mowdie(wort) hill(ock)** a molehill *now SW.*

mowp *see* **moup**

mowrie [rhymes with 'cowrie'] **1** gravel mingled with sand, shingle. **2** a gravelly sea-beach.

mows [rhymes with 'cows'] *now NE, plural noun* banter; a joke, a laughing matter.
adjective safe, harmless, circumspect.
nae mows no laughing matter; serious, dangerous, uncanny.

moyen, myane *noun* **1** power to exert influence; influence, mediation, steps taken *now NE.* **2** forewarning, news in advance, *usually* **get (a) moyen(s) o** *NE.*
verb **1** direct, guide (something); persuade, induce (someone) *NE.* **2** recommend, back (a person) *now NE.*
mak moyen(s) take steps (towards some objective), use influence *now NE.*

moze decay, become musty or mouldy *Shetland Orkney Caithness.*
mozie decayed, fusty, mouldy.

much *see* **mich**

muck *noun* **1** dung, farmyard manure. **2** dirt, filth; refuse, rubbish.
verb **1** clear of dirt, clean out; clean dung out of (a **byre** etc). **2** spread with dung, fertilize. **3** clutter up, spoil the appearance of *Shetland NE.*
muck flee a bluebottle; a dung-fly. **muck midden** a dunghill.
as drunk as muck very drunk. **Lady Muck** name for a person who puts on airs. **muck-the-byre** contemptuous term for a farmer. **wet as muck** soaking wet.

muckle, meikle, mickle *adjective* **1** large, great. **2** applied to the larger of two farms etc of the same name. **3** much, a great deal of. **4** full-grown, adult. **5** of high rank or social standing; self-important. **6** *of letters of the alphabet* capital *Shetland NE.*

adverb much, greatly, very.

noun a large quantity, a great deal.

Mucklie the fair held on **Muckle Friday.**

muckle-boukit 1 physically big and broad, burly. **2** pregnant. **muckle chair** a large armchair. **muckle coat** an overcoat. **muckle deil** the Devil, Satan. **muckle feck** the greater part. **Muckle Friday** the Friday on which the half-yearly **hiring market** (*see* **hire**) was held; the market itself *NE.* **muckle furth** the open air, the outdoors *NE.* **muckle hell** the depths of hell *now Shetland.* **muckle kirk** the parish church; the **Church of Scotland** (*see* **church**) *now Shetland Orkney NE.* **muckled-kited** pot-bellied *NE, Fife.* **muckle pot** the largest cooking pot, a cauldron *now Shetland Orkney NE.* **muckle tae hae, muckle tohoi** a gawky empty-headed fellow. **muckle wheel** a spinning wheel.

I've seen as muckle as I would not be surprised if. **man muckle, woman muckle** grown-up. **mony a mickle maks a muckle** every little helps. **muckle aboot it** much the same, without change *now NE.* **muckle an a nae little** no small amount of *now NE.* **not to mak muckle o't** show little improvement in an illness *now Shetland NE.*

mud a stud for the heels of boots or shoes.

muddle grub about in soil etc with the fingers, especially work (potatoes) away from the root by hand.

mud fish codfish preserved by being salted wet in bulk in the hold of a fishing boat *Shetland Orkney N.*

mudge, midge *verb* (cause to) move, stir, shift.

noun **1** a movement. **2** a sound, a whisper; a rumour.

mudgins movements, especially of the features, grimaces.

mudge *see* **midge**

mug[1], **moog** *N* a mug.

mugger a tinker.

mug[2] *marbles* **1** a hole in the ground used as a target. **2** *usually* **muggie** the game itself *now WCentral.*

mug[3] beat, thrash (as a punishment).

mug[4] *noun* drizzling rain, often with mist or fog *now NE.*

verb, also **muggle** drizzle *now NE.*

muggy drizzling, wet and misty *NE.*

muggart, muggart kail, muggins mugwort.

muid, meid *NE,* **meed** *NE* mood.

muif *see* **muith**

muild[1], mould, **meall** *NE,* **meel** *NE,* **mool, moud** *noun* **1** mould, earth etc. **2** loose soil, lumps of earth. **3** *usually* **muilds** the earth of the grave. **4** the grave.

verb **meall, mool 1** crumble (one substance in with another) *now NE.* **2** crumble down, reduce to small pieces *now NE.* **3** *usually* **muild in** mix well together, associate (with); curry favour with.

mealock, moolock, meelackie a crumb, a small fragment *now NE.* **moolie** *noun* a marble of burnt clay *now WCentral.*

adjective liable to crumble, crumbling.

muildie, moolie 1 *of earth* crumbled, finely broken up *now Shetland Orkney.* **2** earthy, deep in the soil. **moolin(g), millen** a crumb, a small piece.

muild bred a mouldboard. **mould furrow, meel fur** the last furrow of a **rig**[1], ploughed on soil from which the sod has already been turned over.

abune the muild alive, in this world *Shetland Orkney NE.*

muild[2], mule, mould **1** a mould, a pattern etc. **2** *also* **meelie** *NE* a button-mould; a button made of such a mould covered with cloth; latterly a flat linen-covered button.

muilder, moulder, mooler *verb* moulder.

noun crumbled fragments of oatcake *now Shetland Ulster.*

muin *see* **mune**

muir, mure, moor, meer *NE,* **mair 1** a moor. **2** rough, uncultivated heathery land considered as part of an estate. **3** open ground held (usually) by a community, the common; latterly often the market green. **4** peat, peaty soil; a layer of peat *now Shetland Orkney.*

moorband a hard subsoil of sand and clay with embedded stone, impervious to water. **muirburn** the controlled burning of moorland to clear the way for new growth. **muircheeper** a meadow pipit. **muircock** a male red grouse. **muir duck** a wild duck, a mallard. **muir fowl** a red grouse. **muirhen** a (female) red grouse. †**muirill** red-water, a disease of cattle. **muirland** moorland; moorland-bred, rustic, uncouth. **muir pout** a young red grouse. **muirstone** the stone from outcrop rock on moorland, often granite *now NE.*

throu the muir a severe scolding.

†**muist, moost** *noun* **1** musk; *eg* **muist ball** a pomander. **2** hair powder.
verb powder (a wig).

muith, †**meef** *Shetland Orkney Caithness,* **muif** *Shetland Orkney S,* †**meeth** *noun* a warm moist atmosphere, oppressive humid weather, oppressive heat *Shetland Orkney.*
adjective **1** *also* **muithy, meefy, meichy** [-ch- as in 'dreich'] *of the atmosphere* oppressively close and humid. **2** *of people* oppressed or exhausted by heat *now Caithness.*

moothlie in a soft, smooth way.

muive *see* **muve**

mulberry 1 a mulberry. **2** white beam.

muldoan a basking shark.

mule *see* **muild**²

mulk *see* **milk**

mull¹ a headland, promontory.

mulloch a cow without horns *WCentral, SW.*

mull² the mouth or muzzle of an animal or a person *mainly Shetland Orkney, now Fife.*

mull *see* **mill**

mullach [-u- as in 'but'] my dear *Caithness.*

mulligrumph *see* **molligrant**

multiplepoinding [-pinding] *law* an action which may be brought by or in the name of the holder of a fund or property, to determine which of several claimants has preferential right to the fund or property or in what proportions it is to be divided.

multure, mouter [mooter] *noun* †a duty consisting of a proportion of the grain or meal payable to the proprietor or tenant of a mill on corn ground there; the right to this duty.
verb pay **multure** on (grain); charge **multure** against (a person); levy **multure** on (grain) (at a particular rate).

mum *noun* a word, a murmur.
verb utter the least sound; mutter, mumble.

mummle, mumble mumble.

mumbler an implement for breaking clods, a kind of heavy harrow.

mump *verb* **1** nibble like a rabbit. **2** mumble, mutter. **3** grumble, complain peevishly. **4** sulk, mope around; loaf around. **5** gesture and grimace *now NE.*
noun a word, a whisper, the merest suggestion *now NE.*
adjective depressed, sullen.

mun *cant or gipsy, mainly* **muns** the mouth.

mun *see* **munn**

mundheri *sheep-counting,* **methery** *children's rhymes* four.

mundy a heavy hammer used especially by shipwrights.

mune, muin, moon, meen *NE,* **min 1** a moon. **2** a (lunar) month *now S.* **3** a very long period of time. **4** a goldcrest *S.*

mune bow, mune broch a halo round the moon, believed to be a sign of an approaching storm. **munelicht flitting** a secret removal during the night.

the auld mune in the airm(s) o the new the disc of the full moon faintly shining within the crescent moon, believed to be a sign of an approaching storm. **at the back of the mune** at a very great distance. **a month o munes** an impossibly long time.

munge, mounge [moonje] grumble; sulk.

munk *see* **mink**

munn, mun a short-handled horn spoon.

Munro *mountaineering* name for any Scottish peak of 3000 feet (914.4 metres) or more.
Munro-bagger a person who aims to climb every **Munro.**

munsie *NE* **1** an odd-looking or ridiculously-dressed person. **2** a person who is in a sorry state, who has been knocked about. **3** the jack or knave in a set of playing cards.
mak a munsie o reduce to a ridiculous or sorry state, spoil.

munt[1], **mount** *verb* **1** mount. **2** decorate (a garment etc). **3** prepare to set off; depart.
noun **munts** fittings, decoration, especially of metalwork on wood.
munting equipment, dress, especially a bride's trousseau.

munt[2], **mount** *noun* **1** a mount, a hill. **2** a low tree-covered hill.

muntain *see* **mountain**

mup-mup *see* **moup**

murder *see* **murther**[1]

mure *see* **muir**

murgeon, murgon [murjon] *noun* a contortion, a grimace.
verb mock; grimace, posture.

murk *see* **mirk**

murl, mirl *verb, often* **murl doon 1** crumble, reduce to fragments, ruin. **2** crumble away as from decay, moulder.
noun, also **murlack** a crumb, fragment.
murlie crumbly, friable. **murlin** *noun* a crumb, fragment. *adjective* crumbling, mouldering.

murlin a basket used mainly by fishermen *now NE.*

murlin *see* **murl**

murmell grumble at; mutter, mumble.

murmichan [murmichan] a **bogle** or wicked fairy used to frighten children *now Angus.*

murmur complain against; *law* cast doubt on the character or integrity of (a judge).

murn, mourn 1 mourn. **2** complain, show resentment, grumble.
murning *noun* **1** mourning. **2 murnings** the black garments worn to show grief.
murning letter a black-edged letter of invitation to a funeral.
mak (a) murn for lament, bewail *now NE.*

murr make a continuous vibrating, murmuring sound; *of a cat* purr; growl *now NE.*

murther[1], **murder** *noun* murder.
verb **1** murder. **2** harass, torment, distress.
murtherer 1 murderer. **2 murderer** a device for catching deep-sea fish.

murther[2] *of a child* murmur, whimper, sob quietly.

Muscovy cat a tortoiseshell cat *SW.*

musken *see* **mutchkin**

mush[1] the mixture of oak sawdust and chips burned when smoking herring to make kippers.
mush house a store for the mixture *Shetland NE.*

mush[2] *sewing* gather, flounce, puff (out); scallop, cut into a pattern with a stamp.

musicianer a musician *now SW, Ulster.*

muslin kail a thin soup made from barley and vegetables without any meatstock.

mussel: mussel midden a rubbish heap where mussel-shells are thrown *now Fife.* **mussel scaup** a mussel-bed.

mutch 1 a kind of hood or coif, usually of linen etc, worn *eg* by women by night or day, especially a close-fitting cap worn by married women. **2** an old woman.
grannie('s) mutches, grannie mutchie *see* **grannie. night mutch** a nightcap *now*

Orkney.

mutchkin, musken *now SW* a measure of capacity equal to = three-quarters of an imperial pint (.43 litre) or 1 pint (.848 litre) (see p 359).

mute *see* **moot**

muttie a measure for grain; a container holding this amount *N*.

mutuum *law* a contract by which the borrower of goods for consumption, *eg* food, agrees to repay a like quantity of the same goods instead of the actual goods borrowed.

muve, muive, meeve *NE* move.

muzzle, †mizzle 1 a muzzle. **2** the bridle of a plough.

my, ma, mi my; used with certain nouns where English omits: *"I am going to my bed"*.

myane *see* **moyen**

myave [mee**av**] maw, stomach *NE*.

myowt [mee**owt**] a sound, a whisper, especially of complaint or protest *NE*: *"not a myowt out of the children"*.

mysel, masel(l) myself.

N

na[1] no.

na[2], **nae, ne** *mainly used with verbs* not, *eg* **canna, dinna.**

na[3], **nae, no** *NE* now, then.

na[4] than.

na[5] really, indeed.

naar *see* **nar**

nab a peg or nail on which to hang things.

nab *see* **knap**[2]

nabal, nabble, nabald *Shetland Orkney noun* a miser.

adjective grasping, mean, churlish *now NE.*

nabb, knab(b) a hillock, summit.

nabb, nabbie *see* **knab**[2]

nabble 1 nibble *now Shetland.* **2** *mainly clothmaking* work with speed and deftness.

nabble *see* **nabal**

nack *see* **knack**

nacket[1], **nocket 1** a type of small fine loaf. **2** a packed lunch, a snack.

nacket[2] **1** †a boy, youngster. **2** a small, neat person; a pert or precocious child. **3** a little ball.

nackety neat.

nacky *see* **knackie**

nadir *see* **nedder**

nag *see* **knag**[1]

nae[1] no, not any.

nae[2] *NE* not.

nae bit no more than, just.

nae[3] nay, no.

nae *see* **na**[2], **na**[3]

nael, nile, nyvle the navel *mainly SW.*

naesay *see* **na-say**

naether *see* **naither**

naff *see* **nyaff**

nag a hard ball used in **shinty.**

nag *see* **naig**

†**nags** *marbles* a game in which the loser is struck on the knuckles by the other players' marbles; the blows so struck.

naider *see* **naither**

naig, nag 1 †a nag, a small horse. **2** a horse in general.

nail 1 clinch (an argument or bargain). **2** hit, kill.

aff at the nail deranged.

nain, nane *adjective, also* **nawn** (one's) own.

noun †what is one's own, one's due.

nainsell 1 = **ainsel** (*see* **ain**) *mainly NE.* **2** *mainly* **her nainsell** *pronoun* a Highlander's supposed way of speaking of himself; *noun* a Highlander.

by one's nain alone.

†**naiphouse, nepus** a dormer.

naipkin, napkin, nepkin, neepyin 1 a pocket-handkerchief; a neckerchief. **2** a napkin.

nairra, nerra, narrow narrow.

nairra-begaun miserly. **nairra-boukit** thin, lean. **nairra-nebbit** sharp-nosed, bigoted, strict *now Ulster.*

naisty *see* **nestie**

naither, naether, naider, nedder *Shetland N* neither.

naitherins *with another negative* either *now NE:* "A dinna like naitherins o them".

naitur *see* **nature**

nakit, naked, nyakit *NE* [neeakkit] **1** naked. **2** thin, lean. **3** *of alcoholic drink* neat.

nam, nyam [neeam] **1** seize, grab. **2** eat up greedily *mainly S.*

name, neem *Shetland Caithness,* **nem 1** a name. **2** †those bearing a particular name, especially a family or clan.

namely noted, famed. **namer, namie** one of the two chief players in a children's guessing game.

name dochter, name son a girl or boy who has been called after someone *now Shetland Orkney.* **name faither, name**

mother the man or woman after whom someone is named.

ca (someone) out of his name 1 call (someone) names. **2** give a nickname to *mainly Ulster*. **get the name** have a child named after one. **gie in the names** supply the names for the proclamation of marriage banns.

nane, none, neen *pronoun* **1** none. **2** neither (of two).

adjective none.

adverb not at all.

nane *see* **nain**

nap¹, knap, nappie a bowl, a drinking vessel.

nap²: tak the nap aff make fun of, mock.

nap *see* **knap¹**

napery table linen.

napkin *see* **naipkin**

nappie *adjective* **1** *of ale etc* foaming, strong. **2** †slightly drunk.

†*noun* (strong) ale.

nappie *see* **nap¹**

nar, nerr, naur, naar *Shetland NE adjective* **1** near, close *now SW, Ulster*. **2** near or left-hand (side). **3** nearer, closer to the speaker.

adverb **1** nearer, closer. **2** near, close by *now NE*. **3** nearly, almost.

preposition close to, beside.

narrer nearer. **narrest** nearest.

nar *see* **nor¹**

narg, nyarg [neearg] keep grumbling, nag *now Shetland Orkney Caithness*.

narr, nyarr [neearr] *mainly NE* **1** *of a dog* snarl. **2** *of people* be discontented or complaining.

narration an uproar, fuss *mainly SW, S*.

narrative *law* that part of a legal deed which states the relevant essential facts.

narrer, narrest *see* **nar**

narrow *see* **nairra**

na-say, naysay, naesay *noun* a refusal, denial.

verb refuse, deny.

nash *mainly S* impudent or caustic talk.

nash-gab garrulous or impudent talk.

natch 1 a notch, indentation. **2** *curling* a cut in the ice to hold a player's foot. **3** †small scissors used by tailors.

nate, natie *see* **neat**

nation one of the regional divisions of the student body of some Scottish Universities.

natter, nyatter *mainly NE* [neeatter], **nitter** *mainly Shetland Orkney verb* chatter, nag, grouse.

noun **1** grousing, nagging talk; aimless chatter. **2** a bad-tempered, nagging person; a chatterer.

nattle nibble, chew awkwardly, mumble toothlessly.

natural philosophy *Scottish Universities* physics.

nature, naitur nature.

nature grass grass which grows wild and luxuriantly *now NE*.

nauchtie *see* **nocht**

naur *see* **nar**

nawn *see* **nain**

naysay *see* **na-say**

ne *see* **na²**

near *adverb* **1** nearly, almost. **2** narrowly, only just.

adjective closely related by blood or kinship.

verb draw near (to), approach.

nearlins almost *now Shetland NE*.

near about(s) 1 close by. **2** almost, by and large. **near-begaun** miserly. **nearby** *adverb* **1** close at hand. **2** nearly. *preposition* near, beside. **near cut** a short cut. **near gaun = near begaun. near hand** *adverb* **1** near at hand, close by. **2** almost, all but. *adjective* close, near, neighbouring. *preposition* near, close to. **near-hand cut = hand cut.**

as near nearly (as good), near enough. **near the bane** miserly. **near the bit 1 = near the bane. 2** pretty well correct.

near *see* **neir**

neat, nate 1 neat. **2** *of people* trim, smart. **3** exact, precise; nett.

†**nettie, natie** sheer, pure, unmitigated *NE*.

neb *noun* **1** the beak of a bird. **2** a person's nose; the whole face. **3** any projecting tip or point, *eg* of a finger or toe, the tongue, a piece of land, the point of a pencil.

verb **1** *of birds* tap with the beak. **2** put a point on (a quill-pen or pencil).

nebbie 1 biting, nippy, sharp; smart. **2** brusque. **3** cheeky. **4** inquisitive.

nebfu a beakful; a small quantity, a drop.

necessar necessary.

necessitate compelled mainly by circumstance.

neck *noun* **1** the collar of a coat or shirt. **2** the throat, gullet. **3** *mining* the upper part of a shaft, above the coal.

verb **1** break the neck of. **2** embrace.

(in) spite o one's neck in defiance of one's efforts, wishes etc.

nedder, †nadir place an extension below a beehive to give extra room for breeding.

nedder *see* **naither, nether**[1], **nether**[2]

neeber *see* **neibour**

need: †needfire fire said to have magical properties.

hae mair need to do ought rather to do, would be better to. **not out of (the) need o** still in need of. **he will need to** he had better.

needcessity necessity, need.

needle move like a needle rapidly through, or in and out.

neefer *see* **niffer**

neeger 1 a nigger. **2** a hard or reckless person; a savage, barbarous person.

neem *see* **name**

neen *see* **nane, nune**

neep *noun* **1** a turnip; *in Scotland*, usually a swede. **2** a head. **3** a turnip watch.

verb **1** feed (cattle) with turnips. **2** sow (land) with turnips.

neep brose: brose made with the liquid in which turnips have been boiled. **neep heid** a stupid person. **neep lantern** a turnip-lantern. **neep re(e)t** land on which a turnip crop has been grown *NE*.

neeper *see* **neibour**

neepyin *see* **naipkin**

neer *see* **neir, never**

Neer *see* **New-year**

neerice *see* **nourice**

neese, neeze sneeze.

neese *see* **niz**

neet, neetie *see* **nit**[2]

nefe *see* **nieve**

neffie *see* **nevoy**

negleck neglect.

neibour, neeber, neeper, neiper, neighbour *NE,* **†nichbour** *noun* **1** a neighbour. **2** a husband or wife, a bedfellow, partner. **3** *of people or things* a match, one of a set or pair.

verb **neibour wi** be near; co-operate with; associate with; match, form a set with.

neibourheid 1 friendly relations between neighbours. **2** neighbourly relations within a community. **3** a neighbourhood. **neibourless** *of one of a pair* lacking the other.

neir, neer, near a kidney.

neir leather the back or belly-band of a horse's harness.

neist next, nearest.

nem *see* **name**

nephew *see* **nevoy**

nepkin *see* **naipkin**

nepus *see* **naiphouse**

nerr *see* **nar**

nerra *see* **nairra**

nervish nervous, easily agitated.

nesh soft.

ness a headland.

nestie, naisty nasty.

nether[1] *now Caithness,* **nedder** an adder.

nether[2], **nedder** *now Shetland Orkney* lower, under.

nettercap, netterie = **attercap.**

†nettie a woman who goes about collecting wool *mainly S.*

nettie *see* **neat**

nettle: nettle brose: brose made with the juice of boiled young nettle-tops *NE*.

on nettles on tenterhooks, impatient, ill-humoured.

nettle-earnest dead earnest *S, Ulster*.

neuk, newk, nook 1 a nook. **2** a projecting point of land, especially into the sea. **3** an external angle of a building; the corner of a street. **4** an outlying or remote place.

neukit 1 having corners; crooked. **2** cantankerous *NE*.

the East Neuk the eastern corner of Fife. **hold in his ain neuk** keep under strict control *Shetland NE*.

nevel, †knevell *noun* a sharp blow with the fist, a punch.

verb **1** punch, pummel, batter. **2** squeeze, pinch *now Shetland*.

never, niver, neer never.

never a not a single.

nevie- *see* **nieve**

nevoy, nephew, neffie 1 a nephew. **2** a grandson; a great-grandson.

new newly, recently, just.

newin(g) the working of yeast in the making of ale. **newlins** newly, recently. **new fangill** *adjective* †(too) fond of novelty. *noun* novelty, innovation. **new farrant** novel, new-fangled *NE*.

newk *see* **neuk**

news a talk, conversation; a gossip.

newsie gossipy, talkative *mainly NE*.

New-year, Neer 1 the New Year. **2** a gift, or a drink or food given in hospitality at the New Year.

New-year('s) day, Noor's Day 1 New Year's Day. **2** = **New-year** 2. **New-year('s) even** New Year's Eve.

next, nixt 1 next. **2** *with names of days or months* the next but one: *"Friday first .. Friday next"*.

nib 1 = **neb**. **2** a nip; a prod.

nibbie a walking stick with a hooked handle *mainly SW, S*. **†niblick** the golf club corresponding to the No 8 or 9 iron.

nibble fiddle with.

nichbour *see* **neibour**

nicher [-ch- as in 'dreich'], **nicker, nikker**

1 *of a horse* snicker, neigh. **2** snigger.

nicht, night *noun* night.

verb **1** be nichted be overtaken by night *now NE*. **2** pass the night *now NE*.

the nicht afore the morn the eve of an important occasion, *eg* one of the **Common Ridings** (*see* **common**).

nick *noun* **1** one of the notches or growth-rings on an animal's horns. **2** a narrow gap in a range of hills. **3** a broken-off piece, a scrap.

verb **1** cut off, sever; cut short. **2** catch, seize. **3** imprison. **4** cheat, trick.

nickie an oatcake or bun with an indented edge.

†nick stick a tally, a notched stick for keeping accounts.

†nick the thread kill.

nick *see* **knick**

nicker *see* **nicher**

nickie-tams a pair of straps or pieces of string, used by farmworkers to tie their trousers below the knees, to keep the legs above their knee clean.

nickle *see* **knuckle**

nickle naething the term represented by the letter N on a **totum**[1] meaning 'nothing' for the player to whom it fell.

nickum a scamp, a rogue, a mischievous boy.

nidder *see* **nither**

niddle 1 *of the fingers* do intricate or laborious work quickly or persever-ingly. **2** fiddle, potter *now NE*.

nidge dress (a building stone) roughly.

nid (nid) nodding nodding repeatedly, as when dozing.

nieve, †nefe, nive *noun* **1** a fist. **2** nieves fisticuffs *now Shetland Orkney*. **3** †a hand's breadth.

verb †**guddle** (fish) *SW*.

nievie-nievie-nicknack, †**nevie-nevie-nak** first line of a rhyme in a children's guessing game.

niffer, neefer 1 barter, trade. **2** haggle, bargain.

niffler *weaving* a comb-like appliance, an evener.

niffnaff, nyiffnyaff [nee**iff**nee**aff**] *verb* trifle, dilly-dally.

noun a small, unimportant person or thing.

niggar *noun* a miser.

nigh hand nearly, almost *now NE*.

night *see* **nicht**

†**nig nay** a nicknack, trifle.

nikker *see* **nicher**

nile *see* **nael**

nimious *law* excessive, vexatiously burdensome, *now mainly* **nimious and oppressive.**

nimm *exclamation by or to a child* yum-yum.

nimmle nimble.

nimp, nyim [nee**imm**] a morsel.

nimsh, imsh a tiny piece.

nine: ninesie the ninth movement in the game of **chuckies** (*see* **chuck**²) ninth *now NE*. **nineteen** *adjective* = nineteenth. *noun* a lease of a farm for nineteen years.

nine holes the cut of beef below the breast.

(**up**) **to the nine(s)** to perfection.

nip *noun* **1** sharpness of taste, pungency. **2** an advantage, especially in bargaining *NE*. **3** a fragment, piece, a pinch. **4** a sheepmark, a notch cut in the ear.

verb **1** *baking* pinch dough at its edges, make indentations round pastry etc. **2** *especially of animals* nibble; graze. **3** (cause to) tingle or smart. **4** get the better of (in bargaining), cheat *now SW*. **5** seize, catch; snatch.

nippit 1 curt, bad-tempered. **2** pinched with hunger. **3** mean, niggardly. **4** narrow in outlook. **5** *of clothes* tight-fitting. **nippity** quick and jerky. **nippy** = **nippit** 1, 3.

nip-lug backbiting, squabbling. **nip-nebs** Jack Frost. **nipscart** a niggardly person.

nir *see* **nor**¹

nirl, nurl *noun* **1** a fragment, crumb, a small object *now Ulster*. **2 the nirls** a disease characterized by inflamed pustules, a rash.

verb **1** shrink, shrivel, stunt, pinch with cold. **2** shrivel up in oneself, cringe with cold *now Shetland*.

nirlie 1 dwarfish, stunted *now Shetland Orkney*. **2** *of cold* pinching, nipping.

nit¹ a nut.

†**nitmug** a nutmeg.

nit², **neet** a nit, the egg of a louse, now mainly a head louse.

neetie *noun* a mean or disobliging person. *adjective* stingy.

nitch a notch, small cut.

nither, nidder 1 oppress, vex. **2** pinch or stunt with cold or hunger *now S*. **3** shrink or huddle as with cold, shiver.

nitter *see* **natter**

nive *see* **nieve**

niver *see* **never**

nixt *see* **next**

niz *mainly NE*, **neese** *now humorous* the nose.

nizwise far-seeing, perceptive *now NE*.

njirr *see* **nurr**

no *adverb* not.

no bad pretty good. **no canny** risky, unlucky. **no weel** ill.

no *see* **na**³

nob 1 the nose. **2** the toe of a shoe *Edinburgh*.

nobile officium [**no**bilay o**fish**ium] *law* the **Court of Session** (*see* **session**) power of equitable jurisdiction in cases where the law itself does not provide a clear remedy.

nocht, noucht, noth *NE noun* nought, nothing.

adverb not.

nochtie, †**nauchtie 1** *of people* good-for-nothing, insignificant. **2** *of things* small, worthless, unfit. **nochtifie** disparage. **nochtless** worthless, of no account.

nock *see* **knock**²

nocket *see* **nacket**²

†**noddy** a kind of light two-wheeled carriage.

nodge nudge, push *now Shetland*.

noit *see* **knoit**²

nolt *see* **nowt**[1]

nominal raiser *see* **raiser** (*under* **raise**).

nominate *law* **executor nominate** *or* **tutor nominate** an executor or **tutor** named and appointed in the will of the testator or parent.

none *see* **nane**

†**non-entry** *law* the failure of an heir to a deceased **vassal** to obtain **entry** (*noun* (5)); the **casualty** payable to the **superior** in the case of such failure.

noo, now 1 now. **2** under the present circumstances, in view of these facts.
noo(s) an than(s) now and then, from time to time *now NE*. **noona** well then!, now then!, really! **the noo** just now; just a moment ago; in a moment, soon.

noof *see* **nuif**

nook *see* **neuk**

noop a cloudberry *N, S*.

Noor's Day *see* **New-year**

noos *see* **than**

noose *see* **knuse**

noost *see* **knoost**

noozle one of a row of cords attaching the mesh-work to the headrope of a fishing-net.

noozle *see* **knuse**

nor[1], **nar** *NE, S*, **nir** *mainly NE* **1** nor. **2** than. **3** that .. not, (but) that *now NE*: *"nae wonder nor you're thin"*. **4** (**God**) **nor, Deil nor, fient nor, shame nor, sorrow nor** would that, (God) grant that, would to the devil etc: *"God nor that I hang"*; *"sorrow nor the drink wad chock ye"*.

nor[2] **1** used to emphasise negative answers: *"is it sore? - no, nor sore"*. **2** followed by another negative: *"ye nor me havena been there"*.

nor-, norat *see* **north**

norie[1], **norrie** a whim, a fancy *mainly S*.

norie[2] a puffin *now Shetland*.

norlan(d) *see* **north**

Norn (of) the Norse language formerly spoken in Shetland and Orkney, now surviving only in their dialect.

norrie *see* **norie**[1]

Norroway Norway *now Shetland Orkney NE*.

Norse *adjective* Norse; Norwegian.
noun **1** the Norwegian language. **2 the Norse** the Norwegians.

norter, nurture *noun* **1** nurture. **2** rigorous discipline, rough treatment *NE*.
verb **1** nurture. **2** discipline, chastise, punish *now NE*.

north, nor- 1 the north. **2** the north and north-east of Scotland.
northart, norat *adverb* northward, to the north *now Shetland Orkney NE*.
noun the north *now Shetland Orkney NE*. **northerlie, northlins** *now Shetland Orkney* towards the north, in a northerly direction. **Northern Isles** *see* **isle**.
norlan(d) 1 = **north** 2. **2** a person from the north or north-east of Scotland *now Fife*. **north ower** northwards *now Shetland*.

nose *mining* coal left protruding where it has been inadequately stripped.
nosie a throw in the game of **knifie**. **nosethirl** a nostril *now Shetland N*.

not *see* **note**[1], **note**[2]

notarial instrument *law* a formal document made out by a notary, declaring that certain things have been done.

notarial protest a **notarial instrument** in which the notary protests that a debtor shall be liable on non-payment to the consequences set forth in the instrument.

note[1], **not(t) 1** a note. **2** *law* a formal record, especially in a court register, especially an appendix to a **decree** in which a judge gives the reasons for his decision; a step in **Inner House** (*see* **inner**) proceedings used for making an incidental application. **3** a one-pound banknote.

note[2] *verb* **1** †make use of, need. **2** *in past tense and past participle also* **not(t)**, **nott(en)** needed *NE*.

noth *see* **nocht**

notice *verb* heed, watch; tend, see to *now Shetland Orkney NE*.

noun **1** notice, information; heed. **2** care, attentive help *Shetland NE*.

notion: a notion o a liking or affection for (a person).

notionate full of whims or caprices *now SW*.

notorious great(ly), exceeding(ly) *now Ulster*.

notour [no**toor**] *adjective* **1** *of wrongdoers* known by common knowledge, notorious; openly admitted, *eg* **notour bankrupt** *now only law*. **2** *of facts* commonly known or manifest, *mainly law* of crimes etc: *"notour adultery, notour bankruptcy"*.

nott *see* **note**[1], **note**[2]

notten *see* **note**[2]

noucht *see* **nocht**

noup [-oo-] *especially of the elbow* a knob or protuberance.

nourice [-oo-], **neerice** *NE noun* a child's nurse, especially a wet-nurse or foster-mother.

verb nourish.

nouther *see* **nowther**

novation *law* the substitution of a new debt or debtor for a former.

novelle a novel.

novodamus *law* the formal renewal of a grant by a feudal **superior** in order to alter or correct a former grant.

now *see* **noo**

nowt[1], **nolt** **1** cattle. **2** an ox, steer *now NE*. **3** a big unwieldy person, a blockhead. **nowt beast** a cow, bull, calf or ox *now NE*. **nowt('s) feet** calves' feet, cow-heels as a dish.

nowt[2] **1** nought, nothing *S*. **2** **nowts** *marbles* a shout by an opponent preventing the player from firing from any spot he chooses *SW, S*.

nowther, nouther [-ow-, -ou- as -ow- in 'cow'] neither.

nowther nor neither.

†**noy** *verb* **1** annoy, vex, irritate. **2** be troubled, be incensed, angry.

noun **1** vexation, harm. **2** **noys** wrongs, injuries.

nub *noun*, †*also* **nubbie** nickname for a club-footed person.

nub berrie a cloudberry *S*.

nuif, noof neat, spruce *SW*.

nummer number.

nummerable numerable, capable of being numbered.

nuncupative [**nuncy**oo**pay**tive] *law, usually of a will* oral as opposed to written.:

nune, neen *N* noon.

nurl *see* **nirl**

nurr, njirr [nee**irr**] *Shetland Orkney Caithness verb* **1** growl like an angry dog, snarl like a cat *now Shetland Caithness*. **2** *of a cat* purr *mainly Shetland*.

noun the growl of an angry dog *now Shetland S*.

nurring growling, snarling; fault-finding *now Shetland Caithness*.

nurture *see* **norter**

nyaff [nee**aff**], naff, gnaff *verb* **1** *of a small dog* yelp, yap. **2** talk senselessly or irritatingly *now Shetland*.

noun **1** a small, puny, unimportant person; a small, conceited, impudent person. **2** a worthless person.

nyakit *see* **nakit**

nyam *see* **nam**

nyarb [nee**arb**] be discontented or complaining *NE*.

nyarg *see* **narg**

nyarr *see* **narr**

nyatter *see* **natter**

nyiffnyaff *see* **niffnaff**

nyim *see* **nimp**

nyod [nee**od**] *exclamation* God! *NE, Fife*.

nyowl [nee**owl**] howl like a cat *Shetland NE*.

nyvle *see* **nael**

O

o of.

O *see* **ordinar**

oam, yoam *noun* **1** steam. **2** a warm smell, *eg* from cooking. **3** a warm stuffy atmosphere.

oath: oath of calumny an oath taken at the outset of an action by which both parties swear that the facts pleaded are true. **oath of verity** an oath as to the truth of the allegation of debt required to be made by a creditor petitioning for or claiming in **sequestration** (*see* **sequestrate**).

obligant *law* a person who binds himself or is legally bound by a contract, bond or some other obligation.

obligement 1 a formal contract or agreement; an obligation. **2** an act of kindness, a favour.

observe an observation; a remark, comment.

och expression of sorrow, pain, regret, or of annoyance, weariness etc.

ochie *see* **eechie**

ocht[1], **owt** aught, anything; nothing.

ocht[2] ought.

od, odd *in mild oaths* God: *"Od save us a"*.

oe, oy(e) [rhymes with 'go' or 'boy'] a grandchild.

oen *see* **une**

o'er *see* **ower**

o'ercome *see* **owercome**

of, off *see* **aff**

offer threaten; make as if (to..); try : *"And if he offers to rebel"*.

officer an official of a court etc whose duty is to keep order at meetings, deliver messages etc.

    officer of state one of the important officials of state in Scotland, *eg* the **Lord Lyon, Lord Advocate** (*see* **Lord**).

O Grade *see* **ordinar**

oil, ile, uilie, ulyie, eelie oil.

    eelie dolly an oil lamp *NE*. **uilie pig** an oil barrel etc.

old *see* **auld**

Old Hundredth *see* **hunder**

oman *see* **woman**

on 1 about, concerning: *"Dae ye mind on that man?"* **2** supported by, with: *"go on a stick"*. **3** to: **cry** *etc* **on** attract the attention of (someone) by calling out. **4** for: *"Wait on me!"*

    on about talking about, harping on. **on for** eager for. **on oneself** on one's own, independent(ly). **on wi = on for.**

on- = un-.

oncairry a fuss, carry-on.

oncanny *see* **uncannie**

oncome 1 the beginning of something; progress in something. **2** a heavy fall of rain or snow. **3** a sharp attack of illness *S*.

ondeemous *see* **undeemous**

onder *see* **under**

onding 1 a heavy continuous fall of rain or snow. **2** an attack, outburst.

ondocht *see* **undocht**

one *see* **un-**

onerstan(d) *see* **unerstan(d)**

onfa 1 a heavy fall of rain or snow. **2** an attack of a disease.

onfeirie *see* **unfeary**

ongaeins, ongoings, ongauns goings-on, (wild or rowdy) behaviour.

ongang 1 the setting in motion of machinery, especially a mill *NE*. **2** rowdy behaviour *now NE*.

onie, ony 1 any. **2** in any way, at all: *"can ye fish ony?"*.

onkent *see* **unken**

onless *see* **unless**

onricht *see* **unricht**

onset a dwelling site, especially a farm with its house and outhouses, a small cluster of houses.

onstead the houses and building of a farm.

ontil *see* **until**

onwait the act of waiting, a long wait; a person, *eg* an invalid, requiring constant attention; a person who causes a long wait *NE*.

ony *see* **onie**

oo¹, oull [-oo-], wool 1 wool. 2 oose, ooze woollen fluff; fluff from cotton etc.
  oosie, oozie fluffy; furry; having a good nap or pile. **oother, ouder** fluff from wool, cotton etc when it begins to fray. **a(w) ae oo** all one wool; all the same; equal.

oo² woo.

oo³, ou: *in street cries* **caller oo** fresh oysters.

oo⁴ we, us.

oobit, oubet, †woubit [-oo-]: **hairy oobit** a hairy caterpillar.

oof, ouf a wolf.

oof *see* **ouf**

oogly *see* **ugly**

ook *see* **ouk**

ool *noun* an owl.
  verb 1 treat harshly, bully; wreck the health of. 2 feel low or depressed.

oolet an owl.

oon *see* **une, woun**

oon- *see* **un-**

ooncanny *see* **uncannie**

oon(d)er *see* **under**

oon(d)erstan(d) *see* **unerstan(d)**

oon-egg *see* **wind¹**

oonken *see* **unken**

oop, oopie stiffie, oopsie doopsie *see* **up**

oor an hour.

oor *see* **our**

oorit cold, shivery; tired or ill-looking.

oorie, ourie [-oo-], **oorich(ie)** 1 dismal, gloomy, miserable-looking from cold, illness etc; *of weather* dull and chilly, raw. 2 uncanny, strange.
  oorlich miserable-looking from cold, hunger or illness; damp, raw, bleak; *of things* sad and depressing, eerie.

oose, oosie *see* **oo¹**

oot *see* **out**

ootby *see* **outby**

ootcast *see* **outcast**

ootcome *see* **outcome**

ooten *see* **out, outen**

ootfield *see* **outfield**

ootgae *see* **outgae**

ootgang *see* **outgang**

ootgate *see* **outgate**

oother *see* **oo¹**

ootland *see* **outland**

ootlier *see* **outlier**

ootmaist *see* **outmost**

ootrel *see* **outrel**

oot-rin *see* **outrun**

ootset *see* **outset**

ootwale *see* **outwale**

ootwuth *see* **outwith**

ooze, oozie *see* **oo¹**

open, apen, wuppen *adjective* 1 open. 2 free (to do..).
  noun an opening, gap, space.

or *preposition* 1 before. 2 until.
  conjunction 1 before; until. 2 sooner than, rather than.

or *see* **ower**

oranger an orange.

ordeen, ordain 1 ordain. 2 **ordain** *Presbyterian churches* admit (an **elder** or **deacon²**) to office.

orders one's gear, all that one needs for some purpose.

ordinar, ordinary, ordnar *adjective* 1 ordinary. 2 **ordinary** *Scottish Universities* in the Faculties of Arts and Science, of the general courses in any particular subject, passes in a certain number of which lead either to an **Ordinary Degree** or to the higher classes of an Honours course; *also* **Ordinary Degree** an academic degree gained by a number of passes in **ordinary** courses. 3 **Ordinary, O** *secondary education* at a less advanced level, of a state examination, the course leading to it or the certificate awarded to successful candidate; **O (Grade)** one of these

examinations, courses or certificates.
noun 1 ordinary. 2 the usual state of things; what is normal or usual to a person etc.

nae ordinar unusual(ly), extraordinar(il)y: *"there was a fuss nae ordinar"*.

orishon a wild person; an odd-looking person.

Orkney *see* **Islands Council**

orp grumble, complain.

orra, †**orrow** *adjective* 1 spare, unemployed; *of one of a pair* without a partner; unmatched, odd; extra, superfluous. 2 occasional, appearing here and there; *of a job* casual, unskilled; *of a person or animal* doing casual or unskilled work. 3 miscellaneous, odd. 4 strange, uncommon. 5 worthless, shabby, disreputable.
noun what is left over; an article not in use; **orras** odds and ends.

orral a scrap, fragment; **orrals** bits and pieces, odds and ends; leftovers.

orraman a person who does odd jobs, especially on a farm.

ort *noun, usually* **orts** what is useless and has been thrown away; leavings, leftovers. *verb* throw away; refuse; use wastefully.

osel, oz(z)el one of the short cords by which a herring-net is attached to the head-rope.

other *see* **ither**

ou *see* **oo**[3]

oubet *see* **oobit**

ouder *see* **oo**[1]

ouer *see* **ower**

ouf [-oo-], **oof** a small unimportant creature; a stupid fool, idiot.

ouf *see* **oof**

oug *see* **ug**

ought *see* **aucht**[3]

ouk [-oo-], **ook, wick** *now NE,* †**wook** a week.

oull *see* **oo**[1]

oun *see* **woun**

oup *see* **up**

our, oor, wir, wur, weer *NE* our.

our ane my wife; my husband.

ourie *see* **oorie**

oussen *see* **ox**

out, oot *adverb* 1 out. 2 *of a cup etc* emptied: *"is your cup out?"*. 3 *of a gathering of people etc* away and out of the building; *of the meeting itself* over, finished: *"the school was out"*. 4 *especially of one's age* fully, quite *now NE: "I'm fifty out."* 5 *referring to the Jacobite Risings of 1715 or 1745* in arms against the Hanoverian Government. 6 *referring to the* **Disruption** *of 1843* having left the established Church for the **Free Church** (*see* **free**).
preposition 1 out of, from. 2 along, up (a road) in an outward direction away from the speaker: *"out the way homeward"*.
adjective 1 out, outlying etc: *"the out glens"*. 2 (working) out of doors or in the fields, *eg* **outwork(er), out-girl.**

out about out of doors, out in the garden or fields, quite far from one's home. **out at** out of, from (a door, window etc). **out on, ooten** out of, outside. **out o** out of, from out of, beyond. **out ower** *preposition* 1 *of motion* outwards and over; over the top of; over to the other side of; across; out of. 2 *of position* above, over, on top of; bent over (a drink, task etc); on the other side of, on either side of. *adverb* 1 at a distance; aside; apart. 2 out of bed, up. **out ower the door** out of doors.

outs and ins ins and outs, details (of something).)

outby, ootby *adverb* 1 outwards; out and a little way off; away from the shore, out at sea etc. 2 out of doors, outside, out in the fields. 3 away from home, not at hand. 4 in the outer part of a room, away from the fire.
adjective outlying, out of the way, distant, away from the main or central part, *eg* from a farm's main buildings.

outcast, ootcast a quarrel.

outcome, ootcome 1 a coming out, appearance, escape. **2** the result, effect. **3** produce, product; profit.

outen, ooten *literary* without, lacking.

outeral *see* **outrel**

Outer House *law* that part of the **Court of Session** (*see* **session**) in which cases of first instance are heard.

out-farm an outlying farm, usually one worked by a manager or subtenant.

outfield, ootfield *before enclosures and crop-rotation* the more outlying and less fertile land (of a farm); *compare* **infield**.

outgae, ootgae: outgane *of a time or age* past, fully: *"a youth, no twenty-twae outgaen"*. **outga(u)n, outgoing 1** *of a tenant* outgoing, removing, leaving. **2** *of the tide* ebbing.

outgang, ootgang 1 a way out, a means of getting out. **2** an outgoing, departure, *eg* the end of a season, one's removal (from a tenancy). **3** expense, outlay.

outgate, ootgate a way out.

outgaun, outgoing *see* **outgae**

outland, ootland, outlin an outsider, stranger, outcast.

outlay *of a hen* lay away from the regular nest.

outlier, ootlier [oot liyer] **1** *also* **outler** a farm animal which remains outside during the winter. **2** a person from a different or distant place.

outlin *see* **outland**

outmost, ootmaist furthest away.

outrel, outeral, ootrel a person from a different place or family; a stranger, incomer.

outrun, oot-rin 1 an area of outlying grazing land on an arable farm. **2** the way in which a dog runs out and round sheep to gather them for penning.

outset, ootset a patch of reclaimed and newly-cultivated land.

out-stair an outer stair on a house up to an upper flat.

outwale, ootwale, outwyle 1 †an outcast, an unworthy person. **2 outwale(s)** the remainder, rejects, leavings.

outwinter keep (cattle) out of doors throughout the winter.

outwith, ootwuth *preposition* outside, out of, beyond; out of the control of; away from.
adverb outside; out of doors; outwards.

outwyle *see* **outwale**

oven *see* **une**

over *children's rhymes* a numeral, *probably* eight.

over, †uver upper, higher, especially in place-names, *eg* the upper or higher of two farms of the same name.

over *see* **ower**

over-by *see* **owerby**

overgo *see* **owergae**

overhead *see* **owerheid**

overins *see* **ower**

overly *see* **ower**

oversman *see* **owersman**

overtaken *see* **owertaen**

overturn *see* **owerturn**

owe *see* **awe**[2]

ower, over, ouer [-ow-], **o('e)r** *preposition* **1** over. **2** (down) from, out of, out at (a door, window *etc*). **3** beyond, too much for.
adverb **1** over. **2** too, overmuch. **3** showing position or direction, *eg* **ower abune** over there above. **4** *of time* well on, late. **5** off to sleep.

owerance control. **owrins, overins** odds and ends, remnants. **overly** *adverb* **1** carelessly, in a casual way, by chance. **2** too (much). *adjective* **1** superficial, casual, careless. **2** excessive, exaggerated; unusual.

ower all 1 all over, everywhere. **2** above all else, most of all.

ower somebody's heid in spite of someone, without consulting the wishes or rights of someone.

owerby, over-by over, across at or to a place (at a distance from the speaker), over there.

owercome, o'ercome 1 †a surplus, extra, excess. **2** a sudden attack of illness. **3** a refrain (of a song), a chorus; a phrase or a saying which is often repeated.

owerend turn up, set on end, tip up; turn topsy-turvy.

owergae, †**overgo 1** †go over, pass through or over, cross. **2** overflow, cover over (with weeds, dirt etc). **3** overpower, get the better of. **4** *of time* pass.

owergaing 1 a crossing, a way. **2** the act of working over an area etc, *eg* in cleaning, painting. **3** a severe scolding.

owergang *verb* **1** be too much for, dominate. **2** be more or better than.
noun a going over, putting something onto a surface, *eg* a coat of paint.

owerheid, overhead 1 at an average rate per item; overall: *"1 per 100 overhead"*. **2** in confusion; untidily *now Shetland Orkney NE*.

owerplus an excess, what is left over.

owersman, oversman 1 an overseer or inspector in a coalmine. **2** a chief **arbiter**, appointed to have the final decision in the event of deadlock.

owertaen, overtaken made helpless, overcome, stupefied, especially by drink.

owerturn, overturn 1 a chorus of a song; a repetition of a story. **2** *in a business* turnover.

owerword a chorus of a poem or song; a repeated saying.

owld *see* **auld**

own, awn 1 own. **2** recognize as a relation or friend; have to do with; attend to; come into contact with.

owrins *see* **ower**

owt *see* **ocht**[1]

owther either.

ox *noun, plural also* **oussen** an ox.
oxgang a measure of land, a division of a **ploughgate** (*see* **pleuch**) or of a **davach**.

oxter *noun* **1** the armpit; the under part of the (upper) arm. **2** the corresponding part of an animal, the underside of its shoulder. **3** the corresponding part of a garment; the armhole.
verb **1** take, lead, support by the arm. **2** hold, carry under the arm. **3** embrace, cuddle. **4** elbow, shove, jostle.
oxter pouch a breast-pocket.
under one's oxter under one's arm, in one's armpit.

oy(e) *see* **oe**

oz(z)el *see* **osel**

P

†**pa, pall** a pall, a rich cloth.

paal *see* **pall**

pace *see* **paise, pass, peace**

Pace, Paice, Pasch, Pask, Pes, Pesch, Peace Pasch, Easter.

pack[1] **1** a pack. **2** one's worldly goods, property, fortune. **3** †a measure of wool or cloth. **4** a number of sheep owned by a shepherd which are allowed to pasture along with his master's.

   packman 1 a pedlar, a travelling merchant. **2** a type of cloud formation.

pack[2] on close and friendly terms, linked by mutual feeling or understanding.

paction an agreement, bargain, understanding; *law* an unofficial agreement as distinct from a legally binding contract.

pad *noun* **1** a footpath, a narrow, unsurfaced track or way. **2** a pass through hills etc.
   verb **1** travel on foot, trot along steadily and purposefully. **2** leave (hastily), *eg* after being dismissed.

paddle *see* **paidle**[1], **paidle**[2], **paidle**[3]

paddo, paddock, paddy *see* **puddock**

Paddy: Paddy barrow a barrow without sides for carrying large stones. **Paddy's Market 1** a street market in Glasgow (originally much used by the Irish). **2** any confused scene, an untidy room etc. **Paddy's Milestone** name for Ailsa Craig, a rocky island in the Firth of Clyde.

paewae, pauw-wauw *S* [powwow] pale, sickly; drooping, spiritless.

paffle, poffle a small piece of land, a croft, an allotment.

paice *see* **peace**

Paice *see* **Pace**

paich *see* **pech**

paidle[1], **paddle 1** paddle. **2** move with short quick steps, toddle, walk slowly or aimlessly. **3** press or beat with the feet, trample, tread down.

paidle[2], **paddle** *noun* a long-handled tool for weeding, scraping earth etc; a hoe.
   verb scrape (floors etc) clean; use a hoe, clean or clear by means of a hoe.

paidle[3], **paddle** a lump-fish or lump-sucker.

paik, pake *verb* **1** beat, strike, thrash, punish. **2** trudge, tramp along, stump.
   noun **1 get one's paiks** get the punishment one deserves. **2** a blow, stroke, thump. **3** a worthless person or animal, especially a female.

pail 1 †a pall, a cloth to cover a coffin. **2** a hearse.

pail *see* **pale**[2]

†**pailace** a palace.

pailie *see* **palie**

pain: (the) pains chronic rheumatism, rheumatic twinges.

painch, pench, paunch 1 a paunch. **2 painches** the bowels or guts of a person or animal.

paint, pent, pint [rhymes with 'dint'] *verb* paint.
   noun **1** paint. **2** the painted woodwork of a room or building, the paintwork.

paip, pape 1 the stone or kernel of a fruit; a dried cherrystone used as a counter and as currency in children's games. **2 the paips** a game played with cherrystones as counters and stakes.

paip *see* **pape**

pair, perr 1 a pair. **2** a set, not limited to two, of related objects, *eg* **pair of bagpipes, pair of beads, pair of cards. 3** a single object viewed as a collection *eg* **pair of blankets** one large blanket used folded in two; **pair o taws(e)** a teacher's strap with several thongs. **4** a team of two horses for ploughing etc.

an ae pair (horse) place a farm with one team of horses *now NE*.

paircel, parcel, persell 1 a parcel. **2** a small company; a group, herd, flock.

pairish, perrish a parish.

pairls, perils: the pairls paralysis; a paralytic shake or weakness *now S*.

pairple, parpall, †perpell a partition, especially of wood or a similar light material.

pairt, part, †pert *noun* **1** a part. **2** †a portion of land, one of a number of pieces into which an estate might be divided. **3** a place, area, neighbourhood *now Shetland Orkney NE*. **4** a site, a clearly-defined spot.

verb **1** part. **2** divide into parts or portions, share.

pairt-tak 1 partake. **2** †support, side with, defend.

be guid one's pairt be consistent with one's duty, worthy of one *now NE*.

pairt wi bairn give birth to a premature or stillborn baby; suffer a miscarriage.

pairtner a partner.

pairtrick *see* **paitrick**

pairty, perty a party.

†paise, pas, pace *verb* assess the weight of something by holding it, estimate.

noun a stone or metal weight, *eg* one in a pendulum clock.

Paisley with reference to the thread and textile industries of Paisley, the town near Glasgow, or shawls of the **Paisley pattern**; the pattern itself or any fabric bearing it.

Paisley bodie a native of Paisley. **Paisley pattern** an elaborate colourful design based on Hindu and Arabic motifs, used in the **Paisley shawl** and later copied throughout the world. **Paisley screwdriver** a hammer *West Central*. **Paisley shawl** a shawl of the **Paisley pattern** made of cashmere and wool or silk, or cotton and wool, very popular in the 19th century.

paitrick, partrik, patrick, pairtrick a partridge.

paittern, patron a pattern.

pake *see* **paik**

palaver, palaiver *noun* **1** a palaver. **2** a fuss.

verb behave in a silly way, fiddle about; waste time.

pale¹ a small shovel or scoop for taking samples of food, especially cheese.

pale², pail 1 a pale, a stake. **2** †a peg used as a stopper.

pale ale, India Pale Ale a kind of beer less strong than **heavy**.

palie, pailie, pallie, †paulie 1 thin, pale and sickly-looking, listless. **2** stunted, underdeveloped, delicate; not thriving. **3** defective, deformed, lame; paralysed.

pally-handit, pally-fittit 1 having a damaged or useless hand or foot. **2** left-handed. **3** †splay-footed, flat-footed.

pall, paal, pawl *noun* **1** a pole, a strong post, a beam, especially a mooring post. **2** a prop or stay, a support.

verb **1** puzzle, perplex, thwart *Shetland Orkney N*. **2** surprise, astonish *Shetland Orkney NE*. **3** go beyond, surpass, beat *Shetland Orkney NE*.

pall *see* **pa**

pallack *see* **pellock**

pallall, pallie 1 *also* **pallalls** the game of **peever**¹, hopscotch. **2** the counter with which it is played *ECentral*.

pallet 1 †the head, pate. **2** a ball, especially the glass or metal float on a fishing net.

pallie *see* **palie, pallall**

pallion¹ **1 pallions** rags, tatters. **2** a big, clumsy, rough person *NE*.

†pallion² a large and stately tent, a pavilion.

pallo *see* **pellock**

pally *see* **palie**

palm¹ **1** the grippers or claws of a pair of tongs. **2** †the hand of a clock.

palm² one of the various native trees or shrubs, especially the willow, used by Roman Catholics or Episcopalians to represent the palm on Palm Sunday.

palmer, paumer, pawmer *noun* a palmer,

a pilgrim.
verb **1** walk about aimlessly, saunter. **2** move or walk clumsily and noisily *now NE*.

palmie, paumie, pawmie a stroke with a strap or cane on the palm of the hand.

pan[1] *noun* the skull, the cranium.
verb, of soil become solid so that rain does not flow through.
pannie kindling, firewood.
pan bread bread baked in a pan or tin. **pancake** a small, round, flat cake, made by dropping thick batter onto a **girdle**, frying pan etc, smaller and thicker than an English pancake, usually eaten cold with butter, jam etc. †**pandoor (oyster)** a large oyster found in the Forth. **pan drop** a round peppermint **sweetie**, a mint imperial. **pan-jotral(s) 1** (a dish made from) odds and ends of food. **2** a cake made from scraps of other cakes (and fruit). **pan loaf 1** a loaf with a hard smooth crust, baked in a pan or tin. **2** an affected way of speaking to impress others. **pan-wood** small coal or **dross**.
knock one's pan in work very hard, exert oneself to the point of exhaustion.

pan[2] a purlin, horizontal roof-beam *now SW*.

pand, paund, pawn a flounce draping the legs of a bed; the canopy above it, a valance.

pander, paunder wander about aimlessly, drift around.

pandie a stroke with a cane etc on the palm of the hand.

panel, pannel *law* a prisoner at the bar, the accused.

pang 1 pack tight, cram full, stuff. **2** cram (the stomach) with food.

pani water; rain *S*.

pannell *see* **panel**

panshit a state of excitement, panic, muddle *now NE*.

pant[1] (the mouth of) a public well, fountain etc *mainly S*.

pant[2] a prank, a lark, a piece of fun.

pap[1], **paup 1** a pap, teat, nipple. **2** the uvula: *"pap o the hause"*. **3** a conical hill. **4** one of the segments of an orange. **5** a sea anemone.

pap[2], **pop 1** pop. **2** touch or strike lightly and smartly. **3** beat, thrash. **4** aim, throw, shoot; strike with a missile.

pape, paip 1 the pope. **2** *impolite* a Roman Catholic.

pape *see* **paip**

paper, †peper *noun* **1** paper. **2** the manuscript of a sermon. **3** a printed proclamation or notice *now Shetland*.
verb set down on paper for publication, issue a bill or insert a notice in a newspaper.
paper note a (one-pound) banknote *now Shetland Orkney N*.

papingo 1 †a parrot. **2** a parrot-shaped archery target.

papple, popple 1 flow, bubble up. **2** *of fat* sizzle, sputter. **3** †*of people* stream with perspiration; be extremely excited.

parade *see* **parawd**

†**paraphernals** the personal belongings of a married woman, which remained her own property after her marriage.

paraphrase *Presbyterian Churches* one of a collection of metrical versions of scriptural passages printed with the metrical psalms at the end of the Scottish Bible.

parawd, paraud, parade 1 a parade. **2** a procession, march.

parcel *see* **paircel**

Paris bun a sweet, sugar-topped, sponge-like bun.

park, perk *noun* **1** a park. **2** an area of enclosed farmground, a field.
verb **1** enclose (with a wall or ditch) *now Shetland*. **2** rear (animals) in a field or enclosure *now Shetland*.
parkie child's word for a park-keeper or attendant.

parkin, perkin a hard, round, spiced biscuit.

parley *games* a truce, respite.

parpall *see* **pairple**

parpen *noun* a stone which passes through the entire thickness of a wall.
adjective, of a door etc in exact alignment, true *now NE.*

parr a young salmon with dark stripes on its side before the **smolt** stage (*see* **smowt**[1]).

parritch, porridge, †porritch 1 porridge. **2** food in general, one's daily bread.
as plain as parritch as clear as crystal. **auld claes an parritch** one's usual daily routine, the daily grind. **save one's breath to cool one's parritch** save one's breath; hold one's tongue.

parrock, parreck, parroch [-ch as in 'loch'] **1** a small enclosure or pen; a pen in which a sheep is familiarized with a strange lamb *now SW, S.* **2** a group closely packed together *NE.*

parrot (coal) a kind of coal which lights easily and burns with a clear bright flame and a crackling sound.

parry 1 waste time, dawdle or delay in order to avoid action. **2** meddle with, have dealings with.

part *see* **pairt**

partan 1 the common edible crab. **2** an ugly, bad-tempered or stupid person.

particular, parteeklar *now Shetland adjective* **1** particular. **2** private, confidential. **3** remarkable, exceptional; odd. **4** clean, hygenic, especially in cooking.
adverb particularly.

partrik *see* **paitrick**

pas *see* **paise**

Pasch *see* **Pace**

†pash *humorous* the head.

Pask *see* **Pace**

pass[1]**, pace 1** a pace, a step. **2** an indoor passage or corridor, *eg* between the pews in a church or machines in a factory.

pass[2] **1** give up, abandon. **2** †overlook, disregard.
pass-ower an intentional omission.

†passenger a (passing) traveller, a passer-by.

passment decorative edging.

past *adverb* on one side, out of the way; over, done with.
adjective **1** *after a date etc* last: *"I haena seen him this year past".* **2** having reached a specified age on one's last birthday: *"Wee Bob's nine past".*
lay past, put past, set past put away, set aside for later use. **not to (be able to) see past someone** be obsessed with someone's virtues or merits, favour someone to the exclusion of all others. **past a** unspeakable, beyond belief, intolerable *now Shetland Caithness.* **pit-past** a hasty meal, a quick snack.

paster the pastern.

pat *see* **pit, pot**

pate *see* **peat**

path *see* **peth**

†pathit paved.

patience passion.
ma patience! exclamation of wonder or disbelief.

patrick *see* **paitrick**

patron *see* **paittern**

pattle, pettle a small spade-like tool for clearing the mould-board of a plough.

pauchle[1]**, pochle** *noun* **1** a bundle, a small load. **2** a small bundle or parcel, a quantity of something; now especially something taken by an employee from his employer, with or without permission. **3** a swindle, a piece of trickery, a fiddle.
verb **1** be guilty of a minor dishonesty, cheat; rig (an election etc). **2** steal, pocket. **3** shuffle (playing cards).

pauchle[2] **1** move feebly but persistently, struggle along. **2** use up effort and energy. **3** work ineffectually, bungle, potter.
be in in a pauchle be in a disorganized state, be behind with one's work.

pauchtie, paughty [-ch-, -gh- as -ch in 'loch'] **1** supercilious, conceited, insolent, self-important. **2** †stout-hearted, gallant.

paukie *see* **pawk, pawkie**

paullie *see* **palie**

paumer *see* **palmer**

paumie *see* **palmie**

paunch *see* **painch**

paund *see* **pand**

paunder *see* **pander**

paup *see* **pap**[1]

paut *see* **pawt**

pauw-wauw *see* **paewae**

pavey-waveys a girls' skipping game in which the rope is made to wave.

pavie, pavee 1 †a caper, a fantastic movement of the body. **2** †a trick, practical joke. **3** a fuss about nothing, a great state of excitement.

paw[1] a slight movement *now Shetland*.

paw[2] pa, dad.

pawk †a trick, a wile.

   pawkie, paukie 1 wily, shrewd, stubborn. **2** having a matter-of-fact, humorously critical outlook on life, with a sly, quiet wit. **3** roguish, coquettish; lively, merry.

pawkie, paukie a mitten.

pawl *see* **pall**

pawmer *see* **palmer**

pawmie *see* **palmie**

pawn, pawnd 1 a pawn, a pledge. **2** a pawnshop.

pawn *see* **pand**

pawpie child's word for grandfather.

pawt, paut 1 strike the ground with the foot, stamp in rage; *of a horse etc* paw (the ground). **2** walk heavily, stamp around angrily *now Caithness*.

pay *see* **pey**

peace, pace, paice 1 peace. **2** *in phrases eg* **I wish to peace;** I wish to God **surely to peace** surely to God.

   sit at peace *to a child* sit still, don't fidget. **give me peace** leave me alone, don't disturb me.

Peace *see* **Pace**

pear *see* **peer**

pearl purl, a stitch in knitting.

   pearlin(g)s lace (trimming), edging.

pearlins a string of pearls.

pease, pis pease.

peasie a small marble.

pease-brose a dish made of **pease-meal** and boiling water. **pease-meal** a flour of ground pease.

peat, pate 1 peat; a piece of this dried for fuel. **2 the peats** the work of digging and preparing peat for fuel. **3** something resembling a peat, *eg* a coping-stone.

   peat-bank the bank or vertical face from which peats are cut. **peat bree** the water which drains from peat soil, peaty water *now NE*. **peat-caster** a person who cuts peats and lays them out to dry. **peat-coom** peat dust. **peat hag** a hole or pit left in an old peat-working. **peat-moss** a peat-bog, the place where peats are dug. **peat muild** = **peat-coom**.

pech, †pegh, paich *verb* **1** puff, pant, gasp for breath. **2** move or work so as to pant or gasp with the effort. **3** breathe slowly, sigh, groan.

   noun **1** a pant, gasp; one's breath. **2** an asthmatic wheeze, a breathless cough. **3** a sigh of weariness, relief, satisfaction etc.

   pechie short-winded, asthmatic, wheezy.

   a sair pech a weary effort, an exhausting struggle.

†pechan, peghan [-ch-, -gh- as -ch- in 'loch'] the stomach, the belly.

pecht, picht, pict, pech 1 Pict one of an ancient people who inhabited Scotland north of the Forth. **2** contemptuous term for a small undersized person.

peck a small quantity of something edible, what can be pecked, a scrap of food.

pedder, pether a pedlar, packman.

peeack *see* **peek**[1]

pee-the-bed a dandelion.

peedie *see* **peerie**

†peefer, piffer 1 complain, moan. **2** work ineffectually, trifle.

peek[1], **peeack** *noun* **1** the cry of a small animal or bird, a piping noise, a cheep. **2** †a person with a weak piping voice;

an insignificant person *NE*.

verb 1 cheep, chirp, cry feebly. 2 complain, whimper *NE*.

peek² a tiny point of light, a little tongue of flame.

peel¹ *verb* 1 †plunder, rob, cheat. 2 skin (one's leg, arm etc), usually by accident.

peeler a small crab at shell-casting time.

peel-an-eat *noun* potatoes cooked in their skins. *adjective, of a person* unhealthy-looking, sickly

peel² equal, match; *in curling, bowls etc* tie, have equal scores.

peel³ a stockade; the ground enclosed by it; a fortified house or small defensive tower.

peel⁴ a pill, a tablet.

peel *see* **puil**

peelie: peelie-wally sickly, feeble, thin and ill-looking. **peelie-wersh** sickly, delicate; insipid *now S*.

peen, piend a pane, a sheet of glass *now NE*.

peen *see* **pin**

peenge, pinge *verb* 1 whine, complain, whimper. 2 droop, mope, look cold and miserable.

noun a feeble, sickly-looking person; a fretful child.

peengie 1 peevish, fractious. 2 sickly-looking, puny.

peenie 1 a pinafore, especially one worn by children; an apron. 2 *child's word* the tummy.

peeoy a schoolboy's home-made firework.

peep 1 a **peek²** (of a gas jet). 2 a small opening, a crack.

put someone's gas at a peep put someone in his place.

peer, pear a pear.

peerie 1 a child's spinning top. 2 a fir cone *S*. 3 a small stone marble *NE*.

peerie heel a high, sharply-pointed heel of a shoe, a stiletto heel. **peerie-heidit** in a state of mental confusion.

peer *see* **puir**

peerie *now Shetland Orkney*, **peedie** *now Orkney Caithness* small, little, tiny.

peerie-weerie *adjective* = **peerie**. *noun* a tiny creature. **peerie-winkie** *in nursery rhymes* the little finger or toe.

peesie *slang and child's word* excellent.

peesweep, peewee, peeweet, peesie a lapwing.

peesie-weesie sharp-featured, gaunt; shrill-voiced, complaining.

peety, pity pity.

it's a peety o 1 it's a pity about. **2** it's a bad lookout for; it serves you right. **peety me!** exclamation of surprise, disgust etc.

peever¹ 1 the flat stone used in the game of hopscotch. 2 **peever(s)** the game itself. **peever(ie) beds** the chalked square on which the game is played.

peever² a very small marble.

peewee(t) *see* **peesweep**

peg *slang* a policeman.

peggin a beating, drubbing.

pegh *see* **pech**

peghan *see* **pechan**

pell *mainly Shetland Orkney Caithness* 1 a matted tuft of hair; a rag. 2 a dirty person, a tramp.

pellet a pelt, a(n undressed) sheepskin *now S*.

pellock, pallack, pallo *Orkney* 1 a porpoise; *formerly also* a dolphin. 2 something bulky and clumsy; a short fat person.

pelt 1 †a person or thing of little value; trash, rubbish. 2 a low-grade type of coal.

pen¹ 1 a plume, feather. 2 a small spoon for taking snuff. 3 the stalk of a plant or vegetable.

pen-gun a kind of pop-gun or peashooter made from a bird's quill.

talk like a pen-gun chatter on.

pen² a pointed conical hill *S*: "Ettrick Pen".

pench *see* **painch**

pend, pen(n) 1 an arch (of a bridge, gateway etc). **2** an arched passageway or **entry,** especially one leading into the back-court of a block of houses. **3** a covered drain or sewer; the grating over it.

pendicle something dependent on or subordinate to something else, *eg* **1** †a piece of land etc regarded as subsidiary to a main estate; **2** a small piece of ground forming part of a larger holding or farm.

penny money in general; a sum of money (see p 358).

†**penny-book(ie), penny-buff** a child's first school book; *hence* the first class in a school. **penny-fee** cash, earnings. †**pennyland** a measure of land, varying in size. †**pennystane** a round flat stone used as a quoit. **penny wedding** a wedding at which a guest contributed a small sum of money (or food and drink) towards the cost, the surplus being given to the couple as a gift. **penny wheep** a kind of weak ale. **get one's penny(s)worths o** get one's own back on, get the better of.

a bonnie penny a considerable sum of money.

pense think; consider; call to mind.

pensefu thoughtful, pensive. **pensie 1** responsible, respectable *NE*. **2** self-important, pompous, prim.

pent *see* **paint**

penure-pig, pin(n)er pig a (children's) earthenware money-box.

penurious 1 bad-tempered, whining *NE*. **2** attentive to detail, fastidious *NE*.

peper *see* **paper**

†**peppin** petted, spoilt, pampered *NE*.

perconnon, precunnance: perconnon that on the understanding that *NE*.

peremptor 1 †peremptory. **2** *of people* excessively careful, fussy *now Shetland*. **peremptory defence** *law* a defence put forward by a litigant which, if established, bars further proceedings forever.

perfit perfect.

perils *see* **pairls**

perish 1 destroy, kill: *"perished with cold"*. **2** squander (money), wreck (a ship etc); finish (food or drink).

perjink 1 trim, neat, smart in appearance. **2** prim, strait-laced. **3** exact, precise, fussy.

perk a pole or rod, especially one projecting from a wall or window on which clothes were hung to dry; latterly, an indoor drying rail or rope.

perk *see* **park**

perkin *see* **parkin**

perlaig trash, rubbish, rubbishy food *NE*.

perlicket a trace, scrap *Caithness NE*.

pernicketie 1 very precise, obsessed by detail, fussy. **2** cantankerous, touchy, bad-tempered. **3** *of things* requiring close attention or great care, fiddling, troublesome.

perpell *see* **pairple**

†**perqueer, prequeer** *adverb* **1** by heart; perfectly, accurately. **2** exactly, without hesitation.
adjective **1** word-perfect, expert, knowledgeable. **2** clear, distinct, skilfully made. **3** clearly seen, distinctly visible.

perr *see* **pair**

perrish *see* **pairish**

†**persel** parsley.

persell *see* **paircel**

perskeet fastidious, precise; hard-to-please *now Shetland*.

personal bar, personal exception *law* an impediment to a legal right or action due to a person's own previous statements or behaviour, *corresponding to English* estoppel.

pert *see* **pairt**

pertinents *law* anything connected with or forming part of a piece of land or **heritable** property that is not specially reserved from the grant, *eg* buildings on a piece of land, a right of pasturage.

perty *see* **pairty**

Pes, Pesch *see* **Pace**

pet *see* **pit**

pet (day) a day of sunshine in a spell of bad weather.

pettle pet, pamper, fondle *now S*.

peter: come the peter ower act in a domineering way over, dictate to. **pit the peter on** put a firm and sudden stop to.

Peter: peter(ie)-dick, peter(-a)-dick a rhythmic pattern of two or three short beats followed by one long, *eg* in a dance step.
    Peter's thoom, Peter's mark one of the black marks behind the gills of a haddock.

peth, path 1 a cleft on a steep hill; a steep track into a ravine and up the other side. **2** a path.

pether *see* **pedder**

petition *law* one of the methods by which proceedings can be brought before the **Court of Session** (*see* **session**) or the **High Court of Justiciary** (*see* **justiciary**).
    petition and complaint an application to the **Court of Session** for redress of *eg* complaints of breach of **interdict**.

petticoat tails triangular shortbread biscuits.

pettle *see* **pattle**

peuch, pyoch [peeooch, peeoach] **1** *imitating the sound of the wind etc* puff! **2** *expressing impatience, disgust, disbelief etc* pooh! **3** a light blast of air, a puff of wind or breath.
    peuchle, pyocher 1 fuss about or work ineffectually *now Shetland*. **2** cough in a choking, asthmatic way.

peuch *see* **pleuch**

peul *see* **pewl**

peuther, †pewter 1 fuss about doing nothing. **2** bustle about trying to win favour.

pew, pue 1 a stream of air, a breath *now Shetland*. **2** a puff of smoke, wind etc. **3** a small quantity of a substance *now Shetland*.
    †not play pew stop breathing; have no effect; be unable to compete.

pewl, peul, pule *verb* **1** pule, whine, complain. **2** *of animals* be in a weak state; *of people* be only half-alive, scrape a bare living. **3** *of snow or rain* fall thinly, or in small amounts *S*.
    noun **1** a wailing cry; a moan. **2** a seagull.

pewter *see* **peuther**

pey [rhymes with 'gey'], **pay** *verb* **1** pay. **2** beat, punish. **3** yield or provide (a certain payment). **4** pay for: *"it'll help tae pey the coal"*.
    noun **1** pay. **2** a blow, punishment.
    pey aff pay for others' drink etc.

phrase, fra(i)se *noun* **1** a phrase. **2** an elaborate flowery speech, flattery *now NE*. **3** a great talk about something. **4** something false and misleading *now NE*.
    verb **1** phrase. **2** flatter, praise, often insincerely *NE*.
    phrasie *now NE* **1** gushing. **2** fussy, fastidious.

pibroch [peebroch] the music of the Scottish bagpipe, now limited to traditional marches, salutes, laments etc; a piece of this, consisting of a theme (the **urlar**) and a series of variations.

piccatarrie *see* **pictarnie**

picher [-ch- as in 'dreich'] *now NE noun* **1** a state of confusion or muddle. **2** a useless, person, a person who is usually in a flap.
    verb work in a disorganized way, muddle along.

picht *see* **pecht**

pick¹ *verb* **1** be a petty thief, pilfer. **2** question (someone), pick someone's brains.
    noun **1** a pecking; (a quantity of) food. **2** a small quantity.
    pickie-say (hat) the narrow-brimmed hat, worn as a badge of authority by a foreman on a farm *NE*. **pickle in one's ain pock neuk** rely on one's own resources.
    pick-thank *noun* a person who curries favour, a sneak. *adjective* ungrateful, unappreciative.
    pick someone up get someone's meaning.

pick²: pickit roughened, pitted, uneven.

   pick(ie)man a man who dresses millstones.

pick³ *verb* **1** throw, hurl; thrust, drive. **2 pick on** pitch on, choose. **3** *of a (farm-) animal* abort (her young), give birth to prematurely.

   noun **1** a marble, thrown instead of being rolled *NE*. **2** an aborted or stillborn animal.

   picker(stick) *weaving* a mechanism for shooting the shuttle across the loom.

pick⁴ †pique.

   pickant piquant *now NE*.

   hae a pick at have a dislike for, bear (someone) a grudge.

pick⁵ pitch.

pick⁶ a spade in playing cards *NE*.

pickle, puckle 1 a grain of oats, barley or wheat. **2** a small particle or grain ; a speck *now Shetland*. **3** a small amount, a little, a few.

pickmaw a black-headed gull.

pict, Pict *see* **pecht**

pictarnie, piccatarrie 1 a common or arctic tern. **2** a black-headed gull. **3** a thin wretched-looking person; a bad-tempered person.

pie peer closely, squint.

   pie-eyed cross-eyed; drunk.

piece 1 a (short) distance. **2** a piece of food, a snack, now usually a piece of bread, scone etc with butter, jam etc. **3 the piece** each. **4 a piece** a little, rather.

   piece box a box for a (lunchtime) snack. **piece denner** a lunchtime snack of sandwiches etc. **piece poke** the paper bag etc in which a snack is carried.

   piece time a break for a meal or snack.

   baby's piece, christening piece a slice of cake, cheese and a coin offered to the first person to see a baby after its christening.

pie-hole a hole to allow a lace or cord to pass through, an eyelet.

piend *see* **peen**

piet *see* **pyot**

piffer *see* **peefer**

pig 1 a(n earthenware) container, a pot, jar, pitcher. **2** an earthenware moneybox, now sometimes shaped like the animal. **3** an earthenware hot-water bottle. **4** earthenware as a material; a piece of this.

   pigman a pottery merchant, a **pig-an'-ragger.**

   pig-an'-ragger a travelling hawker giving crockery in exchange for rags *NE*.

   †**pigs an(d) whistles** odds and ends, trivialities. **to pigs an' whistles** to pieces, to ruin.

piggin a kind of tub *now Ulster*.

pike *noun* **1** †a pick(axe). **2** a pointed tip or end; a spike. **3** a thorn or prickle on a plant; a spine or quill of an animal *now Orkney*. **4** a conical-topped hayrick for drying hay before stacking.

   verb **1** steal, pilfer *now NE*. **2** make thin, reduce to skin and bone *now Orkney*. **3** nibble, pick (at food). **4** provide with a pike or with a spike or spikes.

   pikie spiked, jagged, barbed.

   pike-thank a person who curries favour, a sneak.

pile¹ 1 a blade (of grass etc). **2** a grain (of corn etc); a leaf (of tea etc).

pile² increase the speed of a swing, scooter etc by moving the body or feet.

   piler a boy's home-made cart, propelled this way.

pilget [-g- as in 'get'] **1** a quarrel, a fight, struggle *NE*. **2** a state of distress or excitement *now NE*.

pilk 1 pick out, shell, peel. **2** pilfer, steal.

piller, puller, pillan a small crab at the shell-casting stage, useful for bait.

pilliedacus [pilliedackus] the person in command.

piltock a coalfish in its early stages *now Shetland Orkney*.

pin, peen *noun* **1** a pin. **2** a kind of door-knocker consisting of a ring rattled up and down a serrated rod. **3 pins** small wedging stones in a wall. **4** a small, neat person or animal *NE*. **5** a mood, frame of mind *now Shetland Orkney:* *"in an angry pin".*

verb **1** pin. **2** fill up (masonry) with **pins** *noun* 3. **3** strike as with a small sharp-pointed missile. **4** beat, thrash. **5** grab, seize *now NE.* **6** move with speed and vigour.

peen-heid the young fry of the minnow or stickleback. **pin-leg** a wooden leg.

pinch *verb* **1** spend or give meanly, stint. **2** move (a heavy object) by levering.

noun a crowbar.

pincher 1 pinchers tweezers, pliers etc. **2** a crowbar.

pind *see* **poind**

pine *noun* suffering, distress, pain *now Shetland Orkney NE.*

verb **1** †cause pain and suffering, torment. **2** waste away from disease. **3** *of fish, hay etc* shrink by drying in the open air.

†piner, pynor [rhymes with 'miner'] a labourer or porter; *in Aberdeen* a member of a society of porters.

piner-pig *see* **penure-pig**

pinge *see* **peenge**

pingle *verb* **1** †compete; quarrel, disagree. **2** struggle, exert oneself, work hard. **3** trifle, dabble or meddle with, work in a lazy, ineffectual way *now S.*

noun **1** a contest; disagreement. **2** an effort, struggle *now Fife.*

pingle(-pan) a small, shallow cooking-pan.

pink¹, pinkie a primrose.

speak pink speak in a very affected over-refined way.

pink² **1** drip (with a sharp, tinkling sound) *now Orkney NE.* **2** strike making a tiny sharp sound, a ping.

pink³ dress up, adorn *now Shetland Orkney Ulster.*

pinkie 1 something very small. **2** the little finger.

pinner-pig *see* **penure-pig**

pint *see* **paint, point**

pintle the penis.

pipe *noun* **1** *also* **the pipes** the Scottish bagpipe(s). **2** a large ripe acorn with its stalk *S.*

verb **1** pipe; play (a tune) on the bagpipes. **2** flute (cloth), frill with a special iron.

piper 1 a piper, especially one who plays the bagpipes. **2** an unsplit, half-dried haddock *NE.* **piper's bidding** a last-minute invitation. **piper's news** out-of-date news. **pipie** informal name for a **pipe major.**

pipe band a band made up of **pipers** and drummers with a drum-major.

pipe major the leader of a **pipe band**; as a military title, the equivalent of the regimental bandmaster in an English regiment.

pirk a sharp point, thorn, prickle.

pirl, purl *verb* **1** twist, twirl, coil, curl; roll, whirl. **2** *in football etc* drive (the ball) with quick light strokes or kicks, dribble *NE.* **3** stir, mix, poke (a fire) *Shetland NE.* **4** spin, whirl round, rotate; swirl, eddy. **5** fumble. **6** move or work idly or half-heartedly *now NE.*

noun **1** a curl, twist, coil. **2** a knot of hair, a bun. **3** an eddy or swirl, a ripple, gentle breeze.

pirlie *adjective* curly, curled, twisted *now S. noun* anything very small. **pirlie pig** a circular, earthenware money-box.

pirlicue 1 a flourish at the end of a hand-written word. **2** †a follow-on, sequel; *Presbyterian Churches* a summary of the sermons preached during the four-day Communion season.

pirn, pirm *Shetland Orkney* **1** a small spool, a reel of or for thread. **2** *weaving* a spool for holding the weft yarn in the shuttle, a bobbin. **3** the reel of a fishing rod.

pirn-mill a mill where weavers' bobbins are made.

pirr¹ a tern.

pirr-maw a black-headed gull.

pirr² *noun* **1** a sudden sharp breeze; a gentle breath of wind *now Shetland NE.*

2 a sudden burst of activity; a panic, rage.

verb **1** *of liquid* ripple; flow, stream. **2** tremble with anger, fizz with rage.

pirrie unpredictable, unreliable; quick-tempered.

pis *see* **pease**

pish 1 piss. **2** gush, rush, splash.

pish-minnie *SW, S*, **pismire** an ant. **pish-the-bed** a dandelion.

Piskie informal name for a member of the Scottish Episcopal Church.

pismire *see* **pish**

piss a call to a cat or kitten.

pit, put, pet *verb, past tense also* **pat, pit**. *past participle also* **pit, putten, pitten, potten 1** put. **2** *used where English has* send, make, take etc: *"A wis juist pittin aff ma claes"*.

pit awa 1 dismiss, sack. **2** bury. **3** commit suicide. **pit by 1** put by, set aside. **2** do away with; bury. **3** complete; spend time, stay. **4** make do with, tide (oneself) over with. **pit on** impress, impose on, fool. **pit-on** insincerity, pretence, falseness. **pitten on** affected, conceited, insincere. **weel pit(ten)-on** finely dressed.

pitawtie, potato a potato.

pitawtie bogle a scarecrow. **potato scone** = **tattie scone** (*see* **tattie**).

pitcher 1 the flat stone etc used in the game of hopscotch; the game itself. **2** a marble which is thrown rather than rolled *NE*.

pithy strong, solid; prosperous.

pitten *see* **pit**

pity *see* **peety**

placad, placard *noun* a placard.

verb make or publish derogatory statements about, tell tales about.

plack †1 a small coin. **2** money, cash; one's worldly wealth.

plackless hard-up.

not worth a plack worth nothing.

plagium [playjium] *law* the offence of child-stealing or kidnapping.

plaid, †plyde 1 a length of (tartan) woollen cloth, formerly worn as an outer garment, now part of the ceremonial dress of members of **pipe bands** (*see* **pipe**). **2** a **plaid** used as a blanket or bed-covering.

plaiding the cloth of which **plaids** are made.

plaid-neuk a fold or flap in a **plaid** used as a pocket, especially by shepherds for carrying young lambs.

†belted plaid(y) a long **plaid** wound round the middle of the body and held in place with a belt, probably an early form of kilt.

plaik *see* **play**

plain, plenn 1 plain. **2** *of ground* without hills, water etc; open; *of any surface* flat, level *now Shetland*.

plainie *games* a movement in its simplest form, before variations etc are introduced.

plain bread bread baked as a **plain loaf**. **plain loaf** a flat-sided white loaf with a hard black crust on top and a floury brown crust at the bottom, a batch loaf. **plain stanes** a pavement; a paved area surrounding a town's market or **Town House** (*see* **toun**).

plaint a complaint, protest, grievance; an expression of distress or grief.

plainyie *see* **pleen**

plaister, plaster, plester 1 plaster. **2** a beating; a dressing-down *now Shetland Caithness*. **3** a person who thrusts himself on the attention or company of others, a fawning person or animal; a flatterer. **4** a mess, shambles. **5** excessive jewellery, frills etc in one's dress.

plait *see* **plet**

plane a sycamore.

plank 1 set down, place (decisively, with a thump). **2** put in a secret place, hide for later use.

plapper *NE* **1** *of a liquid* bubble and plop when boiling. **2** splash about in water.

plash *noun* **1** a splash *now Shetland NE*. **2** a sudden sharp downpour of rain, a heavy shower. **3** a weak tasteless liquid

or drink; a large quantity of a liquid.
verb **1** splash, squelch; *of rain etc* fall in torrents, lash. **2** splash with liquid, wet, drench. **3** walk on waterlogged ground, squelch along. **4 plash** at work in a messy way, mess about in liquids *now Shetland*.
adverb splash!, with a splash *now Shetland NE*.
plashy 1 causing splashes; waterlogged, soaking wet. **2** rainy, showery.
plaster *see* **plaister**
plat, plet *adjective* **1** flat, level, even. **2** direct, clear, downright.
adverb **1** flat; flat on the ground. **2** straight; directly.
noun a landing (on a stair).
verb flatten down (the point of the nails attaching the shoe to a horse's hoof), clinch (a nail) *now Shetland*.
platch[1] *noun* **1** a splashing, stamping in water or mud; a splash of mud etc. **2** a large spot; a patch (of cloth).
verb **1** splash, cover with mud *now Shetland NE*. **2** go about or work in a sloppy way, potter.
platchie wet, muddy. **platchin** soaking *S*.
platch[2] walk in an awkward flat-footed or heavy ungainly way.
play 1 play oneself amuse oneself. **2** *of a liquid or its container* boil. **3** *where English uses* go: *"the door played clink"*.
noun **1** a game, sport, pastime *now Shetland*. **2 the play** time off school or work.
playock, †**plaik** a toy. **play piece** a mid-morning snack at school.
plea, pley [rhymes with 'gey'] **1** *law* a plea. **2** a quarrel, argument.
plead *verb, past tense also* **pled 1** plead. **2** contend, argue, debate in a court of law.
†**pleasance 1** the feeling of pleasure, happiness. **2** a pleasure-ground or park, sometimes attached to a castle *now in place names*.

pleasant, pleesant 1 pleasant. **2** humorous, witty, merry.
pleasure, pleesure *noun* pleasure.
verb please, give pleasure to, satisfy.
pleat a pigtail, plait.
pled *see* **plead**
pleen, †**plainyie,** †**plenye** *verb* **1** make a formal complaint. **2** complain, grumble, mourn.
noun a complaint, an objection.
pleep a sea-bird with a thin, high-pitched cry, *eg* an oyster-catcher, a redshank.
pleesant *see* **pleasant**
pleesure *see* **pleasure**
pleiter *see* **plowter**
plenish 1 †provide (with), fill; stock. **2** furnish (a house etc).
plenishing furniture, household equipment, often that brought by a bride to her new home.
plenn *see* **plain**
plenty a great number of: *"plenty of them play football"*.
plenye *see* **pleen**
plester *see* **plaister**
plet, plait *verb* **1** plait. **2** cross or fold (one's legs or arms). **3** fold. **4** twist, cross.
noun a pleat in a garment, a fold, crease.
plet *see* **plat**
pleuch [pleeooch], **plew, plough, ploo, peuch** [peeooch], **pue** plough.
ploughgang, †**ploughgate** a measure of land (based on what could be ploughed by eight oxen in a year). **pleuch slings** the hooks connecting the swingle-trees to the plough. **pleuch sock** a ploughshare.
pleuter *see* **plowter**
plew *see* **pleuch**
pley *see* **plea**
plink a short sharp sound like that made by a taut string.
plipe *see* **plype**
pliskie 1 a practical joke, a trick. **2** a plight, predicament. **3** a wild idea, a bee in one's bonnet.

pliv(v)er a plover.

ploiter *see* **plowter**

ploo *see* **pleuch**

plook *see* **plouk**

ploom, ploum, plum 1 a plum. **2** the fruit of the potato-plant.

plooster *see* **plowster**

ploot *see* **plowt**

plot, plout *verb* **1** scald something with boiling water to clean it; put (the carcass of a fowl, pig etc) into boiling water to ease plucking or scraping; remove hair, feathers etc from (skins) by scalding; bathe (a sore) in very hot water; overheat, burn, scorch, boil; pluck *eg* feathers from (a bird). **2** become very hot.

noun **1** a scalding, an immersion in boiling water. **2** an overheated state, a sweat, swelter.

plottie a hot drink, especially mulled wine.

ploud *see* **plowd**

plough *see* **pleuch**

plouk [-oo-], **plook, pluck 1** a pimple; a boil. **2** a growth, a swelling. **3** a knob, especially a small knob marking a measure on the inside of a container.

ploum *see* **ploom**

plout *see* **plowt**

plouter *see* **plowter**

plowd, ploud *verb* **1** *also* **plowder** walk in a heavy-footed way, plod along, paddle around. **2** work perseveringly, strive, plod *now NE.*

plowster, pluister, plooster work messily in mud etc, flounder about *now S.*

plowt, plout, ploot *verb* **1** plunge into (a liquid) *now WCentral.* **2** set down suddenly and heavily *now NE.* **3** fall heavily. **4** squelch along; dabble in water or mud *now Shetland NE.* **5** fall with a splash, pelt down.

noun **1** a noisy fall or plunge; a splash, plop. **2** a heavy shower or cascade, a downpour of rain. **3** a punch, thump.

plowt *see* **plot**

plowter, plouter, pleuter, ploiter, pleiter

verb **1** dabble with hands or feet, usually in a liquid, splash aimlessly in mud or water. **2** work or act idly or aimlessly, potter or fiddle about. **3** fumble about, rummage in the dark.

noun **1** the act of working or walking in wetness or mud; a messy task; a botched job. **2** a splash, dashing of liquid. **3** a wet, muddy spot. **4** a sloppy or sticky mess of food etc. **5** a messy inefficient worker.

ploy 1 an undertaking; a piece of business, a scheme. **2** a light-hearted plan for one's own amusement, a piece of fun, a trick. **3** a social gathering, party *now Shetland.*

pluck 1 a mouthful of grass etc taken by an animal as food. **2** a moulting state in fowls or animals. **3** a two-pronged tool for taking turnips from hard ground etc *now NE.*

pluck *see* **plouk**

pluff, pyuff *NE* [pee**uff**] *adverb* with a puff, whoof!

noun **1** a mild explosion, a whiff or puff of air, smoke. **2** a tube used as a peashooter or as a simple form of bellows *now Shetland.* **3** a piece of padding, especially used in a garment.

verb **1** discharge (smoke, breath etc) with a small explosion; blow out by puffing air. **2** swell up, puff out.

pluffer a pea-shooter. **pluffy** *adjective* plump, puffy, fleshy. *noun* a kind of toffee made fluffy and brittle by the addition of bicarbonate of soda, puff candy.

plug dodge (school), play truant.

pluister *see* **plowster**

plum *see* **ploom**

plumb a deep pool in a river or on the seabed.

†**plummet** the pommel on the hilt of a sword.

†**plump**[1] a collection; a group, flock; a clump, cluster.

plump[2] *verb* **1** *of rain* fall heavily, pour. **2** *of a (semi-)liquid* make a loud bubbling noise *now Ulster*.

noun a heavy downpour of rain, often following thunder.

plunk[1] *adverb* with a dull, heavy sound, plump!; in a sudden way, quickly.

noun **1** a heavy fall, plump or plunge; the sound of this. **2** a popping sound, *eg* of a cork being drawn from a bottle. **3** a sharp forward jerk or thrust, a flick, *eg* with the forefinger and thumb on a marble.

verb **1** fall with a dull heavy sound, usually into water etc, plop. **2** make a plopping or gurgling noise. **3** drop into water, plop, put down with a thump. **4** propel (a marble) with a thrust or jerk. **5** strike with a dull thud, thump. **6** pluck (the strings of a musical instrument) to make a popping or twanging noise.

plunker a heavy clay, glass or metal marble. **plunkie 1** a game of marbles played as in **plunk**[1] *noun* 3. **2** a kind of **sweetie** made of treacle or syrup and flour *NE*.

plunk[2] dodge (school), play truant.

ply 1 a fold, a layer or thickness, a strand or twist of rope, wool etc. **2** *fishing rivers* condition: *"in good ply"; "oot o ply"*.

plyde *see* **plaid**

plype, plipe *noun* (the noise of) a sudden dash of water; a sudden heavy shower of rain *now NE*.

verb **1** drop suddenly into a liquid, plunge or splash in mud or water *NE*. **2** dabble or work messily and carelessly *NE*. **3** walk on wet or muddy ground *NE*.

poach [poatch] **1** stir or poke, push, prod. **2** reduce to mush by messing about with *NE*: *"the baby's poaching his porridge"*. **3** mess about *now S*.

pob (tow) the refuse of flax or jute; rope teased into fibres *now NE*.

pochle *see* **pauchle**[1]

pock 1 pock, an eruption on the skin. **2** the disease causing this, *eg* chicken-pox.

pock *see* **poke**

†**pockmantie** a travelling-bag, portmanteau.

pod *see* **pud**

poddock *see* **puddock**

podlie 1 the young of the coalfish; a pollack, a lythe. **2** a tadpole. **3** a red-breasted minnow.

poffle *see* **paffle**

poind, †**pind** [pinned] **1** *law* seize and sell the goods of a debtor; impound. **2** impound (stray animals etc) as surety for compensation for any damage they do.

point, pint *noun* **1** a point. **2** a tagged length of cord etc, *eg* a shoe- or boot-lace.

verb **1** point. **2** *building* indent a stone face with a pointed tool.

pointed precise, (over-)attentive to detail, exact.

poke, pock, pyock *NE* [peeock] **1** a bag, a small sack; a shopkeeper's paper bag; a beggar's bag for collecting meal. **2** a kind of fishing net. **3** a swelling under the jaw of a sheep caused by sheep-rot; the disease itself.

be on one's own pock neuk be relying on one's own resources. **pock puddin 1** a **dumpling** or steamed pudding cooked in a bag. **2** nickname for an Englishman. **pock shakings 1** the last child of a large family. **2** the smallest pig in a litter.

pokey-hat an ice-cream cone.

pole *see* **powl**

police, polis 1 the police. **2** a policeman. **3** †the civil administration of a community, the public services and the preservation of law and order.

policies the enclosed grounds of a large house, the park of an estate.

polis *see* **police**

poll *see* **pow**[1]

pollywag a tadpole.

pony *see* **pown**

poo *see* **pou**

pooch *see* **pouch**

poochle, †**puchal** proud, self-assured, cocky *NE*.

pooder *see* **pouther**

pook *see* **pouk**, **powk**

poolie *see* **poulie**

poon *see* **pund**[1], **pund**[2]

poopit *see* **pupit**

poor *see* **pour**, **puir**

poortith *see* **puirtith**

pooshin *see* **pushin**

pooss *see* **pouss**

poost *see* **poust**

pooster *see* **poustie**

poot *see* **pout**

poother *see* **pouther**

pop *see* **pap**[2]

popple *see* **papple**

poppy show *see* **puppie show**

pork prod, poke, push *now SW, S*.

porr, purr prod, poke, thrust at.

porridge, porritch *see* **parritch**

port 1 a gateway, entrance, especially of a walled town or a castle *now only in place-names*. **2** a piece of open ground near a town gate used as the site of a **hiring market** (*see* **hire**) for farm-workers.

port-a-beul [*Gaelic* porshtabeeal] a fast tune to which repetitive Gaelic words have been added to make it easier to sing, sometimes used as an accompaniment to dancing in the absence of instrumental music.

porter biscuit a large round flattish bun.

pose *verb* place (an object) in a particular position, *eg* with the aim of hiding it; save up.
noun, also **posie** what has been laid down, a quantity, pile, collection, *eg* of money or valuables.

posh(ie) child's word for porridge.

positive determined, obstinate.

poss 1 †strike, hit. **2** press, squeeze (*eg* clothes etc in washing).

post, postie a postman.

postpone *law* relegate the claims of (a creditor) by giving others priority of repayment.

pot, pat *noun* **1** a pot. **2** †a kind of whisky still in which heat was applied directly to the pot. **3** hopscotch *NE*. **4** *also* **pottie** a clay or earthenware marble *now NE*. **5** a pit or hole in the ground, *eg* one from which peats have been dug; a (deep) hole in a river, a pool.
potted heid, potted hoch a dish made of meat from the head or shin of a cow or pig, boiled, shredded and served cold in a jelly made from the stock.
pot barley barley from which the outer husk has been removed in milling, used for making **broth**[1] etc. **stick out like a pot fit** stick out like a sore thumb *NE*. **pot-still** = **pot** *noun* 2.

potato *see* **pitawtie**

potestater [potestatter]: **in one's potestater** at the height of one's career, in one's prime *Shetland NE*.

pottage, pottich 1 pottage. **2** porridge; one's breakfast, food in general *now NE*.

potten *see* **pit**

potterlow a broken or ruined condition, smithereens, pulp *NE*.

pottie putty.

†**pottingar** an apothecary.

pou, pow, pull, pu, poo 1 pull. **2** pluck (fruit, flowers etc). **3** strip (a bird) of feathers, pluck (a fowl). **4** extract (a tooth). **5** *of a chimney etc* have a strong draught, draw.
like pulling teeth extremely difficult (to get a response etc).

pouch, pooch *noun* **1** a pouch. **2** a pocket in a garment. **3** the pocket as containing one's money, one's purse or finances.
verb **1** put into one's pocket; steal, pocket. **2** eat greedily, gulp down *NE*.

pouk [-oo-], **pook**, †**puke** *verb* **1** pluck, twitch, tug. **2** remove the feathers from (a bird), pluck (a fowl).
noun **1** a plucking motion, a twitch, tug. **2** what is to be plucked (off), *eg* wool from a sheep, fluff; a mouthful,

bite; a small quantity, a little. **3** a moulting condition in birds.

poukie dejected-looking, thin and unhealthy-looking. **poukin** the moult. **poukit** plucked; having a miserable appearance, thin-looking; shabby.

in the pouk 1 *of birds* moulting. **2** not very well, below par.

poulie [-oo-], **poolie** a louse.

poun *see* **pund**¹

pounce *see* **punce**

pound *see* **pund**¹, **pund**²

pour, poor *verb* **1** pour. **2** empty (a container) by pouring out its contents; pour the liquid from (boiled food, especially potatoes).
noun **1** a small quantity *now Ulster*. **2** a heavy shower of rain.

pourie 1 a jug, especially a cream jug. **2** a small oil can with a spout.

pour out! the shout by children at a wedding for coins to be scattered in the street. **pour-out** such a scattering of coins. **pour (the) tea** pour out tea.

pouss [-oo-], **push, pooss 1** push. **2** urge, egg on. **3** †poke; prod, strike, punch.

poust, poost, powst strength, power, force *now S*.

poustie [-oo-], **pooster** *Shetland Orkney* power, strength, authority.

pout, poot, powt 1 a poult, a young (game-)bird. **2** *also* **poutie** a small haddock; a child or young person.

pout *see* **powt**

pouter *see* **powter**

pouther, poother, powther, powder, pooder *noun* powder.
verb **1** powder. **2** sprinkle (food) with salt or spices to preserve it.

povereese reduce to poverty, exhaust (land etc) by overworking.

pow¹ [rhymes with 'cow'], **poll 1** the head of a human being or an animal. **2** poll, a person as a unit; voting etc. **3 pow** the end part of something, *eg* the rounded part of an axe-head.

pow² [rhymes with 'cow'] **1** a slow-moving stream flowing through flat land. **2** a creek or inlet used as a wharf for boats *now SW*. **3** a pool of water; a puddle.

pow *see* **pou**

powder *see* **pouther**

powheid, †**powat** [-ow- as in 'cow'] a tadpole.

powk [-ow- as in 'cow'], **pook 1** poke. **2** dig in a careless, clumsy way *NE*.

powl [-ow- as in 'cow'], **pole 1** a pole. **2** a walking stick, stilt, crutch.

†**pown** [-ow- as in 'cow'] a peacock.
pownie, pony a (female) turkey. **pownie cock** a turkey cock.

pownie [-ow- as in 'cow'] **1** a pony. **2** a carpenter's trestle.

powsowdie [-ow- as in 'cow'] **1** thick soup made from a sheep's head. **2** a mixture, a messy hotchpotch, a mush.

powst *see* **poust**

powt, pout [-ow-, -ou- as -ow- in 'cow'] **1** poke, prod *now S*. **2** walk heavily, plod *NE*.

powt net a stocking-shaped net on poles, used to force out or catch fish resting under river-banks *now S*.

powt *see* **pout**

powter, pouter [-ow-, -ou- as -ow- in 'cow'] **1** poke or prod repeatedly. **2** potter. **3** paddle or poke about in a liquid.

powther *see* **pouther**

practick *see* **prattick**

†**praecipuum** [preesipyooum] *law* an indivisible right, *eg* to a peerage, which went to the eldest and not jointly to all **heirs portioners** (*see* **heir**).

praepositura [preepositeeoora] *law* the right of a wife to incur debts on behalf of her husband for food and household requirements.

pram press, squeeze.

pran *NE* **1** crush, squeeze, pulp, pound. **2** bruise, beat, punish.

prap, prop *noun* **1** a prop. **2** something set up as a marker, *eg* as a boundary-mark, a memorial, a target for shooting at, a guide in ploughing.

verb **1** prop. **2** mark (a boundary etc) by means of **praps**.

prat, prot *N* **1** a trick, practical joke, piece of mischief *now Caithness.* **2** an act of disobedience or a bad habit in a horse.

prattick, practick, prottick *NE* **1** †an act, practice, way of doing things; a custom, habit. **2** †a feat of daring or skill, a caper. **3** a piece of mischief, trick *now NE.* **4** an undertaking; scheme, trick, dodge *now NE.*

pratty *see* **pretty**

preceese *adjective* precise.

adverb exactly, precisely.

precent [pres**ent**] lead the singing in a church, act as **precentor**.

precentor [pres**ent**or] in Presbyterian churches where instrumental music is not approved, a person who leads the singing by singing the line for the congregation to repeat *now mainly Hebrides, Highland.*

†precept *law* a document instructing or authorizing a certain action, a warrant granted by a judge to give possession of something or to confer a privilege.

precognition *law* the process of **precognoscing**; a statement made by a witness during this investigation.

precognosce [preecog**nose**] *law* interview potential witnesses with a view to discovering what evidence they will be able to give in court.

precunnace *see* **perconnon**

pree[1] **1** try out, sample. **2** try by tasting.

pree (someone's) mou kiss.

pree[2] call-name for a cow or calf.

preen, prin *noun* a metal pin; something of very little value.

verb fasten with a pin, pin.

preen-cod a pin-cushion. **preen-heid 1** a pin-head; something of very little value or importance. **2** the young of the minnow. **preen-heidit** stupid, of low intelligence.

preen-tae 1 a person or thing attached to another. **2** an unlawful sexual partner, a mistress.

be sittin on preens be very nervous, be on tenterhooks.

preeve *see* **pruive**

preliminary: preliminary defences *law* a defence which is purely technical, not touching the merits of the case. **preliminary examination,** *informal* **prelim 1** an examination for entry to a Scottish University. **2** *unofficially* a class examination taken before the **Highers** (*see* **heich**) etc to provide an estimate of the candidate's ability.

prent, print 1 print. **2** a pat of butter.

speak like a prent buik speak with an air of knowledge; speak in an affected way.

prentice *noun* an apprentice.

verb apprentice (a youth) to a trade or craft.

preparatory service a service held on a weekday, usually Friday, in preparation for the communion service on the following Sunday.

prequeer *see* **perqueer**

presbytery an ecclesiastical court above the **kirk session** (*see* **kirk**); the area represented by such.

prescribe *law, of an action, a right etc* become invalid through the passage of time, lapse; *of a debt, crime etc* be immune from prosecution through lapse of time.

prescription the lapse of time after which a right is either established or rendered invalid or a debt etc annulled, if previously unchallenged or unclaimed.

present *verb, Presbyterian Churches* offer (a child) for baptism.

noun a white speck on the fingernail, commonly believed to foretell the arrival of a gift.

give in a present give as a present, make a present of.

presently now, at this moment, at present.

preserve: preserves weak spectacles intended to preserve the sight.

Guid preserve us (a) goodness gracious!

preses [**pree**siz] the person who presides at a meeting etc, the chairman, president; the leader.

press a large (wall-)cupboard.

pretty, pratty, protty *NE* **1** pretty. **2** *of people* fine, good-looking, dignified; *of men* courageous, manly; *of women* well-built, buxom; *of animals* sturdy, in good condition; *of things* well-made, attractive.

price: be the price o someone serve someone right. **three** etc **prices** three etc times the market or former price.

prick *verb* **1** *of cattle* stampede to escape from insects. **2** †fasten with a pin etc. *noun* a pointed implement, *eg* a skewer, a knitting-needle.

prick-the-louse contemptuous term for a tailor. **prick-me-dainty** affected; over-refined.

prickle a prickling or stinging sensation.

prief *see* **pruif**

prieve *see* **pruive**

prig 1 haggle over a price; drive a hard bargain; beat down a price. **2** plead with (someone) for (something). **3** beg, entreat.

prime fill, stuff, load.

primp *verb* **1** make prim and over-neat, arrange in a stiff, affected way. **2** behave or talk affectedly. *adjective* straight-laced, prim; haughty, conceited.

primsie self-consciously correct, demure, straight-laced, old-maidish.

prin *see* **preen**

principal *adjective* **1** excellent, first-rate. **2** *of a document* original, not in the for..n of a copy. *noun* **1** the head of a university (who also acts as Vice-Chancellor). **2** the original of a document.

prink, prunk *Shetland Orkney* **1** make smart or pretty. **2** strut, move with a swagger.

prinkie fussy, ostentatious, conceited.

prinkle 1 have pins and needles, tingle, thrill. **2** twinkle, glitter, sparkle; *of a*

boiling pot bubble, simmer.

print *see* **prent**

prior rights the statutory rights of the spouse of a person dying without a will to the deceased's dwelling-house with furnishings and **plenishings** (*see* **plenish**) and a financial provision out of the remaining estate.

privative *law, of the jurisdiction of a court* exclusive, not shared or exercised by others.

privileged debt *law* a debt owed by the estate of a deceased person, *eg* for funeral expenses, which takes precedence over the debts of ordinary creditors.

privy privet.

prob 1 an instrument for piercing the stomach of swollen cattle to release gas. **2** a prod, poke, jab.

probation *law* the hearing of evidence in court before a judge; evidence, proof and the procedure for demonstrating it.

probationer 1 *law* a newly-appointed judge of the **Court of Session** (*see* **session**) after he has presented his letter of appointment and before he takes the oath. **2** *Presbyterian Churches* a student **minister** during the period between his licensing (*see* **licence**) and his ordination.

probative *law, of a document* having the quality or function of proving or demonstrating, carrying evidence of its own validity and authenticity.

process *law* the legal papers in an action lodged in court by both parties.

procurator a solicitor or lawyer practising before the lower courts.

procurator fiscal the public prosecutor in a **Sheriff Court** (*see* **sheriff**), who also carries out some of the duties of an English coroner.

procuratory *law* the authorization of one person to act for another.

procure *law* prevail upon, induce, persuade (a person to do something criminal).

Prod(die) contemptuous term for a Protestant.

production *law* the exhibiting of a document in court; an article or document produced as evidence, an exhibit.

professional examination one of a series of examinations, called the **First, Second** *etc* **Professional Examination**, taken by students of medicine and veterinary medicine.

profit natural produce, *eg* milk, grain, the yield of a cow.

prog, progue *noun* **1** a piercing weapon or instrument *now Shetland Orkney Caithness*. **2** a thorn, spine, prickle. **3** a stab, thrust, poke etc.
verb stab, pierce, prick; poke, prod, jab.

progress: progress (of title(s)), progress (of title-deeds *etc*) *law* the series of title-deeds, extending over at least ten years, which constitute a person's title to land.

pron the residue of oat husks and oatmeal from the milling process.

proo 1 a command to a horse to stop. **2** *also* **proochie(-leddy)** a call to a cow or calf.

prood *see* **proud**

proof *see* **pruif**

prop *see* **prap**

†**propine** drink-money; gift, reward.

propone *law* advance or state in a court of law.

prorogate *law* **1** defer the termination of (a period of time), extend, prolong (especially a lease). **2** extend (the jurisdiction of a judge or court), usually by waiving objection to an incompetent jurisdiction.

prot *see* **prat**

protestation *law* the procedure by which a **defender** in the **Court of Session** (*see* **session**) compels the **pursuer** (*see* **pursue**) either to proceed with his action or to end it.

prottick *see* **prattick**

protty *see* **pretty**

proud, prood 1 proud. **2** pleased, glad. **3** *of fish* slow to take the bait, difficult to catch. **4** *of crops* (over-)luxuriant; *of the sea or a river* running high, swollen; *of an object or surface* set higher than its immediate surroundings: *"a proud roof"*.

prove *see* **pruive**

providing the household articles laid aside by a young woman for her bottom drawer.

provoke 1 †a provocation, challenge. **2** a nuisance, pest.

provost 1 the head of a Scottish **burgh**; since 1975 used only in the title **Lord Provost** (*see* **lord**) and as a courtesy title in some authorities. **2** *Scottish Episcopal Church* the minister of a cathedral church.

pruif, proof, prief 1 proof. **2** the estimating of a grain-crop by examining a random sample; the sample itself. **3** *law* a trial of the disputed facts in a civil court before a judge sitting without a jury.

pruive, prove, prieve, preeve *verb, past participle* **proven 1** prove. **2** try out, put to the test, sample; try by lasting.
not proven *law* one of the two verdicts of acquittal available in a Scottish criminal court. Appropriate where the accused's guilt has not been established, but jury (or judge where there is no jury) is not convinced of his or her innocence; the person cannot be tried again.

prunk *see* **prink**

pry prise, move by leverage.

pu *see* **pou**

public: public room a room in a house in which visitors are received and entertained, *eg* a sitting room, dining room.
†**public school** a state-controlled school run by the local education authority.

puchal *see* **poochle**

puckle *see* **pickle**

pud, pod 1 a small, neat, often plump person or animal. **2** name for a pigeon *now Angus Perth.*

puddin(g) 1 a kind of sausage made from the stomach or guts of a sheep, pig etc, oatmeal, onions, seasoning, etc. **2 puddins** guts (of people or animals). **3** a stupid or clumsy person.

pudding supper *see* **supper.**

keep the puddin het keep the pot boiling.

puddle 1 a street gutter *NE*. **2** †a muddle, mess, confusion. **3** an untidy or disorganized worker *now Angus.*

puddock, paddock, poddock, paddo, paddy 1 a frog, a toad. **2** a spiteful arrogant person; a clumsy, ungainly or ugly person. **3** a flat, wooden platform for transporting heavy loads of hay etc.

puddock('s) crud(d)les frogspawn. **be in the puddock hair** be very young.

pue *see* **pew, pleuch**

puff boast, brag.

puffer a small steamboat which carried cargo around the west coast of Scotland. **puffy (dunter)** a porpoise.

puggie[1] **1** a monkey. **2** contemptuous term for a person *now Perth.*

as fou as a puggie extremely drunk. **lose one's puggy** lose one's temper.

puggie[2] **1** *marbles* a hole into which the marbles are rolled. **2** the bank, jackpot or pool in a game of cards etc *WCentral.*

puggled exhausted, done for, at the end of one's resources.

puil, peel *NE* a pool.

puir, poor, peer *NE* poor.

mak a puir mou(th) plead poverty as an excuse for meanness, claim to be poor when in fact one is quite well off.

†**puirtith, poortith** poverty.

puist *verb* cram, stuff full.

adjective comfortably off *now SW.*

puke *see* **pouk**

pule *see* **pewl**

pull *see* **pou**

puller *see* **piller**

pulleyshee a pulley, especially a rope on a pole, used to hang clothes out of a window to dry.

pump *noun* breaking of wind.

verb break wind.

pumphal *now NE* **1** an enclosure for animals. **2** a kind of square church pew.

pun *see* **pund**[1]

punce, pounce *noun* **1** pounce. **2** a light blow, a nudge, poke.

verb **1** pounce. **2** poke, jog.

pund[1]**, pun, pound, poun 1** a pound, a measure of weight; until early 19th century varying in value. **2** a pound in money, a **pound Scots** (see p 358).

pund[2]**, pound, poon** a pound, an enclosure for animals.

pundie a strong type of beer; alcoholic drink in general.

pupil *law* a child under the age of minority (*see* **minor**), 12 for girls and 14 for boys.

pupit, poopit a pulpit.

puppie a poppy.

puppie show, poppy show a puppet show, a Punch-and-Judy show.

mak a puppy-show o anesel make a fool of oneself.

purfled fat and asthmatic, plump and wheezing.

purge *law* clear off an **irritancy** (*see* **irritant**) by remedying the failure which produced it.

purify *law* fulfil or carry out (a condition), bring an agreement etc into operation by complying with a proviso in it.

purl *see* **pirl**

purls small balls of sheep or rabbit dung.

purpie purple.

purpose well-ordered, tidy, methodical; tidy-looking.

purr *see* **porr**

pursue *law* carry on (an action), prosecute (a case), claim (damages), raise an action.

pursuer the active party in a civil action, the plaintiff, prosecutor.

push *see* **pooss**

pushion, pooshin 1 poison. **2** a nasty person or thing.

adjective unpleasant, detestable.

verb **1** poison. **2** make unpleasant, spoil: make (food) uneatable.

puss a hare.

put *see* **pit**

putt[1], **put** *verb* **1** push, shove; nudge gently, prod; butt. **2** *athletics* hurl (a stone or heavy metal ball). **3** *golf* strike (the ball) as in **putt**[1] *noun* 2.

noun **1** a gentle touch or push. **2** *golf* the gentle tapping stroke used to move the ball across the **green**[1] and into the hole. **3** *athletics* the movement by which a weight is propelled.

mak one's putt guid succed, gain one's object.

putt[2] a jetty or stone structure projecting from a river bank.

putten *see* **pit**

pynor *see* **piner**

pyoch *see* **peuch**

pyock *see* **poke**

pyot, piet *noun* **1** a magpie. **2** applied to other birds with pied plumage, *eg* **sea pyot** an oyster-catcher. **3** nickname for a person. **4** a chattering, irresponsible person.

adjective **1** like a magpie in colouring, multi-coloured. **2** *of speech* loud, empty.

pyuff *see* **pluff**

Q

qua *see* **quaw, twa**

quader [-a- as in 'cat'] *NE* **1** make square. **2** agree.

quadriennium utile [kwodriennium **yoot**-ily] *law* the four years following on the attainment of majority during which a person may by legal action seek to withdraw from any deed done to his prejudice during his minority.

quaestor [**kweest**er] *St Andrews University* the chief financial officer of the University, the University Treasurer.

quaich, quaigh, †**quech** *noun* [-ch, -gh as -ch in 'dreich'] a shallow two-handled cup, originally made of wood, sometimes decorated with or made entirely of silver, now mainly ornamental and used for trophies etc.

quaiet *see* **quate**

quair 1 †a quire (of paper). **2** a literary work (of any length).

quaisteen *see* **question**

quait *see* **quate**

quak quake.

quakin-bog a quagmire. **quakin a(i)sh** an aspen.

qual *see* **twal**

qualify 1 †get or give legal sanction to by means of an oath, especially in regard to the Scottish Episcopalians who until 1792 were not permitted to practise their faith until they renounced allegiance to the Jacobite monarchy. **2** †pass the **qualifying examination** for admission to secondary education.

†**qualifying examination,** *informally* the **quallie** an examination at the end of primary education which decided which type of secondary education pupils should have.

quall [-a- as in 'cat'] *of wind etc* calm down *now NE*.

quallie *see* **qualify**

quarrel¹ [-a- as in 'cat'] **1** a stone-quarry. **2** stone etc taken from a quarry.

quarrel² [-a- as in 'cat'] **1** find fault with, tell off. **2** †dispute (a fact or claim), challenge the truth of, take objection to.

quarter 1 a division of a **burgh** or parish, a locality, district *now Orkney*. **2** a fourth part of a round of oatcakes *Shetland*. **3** a quarter-pound. **4** the fourth part of a year, especially referring to a school term etc.

quarterly an examination held at the end of a school term.

quarterman a farm-worker who does odd jobs and errands. **quarter moon** the crescent moon.

quat [-a- as in 'cat'], **quett 1** leave, abandon; give up. **2** stop.

quattin time time to stop work, 'knocking-off time'.

quat *see* **quit**

quate, quait, quiet, quaiet 1 quiet. **2** secret, private. **3** *of weather* still, calm.

quate wi ye! be quiet!

quate *see* **quit**

quaw, qua a bog, quagmire, marsh.

queak, queek squeak, cheep.

quean *see* **quine**

quech *see* **quaich**

queel *see* **cuil**

queem 1 close- or well-fitting, snug, neat. **2** friendly. **3** smoothly, calmly.

queen: make a queen's chair carry a girl seated on the crossed and joined arms of two other people. **Queen Mary** a girls' ring dance accompanied by a song beginning with these words. **Queen of (the) meadow** meadowsweet. **Queen of the South 1** nickname for the town of Dumfries. **2** official name for the Dumfries football team. **3** the Dumfries schoolgirl chosen as the festival queen at the annual local **Riding of the Marches** (*see* **ride**).

queen *see* **quine**

queer 1 considerable, very great: *"a queer lot o money"*. **2** †amusing, funny.

queery *adjective* rather strange *NE*. *noun* an oddity, a queer thing or person.

queeriosity a curiosity, something strange.

queern *see* **quern**[1]

queesitive inquisitive.

queet *see* **coot, cuit**

queeth *see* **cuithe**

queir a choir (of a church), usually a chancel; *latterly* a pre-Reformation cruciform church or its ruin.

quern[1], **queern 1** a quern. **2** the stomach of a fowl, the gizzard.

quern[2] a granule, small seed.

querny *of honey, sugar etc* granular, coarse.

question, quaisteen, queystion 1 a question. **2** *Presbyterian Churches, usually* **questions** (the questions in) the **Shorter Catechism** (*see* **short**). **3** *expressing doubt or wonder* I wonder, goodness knows: *"quaisteen if he can find the road"*.

quett *see* **quat**

quey, queyock a heifer.

queystion *see* **question**

quick swarming, infested *Shetland Orkney Ulster*.

quick water the current (of a river), running water *SW, S*.

quicken(s) couch grass.

quid *see* **cood**[1]

quiet *see* **quate**

quigger *see* **keeger**

quile, quoil, kyle, coil *noun* the small heap into which hay is gathered after being cut.

verb rake (hay) into heaps.

quine, quean, coin, †**queen** *noun, now NE* **1** a young (unmarried) woman, a girl; a female child; a daughter. **2** a female servant. **3** a female sweetheart. **4** a bold, impudent woman, hussy, slut.

quinie *see* **cunyie**

quink goose a brent goose; a greylag goose *now Orkney*.

quinkins 1 dregs or leavings, scum of a liquid, charred traces of food stuck to the saucepan. **2** a worthless trifle.

quinter *see* **twinter**

quintra *see* **countra**

quinzie *see* **cunyie**

quirk *noun* a riddle, catch question, an arithmetical problem.

verb trick, get the better of, cheat.

quirky 1 intricate, twisted, complicated. **2** cunning, resourceful, tricky.

†**quisquous** doubtful, dubious.

quit, quite *now Orkney verb, past tense also* **quat, quate 1** cease, give up, stop. **2** free, acquit.

adjective, also **quat** quit, free.

quittance the discharge of a debt etc, a receipt, payment; an account, a valid explanation.

quite *see* **coat**

quo, co quoth.

quoad ultra [kwoaad-] *law* used in the written pleadings of an action to indicate the point beyond which the **defender** (*see* **defend**) makes no further admission of the **pursuer's** (*see* **pursue**) allegations.

quoil *see* **quile**

quoit, coit, cute *WCentral* play at the game of curling, play a curling stone.

quorum, coarum *NE* **1** a quorum. **2** a gathering, especially of friends for social purposes, a company *NE*.

R

ra *see* **raw**[1], **raw**[2]

raan a disease of turnips.

raan *see* **rawn**

Rab *see* **Rob**

rabbit: rabbit's sugar child's word for the seeds of the common sorrel *NE*. **rabbit thissle** a kind of thistle.

rabble *see* **raible**

†**rabiator** a scoundrel, villain; a lout, boor.

race[1] a run, journey at speed; a flying visit; the act of running; a short run before jumping.

†**racer** nickname for a loose woman.

race[2] a set (of articles used together) *NE*.

rachan *see* **rauchan**

rachle *see* **rauchle**, **raucle**

rack[1] 1 a framework on a wall for crockery and cutlery. 2 †**racks**, *also* **rax** a set of bars to support a roasting spit.

rack[2] *verb* 1 stretch, pull, increase in length. 2 reach, extend. 3 wrench, dislocate, twist. 4 worry needlessly, be over-anxious.

noun 1 a sprain, wrench, dislocation. 2 a frame for stretching wet cloth in the process of fulling. 3 a stretch or reach of a river *now Angus*. 4 a ford in a river, a ridge of gravel or a shallow place *now SW*. 5 a path, track. 6 *curling* = **rink** *noun* 5,6 *WCentral*.

rack pin a stick used to tighten a rope or chain.

rack[3] 1 †a heavy blow, a crash. 2 driving mist or fog.

rack up *of weather* clear.

rack[4] a stay, strut.

rack *see* **wrack**

rackle 1 a chain. 2 the rattling, jingling noise made by a chain *now NE*.

rackle *see* **raucle**

rackless reckless.

rackon reckon.

†**rad, red, rede** frightened, afraid, alarmed.

rade *see* **raid**, **redd**[1], **ride**

radge *adjective* 1 *also* **radgie** mad, violently excited, furious. 2 sexually excited. 3 silly, weak-minded.

noun a loose-living woman.

radical a wild, unruly person, a rogue, rascal.

radical right *law* the ultimate proprietary right of a **truster** which survives if the fulfilment of the trust purposes does not exhaust the whole estate.

radical *see* **reticule**

rae[1], **ray** a roe (deer).

rae[2], **ray** a sailyard *now Shetland*.

rael, rale, real *adjective* 1 real. 2 *of character* honest, forthright, genuine.

adverb very, extremely.

rael *see* **raivel**

raem, raemikle *see* **ream**

raep reap.

raep *see* **raip**

raff[1], **raft** *SW* 1 plenty, a large number. 2 rank growth *now NE*.

raffie *now NE* 1 abundant, generous. 2 thriving, flourishing.

raff[2] a short sharp shower *now NE*.

raffin merry, boisterously hearty *now Perth*.

raffle *see* **raivel**

raft a rafter.

raft *see* **raff**[1]

rag[1] *noun* 1 a rough projection on a surface, *eg* after sawing. 2 a lean, scraggy animal or fish. 3 the poorest pig in a litter *SW*, *S*.

verb †winnow partially.

ragger a rag-collector *N*. **raggie** *adjective*, *also* **raggety** ragged. *noun* a (diseased) salmon *S*. **raggie biscuit** a locally-made biscuit with an uneven edge

ECentral. **raggit** ragged. **raggle** make an uneven cut in, cut jaggedly. **ragglish** erratic; uncertain; wild, unreliable *NE*.

ragnail a loose piece of skin or broken nail at the side of a fingernail, a hangnail. **ragweed** ragwort.

lose the rag lose one's temper.

rag² scold severely.

hae a rag oot o enjoy a joke at the expense of, get a laugh out of. **tak the rag o** make fun of, make a fool of.

rag³ a wet mist, drizzle *Shetland Orkney NE*.

rag⁴ a whetstone.

ragabash, ragabrash *SW* **1** a good-for-nothing, a ragamuffin. **2** a ragged, motley crew, riff-raff.

raggety *see* **rag¹**

raggle¹ cut a groove in stone (or wood) to receive another stone etc, *eg* in the steps of a stair. **2** *mining* cut into the coal-face.

rag(g)lin(s) the space for the edges of the slates under the coping-stones of a gable.

raggle² wrangle, dispute *NE*.

raggle *see* **rag¹**

raible, rabble *noun* **1** a disorganised rigmarole; nonsensical talk. **2** a carelessly-built or ruinous building etc.
verb utter (a torrent of words), speak or read hastily and indistinctly.

raid, rade 1 a foray on horseback; a sudden or surprise attack. **2** a roadstead for ships.

raik, reck *verb* **1** move, go forward, especially with speed. **2** journey, go; walk, stroll; gad about. **3** *of grazing animals* spread out in a line, straggle. **4** range over, wander through. **5** work energetically and speedily *NE*.
noun **1** the act of going; a journey; a long or tiring walk; a stroll. **2** a journey; a trip, run. **3** as much as can be carried in one load; *mining* a train of loaded **hutches**. **4** *of food* a spoonful; a helping. **5** speed, rate *now S*. **6** a cattle- or sheep-walk, a pasture. **7** †a stretch

of river used for salmon-fishing. **8** a roving person or animal.

raik *see* **reak, reck**

rail¹ fit (a stair) with a handrail *now NE*. **railing** a handrail. **rail stair** a stair with a **railing**.

†rail² a woman's short-sleeved bodice.

†traing a range, rank, row.

raing *see* **ring¹**

raip, rape, raep, rope 1 rope. **2** a straw or hay rope. **3** a clothes-line. **4** the ropes securing thatch on a roof or on a cornrick.

a whaup in the raip a snag, drawback, unforeseen difficulty.

raip *see* **rip¹**

rair, roar *verb* **1** roar. **2** *of animals or birds not thought of as roaring* call loudly. **3** call, summon with a loud shout; pay a flying visit. **4** †*of ice etc* make a resounding, cracking noise. **5** *of a curling stone* make a roaring noise as it moves on the ice. **6** weep, cry, usually, but not necessarily, loudly, *often* **roar and greet**.
noun **1** roar. **2** a call, as to a neighbour in passing, a doorstep visit. **3** a loud report; a belch *now NE*.

roarie 1 loud, noisy, roaring. **2** drunk. **3** *of colours* bright, showy; glaring, garish, loud. **rairing buckie** a kind of whelk shell which when held to the ear makes a sound thought to be like the sea.

rairing game the game of curling.

raird *see* **reird**

raise *verb* **1** *law* draw up (a summons, **letter** etc), bring (an action). **2** *curling* strike and move forward (another stone of one's own side) towards the **tee**. **3** arouse, rouse from sleep. **4** infuriate, enrage, drive into a frenzy.
noun a state of extreme bad temper, a frenzy.

raised infuriated, wild, over-excited. **raiser** *law* the holder of the disputed property in a **multiplepoinding**.

raisin Monday *St Andrews University* a Monday in the winter term when senior students demand of first-year students a pound of raisins (in return for their protection).

raison *see* **rizzon**

raith, †reath 1 a period of three months. **2** a term at school, three months of full-time education.

raither, rether, redder *Shetland NE* rather.

raivel, ravel, reavel, raffle *Orkney,* **rael, rile** *SW,* **reul** *verb* **1** get into a tangle or confusion; muddle, disorder. **2** *of thread or yarn* unwind itself from a reel. **3** speak incoherently, ramble, be delirious. **4** confuse, perplex. **5** bamboozle, outwit *Shetland Orkney NE.*
noun **1** a muddle, tangle, confusion. **2** a broken or frayed thread, a loose end. **raiveled** tangled, confused, in difficulties; rambling, delirious. **raiveled hesp** a knotty problem, a state of confusion.

rake *verb* **1** rake, especially stalks of corn left on a harvested field. **2** turn over and smooth out (seaweed) in the last stages of kelp-burning *now Shetland Orkney.* **3** bank up, cover (a fire) so that it will smoulder all night. **4** search (a person). **5** *also* **rauk** rub (the eyes); scratch *Shetland NE.*
noun **1** a hoard, what has been gathered together. **2** a grasping, hoarding person. **3** a very thin person. **4** *only* **rauk** a scratch, groove, rut; the sound of a sharp point scratched on a hard surface.

rale *see* **rael**

rally, ralyie scold, speak angrily to.

ram¹: ram race 1 a headlong rush. **2** a short burst of speed. **ram reel** *now freemasonry* a **reel** danced by men only.

ram² *verb* **1** push, shove, clear one's way by pushing and shoving. **2** punish by bumping the buttocks against a wall or by caning the soles of the feet.

ramble *see* **rammle**

rame, rhame, rhaim 1 †cry aloud, shout, roar. **2** repeat, recite something; drone on monotonously *now Ulster.* **3** dwell

on something, harp on. **4** talk nonsense, rave.

ramfeezle, ramfoozle muddle, confuse; exhaust.

ramgunshoch bad-tempered, rude and boorish *now SW.*

†rammage untamed; violent, wild, unruly.

rammel small or crooked branches; brushwood.

rammish, ramsh, ramse *Orkney* mad, crazy; impetuous, uncontrolled *now Orkney.*

rammle, ramble 1 ramble. **2** wander about aimlessly, especially under the influence of drink.
on the rammle drinking heavily.

rammock *now NE* **1** a big rough piece of wood; a worthless object. **2** a big, coarse person; a large, worthless animal.

rammy a free-for-all, violent disturbance, scuffle.

ramp¹ 1 *of plants* climb, ramble. **2** romp boisterously. **3** stamp, beat the floor with the feet.

ramp² 1 †wild, bold, unrestrained. **2** having a strong, coarse flavour or smell.

†ramper (eel) a sea or river lamprey; any large eel.

ramps wild garlic.

ramscooter trounce, drive off in terror.

ramse *see* **rammish**

ramsh¹, ransh munch, crunch.

ramsh² 1 *of food* rank, unpleasant, coarse. **2** *of people* brusque, bad-tempered *NE.* **3** *of yarn* rough and coarse-textured.

ramsh *see* **rammish**

ram-stam, †ram tam *adjective* headstrong, rash, heedless.
noun **1** a headstrong, impetuous person or action. **2** †the strongest kind of ale, that drawn from the first mash.

ramstougar [ram **stooger**] rough in manner, boisterous, disorderly.

ran *see* **rand¹**

rance *noun* **1** a prop, wooden post or bar used *eg* as the stretcher of a table or chair. **2** a bar used for securing a door or as a crossbar of a fence. **3** *mining* a prop to strengthen a wall of coal or the roof of a working; a pillar of coal left for this purpose.

verb **1** prop up, brace, stay (a building etc). **2** make fast, close up, fasten firmly to prevent movement.

rand, ran 1 a border, rim *now Shetland*. **2** a strip, a narrow section *now Perth*. **3** a stripe or section of a different colour or texture *now SW*.

rander, render *verb* **1** render. **2** talk idly or nonsensically, ramble. **3** *of a wound* discharge pus.

noun **1** a great talker. **2** senseless, incoherent talk. **3** order, restraint, conformity. **4** clarified fat, dripping.

randie *adjective* **1** rough, belligerent, aggressive. **2** *of a woman* loud-voiced, coarse and aggressive. **3** boisterous, wild. **4** lustful; sexually excited. **5** *of language* coarse, uncouth; obscence.

noun **1** a (rude) beggar, a ruffian. **2** a beggar-woman; any foul-mouthed, brawling, bad-tempered woman; a loose-living woman. **3** a boisterous, mischievous person. **4** a romp, frolic.

rane, rone something repeated over and over again *now Angus*.

ranegill [**ran**nigil] a rough character, especially a tinker.

range 1 = **reenge** *verb* 2, 3. **2** agitate (water) to drive fish from a hiding place *S*.

range *see* **rinse**

†rangle a rabble; a crowd, group.

rank 1 *law* place (a creditor) in his due place on the list of accredited claimants to the realized estate of a bankrupt; *of a creditor* be placed thus. **2** get ready, prepare, dress before going out *NE*.

rannle *see* **rantle**

rannoch fern; bracken *now Perth*.

ransh *see* **ramsh**[1]

ranshackle search minutely, ransack.

ransom a very high price or rent.

rant *verb* **1** romp, make merry. **2** play or sing a lively tune, especially for a dance. **3** make a great fuss, complain at length.

noun **1** a romp, boisterous or riotous merry-making *now NE*. **2** a festive gathering with music and dancing. **3** a lively tune or song, especially one for an energetic dance.

†rantie frolicsome, full of boisterous fun. **rantin 1** roistering, merry, uproarious. **2** †*of a fire* burning strongly, blazing. **†rantinlie** merrily, unroariously.

ranter sew together, darn, mend (hastily or roughly).

rantle, rannle †a wooden or iron bar across a chimney from which the chain and pot-hook were hung.

rantle tree 1 = **rantle**. **2** †a roof-beam, rafter.

ransh *see* **ramsh**[1]

rap[1] **1** dash, thump, knock, strike or fall with a sharp thud. **2** fall rapidly in a shower or in drops *now Shetland Orkney*. **3** make a rapping or banging noise *Shetland NE*.

in a rap in an instant, in a moment.

rap[2] a good-for-nothing, a cheat, a rake *now Fife*.

rap[3] rape, the plant.

rape *see* **raip**

raploch *noun, also* **raploch grey** coarse, homespun, undyed, woollen cloth; a garment made of this.

adjective **1** †made of **raploch**. **2** †homemade, crude, rough-and-ready. **3** ordinary, undistinguished; uncouth *now Angus*.

rapple 1 grow rapidly, shoot up. **2** make or mend hurriedly and roughly.

rapture a fit, especially of rage.

rash[1], **thrash, resh, thresh 1** a rush, the plant. **2** †a peeled rush used for a lamp wick *N*.

rashie *noun* = **rash**. *adjective* made of rushes; overgrown with rushes. **Rashiecoat** name of the heroine of a Scottish version of *Cinderella*, who wore a coat of rushes.

the rash bush keeps the cow *proverb* referring to a time of peace and security.

rash² *verb* **1** †rush violently or hastily. **2** *of rain* pour, come down in torrents *now Orkney Caithness*. **3** produce a stabbing or searing pain, throb.
noun a sudden downpour.

rash³ active, agile, vigorous *now S*.

rasp 1 a raspberry. **2** a mole; a birthmark *Perth Fife*.

rat¹: rat('s) tail greater plantain; its seedhead.

rat² a rut, groove, deep scratch *now S*.

ratch¹ *noun* †a gundog, hound.
verb range about ravenously; prowl *now S*.

ratch² damage by rough usage, tear, scratch *now S*.

†rat-rhyme a piece of doggerel verse; a nonsensical rigmarole.

rattle 1 strike or beat repeatedly. **2** speak with a burr. **3** do with great haste and without care.
†rattlescull a thoughtless, emptyheaded person. **rattlestane** *children's rhyme* a hailstone.

ratton, rottan 1 a rat. **2** term of contempt or endearment for a person.

rauchan, rachan a **plaid** or wrap, a clumsy garment *now Perth*.

rauchle, rachle a loose, untidy heap; something ramshackle.

raucle, rackle, rauchle, rachle 1 bold, rash *now Fife*. **2** strong, sturdy, robust; hard, stern, grim, unbending. **3** rough, crude, tough.

rauch, raught *see* **reak**

raught *see* **reak**

rauk clear the chest or throat of phlegm *Angus Fife*.

rauk *see* **rake, rouk**

raun *see* **rawn, rowan**

rave a person who talks too much and nonsensically, a windbag.

rave *see* **rive**

†ravel, revel 1 a rail, railing; a balustrade; a bridge parapet. **2** the horizontal beam in a **byre** fixed to the ropes of the stakes for the tethers.

ravel *see* **raivel**

raverie, reverie *noun now NE* **1** raving, furious or deranged speech; nonsense, foolish talk. **2** a rumour, a piece of gossip.

raw¹, ra, row *noun* **1** a row, a line. **2** a ring of people *now SW*. **3** a row of houses, especially of miners' or farm-workers' cottages; a street of such houses.
verb set up in a row, arrange in a line.

raw², ra *Shetland Orkney NE* **1** raw. **2** *of sheaves* damp, not fully dried out *now Shetland*.

rawn, raun, raan *N*, **rown** [rhyme with 'down'] **1** the roe of a fish. **2** a turbot *now NE*.

rawner an unspawned salmon.

rax, rex *Shetland Orkney verb* **1** stretch oneself after sleep etc; stretch (a cramped limb etc). **2** put (oneself) to great effort, over-exert, strain; sprain (a limb). **3** stretch in order to lengthen etc, pull out; stretch (a person's neck), hang (a person); stretch or extend (something) fully. **4** raise (the head or eyes) in order to look or listen; reach out (the hand or arm); stretch out, crane (the neck). **5** reach, stretch out to take or grasp (something); help oneself to (food). **6** hand (a person an object); give (a person one's hand); deal (a person a blow). **7** stretch, expand; *of the day, time* stretch out.

rax *see* **rack¹, rex**

ray *see* **rae¹, rae²**

reach retch, try to vomit.

read *verb* **1** *of a preacher* read a sermon, rather than preach without notes. **2** interpret (a dream, riddle etc), foretell the future.
noun a loan (of a book etc) for the purpose of reading it.
reader a person appointed to read Scriptures etc in the absence of an ordained minister. **reediemadeasy** a first school reading book. **readin swee-**

tie a conversation lozenge.

ready *adjective* apt, liable, likely to: *"ready makin mistakes"*.
verb 1 make ready, prepare. 2 cook (food), prepare (a meal).
readily probably; likely; naturally.

reak, reek, reik, raik, reck *Shetland,* †**rike** *verb, past participle also* **raucht, raught** [rocht] 1 reach. 2 reach for. 3 deliver (a blow).

real *see* **rael**

ream, reem, raem *mainly Shetland noun* 1 cream. 2 the froth on top of ale *now NE*.
verb 1 *of milk* form cream. 2 skim the cream off (milk). 3 form a froth or foam. 4 *of liquor* rouse confusion (in the mind). 5 be full of a frothy liquid; bubble over.
reamer, †**reaming dish** a shallow dish for skimming cream off milk. **reamy** 1 creamy; made of or with cream. 2 frothing.
raemikle a round wooden tub for holding milk etc; a pail *now Shetland*.

rearie *see* **reerie**
reason *see* **rizzon**
reath *see* **raith**
reave *see* **reive**
reavel *see* **raivel**

rebat [rebat] give a brusque or discouraging reply *NE*.

rebel *law* a person who disregards or flouts authority; a lawbreaker, a person, especially a debtor, declared outside the law by being **put to the horn** (*see* **horn**).

rebound, reboon *NE* 1 rebound. 2 a loud explosive noise as of gunshot. 3 a reprimand, scolding.

receipt, †**ressait** 1 a receipt. 2 a (medical) prescription or preparation. 3 a recipe.

receive, †**resaive** 1 receive. 2 seize, carry off, *as in* **God receive me.**

†**reck, raik** reckon, consider.
what reck(s) what does it matter?

reck *see* **raik, reak**

reclaim *law* appeal, now from the **Outer House** to the **Inner House** (*see* **inner**) of the **Court of Session** (*see* **session**).
reclaiming motion *etc* the procedure by which an appeal is made as above.

recompense a non-contractual obligation by which a person is obliged to restore a benefit derived from another's loss.

record *law* the statements and answers of both parties to an action.
Keeper of the Records the official responsible for the preservation of the public registers, records and rolls of Scotland.

recrimination *law, in a divorce action* a counter-charge on grounds of adultery.

rector 1 a high-ranking university official; now a public figure elected by the students. 2 a headteacher of a secondary school. 3 a clergyman in charge of a full congregation of the Scottish Episcopal Church.

red *see* **rad, reid**

redd[1], †**rade** *verb, past tense, past participle* **red(d)** 1 †save, rescue. 2 save from burning; put out (a fire). 3 free, rid, relieve. 4 clear (a space, the way), make room; clear (land) by reaping, ploughing etc; clear out (a ditch, channel etc); clear (the throat, nose, stomach etc) (*N*); clear (a fireplace, tobacco pipe) of ashes, poke up or out. 5 *law* leave (a house etc) ready for the next occupant, *often* **void and redd.** 6 clear away, remove (from). 7 disentangle, unravel, sort out. 8 *also* **redd up** arrange; settle (affairs etc); clear up, sort out (problems, difficulties etc). 9 fix exactly, determine (the boundaries of a piece of land). 10 separate (combatants); put an end to (fighting) *now NE*. 11 *also* **redd up** put in order, tidy up.
noun 1 the act of clearing away or tidying up; a putting in order; a cleaning, tidying. 2 the power to clear or sweep aside obstacles; energy, drive *now Shetland Orkney*. 3 rubbish etc which has been or is to be cleared away. 4 a comb-

ing and arranging of the hair.

redder's lick, reddin straik *etc* a blow received by a person trying to stop a fight *now NE*. **redding-up** a scolding.

redd bing a mound of waste at the surface of a mine or quarry. **redd box** *mining* a truck for carrying rubbish to a pit-head. **redd han** a freeing, a clearance, a free hand. **redland** *etc* land cleared of its crop, bare after cropping or ploughing.

redd the hoose *curling* clear the **tee** of stones with a fast, forceful shot. **redd up 1** = **redd** *verb* 8. **2** = **redd** *verb* 11. **3** scold, give a dressing-down to; speak critically. **redd-up** a scolding.

redd² 1 fish- or frog-spawn. **2** the rut in a riverbed made by salmon for spawning in.

†redd³ 1 prepared, willing. **2** quick and skilful (with one's hands).

redd *see* **rede**¹

reddendo [re**den**do] *law* the duty or service to be paid by a **vassal** to a **superior** as set out in a **feu charter** (*see* **feu**); the clause in which this is set out.

redder *see* **raither, redd**

reddicle *see* **reticule**

rede, †reed, †redd *verb* **1** advise, counsel; warn. **2** interpret, explain. **3** †think, consider.

†*noun* **1** advice, counsel; plan. **2** a tale.

rede *see* **rad**

redland *see* **redd**¹

reduce *law* annul, set aside by legal process.

ree¹, reeve, reed 1 a yard for storing coal and from which it may be sold retail. **2** an enclosure or pen for animals. **3** †*mainly* **reeve** a prehistoric hill-fort.

ree² 1 tipsy *now Orkney*. **2** over-excited, delirious, crazy.

ree³ a medium-sized sieve or riddle for cleaning grain, peas, etc.

reebal(d), ribald a good-for-nothing, a scoundrel *now Shetland Orkney*.

reed¹ 1 the grain in wood, stone or metal. **2** the line in a coal seam along which

the strata split off. **3** a defect along the length of a lead pipe *WCentral*.

reed² the fourth stomach of a ruminant.

reed *see* **rede, ree**¹**, ruid**

reediemadeasy *see* **read**

†reef a skin disease.

reef *see* **ruif**

reefort, †rifart a radish.

reeg *see* **rig**¹

reek, reik, rick *NE noun* **1** smoke, vapour. **2** a house with a fire burning on the hearth, an inhabited house *now Shetland Orkney*. **3** mist, especially a morning mist rising from the ground. **4** the act of smoking a pipe etc, a smoke, a whiff, puff.

verb **1** *of a house etc* have smoke coming out of the chimney. **2** *of a chimney* give out smoke; fail to give out smoke properly, sending it back into the room. **3** reek. **4** *of hot liquid, damp hay etc* give off vapour or steam. **5** show anger, fume *now Ayr*.

reekie 1 smoky, smoke-filled; blackened by smoke. **2** of or like smoke; misty, damp. **reekie-mire** a hollowed cabbage-stalk packed with oily waste, used to blow smoke into a house as a prank *NE*. **reeking** inhabited *now Shetland Orkney*. **reekit 1** blackened with smoke or soot. **2** *of food* smoke-cured; smoke tainted.

reek *see* **reak, reik**

reel *noun* **1** a lively dance for two, three or four couples; the music to which it is danced. **2** a noise, crash, peal.

verb **1** wind (yarn etc) on a reel; fill (a spool) with thread. **2** *of the eyes* roll with excitement, greed etc. **3** *of the head* be in a whirl, become confused. **4** dance a reel; do a figure-of-eight travelling movement.

reel-fitted having a club-foot. **reel-rall** a state of confusion.

reem *see* **ream**

reemage, reemish *see* **rummage**

reemis, reemish *noun, NE* **1** a resounding crash or rumble. **2** a scuffle, din, clatter.

3 a heavy blow or beating.

reen see **rind**[1]

reenge, reinge, ringe verb **1** wander over, travel through. **2** search (a place) widely and thoroughly. **3** also **reenge the ribs** poke ashes from (a fire). **4** bustle about noisily.

noun **1** range, distance, bounds now NE. **2** a thorough search.

reenge see **rinse**

reerie, rearie a row, uproar NE.

reese see **ruise**

reeshle, reestle see **reesle**

reesk, reisk 1 a piece of moor covered with natural grass. **2** a growth of natural coarse grasses or rushes on rough or marshy ground.

reesle, reestle, reistle, reeshle, rissle 1 rustle. **2** of wind etc whistle. **3** of doors, crockery etc clatter, rattle. **4** rap at (a door). **5** move about noisily or with a clatter, crash about. **6** go through with a scuffling noise, rummage through. **7** move or shake (an object) so as to make it rustle or rattle. **8** beat, thrash. **9** shake, stir, agitate.

reest[1], **reist, wrest** cure (fish, ham etc) by drying or smoking.

noun a framework on which fish, meat etc is smoked now Shetland.

reest[2], **reist, wrest** verb **1** arrest, seize (goods), especially for debt now S. **2** bring to a halt. **3** cover or damp down (a fire) for the night. **4** stop and refuse to move, jib, balk.

reest[3], **reist** the mould-board of a plough.

reet see **ruit**[1], **ruit**[2]

reeve[1] verb, past tense, past participle **reft** tear, grab, snatch forcibly (at) now Orkney.

reeve[2] blaze NE.

reeve see **ree**[1], **reive**

reezie light-headed, especially from drink, tipsy now S.

reeve see **ree**[1], **reive**

refase, refeese see **refuise**

refer law **refer a matter to an oath** submit a fact at issue to proof by the oath of

a **defender** (see **defend**).

reft see **reeve**[1], **reive**

refuise, refase, refeese NE refuse.

regaird, regard regard.

   regairdless 1 heedless, uncaring. **2** regardless.

†**regality** a jurisdiction almost co-extensive with that of the Crown, granted by the sovereign to a powerful subject; land or territory subject to such.

regent 1 †a university teacher who took a class through the full four-year arts course. **2** St Andrews and Aberdeen Universities a lecturer etc who acts as adviser and consultant to students assigned to him.

regibus [rejibus] a boys' game, involving one side trying to capture the other side's caps NE.

regimentals formal dress or livery; one's best clothes.

region one of the nine larger units into which Scotland (except Orkney, Shetland and the Western Isles) was divided for local government purposes in 1975; compare **district**, **Islands Council** and **Borders, Central, Dumfries and Galloway, Fife, Grampian, Highland (Region)** (see **hieland**), **Lothian, Strathclyde, Tayside.**

register the collection of State and official papers, including parliamentary and judicial records and private deeds, latterly especially those concerned with the transfer of **heritable** property.

   (General) Register House, †**Register Office** the various buildings in Edinburgh in which the **register** has been kept.

   Lord Clerk Register the official responsible for the framing and custody of the main state registers and records; latterly a titular office only.

reid, red, rid red.

   reidie a red clay marble WCentral.

   red-arsie a bee with red markings behind. **red biddy** slang a mixture of cheap red wine and methylated spirit or other alcohol. **red brae** the gullet. **red face** a blushing face, as a sign of embarrassment or shame. **red fish 1** a male salmon at spawning time when it turns reddish. **2** *used where the name 'salmon' is taboo* salmon in general. **red gown** the scarlet gown worn by an arts undergraduate of one of the four older Scottish universities. **red hand** in the act of a crime. **reid mad** furiously angry. **reid nakit** stark naked. **reid road = reid brae**. **redware** a kind of seaweed. **reid wud** stark staring mad, beside oneself with rage.

†**reif, rief** plunder, booty, spoil; robbery; plundering.

rei interventus [ray-iy-] *law* conduct by one party to an uncompleted and informal contract with the knowledge and permission of the other party, which makes the contract binding.

reik, reek fit or rig out, equip.

reik *see* **reak, reek**

reing *see* **ring**[1]

reinge *see* **reenge**

reird, raird 1 †a roar; a loud uproar. **2** †(a) din, loud noise. **3** a loud outburst *now S*. **4** a noisy breaking of wind *now NE*.

reis *see* **rice**

reisk *see* **reesk**

reist *see* **reest**[1], **reest**[2], **reest**[3]

reistle *see* **reesle**

reive, reave, reeve *verb, past tense, past participle also* **reft 1** rob, plunder, pillage, later especially in the course of a raid. **2** take away; steal.

reiver 1 †a plunderer, robber, especially one riding on a raid. **2** the chief male participant in the annual festival at Duns, Berwickshire. **Reiver's Lass** the female partner of the **reiver** 2.

release a variety of the game of tig in which players who have been touched by the catcher may be released by the touch of an uncaught player.

relevant *law, especially of a charge or claim* pertinent, sufficient to justify the

appropriate penalty or remedy, if the alleged facts are proved.

†**relict** a widow.

relief 1 *law* the right of a person standing security for a debt to reclaim payment from his principal or from his fellow guarantors if he has paid more than his share. **2** *in a variety of the game of tig* a call by which an uncaught player may release one who has been touched by the catcher and made to stand still.

relieve 1 †*law* release from a legal obligation; especially refund the payment of (a guarantor). **2** release from captivity, set free.

reliever(s) = release.

relocation: tacit relocation *law* the assumed continuation of a lease or contract of employment on unchanged terms if no action is taken at the date of expiry.

remainder a remnant of cloth at the end of a bale. **remainder sale** a sale of such remnants at reduced prices.

†**remarkin** observation, notice; a spectacle.

remeeve *see* **remuve**

remeid, remead remedy, redress.

remember 1 remember of, remember on have memory of, recollect. **2** remind (a person) of or about. **3 remember something to someone** remember to repay someone for something.

remit *law or formal* the referring of a matter to another authority for opinion, information, carrying out etc; the transfer of a case from one court to another; the terms and limits of such a reference.

remorse express regret or remorse (about) *NE*.

remuve [-u- as in -ui- in 'guid'], **remove remeeve** *NE* **1** remove. **2** *of a landlord*, force (a tenant) to quit his holding. **3** *of a tenant* quit a property.

renaig, renegue, reneeg refuse to do work; shirk; shy away from a responsibility, engagement or challenge.

renchel, renshel a thin, spindly thing or person *now S.*

rendal *see* **rin**

render *see* **rander**

reneeg, renegue *see* **renaig**

renk *see* **rink**

renounce *see* **renunce**

renshel *see* **renchel**

rent rend, tear, crack, split.

rental 1 †a rent-roll, register of tenants. **2** the amount paid or received as rent. **3** †a kind of lease granted on favourable terms by a landlord to a tenant.

†**rentaller** a person who held land by being entered in a **rental**, especially as in 3 above.

renunce, renounce 1 renounce. **2** *law* surrender (a lease, inheritance etc).

†**repair 1** a resort, stay. **2** a gathering of people; a frequent coming or going.

reparation *law* the redress of a civil wrong, usually by award of damages.

repeat *law* repay, refund, make restitution.

repel *law, of a court* reject (a plea or submission); overrule (an objection).

repent: †**place of repentance** the area of a church where penitents stood to be rebuked. †**repentance stool, stool of repentance, repenting stool** a seat in a prominent place in a church, usually in front of the pulpit, on which offenders, especially against chastity, sat to be rebuked.

repone 1 †restore to office or to rights previously held, reinstate. **2** *law* restore (a **defender**) to his right to defend his case after judgment has been given against him in his absence.

reporter: *law* the officer responsible for bringing cases before **children's hearings** (*see* **child**).

†**repree** reprove *NE.*

reprobate *see* **approbate.**

†**repute** reputed, considered.

†**requere, requare** require *now NE.*

request, †**requeesht** request.

resaive *see* **receive**

reset *verb* **1** receive, give shelter or protection to (especially a criminal, enemy, fugitive etc). **2** receive (stolen goods), usually with the intention of reselling.

noun, law **1** †the receiving or harbouring of criminals. **2** the receiving of stolen goods, often **reset of theft.**

resetter a person who **resets.**

resh *see* **rash**[1]

resident: residenter a resident, inhabitant, especially one of long standing. †**residenting** residing, dwelling.

resign *law, of a* **vassal:** surrender his **feu** to his **superior.**

resile 1 draw back, withdraw (from an agreement etc). **2** recoil (from something), shrink away in distaste or disgust.

resolutive clause *law* a clause in an agreement whereby it becomes void if some specified event intervenes.

respeck, respect *noun* **1** respect. **2** affectionate esteem; **show respect** attend the funeral of a friend.

verb **1** respect. **2** regard affectionately, esteem.

ressait *see* **receipt**

rest[1]**, rist** *now mainly NE* **1** rest. **2** *of arable land* lie fallow or in grass.

resting chair a settle *now Shetland.* **resting stane** a stone used as a resting place; one on the road to a churchyard where the coffin was laid while the bearers rested. **ristit** *of land* having lain fallow.

rest[2] **1** *also* **rest unpayt** *of a sum* remain due or unpaid, be overdue *now Shetland Orkney.* **2** *of a person* owe (someone something) *now Shetland.*

resting owing *adjective* **1** †*of a person* owing, in debt. **2** *of a debt* unpaid. *noun* the state of a debt being unpaid.

rest *see* **reest**[2]

restrick *now NE* restrict.

resume *law, of a landlord* repossess (part of a piece of land) in accordance with the terms of the lease.

retention *law* the right not to fulfil one's

own part of a contract until the other party has fulfilled his, *eg* not to deliver goods until the buyer has paid for them.

rether *see* **raither**

reticule, radical, reddicle a reticule.

reticule basket a woven bag for carrying on the arm.

retire †withdraw from currency, pay up (a bill of exchange etc) when due.

retiral retirement from office etc. **retiring collection** an extra church collection for some special purpose taken as the congregation leaves.

retour [retoor] *noun* **1** †a return, a return journey; a return journey at reduced rates in a carriage or on a horse hired by another for the outward journey. **2** a round, a turn, a bout; a second helping of food, round of drinks etc *NE*. **3** *law* the reporting back of a decision to the body or person who requested it.

retrocession *law* a returning of a right to the person who granted it.

reuch *see* **ruch**

reul *see* **raivel**

revel *see* **ravel**

reverence: in the reverence of under an obligation to; in the power or mercy of *now Argyll*.

reverie *see* **raverie**

rew *see* **rue**

rewburd *see* **rhubarb**

rex, rax a children's chasing game.

rex *see* **rax**

rhaim, rhame *see* **rame**

rheumatise [roomateez] rheumatism.

rheums [rooms] rheumatic pains.

rhone *see* **rone**[2], **rone**[3]

rhubarb, rewburd, roobrub rhubarb.

give someone rhubarb give someone a sound thrashing.

rhyme, rime repeat, drone on monotonously; talk nonsense.

rhymeless without reason, meaningless; *of people* irresponsible, reckless, ineffective *now NE*.

rib *noun* **1** a horizontal roof-timber joining rafters. **2 ribs** the bars of a grate. **3** *mining* a wall of solid coal or other mineral.

verb, ploughing plough every alternate furrow, turning the soil over onto the adjacent unploughed strip.

ribald *see* **reebal(d)**

ribble-rabble *adverb* in a state of great confusion.

noun a rabble.

ribe long-legged, a thin person; a painfully thin animal *now SW*.

rice, rys, reis **1** twigs or small branches, brushwood. **2** a branch, a twig; a stick.

stake and rice, stab and rice building or fencing with woven stakes or twigs.

richt, right *adjective* **1** right. **2 not richt** not in one's right mind; simple-minded; abnormal, **uncannie**. **3** sober, living in a well-behaved way.

adverb **1** right. **2** very, exceedingly. **3** thoroughly, very much, very well *NE*. **4** adequately, properly, satisfactorily.

ken the richt side o a shillin *etc* be knowing with money, be good at getting the best value for money. **richt an** very, completely. **richt eneuch** comfortably off, well provided for. **richt now** immediately. **richt oot** outright, unequivocally. **the richt way o't** the true account or story, the genuine version.

rick *see* **reek**

ricket a noisy disturbance, racket, row.

ricketie 1 a kind of wooden rattle, now used by children and football supporters. **2** a ratchet brace or drill.

rickietickie a button etc on a thread, used by boys to rattle on a window.

rickle[1]**, ruckle** *noun* **1** a heap, pile, collection especially an untidy one. **2** an old or miserable building; a ramshackle or broken-down object; an emaciated, broken-down person or animal, *often* **a rickle o banes**. **3** an untidy collection or huddle of buildings *now Shetland Orkney NE*. **4** a dry-stone wall; a layer of small stones placed on top of larger stones as a coping to such a wall. **5** a small temporary stack of grain or seed-hay. **6** a small heap of peats or turfs, stacked loosely for drying.

verb **1** pile together loosely; construct loosely or insecurely. **2** build without mortar *now Fife*. **3** build (grain) into small temporary ricks. **4** stack (peats) loosely for drying.

ricklie badly-built, rickety.

rickle² rattle, move with a clattering sound, rattle down.

rickling, wreckling the smallest, weakest animal in a litter.

rickmatick: the hale rickmatick the whole lot.

rid 1 disentangle, sort out. **2** †fix (the boundaries of land) exactly.

rid *see* **reid**

riddle a measure of claret, thirteen bottles arranged round a **magnum** (*see* **magnum bonum**).

    riddling heids the refuse of corn left after riddling.

ride *verb, past tense also* **rade 1** ride out on a foray, especially in the Borders. **2** fix (the boundaries of land etc) by riding round them. **3** cross (a stretch of water) on horseback, ford (a river). **4** *curling, bowls* **ride out** play a stone with such force that it moves (an opponent's stone which was blocking its path to the **tee**). **5** *mining* travel up and down the shaft in a cage.

    rider 1 †a person who rode as in *verb* 1, a **reiver** (*see* **reive**). **2** *curling, bowls* a shot played as in *verb* 4. **riding** a raid on horseback.

    Riding of the Marches the traditional ceremony of riding round the boundaries of common land to inspect landmarks, boundary stones etc, latterly the focus of an annual local festival in certain, especially Border towns. **riding season** the breeding season of animals. **no tae ride the ford wi** not to be depended on, unreliable, untrustworthy. **ride the marches** perform the ceremony of **Riding of the Marches.**

    ride-out one of a series of rehearsal rides of a section of the boundaries in the weeks before the **Riding of the Marches.**

rief *see* **reif**

rifart *see* **reefort.**

rife *adjective* **1** plentiful, abundant. **2 rife wi** having plenty of, well supplied with, rich in. **3** quick, ready, eager for *now Shetland Orkney*.

adverb plentifully, abundantly.

-rife having plenty of, notable for, liable to, *eg* **cauldrife** (*see* **caul(d²)**), **waukrife** (*see* **wauk**).

riff *see* **ruif**

rift¹ *verb* **1** belch. **2** exaggerate, brag *now NE*.

noun **1** a belch. **2** an exaggerated account; a boast *now NE*.

    riftin fou full to bursting point.

rift² a cleft, split in a rock etc.

rig¹, reeg *Shetland Caithness noun* **1** the back or backbone of a person or animal *now Shetland Caithness*. **2** a (white) strip running along the back of an animal *now Shetland*. **3** a ridge of high ground, a long narrow hill. **4** an extent of land, long rather than broad. **5** *early farming* (*see* **runrig** (*under* **rin**)) each separate strip of ploughed land, usually bounded by patches of uncultivated grazing; now one of the divisions of a field ploughed in a single operation. **6** *also* **corn rig** such a piece of land when planted with a crop or being harvested. **7** a measure of land, usually fifteen feet wide and varying in length *now Argyll*. **8 rigs** *mainly literary* the arable land belonging to one farm or proprietor. **9** †a strip of ground leased for building in a **burgh.**

verb plough (land) in **rigs** 5.

rigged and furred ribbed. **riggin** *noun* **1** = **rig** 1. **2** the ridge of a roof; the roof; the materials of which it is made. **3** the top, the highest part of a wall, a cornstack. **4** the top of a stretch of high ground; a high ridge of land. **5** the central point of a period of time, *mainly* **the riggin o the nicht** *NE*. *verb* roof (a building). **riggin-bane** = **rigbane** *now Orkney*. **riggin divot** a turf used as a ridge-coping for a thatched roof *mainly NE*. **riggin-heid** the ridge of a roof. **riggin stane** a stone used as a ridge stone of a roof. **riggin tree** the ridge-beam of a roof. **ride on the riggin** (**o**) be completely preoccupied (with); be very officious (about). **riglin** a male animal or occasionally a man with one testicle undescended. **riggy** name for a cow with markings as in **rig 2** *now Shetland*.

rig-back *now Shetland*, **rig-bane** the backbone, spine. **rig-end** = **endrig** (*see* **en**). **rigwiddie** *noun* a band passing over the back of a carthorse and supporting the cart-shafts. *adjective, of a person* **1** *especially of an old woman* wizened, gnarled, tough and rugged-looking, misshapen. **2** stubborn, obstinate; perverse.

rig-about the runrig (*see* **rin**) system of land holding. **rig and fur, rig and furrow** *of the pattern on a ploughed field, of knitting* ribbed; corrugated. **rig and rendal** = **rundale** (*see* **rin**) *now Shetland Orkney Caithness*.

rig²: on the rig out for fun or mischief. **play the rig wi** *etc* play a trick on, make fun of. **run the rig(s)** run riot, have fun.

rig³ the smallest animal or weakling of a litter.

right *see* **richt**

riglin 1 an undersized or weak animal or person. **2** the smallest animal in a litter.

rike *see* **reak**

rile *see* **raivel**

rilling *see* **rivlin**

rim †*noun* the peritoneum, the inside wall of the abdomen.

rimburs(t)in, rimburst *now Angus Perth* *adjective* ruptured. *noun* a rupture, a hernia. **rimfu** *now SW*, **rimrax(in)** *NE* a large meal.

rime 1 hoar-frost. **2** a frosty haze or mist.

rime *see* **rhyme**

rimple wrinkle; ripple.

rim-ram confused, higgledy-piggledy, disordered *now NE*.

rimwale a board round the gunwale of a boat.

rin, run *verb* **1** run. **2** *of a dog* move sheep at a brisk pace, range out in herding sheep *SW, S*. **3** be covered with water, mud etc, be awash; leak. **4** *of milk* coagulate, curdle *mainly Shetland Orkney*. **5** hold (the hands etc) under running water, swill. **6** *bowls* drive (another bowl or the jack) away with a strong shot. **7** put (a batch of loaves etc) in the oven for baking *now Fife*. *noun* **1** †a stream, water channel. **2** a flow of water. **3** the course of a river or stream, a river valley. **4** a run.

rinner 1 a runner. **2 runner** a thin cut of meat from the forepart of the flank.

rinnings the main points of a story, sermon etc, the outline, gist *chiefly NE*.

rendal, †rundale a landholding system similar to **runrig** but involving larger portions of land. **run deil** an out-and-out rogue. **run-knot** a slip-knot which has been pulled tight. **run lime** mortar poured liquid into the crevices of stonework and left to set *mainly NE*. **†runrig** a system of joint landholding by which each tenant had several detached **rigs**¹ allocated in rotation by lot each year; such a portion of land *latterly only Hebrides*. **rin-water** a natural flow of water, especially one which will drive a millwheel without a dam *NE*.

rinabout *adjective* runabout, roving. *noun* a tramp, rover; a restless person, a gadabout. **rin ahin 1** run close behind or at the heels of. **2** be in arrears, fall into debt. **rin the cutter** bring home alcoholic drink unobserved. **run errands** go on errands. **rin the hills** roam about in a wild, unrestrained way, rush or gad about. **rin in by, run**

in to pay a short call on (a person). **rin-a-mile** *game* a variation on hide-and-seek. **rin out** *of a container* leak. **rin stockings** strengthen stocking heels by darning them with a running stitch. **rinthereout** a tramp, roving person *now NE*.

rinagate a fugitive, rascal.

rind[1] **1** *also* **reen** *N* a strip or slat of wood, a piece of beading. **2** the edge, *eg* of a strip of land.

rind[2] *verb* melt down, render (fat, tallow), clarify (butter etc).
noun melted tallow.

rind[3] hoar-frost.

rind *see* **ruind**

ring[1], **raing** *NE*, †**reing** *noun* **1** a ring. **2** †a circular ditch and rampart of a prehistoric hill-fort, especially of the early Iron Age. **3** *marbles* **the ring** a circle on the ground used as a target; the game itself.
verb **1** ring. **2** put a metal tyre round the rim of (a wheel).
ringer *curling* a stone which lies within the ring surrounding the **tee. ringie** = **ring** *noun* **3. ringle ee** a wall eye; *of an animal* an eye with a ring of white hair round it.
ring-cutter *curling* an instrument for marking the circles round the **tees. ring-net** a herring net suspended between two boats which gradually sail closer to one another with a circular sweep until the net closes and traps the fish. **ring-netter** a boat used in **ring-netting. ring-netting** fishing with **ring nets.**

ring[2] *verb* **1** give a resounding blow to. **2** *of ice etc* make a ringing sound.
noun **1** the striking of a clock, the stroke. **2** a resounding blow.
ringle a ringing, jingling sound.
ring in 1 *of church bells* speed up before stopping or reducing to a single bell as a sign that a service is about to begin. **2** give way, give up; be near the end of one's powers of endurance; be at death's door.

ring[3] reign.
ringin *adjective* **1** domineering. **2** out-and-out, downright. *adverb* forcefully, with ease *NE*.

ringe *see* **reenge, rinse**

rink, †**renk** *noun* **1** †the ground marked out for a contest, combat, race etc. **2** *curling, quoits* the marked-out area of play. **3** a stretch of ice etc for skating. **4** the team forming a side in a game. **5** *curling* a game, one of a series of games constituting a match. **6** a restless, especially noisy, prowling or hunting *NE*. **7** a rattling noise *NE*.
verb **1** range or prowl about restlessly and especially noisily *now NE*. **2** search thoroughly, rummage (in) *NE*. **3** climb, clamber *now NE*.
rinker a round woollen cap of the type worn by curlers.

rinse, reenge, range, †**ringe** *verb* **1** rinse. **2** clean (a pan etc) by scraping or scrubbing, scour *now S*. **3** *only* **rinse** wash down (a meal) with liquor *now NE*.
noun **1** a rinse. **2** a scourer made of heather twigs.

rinthereout *see* **rin**

rip[1] *verb* **1** *also* **raip** *NE* rip. **2** strip off turf before digging *now Shetland*. **3** **rip out, rip down** undo (a piece of knitting). **4** fish with a **ripper.**
noun the act of sawing wood etc along the grain.
ripper a heavy metal bar fitted with hooks and attached to a fishing line.

rip[2] a handful of stalks of unthreshed grain or hay.

rip[3] a round wicker (or straw) basket used for carrying fish, eggs or fishing lines.

ripe *verb* **1** search thoroughly (especially for stolen property); hunt through. **2** rummage through, turn out the contents of (a pocket, etc); pick (a pocket). **3** rifle, plunder. **4** clear (the bars of a fireplace etc) of ash; clear a pipe of ash. **5** strip (*eg* berries from a bush) *Shetland NE*.

noun a poke, stir to clear an obstruction.

rippet *noun* **1** a noisy disturbance, uproar; the sound of boisterous merrymaking. **2** a row, noisy quarrel.
verb create a row or disturbance, quarrel loudly.

ripples a disease affecting the back and lower part of the body, perhaps a venereal disease.

ripture a rupture.

rise *verb* **1** get out of bed in the morning. **2** cause to rise up, lift up; bring about, produce. **3** go or climb up *mainly SW*.
noun **1** the act of getting out of bed. **2** the layer of new wool next to the skin of a sheep at shearing time. **3** a piece of fun at someone's expense, a joke, hoax.
rising *of a period of time* approaching: *"it's rising fower (o'clock)"*.

risk make a ripping, tearing sound, as of roots being torn up *now SW*.

risp¹ *verb* **1** file, smooth off with a file; cut or saw roughly. **2** grind together, grind (the teeth) *now NE*. **3** make a harsh, grating sound. make a grating noise with a risp¹ 2.
noun **1** a coarse file or rasp. **2** = **pin** *noun* 3. **3** a harsh grating sound.

risp²: **risp(grass)** a kind of sedge or reed.

rissert *see* **rizzar**

rissle *see* **reesle**

rissom 1 a single head or ear of oats. **2 not a rissom** not the smallest amount.

rist *see* **rest**¹

rit, rut *verb* **1** scratch, score, groove. **2** mark with a shallow trench or furrow as a guide in ploughing, draining etc. **3** slit (a sheep) in the ear as an earmark. **4** thrust (a sword etc) through; stab *now Shetland*.
noun **1** a scratch, score, groove. **2** the shallow preliminary cut or furrow made in ploughing, draining etc *now Caithness*. **3** a sheepmark in the form of a slit in the ear etc.

rither a rudder.

rittocks the refuse of melted lard or tallow *mainly SW*.

rive *verb, past tense also* **rave 1** tear, rip. **2** wrench, pull apart, break up (into pieces). **3** wrench or force out, dig up. **4** *also* **rive out** break up (untilled ground) with the plough; cultivate (moorland). **5** pull or tug roughly or vigorously. **6** tear (the hair), especially in grief or anguish. **7** tear at or maul an opponent in a fight. **8** *of wind* blow violently *now Shetland N*. **9** work with a tugging or tearing motion or very hard. **10 rive at** eat voraciously, tear into (food). **11** force one's way forward. **12** burst, crack, split. **13** *of cloud* break up, disperse.
noun **1** a tear, rip, scratch. **2** an uprooting, break; breaking off. **3** a pull, jerk, wrench, grab; a hug. **4** a bite, a large mouthful; a good feed. **5** energy in working, vigorous activity *now Shetland*. **6** a split, crack, fissure *now Shetland*. **7** a large quantity or company *now NE*.

rivlin, rilling *now Caithness,* **rullion 1** a shoe of undressed hide *now Caithness*. **2 rivlins** rags, tatters, cheap cloth *now Caithness*. **3** *mainly* **rullion** a coarse, clumsy, rough-looking person or animal.

rizzar, russle, †**rissert** a redcurrant.
white rizzar a white currant *now Fife*.

rizzered 1 *of haddock* sun-dried. **2** *of clothes* sun-dried, thoroughly aired.

rizzon *now NE,* **reason, raison** reason.
out o (a') rizzon unreasonable, exorbitant *Shetland N*. **out o one's reason** out of one's mind. **rizzon or nane** with or without reason on one's side; obstinately *now NE*.

ro rest *now Shetland*.

road, rod *now Shetland noun* **1** a road. **2** *often* **roadie** an unmetalled road, a track. **3** a hand-cut path round a grain field. **4** a direction, route. **5** a way, method, manner. **6** a condition, state *now NE*.

verb **1** travel on a road, set out on a journey *NE*. **2** send (a person) off (on an errand or in a particular direction) *NE*.

roadit on the road, off on a journey; *of a child* able to walk *NE*.

road-en(d) the junction where a side road meets a main road.

a' roads everywhere. **a' the road** all the way. **get the road** be dismissed. **hae one's ain road** follow one's own inclination. **in the road** in one's way, causing one inconvenience. **nae road** by no means, in no possible way. **on the road** *of a woman* pregnant. **ony road** anyhow, anyhow. **out of one's road** out of one's way. **never out of one's road** always able to turn things to one's own advantage; not easily upset *now NE*. **out of the road of** unaccustomed to. **tae the road** recovered after an illness, able to be about again *NE*. **tak in the road** travel along the road, cover the distance, especially at speed *NE*. **tak the road** set off (on a journey).

roan *see* **rone**¹, **rone**², **rone**³, **rowan**

roar *see* **rair**

roast, rost, *past participle also* **roastin, rossin** roast.

roastit 1 uncomfortably hot. **2** *of cheese* toasted.

Rob, Rab 1 familiar form of Robert. **2 the Rabs** the players in the Kirkintilloch Rob Roy football team.

Robbie-rin-the-hedge goose-grass.

Rob Roy (tartan) a red-and-black checked pattern in cloth. **Rob Sorby** name for various sharp-edged tools, *eg* a scythe, a saw.

robin 1 child's word for the penis. **2** a wren *Shetland*.

robin-rin-the-hedge, robin-roond-the-hedge goose-grass *now SW, S*.

roch *see* **ruch**

rochian [-ch- as in 'loch'] a ruffian *NE Central*.

rock¹, **roke 1** a rock. **2** a curling-stone. **3** *also* **rock partan** the common edible crab.

rocklie pebbly.

rock bool a round, hard, candied-sugar sweet. **rock cod(fish)** a cod which lives amongs rocks. **rock-halibut** a coal-fish *NE*. **rock turbot** the flesh of the catfish or wolf-fish.

rock² stagger or reel in walking.

rockie row, rocketie-row with a rocking or rolling motion.

†**rockin(g)** a gathering of women neighbours to spin and chat together; any convivial gathering of neighbours.

rod *see* **road**

rodden the berry of the **rowan** *now N*.

rodden tree a **rowan**-tree.

as sour as roddens very sour or bitter.

roddikin the fourth stomach of a ruminant; tripe.

rodding a narrow track or path, especially one trodden out by sheep.

roke *see* **rock**¹, **rouk**

†**rokelay** a short cloak.

roll *see* **row**¹

rone¹, **roan, rhone** the horizontal gutter for rainwater, running along the eaves of a roof; a **rone pipe**.

rone pipe the vertical pipe for draining water from the **rone**¹; a **rone**¹.

rone², **roan, rhone** a thicket of brushwood, thorns etc; a patch of dense stunted woodland.

rone³, **roan, rhone** a strip or patch of ice on the ground; a children's slide.

rone *see* **rane, rowan**

roobrub *see* **rhubarb**

rood *see* **ruid**

roof *see* **ruif**

rook¹ *noun* **1** a rook, but in Scotland more usually called a **craw**¹. **2** *especially marbles* a complete loss.

verb **1** plunder, clean out; steal. **2** rob (a bird's nest) of eggs. **3** *marbles* win (all an opponent's marbles).

rookie *marbles* a game in which the winner takes all.

the hindmost rook one's last farthing.

rook² *now Angus noun* **1** a quarrel, uproar,

fuss. **2** a noisy group of people.

rook *see* **rouk**

rooketty, ruckity: rooketty-coo the call of a pigeon. **rooketty doo** a tame pigeon.

room, roum [-oo-] **1** a room. **2** †**rooms** domains, territories. **3** an estate; land rented from a landowner, a farm, a **tack**[2]. **4** *originally* the apartment of a **but and ben** (*see* **but**) not used as the kitchen; *hence* a sitting-room, best room. **5** *mining* the working space left between supporting pillars of coal.

   room-end the end of a **but and ben** (*see* **but**) away from the kitchen.

   room and kitchen a dwelling, usually a flat, consisting of á kitchen(/living-room) and another room.

roon *see* **roun(d)**[1], **ruind**

roon(d) *see* **roun(d)**[2]

roop *see* **roup**[1], **roup**[2], **roup**[3], **roup**[6]

roose *see* **rouse**[1], **rouse**[2], **ruise**

roost, rust, roust [-oo-] **1** rust. **2 not a roost** not a brass farthing.

   roostie 1 rusty. **2** *of the throat or voice* rough, dry; hoarse, raucous. **rustie nail** a drink of whisky.

root *see* **rowt, ruit**[1], **ruit**[2]

roove *see* **ruive**

rope *see* **raip, roup**[1]

roset, rozet *noun* resin, rosin.

   verb rub with resin; rub (a fiddle-bow) with rosin.

   rosetty-en(d) a shoemaker's thread *now SW*. **rosetty ruits** fir-roots used as fuel.

   roset-en(d) a resined thread for sewing leather.

rosidandrum rhododendron.

rosie a reddish marble.

rossin *see* **roast**

rost *see* **roast**

rothick a young edible crab *N*.

rottan *see* **ratton**

rotten drunk.

rouch *see* **ruch**

roudes *see* **rudas**

roug *see* **rug**

rough *see* **ruch**

roughie *see* **ruffie**

rouk, rowk, †roke, †rauk, rook mist, fog.

rouk *see* **ruck**

roul *see* **row**[1]

roule *see* **rule**

roum *see* **room**

rounall *see* **roundel**

†roun(d)[1], **roon 1** whisper, tell or talk quietly or privately. **2** discuss.

roun(d)[2], **roon(d)** *adjective* **1** round. **2** †*of speech* honest, plain.

   noun **1** a round. **2** a round turret. **3** a circular sheep-fold. **4 the round** the surrounding country, neighbourhood. **5 the round o the clock** twelve hours. **6** *also* **round-steak** a cut of meat, especially beef, taken from the hind-quarter.

roundel, rounall [roon(d)el] **1** a roundel. **2** a round turret. **3** a circular sheepfold.

roup[1], **rowp** [-ou-, -ow- as -ow- in 'cow'], **roop, †rope** *verb* **1** sell or let by public auction. **2** sell up, especially turn out (a bankrupt) and sell his effects.

   noun a sale or let by public auction.

roup[2], **roop** *verb* shout, roar; croak.

   noun hoarseness, huskiness, any inflamed condition of the throat.

   roupie, roupit hoarse, rough.

roup[3] [-oo-], **roop** *verb* **1** plunder, rob, deprive of everything. **2** prune very severely. **3** take (the marbles of a defeated opponent) in a game of **roopie**, in which the winner claims all the loser's marbles.

roup[4] [rowp] vomit *NE*.

roup[5] [rowp] a stem of seaweed, especially oar-weed *NE*.

roup[6] [-oo-], **roop** a dense mist *SW*, *S*.

rouse[1], **roose** [rhymes with 'choose'] **1** rouse. **2** move with violence or speed, rush *Shetland Orkney NE*. **3** become agitated, excited or enraged.

rouse[2], **roose** [rhymes with 'choose'] *verb* **1** sprinkle (fish) with salt to cure them. **2** sprinkle with water; water with a watering can *NE*.

   rouser a watering-can.

rouse *see* **ruise**

roust *see* **roost**

rout[1] [-oo-] *of the sea, winds, thunder etc* roar, rumble.

†rout[2] [-oo-] snore.

rout *see* **rowt**

routh, rowth [-ou-, -ow- as -ow- in 'cow'] *noun* plenty, abundance, profusion.
adjective, also **routhie** plentiful, abundant, profuse, well-endowed.

rove[1] wander in thought or speech, be delirious, rave.

rove[2] *of a fire* burn well, blaze *NE*.

rove *see* **ruive**

row[1], **roll, roul** [-ow-, -ou- as -ow- in 'cow'] *verb* **1** roll. **2** wheel, convey in a wheeled vehicle. **3** trundle (*eg a* **gird**[1] *noun* 4) forward. **4** play (a bowl or curling-stone); *of bowls* roll towards the jack. **5** wind, twist, twine. **6** wrap up or in; wrap around. **7** wind up (a clock etc). **8** **be rowed intae** be involved or embroiled in. **9** move about with a rolling or staggering gait, stumble along. **10** move about, fidget, toss and turn restlessly. **11** *of sheep* roll over on the back.
noun **1** a roll. **2** *law, only* **roll** a list of cases, applications, motions etc set down for hearing in court. **3** a roll of tobacco.
rower a rolling pin, often a ribbed or grooved one. **rowie** a flaky bread roll made with a lot of butter *NE*. **rolliepin** *games* a rolling action of the hands between the bouncing and catching of a ball. **rowing 1** rolling. **2** a roll of unspun cotton or wool.
row-chow *verb, especially of children at play* roll, tumble. *adjective* rolling, revolving; mixed-up, tangled. **row-chow tobacco** a game in which a chain of boys coil round a large boy and all sway to and fro shouting the name of the game until they fall in a noisy heap.

row[2] [-ow- as in 'cow'] *of a boat* move along in the water easily or smoothly.

row *see* **raw**[1]

rowan, †rone, †roan, †raun-, *also* **rowan-tree, rowan buss 1** the mountain ash. **2** *also* **rowan berry** the fruit of the mountain ash.

rowk *see* **rouk**

rowl *see* **rule**

rown *see* **rawn**

rowp *see* **roup**[1]

rowst[1] [-ow- as in 'cow'] shout, roar, bellow *now Angus*.
rowsty *of weather* windy, blustery.

rowst[2] [-ow- as in 'cow'] arouse, stir to action, rout out.

rowt, rout [rhymes with 'out'], **root** *verb* **1** *of cattle* bellow, roar. **2** *of other animals* roar, cry. **3** shout, make a great noise. **4** play on (a horn); toot. **5** break wind. **6** †*of wind, water etc* roar loudly.

rowth *see* **routh**

royal: royalty an area of land or a district held by or directly of the Crown.
royal burgh a **burgh** deriving its charter and its lands and privileges directly from the Crown; the **Royal Burghs** formed a separate estate in the Scottish Parliament: *see also* **convention.**

royet *adjective* **1** *especially of children* wild, mischievous. **2** *of weather* wild, stormy, variable *NE*.
noun an unruly, troublesome person or animal.

rozet *see* **roset**

rub *verb* **1** *bowls, curling* move (a stone or bowl) aside by knocking gently against it with another.
noun **1** *golf* accidental factors affecting the resting place of the ball in play which must be accepted by the players. **2** a slight jibe, scolding or teasing.
rubbin stane a piece of pipeclay used to whiten doorsteps.

rubbage rubbish.

ruch, rough, rouch, reuch, roch *adjective* **1** rough. **2** *of sheep* unshorn, unclipped. **3** *of grass or crops* strong, luxuriant, dense. **4** abundant; plentifully supplied, especially with good plain fare. **5** *of a bone* having meat on it. **6** foul-mouthed, indecent, dirty.

noun **1** rough. **2** rough ground. **3** land in an uncultivated state. **4** the major part of something.

rough bear = **bear**[1]. **rough blade** the mature leaf of a plant as opposed to the seed leaf. **ruch dram** enough alcoholic drink to cause drunkenness *N*. **ruch-living** *of a man* living in a dissolute or immoral way. **ruch stane** a natural boulder. **ruch-stane dyke** a dry-stone dyke (*see* **dry**).

ruch and right entirely, taking everything into consideration.

ruck, rouk [-oo-] *noun* **1** a hay- or corn-stack of a standard shape and size. **2** a stack or heap, especially of peats *now NE*. **3** a small temporary haystack to allow the hay to dry.

ruckie a stone; a marble *S*.

ruckity *see* **rooketty**

ruckle[1] make a rattling, gurgling or roaring sound, especially of the breathing of a dying person.

ruckle[2] wrinkle, crease, work into folds.

ruckle *see* **rickle**[1]

rudas, †roudes [rhymes with 'Judas'] *noun* **auld rudas** a coarse or masculine-looking woman; a bad-tempered hag *now NE*.

adjective **1** *of a woman* ugly, cantankerous, witch-like. **2** †*of a man* cantankerous, stubborn, rough-mannered. **3** wild, undisciplined, irresponsible *now NE*.

ruddie a loud, reverberating, often repeated, noise.

rue, rew 1 rue. **2 rue on** have pity on, feel compassion for. **3** regret a promise, bargain etc, withdraw from a bargain or contract.

rue-bargain money given as compensation for breaking a bargain, agreement *now SW*.

mak a rue, tak the rue 1 repent, regret; change one's mind. **2** take offence or a dislike.

ruff *verb* **1** beat (a drum), especially before a proclamation; *of a drum* sound a roll.

2 applaud or show approval by stamping the feet; **ruff down** show disapproval, silence (a speaker) by stamping or shuffling with the feet.

ruffie, roughie a torch or light, a fir-brand, a wick of rag smeared with tallow; a torch used when fishing for salmon at night.

rug, roug *mainly Caithness* [-oo-] *verb* **1** pull vigorously or forcibly, tug, drag, draw. **2** *of pain, hunger etc* ache, nag *now NE*.

noun **1** a pull, a rough, hasty tug. **2** a tug on a fishing line, a bite. **3** *of grazing animals* a bite of grass, a feed. **4** a strong undercurrent in the sea, a strong tide. **5** a twinge of nerves or emotions. **6** a knot or tangle of hair *now Orkney NE*. **7** a bargain, especially one which takes unfair advantage of the seller; a high profit, a cut, a rake-off.

rug and reive rob. **rug and rive 1** pull or tug vigorously; struggle, tussle. **2** rob, plunder.

ruid, rood, reed 1 a rood, the cross of Christ; the measure. **2** a square measure (36 square **ells**. See p 360). **3** a piece of ground belonging to a **burgh** rented or **feued** (*see* **feu**) for building and cultivating.

ruif, roof, reef *NE*, **riff 1** a roof. **2** the ceiling of a room.

ruif-tree 1 the main beam or ridge of a roof. **2** a house, home.

ruind, rind, †roon 1 the border or selvage of a web of cloth; a strip of cloth. **2** †any thin strip of material, a shred, fragment.

ruind shune shoes made of strips of selvages of cloth.

ruise, roose, rouse [-oo-], **reese** *NE*, *verb* **1** praise, extol, flatter.

noun praise, flattery; boasting; a boast. **mak (a) (toom) ruise** give (empty) praise or flattery; boast (unjustifiably).

ruit[1], **root, reet** *N* **1** a root. **2** a dried tree root used as firewood, especially one dug up from a bog. **3** the bottom of a hedge.

at the ruit o one's tongue on the tip of one's tongue. **(the) reet and (the) rise** the source and every aspect of something *NE*.

ruit² **root, reet** *mainly Caithness verb* **1** root, dig up with the snout. **2** rummage, search.

ruive roove, rove *especially boat-building* a burr, a metal washer on which the point of a nail or bolt can be clinched; a rivet.

rule, roule *NE,* **rowl** [-ou-, as -ow- in 'cow'] *NE* rule.

ruling elder *Presbyterian churches* a person who has been ordained as an **elder,** in practice one who is not a **minister.**

rullion *see* **rivlin**

rum boorish, coarse.

rumble *see* **rummle**

rumfordin a sheet of metal used as a lining or casing for the back of a fireplace.

rumgumption commonsense, understanding, shrewdness.

rummage, reemage, reemish search noisily, poke around *NE*.

rummle, rumble *verb* **1** rumble. **2** †make a noise or disturbance; move about noisily or riotously. **3** knock violently or throw stones (at a door) as a prank. **4** strike or beat severely; jolt, handle roughly. **5** toss about restlessly in bed. **6** stir or shake vigorously; mash (potatoes); scramble (eggs) *now SW*. **7** clear (a narrow passage, especially a tobacco pipe) with a rod or wire. **8** feel (in one's pocket) for something.

noun **1** a rumble. **2** a movement causing a rumbling sound; a vigorous stir, a rough jolting; a resounding blow or whack. **3** a rough knocking or beating. **4** a badly-built piece of masonry, a ruin. **5** something ugly or dilapidated, *eg* a piece of furniture *now Shetland NE*. **6** a large clumsy person; a rough reckless boy. **7** a rush. **8** a mixture; something confused or disordered *now Shetland*.

rummlie 1 *of soil* rough and stony; loose and crumbly. **2** *of the mind* disordered.

rummle(de)thump 1 mashed potatoes with cabbage (or turnip). **2** mashed potatoes with milk, butter and seasoning *now SW*. **3** = **skirlie** (*see* **skirl**) *now Angus*.

rummlegarie, rummle-skeerie a wild, reckless, or thoughtless person.

rummle-gumption 1 understanding, common-sense. **2** *often* **rummle-gumptions** wind in the stomach, flatulence.

rump *noun* **1** rump; in Scotland, a cut of beef corresponding to English topside and silverside, now usually called **round-steak** (*see* **round²**). **2** †contemptuous term for a person or animal.

verb **1** cut, clip or crop very short. **2** eat down to the roots. **3** plunder; steal; *marbles* win (all one's opponents marbles).

rumpie a small crusty loaf or roll. **rumple** the rump, tail, haunches (of an animal); the buttocks, seat (of a person) *now Shetland*.

rump and stump completely.

run *see* **rin**

runch¹, runsh a wild radish.

runch², runsh crunch, grind, crush.

runch *see* **wranch**

rung *noun* **1** a strong stick; a cudgel. **2** a blow with a stick; a thump. **3** contemptuous term for a bad-tempered person; a large, ugly person or animal; a thin, scraggy animal.

verb **1** make or fit with spans or rungs. **2** beat with a stick, cudgel.

runk¹ 1 an emaciated, worn-out person, animal or thing. **2** contemptuous term, especially for a bad-tempered woman *NE*.

runk² deprive (a person) of all his money, possessions etc, bankrupt.

runkle 1 wrinkle. **2** crease, rumple, crush. **3** gnarl, twist, distort, curl.

runsh *see* **runch**[1], **runch**[2]

runt[1] **1** an old or decayed tree-stump. **2** the hardened, withered stem of a cabbage or **kail** plant. **3** a short, thickset person; an undersized person or animal. **4** contemptuous term, especially for a coarse, ill-natured person, especially an old woman.
runtit 1 stunted in growth. **2** completely deprived of one's possessions, made bankrupt; *marbles* having lost all one's marbles to one's opponent *now NE*.

runt[2] an ox or cow for fattening and slaughter, a store animal, frequently a Highland cow or ox; an old cow (past breeding and fattened for slaughter).

rural *law, of a lease etc* relating to land as opposed to buildings (whether in the country or in town).

rush *verb* **1** *especially of sheep or cattle* suffer from dysentry. **2** flirt with, court (a girl).
noun **1** †dysentry, especially in sheep or cattle. **2** a skin eruption, rash; scarlet fever. **3** a luxuriant growth of vegetation or hair.

rushyroo a shrew *now Perth*.

ruskie 1 a straw basket etc. **2** a straw beehive.

russle *see* **rizzar**

rust *see* **roost**

rut *see* **rit**

ruther 1 †an outcry, uproar. **2** turmoil, chaos, ruin *NE*.

rybat a rabbet.

rys *see* **rice**

S

s, S *see* **us**

sa *see* **sae²**, **saw²**

sab, sob 1 sob. **2** the noise of a gust of wind or the sea.

Sabbath, Sawbath 1 Sabbath, Sunday. **2** *especially among older speakers* Sunday as a day of the week without reference to its religious significance.

sacket 1 a small sack or bag. **2** a scamp, rascal, cheeky person.

sacrament 1 a sacrament, especially the Communion service of the Presbyterian Churches. **2 the Sacraments** the period Thursday to the following Monday including the Communion and other services *now Hebrides Highland*.

sad, sod *N adjective* **1** sad. **2** solid, dense, hard and compact. **3** *of bread or pastry* not risen, heavy.
verb, of a haystack, soil etc (cause to) sink or settle down, shrink, become solid.
saddit 1 *of earth etc* beaten hard, hard-packed. **2** *of bread* heavy, not fully baked.

sae¹, say, sey a wooden water tub, carried by two people on a pole or rope *now Shetland Orkney Caithness*.

sae², so, †sa, †swa 1 so. **2 so it is** *etc* indeed it is etc: *"you're a wee dodger, so you are!"*; **so it is not** *etc* neither it is etc: *"she never lifted her hand, so she didna"*.
ilka sae lang now and again.
sae bein('s) provided that, since.

safe *see* **sauf**

saft, soft *adjective* **1** soft. **2** *of weather* mild, not frosty; thawing. **3** wet, rainy, damp.
noun a thaw; rain, moisture.
saftie 1 a softie, a weak(-minded) stupid person. **2** *also* **saft biscuit** a kind of plain floury bun or roll with a dent in the middle. **3** *also* **saftick** an edible crab which has lost its shell, often used for bait *NE*. **4** a soft slipper.
up someone's saft side into someone's favour. **have a saft side to** have a special liking for.

saidle, seddle saddle.

saikless *see* **sakeless**

sail *noun* a ride in a cart or other vehicle or on horseback.
verb **1** be covered over with liquid. **2** ride or drive in a vehicle.

sain, sane protect from harm by a sign, especially the sign of the cross, bless.

sain *see* **say**

saint, saunt, sant, †sanct *noun* **1** a saint. **2 the Saints** nickname for **St Johnstone** and **St Mirren** football teams.
verb **1** saint, canonize; play the saint. **2** (cause to) disappear, vanish, especially suddenly or mysteriously.
†St Johnsto(u)n name for the town of Perth, of which St John the Baptist is patron. **St Johnstone** official name for the Perth football team. **St Mirren** official name for the Paisley football team.

saip soap.
saip(y) graith soapy lather.

sair, sore *adjective* **1** sore. **2** causing physical pain, distress or strain: *"It's sair on the back"*. **3** causing mental distress or grief: *"It was a sair sicht"*. **4** hard (to bear): *"a sair disaster"*. **5** involving hardship, danger etc. **6** *of a battle, struggle etc* hard, severe, fierce, now often of life in general: **it's a sair fecht**. **7** *of the weather* severe, stormy. **8** *of something unpleasant etc* serious, considerable, sorry: *"a sair come-doun"*. **9** *of the head* aching, painful, throbbing. **10** *of the heart* aching, sorrowful. **11**

of people harsh. **12 sair on** destructive, harmful, giving hard wear or usage to: *"she's sair on her claes"*.

noun **1** a sore. **2** a grief, a sorrow.

adverb **1** sorely, severely, so as to cause pain or suffering. **2** in a distressed manner. **3** hard, with great effort: *"sair won"*. **4** with all one's strength or feeling. **5** very much, greatly, extremely.

sair aff badly off, very hard up. **sair done** *of meat* well done, overcooked. **sair fit** a time of need: *"lay something aside for a sair fit"*. **sair hand 1** a mess, a piece of badly-done work. **2** a large thick slice of bread with butter or jam (which looks like a bandaged hand). **sair heid 1** a headache. **2** a small plain cake with a paper band round it. **sair hert** a sad state of mind; a great disappointment. **sair teeth** toothache. **sair wame** stomach-ache.

sair awa wi't worn out by illness, hard usage etc.

sair *see* **saur, serve**

sairie, sorry, †serie 1 sorry. **2** sad, sorrowful. **3** in a poor or sorry state.

sairious serious.

saison, sizzon *now NE* a season.

saithe, †seeth a full-grown coalfish in its third or fourth year.

saitin satin.

saitisfee satisfy.

sake: for any sake for Heaven's sake.

sakeless, saikless 1 innocent (of). **2** simple; harmless, silly; lacking drive or energy.

sal *see* **saul**

sald *see* **sell**¹

sall shall.

past tense **suld, sud** *now Shetland,* **sid** *now NE,* **shid** *now NE* should. **sanna, shanna** shall not.

salmon, salmond *see* **saumon**

salt *see* **saut**

same, seam fat, especially of pigs, grease, lard.

sammy dreep *see* **dreep**

sanal *see* **sand**

sanct *see* **saint**

sand: san(d)al, san(d)le a sand-eel. **sannie** a sandshoe. **sandy laverock** a ringed plover.

sand bed a very heavy drinker. **sand lowper** a sand flea. **sandshoe** a plimsoll, a gym shoe.

Sandie, Sawnie, Saunders 1 shortened forms of Alexander. **2** a young man, especially a countryman. **3** *often* **auld Sandie** the Devil.

sandle *see* **sand**

sane *see* **sain**

sang, song 1 a song. **2** the noise of the sea breaking on the shore. **3** a fuss, outcry: *"mak a sang aboot"*.

an auld sang an old story or saying, a proverb. **the end o an auld sang** the last of an old custom, institution etc, the end of an era.

sanle *see* **sand**

sanna *see* **sall**

sannie *see* **sand**

sanshach 1 wily, shrewd. **2** disdainful, surly *NE*. **3** irritable. **4** *of people* pleasant *NE*.

sant *see* **saint**

sap¹ (an amount of) something to drink, to be taken with food.

sap² *noun* **1** a sop. **2 saps** pieces of bead etc soaked or boiled in milk etc.

verb sop, soak, steep.

sapsy *adjective* like **saps,** soft, sloppy; effeminate. *noun* a soft, weak-willed, person.

sappie 1 *of meat etc* juicy. **2** *of people* plump. **3** wet, soppy, sodden. **4** *of food* soft, soggy, like **saps** (*see* **sap**²). **5** *of a kiss* soft, long-drawn out.

sapple *verb* soak with water, rain etc; steep (clothes) in soapy water.

noun, also **sapples** soapsuds, lather for washing.

sapsy *see* **sap**²

sar *see* **saur**

sark, serk *noun* **1** a man's shirt. **2 †**a woman's shift or chemise.

verb **1** clothe in or provide with a shirt.

2 line (a roof) with wood for the slates to be nailed on.

sarket an undershirt, a woollen vest *NE*. **a sarkfu o sair banes** a person stiff or sore from hard work or from a beating. **sarking 1** shirting(-material). **2** roof boarding.

sasine, †seisin [**sayzin**] *law* the act of giving or registering possession of feudal property.

Sassenach *adjective* English(-speaking); formerly also used by Highlanders of Lowlanders.
noun an English person.

sassenger a sausage.

sat *see* **saut**

sate a seat.

sattle, settle *verb* **1** settle. **2** *Presbyterian Churches* install (a **minister**) in a charge.
noun a settle, a bench.
settlement 1 *law* the settling of one's property by will. **2** the placing of a **minister** in a charge.
sattlebed a bed which can be folded up to form a seat during the day; a divan bed.

Saturday *see* **Setterday**

saucy 1 vain, conceited. **2** fussy about food or dress.

sauch, saugh [-ch, -gh as -ch in 'loch'] sallow, a willow; a willow rod, willow wood.
sauchen 1 of willow. **2** tough as willow; **dour**, stubborn and sullen. **3** soft, yielding as willow, lacking in energy or spirit.
sauch buss a (low-growing) willow tree. **sauch wan(d)** a twig or branch of willow. **sauch willie** a willow.

sauf, safe *adjective* safe.
verb save.

saul, sal, sowl [-ow- as in 'cow'] *noun* **1** a soul. **2** spirit, courage.
exclamation upon my word!
the (wee) sowl term of familiarity, pity etc.

sauld *see* **sell**[1]

†saulie a hired mourner at a funeral.

saumon, sawmont, salmon, †salmond a salmon.
saumon lowp 1 a salmon leap. **2** a kind of leapfrog.

Saunders *see* **Sandie**

saunt *see* **saint**

saur, sar, †sair *verb* **1** savour. **2** have a certain taste or smell.
noun **1** savour. **2** a slight wind, gentle breeze.
saurless 1 tasteless. **2** lacking in wit, spirit, energy *NE*.

saut, sat, salt *noun* salt.
adjective **1** salt. **2** *of experience etc* painful, severe, bitter. **3** *of prices etc* dear, stinging. **4** *of speech, manner* harsh, unkind *SW*.
verb **1** salt. **2** punish, treat severely; over-charge, sting.
sauter 1 a bad-tempered woman. **2** severe punishment. **sautie bannock** an oatmeal **bannock** with a fair amount of salt, baked on Shrove Tuesday.
saut backet a salt-box, especially one made to hang on the wall. **saut fat** a salt cellar.

saw[1], **shaw** *NE*, **shaave** *NE verb, past tense also* **sew** *now NE*, **schew** *now Shetland NE. past participle also* **sawed** sow.

saw[2], **sa** a salve, a healing ointment.

Sawbath *see* **Sabbath**

Sawmont *see* **saumon**

Sawnie *see* **Sandie**

sax, six, †sex six.
sixsie a move in the game of **chuckies** (*see* **chuck**[2]). **sixsome** a group of six (people), *eg* in a dance. **saxt** sixth.
six(es) and sax(es) very much alike, six and half a dozen.

say *verb, past participle also* **sain** say.
noun **1** what is said; a remark, piece of gossip. **2** a saying, proverb *Shetland Orkney N*.
say ae wey (wi) agree (with). **say awa(y)** *verb* **1** say on, speak one's mind. **2** say grace before a meal. *noun* a long rigmarole. **say wi** agree with.

say *see* **sae**[1], **sey**[1]

scab: **scabbert** *noun* a bare, stony piece of land *NE. adjective* scabbed, bare.
scabbie-heid a person with head lice.
scabbit 1 scabbed. **2** *of land* bare, infertile. **3** *of a person* mean, worthless.

scad *see* **scaud**

scaddin 1 a thin flaky turf, a peat used for thatching. **2** a worthless person or thing.

scaff[1], **skaff** a light boat, skiff.

scaff[2], **skaff** *verb* **1** scrounge, go about looking for (food) to pick up. **2** wander about. **3** eat or drink greedily.
noun **1** food. **2** rubbish; riff-raff. **3** roaming about idly.

scaffie a street-sweeper, refuse collector.
scaffie cairt a refuse-collector's cart or lorry.

scailie, scallie, skylie, skeely 1 (a) slate. **2** a slate pencil.

scaith *see* **skaith**

scal(d) *see* **scaul(d)**

scald *see* **scaud**

scale a shallow dish.

scale *see* **skail**

scale stair a straight (as opposed to a spiral) stair.

†**scallag** [ska**lack**] a farm labourer; latterly form of address to a boy *Highland.*

scallie *see* **scailie**

scallion a spring onion.

scalp *see* **scaup**

scam, scaum *verb* **1** burn slightly, scorch, singe. **2** *of frost* scorch, blight (plants). **3** scold severely.
noun **1** a burn, singe. **2** a withering or scorching of plants. **3** a hurt to one's feelings. **4** a spot, crack, injury. **5** a haze, mist, shadow.

scance, scanse *verb* **1** scan, analyse, look carefully and critically at. **2** criticize, reproach. **3** gleam, glitter, shine.
noun **1** a quick look. **2** a gleam, a brief appearance.

scant lack, scarcity.
scantlins scarcely, hardly.

scap *see* **scaup**

scar, scaur, sker *adjective, also* **skair** timid, shy, wild, apt to run away.
noun a fright, scare.
verb **1** scare, frighten. **2** take fright, run away in fear.

scar *see* **scaur**[1]

scarf, skarf, skart, scart, scrath *NE* a cormorant, a shag.

scarrow *SW* **1** a faint light. **2** a shadow, shade.

scart[1], **skart 1** scratch, scrape. **2** strike (a match). **3** mark (a paper) with a pen, scribble (a note etc). **4** make a scraping, grating, rasping noise.
noun **1** a scratch. **2** a mark or scrape of a pen, a scribble. **3** a furrow or mark on the ground. **4** a grain, trace.
scartle scrape together in little bits; make little scratching movements.
scart free, scart hale unscathed, scot free.

scart[2] **1** a sexually malformed animal; a monster. **2** a thin, shrunken person.

scart *see* **scarf**

scash *NE* **1** quarrel, squabble. **2** twist, turn to one side; shuffle along with the toes turned out.

scathe *see* **skaith**

scattan a herring.

scatter *at a wedding* throw handfuls of coins or sweets in the street for children to scramble for.

scaud, scald, scad *verb* **1** scald. **2** make (tea). **3** *mainly* **scad** *of cloth* (cause to) become faded or shabby. **5** cause grief or pain, punish.
noun **1** a scald. **2** a sore caused by chafing of the skin. **3** tea. **4** a hurt to the feelings. **5** **scad** a faint appearance of colour or light.
scalder a jellyfish, medusa.

scaul(d), scal(d), scawl *noun* **1** a scold, a scolding woman. **2** scolding, railing, abuse.
verb scold.

scaum *see* **scam**

scaup, scalp, †**scap 1** the scalp. **2** †the

skull. **3** thin shallow soil; a piece of (bare) stony ground. **4** a bank for shell-fish in the sea.

scaur¹, scar, sker *S* a steep rock, precipice.

scaur² scar.

scaur *see* **scar**

scaw 1 a scaly skin disease. **2** a mass of barnacles.
   scawt, scaut 1 having a skin disease; scabby, scruffy. **2** shabby, faded. **3** scruffy, scanty.

scawl *see* **scaul(d)**

SCE *see* **Scots**

scent, sint 1 scent. **2** a small quantity, drop, pinch.

scheme, housing scheme a local-authority housing estate.

schew *see* **saw¹**

schlorach *see* **slorach**

scho *see* **she**

scholar a school pupil.

schule, scuil [-u, -ui- as -ui- in 'guid'], **school, skeel** *N*, **squeel** *NE* **1** a school.
   learn the schule be a pupil at school.

scibe *see* **skybe**

sclaff, sklaff *verb* **1** strike with the open hand or with something flat, slap. **2** walk in a flat-footed or shuffling way.
   noun **1** a blow from something flat, a falling flat, a thud. **2** *golf* a muffed shot when the club grazes the ground before hitting the ball. **3** a light loose-fitting shoe or slipper; an old worn-down shoe. **4** a thin flat piece of something.
   sclaffert 1 a blow from something flat *N*. **2** a clumsy flat-footed person *NE*.

sclair- *see* **slair**

sclammer¹ clamber.

sclammer² clamour *NE*.

sclatch, sklatch *verb* **1** smear or cover over with something wet or messy. **2** do something messily, clumsily, or carelessly.
   noun **1** a large smudge, smear. **2** a mess. **3** a heavy fall (into water or mud), a slap, smack.

sclate *see* **slate**

sclave *verb* spread (a story) by gossip; slander (a person).
   noun a gossip, scandalmonger.

sclender, sklender, sclinner *NE*, **sclenner** *NE* slender.

sclice slice.

sclidder *see* **slidder**

sclim, sklim climb.

sclinner *see* **sclender**

sclit *mining* slaty coal, coaly **blaes**.

sclither *see* **slidder**

sclore chat, gossip, **blether¹**.

sclutter *see* **slutter**

scly, sly, scloy *verb* slide, skate (as) on ice.
   noun **1** a strip of ice etc used as a slide. **2** the act of sliding on ice etc.

sclype *see* **slype**

sclyster *see* **slaister**

scob¹ *noun* **1** a twig or cane of willow or hazel, especially one bent over to fasten down thatch etc. **2** a slat of wood used as a splint for repairs etc.
   verb put (a broken bone) in splints.

scob² scoop out, hollow, gnaw out with the teeth.

scodge, skodge, scudge, scodgie *noun* **1** a servant who does light, rough or dirty work, especially a kitchen-boy or -girl. **2** *also* **scodgie brat** a rough apron for dirty work.
   verb do rough work.

scodgebell *see* **coachbell**

scoff, scouf [skowf] **1** steal, sponge, scrounge. **2** swallow (food or drink) quickly.

scog *see* **scug**

scomfish, skomfish, scunfis [skumfish] **1** suffocate, choke, overpower with heat etc. **2** disgust, sicken.
   tak a scomfish at take a strong dislike to, be disgusted at.

sconce, skonce a screen or shelter (of stone, wood etc) against the weather, fire, or for defence etc.

scone [skon] **1** a large, usually round semisweet cake made of wheat flour, baked on a **girdle** etc, or in an oven, and cut into four three-sided pieces; one of these pieces; a similar small round individual-sized cake. **2** an oat-cake *now Shetland*. **3** *mainly* **scone bon-net** = **Kilmarnock bonnet** (*see* **Kil-marnock**). **4** a slap (with the flat of the hand), smack.

verb **1** strike the surface of (something) with a flat object. **2** slap with the open hand, smack (especially a child's bottom).

scondies child's work for smacks, a spanking.

scone face nickname for a person or thing with a round flat face.

a scone o the day's baking an average or typical person. **drop(ped) scone** *see* **drap** *and* **pancake** (*under* **pan**[1]).

sconner *see* **scunner**

scoo *see* **scull**

scoop *see* **scuip**

scoor *see* **scour**[1], **scour**[2], **scour**[3]

scoorie *see* **scourie**

scoosh *see* **skoosh**

scoot *see* **scout**[1], **scout**[2]

score[1] **1** a stroke, scratch. **2** *games* a mark or line on the ground, *eg* the starting line. **3** a line, wrinkle on the skin; a scar left by a wound. **4** a parting in the hair.
over the score beyond the bounds of reason, moderation etc.

score[2] a crevice, cleft, gully in a cliff face.

scorn 1 jeer, scoff at. **2** †**scorn (someone) wi** tease about (a lover).

Scot a native of Scotland; originally one of the people who crossed from Ireland to Argyll in the 5th century.

Scots, Scottish, Scotch

A *Forms:* **Scots** is the usual form in Scottish Standard English, except when referring to national or official matters, when **Scottish** is preferred; **Scotch**, originally borrowed from English, has become the usual form in Scots dialect (usually pronounced [skoatch]), but in Scottish Standard English is now used only in a few phrases: *"Scotch broth", "Scotch whisky".*
B *Meanings:* adjective **1** of or belonging to Scotland or the Scots. **2** used in

Shetland and Orkney to refer to the mainland of Scotland. **3** *mainly* **Scots** of the Scottish legal system. **4** used in measures and money; see pp 358, 360. **5** speaking or expressed in **Scots** *noun.*
noun the Scots language, the speech of Lowland Scotland; that treated in this dictionary.

Scottish baronial *see* **baron. Scotch bun** = **black bun** (*see* **black**). **Scottish Certificate of Education, SCE** examinations in individual subjects conducted annually since 1962 by the Scottish Education Department: the **O Grade** (*see* **ordinar**); the **Higher Grade** (*see* **heich**); the **Certificate of Sixth Year Studies, (C)SYS** examinations at a more advanced level than the **Higher Grade. Scotch collops** thin slices of meat stewed with stock and flavouring. **Scotch convoy** the accompanying of a guest a part or all of the way back to his home; compare **Scots Convoy** (*under* **convoy**). **Scotch cousin** a distant relative. **Scotch cuddy** a pedlar, travelling packman. **Scotch flummery** a kind of steamed custard. **Scotch gravat** a hug, cuddle. **Scotch hand** *see* **hand. Scotch horses** a formation of children running etc with arms linked behind their backs. **Scottish Land Court** a court set up by statute with a legally-qualified chairman and members with agricultural expertise; its jurisdiction covers the various forms of agricultural tenancy. **Scots thistle** one of the thistle family (the exact species being disputed) adopted as the national badge of Scotland.

scouder *see* **scowder**

scouf *see* **scoff**

scoug *see* **scug**

scouk [-oo-]**, skook** *verb* **1** skulk. **2** avoid (in a skulking manner). **3** scowl, look (furtively) from under the eyebrows; frown.
noun a furtive look; a frown *NE.*

scoul [-oo-]**, skool** scowl.

scoup *see* **scowp**

scour[1], **scoor**, **scowr** [rhymes with 'poor'] a shower of rain, especially with gusts of wind.

scoury blustery with rain, wet and squally.

scour[2] [-oo-], **scoor** *verb* scour, rush about.

noun **1** a run, rush, quick pace. **2** a blow, stroke, box (on the ear).

scour[3] [-oo-], **scoor**, **skoor** **1** scour, cleanse. **2** clear out (the bowels, stomach). **3** †flush out with liquid; *humorous* drink, wet (one's throat). **4** scold severely.

scourin clout a rough cloth for washing floors etc.

scour-oot the scattering of coins at a wedding for children to scramble for.

scourge the whip of a spinning top.

scourie, scoorie, scowrie **1** *of people* scruffy, disreputable-looking. **2** *of clothes* shabby, worn.

scout[1] [-oo-], **scoot**, **skoot** *verb* **1** make (water etc) spout or spurt out, squirt. **2** *of liquid* spurt or squirt out.

noun **1** a sudden gush or flow of water from a spout etc; the pipe from which it comes. **2** *also* **scooter** a squirt, syringe, especially one used as a water gun. **3** *also* **scooter** a peashooter, especially one made from a plant stem. **4** diarrhoea, especially of birds or animals. **5** contemptuous term for a person.

scoutie worthless, scruffy; small, insignificant.

scout[2] [-oo-], **scoot**, **skoot** one of various seabirds, *eg* a razorbill, a guillemot.

scouth *see* **scowth**

scouther *see* **scowder**

scow[1], **skow** [rhymes with 'cow'] a flat-bottomed boat, *eg* a lighter, barge.

scow[2], **skow** [rhymes with 'cow'] **1** a barrel stave, thin plank. **2** a splinter, sliver of wood; fragments, shattered pieces.

scowder, scouder, scowther, scouther [-ow-] *verb* **1** burn, scorch, singe; over-toast (bread etc). **2** *of frost or rain* wither, blight (leaves etc). **3** become scorched, burn. **4** rain or snow slightly.

noun **1** a scorch, singe, burn. **2** a jellyfish (because of its burning sting). **3** a slight shower (of rain).

scowf *see* **scowth**

†**scowp, scoup** bound, dart, skip, run hither and thither.

scowr *see* **scour**[1]

scowrie *see* **scourie**

scowth, scouth, skouth, scowf [skowth, skowf] freedom, scope.

scowther *see* **scowder**

scrab **1** a crab-apple. **2** a shrivelled or stunted person or thing.

scrachle *see* **scrauchle**

scrae, skrae **1** a stunted, shrivelled, or under-developed person or animal. **2** a shrivelled dried-up thing.

scraffle scramble, claw about with the hands *now Shetland Orkney Caithness*.

scrag *see* **scrog**

scraich, scraigh *see* **skreek**

scran, skran *noun* **1** food. **2** scraps or leavings of food or other rubbish often got by begging or scrounging.

verb scrounge about for (food etc); scrape together.

†**scran bag** a bag in which a beggar collected scraps of food etc.

scrape 1 a scrape of the pen a mark made by a pen; a hasty scribble or letter. **2** the shallow first furrow made in a **rig**[1].

scrat[1] *verb* **1** scratch, claw; make a scratching noise. **2 scrat aff** mark out with shallow furrows the **rigs**[1] to be ploughed in a field.

noun **1** a scratch, slight wound; the noise made by scratching. **2** the shallow first furrow made in a **rig**[1].

scrat[2] a puny or stunted person or animal.

scratcher **1** *slang* a bed. **2** a trawler which fishes as close as possible to the three-mile limit *NE*.

scrath *see* **scarf**

scrauchle, scrachle scramble with hands

and feet, climb hastily and clumsily.

scraw, skraw a thin turf or sod, especially as used for roofing *SW, Ulster.*

scree¹ a mass of loose stones on a steep hillside.

scree² a riddle or sieve for grain, sand, coal etc.

screechan *see* **screich**

screed, skreed *noun* **1** a long narrow strip: (1) of cloth, paper etc; a torn piece; (2) of land. **2** *often contemptuous* a long speech or piece of writing. **3** a tear, slash; a scratch. **4** the sound of tearing etc; a grating, scraping noise. **5** a spell of drinking.
verb **1** tear, rip. **2** tear, come apart. **3** make a shrill screeching noise. **4** *often* **screed aff** read, recite fluently, reel off.

screef *see* **scruif**

†**screen** a shawl, headscarf.

screenge, scringe **1** rub or scrub energetically. **2** whip, flog. **3** search eagerly or inquisitively. **4** wander about aimlessly *NE.*

screeve, skreeve, scrieve *verb* **1** graze (the skin), peel or tear off (a surface etc), scratch, scrape. **2** make a scraping or grating motion or sound.
noun **1** a large scratch. **2** a scraping or grating sound.

screeve *see* **scrieve**²

screich, screechan [-ch as in 'dreich'] *Shetland* whisky.

screw a shrew.

screw *see* **scroo**

scribe *noun* a mark made with a pen; a piece of writing.
verb write.

scrieve¹ *verb* **1** move along quickly and smoothly. **2** talk fluently for a long time *now Shetland.*

scrieve², **screeve** *verb* **1** write, especially fluently and easily. **2** scratch a mark on (wood), *eg* to show the shape in which something is to be made.
noun **1** a piece of writing, a letter or its contents. **2** *thieves' slang* a banknote.

scrieve *see* **screeve**

scriff *see* **scruif**

scrift a long account, a long piece of prose or verse recited or read.

†**scrim, skrim** beat, strike, scrub vigorously.

scrimp *adjective* **1** in short supply. **2** *of clothes* short, tight. **3** *of people* having too little (of something). **4** mean, sparing.
verb **1** stint, not give enough to. **2** cut down in amount; use (up) carefully or meanly. **3** be over-careful, mean.
scrimpit scanty; undersized; mean.
scrimpy scanty, inadequate.

scringe *see* **screenge**

scrocken, skurken dry out (especially peats), shrink up with heat or drought.

scrog, scrag, scrug **1** a stunted or crooked bush or tree a stump of such. **2** a crab-apple (tree).
scroggie full of **scrogs**, covered with undergrowth; *of a tree* stunted or crooked.

scrog *see* **scrug**

scroll a rough draft or copy; a writing-pad etc for rough drafts or notes.

scronach *noun* a shrill cry, outcry, loud lamentation *now NE.*
verb NE **1** shriek, yell, cry out. **2** make a great outcry or fuss, grouse.

scroo, screw *noun* a stack of corn, hay etc, or of corn sheaves *Shetland Orkney N.*
verb build (corn etc) into stacks *now Shetland Orkney.*

†**scrow** [rhymes with 'cow'] **1** **scrows** long strips or thin scraps of hide used for making glue. **2** a long list of people; a crowd, mob.

scrub **1** a pot-scrubber. **2** a mean person, a hard bargainer.

scruff *see* **scruif**

scrug, scrog tug (one's cap) forward so as to make oneself look bold or smart.

scrug *see* **scrog**

scruif, scruff, scriff, screef *NE noun* **1** scruff, scurf. **2** a hardened scab of skin, hair, dirt. **3** a thin surface layer, a film, crust etc, *eg* of vegetation on the ground. **4** the surface of water or the sea. **5** (a) worthless person or people, riff-raff.

verb **1** cover over thinly. **2** scrape (off) the surface of.

scrump something crisp and hard; a crust, hard surface layer *NE*.

scrunt[1], **skrunt** **1** something shrunken or worn down by use, age etc. **2** a thin, scraggy, shrunken person; a poorly-developed plant. **3** a mean miserly person.

scrunty **1** stunted, shrivelled, stumpy. **2** mean, miserly.

scrunt[2], **skrunt** **1** scrape, scrub, scratch, grind. **2** plane (wood) roughly; rough down (pointing) with a handpick.

scry **1** †a cry, yell. **2** a public proclamation *NE*.

scud *verb* **1** throw (a flat stone) so as to make it skip over the water, play ducks and drakes. **2** beat with the open hand or a strap, smack.

noun a blow, smack, a stroke with the **tawse** (*see* **taw**[1]) or cane.

scudder a driving shower of rain or snow *NE*. **scuddie** a game like **shinty** or hockey; the club or the ball used in it *N*.

scuddie *adjective* **1** naked, without clothes, or with one garment only. **2** miserable, scruffy, shabby-looking. **3** stingy, insufficient, too small *NE*.

noun **1** the bare skin, a state of nakedness. **2** *also* **scud** a nestling, a young unfledged bird.

scuddle[1] **1** work in a slatternly way, do housework messily. **2** dirty (one's clothes), make shabby or shapeless *now NE*.

scuddlin claes one's second-best clothes.

scuddle[2] scurry, roam about aimlessly; dodge, shirk work.

scuddler a scullion, kitchen-boy; a maid-of-all-work.

scudge *see* **scodge**

scuff *verb* **1** touch lightly in passing, draw

one's hand etc quickly over; brush off or away. **2** hit with a glancing blow. **3** shuffle, scuffle. **4** wear away (clothes), make worn and shabby.

noun **1** a glancing or brushing stroke of the hand, a slight touch in passing, a hasty wipe. **2** a slight passing shower of rain. **3** riff-raff.

scuffin *of clothes* second-best. **scuffy** **1** shabby, worn, mean-looking. **2** mean, miserly *NE*.

scug, skug, scoug, scog *verb* **1** hide, screen. **2** shelter, protect. **3** take shelter or refuge (from). **4** hide, skulk.

noun **1** shade, shelter, protection (of a rock etc). **2** a pretence, excuse.

scuil *see* **schule**

scuip, scoop, skip, skeep *NE noun* **1** a scoop. **2** a kind of (flat) hat or bonnet with a brim. **3** *mainly* **skip** the front brim of a hat, the peak of a cap.

skippit bonnet a cloth cap with a peak.

sculduddery *noun* **1** unpermitted sex. **2** obscenity, indecency, especially in language.

scull, skull, scoo a shallow, scoop-shaped basket for carrying peats, potatoes, grain; a similar-shaped basket for holding fish or baited lines.

scult, skult strike with the palm of the hand, slap, smack.

scum *noun* a worthless disreputable person.

verb **1** skim, remove scum (from). **2** catch with a small round net (herring fallen back into the sea as the nets are hauled aboard). **3** †slap (someone's face).

scummer **1** a ladle or shallow dish for skimming. **2** a young crew member who **scums.**

scunfis *see* **scomfish**

scunge, skunge, squeenge *NE* prowl or slink about (in search of something), scrounge.

scunner, skunner, †sconner *verb* **1** shrink back, hesitate. **2** get a feeling of disgust or loathing, feel sick, have had more than enough. **3** feel disgust for, be sickened by, be bored or repelled by. **4** cause such feelings in (a person). **5** make bored, uninterested.

noun **1** a feeling of disgust, loathing, sickness, dislike, loss of interest or enthusiasm: *"tak a scunner at something"*. **2** a shudder; a sudden shock. **3** something which or someone who causes loathing or disgust, a nuisance. **scunneration** something which causes dislike or disgust. **scunnered, scunnert** disgusted, bored, fed up. **scunnerfu, scunnersome** disgusting, nauseating, objectionable, horrible.

scur 1 *also* **scurl** a scab on a sore or wound *NE*. **2** a small loose horn in polled or hornless cattle.

scurr slither, slide, skate, skid *NE*.

scurry, squeerie roam about, prowl about like a dog on the hunt *now NE*.

scurryvaig a tramp, vagabond; an idle person, a slut; a lout.

scush *NE verb* shuffle.
noun a shuffling, scuffling with the feet; the noise of this.
scushle *verb* = **scush.**
noun an old worn-down shoe.

scutch¹, skutch 1 graze the surface of one object with another, flick. **2** walk quickly with a light scuffling step. **3** slide on ice, skate, sledge.

scutch² cut with a hook or knife, slash, trim (a hedge).

scutter *verb* **1** do something messily or carelessly; spill or splash about. **2** do troublesome, time-wasting, pointless work, fiddle about. **3** keep back with something unimportant or annoying.
noun **1** the doing of work awkwardly or dirtily, a footling, time-consuming, and annoying occupation. **2** a person who works in a muddled or dirty way. **scutterie** troublesome; time-wasting, footling *NE*.

scuttle refuse water, dishwater, *usually* **scuttle hole or scutter hole** a hole into which this is poured, a sewage pit, a drain.

sea, sey the sea.
sea cat a wolf-fish. **sea dog** a dogfish.X **sea loch** an arm of the sea, especially fiord-shaped. **sea-maw** a seagull. **sea pyot** an oyster-catcher. **sea tangle** = **tang¹**. **sea toun** a seaport town or village. **sea ware** seaweed, especially the coarse kind washed up by the tide and used as manure.

seal *see* **sell²**

seam 1 a row of natural or artificial teeth: *"a seam of teeth"*. **2** the parting of the hair. **3** a piece of sewing or needlework. **4** any task, piece of work. **5** a nail used to fix together the planks of a clinker-built boat, riveted by a **ruive.**

seam *see* **same**

seannachaidh *see* **shenachie**

search *noun* a sieve, strainer.
verb put through a sieve, sift, strain.

secede: Seceder 1 †a member of any of the branches of the **Secession Church. 2** a member of the **Free Presbyterian** (*see* **Free**) Church *Highland*. **secession** the departure from the **Church of Scotland** (*see* **Church**) in 1732 by a group of ministers led by Ebenezer and Ralph Erskine. **Secession Church** the church formed after this event.

sech *see* **sich**

seck sack.

secretar a secretary.

seddle *see* **saidle**

sederunt [se**day**roont] **1** a list of those present at a meeting. **2** †a meeting of an official or judicial body. **3** an informal meeting or sitting. **4** an unpleasant interview, a scolding.

see, sei *S* [rhymes with 'gey'] *verb, past tense also* **seed 1** see. **2** look at. **3** take steps to: *"see to get some mair"*. **4** hand, let (a person) have: *"see me the teapot"*. **5** introducing a person or thing about to be discussed: *"see him, he canny drive"*.

I've seen myself (do(ing) something) I can remember.., I have often... **seestu**

you see, you understand.

see about look after, ask about (a person). **see after 1** look after (a person). **2** make enquiries for. **see at 1** look at. **2** inquire of. **see someone far enough** *expression of annoyance* wish that someone were out of the way, had not appeared. **see thegither** see eye to eye, agree. **see till, see to** = **see at 1**.

seeck sick.

seed 1 *also* **sid** particles of (oat-)bran, frequently used to make **sowans**. **2** a grain (of something).

seedle *see* **saidle**

seek[1], **sik** *verb, past tense, past participle also* **socht, soucht 1** seek. **2** search for, look for. **3** ask for, *eg* by begging or in order to buy or hire etc. **4** search (a place), look through. **5** invite (a person) (to come, do etc); *of a farmer* invite (a servant) to remain for the next half-year. **6** to go, come etc to, in(to), away etc. **7** ask for the hand of (a woman), propose to. **8** wish, desire: *"I'm seeking to go"*. **9** bring, fetch *S*. **socht** exhausted *NE*.

seek[2] soak, ooze.

seel *see* **seil**

seelyhoo *see* **hoo**[3]

seen *see* **see, seeven, sune, syne**

seendil, sinnle seldom.

seerup syrup.

see's a haud o *see* **haud**

seestu *see* **see**

seet *see* **suit**

seeth *see* **saithe**

seeven, siven *N*, **seen** seven.

†**seven night, sennicht** a week.

seg[1] **1** sedge. **2** a yellow flag-iris.
seggan a wild iris. **seg(g)ing** a disease of oat-plants. **seggy** sedgy.

seg[2] sag.

seg[3] *of sour fruit etc* set (the teeth) on edge.

segg an animal, especially a bull, which has been castrated when fully grown.

sei *see* **see**

seich *see* **sich**

seil [-ee-], **seel** happiness, bliss, prosperity, good fortune.
seily blessed, lucky, happy. **seilyhoo** a caul found on the head of a newborn child, thought to be very lucky.

seil *see* **sile**[1]

seip *see* **sype**

seisin *see* **sasine**

sel, self self.
self-contained *of houses or flats* having their accommodation and entrance restricted to the use of one household.

selch [-ch as in 'dreich'] **1** *also* **silkie, selkie** *Shetland Orkney Caithness NE* a seal, the animal. **2** a fat clumsy person.

self *see* **sel**

Selkirk bannock a kind of rich fruit loaf, made as a speciality by Selkirk bakers.

sell[1] *verb, past tense also* **sald** *now Shetland,* **sauld, selt,** *past participle also* **sald, sauld** sell.

sell[2], **seal** the rope, iron loop or chain by which cattle are tied by the neck to their stalls.

semmit a man's vest or undershirt.

semple simple.

Senator of the College of Justice official title of a judge of the **Court of Session** (*see* **session**).

senatus [senaytus] *in full* **Senatus Academicus,** *latterly also (less formally)* **Senate** *in the older Scottish Universities* the body, consisting of the Principal, Professors, and, more recently, a number of Readers and Lecturers, which superintends and regulates the teaching and discipline of the University.

send 1 †a message. **2** a friend of the bridegroom sent to summon the bride to the wedding.

†**senior secondary (school)** a state secondary school providing more academic courses than the **junior secondary school** attended by pupils who were successful in the **qualifying examination** (*see* **qualify**).

sennen *see* **sinnon**

sennicht *see* **seeven**

sense essence, juice *NE*.

sequestrate *law* put (the property of a bankrupt) in the hands of a trustee, by appointment of a court for equitable division among his creditors; make a person bankrupt.

ser *see* **serve**

serie *see* **sairie**

serk *see* **sark**

sermon †divine service, an act of church worship: *"after sermon"*.

ser's, sirs (God) preserve us!

serve, ser, sair *verb* **1** serve. **2** *of clothes* fit, suit. **3** satisfy or content, especially with food or drink; satiate, give too much to: *"to sair a bairn like that!"* *noun* **ser** one's fill, enough.

saired satisfied, full up. **ill-saired** not having had enough food. **weel-saired** well satisfied with food or drink. **server** a salver, tray. **sairin 1** one's fill (especially of food). **2** enough of something unpleasant; a thorough beating.

serve a person heir *law* declare a person heir to an estate through legal process.

service 1 *Presbyterian churches* the serving of the elements at Communion. **2** the serving of refreshments, especially at a funeral or wedding. **3** *law* the procedure by which **heritable** property was transmitted to an heir.

servit a table-napkin, serviette.

servitor a (male) servant; a janitor or attendant at Edinburgh University.

servitude a restriction imposed on the use of **heritable** property, for the benefit of a neighbouring landowner.

session 1 = **kirk session** (*see* **kirk**). **2** *schools and Scottish universities* the part of the year during which teaching is carried on.

session clerk the clerk or secretary of a **kirk session**. **session house** the room in or attached to a church, in which the **kirk session** meets.

Court of Session the supreme civil court in Scotland.

set¹ *verb, past tense also* **setten** *now NE* **1**

set. **2** make to sit, seat, place on a seat. **3** sit, be seated. **4** stack (peats) to dry. **5** dislocate (one's neck). **6** bring (a mill) to a stop by turning off the water from the wheel. **7** *of plants and animals* stop growing, have the growth checked. **8** disgust, sicken *now NE*. **9** *of a horse* jib, refuse to obey the rider or driver. **10** start off, set out *now Shetland Orkney*. **11** guide in a certain direction *now NE*. **12** send (a person or thing). **13** accompany (a person home etc). **14** leave (milk) standing for the cream to rise. **15** let by contract, lease. **16** be hired out. **17** be suitable for, suit: *"It sets us to be dumb a while"*. **18** *of a person* look well in: *"it sets ye weel."*

noun **1** a set, a young plant etc used for planting; a potato for planting. **2** a letting or leasing of a farm etc. **3** *law* **action of set (and sale)** an action in which a part-owner of a ship can request to buy out or be bought out by his partners, or to have the ship sold. **4** a check; a setback, a disappointment. **5** a feeling of disgust *NE*. **6** a carry-on, fuss. **7** a joke, piece of fun. **8** the way in which a thing is set or arranged; a condition, state (of affairs). **9** a twist or warp in a piece of wood. **10** *of a person* build, physique, kind. **11** a person's attitude. **12** the setting of a piece of music. **13** *usually* **sett** a checked pattern in cloth, especially (the arrangement of) the squares and stripes in a tartan.

adjective **1** inclined, determined, obstinate, *often* **well-set, ill-set. 2** pleased *now NE*.

set awa *verb* set off, start on a journey. *noun* a fuss; a row, scolding; a send-off. **set by** lay aside, clear away, set aside for future use. **set down** *verb* cause to sit down, especially for a meal. *noun* a formal meal, a spread. **set on** make and kindle (a fire). **set to** set upon, attack. **set up 1** earth up (a plant). **2** set (a chimney) on fire. **3 set him** *etc* **up**

what a cheek!. **set-up** conceited, stuck up. **set up one's gab** make impudent remarks.

set² a team to build corn-stacks; the number of **rigs**¹ reaped at one time by a band of reapers.

seteesh [seteesh] a schottische *Orkney NE*.

sett, setten *see* **set**¹

setterel *NE* **1** small and thickset. **2** short-tempered, sarcastic.

settle *see* **sattle**

Saturday, Saturday Saturday.
   Saturday's penny *etc* a penny etc given to a child as pocket money.

seuch *see* **souch**

seur *see* **shuir**

seven night *see* **seeven**

sevendle [sevendle] **1** strong, securely made. **2** thorough, extreme.

severals several persons or things.

sew *see* **saw**¹, **shew**

sex *see* **sax**

†**sey**¹, **say** [rhymes with 'gey'] *verb* test, try, attempt.
   noun **1** a trying out, test. **2** *also* **sey piece** a test-piece, sample, especially of a worker applying for entry to a trade incorporation.

sey² [rhymes with 'by'] **1** †*butchering* a cut of beef from the shoulder to the loin, *corresponding to English* shoulder steak and sirloin; *see also* **backsey** (*under* **back**¹) and **foresye**. **2** *tailoring* the armhole of a sleeve.

sey *see* **sae**¹, **sea**, **sye**

sgian *see* **skean**

shaave *see* **saw**¹

†**shabble 1** a curved sword, sabre, cutlass. **2** a little, insignificant person or thing.

shachle *see* **shauchle**

shackle, sheckle 1 a shackle. **2** the wrist. **3** a connecting part of a plough.

shade *see* **shed**

shae, shoe, shee *NE*, plural also **shune** [-u-as -ui- in 'guid'], **shoon, sheen** *noun* **1** a shoe. **2** the shute carrying grain from the hopper to the millstone.

verb **1** shoe. **2** fit with metal rims, studs, tips etc.
   auld shune an old sweetheart. discarded lover.
   cast a shae have an illegitimate child.

shafe *see* **shaif, sheave**

shag the refuse of oats, barley etc.

shaif, shafe, shave a sheaf.

shair *see* **shuir**

shaird, shard, sherd 1 a shard, sherd, a fragment. **2** †the remains of something broken. **3** contemptuous term for a person or animal, especially an under-sized or deformed one *now NE*.

shairn, sharn dung, excrement, especially of cattle.

shairp, sharp, sherp *adjective* **1** sharp. **2** *of soil* gravelly, open and loose.
   noun **1** the act of sharpening (a tool etc). **2** a frost-nail on a horse's shoe.
   verb **1** sharpen. **2** provide (a horseshoe) with frost-nails.
   shairp set keen, eager (for food, sex etc).

shak, shake *verb, past tense also* **shuk, shakit**, *past participle also* **shakken, sheuken, shucken, shooken, shook** shake.
   noun **1** a shake. **2** the shaking of grain from an ear of corn *now Shetland Orkney N*.
   shakers 1 the moving racks in a thre-shing mill. **2** quaking-grass. **3** a fit of shaking, from disease or fear; a state of terror. **shakins** herring which have to be shaken out of the net and are thus damaged. **the shakins o the poke** the last remnants; the last-born of a family.
   shak a fit dance.

shall *see* **shell**

sham, shan twist the face, make a face, grimace.

shammle *now NE*, **shamble 1** shamble, walk awkwardly. **2** twist, strain; twist (the face).

shan 1 of poor quality, bad, shabby. **2** shy, timid, frightened.

shan *see* **sham**

shanna *see* **sall**

shangie[1], †**shangan** *noun* 1 †a stick, can etc put on a dog's tail. 2 **shangies** handcuffs. 3 a forked stick used to make a catapult.
verb put a **shangie** on (a dog's tail).

shangie[2] a row, disturbance, fight.

†**shangie**[3] thin, scraggy.

shank *noun* 1 a leg of meat. 2 the leg of a stocking; a stocking, sock, or any garment, in the process of being knitted. 3 the stem or shaft of a spoon, brush, glass etc. 4 the stem or stalk of a tree, plant, or fruit. 5 the lower part or sides of a cornstack. 6 a chimneystack. 7 the shaft of a mine. 8 a downward slope of a hill.
verb 1 walk, go, or cover on foot. 2 send away on foot. 3 knit stockings etc. 4 fit (a tool etc) with a **shank** or handle. 5 sink (a shaft).
shanks'(s) naig(ie) shanks' pony.

shankie a lavatory.

shap *see* **chap**[2], **shaup**, **shop**

shape *verb* 1 **shape to** turn out, show promise of being etc. 2 **shape to** set out for. 3 cut (cloth) in a certain pattern or shape.
noun 1 a dressmaking pattern, a pattern piece. 2 an attitude; manner.
mak a shape make an effort.

shard *see* **shaird**

share *see* **shear**

sharg, *also* **shargar** a small, stunted, weakly person.

sharn *see* **shairn**

sharp *see* **shairp**

sharrie quarrel, fight *NE*.

shatter *see* **chatters**

shauch twisted, askew, out of shape.

shauchle, shachle, shochle *verb* 1 walk without lifting the feet, shuffle. 2 wear (a garment, shoes etc) out of shape.
noun 1 a shuffling, clumsy walk. 2 an old worn-out shoe, slipper. 3 a weakly, stunted, or deformed person or animal.

shauchlin, *also* **shauchlie** 1 unsteady or weak on one's feet, shuffling; knock-kneed; wearing worn-out shoes. 2 *of shoes* out of shape, down at heel and worn, badly-fitting.

shauld, shaul 1 shallow, not deep. 2 shallow in character, empty-headed.
noun a shallow part in the sea or a river, a shoal.

shaup, shawp, shap *noun* 1 the seed husk of peas, beans etc; a pea-pod. 2 an empty-headed, useless person. 3 **shaups** bits, smithereens.
verb shell (pea-pods), take (peas) from the husks.

shave *see* **shaif, sheave**

shavel *see* **shevel**

shavie a trick, swindle.

shaw[1], **show** *verb* 1 show. 2 cut off the **shaws** of (turnips).
noun 1 a show. 2 **shaws** the stalks and leaves of potatoes, turnips etc. 3 **the shows** a fair with roundabouts, side-shows etc.

shaw[2] a small natural wood.

shaw *see* **saw**[1]

shawlie an urban working woman or girl.

shawp *see* **shaup**

she, scho [-o- as -ui- in 'guid'] she. **hir, hur** her: 1 used by a husband of his wife or by a servant of his or her mistress. 2 referring to a thing, *eg* a mill, bell, church, clock. 3 *literary, supposedly of a Highlander's speech* I, me.

sheal *see* **shiel**[1]

shear, share *verb* 1 shear. 2 reap (corn), cut (crops) with a sickle. *noun* 1 the act of cutting (especially corn). 2 a cut edge, especially of a sheaf of corn *NE*.
shear mouse a shrew.

shears (a pair of) scissors; (sheep-)clippers.

sheath a kind of pad on a belt used to hold knitting needles when not in use.

sheave, shave, shafe 1 a sheave, a pulley(-wheel). 2 a slice of bread, cheese etc.

sheckle *see* **shackle**

shed, shade, sheed *now Shetland Orkney*

NE **1** shed. **2** separate (lambs from ewes). **3** part or comb (the hair, a sheep's fleece etc) to one side or the other.

noun **1** the act of sorting out sheep, *eg* as a test in sheepdog trials. **2** parting the hair on the head or the wool on a sheep's back. **3** a slice, piece. **4** a separate piece of ground.

shee *see* **shae**

sheed *see* **shed**

sheel, shiel, shill *verb* **1** shell (peas, grain etc), take out of the husk or pod. **2** cut (a mussel) from its shell. **3** win money, marbles etc from, rook (a person). **4** shell out (money). **5** throw out or scatter right and left *NE*.

sheelings the grain removed from the husk by milling. **sheelocks** the small grains blown away during winnowing; the chaff and broken straw riddled off in threshing.

sheel *see* **shuil**

sheemach *N* [**shee**mach] **1** a tangled mass of hair. **2** a pad used as a saddle. **3** a worn-out thing, a puny person or animal.

sheen shine, gleam, glisten.

sheen *see* **shae, sune**

sheep: sheepie mae 1 a sheep. **2** a flower of the wild white clover.

sheep drain a drain in pasture land. **sheep eik** the natural grease in a sheep's wool. **sheep fank** a (dry-stone) enclosure where sheep are gathered for shelter, dipping, shearing etc. **sheep shank** the leg of a sheep. **nae sheep shank** a person of some importance.

sheer *see* **shuir**

sheet *see* **shuit**

sheil *see* **shiel**[1]

shelband *see* **shelvin**

shell, shall *Shetland Orkney N noun* **1** a shell. **2** a small saucer-shaped dish, *eg* the bowl of a **cruisie** lamp; a saucer. **3** a fragment, small piece.

†**shelly coat** a water-sprite wearing a shell-covered coat.

shellwing, shelmont *see* **shelvin**

sheltie 1 a Shetland pony, one of a breed of very small horses, originally native to Shetland; also applied to any pony, usually a **garron**[1]. **2** a Shetlander *Shetland N.*

shelvin, shellwing *now Shetland Orkney Caithness*, **shelmont, shelband** a part of the sides of a cart, especially one of the movable boards to allow the carrying of bigger loads.

shenachie, *Gaelic* **seannachaidh** [**shen**achie] originally a professional reciter of family history etc, now a teller of traditional Gaelic heroic tales.

shepherd('s) check, shepherd('s) tartan (a cloth of) black-and-white check.

sherd *see* **shaird**

sheriff, shirra, sherra 1 †the (hereditary) chief officer of a county, responsible to the sovereign for peace and order. **2** the chief judge of a **sheriffdom**. **3** a legal officer who performs judicial and certain administrative duties.

sheriffdom the area under the jurisdiction of a **sheriff** *noun* 2, now a group of **regions** or a division of a **region**.

sheriff clerk the clerk of the **Sheriff Court**. **Sheriff Court** the court presided over by the **sheriff**. †**sheriff depute 1** the lawyer appointed to perform the judicial duties of the **sheriff** 1. **2** = **sheriff** 2. **sheriff officer** an official or messenger who carries out the warrants of a **sheriff**, serves writs etc. **sheriff principal 1** † = **sheriff** 1. **2** = **sheriff** 2. †**sheriff substitute** = **sheriff** 3. **Sheriff of Chancery** the **Sheriff Principal** of Lothian and Borders when performing his duties, throughout Scotland, in connection with **service** of heirs.

sherp *see* **shairp**

sherrack, shirrak *noun* a noisy quarrel, rumpus.

verb raise a riot about (a person); give (a person) a public dressing-down.

Shetland *see* **Islands Council**

sheth a crossbar, especially in the frame of a cart etc; a connecting bar in a plough.

sheuch, sheugh, sough, shough [shooch, shuch] *noun* **1** a trench in the ground, especially for drainage, a ditch, open drain. **2** a temporary trench or furrow for plants. **3** a furrow. **4** a street gutter. *verb* **1** dig, trench, make a ditch or furrow (in). **2** lay (a plant etc) in the ground, especially in a temporary trench.

in a sheuch in a state of misery, ruined.
up the sheuch mistaken, in error.

sheuken *see* **shak**

sheul *see* **shuil**

shevel, showl [-ow-]**, shavel, shile** *SW adjective, of the mouth* twisted.
verb **1** twist out of shape; screw up (the face). **2** twist the mouth, make a face from annoyance, pain, a bitter taste etc.

shew [shoo]**, sew, †sue, †show** *verb* sew.
noun the act of sewing; a spell of needlework.
shewster needlewoman *now NE*.
shew-up the shutting-down of a business, bankruptcy.

shid *see* **sall**

shiel¹, sheil, sheal, shield 1 a temporary or rough hut or shed, especially one used by (salmon) fishermen or shepherds (and their animals), a **shieling. 2** †a summer pasture with a shepherd's hut or huts.
shieling a high or remote summer pasture, usually with a shepherd's hut or huts; one of those huts.

shiel² shield *now NE.*

shiel *see* **sheel, shuil**

shiffle *see* **shuil**

shift *verb* **1** change places with *now NE.* **2** change (one's clothes, shoes etc); change the clothes of (another person), providep (someone) with (fresh clothes). **3** make a move in the game of draughts.

noun **1** a change of situation, home or job. **2** each successive crop in a system of crop-rotation; the land or field on which this is grown. **3** a change of clothing. **4** a move in the game of draughts.
shiftin claes one's second-best clothes, those worn when changing from one's working clothes.
shift one's feet change one's shoes and stockings.

shilagie [shilaggie] coltsfoot, especially its leaves used by juvenile smokers as a substitute for tobacco.

shile *see* **shevel**

shilfa, shilly a chaffinch.

†shill shrill(y)

shill *see* **sheel**

shilling used until the 1950s in the classification of the strength of beer, from the price per barrel, *eg* **forty-shilling ale** a very light beer; later re-introduced (without reference to the price) in the 'real-ale' boom of the 1970s.
shilling land a land measure.
want tippence o the shilling be mentally defective, be not all there.

shilly *see* **shilfa**

shilpie thin, puny, pinched-looking.

shilpit 1 thin, puny, starved- or pinched-looking. **2** *of drink* insipid, thin *now Shetland Orkney.* **3** sour, bitter; no longer fresh *now Shetland Orkney Caithness.*

shim a horse-hoe, a kind of small plough for weeding etc *NE.*

shin a ridge or steep hillface.

shin *see* **sune**

shine¹ 1 a social gathering: *"tea shine, cookie shine".* **2** a disturbance.

shine² throw with force, fling *S.*

shinner *see* **cinner**

shinnon *see* **sinnon**

shinty, shinny *noun* **1** a game like hockey played towards **hails⁴**, now mainly in the Highlands. **2** the club or stick used in the game, a **caman.**

shire *adjective* **1** †bright. **2** †*of liquid etc*

clear, unclouded. **3** †complete, utter. **4** thin; watery; sparse.

verb pour off top liquid, separate a liquid from its dregs.

shirpit thin, shrunken, with sharp, drawn features.

shirra *see* **sheriff**

shirrak *see* **sherrack**

shirramuir, shirramere *noun* **1** †**the Shirramuir** the Jacobite rising of 1715 which ended in the battle of Sheriffmuir. **2** a noisy row; a dressing-down *NE*.

shirrel a (piece of) turf, especially from the surface of a peat bog.

shither shiver, shudder *now S*.

shittle *see* **shuttle**[1]

shive a slice (of bread).

shivering bite a small snack taken after swimming to stop shivering.

shivers splinters of stone (broken off in stone-dressing).

shivereens small bits.

shoad *see* **shod**

shochle *see* **shauchle**

shock a (paralytic) stroke.

shockle an icicle.

shod, shoad *past tense, past participle* shod.

verb, past tense, past participle **shod(d)it** **1** put shoes on; shoe (a horse). **2** fit (a bootlace, spade etc) with a metal tip etc. **3** put iron toe- and heel-pieces on (a shoe), cover (shoe soles) with studs etc.

noun **1** †a shoe. **2** an iron tip etc on a (wooden) object to prevent wear; the metal tyre of a cartwheel. **3** a metal plate on the toe or heel of a shoe; a hobnail.

shoe *see* **shae**

shog, shogue, shug, shoog, showg *verb* **1** shake, jog, cause to swing or rock. **2** *also* **shoggie** sway, swing, rock from side to side, wobble. **3** go at a leisurely but steady pace, jog along.

noun **1** a jog, shake, nudge. **2** *also* **shoggie** a swinging or rocking; a swinging-rope; a child's swing.

shoggie shaky, unsteady, wobbly.

sho(g)gie boat a swing-boat at a fair.

shoggy-shoo 1 a seesaw, the game of seesaw. **2** a swing. **shoggle, shoogle, shuggle** *verb* **1** sway, move unsteadily, rock, wobble, swing. **2** shake, joggle, cause to totter or rock. **3** jog along, move unsteadily, shuffle. *noun* **1** a jog, jolt, shake. **2** a swinging on a rope, tree-branch etc. **shooglie** shaky, unsteady, tottery.

shog bog a soft watery bog.

shoo *see* **shue**

shooder *see* **shouder**

shooer *see* **shour**

shoog, shoogle *see* **shog**

shook, shooken *see* **shak**

shoon *see* **shae**

shoot, shuit suit.

shoot *see* **shuit**

shoother *see* **shouder**

shop, shap, chop, tchop *NE* a shop.

shop door the front flap or fly of trousers.

shore[1] a quay, landing place, harbour: *"the Perth shore"*.

shore[2] a kind of marbles game.

shore[3] *verb* **1** threaten. **2** scold *now Shetland*. **3** †urge; hound (a dog) *S*. **4** †offer as a mark of favour.

short: shortlins, shortly 1 shortly. **2** recently. **shortsome** lively and entertaining, cheerful, making time pass quickly. **Shorter Catechism** *in the Presbyterian Churches* the shorter of two catechisms approved by the **General Assembly** (*see* **General**) in 1648.

shortbread a kind of biscuit made of a short dough of flour, butter and sugar.

shortcome a shortcoming. **short gown** a kind of long loose blouse of strong cloth, worn by women while doing housework. **short-set** small and stockily-built.

short and lang in brief. **short (sin) syne** a short time ago. **short in the trot** (*NE*), **short in the pile** (*SW*) in a bad temper,

Shulpilr

curt and rude.

shot *noun* 1 flow (of blood etc) from the body. 2 *weaving* a single movement of the shuttle carrying the weft across the web. 3 a piece of ground, especially one cropped in rotation. 4 a brief loan; a turn: *"gie's a shot o yer bike"*.
verb 1 shoot. 2 cast (lines or nets) *NE*.
exclamation a warning among children of the approach of a policeman, teacher etc.

shott a young pig after weaning.

shotten *see* **shuit**

shottle, shuttle a small compartment at the top of a trunk, chest etc.

shouder, shoulder, shooder, shouther, shoother [-oo-] 1 a shoulder. 2 the swelling part of a wave rising to the crest.
shouder heid the socket of the shoulder-bone; the shoulder joint.
never look ower one's shouder never look back, go steadily forward. **shouder-the-win** (having) a deformity in which one shoulder is higher than the other.

shough *see* **sheuch**

shour [-oo-], **shooer, shower** 1 a shower (of rain etc). 2 a pang of pain etc.

shouther *see* **shouder**

show the refuse of flax stems broken off in scutching.

show *see* **shaw**[1], **shew**

showd [-ow- as in 'cow'] *now NE verb* 1 swing to and fro, rock.
noun a rocking, swaying motion; a swing.

shower *see* **shour**

showg *see* **shog**

showl *see* **shevel**

shreed a shred.

shrood a shroud.

shrunkled shrunken, shrivelled.

shucken *see* **shak**

shud a large piece or lump *S*.

shue, shoo 1 swing, rock or sway backwards and forwards. 2 row (a boat) backwards, back water *now Shetland Orkney Caithness*.

shuffle *see* **shuil**

shug *see* **shog**

shuggar *see* **succar**

shuggle *see* **shog**

shuil, shiel, sheel, shull, sheul, shuffle, shiffle *noun* a shovel.
verb 1 shovel. 2 take away (someone's) store of something, clean (someone) out. 3 slide; shuffle (the feet).

shuir, seur, shair, sheer *NE* sure.

shuit, shoot, shute, sheet *N verb, past tense also* **sheetit** *NE. past participle also* **sheetit** *NE 1* shoot. 2 position (a fishing-net) in water. 3 push, jerk forward. 4 *especially in buying and selling cattle and sheep* separate the good from the bad. 5 *of walls* bulge; collapse *now Orkney*.
shot *adjective* 1 *of plants* run to seed. 2 *also* **shotten**, *of fish* spawned. 3 **shot of** rid of, free from. *noun* an inferior animal, especially a sheep, left over *eg* after a buyer's selection. **shot blade** the leaf enclosing the corn-stalk and ear. **shot joint** a joint deformed by rheumatism.
shuit by manage somehow.

shuit *see* **shoot**

shuk *see* **shak**

shull *see* **shuil**

shune *see* **shae, sune**

shunner *see* **cinner**

shurf an insignificant person *S*.

shut: shut to close (especially a door) properly.

shute *see* **shuit, suit**

shuttle[1], **shittle** *noun* a shuttle.
verb 1 weave, drive the shuttle in a loom, be a weaver. 2 move to and fro like a shuttle.

shuttle[2] quick, active *NE*.

shuttle *see* **shottle**

shuve [-u- as -ui- in 'guid'] shove.

sib: sib to 1 related by blood to, of the same family as. 2 closely akin to, allied with, of the same sort. 3 bound by ties of affection, familiarity etc.

sibbens *see* **siven**

sic, sich, such such.

    siccan 1 such, of such a kind, of a sort already mentioned. **2** what (a) ..!; how ..!: *"siccan a day."*

    siclike *adjective* **1** suchlike. **2** *of health, quality etc* much about the same; so-so, indifferent. *adverb* similarly, in the same way. **sic-an-sae, sic-an-sic-like** alike, similar, much of a muchness.

siccar *see* **sicker**

sich, seich, sech sigh.

sich *see* **sic**

sicht, sight *noun* **1** a sight. **2** a close look, examination. **3** the pupil (of the eye). *verb* **1** sight. **2** examine, inspect (*eg* a newborn animal for its sex).

    a sicht for sair een a welcome or pleasing sight.

sick a call to a lamb or calf to come to be fed from its bottle *NE*.

    sick (lamb) a pet lamb brought up on the bottle *NE*.

sicker, siccar *adjective* **1** safe, free from danger etc. **2** firm, stable, fixed; held firm. **3** dependable, reliable. **4** careful, cautious, especially with money, wary. **5** *of a blow* hard, severe. **6** certain, sure; assured. **7** *of laws, weather etc* harsh.

    mak siccar make sure or certain.

sid *see* **sall, seed**

side[1] direction, district: *"Dumbartonside".*

    sidelin(s), sidlings *adverb* **1** sideways, side on, to one side. **2** *of speech or look* indirectly. *adjective* **1** sidelong, moving or glancing sideways. **2** sloping, on a slope. *noun* a sloping piece of ground, a hillside. **sidieweys** sideways.

    side legs sidesaddle.

side[2] **1** †*of clothes, hair etc* long, hanging low. **2** hard or severe on *NE*.

sidlings *see* **side**[1]

siege *noun* a (mason's) bench. *verb* scold severely, storm at *NE*.

sieth *see* **suith**

sight *see* **sicht**

signet one of the Crown seals of Scotland, originally used for private and some official documents of the Sovereign, *latterly* used as the seal of the **Court of Session** (*see* **session**); see also **writer** (*under* **write**).

    Keeper of the Signet the custodian of the **signet**, now a titular office, the holder also being **Lord Clerk Register** (*see* **register**); the actual custodian is now the **Deputy Keeper of the Signet**.

sik *see* **seek**[1]

sile[1], **seil** [-ei- as -ey in 'gey'] *verb* pass (a liquid, especially milk) through a sieve, strain. *noun* a sieve, strainer, filter, especially for milk.

sile[2], **sill** the newly-hatched young of fish, especially of herring.

sile[3], **syle** a roof rafter.

silkie *see* **selch**

sill *see* **sile**[2]

siller 1 silver. **2** money.

    sillered wealthy. **siller shakers** quaking grass.

silly *adjective* **1** helpless; weak, sickly, delicate; shaky. **2** mentally deficient.

    silly cuddies the game of leapfrog.

simmen, simmond a rope made of straw, heather, rushes etc, used with stone weights to hold down thatch on houses and stacks.

simmer[1], **summer** summer.

    simmer cowt a heat haze, the shimmering of the air on a hot day.

    simmer and winter go into (something) in great detail, be long-winded in telling a story.

simmer[2] a summer, a beam, especially one in the floor of a corn-kiln.

sin[1] a son.

    Son of the Rock 1 a native of Dumbarton or Stirling. **2 the Sons (of the Rock)** nickname of Dumbarton football team.

sin[2]: **sin one's soul** become guilty of sin (especially by telling lies).

sin *see* **sun, sune, syne**

sinder, sinner 1 sunder. **2** single, hoe out (seedlings) *NE*. **3** part (company from).

sindrins a fork in the road. **sindry, sundry, sinnery 1** sundry. **2** separate, apart, distinct.

sine *see* **synd**

sing[1] a whizzing blow, wallop.

    sing dumb keep silent.

sing[2] *verb, past tense, past participle also* **sung** singe.

    singit stunted, shrivelled, puny.

single *adjective in a fish-and-chip-shop* not served with chips, by itself: *"single fish", "single pudding".*

    noun a handful or small bundle of gleaned corn.

    verb thin out (seedlings, especially turnips).

    single en(d) a one-roomed house or flat.

singular successor *law* a person who acquires **heritable** property by a single title, normally by purchase, as opposed to an heir, whose title is general or **universal.**

sink *mining* a pit-shaft, a coal-pit.

sinner *see* **sinder**

sinnle *see* **seendil**

sinnon, sennen, shinnon a sinew.

sinsyne *see* **syne**

sint *see* **scent**

sipe *see* **sype**

sipper *see* **supper**

sirple *now S,* †**sipple** sip continuously, go on drinking in small quantities, tipple.

sirs *see* **ser's**

sist *verb, law* **1** stop, stay or halt (a legal process or procedure) by judicial decress, both in civil and ecclesiastical courts. **2** summon or cite to appear in a court case. **3** present oneself before a court, appear for trial or as a litigant.

    noun a stay or suspension of a proceeding; an order by a judge to stay judgment or execution.

sister: sister bairn the child of a parent's sister, a cousin *now Shetland Caithness.* **sister('s) son** a nephew, the son of one's sister *now Shetland Orkney.*

sit *verb, past tense also* **sut,** *past participle also* **sitten, sutten 1** sit. **2** *of plants* stop growing, be stunted.

    noun sinking or settling down of the surface of the ground or of something built on it.

    sitten 1 *of tea* stewed, strong and bitter. **2** *of an egg* near to hatching. **sitten-doun** *of a cold etc* persistent, chronic. **sitting doun** a settlement in marriage.

    sit down *verb* settle oneself in a place or situation, make one's home. *noun* **1** a chance or spell of being seated, a seat. **2** a home, settlement, a situation. **sit in** draw one's chair in (to a fire, a table). **sit on** *especially of a tenant at the end of a lease* remain in a place or house; stay on. **sit on a person's coat-tail(s)** depend on or make use of someone else. **sit-ooterie** *humorous* a recess etc where one may sit out a dance etc. **sit-sicker** name for various species of crowfoot *NE.*

sit *see* **suit**

sitherwood southernwood.

sitten *see* **sit**

siven [sivven] **1** a wild raspberry. **2** †**sivens, sibbens** venereal disease with raspberry-like sores.

siven *see* **seeven**

siver *see* **syver**

six *see* **sax**

sizzie *see* **sussie**

sizzon *see* **saison**

skaff *see* **scaff**[1], **scaff**[2]

skaich *see* **skech**

skaik smear, plaster with something soft and wet, streak, blotch *NE.*

skail, scale, skale, skyle, †**skell 1** scatter, throw or spread about (a collection of things). **2** spread (manure etc) over the ground. **3** plough out (a ridge) so that the furrows fall outward on either side of the **hintin** (*see* **hint**). **4** shed, throw (from a container). **5** pour out; spill (accidentally). **6** burst (a garment) at a seam. **7** scatter (a group of people); chase, put to flight; dismiss (a meeting, congregation). **8** *of a group, eg in a school, church etc* break up, separate.

9 *of persons or things* become detached or separated; *of a container or its contents* spill out or over, overflow or leak out.

skainie, skeenie, †skeenzie string, twine.

†skair, skare share, a portion, part.

skair *see* **scar**

skair(d) 1 a slanting cut or notch in a piece of wood by which it can be joined to another of similar shape. **2** a piece of wood so shaped, *eg* a fishing rod.

skaith, scaith, scathe *noun* damage, hurt, harm.
verb harm, injure, damage.
tak skaith be hurt, damaged etc.

skale *see* **skail**

skane *see* **skin**

skare *see* **skair**

skarf *see* **scarf**

skart *see* **scarf, scart**[1]

skate 1 a skate, the fish. **2** a stupid or nasty person.

skave, skived over to one side, off the straight, tilted.

skavie, skeevie *noun* a trick, piece of mischief *NE*.
verb rush about (in an idle, silly or showy way) *NE*.

skean, sgian [**skee**an] a Highlander's short-bladed black-hilted sheath-knife or dagger.
skean dhu, sgian dubh [**skee**an **doo**] one now commonly worn in the sock as part of Highland dress.

skech, skaich, skeich *verb* get (something) in an underhand way, scrounge; wander about in search of (food).
noun a scrounger, sponger.
on the skech on the prowl.

skeechan [-ch- as in 'dreich'] a beer-like alcoholic drink produced in the later stages of brewing.

skeeg[1] the smallest amount (especially of liquid).

skeeg[2]**, skeg, skig** *verb* whip, strike, slap *NE. noun* a blow, smack, especially on the bottom *NE*.

skeel[1]**, skill 1** skill. **2** skill in the art of

healing (people or animals), especially by non-professionals.
verb scan expertly, investigate, look carefully, especially for weather signs.
skeely 1 skilled, experienced, practised. **2** having real or supposed skill in the art of healing. **skeely wife** a woman believed to have great or supernatural healing powers.

skeel[2] a kind of wooden tub *now Angus*.

skeel *see* **schule**

skeely *see* **scailie**

skeenie, skeenzie *see* **skainie**

skeep *see* **scuip**

skeer, †skyre *verb* scare.
adjective nervous, fearful, agitated; flighty; mentally unstable.

skeet *see* **skite**[1]

skeetch *see* **sketch**

skeevie *see* **skavie**

skeg *see* **skeeg**[2]

skeich, skeigh [-ch, -gh as -ch in 'dreich'] **1** *of horses* frisky, spirited, restless. **2** *of people* in high spirits, daft; shy, haughty.
skeichen 1 timid, easily, scared, nervous. **2** fussy about food, easily upset *NE*.

skeich *see* **skech**

skeir *see* **skire**

skelb 1 a thin flake, slice, or splinter of wood etc, especially in the skin. **2** any thin slice *NE*.

skelf[1] **1** a shelf *Orkney N*. **2** a shelf above a **box bed** (*see* **box**), (used as a bunk for young children).

skelf[2]**, skelve 1** a thin slice, a flake; a splinter especially in the skin. **2** a small thin person.

skell *see* **skail**

skellet (bell), skillet a small bell, *eg* one used by a public crier.

skellie[1] *adjective* **1** squinting, squint-eyed. **2** lop-sided.
noun a cast in the eye, a squint; a sideways glance.
verb **1** squint, be cross-eyed. **2** make a mistake, exaggerate.

skellie² a ridge of rock running out to sea, usually covered at high tide.

skelloch¹ shriek, scream, cry.

skelloch² charlock or wild mustard.

skellum a scamp, rogue, scoundrel.

skelp¹, skilp *verb* **1** strike, hit, especially with something flat, smack (someone's bottom); hit, drive with blows, kicks etc; beat, hammer. **2** throb; *of a clock* tick. **3** work with energy or gusto. **4** gallop, move quickly.
noun **1** a blow, especially with a flat object, a smack. **2** a blast of wind, downpour of rain. **3** an attempt, try, **shot.**
  skelping big of its kind. **skelpit leathering** a thrashing, spanking.

skelp² **1** a thin slice; a flake; a splinter, especially in the skin. **2** a large slice or chunk. **3** a long strip (of ground).

skelter scurry, scamper, rush.

skelve *see* **skelf²**

skemmels a slaughter-house; a meat or fish market.

skemp scamp.

skep *noun* **1** a basket, especially for grain, meal, or potatoes. **2** a beehive.
verb put (a swarm of bees) into a hive.
  skeppie, skep (bee) a hive- or honeybee. **skeppit** put to bed, tucked up for the night.

sker *see* **scar, scaur¹**

skerrie a rock in the sea, especially one covered at high tide.

sketch, skeetch, skytch [-y- as -ey in 'gey'] *noun* **1** an ice-skate. **2** a turn or spell of skating.
verb **1** skate. **2** *of a stone* skim along the surface of water; play at ducks and drakes.
  skeetcher 1 the flat stone etc kicked in the game of **peever¹**; the game itself. **2** a skimming stone. **3** *also* **skytcher** a skater; an ice-skate.

skew¹ a stone forming part of the coping of the sloping part off the gable; the coping itself.

skew², skyow *NE* [skeeow], **skeuch** *NE*,

skeugh [skeeooch] *verb* **1** go off the straight, move sideways *now NE*. **2** twist, turn sideways, screw round. **3** *of the feet, legs* splay, turn outwards *NE*. **4** *of the eyes or glance* squint naturally or on purpose. **5** fall out, disagree *NE*.
noun **1** a twist, turn, sideways movement. **2** a squint, sidelong glance *NE*. **3** a quarrel, row *NE*.

skew-whiff at an odd angle, off the straight, out of order.

skewl, skyowl [skeeool, skeeowl] turn aside; twist.

skice leave quickly and without being noticed *NE*.

skiddle¹, skittle *verb* splash, squirt, spill.
noun **1** a thin watery liquid, *eg* weak tea. **2** a mess, muddle, especially with spilling of liquid. **3** contemptuous term for a small thing, person, or animal.

skiddle² move quickly and lightly.

skiff¹ *verb* **1** move lightly, skim, glide, skip. **2** rain or snow very slightly. **3** do work carelessly. **4** touch lightly in passing, brush, graze. **5** throw along the surface; make (a flat stone) skip over water, or over the ground.
noun **1** a slight touch or graze in passing. **2** a slight gust of wind. **3** a slight touch (of an illness). **4** a slight shower of rain or snow.
  skiffer a flat stone used in playing ducks and drakes. **skiffin 1** a slight fall of snow. **2** a thin partition or screen. **skiffle** *noun* a slight shower of rain. *verb, eg of a stone on water* skip or skim across. **skifflers** the game of ducks and drakes.

skiff² a type of small fishing boat with oars and a lugsail.

skift *verb* **1** move lightly, skim, skip. **2** *of rain or snow* fall lightly.
noun **1** a light shower of rain or snow. **2** a hurried dusting.
  skifter 1 = **skift 1**. **2 skifters** the game of ducks and drakes.

skifting board skirting-board.

skig *see* **skeeg²**

skill *see* **skeel**[1]

skillet *see* **skellet**

skilp *see* **skelp**[1]

skilt move about quickly and lightly, dart, skip.

skime 1 a glance, a quick or angry look. **2** a gleam of light, flash; a brief glimpse.

skimmer *verb* **1** twinkle, gleam; be bright. **2** glide along easily and quickly.

noun a light sprinkling, especially of snow or rain.

skin, skane *Shetland noun* **1** skin. **2** *slang* a robbery; a swindle.

verb **1** skin. **2** take the surface layer of soil etc off (land).

skinnin a small amount (taken or saved).

skin and birn *see* **burn**[2]. **skin-the-cuddy** a kind of leapfrog.

skink[1] **1** a shin, knuckle, of beef. **2** a soup, especially one made from this (but *see* **Cullen skink**).

skink[2] *verb* pour.

noun **1** drink, especially of a weak, wishy-washy kind. **2** a kind of thin, oatmeal-and-water gruel.

†**skinkin** easily poured, thin, weak.

skink[3] crush, squash by weight or pressure.

skinkle glitter, gleam, sparkle.

skinny[1] a bread roll.

skinny[2]: **skinnymalink(ie)** a thin, skinny person or animal. **skinny tatie** a potato boiled in its skin.

skip[1]: **skippie** *of roads etc* slippery, icy. **skip rape** a skipping rope.

skip[2] *noun, curling and bowls* the captain of a rink or side.

verb act as **skip** to a team.

skip *see* **scuip**

skipe *see* **skybe**

skippie, skippack the game of tig *N*.

skire, skyre, skeir [-ee-] *adjective* clear; bright.

adverb absolutely, altogether: *"skire mad"*.

verb shine brightly, glitter; be gaudy; garish.

skirl *verb* **1** scream, screech; cry out with fear, pain or grief; shriek with excitement or laughter; cry or sing shrilly. **2** *of bagpipes etc* make a shrill sound. **3** crackle, sputter; *especially in frying* sizzle.

noun **1** a scream or shriek of pain, fear etc. **2** a shriek of laughter etc. **3** the loud cry or whistle of a bird. **4** the shrill sound of bagpipes; a wrong note accidentally played. **5** the sound of a strong wind; the wind itself; a flurry (of snow or hail). **6** a screeching, whirring or whistling noise.

skirlie, skirl-in-the-pan a dish of oatmeal and onions fried in a pan. **skirly wheeter** an oystercatcher *NE*.

skirl naked completely or stark-naked.

skirp *NE verb* **1** sprinkle (water etc), splash in small drops or squirts. **2** *of water, mud etc* splash, fly up in small drops; rain slightly, spit.

noun **1** a small drop, splash, or spurt of liquid; a slight shower or spot of rain. **2** a small flying piece of metal, stone etc.

skirr scurry about, rush, whizz *now Orkney*.

skirt run away; elope; play truant from (school).

skirvin a thin covering of soil, snow etc *S*.

skit[1] **1** a trick, hoax. **2** a squirt of water; a sharp short shower.

skit[2] **1** diarrhoea. **2** contemptuous term for a woman.

skite[1], **skyte, skeet** *Shetland Orkney verb* **1** dart through the air suddenly, forcibly and often at a slant. **2** rebound. **3** slip or slide on a slippery surface; skate (on ice). **4** throw, send flying, make (something) shoot off at an angle; cause (a stone) to skip over the surface of water. **5** cause a spray or splash of liquid. **6** act wildly. **7** strike, hit.

adverb with a sharp blow, with force or bounce.

adjective off one's head, daft *now NE*.

noun **1** a sudden sharp blow. **2** the act of shooting out or squirting liquid; a squirt, a syringe; a small amount of water; a short sharp shower of rain; a small amount of liquor, a dram. **3** a spree, blow-out: *"on the skite"*. **4** a slip, skid. **5** a yellowhammer *NE*.

skiter a squirt, syringe; a pea- or water-shooter, especially one made from a plant stem.

skitie slippery.

skite² *verb* have diarrhoea.

noun, also **skiter** *NE* a nasty person.

skitter¹ *noun* **1** diarrhoea. **2** anything dirty or disgusting, a mess.

verb **1** have diarrhoea. **2** waste time doing footling jobs, potter about aimlessly.

skitterie 1 trifling, small or inadequate. **2** *of a task* fiddly, time-consuming.

skittery feltie the fieldfare.

skitter² slither, slip in a jerky awkward way.

skittle *see* **skiddle**¹

skive¹ roam or prowl about (like a dog in search of food).

skive² shave, pare, slice off a thin layer from.

skived *see* **skave**

skiver *noun* a splinter of wood in the skin. *verb* pierce or stab as with a skewer.

skivet a sharp hard blow *S*.

sklaff *see* **sclaff**

sklaik *see* **slaik**

sklait *see* **slate**

sklant *see* **sklent**³

sklatch *see* **sclatch**

skleet *see* **sklute**

skleff 1 shallow, flat; thin and flat. **2** equal, even (in a competition etc) *S*.

sklender *see* **sclender**

sklent¹, **sklint** *verb* **1** *also* **slent** move at a slant, sideways, zigzag. **2** slope, slant, lie to one side. **3** aim (something) sideways, send across. **4** look sideways, squint.

noun **1** a slanting cut; a slope. **2** a sideways movement, change of direction.

3 a sidelong glance.

adjective slanting, to one side.

sklent² tear, rip (especially clothes) *now Shetland*.

sklent³, **sklant** *(Shetland)* a chance, opportunity *now Shetland*.

skleush, sklush [skl(ee)oosh] *verb* walk in a clumsy, shuffling, or weary way *N*.

noun a trailing, shuffling, heavy-footed walk *N*.

skleut *see* **sklute**

skleuter *see* **slutter**

skliff, skluif, skloof *verb* **1** walk with a heavy, shuffling step, drag the feet, scuffle. **2** strike with a glancing blow, rub against. **3** cut away the upper surface or covering of, pare, slice.

noun **1** a shuffling, trailing way of walking. **2** a clumsy, worn-out shoe. **3** a blow with a flat surface, a swipe in passing. **4** a segment, *eg* of the moon, of an orange.

sklim *see* **sclim**

sklint *see* **sklent**¹

sklinter splinter, break off in pieces or flakes.

skloit *see* **sklyte**

sklone a large amount of something soft.

skloof, skluif *see* **skliff**

sklush *see* **skleush**

sklute *now S* [-u- as -ui- in 'guid'], **skleut**, **skleet** *Caithness* walk in a flat-footed, shuffling, or splay-footed way.

sklype *see* **slype**

sklyte, skloit *noun* **1** a heavy fall, a thud *NE*. **2** a soft, wet, half-liquid mass *NE*. **3** a big, clumsy, slovenly person or animal *NE*.

verb **1** fall with a thud or thump; go with a clatter. **2** pour or throw liquid in a careless noisy way *NE*. **3** work messily or clumsily.

skodge *see* **scodge**

skomfish *see* **scomfish**

skonce *see* **sconce**

skook *see* **scouk**

skool *see* **scoul**

skoor *see* **scour**³

skoosh, scoosh *verb* gush in spurts or splashes, squirt; dart or move quickly with a swishing sound.
noun **1** a splash, spurt, jet (of liquid). **2** lemonade etc.
adverb with a splash or swish.
skoosher a device for sprinkling or spraying, a sprinkler.

skoot *see* **scout**[1], **scout**[2]

skouth *see* **scowth**

skow *see* **scow**[2], **scowk**

skrae *see* **scrae**

skraich, skraik screech, shriek, scream.
noun a shriek, screech, shrill sound.

skran *see* **scran**

skrank thin, skinny.

skrankie thin, scraggy, shrivelled.

skrauch utter a shrill cry, scream, shriek, shout.

skraw *see* **scraw**

skreed *see* **screed**

skreek, skreich, scraich, scraigh [-ch, -gh as -ch in 'dreich']: **skreek o day** first light, the crack of dawn.

skreek *see* **skreich**

skreeve *see* **screeve**

skreich, skreigh [-ch, -gh as -ch in 'dreich'], **skreek** shriek, screech, scream.

skreich *see* **skreek**

skrim *see* **scrim**

skrink *verb* shrink, shrivel up.
noun a shrivelled, unpleasant person.
skrinkie thin, wrinkled, shrivelled.

skrunkit shrunk, shrivelled.

skrunt *see* **scrunt**[1], **scrunt**[2]

skug *see* **scug**

skule a mouth disease in horses.

skull *see* **scull**

skulk play truant from (school) *now Orkney NE*.

skult *see* **scult**

skunge *see* **scunge**

skunner *see* **scunner**

skurken *see* **scrocken**

skutch *see* **scutch**

sky *noun* daylight, sunlight, the sun, especially at dawn or sunset.
verb, NE **1** look towards the horizon, shading one's eyes with one's hand. **2** shade (a patch of water) so as to see the bottom. **3** look about one.

skybal(d) *noun* a rascal, rogue; a poor wretch; a ragamuffin.
adjective **1** rascally, tattered, ragged. **2** not having enough, needy; not providing enough *NE*.

skybe, scibe, skipe a mean rogue, a bad-mannered person *S*.

skyle *see* **skail**

skylie *see* **scailie**

skyow *see* **skew**[2]

skyowl *see* **skewl**

skyre *see* **skeer, skire**

skytch *see* **sketch**

skyte *see* **skite**[1]

slab[1] **1** the first slice cut off a loaf. **2** a thin person with a broad frame *NE*.

slab[2] slaver, eat or drink noisily, slobber.
slabber 1 wet or stain with saliva or with food when eating. **2** wet with something messy and semi-liquid. **3** slaver, dribble; eat or drink noisily, sloppily. **4** make a snorting, bubbling sound as in weeping or sleeping. **5** work carelessly, messily or with something wet or messy. **6** talk drivel, babble. *noun* **1** a greedy or noisy mouthful, a slobber *now Angus*. **2 slabs** senseless or foolish talk, idle chatter. **3** mud; muddy, trampled soil *now NE*. **4** something liquid or messy, especially food. **5** a messy person, a slobberer.

slack[1] *adjective* **1** short of money. **2** *of a ewe* past breeding age, about to be sold for meat.
noun a slackening, loosening.
verb slacken off, become less tense or active, weaken.

slack[2] **1** a hollow, especially between hills, a pass. **2** a low-lying, boggy hollow area in the ground *S*.

slade *see* **slide**

slae[1] sloe, blackthorn.

slae[2] a slow- or blindworm.

slag[1] a large blob of something wet, soft,

or messy *now Angus.*

slaiger, slagger *verb* **1** smear with something soft and wet, daub with mud etc. **2** eat or drink messily. **3** walk messily in mud etc, plod wearily or carelessly. *noun* **1** a wet, soggy, or slimy mess, a daub, smear of sloppy food etc. **2** an act of daubing; careless, messy work.

slaigerin dirty, careless and messy.

slag² a marshy place.

slaik, slake, slaich, sklaik *verb* **1** lick, smear with the tongue, slobber on. **2** *especially of a pet animal* lick (dishes) or eat (food) on the sly. **3** kiss, fondle over-sloppily *now Angus.* **4** smear, daub, streak.
noun **1** a lick with the tongue, a slobbering lick or kiss. **2** an act of daubing or smearing; something soft, wet, or messy which has been smeared on. **3** a careless wash, a hasty clean or wipe; a dirty, messy way of working. **4** a person who eats or drinks too much.

slaip, slape slippery, smooth, sleek.

slair, sclair- smear, cover (with something soft, wet, messy).
slairie *verb* = **slair.** *noun* a smear, daub, a lick of paint. *adjective* messy in one's eating habits.

slairg, slerg, slairk *verb* **1** smear, bespatter (with something wet and dirty); smear on or in. **2** drink noisily, slobber at one's food *now S.*
noun a quantity of something messy or semi-liquid, a dollop, smear.

slaister, slester, slyster, sclyster *ECentral* [-y- as -ey in 'gey'] *verb* **1** work messily or splash the hands about in a liquid; work awkwardly, clumsily. **2** wade in mud or water *now Shetland Caithness.* **3** eat or drink messily or greedily. **4** make messy, smear; smear (a substance) on a surface, spread or scatter messily.
noun **1** a state of wetness and dirt, a splashy mess, dirty water, slops. **2** a disgusting mixture of foods etc. **3** a state of confusion. **4** a careless, dirty

worker, a slut; a messy person, especially a messy eater.

slaisterin untidy, careless and messy.
slaistery wet and dirty, muddy, slimy.
slaister kyte a messy eater, a greedy person.

slake, slawk *now Orkney,* **slauk, sloke** name for various kinds of edible fresh- and salt-water algae *now Shetland Orkney Caithness.*

slake *see* **slaik**

slammachs gossamer, spiders' webs *NE.*

slamp slim, supple.

slap¹, slop *N noun* **1** a slap, a smack. **2** a large quantity, a dollop *now Shetland Angus.*
verb **1** a slap, smack. **2** beat, go beyond, exceed.
full slap at full speed.

slap², slop *noun* **1** a gap or opening in a wall, hedge etc. **2** an opening left temporarily in a salmon weir to allow the fish to swim up-river to spawn. **3** a narrow passage or lane between houses *NE.* **4** *often in place-names* a pass or shallow valley between hills. **5** a hole, missing part, a break in a pattern; a lack, want.
verb **1** *building* make a gap or break in (a wall etc) or for (a door, window etc). **2** thin out (seedlings etc) *NE.*
slapped notched, roughened at the edge *now Shetland.*
Saturday('s) slap the period from Saturday night till Monday morning, fixed by law for the free passage of fish up-river.

slap³, slop 1 slaps slops, sloppy food etc. **2** a careless or dirty person.
slap bowl a slop basin.

slape *see* **slaip**

slash *noun* a splash, a violent dash or clash, especially of something wet *now Shetland NE.*
verb **1** throw (liquid) with a splash; hit with something wet. **2** rush violently, dash forward.
adverb with a clash or splash, violently.

slarrie *see* **slaurie**

slatch *verb* work in something messy, potter in mud etc; walk or splash through mud *S*.

noun **1** a messy dirty worker; a dirty coarse woman *S*. **2** a wet and muddy place *S*. **3** a slap, a heavy thud.

slate, sclate, sklait slate.

slater a woodlouse.

slate house a house with a slate roof.

sclate stane *often in proverbs etc concerning money* a piece of slate or stone: *"he's makin siller like sclate steens"*.

want a slate be feeble-minded.

slate *see* **slite**

slauch *see* **sloch**²

slauk *see* **slake**

slaurie, slarrie *verb* daub or splash with mud etc; dirty (one's clothes).

noun a smear, smudge, daub of something soft and sticky.

slaver, slever, sliver *NE verb* **1** slaver. **2** talk nonsense, chatter in a silly way; talk insincerely. **3** *of lovers* cuddle, pet.

noun slaver, saliva.

slaw slow(ly).

slawk *see* **slake**

sled 1 a sledge. **2** a child's cart, usually made of short planks on the frame of an old pram.

sled *see* **slide**

slee, sly 1 sly. **2** *of persons* clever, skilled, expert; wise. **3** *of things* well-made; showing the skill of their creator or user.

sleech [sleetch], **slike** *now Fife,* †**sleek** silt, mud or sludge left behind by the sea or a river.

sleek *adjective* smooth, fawning and deceitful; cunning, self-seeking, sly.

verb **1** smooth. **2** *in measuring* level off (especially grain or fruit) at the top of the container; *of the commodity* fill (its container). **3** slink, sneak. **4** flatter, wheedle, curry favour with.

noun a measure of capacity, especially of grain or fruit.

sleekit **1** smooth, having an even surface or glossy skin. **2** smooth in manner; sly, cunning, not to be trusted.

sleek *see* **sleech**

sleep 1 *of a top* spin so fast and so smoothly that it appears motionless. **2** *law, of an action* lapse through passage of time and failure to bring the case to court *compare* **waken** (*under* **wauken**).

sleepie men, sleepie things the little specks of matter which form in the eyes during sleep.

be sleepit oot have slept one's fill. sleep in oversleep.

sleesh 1 a slice *now NE*. **2** a swipe, cutting stroke; a lash, as with a whip.

slent *see* **sklent**

slerg *see* **slairg**

slerp *verb* **1** slobber, splutter messily, spit. **2** smear or daub with something wet or messy. **3** eat or drink noisily or messily, slurp.

noun **1** a spoonful of liquid taken with a slobbering sound, slurp. **2** a slut, a slovenly woman.

slester *see* **slaister**

sleum *see* **sloom**²

slever *see* **slaver**

slibb(er)ie slippery *now Angus*.

slicht¹ **1** sleight, cunning, skill. **2** the method, trick, or knack (of doing something).

slicht² slight.

slid 1 *of surfaces* slippery, smooth. **2** *of persons or their actions* smooth, cunning.

slidden *see* **slide**

slidder, sclidder, sclither *verb* **1** slip, slide, slither. **2** saunter, walk or move in a casual or lazy way. **3** cause to slip or slide.

noun **1** a sliding, slithering movement, a slip, skid. **2** ice, an icy surface *NE*. **3** a narrow steep hollow or track down a hillside, especially when stony, a **scree** *now S*. **4** a slow-moving person, a lazy person *now WCentral*.

slidderie **1** slippery. **2** *of food* soft, sloppy. **3** insecure, unstable to stand on etc, shaky; changeable, uncertain. **4** *of people or actions* sly, deceitful, unreliable.

slide, *verb, past tense also* **slade, sled,** *past participle also* **slidden 1** slide. **2** tell a mild lie, exaggerate *now NE*.

slider 1 a metal loop on a cart-shaft. **2** an ice-cream wafer. **slid(e)y** slippery, very smooth.

slike *see* **sleech**

slim *adjective* **1** *of clothes, shoes etc* flimsy, thin *now Shetland NE*. **2** sly, crafty, wily.

verb, frequently **slim ower** treat (work) carelessly, rush through (a job).

slim jim a kind of **sweetie** consisting of long strips of coconut or liquorice *WCentral*.

sling *verb* walk with a long vigorous stride, swing along *now S*.

noun **1** the swivels, hooks and chains of the draught-harness of a cart. **2** a swinging vigorous way of walking, a long striding step.

slinger 1 slingers sausages. **2** a dish consisting of bread sops boiled in milk *NE*.

slink *noun* **1** contemptuous term for a person, a smooth crafty person. **2** a premature, or newly-born unfed calf or other animal, one born dead.

adjective thin, scraggy.

slunken weak or starved looking.

slip¹ *verb* allow (a chance etc) to slip, not do something.

noun **1** a loose (protective) garment for slipping over one's clothes, a pinafore. **2** an abortion, miscarriage.

slipper a slippery state or condition; something which causes slipperiness, ice etc *now NE*. **slippy** slippery.

slip body an under-bodice.

slip bolt a (door- or window-)bolt made to slip into a cylindrical socket, a barrel-bolt. **slipshod 1** wearing shoes but no stockings. **2** having one's shoelaces hanging loose.

slip away die quietly. **slip-by** a carelessly-performed task, shoddy work.

slip-ma-labor a lazy untrustworthy person *now Shetland*. **slip the timmers** die *NE*.

slip² a measure of yarn, usually in the form of a two-pound hank.

slipe¹, slype 1 a kind of sledge, a wooden wheelless platform for moving heavy loads. **2** a rail or wooden runner by which barrels etc are unloaded from a lorry.

verb haul (a load) on a **slipe.**

slipe² move in a slanting direction, fall (over) sideways.

slite, *past tense also* **slate,** *past participle* **slitten 1** slit, rip up, split. **2** †make sharp, whet.

slitter, sluiter *verb* **1** work or walk messily in water etc, splash about untidily; eat or drink messily. **2** smear with something wet or messy, make messy or stained.

noun **1** a sloppy mess especially of food; a dirty untidy state. **2** an untidy, or messy person.

slittery wet and messy, sloppy.

slive a thin slice, a sliver *S*.

sliver *see* **slaver**

sloam *see* **sloom¹**

†**sloan** a sharp answer, a snub.

sloch¹, slough, sluch [-ch, -gh as -ch in 'loch'] **1** slough, an outer skin. **2** the outer skin or husk of certain fruits or vegetables. **3** the pelt or coat (taken skin and wool together) from a dead sheep. **4** †a suit (of clothes).

verb **1** slough. **2** remove the wool from a dead sheep by skinning rather than clipping or shearing *SW*.

sloch², slauch swallow (food or drink) in a noisy slobbering way.

noun a noisy gulp of food or drink; a hearty drink, a good swig.

slochy slimy, dirty and disgusting.

sloch *see* **slock²**

slochen *see* **slocken**

slock¹, sloke *verb* **1** quench (thirst etc), *often* **slock one's drouth. 2** satisfy the thirst of (a person, animal); satisfy the wishes or desires of. **3** slake (lime). **4** moisten, soak *NE*. **5** put out (a fire etc). **6** *of fire* go out *now Shetland Orkney Caithness*.

noun a drink.

slockin a drink, enough (drink) to quench one's thirst. **slockit** drunk *Orkney NE*.

slock², sloch 1 *also* **slug** a hollow between hills, a pass. **2** a creek or gully in the sea, a long deep inlet, of the sea between rocks often one which appears only at low tide.

slocken, slochen 1 put out (fire, flame). **2** quench (thirst). **3** quench the thirst of (a person or animal). **4** celebrate with a drink. **5** moisten, soak. **6** slake (lime). **7** make a paste of (meal). **8** †make less, suppress.

slockener a drink, a thirst-quencher.

slogan a war- or rallying-cry, usually the name of a clan chief or clan meeting place used in the Highlands and in the Borders, originally as a signal to take up arms or as a password.

slogger *noun* a dirty or untidy person.

sloggerin dirtily or untidily dressed.

sloit, slowt *Fife* walk slowly, slouch, stroll idly or carelessly about.

sloke *see* **slake, slock¹**

slooch, slouch [slootch] *verb* **1** slouch. **2** crouch, cower, skulk.

noun **1** a slouch. **2** an idle, work-shy person.

sloom¹, sloam *SW, Ulster noun* a dreamy or sleepy state, a daydream, a light or unsettled sleep *now NE*.

verb **1** slip along easily and quietly. **2** †*of plants* (cause to) become soft; (cause to) wilt and decay. **3** *of plants* (cause to) grow or sprout unnaturally *Ulster*.

sloom², sleum a rumour, piece of hearsay or gossip *NE*.

sloomin a secret report, a rumour *NE*.

sloonge *see* **slounge, slunge**

sloosh *noun* **1** a sluice. **2** a dash of water, a splashing.

verb splash with water, flush.

slooster *see* **slouster**

slooter *see* **slouter**

slop, slope a kind of loose-fitting jacket or tunic, formerly worn by field workers or fishermen.

slop *see* **slap¹, slap², slap³**

slope 1 avoid paying *now Fife*. **2** shirk one's work, dodge duty, laze about.

sloper a shirker.

slorach, schlorach *NE verb* **1** eat or drink messily and noisily, slobber. **2** clear the throat loudly, breathe or speak through catarrh.

noun a wet, disgusting mess (of something) *now NE*.

slork *verb* **1** make a slobbering noise, *eg* when eating; suck up (food or drink) noisily. **2** sniff or snort. **3** *of shoes or persons* make a squelching noise in walking *S*.

noun a noisy sucking up of food or drink.

slorp *verb* **1** eat or drink noisily and slobberingly. **2** *of shoes etc* squelch.

noun a noisy mouthful, a slobber, gulp.

slot¹ *noun* **1** a bar or bolt for a door, window etc. **2** a cross-piece or bar, especially in a harrow or cart.

verb bolt, lock (a door, window), secure with a bolt or bar.

slot² **1** the hollow running down the middle of the chest. **2** the seam in which a draw-string runs.

slotch *verb* slouch, drag the feet in walking.

noun a lazy, slouching person, a layabout, ne'er-do-well.

slouch *see* **slooch**

slough *see* **sloch¹**

slounge [-oo-], **sloonge, slunge** *verb* **1** idle or loaf about, walk in a slouching, lazy way. **2** behave furtively and stealthily. **3** hang about in the hope of getting food.

noun **1** a lazy, lounging person. **2** a person or animal always on the lookout for food, a scrounger, a greedy person or animal. **3** a sneaking, sly, trouble-making person *mainly SW*.

slounge *see* **slunge**

slouster [-oo-], **slooster, sluister 1** dabble in water or mud, work untidily or messily. **2** swallow noisily and awkwardly, gulp, slobber.

slouter [-oo-], **slooter** a coarse, slovenly, lazy person.

slouth, slowth carry out (a task) in a lazy, idle, careless way, treat with indifference or neglect *now NE*.

slowt *see* **sloit**

slubber *verb* slobber, swallow sloppy food, eat or drink in a noisy, gulping way.

noun a noisy, slobbering way of eating *now Orkney N*.

sluch a slough, a mire, a wet, muddy, boggy place.

sluch *see* **sloch**¹

sludder, sluther something wet and slimy, mud, filth.

slug¹ a sleep, nap, a rest.

slug² a loose garment worn to protect the clothing.

slug *see* **slock**²

sluister *see* **slouster**

sluiter *see* **slitter**

slump¹ *noun* †a large quantity, great number.

verb treat (several things) as one, lump together, deal with as a whole.

slump number, slump sum a number etc reckoned in round figures.

at the slump, in a slump taken as a whole, in total; by a rough-and-ready calculation.

slump² a marsh, boggy place.

slump³ sink into mud, slush etc *now SW*.

slung 1 a sling (for hurling stones). **2** a tall lanky stupid person; a rascal *NE*.

like a slung-stane like a bolt from the blue *NE*.

slunge, slounge [-oo-], **sloonge** *verb* **1** make a plunging movement or noise. **2** put into water, or throw water over.

noun a plunging movement, a headlong

fall, a splash made by a heavy object.

slunge *see* **slounge**

slunk¹ a wet and muddy hollow, a soft, deep, wet rut in a road, a ditch *now SW*.

slunk² a lazy, sneaking person, a shirker.

slunken *see* **slink**

slush *noun* a speech peculiarity in which *sh* is used in place of the normal *s*.

verb **1** work in a messy or careless way *Shetland Orkney Caithness*. **2** wade messily through wet mud etc, shuffle.

slushy *now Shetland Orkney Caithness* **1** *of drink etc* weak. **2** dirty.

slute a messy, sluggish person.

sluther *see* **sludder**

slutter, sclutter, skleuter *verb* **1** work in a messy, dirty way, or in something messy. **2** slouch. **3** splash; plunge, flounder in mud *NE*.

noun **1** a mess, a mass of dirty (semi-) liquid. **2** a state of confusion, a muddle. **3** a splash, slop.

sly *see* **scly, slee**

slype, sclype, sklype *noun NE* **1** a hard slap or smack, a thud caused by falling heavily. **2** contemptuous term for a lazy, coarse, worthless person, usually a man.

verb NE **1** throw or fall down with a hard smack. **2** walk with a heavy, flat-footed step.

slype *see* **slipe**¹

slyster *see* **slaister**

sma, small *adjective* **1** small. **2** *of people, animals* slim, slender, slightly-built; *of things* narrow, thin. **3** fine, made up of small particles etc: *"small rain"*. **4** *of cloth, mesh* fine in texture. **5** *of the sea, a lake etc* smooth, calm; *of a river* low, not in flood.

noun **1** a small quantity or amount, a little, not much. **2** **smas** small change *NE*. **3** **smas** small (drapery) goods.

adverb quietly: *"speak sma!"*.

smally *of people* undersized, weakly; *of things* small, slight.

sma-boukit small, compact, shrunken.

sma breid = **tea bread** (*see* **tea**). **small debt court** a court set up under a **sheriff** for dealing with debts up to £20; now replaced by the summary courts and small claims procedures. **sma faimily** a family of young children. **small fish** fish such as haddock, herring etc, caught inshore. **sma hours, wee sma hours** the very early hours of the morning, just after midnight. **sma lines** the lines used by inshore fishermen to catch **small fish**. **sma thing** a small sum of money. **sma write** ordinary joined-up handwriting, cursive handwriting *now NE*.

think anesel nae sma drink think oneself to be an important person. **in smas** in small amounts, piecemeal, little by little.

smacherie, smaggrie 1 a large number of small objects or people (especially children), especially in disorder or confusion *now NE*. **2** a hotchpotch or mixture of food, especially **sweeties** *now NE*.

smack 1 kiss, especially in a loud hearty way. **2** move along with speed *now Angus Perth*.

smad, smud *noun* a small stain, smut, dirty mark; a very small quantity of anything *now Shetland NE*.

verb stain, soil *now Shetland NE*.

smaggrie *see* **smacherie**

smaik contemptuous term for a person; a rogue, rascal.

smairg smear with something oily or messy; = **smear** 2.

smairt, smart, smert smart.

smairter, smartie a lively and efficient person, one who is quick to understand and act.

small, smally *see* **sma**

smarrach a confused crowd or collection, especially of children *NE*.

smash a smashed or pulpy state.

smashie a kind of marbles game; a heavy marble used in this game.

smatchet, smatchert a small, worthless person (or animal), a cheeky or mis-

chievous child, a little rogue; *of an adult* an impudent, worthless person, a rascal *now Shetland Orkney N*.

smatter, smather *verb* **1** smash *now SW, S*. **2** work untidily, (appear to) be busy with trivial jobs.

noun **1 smatters** bits and pieces, smithereens; odds and ends, small amounts. **2** a small jumbled collection of people or things, especially of children.

smear, smeer *verb* **1** smear. **2** treat (a sheep's fleece) with a tar-and-grease compound to protect it from damp and pests.

smeerich [-ch as in 'dreich'] *noun* a thin layer (of butter etc) *N. verb* make a mess of *NE*.

smearless *see* **smerghless**

smeddum *noun* **1** fine powder, *eg* a finely ground meal, a medicinal powder. **2** spirit, energy, drive, vigorous commonsense and resourcefulness.

smeech *see* **smiach**

smeek *noun* **1** the fumes from something burning, smoke. **2** an unpleasant smell, a stuffy foul atmosphere. **3** something for smoking out bees. **4** a whiff, stifling puff of fumes; the act of smelling, a sniff.

verb **1** affect or suffocate with smoke or soot, make smoky. **2** give off smoke or fumes. **3** sterilise with smoke. **4 smeek out** drive out (bees) with smoke fumes; smoke out people as a joke.

smeeker something for smoking out bees (or playing practical jokes). **smeekit 1** smoke-stained; stifled or blinded by smoke. **2** drunk.

smeer *see* **smear**

smeerless *see* **smerghless**

smeeth *see* **smuith**

smell a small quantity, a taste (especially of drink).

smelt a smolt, young salmon.

smerghless [smerchless], **smeerless, smearless** lacking in spirit or energy, feckless, stupid; *of things* insipid, uninteresting *N*.

smert *see* **smairt**

smiach [**smee**ach], **smeech** [rhymes with 'dreich'] a sound, whisper, murmur; a trace, a sign of life.

smiddy a smithy.

smiler *humorous* a kind of wide-toothed wooden rake for stubble *N*.

smird a smut, smudge, a spot of dirt, rain etc *Shetland NE*.

smirk[1] *verb* smile in a pleasant friendly way, have a smiling expression; have a flirtatious smile.

noun a pleasant smile, a friendly expression.

smirkie having a good-natured, friendly expression.

smirk[2] a kiss *NE*.

smirked *literary* stained *now NE*.

smirr, smurr *noun* a fine rain, drizzle, *often* **smirr o rain;** sleet or snow.

verb, of rain or snow fall gently and softly in fine clouds, drizzle.

smirtle smile in a knowing way, smirk; giggle, snigger.

smit 1 affect (with) (something bad). **2** *of an infectious disease or patient* affect by contact, infect, taint.

noun **get the smit** infect or be infected by a disease; fall in love.

smittal, smittin, smitsome infectious.

smitch 1 a stain, blemish, smudge. **2** a very small amount; a small person.

smite a small unimportant person, a weak creature *NE*.

smizzle drizzle *SW, S*.

smoch thick choking smoke; thick fog.

smochy smoky; *of the air* close, sultry, stifling *now Fife*.

smoke: (Arbroath) smokie an unsplit smoked haddock.

smoke board a wooden flap over a fireplace to control the draught and prevent the chimney from smoking.

smoke o tobacco as much tobacco as will fill a pipe.

smolt *see* **smowt**[1]

smoochter *see* **smuchter**

smooder *see* **smouder**

smook, smuk slink or sneak (about) (looking for something to pilfer).

smook *see* **smuik**

smool[1]**, smuil** *verb* **1** slink, sneak *now NE*. **2** curry favour, suck up to, wheedle. **3** *literary* remove stealthily, steal.

noun, often of a child a wheedler, a very small or unimportant person *NE*.

smool in wi suck up to *now Angus*.

smool[2] scowl, frown; look scornful and unfriendly *SW*.

smoor *see* **smuir**

smoorach *see* **smurach**

smoost *see* **smuist**

smooth *see* **smuith**

smore *verb* **1** smother, suffocate, stifle (*eg* with smoke) *now Shetland NE*. **2** be smothered or stifled, choke. **3** put out (a fire, light etc) *now NE*. **4** block in or cover thickly with snow. **5** *of snow, smoke etc* fall or come out in a dense stifling cloud; *of atmosphere* be thick with snow, smoke etc.

noun a thick, close, stifling atmosphere full of smoke, snow, fine rain, dust etc.

smorin *of a head-cold* thick, choking, heavy. **be smorin wi the caul** have a very bad cold.

smot mark (sheep) with tar or other colouring as a sign of ownership.

smouder [-oo-]**, smooder** smoulder.

smowt[1]**, smout** [rhymes with 'shout']**, smolt 1** a young salmon (or sea trout) between the **parr** and **grilse** stages. **2** a small unimportant person, a small child, animal or thing.

smowt[2] a term used in games of marbles *WCentral, SW*.

smucht = smuchter *noun* **1** *NE*.

smuchty smoky; misty, close *NE*.

smuchter, smoochter *verb, NE* **1** smoulder, give off thick black smoke, burn slowly. **2** *of rain, snow etc* fall in a fine mist, drizzle.

noun, NE **1** thick smoke, *eg* from damp fuel; slight smoke from a fire not properly lit; a thick stuffy atmosphere. **2** a thin light mist or rain. **3** a thick choking cold, a heavy catarrh.

smud *see* **smad**

smudge *verb* laugh quietly to oneself, smirk.

noun a quiet laugh, a smirk, simper.

smue smile quietly or smugly, smirk; laugh.N

smuggle-the-geg *see* **geg**[3]

smuik, smook *noun* **1** smoke, fumes. **2** fine thick snow or rain *Orkney Caithness NE*.

verb **1** smoke, smoulder with thick smoke. **2** (expose to) smoke; cure (meat) by smoking; smoke out (bees); discolour by smoke.

smuil *see* **smool**[1]

smuir, smoor *verb* **1** be choked, suffocated, die, especially by being buried in a snowdrift. **2** suffocate, smother. **3** bury, cover over thickly in a thick covering of smoke, snow, vegetation etc. **4** damp down (a fire) so that it smoulders quietly. **5** cover with a thin coating, smear (*eg* a sheep with tar). **6** hide, reduce, quench (feelings etc): *"pity smoored his anger"*.

noun a thick atmosphere, a dense cloud of smoke, snow, rain, mist.

smuirich, smoorach kiss, hug, cuddle.

smuist, smoost *verb* smoke without much fire, smoulder, burn slowly.

noun a thick, choking smoke or its smell.

smuith, smooth, smeeth *adjective* smooth. *noun* a smooth or level place, especially the sandy sea-bottom *N*.

smuk *see* **smook**

smurach, smoorach fine dust or powder, *eg* crumbled peat.

smurr *see* **smirr**

smush[1] *verb* break into very small pieces, crush, smash.

noun a mass of tiny crushed pieces, something reduced to pulp or powder, *eg* over-boiled potatoes.

smush[2] a thick cloud of smoke or soot particles, grime, a sulphurous smell.

smyte, smytrie contemptuous term for a

collection of people (especially children) or small objects *now NE*.

snab[1], **snob** a cobbler; a cobbler's boy or apprentice.

snab[2] a steep short slope, a rock that juts out.

snack[1] *noun* a bite, snap, especially of a dog.

verb snap with the teeth, bite.

snack[2] **1** *of people* nimble, active, quick. **2** clever, quick in mind.

snag *verb* snarl (at); nag, grumble, taunt *now NE*.

noun a titbit, especially a **sweetie** *now NE*.

snagger snarl, growl; snore hard *NE*.

snaik, snake sneak, skulk about, do something in a mean, underhand way.

snail a slug.

snake *see* **snaik**

snap *verb* **1** snatch *now NE*. **2** gobble (up), eat quickly or with pleasure.

noun **1** a small piece, scrap, especially of food: *"eat it up, every snap"*. **2** a sharp blow, a rap *Shetland N*.

adjective **1** short-tempered, giving a short reply *now Shetland*. **2** quick, eager, smart.

in a snap like a shot, with no delay *now Shetland Caithness*.

snapper *verb* stumble, trip, fall suddenly *now Shetland NE*.

noun **1** a stumble, jolting motion *now NE*. **2** †a blunder; an unfortunate accident.

snar 1 severe, strict. **2** †sharp (in one's dealings); shrewd, efficient.

snarl snare.

snash *verb* **1** snap, bite *now Orkney*. **2** insult, speak rudely to, sneer at.

noun abuse, cheek.

snashters contemptuous term for **sweeties**, cakes etc; trashy food.

snaw, snow, snyauve *NE* [sneeawve] snow. **snaw bree, snaw broo** slush, often that carried down in rivers. **snaw flake** a snow bunting. **snaw wreath** a snowdrift.

like snaw aff a dyke (disappear) very quickly.

sneck¹, snick *noun* a latch, catch of a door etc.

verb 1 latch, fasten (up) with a latch etc; make (a catch) fast. 2 shut (one's mouth), shut up. 3 lock up or in, catch (something) in (a door), jam or squeeze between two objects. 4 switch or turn off (an electrical appliance). 5 *of a door* close on a latch, shut.

sneck-draw(er) a crafty, deceitful person.

draw a sneck, lift a sneck open a latch, act craftily or stealthily, insinuate oneself into something. **off the sneck** *of a door etc* unlatched, with the catch left off. **on the sneck** latched but not locked.

sneck² *noun* 1 a notch, a slight cut; a mark in an animal's horn as a sign of age. 2 the power or act of cutting; a cutting remark. 3 a dip in the ground, a saddle between hills.

verb 1 cut sharply, cut into or off, prune, notch. 2 beat, be better than *NE*.

sneck³, snick *verb* snatch, seize, steal.

noun a greedy grasping person.

sned¹ the shaft of a scythe, to which the blade is attached.

sned² *verb* 1 chop, lop off (a branch); prune (a tree). 2 cut off the tops (and roots) of (turnips, thistles etc). 3 cut off, trim.

noun a cut, cutting; a slash, slight wound; a lopping or pruning.

sneed *see* **snuid**

sneel *see* **snuil**

sneer snort, twitch the nose, snuffle, breathe heavily or noisily.

sneesh *noun* (a pinch of) snuff.

verb 1 take snuff. 2 sneeze.

sneeshin, snishin(g) snuff, a pinch of snuff; something of little value.

sneeshin mull a snuffbox, originally one which ground the snuff.

sneest *see* **sneist**

sneet *see* **snite¹, snuit**

sneeter 1 giggle, snigger. 2 weep, blubber.

sneevil, snivel *verb* 1 snivel. 2 speak through the nose, whine. 3 cringe, act insincerely.

noun 1 a severe cold in the nose. 2 a nasal twang; a snuffle in one's speech.

sneev(l)ie *see* **hinkum sneev(l)ie**

sneg, snig snip, chop.

sneist, sneest, snist *verb* behave in a contemptuous way, be scornful.

noun a taunt, a look of contempt, cheek.

sneisty cheeky, sneering, sharp.

snell *adjective* 1 severe in manner or speech, sarcastic *now Shetland NE*. 2 *of weather* bitter, severe. 3 *of a blow, fortune etc* hard, severe *now NE*. 4 sharp to the taste or smell, strong *now NE*. 5 clear-sounding, shrill. 6 †nimble, active, clever.

adverb 1 quickly, eagerly. 2 harshly, unfeelingly, vigorously. 3 *of winds* keenly, piercingly, with a nip.

sneyster [-ey- as in 'gey'] burn, scorch, roast.

snib *verb* 1 fasten (a door etc) with a catch. 2 cut (short or off), slice, cut into. 3 †check, restrain, punish.

noun 1 a check, scolding; a calamity, reverse. 2 a catch, small bolt for a door etc. 3 a short steep hill or ascent.

snicher, snichter snigger, titter.

snick *see* **sneck¹, sneck³**

sniffle be slow in motion or action *now NE*.

snifflin slow, lazy *NE*.

snifter *verb* 1 sniff; snivel, snuffle (*eg* with a cold); snort, snore. 2 *of wind* blow in strong gusts.

noun 1 a (noisy) sniff, from a cold, grief etc, a snivel, whimper, snigger. 2 **the snifters** a (severe) head cold, catarrh, stuffed nose. 3 a strong blast, gust, flurry (of wind, sleet etc). 4 a shock, reverse, rebuff, quarrel *now S*.

snifty haughty.

snig *see* **sneg**

snigger *verb* catch (salmon) illegally by

dragging a cluster of weighted hooks along the river bed; fish (a pool) by this method.

noun the grappling hooks used in this way *Caithness NE*.

snip: snippit 1 quick in speech, sharp. **2** mean, giving short measure. **3** *of a horse* with a white patch on its face.
snippy = **snippit** 1.

snipe[1] contemptuous term for a person.
snipie a kind of marbles game.

snipe[2], **snype 1** a smart blow *now S*. **2** a setback, a loss by being cheated, a letdown, fraud, cheat *NE*.
verb **1** strike smartly. **2** cheat, bring loss on *NE*.

snirk *verb* snort, wrinkle the nose, snigger.
noun a snort, snigger.
snirket *of a face* pinched, puckered.

snirl snigger, laugh into oneself.
snirly a gusty biting wind.

snirl *see* **snorl**

snirt *verb* **1** snigger, make a noise through the nose when trying to stifle laughter; sneer. **2** snort.
noun **1** a snigger, suppressed laugh. **2** a snort. **3** contemptuous term for a small person, especially a child.

snishin(g) *see* **sneeshin**

snist *see* **sneist**

snitchers handcuffs.

snite[1], **snyte, sneet** *verb* **1** blow (one's nose), especially with the finger and thumb, wipe the nose *now Shetland Orkney NE*. **2** snuff (a candle), strike off (the burnt tip) *now NE*. **3** hit, strike *now S*.
noun **1** a blowing or wiping of the nose *now Shetland NE*. **2** a sharp blow, especially on the nose.
snite someone's niz tweak someone's nose; take someone down a peg; taunt someone *now SW*.

snite[2], **snyte** *usually contemptuous or insulting* a worthless person, a small unimportant person or thing *now Shetland NE*.

snite *see* **snuit**

snitter laugh into oneself, giggle, snigger *now S*.

snivel *see* **sneevil**

snob *see* **snab**[1]

snocher, †snocker *verb* snort, snuffle.
noun **1** a snort, snore. **2 the snochers** a severe nose cold.

snochter nasal mucus.
snochter-dichter a handerchief.

snocker *see* **snocher**

snod *adjective* **1** smooth, level, evenly cut. **2** neat, trim, tidy. **3** comfortable, snug, at ease.
verb **1** make trim or neat, tidy. **2** prune, cut, smooth, make level.
snod-up, snoddie-up a tidying, smartening.

snog *see* **snug**

snoiter breathe loudly through the nose, snore; snooze *now Angus*.

snoke, snook, snowk *verb* **1** sniff, smell, scent out (as a dog), poke with the nose. **2** hunt, nose one's way, prowl.
noun a smell(ing), sniff.

snood *see* **snuid**

snook *see* **snoke**

snool *see* **snuil**

snoot *see* **snout**

snoove *see* **snuve**

snoozle 1 snooze *now NE*. **2** nuzzle, poke with the nose; snuggle.

snore *verb* **1** *of animals* snort. **2** *especially of wind, fire etc* make a rushing, whirring, droning sound. **3** move at speed with a rushing, roaring sound.
noun a snort, roar, loud roaring or droning noise *now Shetland Caithness*.

snork 1 snort, snore, snuffle. **2** *of things* make a roaring or explosive sound *S*.

snorl, snurl, snirl *noun* **1** a knot, tangle, kink or twist in a thread, rope etc, a mix-up. **2** a difficulty, scrape, muddle, confusion.
verb ruffle, wrinkle, twist, tangle.

snot *noun* **1** the burnt wick of a candle *now NE*. **2** contemptuous term for a person.

verb snub, tell off.

snotter 1 *mainly* **snotters** nasal mucus, especially when hanging from the nose. **2** = **snot** *noun* 1. **3** the red skinny flaps on a turkey-cock's beak. **4** = **snot** *noun* 2. **5** a snub, telling off. *verb* **1** snuffle, snort. **2** snivel, weep noisily. **3** snooze, doze. **snotter box 1** the nose. **2** a soft, stupid, untidy person. **snotter-dichter** a handkerchief. **snottery 1** slimy, running at the nose. **2** tearful, miserable. **3** surly, short, snooty. **snotty** short-tempered, curt, huffy.

snout, snoot 1 a snout. **2** contemptuous term for the face, head. **3** the peak (of a cap). **4** *slang* a detective, policeman. **snoutit** *of a cap* peaked.

snow *see* **snaw**

snowk *see* **snoke**

snubbert 1 *humorous or contemptuous* the nose *NE*. **2** the red skinny flaps on a turkey-cock's beak *NE*.

snude *see* **snuid**

snuff *noun* **1** a pinch of snuff. **2** a very small amount (of something), something of little importance or value. *verb* take snuff.

snuff horn a snuffbox, one made from a horn tip. **snuffmill, snuffmull** a snuffbox.

snuffy sulky, touchy.

snug, snog 1 smooth, sleek, close-cropped *now Shetland Orkney*. **2** neat, trim, tidy *now Orkney Caithness*.

snuid, snude, snood, sneed *NE* **1** a snood, a ribbon etc bound round the brow and tied at the back under the hair, worn especially by young unmarried women; a symbol of virginity. **2** *fishing* the hemp part of a sea-line to which the hook is attached; the twisted loop of horsehair by which the hook is sometimes attached to this.

snuil, snool, sneel *NE noun* a weak or cowardly person; a lazy person. *verb* **1** subdue, humiliate, tell off, snub *now Orkney*. **2** give way, cringe, act meanly, deceitfully or weakly. **3** show

lack of energy, loaf about, move slowly and lazily.

snuit, snite *NE*, **sneet** *NE* move about or work in a lazy, careless or dazed way, laze about, be at a loose end *now NE*.

snurl *see* **snorl**

snuve, snoove 1 twist, twirl, spin, make yarn. **2** move smoothly, easily, or steadily, glide. **3** move carelessly, lazily, slink, sneak, laze about.

snyauve *see* **snaw**

snype *see* **snipe**²

snyte *see* **snite**¹, **snite**²

so *see* **sae**²

soach *see* **souch**

soad *see* **sod**

soam a chain or rope attaching a draught-ox or -horse to a plough etc.

sob *see* **sab**

sober 1 poor, miserable *now NE*. **2** small, slightly-built *NE*. **3** in poor health, sickly, weak.

socher [-ch as in 'loch'] pamper oneself, be fussy about one's health.

socht *see* **seek**¹

sock a ploughshare.

sod, soad 1 a sod. **2** a piece of turf used as fuel.

sod *see* **sad**

sodger, soldier, soger *noun* **1** a soldier. **2** **sodgers** the stems and flowerheads of plantain, especially ribwort plantain; a game played with these. **3** name for various small reddish-coloured creatures *eg* a ladybird, a red-breasted minnow. **4** **sodgers** small sparks, *eg* on the edge of burning paper; smuts of burning soot. **5** a wounded or injured child or animal. *verb* **1** soldier. **2** march in a stolid, dogged way, trudge.

sodger-clad but major-minded *usually complimentary* having a strong sense of pride and self-respect in spite of a humble position. **sunny sodger** a red wild bee.

sodie soda.

sodie heid contemptuous term for a

scatterbrained person.

soft *see* **saft**

soger, soldier *see* **sodger**

sole 1 the lower part, bottom or base of something, *eg* the flat bottom of a golf club; the smooth undersurface of a curling-stone; the lower crust of a loaf of bread; the bottom rope of a fishing net. **2** the surface vegetation of a pasture. **3** a sill, a supporting or strengthening beam, especially in a window or doorcase.

sole shaif the end slice of a loaf. **sole tree** a horizontal beam of wood, usually on the ground, which supports posts, *eg* to make a manger on the floor of a **byre.**

solid 1 sane *now Angus.* **2** *of people* having a large supply, well-stocked with; *of things* plentiful.

solvendie *of things* firm, safe, sure.

some, sum *pronoun, adjective* some.
adverb a little; very, a great deal: *"some glad"; "I'm some to blame"; "I some thocht that".*

somebit somewhere. **somegate 1** somewhere. **2** somehow, in some way. **someplace** somewhere. **something** somewhat, a little. **someway 1** somehow. **2** somewhere *now Shetland NE.*

and some and more so: *"she's as bonny as you and some".*

son *see* **sin**[1]

sonce *see* **sonse**

song *see* **sang**

sonk *see* **sunk**

sonnet 1 a song. **2** a tale, a (tall) story, nonsense *now NE.* **3** a fuss *Angus.*

sonse, sonce abundance, plenty; prosperity, good fortune.

sonsie 1 bringing good fortune; lucky. **2** friendly, hearty, jolly; good, honest. **3** *especially of women* attractive; *of the figure* buxom, plump; *of young children* chubby, sturdy. **4** fine, handsome, impressive; pleasant, cheery. **5** big, roomy, substantial.

soo[1]**, sow 1** a sow. **2** a pig. **3** *also* **soo stack** a ridge-shaped mass, *eg* a large oblong stack of hay. **4** a ballan wrasse *now NE.*

soo('s) cruive, soo('s) crave a pigsty. **soo-mouthed** *of animals* having an upper jaw that sticks out.

soo[2] ache; throb, tingle with pain, etc.

sooans *see* **sowans**

sooch *see* **souch**

sook *see* **souk**

sookan a one-ply rope of straw etc, used mainly for binding straw, thatching ricks etc.

sool *see* **sweel**[3]

soom, soum, swim, sweem, †swoom *verb* swim.
noun an extremely wet state, a flood.

soom *see* **soum**[1]

soon *see* **sune**

soon(d) *see* **soun(d)**[1], **soun(d)**[2], **soun(d)**[3]

soop *see* **soup, sweep**

soople, souple, supple 1 a swipple, the part of a flail which beats the grain. **2** †a cudgel, a stout stick.

soople *see* **souple**

soor *see* **sour**

soord *see* **swurd**

soorldab: gie someone his soorldab, gie something its soorldab put paid to, finish off, spoil.

soose *see* **souse**[1], **souse**[2]

soosh 1 beat, punish severely; deal severely with. **2** swill, splash, wash over *NE.*

sooter *see* **souter**

sooth *see* **south**[1], **south**[2], **suith**

sore *see* **sair**

sorn 1 *also* **sorn on** scrounge or sponge (on), abuse someone's hospitality. **2** scrounge food, forage. **3** †make someone give free board and lodging by force or threats, *often* **thig and sorn.**

sorra, sorrow 1 sorrow. **2** (the) Devil. **3** a rascal, a troublesome child, a pest of a person.

sorrafu 1 sorrowful. **2** troublesome. **sorra a** not a *now Shetland N.* **sorra fa ye** *etc* used as a curse.

not have one's sorra(s) to seek have plenty of trouble on one's hands. **sorra care** too bad!, bad luck!

sorry *see* **sairie**

sort *verb* **1** put in order, arrange, tidy up; tidy (oneself). **2** repair, mend, fix up; heal. **3** castrate *Shetland NE*. **4** provide for, supply (with etc). **5** feed and litter (especially a horse). **6** attend to the wants of (a child or sick person) *now NE*. **7** deal with by punishment etc, put (a person) in his place, scold. **8** bring together, pair, match; come together, keep company, live in harmony (with); come to an agreement.
noun **1** a considerable number, a fair amount (of) *S*. **2** a repair, a tidying up.

sosh a Co-operative Society shop *now Angus Fife*.

soss[1] *noun* **1** a mixture of food or drink, a wet, soggy mess of food. **2** a (very) wet state, a dirty wet mess. **3** a state of dirt and disorder, a muddle, confusion.
verb **1** eat sloppy or messy food; eat in a messy way. **2** mix (especially liquids) in a messy way. **3** make wet and dirty, make a mess of *now Shetland NE*. **4** make a mess, work dirtily or in dirty conditions. **5** nurse over-tenderly, fuss over; pester *now NE*. **6** *also* **soss up** *etc* cuddle *now NE*. **7** take one's ease, lie idle *now NE*.

soss[2] *noun* a thud, a heavy awkward fall, a heavy blow.
verb fall or set down with a thud.

sot[1] a stupid person.

sot[2], **sut** *child's word, after* not = so: *"It is not.—It is sot."*

sotter *verb* **1** boil, simmer, bubble or sputter in cooking. **2** sputter, crackle; come bubbling out. **3** soak. **4** work in a dirty unskilful way; handle in a disgusting way. **5** laze, potter about.
noun **1** the noise made by something boiling, frying or bubbling up. **2** a state of wetness *NE*. **3** a mess, muddle, confused mass, chaos.

souch, sough [-oo-], **sooch, sugh, seuch,**

soach [-ch, -gh as -ch in 'loch'] *noun* **1** the sound of the wind, especially when long-drawn-out. **2** the rushing, roaring or murmuring of water. **3** a rustling or whizzing sound, as of an object moving rapidly through the air; a whizzing blow. **4** a deep sigh or gasp, heavy breathing, panting. **5** a song, tune *now NE*. **6** the sound or pitch of a voice, an accent, way of speaking. **7** a high-pitched way of speaking, a whine, especially in preaching. **8** general feeling or opinion, attitude, style. **9** gossip, rumour, scandal. **10** an uproar, fuss.
verb **1** *of objects moving through the air* whizz, buzz, drone, flap, whirr. **2** *of leaves etc* rustle, whisper; *of water* ripple, gurgle, make a slapping sound. **3** *of wind* make a rushing, moaning, murmuring sound. **4** breathe heavily, sigh, wheeze, splutter, gurgle. **5** **souch awa** die. **6** sing softly, hum, whistle. **7** *of music* sound, waft *now NE*.
keep a calm souch keep quiet, hold one's tongue; keep calm or still.

soucht *see* **seek**[1]

soud *see* **south**[1]

souder *see* **sowther**

souf *see* **sowff**

souflet, sufflet a blow with the hand, a smack.

sough *see* **sheuch, souch**

souk [-oo-], **sook, suck** *verb* **1** suck. **2** flow in a certain direction, as if drawn by suction. **3** suckle (a baby animal), breastfeed (a baby).
noun **1** a stupid person. **2** a cheat, deception, swindle *NE*. **3** a person seeking favour, a toady.
usually **souk souk** a call to an animal, especially to a calf.
auld wifie's soukers mint imperials, **pan drops** (*see* **pan**). **soukie** *noun* **1** a suckling. **2** *contemptuous* a petted or spoilt child. **3** clover; sometimes common red clover *now Shetland. adjective, only* **sucky** *of a wound or blow* painful, stinging. **soukie mae, souky mammy** a

clover flowerhead. **soukie soo** the flower of the clover. **soukie sourocks** wood-sorrel. **soukin teuchit** *NE,* **souk turkey** *etc* a feeble or foolish person.

souk in curry favour, try to get into someone's good books. **souk-the-pappie** *contemptuous* a fairly old but babyish child, a big baby; an effeminate person.

soum¹ [-oo-], **soom, sum** *noun* **1** a sum. **2** the unit of pasturage which will support a certain fixed number of livestock; the number of livestock (usually a cow or a proportionate number of sheep) which can be supported by this unit.

soum² [soom] guess, suspect: *"I soum it was you that did it"*.

soum *see* **soom**

soun(d)¹, soon(d) 1 sound. **2** a rumour, report; gossip.

soundin box a canopy etc over a pulpit to bounce the speaker's voice out into the congregation.

sounstick the sound-post of a violin.

soun(d)², soon(d) 1 sound, in good condition. **2** smooth, even, level.

soun(d)³ [-oo-], **soon(d)** *verb* faint (away). *noun* a faint; faintness, *often* **in (a) sound** *now Shetland Orkney.*

a sound in a faint *now Shetland Orkney.*

soup [-oo-], **soop** a (small) amount of liquid, a sip; *also ironic* a considerable amount, especially of spirits.

soup *see* **sowp¹, sweep**

souple [-oo-], **soople, supple** *adjective* **1** supple. **2** ingenious, cunning, crafty. **3** limp, helpless with laughter etc. **4** †*of speech* fluent, chattering. *adverb* agilely.

souple *see* **soople**

soup tatties potato soup *now NE.*

sour, soor 1 sour. **2** *of weather* cold and wet, miserable. *verb, of water on lime* soften, slake.

sourock 1 name for various kinds of sorrel. **2** a sulky, bad-tempered person.

sour cloot a gloomy, bad-tempered person. **sour dock(en)** common sorrel *SW, S.* **sour dook 1** buttermilk; *now also* yoghurt. **2** a bad-tempered, mean person. **sour face = sour cloot. sour leek = sour dock(en). sour milk** buttermilk. **sour-moued, sour-like-mood** *NE,* **sour-mood-like** *NE* sulky-looking. **sour ploom 1** sour grapes. **2** a native of Galashiels. **3** a sharp-flavoured round green boiled sweet. **4 = sour cloot.**

sourd *see* **swurd**

souse¹, soose, sowse *verb* **1** strike, cuff, thump. **2** fall or sit (down) heavily. *noun* **1** a heavy blow, especially on the head, a thump. **2** (the sound of) a heavy fall. *adverb* violently, heavily, with a thud *now SW.*

sous(t)er something very large, a large amount.

souse² [-oo-], **soose** tell off, put (a person) in his place, silence *now Angus Perth.*

sout [-ow-], **sowt** a sudden bounce, jolt or bump (as when a plough strikes against a stone) *SW.*

souter [-oo-], **sooter** *noun* **1** a shoemaker, cobbler. **2** a native of Selkirk or Forfar. *verb* **1** cobble, make or mend shoes *now NE, SW.* **2** get the better of, trounce; *in games* defeat without one's opponent scoring.

souter('s) ends, sutter's lingles waxed thread used by cobblers *now NE, Perth.*

south¹, sooth, soud *now Shetland* **1** south. **2** characteristic of or belonging to the south.

southert southward. **southie** lefthanded. **southron 1** *of people* belonging to or living in England, English. **2** †*of things* of or characteristic of England or the English. **suddren wud** southernwood.

southland southern, from the south.

south awa, south by(e) in the south.

south², sooth, sowth *noun* quiet singing or whistling, a low murmur (of music). *verb* hum, sing or whistle softly *now*

NE.

souther *see* **sowther**

sow *see* **soo**[1]

sowans, sooans 1 a dish made from oat husks and fine meal steeped in water for about a week; after straining, the liquid was again left to ferment and separate, the solid matter at the bottom being the **sowans**, the liquid **swats**; usually eaten like porridge, boiled with water and salt. **2** *weaving* a flour-and-water size applied to warp threads.

sowans nicht Christmas Eve *NE*. **sowan seeds** the rough husks of oats used in making **sowans** *now Caithness NE*.

drinking sowans, knotting sowans the liquid left after straining **sowans** but before fermenting, usually thickened a little by heating *now NE*.

sowd 1 a (large) quantity or amount of money or possessions; a large amount or number. **2** *also* **sowdie** a large clumsy person *NE*.

sowder *see* **sowther**

sowff, souf [-ow-] *verb* **1** sing, hum or whistle softly or under one's breath *now NE*. **2** *of wind, water etc* murmur; *of a breeze or smoke* puff gently.

noun NE **1** a low whistling, singing or humming. **2** wheezing, heavy breathing; a snooze, sleep. **3** a stroke, blow, smack.

sowl *see* **saul**

sowp[1]**, soup** [-ow-] **1** a (small) amount of liquid, a sip, a larger amount, especially of spirits. **2** a drink; something to drink.

sowp[2] *verb* soak, steep.

noun **1** rain, wet weather. **2** wetness; a bog. **3** water for washing, lather *mainly SW*.

sowse *see* **souse**

sowt *see* **sout**

sowth *see* **south**[2]

sowther, souther, souder, sowder 1 solder. **2** unite in marriage; make (a marriage) *now NE*. **3** settle, patch up (a quarrel, etc). **4** reduce, ease (sorrow, pain,

anger etc). **5** confirm, strengthen (a friendship); seal (a bargain etc) *now NE*. **6** agree, get on well together.

†**soy** silk.

space *noun* a pace, stride, used as a unit of measurement, approximately 1 metre *now Shetland Caithness*.

verb measure by pacing.

spad on walk energetically *NE*.

spade, spead *now NE*, **spadd** *mainly NE*, **spaud** *NE* a spade.

spadin(g) a spade's depth (or breadth) of earth; a trench of one spade-depth. **spade's casting** one of various measurements in peat-cutting.

spae, spe(e), spey [spay] **1** prophesy, predict, tell (fortunes). **2** read (someone's hand) *now NE*. **3** tell the future about.

spaewife a female fortuneteller.

spag, spaig *Caithness* a paw, hand, foot, especially a big clumsy one *now Caithness*.

spagach flat-footed, with clumsy or badly-shaped feet *now N*.

spaik, spake, spyauck *NE* [sewwawk] **1** a spoke (of a wheel etc). **2** a wooden bar, rod or batten; a stake or pale in a wooden fence etc. **3** the perch of a bird's cage, a roosting bar. **4** one of the rungs of a ladder. **5** one of the bars of wood on which a coffin is carried to the graveside.

spaikit made of spokes or bars of wood.

spail, spale, speal, spell *now NE* **1** a splinter, chip or sliver of wood; a wood-shaving; a thin strip or lath of wood. **2** a splinter in the skin. **3** a wooden spill or taper used for lighting etc. **4** a small piece of something; something of little or no value. **5** a shroud-like shape of candlegrease on a guttered candle, thought to foretell the death of the person in whose direction it forms.

spail basket a two-handled (potato-) basket made of thin strips of wood. **spail box** a (usually small) box made of thin strips of wood, used for money, pills etc.

spail *see* **speel**[1]

spain *see* **spean**

spaingie *NE*, **spainyie, spengie** [-ng- as in sing] *NE adjective* Spanish.

noun, also **spaingie wan** *NE* a cane *eg* as used for punishment, as a fishing rod etc.

spairge, sparge, sperge scatter, sprinkle, dash (water, mud etc) (about) *now NE*.

spaiver the opening in the front of trousers.

spake *see* **spaik**

spalder stretch; sprawl.

spale *see* **spail**

spalebone *see* **spaul**

span *see* **spang**

spane *see* **spean**

spang[1], **span** span.

spangie a game played with marbles etc.

a spang nievefu as much of something as can be grasped in the hand. **spang the nose** thumb one's nose.-

spang[2] *noun* a pace, a long vigorous step or bound.

verb **1** stride out, walk with long steps, leap, bound. **2** stride over, leap (over); measure by pacing.

spanghew jerk or catapult violently into the air especially as a way of torturing frogs and birds *now S*.

spang-new, spankie-new brand-new.

spank: spank awa, spank aff *etc* move nimbly and briskly on foot, horseback or in a vehicle.

spanker 1 a spirited fast horse. **2** a person who walks quickly with a brisk regular stride. **spankie** *of animals* frisky, nimble, spirited.

spar, spare *noun* **1** a spar. **2** a wooden bolt for securing a door, a linchpin. **3** a bar or rail of a wooden fence or gate *now NE*. **4** a rung of a chair or ladder. **5** a crossbar or wooden slat in a kitchen dresser.

verb brace (the limbs) in order to resist a strain *now NE*.

sparred slatted.

spare 1 the opening or slit in a woman's skirt, petticoat etc. **2** the opening in the front of trousers.

sparge *see* **spairge**

spark, sperk *now S*, **spirk** *mainly NE noun* **1** a spark. **2** a very small amount (of something liquid or semi-liquid), a drop, *eg* a raindrop, a spot of mud etc. *verb* **1** spark. **2** set alight; light (a match etc). **3** spatter with liquid or mud; spot with mud etc *now Shetland Orkney NE*. **4 spark in** sprinkle, scatter (seed etc) *now Orkney*. **5** throw out a fine spray; sputter; come out etc as or like sparks. **6** rain slightly; spit with rain *now Shetland Orkney NE*.

sparkie giving off sparks; bright, sharp, quick-witted; lively *now NE, Perth*.

sparling *see* **spirling**

sparrow, sporrow *now Shetland Orkney*, **sparra, sparry** a sparrow.

sparrabaldy having thin legs *NE*.

sparrow drift, sparrow hail, sparrow shot shot for shooting small birds.

†**spartle, spurtle** sprawl, struggle; kick about, wriggle.

spat a spot.

spatril a musical note, especially as written on a score.

spatch patch *S*.

spate, †speat 1 a spate, a flood, a sudden rise of water. **2** a heavy downpour (of rain). **3** a flood of tears.

verb rain heavily.

spatril *see* **spat**

spaud *see* **spade**

spaul, spauld, †spule 1 the shoulder; the shoulder-bone. **2** a joint, a shoulder or leg (of mutton, beef etc); the wing or leg of a fowl; a shoulder cut of beef, shoulder steak *now NE*. **3** †a limb.

spalebone a cut of beef from the shoulder, blade-bone steak.

black spauld a cattle disease, a form of anthrax.

spave spay, neuter (a female animal).

spavie spavin; *also humorous* a human

rheumatic disease.

spe *see* **spae**

spead *see* **spade**

speak, speik, spek, spike *NE,* **spick** *NE*
verb **1** speak. **2** *often as a command etc*
listen to, attend to: *"speak a meenit,
Mistress'.* **3** order (goods): *"I'll speak
a new pair o boots'.*
noun **1** a chat, conversation *now Shetland.* **2** a speech, statement, comment;
a popular saying *now NE.* **3** a story
without much truth in it, a piece of
make-believe; hot air, nonsense *Shetland NE.* **4** gossip, scandalmongering.
5 a subject of conversation, especially
of current gossip or rumour, the talk
(of a place).
speaking time the time of year at which
employers, especially farmers, renew
or end workers' contracts.
speak back reply (in argument); talk
back. **speak in** visit briefly. **speak to** *of
a farmer etc* engage (a worker) for a
further term.

speal *see* **spail**

spean, spain, spane, spen 1 wean (an infant
or suckling animal). **2** put (a person or
animal) off food through disgust, fear
etc. **3** draw (a person) away from (a
habit, idea etc); separate, part from. **4**
be (being) weaned *now Angus Perth.*
new speaned newly weaned, just weaned.

speat *see* **spate**

special *of beer* a carbonated version of
heavy.

spee *see* **spae**

speeach [-ch as in 'loch'], **speeock** an (oak)
log; a stake, stick.

speed, success, prosperity, good fortune.
come speed be successful: *"he never cam
muckle speed".*

speeder, speedart *SW,* **spider 1** a spider. **2**
the Spiders nickname for Queen's Park
football team. **3** a trout-fly without
wings. **4** †a pennyfarthing bicycle
Orkney NE.
speeder jenny *now SW, S,* **speederlegs** a

cranefly, daddy-long-legs. **spider webs-
ter** a spider.

speel¹, spail, spell *noun* **1** a spell (of time).
2 a time of rest or relaxation, a break
in work.
verb **1** take a turn at work for (someone), relieve (someone) at work, substitute for (someone). **2** *often* **speel on**
work or walk with great energy *now
SW.*

speel², speil *verb* climb, clamber up,
down.
noun the act of climbing; a climb.

speen *see* **spune**

speendrift *see* **spindrift**

speeock *see* **speeach**

speer *see* **speir**

speerit, spreit spirit.

speeshal special.

speet, spit *noun* **1** a (roasting-)spit. **2** a
pointed stick on which fish are hung
up to dry.
verb **1** spit. **2** hang (fish) up by the
heads or gills on a spit to dry.

speik *see* **speak**

speil *see* **speel²**

speir, speer, spier *verb* **1** ask a question,
inquire, make inquiries; ask too many
questions. **2** **speir for** ask after
(someone's health). **3** ask for. **4** ask,
put a question to (a person). **5** *also*
speir for make a proposal of marriage
to, ask for the hand of. **6** invite. **7**
speir out search, track down, trace (by
inquiry).
noun **1** a question(ing), investigation.
2 a person who is continually asking
questions; a prying inquisitive person.
speirin inquisitive, searching. **speirins 1**
questioning, investigation, asking too
many questions. **2** information, news.
speir someone's price make a proposal
of marriage to someone.

spek *see* **speak**

spel(d) lay flat, spread out; split, cut, slice
open (especially fish to dry) *now Shetland Caithness.*
spelder 1 spread or pull open or apart.

2 wrench oneself or pull one's muscles by falling with the legs apart. **3** stretch out, sprawl; thrash about awkwardly.
spelding now Shetland N, **speldrin** a split and dried (or smoked) fish, especially a haddock or whiting.

spelk, spyolk Shetland [speeolk] **1** a sharp splinter (of wood, glass etc); a small strip of wood. **2** a surgical splint.
verb **1** splinter; fly about like splinters. **2** bind (a broken limb) with splints, repair (something broken) with splints etc.

spell[1] spelling, a spelling lesson.

spell[2] **1** state falsely; exaggerate now SW. **2** swear.

spell see **spail, speel**[1]

spen see **spean**

spence, spense an inner room of a house, used as a sitting room, small bedroom etc, or for storage.

spend: spent of a fish, especially a herring spawned, in poor condition after spawning.
spendrife spendthrift NE.

spengie see **spaingie**

spense see **spence**

spent see **spend**

spentacles spectacles.

sperge see **spairge**

sperk see **spark**

sperling see **spirling**

speshie [speeshie] a species.

speuchan see **spleuchan**

speug see **spug**

spew see **spue**

spey see **spae**

spice pepper now Shetland Orkney N.

spick see **speak**

spicket, spigot, also **spriggit** an outdoor tap, often one supplying water for a neighbourhood.

spider see **speeder**

spiel a curling match.

spier see **speir**

spigot see **spicket**

spike see **speak**

spirk see **spark**

spile[1] a wooden plug for stopping up a cask, a spigot.
spile tree a pole on which fishing lines are hung to be cleaned or baited NE.

spile[2] spoil.

spilk shell (peas) NE.

spin go well NE.
spinner 1 a cranefly, daddy-long-legs. **2** a garden spider. **spinnin jenny 1** = **spinner** 1. **2** a home-made spinning toy. **spin(nin) maggie** = **spinner** 1.
spin the knife a party game.

spindrift, speendrift NE, **spunedrift 1** spray whipped up by wind and driven across the tops of waves. **2** snow blown up from the ground by gusts of wind, driving snow NE.

spink[1] name for various flowers, eg lady's smock, common primrose, maiden pink.

spink[2] a chaffinch.

spinle a spindle.

spire wither, fade, dry up.

spirk see **spark**

spirl 1 a small slender shoot. **2** a tall thin person.
spirlie adjective slender, thin, spindly. noun a slender person.

spirling, sparling, sperling a smelt.

spirtle see **spurtle**

spit: spitten image the exact likeness of.
spitter noun **1** a slight shower of rain or snow. **2 spits** small drops of wind-driven rain or snow. verb, of rain or snow fall in small drops or flakes, drizzle. **spittin 1** spittle. **2** a small hot-tempered person or animal NE. **spittle** a quantity of saliva spat out at one time.
spit and gie (it) ower give in, admit defeat now NE.

spit see **speet**

spite a disappointment, a cause for annoyance or grief.

splairge verb **1** slander. **2** spatter, splash (a person etc). **3** sprinkle, splash (a liquid etc). **4** fly or splash in all directions. **5** move clumsily through water, mud etc.

6 run wild, waste one's resources or talents heedlessly.

noun a splash, sprinkling, splodge of water, mud etc.

splash, splashack a plaice *N*.

splatch *noun* a splodge, blot, *eg* of something sticky, a patch of colour, dirt etc.

verb daub, splash.

splatter *verb* **1** scatter, splash, spatter. **2** blurt out, babble *now WCentral*. **3** spatter, daub, splash with liquid, mud etc. **4** splash noisily; walk or run with a clattering or rattling noise.

noun **1** a splashing, clattering or rattling sound; a commotion. **2** a splash of liquid, mud etc. **3** a thin sprinkling.

splay *sewing* finish a seam by hemming the upper edge down over the lower one.

spleet split.

spleeter a person who splits fish and removes the backbone.

spleet new brand-new *now Shetland Orkney N*.

spleiter, spleeter, spleyter [rhymes with 'tighter'] *noun* **1** a splash of spilt liquid, a blot *now NE*. **2** a wind-driven shower of rain, snow etc *now NE*.

verb spill, spatter messily over an area *NE*.

spleuchan, speuchan a (leather) pouch for tobacco or for money.

spleut the noise caused by a sudden spluttering gush; liquid shed or spilled in this way.

spleuter burst or gush out with a spluttering noise *NE*. **spleuterie 1** weak and watery *now NE*. **2** *of weather* wet, rainy.

spleyter *see* **spleiter**

splice a sliver of wood, splinter.

splicer an instrument for twisting straw ropes.

splinder *now Shetland Orkney* a splinter, fragment.

splinder new brand new.

splint new brand new.

split part (the hair).

split new brand new, as new as split wood.

splitter *noun* (the noise of) a splashing or splattering of liquid; a hubbub.

verb splutter, make a spluttering noise; make a mess by splashing liquid about.

splore 1 a party, spree, often with drinking. **2** a quarrel; a state of excitement or commotion, a fuss. **3** an exploit, escapade.

verb **1** make merry, have a good time. **2** show off, boast (about).

splunt *SW, S*, **sprunt** *mainly S* go wooing or courting.

splurt squirt, spit liquid from the mouth in a splash.

spoach *mainly S* [spoatch] **1** poach. **2** sponge, scrounge around for favours. **3** pry, rummage, poke about in.

spoon *see* **spune**

spoonge, spounge [-oo-] sponge.

spoot *see* **spout**

sporran a purse or pouch, especially the (ornamented) leather pouch worn in front of a man's kilt, used to hold money etc.

sporrow *see* **sparrow**

spoucher [spootcher] a (long-handled) wooden ladle or scoop, especially for baling a boat or lifting fish from a net.

spounge *see* **spoonge**

spout, spoot *noun* **1** a spout, a pipe. **2** a natural spring of water streaming from the ground or from a cleft in a rock; *latterly also* an outside tap. **3** a waterfall. **4** a narrow enclosed pathway; a gully in a cliff-face. **5** a horizontal roof gutter. **6** a razor-fish, a razor-clam. **7** a squirt, a toy (water-)gun, usually made from a plant stem. **8** a small quantity of liquid. **9** a rush, dart, sudden movement *now Shetland Caithness*.

verb **1** spout. **2** dart, spring, bound out suddenly.

spoutie *of soil* full of springs, marshy, undrained.

spout fish = **spout** 6. **spout gun** a popgun.

sprachle *see* **sprauchle**

sprack lively, alert *now Caithness*.

sprackle *see* **sprauchle**

sprag a brad (nail).

spraich, spraigh, sprauch, sprech [-ch, -gh as -ch in 'dreich'] *verb* cry shrilly, scream, shriek *now NE*.
noun a scream, cry, shriek; the sound of weeping or wailing.

spraikle *see* **spreckle**

spraing, †sprang a stripe, streak.

spraith *see* **spreath**

sprat, spret, sprit a coarse reedy rush or grass growing on marshy ground and sometimes used in rope-making and stack-thatching.

sprattle scramble, struggle, sprawl.

sprauch *see* **spraich**

sprauchle, sprachle, sprackle *verb* move laboriously or in a hasty, clumsy way (especially upwards), clamber; struggle (especially to get out of something), flounder about.
noun **1** a scramble, struggle. **2** a stunted feeble creature, a weakling *SW*.

sprawlach sprawl, flail about, flounder *NE*.

spread, spreid, spreed 1 spread. **2** spread butter etc on (a slice of bread etc). **3** turn the top covers of (a bed) down or up.

spreath [rhymes with 'faith'], **spraith, †spreach** [rhymes with 'laich'] **1** cattle; a herd (of cattle) stolen and driven off in a raid, especially by Highlanders; booty, plunder. **2** driftwood, wreckage from ships *now NE*.

sprech *see* **spraich**

spreckle, †spraikle a speckle, spot, freckle.
spreckled speckled, mottled, flecked.

spree, spry *adjective* **1** spry. **2** neat, smartly dressed.
verb smarten up.

spreed, spreid *see* **spread**

spreit *see* **speerit**

sprent spring (forward), run, sprint.

spret *see* **sprat**

sprig a (dance) tune, a snatch of song.

spriggit *see* **spicket**

spring *verb* burst, split *Shetland Orkney Caithness*.
noun **1** the rise, slope, height (of an arch). **2** a lively dance(-tune).

sprit *see* **sprat**

sprit-new brand new.

sprittled speckled, spotted *now S*.

sprool *noun, fishing* a short length of wire etc pushed through the sinker of a hand-line, with a hook attached at either end.
verb fish offshore with a **sprool.**

sprose, sprowse boast, swagger *WCentral*.

sproosh *see* **sprush**

sproot *see* **sprout**

sprot a rush, name for various reeds.

sproug *see* **sprug**

sprout, sproot *verb* **1** sprout. **2** rub or break off the sprouts of (potatoes) *Shetland Orkney N*.
noun **1** a sprout. **2** a child.

sprowse *see* **sprose**

sprug, sproug [-ow-], **spurdie, spurg, spur-gie** *NE* **1** a house- or hedge-sparrow. **2** a small (lively) person, a child.

sprunt *see* **splunt**

sprush, sproosh *adjective* **1** spruce. **2** brisk, smart in one's movements, spry.
noun **1** spruce (fir). **2** a smartening up, a tidying or setting in order. **3 sproosh** lemonade *NE*.

spry *see* **spree**

spue, spew *verb* **1** spew. **2** *of a* **pudding** burst, split open *Shetland NE*. **3** *of liquid, smoke etc* flow, pour (out etc), billow out.
noun **1** spew. **2** (a puff of) smoke *now Shetland Angus*. **3** a retch.
spuin fou full, especially with drink, to the point of vomiting.

spug, speug, spyug [sp(ee)**ug**] **1** *humorous or child's word* a house-sparrow. **2** a child, a small person etc.

spule *see* **spaul**

spulyie, spulzie, spulie [**spool**(y)ie] *verb* **1** rob, plunder (person or place). **2** (take (something) away from (someone) by stealing. **3** take as plunder, steal *now NE*. **4** plunder. **5** spoil, harm.

noun **1** the act of plundering. **2** booty, plunder. **3** jetsam, anything washed ashore *now Orkney*.

spune [rhymes with 'muin'], **spoon, speen** *NE* a spoon.

spune-gabbit having a thick lower lip that juts out. **spune meat** soft or liquid food eaten with a spoon.

have mair than what the spune pits in (the heid *etc*) be more than usually clever. **hae nothing but what the spune pits in (the heid** *etc*) be more stupid than usual. **mak a spune or spoil a horn** succeed or fail in a big way. **pit in one's spune** interfere in another's affairs.

spunedrift *see* **spindrift**

spung 1 a purse, pouch for money, often with a spring clasp. **2** a watch-pocket in trousers.

spunk 1 a spark (of fire), quick flicker of light, glimmer. **2** the least bit: *"spunk o sense"*. **3** a splinter, chip. **4** a match. **5** a tiny, poor, miserable fire.

verb spark (in all directions).

spunkie 1 = **spunk** *noun* 1, 5. **2** a will-o-the-wisp. **3** a lively young person.

spunk out *of news, scandal etc* leak out, become known. **spunk up 1** flare up in anger or passion. **2** cheer up.

spurdie, spurg, spurgie *see* **sprug**

spurl struggle, sprawl, kick.

spurtle, spirtle, spurkle 1 a short round stick for stirring porridge, soup etc. **2** *baking* a long-handled, flat-bladed implement for turning oatcakes, scones etc.

spurtle leg, spurtle shank a thin leg like a porridge stick.

spurtle *see* **spartle**

spyauck *see* **spaik**

spyog [speeog] a paw, hand, foot, or leg.

spyolk *see* **spelk**

spyug *see* **spug**

†**squabash** [squabash] silence (a person) by demolishing his arguments, pretensions etc, squash.

squaik, squeck, squak, squach, squaich [-ch as in 'dreich'] *of birds or trapped animals* squeal, squeak, screech, squawk.

squalloch [-a- as in 'cat'] *verb* scream, make a noise and disturbance *NE*.

noun the noise of children playing.

square, squar 1 a square. **2 the square** farm buildings, a farm, especially when forming the four sides of a square.

squatter [-a- as in 'cat'] *verb* **1** flutter in water like a duck, flap about in mud or water, splash along. **2** scatter about, waste.

noun a large number of small creatures or objects, a confused crowd.

squeak *humorous* a local newspaper.

squeck *see* **squaik**

squeeb 1 a squib. **2** contemptuous term for a person *NE*.

squeef contemptuous term for a person.

squeegee twisted, at the wrong angle, out of shape.

squeel *see* **schule**

squeenge *see* **scunge**

squeerie *see* **scurrie**

squeeter spatter, (cause to) fly in all directions *NE*.

squint off the straight, set at a slant, oblique.

squirk squirt out suddenly.

squirl *in writing* a flourish at the end of a letter; *in clothes etc* a piece of trimming, a flounce.

sta, stall, staw *noun* **1** a stall. **2 staw** a feeling of sickness or disgust caused *eg* by eating too much, often **get a sta. 3** an annoyance, nuisance; a pest, a bore.

verb **1** stall. **2** become sickened by food etc; become bored or fed up. **3** sicken or disgust with too much food. **4** tire, weary, bore.

sta *see* **steal**

stab *verb* a prickle, thorn, a piece of wood in the skin.

stab *see* **stob**

stab and rice *see* **rice**

stacher, staucher stagger, stumble.

staucherie unsteady in walking.

stack a tall column of rock rising out of the sea, separated from the cliffs by weathering *Shetland Orkney N*.

stack *see* **stick**[1]

stack rope *see* **stalk**

stad(d)le *see* **stathel**

staelt *see* **steal**

staff a walking-stick.

  ding in staves, fa in(to) staves smash or fall to pieces.

staig 1 a young horse of either sex, of one to three years old, not broken to work. **2** a stallion. **3** a young castrated horse, a gelding.

  staiger a groom who accompanies a stud-horse.

stainch *see* **stench**[1], **stench**[2]

stainchel, stanchel, stenchel [**stain**shel] **1** an iron bar, usually as part of a grating for a window etc. **2** a bar for securing a door or gate.

staincher [**stain**sher] an iron bar forming part of a window-grating.

stair 1 a staircase. **2** = **common stair** (*see* **common**).

  stairheid 1 the landing at the top of a flight of stairs or at the top of a **stair** 2. **2** used to describe something, *eg* a quarrel, which takes place on a **stairheid** among neighbours: "*stairheid rammy*".

stairt *see* **start**

stairve *see* **sterve**

stake a young ling *NE*.

  stake net a salmon-fishing net fixed on stakes in tidal waters.

stake and rice *see* **rice**

stakey *marbles* a game in which stakes are laid.

stale[1] a foundation of a stack.

stale[2] urine, especially that collected for making bleach or manuring.

stalk a chimney-stack.

  stalk raip, stack rope a rope passed through a ring on a stable manger, weighted at one end and tied to the horse's stall halter at the other.

  be ca'ed off the stalk *of the heart* be stopped by a sudden fright etc.

stall *see* **sta**

stam walk heavily, stamp along.

stamack, stomach the stomach.

  find the bottom o one's stamack feel ravenously hungry. **hae a good stamack** have a hearty appetite.

stamagast, stammygaster *noun* an unpleasant surprise, a shock *NE*.

  verb **1** surprise, shock, disappoint. **2** sicken, disgust.

stame *see* **steam**

stammer stumble, stagger.

stamp a trap for animals.

stan *see* **stand**

stance *noun* **1** a site, foundation; a building-site; a site for an open-air market, fair etc; a space for a single stand, side-show etc, a street-trader's pitch. **2** an overnight stopping-place for a drove of cattle. **3** a station terminus for buses etc, a place where public vehicles stand waiting for passengers: "*taxi stance*". **4** a stall etc for an animal in a stable.

  stanced placed on a certain spot; *of an animal* exhibited for sale at a market *NE*.

stanch *see* **stench**[1]

stanchel *see* **stainchel**

stand[1], **staun, stan** *verb* **1** stand. **2** *in calls to a horse* stop!, stand quiet!

  noun **1** a stand. **2** a stall or booth at a market etc. **3** a complete set or outfit *eg* of ropes, knitting needles.

  standing constant, permanent.

  stan-tae a set-to, a tussle. **stand to the wa** *of a door* be wide open.

stand[2], **staun** *noun* an upright tub, barrel etc.

standard Habbie *see* **habbie**

standart, standard, stannert 1 a standard. **2** an upright pole or post.

  standard-bearer the chief male participant in the Selkirk **Common Riding** (*see* **common**), who carries the **burgh** flag round the town's boundaries. **Standard Grade** applied to a certificate, examination or course (replacing the **O Grade** (*see* **ordinar**) in stages from 1984 on) awarded to all pupils in secondary schools at the end of the fourth year. **standard security** the form of **heritable** security which is now the only way of creating a security over land.

stane, stone, steen *Orkney N* **1** stone. **2** a testicle.

stondie, stoner a large brown earthenware marble. **stonie** a small coloured marble.

stane blind completely blind. **stane chack(art)** a stonechat; a wheatear. **stane chipper** a wheatear. **stane (k)napper** a person who breaks stones.

stanelock *see* **stenlock**

stang[1] *verb* **1** sting. **2** shoot with pain, throb, ache.

noun **1** a sting (of an insect etc). **2** something which hurts. **3** a sharp pain.

stang[2] **1** a pole, wooden bar or rod. **2** a spike, prong etc of metal.

the stang o the trump the best of the bunch *NE*.

stank 1 a pond, pool; a swampy place. **2** a ditch. **3** an obstacle, difficulty. **4** a street gutter.

doun the stank lost; *of money* squandered.

stankle a small temporary hay-rick.

stanlock *see* **stenlock**

stannert *see* **standart**

stap[1], **staup** *S* step.

stap[2], **stop 1** stop, block up, halt. **2** push, cram (in(to)). **3** stuff, pack with. **4** stuff oneself with food. **5** tuck bedclothes around (someone) *NE*.

stappit haddie a stuffed haddock *N*.

stap[3] a stave of a wooden cask or pail etc.

gae to staps fall to pieces.

stap-faither, stappy a step-father.

stapple[1] a stopple, stopper, plug, bung.

stapple[2] a bundle of straw used for thatching.

stapple[3] the stem of a (clay) tobacco-pipe.

star name for various kinds of grass growing on moor or boggy ground.

stark strong, sturdy; strongly made.

starn[1], **stern 1** a star. **2** a grain, a small amount.

the starn o the eye the pupil of the eye.

starn[2] the stern (of a boat etc).

start, stert, stairt *verb* **1** start. **2** startle, disturb.

noun **1** start, a leap, sudden movement. **2** a short time, a moment.

startle, stertle 1 startle. **2** rush about wildly, stampede.

starve *see* **sterve**

stashie, stushie, stishie an uproar, commotion, quarrel; a fuss, bother.

state a statement of facts or figures, *eg* in the pleas of a law-suit or in financial transactions etc.

stathel, stad(d)le 1 the foundation of a stack, built of stone etc. **2** the main part of a stack.

staucher *see* **stacher**

staun *see* **stand**[1], **stand**[2]

staunch *see* **stench**[2]

staup *see* **stap**[1]

stave *noun* a sprain or wrench of a joint. *verb* **1** thicken (iron) by heating and hammering. **2** sprain or bruise (a joint). **3** stagger, totter.

stavel, †stevel stumble.

staver stagger, stumble.

staves *see* **staff**

staw *see* **sta, steal**

stay *see* **stey**[1], **stey**[2]

stead, steadin(g) *see* **steid**

steady, steedie, studdie 1 steady. **2** continuously, all the time.

steal *verb, past tense also* **staw, sta, stule, stealt** *now NE,* **staelt** *Orkney NE. past participle also* **stow(e)n** *now Shetland NE,* **stealt** *now NE* steal.

steam, stame *NE* steam.

steamie a public wash-house. **steamin** very drunk.

stech, steigh, stoich [-ch, -gh as -ch in 'dreich'] *verb* **1** stuff with food. **2** fill with bad air or fumes, stink. **3** gasp, pant, puff.

noun **1** a gasp, a grunt. **2** a stuffy atmosphere, a fug. **3** smelly or dirty rubbish.

stechie stiff-jointed, slow-moving.

sted, steed *see* **steid**

steedie *see* **steady**

steek[1], **steik, steck** *now Shetland* **1 steek someone** *etc* **out** close a door on someone etc so as to keep him etc out. **2** close, shut, fasten.

steeker 1 a boot-lace. **2** the back-board of a cart. **steekit nieve** the clenched fist. **steek and hide** the game of hide-and-seek. **steek one's nieve on** keep quiet about; settle for (a price) *NE*.

steek[2], **stick** *verb* stitch, sew.

noun a stitch.

keep steek(s) wi keep pace with. **let doun a steek** make a mistake.

steel *see* **stuil**

†**steelbow** [**steel**boo, but now usually pronounced **steel**boa] a form of land-tenancy whereby a landlord provided the tenant with stock, grain, implements etc under contract that the equivalent should be returned at the end of the lease.

steen *see* **stane**

steenge a sharp pain.

steepend *see* **stipend**

steepid *see* **stupit**

steer 1 stir. **2** disturb, pester. **3** plough, especially for a second time in a year. **4** start off on a journey, set out.

noun a stir, movement, bustle.

steerie lively, bustling, busy. **steering** active, restless, lively; full of activity or commotion.

cauld steer(ie) oatmeal stirred in cold water.

steet *see* **stuit**

steeth *see* **steid**

steeve *see* **stieve, stive**

steg[1] a hold-up of work in a factory *WCentral*.

steg[2] walk with long heavy steps, stride.

steich *see* **stey**[1]

steid, stead, steed, sted, steeth *Shetland Orkney Caithness noun* **1** stead. **2** a site, foundation, base. **3** a **steading** (*noun* 1).

4 a mark, a track *now SW*. **5** profit, service.

verb **1** place. **2** make the base of (*eg* a peat-stack or building) *Shetland Orkney*.

steadin(g) 1 the buildings on a farm, sometimes but not always including the farmhouse. **2** a building site; the site of the buildings on a farm.

steigh *see* **stech**

steik *see* **steek**[1]

stell[1] *verb* **1** place in position, set up. **2** steady (oneself or one's feet) by planting the feet against something firm. **3** keep (the eyes) rigid, fix (the eyes). **4** halt, stop.

noun **1** a place in a river over which nets are drawn to catch salmon. **2** an open enclosure for sheep on a hillside. **3** a clump of trees used as a shelter for sheep. **4** *mining* a prop for underpinning a roof.

stell[2] a still (for whisky).

stell[3] go with a firm, purposeful step, stride.

stellionate *law* a crime for which there is no specific name, *eg* a kind of fraud in which the same right is granted to two or more different people.

stem the peak of a cap.

stench[1], **stanch, stainch 1** stanch, check the flow of. **2** satisfy with food.

stench[2], **staunch, stainch, stinch 1** staunch. **2** serious, severe-looking, rigid *now NE*. **3** strong, firm; in good health.

stenchel *see* **stainchel**

stend, sten *verb* **1** leap, spring up. **2** *of animals* rear, start. **3** stride, walk or march purposefully *now Shetland*.

noun **1** a leap, spring, bound. **2** a long firm bouncing step, a stride. **3** †a sudden start, a thrill of excitement, fear etc.

stenlock, stan(e)lock a coalfish *now WCentral*.

stent[1], **stint** *verb* **1** stretch out (a sail, net etc); pitch (a tent); make taut. **2** exert oneself, make an effort.

stenter a clothes prop. **stenting post** a strainer in a wire fence.

†**stent²**, **stint** a tax, especially on land held of the king.

stent³ *noun* **1** the limit to which one is prepared to go. **2** the proportion of pasture in a common allocated to each tenant. **3** an amount of work to be covered in a given time.

verb **1** limit, check; stint. **2** give an amount of work to (a person); make (a person) work hard.

step 1 a patch (of road). **2** a stepping-stone in a river.

tak a step walk, make a short journey.

stern *see* **starn¹**

stert *see* **start**

stertle *see* **startle**

sterve, stairve, starve 1 starve. **2 sterve wi cauld** feel chilled.

stevel *see* **stavel**

stew, stue, steuch [-ch as in 'dreich'] *noun* **1** (a cloud of) dust. **2** an uproar; trouble. **3** a stench; a suffocating cloud. **4** a coating or sprinkling of dust or powder.

verb stick, cause a stench.

stey¹, stay, sty [rhymes with 'gey'], **steich** [rhymes with 'dreich'] *of a hill, road etc* (very) steep; difficult to climb.

set a stout heart to a stey brae face difficulties with courage and determination.

stey², stay [rhymes with 'gey'] **1** stay, stop. **2** live, dwell, reside.

stey³ [rhymes with 'gey'] a stay, support.

steyband a crossbar of a door; a bar to fasten a double door from the inside.

stibble stubble.

†**stibbler 1** a harvest-worker who gathers up odd straws. **2** a **probationer** (*see* **probation**) in the Presbyterian church who preaches here and there as required.

stibble butter high-quality butter made from the milk of cows grazed on stubbles.

stichle [-ch- as in 'dreich'] rustle, stir, bus-

tle *now NE*.

stick¹ *verb, past tense also* **stack** *now NE,* **stickit.** *past participle also* **stucken 1** stick. **2** stab, thrust a knife into, finish off. **3** *of a horned animal* gore, stab or butt with its horns. **4** stop in the middle of (a job etc).

stickers goose-grass. **stickin** stiff in manner, obstinate. **stickit 1** *of a task etc* left spoilt or unfinished. **2** *of people* failed, insufficiently qualified: *"stickit minister"*. **3** *of plants* stunted, checked in growth. **sticky-fingered** apt to steal. **sticky-Willie** goose-grass.

stick in work hard, go energetically (at). **stick up to 1** pay court to. **2** stand up to.

stick² wooden, made of timber.

nae great sticks at not very good at *Shetland NE.*

stick *see* **steek²**

stiddie *see* **studdie**

stieve, steeve, stive 1 firmly fixed, rigid, stiff. **2** firm, strong, sturdy. **3** steady, loyal, dependable. **4** hard-hearted, obstinate. **5** shrewd in business, slightly mean. **6** *of a struggle* hard, grim. **7** *of a road* difficult, steep and rough. **8** *of food or drink* strong, full of body.

stife a suffocating atmosphere, smoke *now S.*

stiff: stiffen starch (clothes). **stiffing, stiffening** starch.

still, stull *adjective* **1** still. **2** reserved, not saying much.

verb **1** still, (become) quiet. **2** remain quiet and silent *now Shetland.*

still and on 1 yet, nevertheless. **2** always, continuously.

stilp *now NE* walk with long stiff steps, stump about.

stilpert *noun* **1** a stilt. **2** a tall lanky person or animal. *verb* walk with long stiff strides.

stilt *noun* **1** one of the handles of a plough. **2** a crutch.

verb **1** go on stilts or crutches. **2** walk

stiffly, haltingly.

stime, styme 1 a tiny amount, particle, jot. **2** a glimmer or glimpse of light.

stimpart 1 a dry measure, the fourth part of a **peck** (see p 358). **2** a measure of land, the fourth part of a **rig**¹.

stinch *see* **stench**²

sting a pole, *eg* **1** used to push off a boat; **2** †one carried on the shoulders of two men, with a load hung from it. **3** †used by thatchers to push straw into the roof.

stink fill (a place) or affect (a person) with a bad smell.

stinking haughty, snobbish, supercilious. **stinking Billy** sweet william. **stinkin Willie** ragwort.

stint stop, halt *now NE*.

stint *see* **stent**¹, **stent**²

stipend, steepend the salary of a Presbyterian minister.

stippit *see* **stupit**

stirk, stırk 1 a young bullock or (sometimes) heifer kept for slaughter at the age of two or three. **2** a stupid idiot. **3** a sturdy young man.

be (putten) in the stirkie's sta *of a child* lose some of its parents' attention after the birth of a new baby.

stirlin(g) a starling.

stirrah 1 a (sturdy) young lad. **2** contemptuous term for a man; a rough unmannerly youth *now S*.

stishie *see* **stashie**

stive, steeve stuff, pack, cram with food.

stive *see* **stieve**

St Johnstone, St Johnsto(u)n, St Mirran *see* **saint**

stob *noun* **1** *also* **stab** a stake, a (fence) post. **2** a short thick nail. **3** a stout thickset man. **4** a prickle, a thorn; a splinter in the skin. **5** a bradawl. **6** a Y-shaped stick used in thatching.
verb **1** prick or jab with a pointed object *now NE*. **2** *also* **stab** fence with stakes, mark with posts. **3** prop up (plants) with stakes. **4** thatch with **stobs** (*noun* 6). **5** trim (a stack) with a hay-

fork *Orkney NE*.

stobby rough and spiky, prickly, bristly.

stock¹ *noun* **1** a block of wood, log; a tree-stump. **2** the hard stalk of a plant, especially of a cabbage etc; the whole plant. **3** the rail of a bed, the side of a bed away from the wall. **4** a chap, bloke, creature *now NE*.
verb **1** *of the body* become stiff or cramped. **2** *of plants* send out shoots, sprout *now N*.

stocking the livestock and gear needed to run a farm. **stockit** obstinate, stubborn *NE*.

†**stock**² a kind of (clarinet-type) wind instrument.

stockin(g) a stocking used to store one's savings.

stocking needle a darning needle.

stodge walk with a long slow step, stump.

stog *see* **stug**¹, **stug**²

stoich *see* **stech**

stoit, styte *verb* **1** bounce. **2** stagger from drink etc. **3** walk in a casual easy way, saunter *NE*.
noun **1** a buffet, blow. **2** a stagger, tottering step *now NE*. **3** a stupid, clumsy person. **4** foolish talk, nonsense *now Orkney Caithness NE*.

stoiter 1 walk unsteadily, totter. **2** stumble or falter in speech.

stole *see* **stuil**

stolum a pen-nibful of ink *now N*.

stomach *see* **stamack**

stondie, stone *see* **stane**

stoo, stow [rhymes with 'moo'] **1** cut (off) (an animal's tail or part of its ear as a mark of ownership). **2** cut off (the stem or shoots of a plant or tree) *now Shetland NE*.

stook 1 a shock of cut leaves, set up to dry in a field. **2** a bundle (of straw).

stookie *noun* **1** stucco, plaster of Paris; a plaster-cast for a broken limb. **2** pipeclay. **3** a stucco figure. **4** a slow-witted, dull, or shy person. **5** **stookies** a children's game in which the players try to remain motionless as long as possible.

stookie eemage *etc* a plaster statue.

stand like a stookie stand as if unable to move.

stookit having short upright horns; peaked, crested.

stool *see* **stuil**

stoon(d) *see* **stoun(d)**^{1}, **stoun(d)**^{2}

stoop *see* **stowp**

stoop and roop *see* **stoup and roup**

stoopit *see* **stupit**

stoor *see* **stour, sture**^{1}

stoot *see* **stout, stuit, stut**

stoothe make or cover (a wall etc) with lath and plaster *SW, S.*

stop *see* **stap**^{2}

store: the store the Co-op, popular name for a Co-operative Society shop.

not store the kin not survive, not last out.

storm fallen snow, especially lying for a long time; a period of wintry weather. **storm cock** the missel-thrush. **storm window** a dormer window.

story *see* **torie**

stot^1 **1** a bullock. **2** a stupid clumsy person.

stot^2 *verb* **1** bounce; jump up; walk with a springy or stately step; bound, go by leaps. **2** stagger, walk unsteadily. **3** stutter, stammer.

noun **1** a bounce, a spring, hop in a dance. **2** a sharp blow. **3** a sudden movement, a stumble, stagger *now Shetland.* **4 the stots** a fit of the sulks *now Shetland.* **5** the beat of a tune, rhythm (of speech or dance). **6** the events in a story, the thread of a speech etc. **7** a stroll, saunter *now NE.* **8** a stammer, stutter, speech impediment *now Orkney.*

stotter 1 stagger, stumble. **2** *term of admiration for women* a smasher.

aff the stots out of the rhythm; off one's stride; off the mark.

stoun(d)^1 [-oo-], **stoon(d)** *noun* **1** a period of time, a while. **2** a sharp throb of pain; an ache. **3** a pang of mental pain

or emotion, a thrill of pleasure or excitement. **4** a mood, a fit of depression etc.

verb throb, ache, smart.

stoun(d)^2 [-oo-], **stoon(d)** *verb* **1** stun, stupefy. **2** resound, ring with *now Angus.*

noun **1** a stunning blow. **2** a stupefying din *now Angus.* **3** a stunned state.

stoup, stoop 1 a wooden post, prop, *eg* a table-leg, gatepost. **2** the end of the under-rail of a farm cart; the handle of a plough. **3** *mining* a pillar of coal left to support the roof of the working. **4** a loyal supporter, a pillar: *"a stoup o the Kirk".*

stoup-and-room pillar-and-stall, a method of working coal by leaving pillars of coal to support the roof.

stoup *see* **stowp**

stoup and roup, stoop and roop completely, absolutely.

stour [-oo-], **stoor** *noun* **1** strife, conflict, battle. **2** commotion, fuss, disturbance. **3** a storm, wild weather; a blizzard *now Shetland Orkney.* **4** dust in motion, flying, swirling dust; (a layer of) dust; any fine powdery substance, especially produced by grinding etc. **5** a (cloud of) fine spray. **6** a pouring out of liquid *now NE.*

verb **1** run, rush (on), bustle (about). **2** *of dust, spray etc* swirl, rise in a cloud. **3** spray with dust etc. **4** gush out in a strong stream.

stourie *now Orkney*, **stoorin** *NE noun* a kind of liquid fine-oatmeal gruel.

adjective **1** dusty. **2** *especially of a young child* active, restless.

like stour like a whirl of dust, with a rush.

stour *see* **sture**^{1}

stoussie [stoossie] a plump sturdy little child.

stout, stoot 1 stout. **2** in good health, robust. *See also* **stey**^{1}.

stoutherie [stootherie] theft; stolen goods; gear.

stove *cooking* a stew.

verb **1** *cooking* stew. **2** steam; *of smoke* billow out in clouds; *of people* reek with alcoholic fumes.

stovies, stoved tatties dish of stewed potatoes, onions etc, sometimes with small pieces of meat etc.

stow [rhymes with 'cow'] fill (the stomach) with food.

stow *see* **stoo**

stow(e)n *see* **steal**

stowff [-ow- as in 'cow'] walk with a slow dull heavy step *NE*.

stow(n)lins [-ow- as in 'cow'] in a hidden or secretive way.

stowp, stoup [-ow-] **1** a wooden pail, especially one for carrying water from a well. **2** a tankard, decanter, mug etc: *"a pint stoup"*. **3** a (milk or cream) jug *now NE*.

stoy[1] a cork float marking the position of fishing-lines or crab-traps *now NE*.

stoy[2] saunter, stroll *now NE*.

strab a stalk of corn missed by the reaper; any odd or loose straw *NE*.

strabush *see* **stramash**

strachle, strauchle 1 move or walk with difficulty, struggle *SW*. **2** straggle, grow in a loose untidy way.

stracht *see* **straucht**

strae, straw, stray *noun* straw.
verb supply with straw.
straw crook a rope-twister, **thrawcruik** (*see* **thraw**). **strae death** natural death (in one's bed). **strae mouse** a shrew.

strag 1 a thin, straggly crop; thin wispy hair. **2** a roaming person; a loose woman. **3** a stray pigeon.

straik, strake, strak *noun* **1** a stroke, a blow etc. **2** the motion or marks of a harrow; the ground covered by one journey of a harrow. **3** a stroking, caressing movement of the hand. **4** a stripe of colour, ray of light etc. **5** a small amount. **6** a rounded stick with one straight edge for levelling, *eg* corn in a measure. **7** a tool for sharpening scythes etc. **8** a (long, narrow) tract of land or water; a sheep-walk. **9** a

journey, long walk.
verb **1** stroke. **2** harrow (a piece of ground). **3** smear, sprinkle, spread, streak. **4** streak, mark with streaks of a different colour. **5** level off (grain etc) in a measure. **6** fill (a road etc) with snow up to its fences etc. **7** sharpen (a scythe etc) with a **straik**. **8** stretch. **9** lay out (a corpse).

straik *see* **strik**

strait, stret *now NE* **1** strait, narrow; strict. **2** tight, close-fitting. **3** tense, taut, rigid; full to bursting. **4** *of mountains etc, of a bargain* steep.

straiten tighten (a knot etc) *Shetland NE*.

strak *see* **straik, strik**

strake *see* **straik**

stramash [stramash], **strabush** [strabush] *Fife* **1** an uproar, commotion, row. **2** a state of great excitement or rage *now Shetland Caithness*. **3** a smash, crash, accident, disaster. **4** a state of ruin.

stramlach *NE* [stramlach] **1** something long and trailing. **2** a tall, lanky person.

stramp stamp, tread, trample (on); stump about.

strand[1] a beach or shore of the sea; a sandbank etc exposed at low water *now Orkney Caithness*.

strand[2], **straun 1** a little stream. **2** an artificial water-channel, a (street-)gutter.

strang *adjective, adverb* strong.
noun urine which has been allowed to stand for some time, used as a bleach or in making manure *now Shetland Orkney N*.

strange, strynge 1 strange. **2** aloof; *especially of children* shy, self-conscious.
stranger anything thought to foretell the arrival of an unexpected visitor, *eg* a tea-leaf on the surface of a cup of tea.

strap, strop *noun* **1** a strap, a strip of leather etc. **2** a string or bunch of objects linked together; a cluster of berries, especially currants *now S*. **3** the band of corn-stalks used to tie up a sheaf at harvest *SW*. **4** a strip of wood to which something else may be nailed. **5** black treacle, molasses.

verb **1** fix strips of wood on (a wall) as a base for lath, skirting etc. **2** *only* **strap** groom (a horse).

strath a river valley, especially when broad and flat.

strathspey a kind of dance, slower than a **reel**; a tune for such.

Strathclyde (Region) a **region** formed from the former counties of the City of Glasgow, Bute, Dunbarton, Lanark, Renfrew and Ayr and parts of the former counties of Argyll and Stirling.

strauchle *see* **strachle**

straucht, straught, stracht, strecht [-ch-, -gh- as -ch in 'loch'] *adjective* straight. *adverb* **1** straight. **2** immediately, without delay.

verb **1** stretch. **2** straighten; smooth, set to rights. **3** lay out (a corpse) by straightening the limbs *now NE*.

strauchten straighten the limbs of, lay out (a corpse).

straun *see* **strand**²

stravaig, stravague [stravaig] *verb* **1** roam, wander aimlessly. **2** go up and down (a place).

noun a roaming about, a stroll.

strave *see* **strive**

straw strew, scatter, sprinkle.

straw, stray *see* **strae**

streak *see* **streek**¹

streamer 1 streamers the aurora borealis, northern lights. **2** a male minnow near spawning time.

strecht *see* **straucht**

streck *see* **strik**

streek¹, **streik, streak** *verb* **1** stretch. **2** lay out (a corpse). **3** put (a plough etc) into action; start work, get going *now NE*. **4** question closely. **5** reach out, be stretched out. **6** hurry; go at full speed.

noun **1** a stretch. **2** a continuous extent of time or space, a spell.

streeker a very tall thin person *now NE*.

streekin tall and agile *S*. **streekin buird** the board on which a corpse is laid out for burial *now NE*.

streek²: **streek o day** daybreak, the first light of day.

streel *see* **strule**

streen strain.

streen *see* **yestreen**

street: on the street(s) 1 in the street, out-of-doors. **2** roaming the streets; homeless, down-and-out.

streetch 1 stretch. **2** stretch the legs, take exercise by walking or dancing.

stretcher a clothes-prop.

streeve *see* **strive**

streik *see* **streek**¹

strenth strength.

stress overwork, fatigue.

stret *see* **strait**

strib *see* **strip**²

strick¹ strict.

strick² *of running water* rapid, swift-flowing.

stricken *see* **strik**

striddle *verb* **1** straddle. **2** walk with long steps, stride, step out.

noun the spreading of the legs in walking etc; a wide stride or pace.

strideleg(s) astride.

stridlins astride, with the legs apart.

striffin a thin skin; a long thin strip *now Shetland Orkney Caithness*.

strik, strike, †streck *verb, past tense also* **strak** *now NE*, **straik, strook.** *past participle also* **stricken, strucken 1** strike. **2** *of fish* become enmeshed in a net.

noun a disease of sheep caused by maggots.

strucken hour a whole hour by the clock, a long boring time.

strind, strynd [rhymes with 'mind'] descent; inherited qualities.

strin(d) [rhymes with 'pin(ned)] **1** a very small stream; a trickle. **2** the jet of milk from a cow's teat *NE*.

string a section of a fishing-line.

strinkle scatter, sprinkle.

strintle sprinkle, scatter, spurt; trickle

now Caithness.

strip¹ 1 a stripe, a long thin line of colour, light etc. **2** a long narrow belt of trees. **3** a young fellow, a youth. **4** a single journey of harrows over a ploughed field.

    strippit ba a round peppermint **sweetie** with black and white stripes.

strip² 1 *also* **strib** squeeze the last drops of milk from (a cow).

    strippin(g)s the last milk drawn off at a milking; the pickings, gleanings.

stripe¹, strype 1 a small stream. **2** a street gutter.

stripe², strype pull, or draw (an object, *eg* between the fingers to wipe it).

strive *verb, past tense also* **strave, streeve** *now NE* **1** quarrel, dispute; take a dislike (to) *now Shetland NE.* **2** scatter coins or sweets at a wedding for children to scramble for *S.*

    striven having quarrelled.

strod, strodge stride or strut along *S.*

strone, stroan 1 *often of dogs* urinate. **2** *of water etc* spout, spurt, gush.

strook *see* **strik**

stroonge *see* **strounge**

stroop *see* **stroup**

stroosh *see* **strush**

strop *see* **strap**

strounge [-oo-], **stroonge, strunge 1** harsh to the taste, bitter. **2** *of people* gruff, sullen.

stroup [-oo-], **stroop 1** the spout or mouth of a kettle, jug, pump etc. **2** the spout or outlet of a spring or well, a water-tap.

    stroupach, stroupan a drink of tea *Highland.* **stroupie** a teapot *now Shetland.*

strow¹ [rhymes with 'cow'] *verb* strew.

    noun struggle, quarrel; a commotion.

strow² [rhymes with 'cow'] a shrew *SW.*

strowd *NE* [-ow- as in 'cow'] **1** a popular, often nonsensical song, a street ballad. **2** a piece of nonsense.

strucken *see* **strik**

struissle, strussel a struggle; a hard or demanding task.

strule, streel a stream.

strum¹ a bad mood; the huff: *"tak the strum(s)."*

strum² *mining* the fuse of a shot or explosive charge.

strunge *see* **strounge**

strunt¹ *noun* a huff, the sulks: *"tak the strunt(s)."*

    verb offend, sulk.

strunt² strut, walk about in an affected way.

†strunt³ spirits, especially whisky, toddy.

strush, stroosh 1 a disturbance, squabble; a commotion. **2** a bustling, swaggering walk *Caithness.*

    strushlie untidy, slovenly *NE.*

strussel *see* **struissle**

strynd *see* **strind**

strynge *see* **strange**

strype *see* **stripe¹, stripe²**

stucken *see* **stick¹**

stuckie, stushie a starling.

stuckin a stake.

studdie, stiddie a stithy, an anvil.

studdie *see* **steady**

stue *see* **stew**

stuff 1 provisions, a store of food. **2** corn, grain, a crop.

    stuffie *NE* **1** in good health, sturdy, full of vigour. **2** spirited, plucky, game. **the stuffie** whisky.

stug¹, stog 1 stab, prick, jab. **2** dress (stone) roughly with a pointed chisel.

    noun a prick, stab with some pointed object; such an object, a dart.

stug², stog *noun* **1** a jagged or uneven cut, anything left rough by careless cutting. **2** a stocky, coarsely-built, clumsy person or animal.

    verb **1** cut roughly or unevenly. **2** walk heavily, plod, stump.

stuil, stool, stole, steel *NE noun* **1** a stool; *see also* **repent.** **2** a bench, counter, trestle. **3** a tree-stump; a new shoot rising from a group of such stumps after cutting. **4** a stall (as in finger-stall, head-stall).

stuir a penny *now Shetland*.

stuit, stoot, steet *N* prop, support.

stule *see* **steal**

stull *see* **still**

stummer stumble, stagger *now Orkney*.

stump 1 the core of an apple, what is left after the flesh has been eaten. **2** a short stocky person or animal; a stiff, slow-moving person *now Shetland*. **3** a stupid person *now S*.

stumpart walk heavily, clumsily *NE*. **stumparts** legs *NE*. **stumper** walk clumsily, heavily *NE*. **stumpie 1** the stump of something, *eg* of a quill pen. **2** a short, stocky or dumpy person. **stumpit** short, stunted; stocky, dumpy. **stump and rump** completely, absolutely.

stunk sulk, go into a huff *NE*.

stunks the stake in a game of marbles; the game itself.

stunkard sulky, surly, obstinate.

stunt bounce, walk with a springy step.

stupe [-u- as in 'stupid' or like -ui- in 'guid'] a fool, stupid person.

stupit, stippit, stoopit, steepid *NE* stupid.

sturdy *adjective* giddy-headed *now Shetland Caithness*.

noun **1** a brain disease in sheep, causing giddiness, staggering and collapse. **2** a fit of sulks: *"tak the sturdies"*.

sture, stour, stoor [rhymes with 'puir' or 'moor'] **1** big, stout, burly *now Shetland*. **2** strong, sturdy *now Shetland*. **3** rough in manner or appearance; grim, stern; hard, determined *now S*. **4** *of a sound* deep and hoarse, harsh, rough.

sturk *see* **stirk**

sturken recover one's strength.

sturt *noun* strife, trouble, annoyance.
verb trouble, disturb, annoy.

stushie *see* **stashie, stuckie**

stut, †stoot stutter, stammer.

sty *see* **stey**[1]

style *law* the approved form or model for drawing up a legal document.

styme *see* **stime**

styte *see* **stoit**

subject *law* a piece of **heritable** property, *eg* a piece of land, a house.

submission *law* a contract, or the document embodying it, by which parties in a dispute agree to submit the matter to arbitration.

substitute *law, noun* a beneficiary who will take a gift of property after the death of the first beneficiary.
adjective †nominated to act in place of another, as a deputy; nominated to replace a predeceasing person in an inheritance. *See also* **sheriff.**

substract, subtrack subtract.

succar, sucker, sugar, shuggar sugar.

sugarallie liquorice, especially when made up as a **sweetie**; a stick etc of liquorice. **sugarallie hat** a top hat. **sugarallie water** a children's drink made by dissolving a piece of liquorice in water. **sugar bool, sugardoddle** a round, striped boiled **sweetie**. **sugar piece** a slice of bread buttered and sprinkled with sugar.

such *see* **sic**

suck *see* **souk**

†sucken an obligation on tenants on an estate to use a certain mill; the payment due for the use of the mill; the lands of an estate on which there was a **sucken**.

sucker *see* **succar**

suckler 1 *of farm animals* a suckling; a cow giving suck. **2 sucklers** the flowerheads of clover.

sud *see* **sall**

suddenty suddenness: **on a suddenty** all of a sudden *now N*.

suddle dirty, soil.

suddren wud *see* **south**[1]

sue *see* **shew**

sufficient *of things* substantial, solid, of good enough strength or quality.

sufflet *see* **souflet**

sugar *see* **succar**

sugg a fat, easy-going person *Orkney NE*.

sugh *see* **souch**

suin *see* **sune**

suit, seet *NE,* **sit** *NE,* **shute** soot.
> **Auld Suitie** nickname for the Devil.
> **suit drap** a flake of soot, especially when hanging from a ceiling.

suith, sooth, †**sieth** *(NE)* sooth.
> **(by) my suith** upon my word, to tell the truth.

suld *see* **sall**

sum *see* **some, soum**[1]

summar roll *law* a roll of cases which require speedy disposal, going before the **Inner House** of the **Court of Session** (*see* **session**).

summary *law* applied to procedures which dispense with the full formalities of the law.

summer *see* **simmer**[1]

summons *noun, law* the document whereby a **pursuer** (*see* **pursue**) raises a **Court of Session** (*see* **session**) action or a **Sheriff Court** (*see* **sheriff**) summary cause.
> *verb* take out a **summons** against, especially in actions of removal from a tenancy.

sumph *noun* **1** a stupid, slow-witted person. **2** a surly, sullen, sulky person.
> *verb* act like a **sumph**; sulk, be sullen

sun, sin the sun.
> **sun blink** a gleam of sunshine. **sun broch** a halo round the sun. **sungates** *now Shetland,* **sunways** following the sun, from east to west. **sun side** the side of a place facing the sun, the south side.

Sunday: Sunday blacks the black suit formerly always worn by men for attending church on Sunday. **Sunday('s) claes** one's church-going clothes, one's best clothes. **Sunday('s) face** a (very) solemn, somewhat sanctimonious look. **Sunday Monday** name of a ball game *NE.* **Sunday name** one's formal first name, as opposed to a familiar form of it. **Sunday strae** an extra amount of straw threshed to tide the animals over the weekend and so avoid threshing on Sunday *Shetland Orkney NE.*

sundry *see* **sinder**

sune, soon, suin, seen *NE,* **sin, shune, shin, sheen** *Caithness* [-u-, -ui- as -ui- in 'guid'] **1** soon. **2** early, before it is late.
> **sune as syne** sooner rather than later, soon for preference. **sune or syne** sooner or later.S

sung *see* **sing**[2]

sunk, †**sonk 1** a turf seat, a kind of sofa made of layers of sods, often at a fireside or against a sunny gable. **2** an overweight person, with a sack-like figure.
> **sunkie** a little bench or stool, *eg* a milking-stool *S.*

sunkets eatables, especially titbits or delicacies.

sup *noun* **1** a mouthful, enough to satisfy for the time being; a drink: *"a sup tea".* **2** a quantity, amount (of other liquids, especially rain).
> **suppable** fit to be supped, eatable. **suppin sowans: sowans** thick enough to eat with a spoon.

superannuate mentally deranged, senile; stupefied, dazed.

superior *law* a person who has made a grant of land in feu to a **vassal** in return for a **feu duty** (*see* **feu**) or (formerly) for the performance of certain services.

supersede *law* postpone, defer, put off.

supper, †**sipper** *noun* **1** supper. **2** the last meal of the day given to an animal.
> *verb* **1** give (an animal) its last meal of the day. **2** do for the supper of.
> **fish-supper** fish-and-chips especially when bought from a fish-and-chip shop. **pudding-supper** a **pudding** and chips, especially when bought from a fish-and-chip shop.

supple *see* **soople, souple**

supply assistance, support, giving food etc to someone in need.

suppose if, even if, although: *"I wadna tell you suppose I kent."*

surcoat a kind of undershirt or waistcoat; a fisherman's jersey *now NE.*

sure assure, tell (a person) for certain *NE:* *"I sure ye."*

surree, swaree a soiree, a social gathering, especially one organized by a church, Sunday school etc.

surrogatum [surroga**y**tum] *law* something which stands in the place of another, *eg* the price of a thing instead of the thing itself.

suspend *law, of a court* defer or stay (execution of a sentence etc) until the case has been reviewed; *a litigant or convicted person* ask for **suspension** as a form of appeal.

suspension *law* a warrant for stay of execution of a **decree** or sentence until the matter can be reviewed, used when ordinary appeal is incompetent.

sussie, sizzie care, trouble, bother, often in dealing with a drunk person.

sut *see* **sit, sot**

sutten *see* **sit**

sutter *see* **souter**

swa *see* **sae**²

swab [rhymes with 'stab'] a pea- or bean-pod *S, SW*.

swabble *S* [rhymes with 'rabble'] *verb* beat, thrash.
noun a long supple stick; a tall thin person.

swack¹ **1** (the sound made by) a heavy blow or fall; a sudden or powerful movement. **2** a big mouthful.

swack² **1** soft, moist and easily moulded; *of cheese* not crumbly *N*. **2** easily bent or stretched *N*. **3** active, supple.
swacken make or become soft and supple, loosen *Shetland Orkney N*.

Swade, Swad 1 a Swede *NE*. **2 swade, swad** a swede, the variety of turnip.

swag *verb* sway from side to side, wag to and fro; hang down heavily.
noun **1** (the act of) swinging or swaying. **2** a quantity of liquid, a long drink *now Shetland Orkney*.

swage 1 [swadge] subside, settle down, shrink. **2** take in and digest (food) *Shetland Caithness*. **3** relax after a good meal.

swail, swell, swyle a wet hollow, a boggy place *now NE*.

swaips *noun* a slanting direction, a slope.
adjective slanting or sloping.
verb, of a road rise or descend at a slant.

swaird a sward.

swall [rhymes with 'pal'] swell.

swalla [-a- as in 'cat'], **swallow 1** a swallow, the bird. **2** a martin.

swallie [rhymes with 'pally'] swallow.

swamp [rhymes with 'lamp'] *especially of a formerly plump person* thin.

swander [rhymes with 'gander'] become giddy or faint; reel about, stagger; hesitate.

swang *see* **swing**

swank agile, strong; *especially of a young man* smart, well set-up.
swankie adjective = **swank.** *noun* a smart, active, strapping young man.

swap¹ [rhymes with 'cap'] *verb* **1** strike, hit *now Shetland*. **2** move briskly or forcibly, fling *now Shetland*. **3** brandish (a weapon), make a swipe with (a sword etc), wave about *now Shetland*. **4** fold or wind (a rope, strip of cloth etc) over on itself, criss-cross *Shetland NE*. **5** rope (a stack) *NE*. **6** swirl, swing, move violently. **7** exhcange, barter.
noun **1** a blow, stroke, slap *Shetland*. **2** an exchange, a give-and-take. **3** a sudden gust of wind *Shetland Orkney Caithness*.

swap² [rhymes with 'cap'] *noun, also* **swype** the face or a feature of it, especially as it resembles someone in one's family.
verb resemble in appearance, show a family likeness to.

swap³ [rhymes with 'cap'] the shell or pod of peas or beans before they begin to swell; the peas or beans themselves.

sware *see* **sweer, swire**

swaree *see* **surree**

swarf, [rhymes with 'scarf'], †**swerf** *verb* **1** faint *now Shetland*. **2** cause to faint; stupefy.

swarrach [-ch as in 'loch'] a crowd, swarm (especially of young children in a family) *NE*.

swash [rhymes with 'mash'] *verb* **1** dash down, cast against the ground; slash; beat. **2** dash or splash (liquid) about or over *now Shetland Orkney*. **3** swagger, show off *now NE*.

noun **1** a splash or plunge in water; a dash of water, the wash of waves against something *now Shetland Orkney*. **2** a large amount, *eg* of food. **3** affected, showy behaviour; a swagger; a strutting, haughty manner.

swat *see* **sweet**[1]

swatch [rhymes with 'match'] **1** a typical piece, example, selection etc. **2** a similarity, a feature in common. **3** a glimpse, a partial view. **4** a short spell, turn.

tak (a) swatch o take a critical look at, scrutinize. **tak the swatch o** take the measure of, be a match for *NE*.

swats [rhymes with 'cats'] **1** newly-brewed weak beer; a substitute for this, made of molasses, water and yeast. **2** the liquor resulting from the steeping of oatmeal husks in the making of **sowans** *Shetland Orkney N*.

swatter [rhymes with 'batter'] *verb* flutter and splash in water, flounder about.

noun a large collection or crowd, especially of small creatures, a swarm *now NE*.

swaver *verb* totter, sway, move unsteadily *Shetland Orkney NE*.

noun a bending to one side, a lurch, stagger *NE*.

swaw ripple.

sway a swathe, a row of cuts of grass made by a scythe.

sway *see* **swey**

sweamish squeamish.

swear *see* **sweir**

sweat *see* **sweet**[1]

swedge a tool for making the grooves and nail-holes in a horseshoe.

swee *see* **swey**

sweek *see* **swick**

sweel[1], **sweil**, **swill** *verb* **1** swill. **2** wash

(the throat) down with liquor. **3** wash away; wash (food) down with a drink. **4** dash or throw (water) about, swirl round, swallow in large gulps. **5** *of water, waves* roll, flow with a swirling motion. **6** swirl, spin (quickly), roll; *of dancers* whirl, spin round.

noun **1** swill. **2** a large amount of drink *now NE*: *"a guid sweel."* **3** a rinsing, washing or swilling. **4** a swirl, spin, twist.

sweel[2], **swyle** **1** wrap (a person) in cloth or clothing, swathe. **2** wrap, wind, tie or bind round.

sweeler a cloth body-belt, a binder, especially for a baby.

sweel[3], **sweevil**, **sool**, **swill** **1** a swivel. **2** *only* **sweevil** a gust of wind, a short, sharp gale *Shetland Orkney*.

sweem *see* **soom**

sweeng *see* **swing**

sweep, soop, soup [-oo-], **swoop, swype** *NE* **1** sweep. **2** **soop** *curling* sweep (the ice) in the path of a curling-stone.

sweep-the-fluir a move in the game of **chucks.**

sweer, sweir *verb, past tense also* **swure, sware** swear.

noun **1** a bout of swearing. **2** a swear-word.

sweer *see* **sweir**

sweesh swish.

sweet[1], **sweat**, **sweit**, **swat**, **swite** *NE* **1** sweat. **2** stress, exertion; a state of anxiety or excitement.

sweet[2] *of milk* fresh, untreated, not skimmed or sour; *of butter* fresh, unsalted.

sweeten **1** sweeten. **2** bribe.

sweet-bread fancy cakes, pastries *now Shetland Orkney*. **sweet-milk cheese** cheese made from unskimmed milk, **Dunlop** cheese *N*.

sweetie **1** a sweet, a small piece of sweet food. **2** darling. **3** a large sum of money *NE*.

work for sweeties work for very little money.

sweevil *see* **sweel**[3]

sweil *see* **sweel**[1]

sweir, sweer, swear lazy, unwilling (to work).

sweirt = **sweir**. **sweirtie** laziness *Shetland NE*.

sweir-arse, sweir-draw, sweir-tree a game in which two people sitting on the ground, holding a stick between them, each try to pull the other up.

sweir *see* **sweer**

sweit *see* **sweet**[1]

swelchie [-ch- as in 'dreich'] a whirlpool in the sea *Orkney Caithness*.

swell *see* **swail**

swelt become faint with weakness or emotion, be physically overcome.

sweltry oppressively hot, sultry.

swerd *see* **swurd**

swerf *see* **swarf**

swey, sway, swee, swy(e) *Shetland NE* **1** sway. **2** continually change one's opinions etc. **3** make to sway or swing, move (an object) to one side.
noun **1** a sway. **2** a swinging semi-circular motion; a swerve; a swinging blow; a changing of the direction of a wind. **3** a swing for children. **4** a lever, crowbar. **5** a movable iron bar over a fire, on which pots, kettles etc can be hung.

swey boat a swingboat at a fair.

swick, sweek *noun* **1** (a piece of) deceit, a trick, swindle. **2** a cheating rogue.
verb cheat, swindle, deceive.

the swick o 1 the responsibility for (something bad or unfortunate) *NE*. **2** the knack or ability to do (something).

swidder *see* **swither**[1]

swiff, swuff the motion itself or the hissing or whizzing sound of an object flying through the air, a rush of air, a whirr *now Shetland NE*.

swig go with a swinging motion, rock, jog.

swill *see* **sweel**[1], **sweel**[3]

swim *see* **soom**

swine a pig, pigs.

swine crue, swine cruive a pigsty. **swine meat** pigswill. **swine pot** a pot in which pigs' food is boiled. **swine('s) same** lard, pig's fat.

the swine has run through it the plan, affair etc has come to nothing, been completely ruined.

swing, sweeng *verb, past tense also* **swang** *now Shetland NE* swing.
noun **1** a swing. **2** *also* **swing rope** a rope for tying up a boat; *herring-fishing* the line of nets to the stern of the boat.

swinge *verb* beat, flog, drive with blows *now Shetland*.
noun a heavy blow, a dash or clash.

swink work hard; struggle hard.

swipper(t) quick, nimble, active *NE*.

swird *see* **swurd**

swire, †sware a hollow or slope between hills, often one with a road; a hollow or level place near the top of a hill.

swirl, sworl, swurl *noun* **1** a swirl. **2** a twist, twirl, coil; a twisted or tangled state.
verb (cause to) move round and round, whirl, eddy, wave, brandish.

swirlie 1 *especially of the hair* having a marked curl or coil, curly, frizzy. **2** *of wood* with twists in the grain, knotty; *of rock* knobby, with an uneven grain. **3** tangled, twisted.

switchbell *see* **coachbell**

swite *see* **sweet**[1]

swith, swythe *adverb* quickly, rapidly; at once.
adjective quick, speedy.

swith awa *often as an order to a dog* quick!, away!

swither[1], **swidder** *NE*, **swuther** *verb* **1** be uncertain, hesitate, dither. **2** *of things* be uncertain, have a doubtful appearance.
noun **1** a state of indecision or doubt, hesitation, uncertainty. **2** a state of nervousness, a panic, fluster. **3** a state of confusion. **4** a dithering, undecided person.

swither[2] rush, swirl *now Shetland*.

swither[3] *of weather* be very hot, swelter

Shetland NE.

switherel a jellyfish, medusa.

switter struggle like a drowning person, splash or flounder about.

swoof make a rustling, swishing sound, as the wind etc *now Shetland.*

swoom *see* **soom**

swoop *see* **sweep**

sword *see* **swurd**

sworl *see* **swirl**

swuff *see* **swiff**

swurd, sword, swourd, swird, sourd, soord, †swerd 1 a sword. **2** a crossbar, *eg* in a barred gate *now Caithness.* **3** a slat of wood or tang of metal on the end of a ladder, used to stop it slipping.

sword dance a Highland dance, usually solo, consisting of a series of steps between swords laid cross-wise on the ground.

swure *see* **sweer**

swurl *see* **swirl**

swuther *see* **swither**[1]

swy(e) *see* **swey**

swyle *see* **swail, sweel**[2]

swpe *see* **swap**[2], **sweep**

swythe *see* **swith**

sybow, syboe, sybie a spring onion.

sye, sey *verb* pass (liquid) through a sieve, drain, filter.

noun a strainer or sieve, especially for milk.

sye-dish, sye-milk *now NE* a milk-strainer.

syes chives *NE.*

syke 1 a small stream etc, especially one in a hollow or on flat, boggy ground, and often dry in summer. **2** a marshy hollow, especially one with a stream, a cleft in the ground.

syle *see* **sile**[3]

synd, syne, sine [rhymes with 'mind' or 'mine'] *verb* **1** rinse (a container etc),

swill, wash out. **2** wash (the face, clothes etc), give a quick swill to (something) by drawing it through water. **3** wash (food) down with drink, swill (something) away or out with water etc.

noun a washing or rinsing out, a swill, a hasty wash.

syne, sin, seen *NE adverb* **1** directly after, next, afterwards. **2** in that case, so, then: *"and syne, ye're no gaun".* **3** ago, since, before now. **4** from then, since, thereafter.

noun that time, then: *"fae syne".*

conjunction **1** since, from the time that. **2** *only* **sin** since, because, seeing that.

preposition since (the time of).

sinsyne since then, after that time.

synod *Presbyterian Churches* a court between the **presbytery** and the **General Assembly** (*see* **general**); in the smaller churches with no **General Assembly**, the **synod** is the supreme court.

sype, sipe, seip *verb* **1** = **seep**. **2** *of a container* drip, leak. **3** cause to drip or ooze; draw liquid from, drain; drip-dry (clothes).

noun **1** an oozing, leakage. **2** a small trickle of water; a drip; a small quantity of liquid, that which drips from an emptied bottle.

sypin, sypit soaked *now Shetland NE.*

sypins oozings, leakage; the last drops from a container.

SYS *see* **Scots**

sythe strain (especially milk) through a sieve, filter.

syver, siver, syre 1 a ditch, drain, water-channel, a (covered-in) stone-lined field-drain. **2** a street gutter. **3** the opening of the drain-trap in a street gutter, often including the grating which covers it.

T

ta *see* tae³

taa *see* taw²

tabacha *see* tobacco

tabbie a cigarette stub *ECentral.*

table *noun* 1 *church, often* the table, the tables the Communion table; Communion; a series of celebrations of Communion by relays. 2 *mining* a platform on which coals are screened and picked.
verb, law lodge a summons before a court as a preliminary to its being called.

tabling the stone coping of a wall or gable.
table heid the surface of a table, a tabletop. table stone, table tombstone a horizontal gravestone.

tablet, taiblet 1 a tablet. 2 a kind of hard fudge.

tabour, toober beat, thrash.

tac tact *now Shetland NE.*

tach *see* tyach

tacit *see* relocation

tacht taut *now N.*

tack¹ tack.
tongue-tackit tongue-tied, having a speech impediment, dumb.
hing by a tack hang by a thread. keep tack till keep pace with, keep up with.

tack² 1 a lease, tenancy, especially the leasehold tenure of a farm, mill, mining or fishing rights, tax-collecting etc; the period of tenure. 2 the farm or land held on a lease. 3 an agreement, bargain. 4 a specific period of time, *eg* a lease (of life), a spell (of weather).
tacksman 1 a person who holds a tack², a tenant *now N.* 2 †a chief tenant, often a relative of the landowner, who leased land directly from him and sublet it to lesser tenants *mainly Highland.*

tacken *see* take

tacket a small nail, now often on the sole of a shoe.
tacketed, tackety studded with tackets, hobnailed: *"tackety boots"*. tackety jock a shoemaker's last.

tacksman *see* tack²

†taddy a kind of snuff.

tade *see* taid

tadge *see* targe

tae¹, toe 1 a toe. 2 a prong of a fork, salmon spear etc. 3 one of the thongs at the end of a tawse (*see* taw¹) *now Shetland Orkney N.*
tae-bit the iron toe-plate on a boot sole. tae('s) length the length of one's toe; a very short distance.

tae² one (of two): *"it gaes in at the tae lug and oot at the tither"*.

tae³, ta, te, tee *now NE*, ti, to, tu (*see also* till) *preposition* 1 to. 2 *of food* with, for: *"an egg to his tea"*. 3 *with verbs of looking* at: *"look to that picture"*. 4 by: *"he's a joiner to trade"*. 5 with (a specified person) as the father, by: *"she had a child to her cousin"*. 6 compared with: *"I'm but a puir man to you"*. 7 for, on behalf of, for the use of: *"he worked to Mr G"*. 8 for, as (being): *"having had an outlaw to his father"*. 9 *expressing family relationship* of: *"son to the Sheriff"*. 10 (hatred etc) towards, against: *"he had a mortal hatred to his son."*
adverb 1 to. 2 *implying direction towards, closeness or contact* (1) *of a door* so as to shut or close, closed: *"close the door to"*; (2) close, on, together, in contact *NE*. 3 too, also, as well. *conjunction* till, until.

tobackie one of the actions in a children's ball-game. tae-bread an extra loaf etc given free as a discount. tae-fall 1 a lean-to porch or outhouse. 2 an addition; an extra charge, burden. tae-

name an additional name, a nickname or additional surname, especially one used in a community where many have the same surname *now NE*.

be tae have gone to: *"arena ye tae yir bed?"* **be tee** be up to schedule *NE*. **easy tae** easy for *Shetland NE*. **weel tee** up to time, well in hand *NE*.

tae *see* **dey**², **tea**

taed *see* **taid**

taen *see* **tak**

taffie toffee.

taft a toft, a homestead and its land etc.

taft *see* **thaft**

tag 1 a tag. **2** a long thin strip or slice of flesh etc. **3** the strap used for punishment in schools.

taibet, tebbit, tibit, tapet †physical sensation, feeling; energy, strength.

taibetless 1 without feeling, numb; dull, spiritless. **2** foolish, silly.

taiblet *see* **tablet**

taickle tackle.

taid, tade, taed, ted 1 a toad. **2** term of endearment *NE*. **3** a sheep-tick.

taigle *verb* **1** tangle, entangle, confuse, muddle. **2** get in the way of, keep back, harass. **3** get the better of (in an argument), bamboozle; perplex. **4** delay, dawdle, hang about. **5** drag (the feet), walk along slowly.

noun a tangle, muddle.

taigled tired, harassed.

taiglesome 1 time-consuming, causing delay. **2** tiring, tedious.

taigle the cleek hold things up, hinder progress.

taik 1 tack (of a ship). **2** stroll, saunter *Shetland N*.

taiken, token 1 a token. **2** a small piece of stamped metal used as a pass to the Communion service (now replaced by a printed card).

tail 1 a long narrow piece of land jutting out from a larger piece. **2 tails** onion leaves. **3** the end (of a period of time or of an activity). **4** †the retinue or entourage of a Highland **chief. 5** a

prostitute.

tailer(t) a hand turnip-cutter *Orkney N*. **tailie** (**day**) 2 April, when children fix paper tails with various messages to the backs of unsuspecting victims.

tailsman a sawmill worker who takes and sorts the timber from the saw.

tailor, tailyour, teylor, tylor a tailor.

tailor's gartens ribbon-grass.

taiiyie, tailz(i)e, taillie 1 a cut or slice of meat for boiling or roasting, now especially of pork. **2** †*law* an entail, the settlement of **heritable** property on a particular line of heirs.

taim *see* **tume**

tainchel *see* **tinchel**

taing *see* **tang**²

taings *see* **tangs**

taint *see* **tint**

tair *see* **tear**

taird *see* **tuird**

tairge *see* **targe**

tairm *see* **term**

tairt, tert 1 a tart. **2** a girlfriend.

taisch †a vision seen in **second sight**, especially an apparition of a person about to die.

taise *see* **tease**

taisle, †teazle, †tassel *verb* **1** entangle, mix up. **2** toss, throw about; stir up. **3** tease, irritate.

noun a knocking about; a tussle.

tait, tate, teat, tit *NE* **1** a small tuft or bundle of hair, wool etc. **2** a tuft of grass, a small bundle of hay or corn. **3** *also* **a** (**wee**) **tait** a small amount (of something); somewhat: *"a wee tait bacon"; "a wee tate tipsy"*.

taiver, taver *verb* **1** wander about aimlessly; waste time. **2** wander in mind or speech, rave. **3** annoy; bewilder with talk or questioning.

noun **taivers** foolish talk, nonsense.

taivert bewildered.

taivers, tavers rags, tatters, shreds, *often of meat* **boiled to taivers.**

tak, take *verb, past tense also* **tuk, teuk** [tee**ook**]. *past participle also* **tane, ta'en,**

teen *now Shetland N,* **tacken, tooken 1** take. **2** catch (one's foot) on; be tripped by. **3** *of water* come up as far on a person as, reach up to (a certain height) on a person: *"that pool will take you over your head."* **4** stop oneself from doing or saying something which one might later regret. **5** marry. **6** lease, take on lease. **7** take over (a crop) for the grazing of livestock. **8** need the utmost strength and effort from: *"It'll tak ye to jump that burn".* **9** make for, go to. **10** catch fire.

noun **1** an act of seizing, a capture, catch; a catch of fish. **2** a state of excitement, agitation, rage etc. **3** a state of growth, the sprouting of a crop.

taen(-like) surprised, embarrassed.
takkie the game of tig; the pursuer in the game *NE*.
tak about 1 take care of; handle, manage. **2** prepare (a corpse) for burial. **3** harvest successfully. **tak aff** resemble. **tak the air, tak the lift** *of frost* rise, disappear. **tak awa 1** eat or drink up. **2** *of the fairies* take away (a human child) and substitute one of their own; **ta'en-awa** a fairy changeling. **tak back** go back. **tak someone's breath** choke someone. **tak one's death** die *Shetland NE.* **tak the door after oneself, tak the door wi oneself, tak the door tae** leave a room, closing a door behind one. **tak doun 1** weaken, cause to lose weight. **2** dilute (spirits). **3** make (one garment) from another. **4** make poor, bankrupt. **tak one's hand aff (someone's face** *etc)* slap, smack someone. **tak someone's head** go to someone's head, make someone giddy. **tak ill** become ill. **tak in 1** house (farm stock), bring under cover. **2** dismantle (a cornstack) and carry the sheaves to be threshed. **3** arrest, take into custody. **4** *of a boat* let in (water), leak. **5** bring in, welcome (a new day, year etc). **6** get over (a road), cover (a distance) *NE.* **tak in about** take (a person) in hand, discipline. **tak on**

1 buy on credit or account. **2** affect physically. **3** have (a person) on, tease. **4** get excited or emotional, be worked up; mope. **tak on with** take a liking to, be attracted by. **tak out 1** enrol in (a class) or for (a subject) at a university. **2** drink up, drain (a glass) *now Shetland.* **tak tae oneself** admit the truth of (an accusation), feel guilt or remorse, be sensitive about. **tak up 1** take (a collection) at a meeting. **2** raise or lift (one's foot) to kick. **3** *of a school or college* reopen after a holiday. **4** understand, get the meaning of. **5** run into debt, live on credit. **6** *of wind* rise, begin to blow. **be taken up about, be taken up wi** be charmed by, be pleased with. **tak up house** set up house; become a householder. **tak wi 1** admit; admit that one is the father of *now NE.* **2** find agreeable, take kindly to.

tald *see* **tell**
tale: talesman a storyteller *now Shetland.* **tale-pyot** a tell-tale.
   with his tale according to his story, as he would have others believe.
Tallie *humorous or contemptuous, especially of a seller of ice cream, fish and chips etc* an Italian.
   tallie iron a goffering iron.
tallon, tallow, tally *see* **tauch**
Tam Tom.
   Tam o' Shanter a round, flat woollen cap often with a **tourie** (*see* **tour**[1]). **trimmlin Tam 1** = **potted heid** (*see* **pot**). **2** a fruit jelly.
Tammie 1 Tommy. **2** a kind of beret; *compare* **Tam o' Shanter** (*see* **Tam**).
   Tammie-a'thing a general shop (keeper). **Tammie cheekie** *NE,* **Tammie norrie** a puffin. **tammie reekie** a kind of smoke gun made from a cabbage stem. **trimmling Tammie** a fruit jelly.
tammock *see* **tummock**
tane, teen *NE* one (of two): *"the tane wad tell a tale, the tither sing a song".*
tane *see* **tak**
tang[1] large, coarse seaweed growing

above low-water mark *Shetland Orkney*.

tangle 1 *also* **sea tangle** = **tang**¹. **2** a tall, lanky person. **3** an icicle.

tang², taing *Shetland noun* **1** a tang, a spike of metal. **2** the prong of a digging- or pitchfork. **3** the tongue of a Jew's harp.

tangs, taings, tings, teengs, tyangs [tee-angs] *NE* tongs.

tanker a tankard.

tanker-backit round-shouldered and hollow-backed.

tannel, tawnle a beacon; a bonfire, especially at certain festivals.

tanner *see* **tenor**

tansy ragwort.

tantersome exasperating, annoying *NE*.

tap¹, top *noun* **1** the top. **2** a tuft of hair, feathers etc; a forelock; a bird's crest. **3** †*spinning* the tuft of flax or tow put on a distaff at one time. **4** the head. **5** the tip, end. **6** a fir cone. **7** the surface of water. **8 taps** a framework fitted round a cart so that large loads of hay etc may be carried. **9 tops** the best sheep or lambs in a flock.
verb **1** top. **2** cut the tip of the ear of (an animal) as an ownership mark. **3 top** *golf* hit (the ball) on its upper part, making it spin rather than fly forward. **tappin 1** a tuft or crest on a bird's head. **2** the peaked top of a hill; a cairn on a hilltop. **tappit** crested, tufted. **tappit hen 1** a tufted hen. **2** a kind of (pewter) decanter, containing a standard measure, its lid knob shaped like a fowl's tuft.

tapsman the chief man in charge of a drove of cattle, the head drover. **tap pickle** the highest ear on a stalk of oats, usually considered to be of the best quality. **taptaes** tiptoes.

never aff someone's tap always criticizing, continually quarrelling with someone. **on someone's tap** attacking, severely scolding someone. **take one's tap in one's lap** pack up and go, leave

in a hurry. **tap o lint, tap o tow 1** † = **tap**¹ *noun* **3**. **2** a head of flaxen hair. **3** a fiery-tempered person. **the tap o the road** the middle of the road. **the tap o the water** high water, full tide.

tap² a top, the toy, especially a whipping top.

tape measure exactly (with a tape-measure); deal out or use sparingly.

taper use (food) sparingly.

tapet *see* **taibet**

tapner *see* **taupin**

tappietourie [-oo-], **tappie-toorie** something which rises to a peak; an ornament on top of something *eg* a turret; a knot of ribbons, a tassel, pompom, a bonnet with this.

tapsalteerie, tapsie-teerie upside down, topsy-turvy; chaotic, muddled.

tapsman *see* **tap**¹

tar, ter tar.

tarry, taurie 1 tarry. **2** *also* **tarry-fingered** light-fingered, likely to steal. **tarry breeks** nickname for a sailor.

tar buist a box containing tar for smearing and marking sheep.

tarbet, tarbert *in place-names* an isthmus or neck of land between two stretches of water, often one over which a boat could be drawn.

tards, tawrds, targe a school punishment strap *N*.

tare *see* **tear**

targe, tairge, tadge *verb* **1** treat strictly or severely; question closely, cross-examine; scold severely. **2** bustle about, hustle, do something vigorously.
noun a violent, scolding woman, a shrew.

targer 1 a violent, quarrelsome, domineering person, especially a woman. **2** nickname for a big, active, bustling person.

targe *see* **tards**

target 1 a long narrow shred of cloth, a tatter; an oddly- or untidily-dressed person. **2** a thin strip of flesh, especially from a wound; a long thin strip of dried skate.

tarledder, †tarleather a strong strip of hide, taken from the belly of the animal, dressed and used as a thong, strap etc.

tarloch a small, weak or worthless person, animal, or thing *now NE*.

tarmagan, †tarmachan a ptarmigan.

tarragat question closely, pester.

tarraneese *see* **tirran**

tarrie(-dog), terrie(-dog) a terrier.

tarrock, tirrick 1 a tern. **2** a (young) kittiwake.

tarrow 1 delay, linger, hesitate. **2 tarrow at, tarrow on** feel or show reluctance for, show hesitation at, spurn, refuse. **3** complain.

tarry *see* **tar**

tartan 1 a woollen cloth with a pattern of stripes of different colours crossing at right angles; such a pattern, especially one associated with a particular **clan** (although the ascribing of particular tartans to clans is largely unhistorical). **2 †**a tartan garment, especially a Highland **plaid.**

fireside tartan, Grannie's tartan, tinker's tartan mottled skin on the legs caused by sitting too close to a fire. **tear the tartan** speak Gaelic.

tartle[1] hesitate, be uncertain.

tartle[2] **1** a matted tuft of hair or wool at an animal's tail. **2 tartles** tatters, torn or trailing edges of (dirty) cloth.

tary, terry 1 †trouble, harm. **2** the Devil *NE.*

tash *noun* a stain, smudge; damage; a blot on one's character.

verb **1** stain; spoil (flowers or clothes) by rough or careless handling. **2** weary (with hard work).

tashy tattered, slovenly in appearance, untidy.

task a set lesson to be prepared, a piece of school homework.

tasker a pieceworker; especially a thresher of corn. **taskit** exhausted by hard work; stressed, harassed.

tass, tassie a cup, goblet etc, especially for spirits.

tassel *see* **taisle**

taste *verb* drink alcohol in small amounts, tipple.

noun **1** a small quantity of alcoholic drink, a **dram. 2** a small quantity.

lose taste o lose interest in or liking for. **taste one's gab, taste one's hert** cause a pleasant taste in one's mouth, whet the appetite.

tat *see* **taut, that**

tate *see* **tait**

tathe, toth, †tath 1 †the dung of cattle or sheep left for manure on their grazing land. **2** coarse rank grass which grows on ground thus manured.

tatie *see* **tattie**

tatter talk idly; scold.

tatterwallop 1 a rag, tatter. **2** a ragged person, ragamuffin *Orkney NE.*

tattie, tatie, tawtie, tautie 1 a potato. **2** *contemptuous* the head; a stupid person.

tattie-ait a kind of oat, the potato-oat. **tattie-bannock** = **tattie scone. tattie-bing** a clamp of potatoes. **tattie-bogie, tattie-bogle, tattie-boodie** *NE* **1** a scarecrow. **2** a ragged, untidy or strangely-dressed person. **3** a large raw potato with matchsticks stuck in it as a toy. **4** a turnip-lantern used at **Halloween. tattie-bree, tattie-broo** water in which potatoes have been boiled. **tattie-broth** potato soup. **tattie-champer, tattie-chapper** a potato-masher or pestle. **tattie-claw** potato soup. **tattie deevil** a machine for digging potatoes *NE, Angus Fife.* **tattie doolie** a scarecrow; a ragamuffin. **tattie holidays** an autumn school holiday to allow children to help with the potato harvest. **tattie holin** = **tattie howkin** *NE.* **tattie howker** a person who works at the potato harvest, especially a temporary worker from Ireland. **tattie howkin, tattie-liftin** the potato-harvest. **tattie-parer** a potato-peeler. **tattie-peelin 1** a potato

peeling. **2** *of speech* affected, prim. **tattie pit** = **tattie bing**. **tattie-ploom** the
seed-box of the potato plant. **tattie-
poke** a sack for potatoes. **tattie pourins**
= **tattie bree**. **tattie-scone** a (flat) **scone**
made of flour, milk and mashed
potato. **tattie-trap** *insulting* the mouth.
tattie weather weather favourable for
the potato harvest.

the (clean) tattie the right person, one
who can be trusted or relied on. **tatties
and dab** potatoes boiled in their skins
and dipped in melted fat, gravy etc.
tatties and point a meal of potatoes
only (the non-existent meat being
pointed at). **the vera tattie** the very
thing.

tauch, tallon, tallow, tally tallow, **tauch**
being sometimes used for the sub-
stance in its natural state and **tallow**
when it has been melted down.

tauchie smeared with tallow or fat,
greasy.

tally lamp a miner's lamp.

tauld *see* **tell**

taum a fit of rage, bad temper, a sullen,
sulky mood.

taupie, tawpie *noun* a scatterbrained,
untidy, awkward or careless person,
especially a young woman.
adjective foolish, awkward, slovenly.

taupin a main branch of a root; a tap-
root, especially of a turnip.

taupiner, tapner a curved knife with a
hooked tip for harvesting and topping
and tailing turnips *NE*.

taurie *see* **tar**

taut, tawt, tat *noun* a tangled, matted tuft
or lock of wool, hair etc.
verb mat, tangle.

tautie, tautit matted, tangled, shaggy,
untidy; having a rough, shaggy head
or coat.

tautie *see* **tattie**

taver *see* **taiver**

tavers *see* **taivers**

taw[1] *verb* **1** knead, draw out, twist (*eg*
dough, toffee); pull and tug at. **2** work

with great effort, struggle. **3** *also* **tawse**
beat, whip with a **tawse** (*noun* 1).
noun **1** **taws(e)** a leather punishment
strap with thongs, used in schools, a
whip with tails; the lash for a whipping
top. **2** *child's word* the penis.

taw[2], **taa, tyave** [teeaave] a fibre of a plant
or tree, a fibrous root, a conifer preserved in peat.

tawnle *see* **tannel**

tawpie *see* **taupie**

tawrds *see* **tards**

taws(e) *see* **taw**[1]

tawt *see* **taut**

tawtie *see* **tattie**

Tayside, *also* **Tayside Region** a **region**
formed from the former counties of the
City of Dundee, Angus and Kinross
and part of the former county of
Perth.

tazie *see* **tease**

tchick 1 tut-tut. **2** sound made to urge on
a horse.

tchop *see* **shop**

te *see* **tae**[3]

tea, tae 1 tea. **2** *also* **high tea** a meal eaten
in the early evening, usually consisting
of one cooked course followed by
bread, cakes etc and tea.

tea-bread buns, **scones** etc, eaten with
tea. **tea-hand, tea-jenny** a person (male
or female) who drinks a lot of tea.

tea and till't tea served with a cooked
meal, **high tea.**

teal coax, wheedle, flatter.

tear [rhymes with 'beer' or 'bare'], **teir,
tair, terr** *verb*, *past tense also* **tare, tuir
1** tear, rip. **2** *of wind* blow hard, gust,
rage. **3 tear awa, tear on** work energetically and with speed (at). **4** rage
(at).
noun **1** a tear, a rip. **2** *of a plough* the
set of the ploughshare, which regulates
the cut in the furrow. **3** a piece of fun,
a spree, joke. **4** a lively entertaining
person, a comic. **5** a (great) quantity,
a (large) amount of.

tearer a passionate, bad-tempered person; *of a woman* a shrew. **tearin** *noun* an angry scolding, a thorough dressing-down. *adjective* rowdy, boisterous. **tornbellie** a herring split or broken by careless handling. **torndoun** disreputable, broken-down. **torn face** (a person with) a bad-tempered, sulky, glum face.

tear at, tear up go at, set about, tackle with great energy. **tear in** reclaim (waste ground).

tear *see* **teer**[2]

tease, taise tease.

tazie, teesie a struggle, strenuous effort.

teat *see* **tait**

teazle *see* **taisle**

tebbit *see* **taibet**

ted *see* **taid**

tedder *see* **tether**

tedisome, teedisome tedious, tiresome, boring.

tee 1 *golf* the peg or (formerly) the small heap of sand from which the ball is driven at the start of each hole; *now also* the patch of ground from which this is done. **2** *curling* the target, a mark on the ice in the centre of several concentric circles. **3** *quoits, carpet bowls* the target or goal.

tee *see* **tae**[3]

teedisome *see* **tedisome**

teedle sing or hum a tune without the words; sing softly.

teedy, teethy cross, fractious; bad-tempered.

teef *see* **thief**

teeger 1 a tiger. **2** a fierce quarrelsome person.

teel till (land).

teel *see* **tuil**

teem *verb* **1** empty (a container); empty out (the contents) from a container. **2** drain water from (potatoes). **3** *of rain* pour, come down in torrents. **4** *of water* flow or gush.

noun a very heavy, long-lasting downpour of rain.

teemie *child's word* urinating.

teem *see* **tume**

†**teen**[1], **teend** harm, hurt; sorrow, grief.

†**teen**[2] = **at een** (*see* **even**) in the evening.

teen *see* **tak, tane, tune**

teenge 1 a tinge. **2** colic.

teengs *see* **tangs**

teenie *contemptuous* a junior domestic servant; an effeminate man.

teenie-bash familiar, often insulting term for a woman or girl *ECentral*.

greeting Teenie a weepy, complaining person (male or female). **Teenie f(r)ae Troon, Teenie f(r)ae the neeps** an odd-looking, oddly-dressed or over-dressed woman.

teenty *children's rhymes* two.

teep, type *noun* a type, a representation; stamp; letters in printing.

verb stamp (a letter, figure etc) on wood or metal with a die.

teep *see* **tuip**

teepical typical.

teer[1] tare, wild vetch.

teer[2], **tear: a' by teer, a' the teer** barely, by the skin of one's teeth, touch and go.

teerie-orrie throwing a ball against a wall, catching and bouncing it in various ways *ECentral*.

teesie *see* **tease**

teet[1] *verb* peep, peer, glance slyly.

noun a shy peep, a sly, secretive glance. **teet(ie) bo** (the game of) peep-bo.

teet[2] the smallest sound, a squeak.

teeter hesitate.

teeth *see* **tuith**

teethe 1 set teeth in, provide with teeth or spikes. **2** face, stand up to.

teethy *see* **teedy**

teetle, title 1 a title. **2 titles** the title-deeds of land or property.

teet-meet *see* **toot-moot**

teetotum a very small, unimportant person.

teewheet, teewhip *see* **teuchit**

teh expressing impatience or derision.

te-hent [teehint] behind.

teind, tiend *church law* an allocation of a

tenth of the produce of a parish for the support of religion, after the Reformation granted to landowners by the Crown, now an amount payable by the owner to the **Church of Scotland** (*see* **church**) and used as part of the parish minister's **stipend.**

Clerk of Teinds the principal clerk to the **Court of Teinds. Commission(ers) of Teinds, Court of Teinds** the names (at various dates) of the body administering the **teinds,** since 1707 as part of the **Court of Session** (*see* **session**).

teir *see* **tear**

teistie, †toist a black guillemot *Shetland Orkney Caithness.*

tell, tol(l) *verb, past tense, past participle also* **tald, tauld, telled, telt** tell.

   telling a warning, lesson: *"let that be a telling tae ye"; "take a telling".* **it would be telling** it would be to the advantage of (a person), it would be better for (a person).

   tell down count out (money) in payment. **tell on** tell tales about, inform against.

tenaby *children's rhymes* ten *now Shetland Orkney Caithness.*

tend attend (to), look after, see (to).

tender[1] in poor health, weakly.

tender[2] *law* an offer of a sum in settlement made during an action by the **defender** to the **pursuer** (*see* **pursue**); (the English *tender* is an offer before an action).

tenement 1 a tenement, a holding of land with buildings on it. **2** a large building, usually of three or more storeys divided into flats for separate householders; the section of such a building served by one stair.

tenon a tendon.

tenor, tanner *carpentry* a tenon.

tent *noun* attention, heed, care.

   verb **1** pay attention to, listen to. **2** watch over, take good care of; take charge of, look after (animals or children).

   tentie 1 watchful; attentive. **2** cautious, careful.

   tak tent 1 be careful, beware. **2** notice, take note. **tak tent o 1** take (good) care of, heed. **2** pay attention to, keep watch on. **3** beware of, be on one's guard against.

   tak tent listen to.

tenter a bar of wood fitted with hooks on which fish are hung to dry *NE Fife.*

ter *see* **tar**

terce *law* the right of a widow to the **liferent** (*see* **life**) of one third of her husband's **heritable** estate, if no other provision has been made for her.

term, tairm 1 a term. **2** *law* one of the four days of the year on which certain payments, *eg* rent or interest, become due, leases begin and end, and (formerly) contracts of employment, especially on farms, began and ended, **Candlemas, Whitsunday, Lammas, Martinmas;** latterly removal **terms** only were fixed as 28 May and 28 November.

term *see* **thairm**

terr *see* **tear**

terrible, terrel 1 terrible. **2** very much, awfully: *"It's terrible wet".*

terrie *see* **tarrie**

terry *see* **tary**

tersie versie topsy-turvy.

tert *see* **tairt**

testament that part of a will in which an executor is appointed.

testament(ar) *see* **tutor**

tether, tedder *noun* **1** a tether. **2** scope, the limits: *"his mither gied him ower lang a tether."* **3** †a hangman's noose.

   verb **1** tether. **2** restrict the freedom of, tie down. **3** *sarcastic* marry.

tethery *children's rhymes* three.

teuch, tough, tyeuch, tyoch, teugh, cheuch [tee**ooch**, tee**uch**, tchooch, tchuch] **1** tough. **2** *of people* rough, coarse. **3** *of weather* rough, wet and windy.

   teuch Jean a kind of sticky, chewy **sweetie.**

teuchit [tee**ooch**it], **teewheet, teewhip**

Orkney, **tuchit** [-ch as in 'loch'] a lapwing, peewit.

    teuchit('s) storm a period of bleak wintry weather in March (when the **teuchits** arrive and begin to nest).

teuchter [tee**ooch**ter] contemptuous term for a Highlander, especially a Gaelic-speaker, or for anyone from the North; a countrified person.

teug *see* **tug**

teugh *see* **teuch**

teuk *see* **tak**

teulie *see* **tulyie**

teven *children's rhymes* seven.

tew = **taw**¹ *verb* 2.

    tewed 1 *of food* tough, shrivelled. **2** exhausted.

tew *see* **tyauve**

tewk *see* **tuck**

teylor *see* **tailor**

Teysday *see* **Tysday.**

thack, theck, thaik thatch.

    thack and raip the thatch of a house, stack etc and the ropes tying it down; something tidy, comfortable, well-secured.

thae, they, thea those.

thaft, taft *Shetland* a rower's bench, thwart.

thaik *see* **thack**

thaim *see* **them**

thairm, therm, term *Shetland* **1** a human or animal bowel, gut, intestine; a gut used as the skin of a sausage etc. **2** gut dried and twisted into a string or cord for various purposes, catgut, *eg* as a cord for a pendulum clock; as a fiddle-string.

than, an *adverb* then.

    conjunction than.

    noos an thans now and then. **or than, or thance** or, if not, then; or else; or even: *"come hame sure or than I'll be angry".* **than-a-days** in those days, at that time. **weel than** in that case; yes indeed, very much so.

thane *in the Middle Ages* a minor noble who acted as an official of the Crown.

thank: thankrife full of thanks, grateful.

    thanksgiving (service) *Presbyterian Churches* the service after Communion, in which special thanks are given to God.

    give thanks say grace after (and later also before) a meal.

that, dat *Shetland Orkney,* †**tat** *representing Highland speech, pronoun, also* **at** *N* **1** that. **2** this: *"that's a braw day".* **3** *also* **aa that** used to emphasize a previous phrase: *"It's very cold. It is that."* *adjective* **1** *also* **at** *N* that. **2** those: *"that men".* **3** *also* **thattan, that a ..** such, so much: *"she had that a cauld".*

    conjunction that.

    adverb so, to such a degree; to that extent; very: *"he was that frightened".*

    relative pronoun **1** that, who(m), which; often left out in Scots: "wha was the leddy gaed doon the road afore ye?" **2** *as possessive* (1) **that** *with possessive adjective, now NE:* "the crew that their boat wis lost"; (2) **that's:** *"the woman that's sister mairriet the postie;* (3) *not used of persons* **that .. o't, that o them:** *"the hoose that the end o't fell".*

    and that and so on, et cetera: *"he'll bring the milk and that."* **like aa that** like anything, at full speed: *"singing like aa that".* **or that** or the like, or something similar: *"a visitor and maybe a painter or that."*

thaw *see* **thow**

the, de *ECoast,* **da** *Shetland,* **ee** *N* **1** the. **2** used with names of relatives: *"the wife".* **3** used with the names of parts of the body: *"keep the heid".* **4** used where English leaves out, *eg* referring to public institutions: *"he's at the school now";* in the home: *"up the stair", "sit at the table", "fish for the tea";* commodities: *"the price of the milk";* a fit of temper: *"take the huff";* with names of diseases etc: *"he's got the measles", "he was a terrible man for the drink", "the dry rot";* with names of activities: *"you've been at the smoking";* trades or crafts:

"they're at the fishing"; of languages etc: *"the Gaelic", "a minister's no muckle worth withoot the Greek";* of sports, games etc: *"they were playing at the chess";* before a surname to indicate the leading member of a family: *"Robert the Bruce", "the Chisholm",* and to indicate the chief of a Highland clan: *"the Mackintosh";* certain place-names: *"the Langholm";* before the names of schools or colleges: *"at the Waid Academy";* **the baith:** *"the baith of them";* **the maist:** *"the maist fouks".* **5** used where English leaves out or uses **a**: *"he wears the kilt"; "they tell me you're to be the great surgeon".* **6 the noo** now: *"he's here the noo".* **7** there: *"the ben".* **8 the day** today, **the morn** tomorrow, **the nicht** tonight, **the year** this year.

the *see* **there**

thea *see* **thae**

theat, theet 1 theats the traces (attaching a horse to a vehicle, plough etc). **2** a tow, pull by a trace-horse.
   out of (the) theat(s) *NE* **1** disordered; out of control; going beyond normal limits. **2 out of theat** in addition to what is expected or needed.

theck *see* **thack**

thee, thei the thigh.

thee *see* **thou, thy**

theedle *see* **theevil**

theek, thick *verb* **1** †roof (a building) with (stone, slate, lead etc). **2** roof, cover (a building, hay- or peat-stack) with (thatch). **3** cover, protect with a thick covering of hair, clothes etc.
   noun **1** thatch. **2** any thick covering of hair etc.

theel *see* **theevil**

theer *see* **there**

theet *see* **theat**

theevil, theedle, theel *Fife* a short tapering stick used to stir food as it cooks; used in certain areas, *compare* **spurtle.**

thegither, thegidder, thegether together.

thei *see* **thee**

their, thir, der *Shetland* their.

theirsel, theirsels themselves.

them, thaim, dem 1 them. **2** those: *"them 'at sent it kens best".*

themselves two just the two of them.

there, theer *S,* **der(e)** *Shetland Orkney* **1** *also* **the, they, de(y)** there: *"they'll be nae peace"; "dey wir no a flooer ta be seen".* **2** *also* **dir** *Shetland Orkney* there is, there are: *"there naebody in".*
   there awa(y) away to or in that place; in that general direction. **or thereby** *of a number or amount* or round about the figure mentioned. **there out 1** †outside that place. **2** out of doors, in the open. **3** out of that; out of that place.

thereckly directly *SW, S.*

therm *see* **thairm**

therteen *see* **thirteen**

therty, thretty, tretty *Shetland Orkney* thirty.

these *see* **this**

the streen *see* **yestreen**

thewless *see* **thowless**

they *see* **thae, there**

†**thibet** (cloth made from) a kind of fine wool, used for women's dress aprons.

thick thickset, muscular, burly.
   thickness a dense fog or sea-mist. **thick black** a brand of strong tobacco.
   thick and three-fauld 1 in large numbers, in a crowd. **2** very friendly.

thick *see* **theek**

thief, teef *Shetland Orkney noun* **1** a thief. **2** general term of contempt; a rascal, scoundrel. **3 the auld thief, the black thief** the Devil, Satan *now Shetland Orkney.*
   verb steal.
   thieflike, theif(t)ie like a thief, rascally; stealthy.

thieveless *see* **thowless**

thig beg, cadge; ask for free gifts from friends, *eg* when setting up house or a business.

thig *see* **sorn**

thight tight, close in texture, watertight *Shetland Orkney.*

thimble, thimmle *see* **thummle**

thimmle *see* **thummle**

thin, tin *Shetland* **1** thin. **2** *of wind, weather* cold, bitter, piercing.

    the thin(s) diarrhoea *NE*.

thing, ting 1 a thing. **2** *referring back to a previous noun* kind, sort, stuff: *"some black ink, or some blue thing", "I dinna like saut butter; hae ye nae sweet thing?"* **3** amount, number: *"an awfu thing o port".*

    a wee thing(ie) rather, a little: *"a wee thing earlier".*

think, tink *Shetland Orkney* think.

    I'm thinking I presume, it's my opinion. **my ain think** my own private thoughts or opinion. **think lang** long (for). **think on** think of or about.

thir *see* **their, this**

third, trid *Shetland* **1** third. **2 thirds** what is left of grain after milling or brewing, third quality flour.

thirl[1]**, tirl** *Shetland Orkney* **1** pierce, bore through, make holes in. **2** *mining* cut through (a wall of coal). **3** thrill. **4** vibrate, quiver.

    noun **1** a hole. **2** *mining* a hole connecting one working with another. **3** †a thrill.

thirl[2] **1** †hold in bondage or servitude. **2** †*law* bind (lands or tenants) to have grain ground at a particular mill. **3** bind with ties of affection, sense of duty or loyalty, force of habit etc.

    ʼhirled bound by ties of affection, duty etc; hidebound by an idea, belief etc.

thirstle, thistle *see* **thrissel**

thirteen, thretten, therteen, tretten *Shetland* **1** thirteen. **2** thirteenth.

    thirteent thirteenth.

this, dis *now Shetland,* **is(s)** *now N, pronoun, plural also* **thir 1** this. **2** this time, this place, now, here: *"he gaed fae this tae Ayr".* **3** these *Shetland NE: "this is them", "this is the effects of the war".* *adjective* **1** this. **2** these: *"this bonny boys".* **3 these** those *now NE: "these seeds in my hand are better than these on the table".* **4 this day** today; **this nicht** tonight.

    adverb so, to such a degree or extent *now Shetland NE: "this auld".*

    this oʼt this state of affairs.

tho, to *Shetland Orkney* though.

thocht, thought, thoucht, tought *Shetland Orkney* [-ch-, -gh- as -ch in 'loch'] **1** thought. **2** care, trouble; (a cause for) anxiety, worry. **3 a (wee** *etc)* **thocht** a very small amount (of), a little; rather.

    thochtie *adjective* heedful, attentive; serious-minded; anxious. *noun* = **thocht** *noun* **3**. **ill-thochted** having nasty or suspicious thoughts, nasty-minded.

thole 1 suffer, have to bear (pain, grief etc). **2** suffer with patience or bravery, put up with. **3** be able to endure; manage. **4** be patient, wait patiently.

    tholeable bearable.

    thole wi put up with, tolerate.

thon *indicating a thing or person further away from the speaker than another or others* that; those.

thonder, thonner over there, at some distance, yonder.

thoo *see* **thou**

thoom *see* **thoum**

thorn, torn *Shetland* a thorn.

    thornie (back) a thornback ray *now Shetland.*

thorow, thorough *preposition* through.

    adjective **1** thorough. **2** mentally alert, sane *now SW, S.*

    verb clean thoroughly.

    noun a thorough cleaning or tidying.

    thorough-band a stone which goes through the whole thickness of a wall.

thort, twart *Shetland Orkney* across, from side to side.

thorter *preposition* on or to the other side of, across, over *now Shetland.*

    verb **1** cross the path of; thwart, oppose. **2** do something in a direction at right angles to what one has done before, *eg* in ploughing, in spreading butter on bread *now NE.*

    thorter ill a kind of paralysis in sheep causing distortion of the neck.

thou, du *Shetland Orkney,* **tou, thoo** *now Orkney* [rhymes with 'moo'] thou. **thee, dee** thee: used *eg* between close friends, or by adults to children etc, now limited mainly to *Shetland Orkney.*

thoucht, thought *see* **thocht**

thoum [-oo-], **thumb, thoom, toom** *Shetland Orkney noun* **1** the thumb. **2** in reference to the practice of confirming a bargain etc by licking and joining thumbs: *"there's my thoum"; "wet thoumbs".*
verb **1** thumb, touch with the thumb. **2** rub or massage (a sprain) with the thumb *Shetland NE.* **3** dab or press (butter on bread etc) with a moistened thumb.

thoumie a wren *NE.* †**thumbikins** a thumbscrew used to torture **Covenanters** (*see* **covenant**).

thoum-hand the right hand *NE.* **thumb note** *piping* high A, the top note of the bagpipe scale. **thoum-piece** a slice of bread with butter spread on with the thumb. **thoum-raip** a hay- or straw-rope made by twisting the strands under the tip of the thumb.

put one's thoum on keep secret, keep silent about. **crack one's thoums** snap one's fingers in pleasure or derision *now Shetland NE.* **not fash one's thoum** pay no heed, never worry or concern oneself. **no be able to see one's thoum** be unable to see ahead of one (in the dark). **turn one's thoum** make an effort.

thoumart *see* **foumart**

thow, thaw, tow *Shetland Orkney* [rhymes with 'cow'] thaw.
dirty thow a thaw brought on by rain. **dry thow** a thaw after a high wind. **weet thow** a thaw without wind or rain.

thowl, thow [-ow- as in 'cow'], *also* **thowl pin** a thole, a pin which holds an oar.

thowless [-ow- as in 'cow'], **thewless, thieveless** lacking energy or spirit, listless, inactive; lacking initiative, ineffectual.

thrae, tray obstinate, unwilling.

thrae *see* **fae**

thrain *noun* †a (sad) refrain.
verb talk on and on about, keep asking (for) *Fife.*

thraip *see* **threap**

thram thrive *N.*

thrammel the rope or chain by which cattle are tied in their stalls; the part linking the post to the part round the animal's neck.

thrang, throng, trang *Shetland Orkney noun* **1** a throng. **2** a large quantity or number *now NE.* **3** pressure (of work or business), (a time of) great activity.
adjective **1** crowded (closely together); full, well-packed. **2** numerous, in crowds. **3** *of places* thronged, crowded with people. **4** busy, fully occupied. **5** on very friendly terms (with).
adverb **1** †closely, in large numbers. **2** busily, carefully.
verb throng.

thrangity 1 a bustling crowd, a press of people. **2** busyness, pressure of work; bustle.

thrapple[1], **thropple, trapple** *Shetland Orkney noun* the windpipe, the throat, the gullet.
verb throttle, strangle.

weet one's thrapple have something to drink, quench one's thirst.

thrapple[2], **thropple** draw (a hole in cloth) roughly together, instead of darning *S.*

thrash, thresh, tresh *Shetland Orkney verb, past tense also* **thruish, throosh, thrush, treush** *Shetland Orkney,* **threesh** *NE. past participle also* **thrashen, thrushen, treshen** *Shetland Orkney* thresh, thrash. English distinguishes between *thresh* beat (corn) and *thrash* beat, punish; in Scots the distinction is not made and the form is now usually **thrash.**

thrash *see* **rash**[1]

thrashel, treshel *Shetland* a threshold.

thrashen *see* **thrash**

thratch *verb* twist the body about, writhe (in the death agony).
noun a jerk, twist of the body (in the

death agony).

thrave *see* **threave**

thraw, throw, traa *Shetland Orkney verb, past tense also* **thrawed.** *past participle also* **thrawn, traan** *Shetland Orkney* **1 thraw** (1) twist, turn; wring; distort. (2) turn (a key) in a lock, (a knob) on a door etc. (3) twist (straw etc) together, make (a rope) thus. (4) twist (a part of the body), wrench, sprain. (5) distort the meaning of. **2 thraw** turn, twist; curl, become warped or twisted. **3 thraw** (1) thwart, oppose, cross. (2) be contrary, quarrel, grumble. (3) quarrel with. **4** throw. **5** throw throw up, vomit. *noun, only* **thraw** *in all senses except 1 and 6:* **1** a throw. **2** a turn, twist; a turn, distortion, tilt, warp. **3** a wrench of a muscle etc, a sprain. **4** a twisting of the face, a wry expression. **5** a twisting of the body in pain, a convulsion, spasm. **6 throw** *piping* a series of gracenotes preceding a melody note of higher pitch. **7** *mining* a fault in a vein or stratum. **8** a fit of obstinacy or bad temper, the sulks. **9** a dispute, quarrel. **10** a reverse, setback *now NE.*

be thrown back suffer a relapse in an illness.

thrawcruik, thrawhuik 1 an implement for twisting straw etc into rope. **2** a twisted straw rope. **thraw-mouse** a shrew *NE.* **thraw-rape** = **thrawcruik.**

heads and thraws lying in opposite directions; higgledy-piggledy. **out o thraw** *masonry, of a stone* into alignment, squared. **thraw one's face** screw up, twist the face as a sign of pain etc. **thraw the neck of** wring the neck of.

thrawart, traaward *Shetland Orkney* contrary; unfavourable *now Shetland Orkney.*

thrawn, trawn *Shetland Orkney Ulster* **1** twisted, crooked, distorted. **2** *of the mouth, face* twisted with pain, rage etc, surly. **3** obstinate, contrary; cross, sullen. **4** *of the weather* disagreeable, bad *now NE.*

thrawn *see* **thraw**

thread *see* **threid**

threap, threep, threip, thraip, traep *Shetland Orkney verb* **1** argue, quarrel. **2** keep saying (something) very firmly. **3 threap at** nag at, be insistent with.

noun **1** an argument; a quarrel. **2** strongly held opinion, an aggressive statement of one's beliefs. **3** an old superstition, idea or saying. **4** *ploughing* (1) the angle between the points of the coulter and of the share *Angus Perth;* (2) a swingletree *SW.*

keep (up) to one's threap keep to one's opinions, stick to one's guns. **threap down someone's throat, threap on someone** force one's opinion(s) on someone, try to make someone believe.

threat, threet, threit *noun* a threat.

verb threaten.

threave, thrave, trave *Shetland Orkney* **1** a measure of cut grain, straw or thatching material, consisting of two **stooks**, usually with twelve sheaves each, but varying locally. **2** a large number or quantity, a crowd *now Shetland.*

three, chree *now Fife,* **threy** *S,* **tree** *Shetland Orkney,* **hree** *now WCentral* three.

threesie 1 a move in the game of **chucks** (see **chuck**[2]). **2** *also* **threeie** the third square or box in the game of **peever**[1].

threesome (of) a group or company of three.

three four three or four, a few.

threed *see* **threid**

threep *see* **threap**

threeple *adjective* triple, three times over *now NE.*

verb treble *NE.*

threeplet a triplet.

threesh *see* **thrash**

threesie, threesome *see* **three**

threet *see* **threat**

threid, threed, thread, treed *Shetland Orkney* thread.

threid dry completely dry.

get the richt threid o have a correct understanding of, get the hang of.

threip *see* **threap**
threit *see* **threat**
thresh *see* **rash**[1], **thrash**
thretten *see* **thirteen**
thretty *see* **therty**
threy *see* **three**
thrift, trift *Shetland Orkney* **1** thrift. **2** †prosperity, success, good luck. **3** work, industry, profitable occupation. **4** willingness to work, energy, enthusiasm *now Orkney*.

thriftie a child's moneybox.

thrimmle *see* **thrummle**
thrissel, thistle, thirstle *now Caithness*, **thrustle, thustle, tistle** *Shetland Orkney* a thistle; the emblem of Scotland.

thrist *now Shetland Orkney NE*, **trist** *Shetland Orkney* thirst.

thrive, trive *Shetland Orkney verb* thrive. *noun* prosperity, a thriving state, boom *now SW*.

ill-thriven badly-nourished, scraggy.

throch *see* **throu, thruch**
throm from.
throng *see* **thrang**
throosh play truant from (school) *SW*.
throosh *see* **thrash**
thropple *see* **thrapple**[1], **thrapple**[2]
throstle a song-thrush.
throttle the throat, gullet, windpipe.
throu, throw, trou *Shetland Orkney*, **throuch, through, throch** *preposition* **1** through. **2** further into, inside, in another part or end of: *"she was sometimes with him and sometimes through the house"*. **3** across: *"through the bridge"*. **4** on the other side of (a wall), in the next room, next door. **5** during, in (the course of): *"through the day"*.
adverb **1** through. **2** *referring to the length or direction of a journey* across country, from start to destination; having completed one's journey, arrived: *"they came through from Ayr"*. **3** at or near one's end, done for.
verb **1** †complete. **2** succeed, win through *mainly SW*.

throu-band a stone which goes through the whole thickness of a wall. **through bearing** support, livelihood, maintenance; a way out of difficulty or hardship *now Shetland*. **through-ca** energy, drive *now NE*. **throucome** what one has to come through, an ordeal, hardship *Shetland NE*. **througang 1** a way through *now Shetland Orkney*. **2** a passage(way), thoroughfare, lane. **througate** a passage(way), lane. **through-gaun, throu gaen** *adjective* **1** passing through. **2** connecting one street, house etc to another. **3** energetic, active. *noun* **1** a passageway. **2** a strict and critical examination of a person's conduct. **through-hochie** *marbles* a throw in which the marble is thrown through the legs from behind *NE*. **through house** a house whose rooms lead off one another, with no lobby. **through-pit 1** production, output. **2** energy, activity, capacity for or progress at work. **through-pittin** a rough handling, a severe scolding or questioning.

gang throu it go bankrupt *NE*. **through the boil** up to boiling point and allowed to boil for a short time. **through the cold** *of speaking* thickly, in a choked manner. **through the floor** from one side of the room to another. **throu-the-muir** *noun* a severe dressing down, a violent row. *adjective* untidy, heedless, devil-may-care *NE*. **through time** in time, eventually. **through the week** during the week: on a weekday; on weekdays.

througal [-oo-] frugal *SW*.

through *see* **throu, thruch**

throuither, through other, throuther *adverb* mingled or mixed up (together), higgledy-piggledy.
adjective **1** *of people* untidy, disorganized, unruly. **2** *of things* confused, untidy.
noun **1** a confusion, row; a muddle *now NE*. **2** an unmethodical person.
throuitherness muddle-headedness, lack of method *now NE*.

throw *see* **thraw, throu**

thruch, through, throch, trouch [-ch, -gh as -ch in 'loch'] a flat gravestone, strictly one resting on the ground, but also applied to one resting on four feet.

thruish *see* **thrash**

thrum[1] *noun* **1 thrums** thrums, the ends of (warp-)threads, scraps of waste thread. **2** a(n obstinate) streak in a person's character; a whim, fit of bad temper.
thrummie covered with or made of **thrums**, like **thrums**, frayed *NE*. **thrummy (caip)** the Devil *NE*.
sing (gray) thrums *of a cat* purr. **three threeds and a thrum** a cat's purr *now Orkney*.

thrum[2] *of a cat* purr *now NE*.

thrummle, thrimmle 1 †press. **2** press, rub or twist between the fingers; grasp (something) by fumbling or groping. **3** fumble or grope with the fingers; work (with) the fingers in a cramped or awkward way *NE*.

thrumple crumple up, crush *NE*.

thrush *see* **thrash**

thrushen *see* **thrash**

thrustle *see* **thrissel**

thud, tud *Shetland Orkney verb* **1** thud. **2** *of wind* come in noisy blasts, bluster *now Shetland*.
noun **1** a (noisy) blast of wind, a sudden squall, gust *now Shetland Orkney*. **2** a thump, blow with the fist *now Orkney Caithness*.
thuddin a beating; a severe scolding.

thumb, thumbikins *see* **thoum**

thummle, thimble, thimmle 1 a thimble. **2 thummles** name for various plants, *eg* the foxglove, raspberries.
wha's got the thimble a variety of hunt-the-thimble.

thunner, thunder, tunnir *Shetland* thunder.
thunnered *of liquids, especially milk* tainted, soured, affected by thundery weather.
thunder-plump a sudden heavy thunder-shower. **thunner spale** a thin piece

of wood whirled round on a string to make a thunderlike noise.
thunner-an-lichtenin lungwort or other plant with white-spotted leaves.

thustle *see* **thrissel**

thwang *see* **whang**

thy, dy *Shetland*, **dee** *Shetland Orkney*, **thee** thy (used between *eg* close friends or by adults to children).

ti *see* **tae**[3]

tial a tie, fastening, something used for tying, *eg* a cord, ribbon *now Shetland Orkney*.

Tibbie Thiefie a sandpiper *NE*.

tibit *see* **taibet**

tice, tyse *now Shetland Orkney* coax, wheedle, entice.

ticht, tight [rhymes with 'licht'] *adjective* **1** tight. **2** capable, alert, vigorous. **3** *of people* close-fisted; *of things* in short supply. **4** short of money. **5** neat in build, well-made, shapely. **6** *of people* neat, smart, carefully dressed; *of things* neatly kept or arranged, snug. **7** strict, severely critical *now Caithness*.
adverb tightly, closely, neatly.
verb tighten, make close, secure or watertight.
noun a tightening.
tichten *verb* tighten. *noun* a tightening.
ticht-hauden hard-pressed, harassed *SW, S*.

tick[1] *noun* **1** *also* **tickie** a small quantity, a grain, drop. **2** the game of tig *now Shetland*.
verb tap lightly, especially in the game of tig.
tickie-tak = **tick**[1] *noun* **3** *now NE, Perth*.
†**tic-tac-toe** a game played with a slate and slate pencil.

tick[2]: **play the tick** play truant *Fife*.

tick[3], **tickie, tick tick** a call to chickens to come for food.
tickie *child's word* a hen or chicken *NE*. **tickie-taed** pigeon-toed.

ticket 1 *church* a Communion **token** (*see* **taiken**). **2** a person dressed in a slovenly, untidy or odd way, a sight.

tickie *see* **tick**[1], **tick**[3]

tickle[1] puzzle.

tickler a problem, puzzle. **tickly 1** tickly, ticklish. **2** puzzling, difficult.

tickle[2] catch, tangle, become entangled in *ECentral*.

tic-tac-toe *see* **tick**[1]

tid 1 a favourable time or season, an occasion or opportunity. **2** the proper or favourable season for ploughing etc. **3** a suitable condition of the soil for cultivation. **4** a mood, humour.

tidder *see* **tither**

tide *noun* **1** (a) time. **2** the sea, ocean. **3** the foreshore, the land between high and low water marks.
verb **1** †befall, happen. **2** leave (fishing lines) for sufficient time to let fish take the bait.

tidy, tydy 1 in good condition, shapely, plump *now Orkney*. **2** *of a cow* giving milk; in calf.

tie: tied 1 married. **2** *of people or circumstances* obliged, certain (to be), inevitable.
tie-back a short rope tied between two horses of a plough team to prevent their heads moving to the side.

tiend *see* **teind**

tift[1] order, state, condition; humour, frame of mind *now SW, S*.

tift[2], **tiff** *noun* **1** a tiff, a quarrel. **2** a fit of bad temper, the sulks. **3** †a sudden breeze, gust of wind.
tifter = **tift**[2] *noun* 1 and 2. **tifty** quarrelsome, touchy.

tig *verb* **1** amuse oneself with, keep company with, flirt with *now Shetland NE*. **2** touch, pull playfully, teasingly or amorously *now Shetland*. **3** touch lightly with the hand, especially in the game of tig. **4** *of cattle* run up and down, dash about when tormented by flies. **5** take a sudden whim, go off in a huff.
noun **1** a light playful touch, slap; the tap given in the game of tig, usually

accompanied by the call **tig. 2** a sudden whim, mood or humour; a fit of sullenness. **3** used as a call in the game of **tig** when the pursuer touches someone.

tiggie cross *now Angus Perth*.

tig-tag dally; haggle *now Shetland*. **tig-tire** a state of suspense. **tig-tow** play at tig; romp, flirt *now SW*.

chain(y) tig, high tig, lame tig variations of the game of tig. **tak the tig** take a sudden whim or notion; get a fit of the sulks.

tight *see* **ticht**

tike[1], **tyke 1** contemptuous term for a dog. **2** a rough person, a clumsy, bad-mannered boor. **3** a mischievous child; a fellow, chap.
tike-auld very old *now NE*. **tike-tired** dog-tired, worn out.

tike[2], **tyke** a tick, a mattress cover, ticking.
tyking 1 = **tike**[2.] **2** the mattress itself.
tike-o-bed a mattress.

tile, *also* **tile hat** a top hat.

till, tull (*see also* **tae**[3]) *preposition* **1** till. **2** to: *"he'll be a credit till us a'"; "If ye're keen till ken"*. **3** indicating setting about something: *"fauld up yer sleeves, and till't"*. **4** †*often with verbs of looking* at. **5** with (a specified person) as the father, by *now Shetland N*: *"she had a lassie till him"*. **6** for, on behalf of, for the benefit of: *"a cradle till her"*. **7** with, for, as an accompaniment of (food): *"tak some saut till't"*.
conjunction **1** till, until. **2** before, when: *"it was not long till I was cosy in bed"*. **3** in order that: *"give me a match till I light the gas"*.
†**till trade** by trade.

tiller *of corn etc* produce side-shoots from the root or base of the stem.

tillie-pan, tully-pan a flat iron cooking pan; a saucepan *NE*.

tim *see* **tume**

timber *see* **timmer**

time a fuss, great excitement.
timeous, timous [rhymes with 'primus']

1 (sufficiently) early, in good time *now law*. **2** at the proper time, well-timed. **at aa time** at any time, at all times. **at a time** at times, now and again. **in (all) time coming** for all time to come. **this side of time** in this world, while life lasts. **time o day 1** a clock. **2** the appropriate time. **3** a severe manhandling or scolding. **a fine time of day** a pretty pass. **the time that** while, during the time that. **a time or twa** once or twice.

timmer, timber *noun* **1** timber. **2** wood as a material, especially as used for making small articles. **3** †a wooden dish or utensil.

adjective **1** wooden, made of wood. **2** wooden, dull, stupid. **3** unmusical, tuneless.

verb **1** beat, thrash. **2 timmer up** move briskly, go at (something) vigorously *NE*.

timmer-tongue a disease of the tongue in cattle. **timmer-tuned** having a harsh unmusical voice, tone-deaf.

timorsome nervous, timid.

timous *see* **time**

tin *see* **thin, tune**

†**tinchel, tainchel** *deer-hunting* a ring of hunters who surrounded an area and closed in to entrap a deer.

tindle tinder.

tine *see* **tyne**

ting *especially of cattle* eat to bursting point *WCentral*.

ting *see* **thing**

tingle[1] (cause to) tinkle, ring or chime.

tingle[2] patch a leak in the clinkers of a boat *ECoast*.

tings *see* **tangs**

tink *see* **think**

tinker, tink, tinkler 1 *also* **tinkie** a travelling pedlar or trader, living in a tent, caravan etc, and dealing in small metal wares, brushes, baskets etc. **2** *now usually* **tink** contemptuous term for a person, especially a foul-mouthed, quarrelsome, vulgar person.

tinking an abusive scolding, a slanging

NE.

tinker's tartan *see* **tartan**. **tinker's tea** tea brewed in a pan rather than in a teapot. **not to care a tinker's curse** not to care at all.

tinnie 1 a small tin mug, especially one used by children. **2** a tinsmith.

tint, taint 1 †a conviction. **2** proof, information.

tint *see* **tyne**

tip[1] **1** tip, put a tip on. **2** remove the tip of *now Perth*. **3** walk or dance on tiptoe, trip lightly.

tipper walk on tiptoe, trip, teeter. **tippertin** a piece of cardboard pierced by a pointed stick on which it is spun *now NE*. **tippet 1** *fishing* a length of twisted horsehair to which the hook is attached on a line *now NE*. **2** a handful of stalks of straw, used *eg* in thatching; a plait, tuft or handful of hair, wool, straw etc *now NE*. **tippin** *fishing* the horsehair or nylon cord used to attach the hook to the line. **tippit 1** tipped. **2** *of a pipe, sink etc* choked to overflowing. **tippy** fashionable, stylish.

tip up dress up, smarten oneself.

tip[2]: **have a guid tip o onesel** have a good opinion of oneself.

tip[3] *football* kick lightly with the point of the toe *now Shetland NE*.

tip *see* **tuip**

tippence twopence.

tippeny, two-penny, tuppeny 1 tuppeny, twopenny. **2** †*also* **tippeny book** a child's elementary reading book, succeeding the **penny book** (*see* **penny**).

tippeny-nippeny a kind of leapfrog.

tipper, tippertin, tippet, tippin, tippy *see* **tip**[1]

tire tiredness, weariness.

tirl[1] **1** pull or strip off (a covering *eg* clothes, bedclothes, thatch). **2** strip the covering off (a person or thing); take the roof off (a building). **3** take the surface off (a piece of ground).

tirl[2], **turl** *verb* **1** cause to spin, turn, twirl. **2** turn, move (some movable fitting on a door etc) to and fro to produce a rattling, tapping noise; knock, rattle on (a door etc), *eg* with a special moveable device (*see* **pin** 2). **3** turn or bowl over, upset, trip. **4** turn over, spin, roll, swirl, whirl.

noun **1** a turn, twirl. **2** a breeze; a flurry of snow etc *now NE*. **3** a knock, rattle (on a door etc).

tirlie something which curls, twirls, or spins round *now Orkney*. **tirlie-tod** greater plantain *NE*. **tirlie-whirlie 1** an ornament, nick-nack. **2** *singing* a trill, grace-note *now Shetland*. **3** †an intricate device, a gadget.

tirl at 1 = **tirl²** *verb* 1. **2** *often* **tirl at the pin** = **tirl²** *verb* 2.

tirl³ 1 pluck on (the strings of a musical instrument). **2** cause to vibrate; sound (a musical instrument) by plucking the strings.

tirl *see* **thirl¹**

tirless 1 a trellis. **2** *also* **tirlie** a barred gate; a turnstile.

tirn *see* **turn**

tirr¹, tirve *now Orkney Caithness verb* **1** take the top layer off (a piece of ground) so as to allow digging for peat, quarrying for stone etc. **2** strip or tear off (a covering, especially roofing) *now N, Fife*. **3** strip, undress *NE*. **4** strip (a room, bed etc); dismantle. **5** rob (a fruit-tree) *NE*.

noun the layer of turf, soil etc removed from the rock of a quarry.

tirrin 1 the act of **tirring** *now Orkney N*. **2** the layer removed before digging or quarrying *now Orkney N*.

tirr² a passion, a fit of bad temper or rage.

tirran, tyran *now Shetland* **1** a tyrant. **2** a bad-tempered, awkward, or exasperating person.

tirraneese, tarraneese 1 harass with overwork; tease, irritate *NE*. **2** treat roughly, bash or batter about *NE*.

tirrick *see* **tarrock**

tirrivee 1 a fit of rage or bad temper; a wild mood. **2** a state of excitement; a disturbance, fight.

tirr-wirr *noun* a disturbance; a noisy quarrel, scolding match.

verb quarrel, fight noisily; speak sharply.

tirve *see* **tirr¹**

Tiseday *see* **Tysday**

tishie tissue.

tistle *see* **thrissel**

tit¹ pull, tug, jerk, twitch *now Shetland NE*.

tit² strike lightly, tap.

tit³ a nipple or teat.

tit⁴ a fit of bad temper or rage.

tit *see* **tait**

titch touch.

tite quickly, in rapid succession *now Shetland Orkney*.

tither, tother, tidder *Shetland NE*: **the tither 1** (the) other, alternative, second of two (or more), another; previous, recent. **2** additional, yet another, next; *see also* **tae³, tane.**

title *see* **teetle**

titlin 1 a meadow pipit *now Orkney Caithness*. **2** the smallest and weakest in a brood, especially in a litter of pigs.

tittie familiar word for a sister.

tittle gossip, tell someone something, especially by whispering in their ear; whisper, chatter.

to *see* **tae³, tho**

toaster a metal rack or (formerly) a stone for drying and toasting oatcakes in front of an open fire after baking *now NE*.

toatie *see* **tot¹**

tobacco, tabacha *now Shetland* tobacco. **tobacco fleuk** a lemon sole *NE*.

tobackie *see* **tae³**

toby 1 a stopcock or valve in a water- or gas-main, usually in a roadway, at which the supply may be cut off. **2** the penis *NE*.

tocher a marriage portion, especially a bride's dowry.

weel tochered well provided with a **tocher**; well endowed, settled.

tod¹ a fox.

toddie's grund *children's games* a place of sanctuary, a "den".

tod-lowrie a fox. **tod('s) tail(s) 1** stagshorn clubmoss. **2** foxglove *S*.

hunt the tod the game of hide-and-seek *now NE*. **(the) tod and (the) lambs** a draughts-like board game, fox and geese. **tod-i-the-faul(d)** name of various games.

tod², toddie a round cake, scone etc *now S*.

toddle, todle 1 toddle. **2** †*of running water* glide, ripple.

toe *see* **tae¹**

toga *Aberdeen University* the scarlet gown worn by undergraduates.

toil exhaust oneself with hard work *now Shetland*.

toist *see* **teistie**

toit, toyt *verb* **1** walk unsteadily, totter *now NE*. **2** move about doing odd jobs, work steadily but not too hard.

noun an attack of illness, a dizzy turn.

toitle totter; toddle; idle.

token *see* **taiken**

tol *see* **tell**

tolbooth, towbeeth *N* [-ow- as in 'cow'] **1** †a booth or office where tolls, dues etc were collected. **2** †a town prison (formerly often cells under the town hall). **3** a town hall, often including *noun* 1 and *noun* 2; a building originally used as such.

toll a checkpoint on a turnpike road where tolls were collected, a toll-bar.

toll *see* **tell**

tolter unsteady, unstable; insecure *now Orkney*.

tome, toum [-ow-] a cord of twisted horsehair used in a fishing-line, *eg* to join the hook to the line.

tongue *noun* impudence, abuse, violent language.

verb scold.

tonguie talkative.

tongue-tack(it) *see* **tack**¹·

toober *see* **tabour**

tooch [-ch- as in 'dreich'] the sound of a shot, a bang, puff *S*.

tooder *see* **touther**

too-hoo 1 a fuss; a hullabaloo. **2** a useless, wishy-washy person.

took *see* **touk¹, touk², touk³**

tooken *see* **tak**

tool *see* **toul**

tool(y)ie *see* **tulyie**

toom *see* **thoum, tume**

toon *see* **toun, tune**

toontie *see* **twenty**

toop *see* **tuip**

toopie *see* **toupie**

toor *see* **tour¹, tour², turr**

toorie *see* **tour¹**

toosh nonsense word used in children's games.

toosht 1 a loose untidy bundle (of straw etc); a bunch, tuft. **2** a slut; a nasty unpleasant person.

toot, toots *exclamation* nonsense!

toot *see* **tout¹, tout²**

tooter *verb* **1** work unskilfully, potter or mess about. **2** toddle, walk with short prim steps.

noun NE **1** ineffectual working; a botch. **2** a feckless worker. **3** a tottery walk, toddle.

tooth *see* **tuith**

toother *see* **touther**

toot-moot, teet-meet *NE* a low muttered conversation, a whispering together.

top *see* **tap¹**

tore *see* **torr**

torfle *S verb* **1** go down in health; die, be lost. **2** toss or tumble about.

torie *NE*, **story** *Shetland Orkney Caithness* the grub of the cranefly or daddy-long-legs.

toriet full of **tories** *NE*.

torn *see* **tear, thorn**

torr, tore *noun* **1** any ornamental projection or knob. **2** †the bow or pommel of a saddle.

torsk *see* **tusk¹**

torter torture *now Shetland N*.

tortie a tortoise.

tosh *adjective* **1** neat, tidy, smart. **2** intimate, friendly.
verb make neat or tidy, smarten up.

tosie, tozie 1 comfortable, cosy, snug. **2** slightly drunk and merry.

toss a toast, a drink to someone's health; the subject of a toast.

tossel 1 a tassel. **2** a tuft or fringe of hair. **3** the penis.

tot[1] **1** a small child, toddler. **2** *child's word* the penis *N*.
tot(t)ie, toatie *noun* = **tot**[1] 1. *adjective* small, tiny.

tot[2] the sum total, the whole lot: **the hail tot.**

tot[3] toddle; totter.

total teetotal.

toth *see* **tathe**

tother *see* **tither**

tottle *verb* **1** simmer, boil gently. **2** *of running water* ripple. **3** walk unsteadily, totter. **4** totter and fall, topple over.

totum[1] a teetotum, the four-sided top spun in games of chance; the game itself.

totum[2] **1** a small child. **2** any very small neat person, animal or thing.

tou *see* **thou**

tough *see* **teuch**

tought *see* **thocht**

†**touk**[1] [-oo-], **took, tuck** the beat or tap of a drum.
by tuck of drum *of a proclamation* (made) by a public crier with his drum.

touk[2] [-oo-], **took, tuck** *verb* tuck.
noun **1** a tuck, fold. **2** an embankment or jetty built to prevent soil erosion.

touk[3] [-oo-], **took** an unpleasant flavour or aftertaste.

toul, tool a towel.

toum *see* **tome**

toun, toon, town *noun* **1** a town. **2** an area of arable land on an estate, occupied by a number of farmers as co-tenants. **3** a cluster of houses belonging to the tenants of a **toun** *noun* 2, a village. **4** a farm with its buildings and the immediately surrounding area.

toundie the person left in charge of a farm when the rest of the household are away *NE*. **tounie, tounser** a town-dweller as opposed to a countryman.

toun's bodie a town-dweller. **toun end 1** the end of or way out from a town. **2** a row of cottages, usually on a farm.

toun gate the main street of a town or village *S*. †**town guard** an armed group (of ex-soldiers), enrolled for police duties *Edinburgh*. **toun heid** the higher or upper end of a town. **town house** a town hall. **toun-keeper** = **toundie** *NE*. **township** = **toun** 2, especially in the Highlands, of a community of crofters. **toun's speak** the talk of the town, the local scandal.

a clean toun a farm from which all the hired servants have left at one term. **keep (the) toun** act as **toundie** *NE*.

toupie, toopie *Shetland,* **toupican, toupichen** *NE* [-oo-] any high pointed object, a knob on the top of something.

tour[1], **toor, tower** *noun* a tower.
tourie, *often* **toorie 1** a little tower; something rising to a point; a heap (of sand, stones etc). **2** a pompom on a hat. **3** a top-knot or bun of hair. **tourock 1** = **tourie** 1. **2** an ornamental top, tuft etc.
tower house a high tower originally used both as a residence and for defence.

tour[2], **toor, tower 1** one's regular turn or spell. **2** a tour, a circular route.
tour about, tour and turn turn about, alternately.

toure *see* **turr**

touse, towse [rhymes with 'lose'] **1** pull or knock about, handle (especially a woman) roughly. **2** disorder. **3** tease out.
tousie 1 *usually the hair* untidy, tangled. **2** untidy. **3** rough, boisterous, rowdy, violent. **tousie tea** high tea. **tousle, tussle** *verb* **1** tousle, pull about (roughly); rumple. **2** *of lovers* pull one another about playfully, fondle one another. **3**

rummage about in, turn out the contents of; unravel, disentangle.

noun **1** a struggle, tussle, contest. **2** a rough romp with a person of the opposite sex. **touslie 1** *of the hair* dishevelled, ruffled. **2** *of wind* blustery, boisterous.

tout¹, toot [rhymes with 'soot'] *verb* **1** toot. **2** trumpet, make a noise like a horn; speak loudly, shout. **3** †spread (a report).

noun a toot.

touter 1 *also* **touteroo** *NE* a horn, trumpet, often a toy trumpet. **2** gossip. †**touting horn** a cow's horn sounded by a cowherd driving his animals.

tout², toot [rhymes with 'soot'] *verb* **1** drink too much, tipple. **2** drink down, empty (a glass etc) to the last drop.

noun, also **toutie 1** a draught, swig, originally a large single drink, but now rather a small but repeated drink, a tipple. **2** a drinker, tippler.

tout *see* **towt**

touteroo *see* **tout¹**

touther, toother, towther, towder, tooder, tudder *verb* handle roughly.

noun a rough handling; a throwing into confusion; disorder, a mess.

toutherie untidy, slovenly.

toutie *see* **tout²**

tove¹ *mainly S* **1** *of a fire etc* send out (smoke or flames). **2** *of smoke* billow out, rise in the air. **3** rise into the air, soar; hurry along. **4** swarm or stream out. **5** puff up with praise, flatter.

tove² chat, gossip.

tow¹ [rhymes with 'cow'] tow, flax or hemp fibre.

tow-gun a popgun with tow wadding.
hae ither tow on one's rock have other concerns or intentions.

tow² [rhymes with 'cow'] **1** a rope, cord, length of strong twine, string etc. **2** a skipping-rope. **3** a whip, whiplash. **4** a gallows rope, hangman's noose.

lat the tow gang wi the bucket *proverb* give up, get rid of something

impatiently, cut one's losses.

tow *see* **thow**

towbeeth *see* **tolbooth**

towder *see* **touther**

tower *see* **tour¹, tour²**

tow(i)n [-ow- as in 'cow'] **1** †beat; tame by beating. **2** toss and turn, bustle (about), rummage *SW*.

towler [-ow- as in 'cow'] a large marble *S*.

towmond [-ow- as in 'cow'] **1** a year. **2** a sheep or wether in its second year *S*.
†**towmondall** a year-old cow, steer or colt.

town *see* **toun, tow(i)n**

towrow [-ow- as in 'cow'] a noisy uproar, disturbance.

towse *see* **touse**

towt, tout [rhymes with 'shout'] *noun* **1** a slight illness. **2** a sudden (usually bad) mood, huff. **3** a teasing remark, taunt *S*.

verb **1** †toss about, upset, disorder. **2** tease, annoy, taunt.

towtie 1 subject to frequent attacks of slight illness. **2** touchy, irritable. **3** *of things* uncertain, changeable.

towther *see* **touther**

†**toy** a linen or wool cap with a flat crown and a back-flap reaching to the shoulders, worn by married and elderly women.

toyt *see* **toit**

tozie *see* **tosie**

traa *see* **thraw**

traan *see* **thraw**

traaward *see* **thrawart**

trace, tress a trace, a draught rope etc.

tracer 1 a trace-horse. **2** the man in charge of a trace-horse.

trachle *see* **trauchle**

track¹ *noun* a trench.

verb train or break in (a young animal or person) *NE*.

track², tract- 1 track, tow (a boat). **2** make (tea).

trackie = **track-pot** *NE*.
†**track-boat** a boat which is towed.
track-pot a teapot.

track³ a tract, a (religious) pamphlet *N*.

track⁴, tract *noun* **1** a tract (of land, time etc). **2** a continuing or settled state. **3** a period of time; a spell of weather. **4** a feature, trait.

track⁵ a poorly- or untidily-dressed person *NE*.

trackle *see* **trauchle**

tract *see* **track²**, **track⁴**

trade, tred, tread **1** trade. **2** a corporation of master craftsmen in any one trade in a **burgh**. **3** coming and going between people; a fuss. **4** a continued practice, a habit, *often* **mak a trade o. 5** the **Trades** = trades holidays.

    trades holiday(s) the annual summer holiday, originally of the craftsmen of a town, especially Edinburgh, later extended more generally; *compare* **fair**.
    tradesman a person who practices a trade, an artisan, craftsman.
    to trade by profession or occupation: *"a tailor to trade"*.

tradition *law* delivery, handing over.

traep *see* **threap**

traffeck [trafeck], **trafike** *NE* [trafike], **traffic** *noun* **1** traffic. **2** dealings, familiar communication, transactions *now Shetland Orkney N*. **3** work, progress with a job, activity *Shetland NE*. **4** **traffecks** odds and ends; spare parts; trash *now Shetland*.
    verb **1** traffic. **2** deal, have to do, or have relations (with) *now Shetland NE*.

trag 1 something of poor quality or little value, trash *Shetland NE*. **2** riffraff *NE*.

traicle, treacle, tryacle, trykle, trekkle treacle; in Scotland often used of any of molasses, treacle or syrup.
    traicle ale, traicle bendy light ale brewed from treacle, water and yeast.
    traicle gundy candy or toffee made from treacle. **traicle peerie** = **traicle ale. traicle piece** a slice of bread etc spread with treacle. **traicle scone** a scone made with treacle.
    black traicle molasses.

traik *verb* **1** be ill, in poor health; become weak; pine and die. **2** roam, wander about idly or aimlessly, prowl. **3** tramp, trudge, walk wearily or with difficulty. **4 traik after** follow, run after.
    noun **1** an illness, especially of an epidemic type. **2** misfortune, loss, especially that caused by disease in farm animals. **3** the flesh of sheep which have died of exhaustion or disease. **4** the act of **traiking** (*verb* 2, 3). **5** a person or animal who is always roving about; a gadabout. **6** a long tiring walk, a trudge.
    traikit 1 wasted, worn out; fatigued. **2** *of animals* having died of exhaustion or disease.

trail *verb* tramp, trudge; wander about idly.
    noun **1** a large collection of articles, a haul. **2** a long wearisome walk, a tramp, trudge. **3** *also* **trailach** a careless, dirty, slovenly person, especially a woman.
    trail-en(d) the first of a fleet of herring nets to be **shot** (*see* **shuit**) and hence the furthest from the boat *Shetland NE*.

traipse, trapeeze *verb* tramp, trudge wearily; shuffle through mud and dirt; go about, gad about.
    noun a long weary trudge, a tiring walk.

traison treason.

traissle tread or trample down (growing crops or grass).

trait *see* **treat**

traivel *see* **travel**

trallop *see* **trollop**

tram 1 a shaft of a barrow, cart etc. **2 trams** the legs. **3** a very tall, thin, ungainly person (with long leg). **4** a tram, a passenger car on rails; a car in a coalmine.
    tramsach *N* **1** a big, ungainly person or animal. **2** a rough, untidy person.

tramp *verb* **1** stamp or tread heavily on, trample on. **2** tread, press down, crush by treading or stamping. **3** wash (clothes or bedclothes) by treading them in soapsuds. **4** press down compactly by hand, pack firmly.

noun **1** an iron plate on the sole of a boot or shoe used in digging. **2** a strip of iron on the top of a spade blade for the foot to press on. **3** *curling* a piece of spiked iron on a boot sole to prevent slipping on the ice.

trampers the feet. **trampie** a tramp, vagrant.

tramp-cole a cock of hay compressed by **tramping. tramp-pick** a pick or crowbar with an iron bracket for the foot to press on. **tramp-wife** a female tramp *NE.* **tramp on a person's taes** intrude on a person's interests, take advantage of, offend a person.

tramsach *see* **tram**

trance *noun* **1** a narrow passage between buildings, an alley, lane. **2** a passage within a building, especially that connecting the two main rooms of a cottage, a corridor. **3** an aisle in a church.

trance door the door of a passage, especially an inner door leading from the outside door to the kitchen of a cottage.

trang *see* **thrang**

transack, transact *noun* a transaction, matter of business.

verb transact.

translate *church* transfer (a **minister**) from one charge to another.

trantles trifles; odds and ends; miscellaneous bits of equipment etc.

trap[1] correct another pupil's mistake and thus take his place in order of merit in a school class.

trap[2], *also* **trap ladder, trap stair(s)** a ladder, a (movable) flight of steps (leading up to a loft etc).

trapeeze *see* **traipse**

trappin 1 material used to trim or tie garments, lace, tape, ribbon. **2** haberdashery, goods sold by a hawker *now S.*

trapple *see* **thrapple**[1]

trash wear out, exhaust, abuse with overwork.

trashtrie trash, useless rubbish.

trath *see* **trowth**

trattle talk idly; chatter, gossip.

trauchle, trachle, trackle *verb* **1** bedraggle, injure, spoil (by dragging, knocking about etc); trail through mud etc. **2** walk slowly and wearily, drag oneself along. **3** exhaust, overburden, harass; hamper, trouble, worry: *"I'm fair trauchled"*. **4** labour on, toil.

noun **1** a long, tiring trudge or walk. **2** tiring labour, drudgery. **3** a state of complete muddle caused by having too much to do. **4** a source of trouble or anxiety, a burden. **5** a careless incompetent person, an inefficient worker.

trave *see* **threave**

travel, traivel *verb* **1** travel. **2** walk; go about or make a journey on foot; walk back and forth, pace up and down; do (a journey) on foot. **3** go about on foot begging or hawking haberdashery, *often* **travel the roads. 4** drive (cattle etc) from place to place along a road.

noun **1** travel. **2** a walk, journey on foot.

traveller 1 a hawker, tinker, gipsy. **2** a head-louse.

travelly *see* **trevallie**

travise, trevis(s) 1 a wooden partition between two stalls in a stable or cowshed. **2** †*also* **triffice** a stall or loose-box in a stable.

trawn *see* **thrawn**

tray *see* **thrae**

treacle *see* **traicle**

tread *see* **trade**

treadwiddie the draught-chain with hook and swivel connecting a plough or harrow to the swingle-trees.

treat, trait 1 treat. **2** †beg, request.

trebling *piping, in* **pibroch** the form in which the **doubling** (*see* **dooble**) of a variation is sometimes repeated with further development.

tred *see* **trade**

tree 1 †wood, timber. **2** a rod, stick, pole. **3** *mining* a pit-prop. **4** †a wooden barrel, keg, especially for ale.

†**tree-leg** a wooden leg. **tree-speeler** a tree-creeper.

tree *see* **three**

treed *see* **threid**

treelip *see* **trollop**

treeple *now NE* **1** treble, triple. **2** play (a tune) in triple time or dance to it, waltz; beat time with the foot to a dance tune.

treesh *now NE verb* **1** *often* **treesh wi** beg, wheedle, entice in a kind and flattering way. **2** run after, court. **3** call an animal.

exclamation a call to cattle, especially calves, to come.

treetle, trytle 1 trickle. **2** walk with short steps, trot.

trekkle *see* **traicle**

tremendous, tremendious *adjective* tremendous.

adverb very much, extremely.

tremmle, tremble, trimmle tremble.

tremmlin a virus disease of sheep, causing paralysis, tremor etc. **tremmlin tree** an aspen. **trimmlin strae(s)** unthreshed straw *NE*. See also **Tam, Tammie.**

tresh *see* **thrash**

treshel *see* **thrashel**

treshen *see* **thrash**

tress a trestle for holding up a board, table etc, often including the bench it supports.

tress *see* **trace**[1]

tretten *see* **thirteen**

tretty *see* **therty**

treush *see* **thrash**

trevallie, travelly [trevallie, trevellie] a startling noise, a crash; a disturbance, brawl.

trevis(s) *see* **travise**

trew, trow, true believe.

trews [trooze] **1** *formerly* close-fitting trousers made of fine, usually tartan cloth, with the legs extended to cover the feet, worn by Highlanders; *later* tartan trousers worn by certain Scott-

ish regiments; short tartan trunks worn under a kilt. **2** ordinary trousers.

tribble *see* **trouble**

tricker the catch or trigger (of a gun).

trid *see* **third**

triffice *see* **travise**

triffle a trifle, a small amount.

trift *see* **thrift**

trig *adjective* **1** active, nimble, lively, alert. **2** trim, neat, well turned out; tidy. *verb often* **trig up, trig out** smarten up.

trimmle *see* **tremmle**

trimmlin Tam *see* **Tam**

trimmlin Tammie *see* **Tammie**

trindle *see* **trinnle**

trink 1 a trench, channel, ditch, gutter. **2** a narrow coastal inlet. **3** a rut in a road. **trinkit** rutted *NE*.

trinkle 1 trickle. **2** sprinkle, scatter over.

trinnle, trunnel, †**trindle** *noun* a wheel or similar circular object; a wheelbarrow wheel.

verb, also **trintle 1** *of an object, vehicle etc* roll, trundle, bowl along. **2** *of people etc* move along; waddle; straggle. **3** flow, trickle. **4** cause to roll, flow, trickle.

trintlet a small ball or pellet, *eg* of sheep's dung.

tripling *especially in* **pibroch** *or* **strathspey** (*see* **strath**) a melody note divided into three by the insertion of two short grace-notes.

trist *see* **thrist**

trith *see* **trowth**

trive *see* **thrive**

troch, trough, trouch [rhymes with 'loch' or 'cow'] *noun* **1** a trough. **2 trochs**, *latterly* **trows** a (wooden) channel for water, especially one leading to a millwheel. **3** the channel or bed of a river, especially a rough part; a similar channel among sea rocks. **4** †the valley or basin of certain rivers in south-west Scotland. **5** *often* **trochie** a narrow passage between houses. **6** *usually* **trows** a kind of flat-bottomed river barge in two sections with a space through which salmon could be speared *S*. **7** *contemptuous* a person who eats or drinks to excess.

trowmill a watermill. **troch-stane** a stone trough.

trock *see* **troke**

troddle toddle, trot.

troddle *see* **trottle**

trodge trudge *now Shetland Orkney Angus*.

trogger, troggin *see* **troke**

trogs, trugs *exclamation* faith, *often* **by my trogs.**

trois *see* **turse**

troke, truck, trock, trouk [-oo-], **trog** *verb* **1** truck, bargain, barter. **2** trade, deal in a small way with. **3** spread, carry (news, gossip etc). **4** associate with, have evil or unlawful dealings with, be on friendly or intimate terms with. **5** potter or bustle (about) fussily, occupy oneself with trivial matters.

noun **1** truck, barter, exchange; a bargain or business deal. **2** *usually* **trokes** haberdashery, odds and ends, trinkets. **3** any worthless or rubbishy goods; trash. **4** *of people or animals* worthless specimens. **5** truck, improper dealings, association. **6** a small piece of work or business, a task, errand. **7** nonsensical talk, rubbish.

tro(c)ker, trucker, trogger a bargainer, dealer, petty trader, pedlar. **trockerie, troggin** = **troke** *noun* 2.

troll an untidy, slovenly person.

trollie-bags 1 the guts of people or animals. **2** a fat, unshapely person.

trollop, trallop, treelip *NE noun* **1** a trollop. **2** a long, clumsy person or animal. **3** a long, trailing piece of cloth, a tatter; a large, ugly, straggling mass of something.

verb hang or trail loosely or untidily.

tron, †trone 1 †a weighing machine, especially a public one in a **burgh**, set up in or near a market-place for weighing merchandise, especially local produce. **2** the place or building where the

tron stood and the area round it; the market-place; the town centre; sometimes also used in the past as a place of public exposure and punishment. **3** †*also* **tron weight** the standard weight for home-produced commodities, varying in different localities.

trone *see* **troon, truan**

tronie a long story, rambling chat *Angus*.

troon, trone, troo *noun* a truant, *often* **play the troon.**

verb play truant (from).

trooshlach trash, useless things or people.

trooshter 1 useless rubbish *NE*. **2** troublesome children *N*.

troot *see* **trout**

trosk a silly, talkative person; a slow-witted, slovenly person, especially a woman *Caithness*.

trot: trottin *of a stream etc* babbling. **trottle 1** toddle. **2** dawdle, idle.

back-door trot diarrhoea. **short in the trot** *see* **short.**

trot the throat *Shetland Orkney*.

troth *see* **trowth**

trottle, troddle, trottlick a small ball of dung, especially of sheep.

trottle *see* **trot**

trou *see* **throu**

trouble, tribble 1 trouble. **2** sickness, disease; an ailment. **3** *mining* a fault in a seam.

trouch *see* **thruch, troch**

trough *see* **troch**

trouk *see* **troke**

trouker [-oo-], **trucker** a cheat; a rascal, rogue.

troush [troosh] a call to cattle.

trouss *see* **turse**

trout, troot 1 a trout. **2** *often* **troutie** term of endearment to a child.

trow, trowl [-ow- as in 'cow'] roll, spin round.

trow *see* **trew**

trowen *see* **truan**

trowmill, trows *see* **troch**

trowth *now Caithness* [-ow- as in 'cow'], **truth, troth, truith, trith, trath** *Shetland*

Orkney **1** truth. **2** troth, one's pledged word.

truan, trowen [-ow- as in 'cow'], **trone** a trowel; a tool for smoothing cement or plaster.

truck *see* **troke**

trucker *see* **troke, trouker**

trudder rubbish, trash.

true *see* **trew**

truel a trowel.

truff *see* **turr**

trugs *see* **trogs**

truith *see* **trowth**

trump a Jew's harp.

trumph trump, the chief suit in a card game; a splendid person etc.
what's (to be) trumph(s)? what's doing?, how are things?, what's to be done next?

trumphery trash, rubbish.

truncher a trencher.

trunnel *see* **trinnle**

trusdar [**troos**ter] an untrustworthy person *N Highland SW*.

truster *law* a person who sets up a trust for the administration of property or funds.

truth *see* **trowth**

tryacle, trykle *see* **traicle**

trypal a tall, thin, ungainly person.

tryst [rhymes with 'priced'] *noun* **1** †an agreement, a pledge. **2** an appointment to meet at a specified time and place. **3** an appointed meeting or assembly, a rendezvous. **4** an appointed meeting-place; a conspicuous object chosen as a rendezvous, *eg* for huntsmen. **5** a market, especially for the sale of livestock, a fair.
verb **1** make an appointment, arrange a time and place of meeting. **2** meet with by pre-arrangement. **3** engage to be married. **4** order or arrange (something) in advance. **5** fix, arrange (a time or occasion). **6** invite, encourage, entice. **7** **tryst wi** make a fuss of, coax, wheedle *N*.

trysted *of people* hired or engaged in advance; *of things* made to order. **trysting** the place or time for a **tryst**: *"trysting place"; "trysting tree"*.
bide (one's) tryst wait for someone at a prearranged meeting-place. **haud (one's) tryst** do as one has agreed, keep one's word.

trytle *see* **treetle**

tu *see* **tae**³

tub *mining* a **hutch** for carrying cut coal; a measure of coal.

tuchit *see* **teuchit**

tuck, tewk a call to hens to come for food. **tuckie (hen)** *child's word* a hen or chicken.

tuck *see* **touk**¹, **touk**²

tuckie awkward, clumsy; *of a limb etc* disabled, deformed *NE*.

tud *see* **thud**

tudder *see* **touther**

tug, chug, teug tug.
tuggle, chuggle pull (about) roughly and jerkily.

tuil, teel *now NE* **1** a tool; *humorously* any piece of equipment etc. **2** term of contempt for a person.

tuilz(i)e *see* **tulyie**

tuip, tup, toop, tip, teep *NE* **1** a ram. **2** *familiar or slightly insulting* a man.
verb, usually of a ram mate; sire.
tup-yeld *of a ewe* barren, infertile.

tuir *see* **tear**

tuird, taird a turd.

tuith, tooth, teeth **1** a tooth. **2** a part of a rainbow seen near the horizon, regarded as a sign of bad weather *NE*. **tuithfu(l)** a mouthful.
in spite of someone's teeth despite someone's wishes or efforts, in defiance of someone.
granny's tuith *see* **grannie**

tuk *see* **tak**

tull *see* **till**

tulloch a mound, hillock; frequently a fairy mound.

tully *see* **tulyie**

tully-pan *see* **tillie-pan**

tulyie, tuilz(i)e, tool(y)ie [**toolie**], **tully,**

teulie, †**tweelie** *SW noun* **1** a quarrel, fight; a noisy row, a struggle; a verbal quarrel, wrangle. **2** trouble; toil, exertion.

verb quarrel, fight; argue, squabble.

tume, toom, teem *N,* **taim, tim** *adjective* **1** empty; unoccupied, vacant. **2** *of a person or his limbs etc* thin, lank. **3** fasting, hungry. **4** echoing. **5** foolish. **6** *of words etc* vain, hollow. **7** *of machinery* idling, not actually processing material.

verb **1** empty (a container); empty (a glass etc) by drinking. **2** empty (the contents) from a container. **3** fire (a gun). **4** *of rain* pour, come down heavily; *compare* **teem.**

noun a place where rubbish is emptied, a dump.

tume-handit empty-handed, bringing no gifts. **tume-heidit** silly, foolish.

tumfie, tumphie a dull, stupid, soft person.

tummle tumble.

tummle the cat do a somersault, go head over heels *Shetland NE.*

tummock, †**tammock** a small hillock, a tussock; a molehill.

tumphie *see* **tumfie**

tumshie a turnip.

tunder tinder *now Angus.*

tune, toon, tin, teen *NE noun* **1** a tune. **2** intonation (of speech), often associated with a particular dialect. **3** mood, humour, temper.

verb **1** tune. **2** put (an implement) in proper working order, adjust.

tunie moody.

tak a tune to oneself play a tune by oneself.

tunnir *see* **thunner**

tup *see* **tuip**

tuppeny *see* **tippeny**

turbot a halibut.

turf *see* **turr**

turk fierce, truculent, sullen.

turkas a pair of pincers or pliers, especially as used by a blacksmith.

turl *see* **tirl**[2]

turmit *see* **turneep**

turn, tirn *verb* **1** turn. **2** turn (cut hay, peats etc) to dry; dismantle and rebuild (a small stack etc of such) for drying. **3** become, grow, *eg "it was a dark night turned"; "ye're turnin a big boy".*

noun **1** a turn. **2** a stroke or spell of work; a piece of work, duty. **3** a trick: **tak the turn oot o** trick, deceive. **4** a rebuff, setback. **5** a refrain especially in a ballad.

turn-fittin building piles of peats (as *verb* 2). **turnpike,** †**turnpike stair** a spiral stair, a stair revolving round a central axis.

aff the turn *of a door* at rest, still. **the day** *or* **year is on the turn** the days are changing in length of daylight, temperature etc. **do the turn** serve a (useful) purpose, meet a need. **turn someone's hand** provide someone with the money for something, relieve someone of financial difficulties. **turn someone's head** make someone feel giddy or drunk. **the turn of the nicht** midnight, the dead of night. **turn ower in years** grow old, age. **turn to the door** put out of one's house, expel. **turn up the wee finger** have a habit of drinking too much. **turn the (wull) cat** do a somersault, go head over heels. **the turn o the year** the time of year when the days begin to lengthen.

turneep, turnip, turmit a turnip, *in Scotland* usually a swede.

turnpike *see* **turn**

turr, truff, turf, toure, toor *noun* **1** turf. **2** a surface peat or turf cut as fuel. **3** †the turf over a grave; the grave itself.

verb remove surface turf from.

Turra Turriff, the town in Aberdeenshire. **Turra neep, Turra tattie** nickname for a native or inhabitant of Turriff *NE.*

turse, trouss, trois *verb* **1** truss, pack up, make into a bale etc. **2** adjust or tuck up (a garment etc); get dressed.

noun **1** a truss, a bundle, bale, *eg* of

straw, thatch, sticks etc. **2** a tuck, fold, or hem in a garment.

tushilago [-laygo] **1** *also* **dishilago** tussilago, coltsfoot. **2** a butter bur.

tusk[1], **torsk** *Shetland* a ling-like fish of the cod family, found mainly in northern Scottish waters.

tusk[2] *noun, mainly* **tusks**, *also* **tusk stones**, **tuskin(g) (stones)** *building* projecting end-stones for bonding with an adjoining wall, toothing.

verb cut (peat) from above the bank *N*.

tusk[3] empty (out) the contents of (a bag etc); empty one container into another.

tussle *see* **touse**

tutor *law* the guardian and administrator of the estate of a **pupil**.

tutor dative a **tutor** appointed by a court, originally by the Crown. **tutor nominate, tutor testamentar(y)** a **tutor** appointed originally by the father, now by either parent of a **pupil** to act if the parent(s) should die.

tutor at *or* **of law** the nearest male relative on the father's side, who becomes **tutor** of a **pupil** in default of one appointed by the parents.

twa, twae, two, qua, †**tway** two.

twosie the second move etc in various games. **twosome 1** (of or for) a pair, a group or company of two. **2** (a Scottish country dance, especially a **strathspey** (*see* **strath**)) performed by two people. **twa-bedded** twin-bedded. **twa-eyed (beef)steak** *humorous* a herring or kipper. **twa-fanglet** indecisive *NE*. **twafaul(d) 1** twofold. **2** bent double. **3** deceitful, two-faced. **twa-han(d)(it) crack** a conversation between two people. **twa-han(d)it work** work so badly done that it has to be done again. **twahorse ferm** a farm needing only two horses to work it. **twa-pair** *of a farm* worked by two pairs of horses. **(the) twa part** two thirds. **twa-skippet, twasnooted** *of a cap* with a peak back and front, *eg* a deerstalker. **two or three, twa three, twaree, twartree** *Shetland*

Orkney two or three, a few, several. **twa words** a discussion, argument.

nane o the twa neither. **ony o the twa** either.

twad *see* **will**[1]

twae *see* **twa**

twal, twel, twelve, twol, twull, qual 1 twelve. **2** a set or group of twelve persons or things. **3 the twal** twelve o'clock, especially midnight.

twelt, twalt twelfth. **twelvesie** the last move in the game of **chucks** (*see* **chuck**[2]), in which uncaught stones must be laid in a row.

twal hours, twaloors 1 twelve noon (or occasionally midnight). **2** a midday snack or drink; a midday meal. **twal hundred** (of) medium-fine linen woven on a reed of twelve hundred splits. **twalmonth** (the period of) a year.

twang a sudden sharp pain, an acute pang.

twar *see* **be**

twaree *see* **twa**

twart *see* **thort**

twartree, tway *see* **twa**

tway *see* **twa**

tweed a strong, usually rough-textured, twilled woollen cloth, usually of yarn of two or more colours, made usually in the Borders and in the Outer Hebrides (**Harris tweed**).

tweedle[1] †*verb, noun* = **tweel**[1].

tweedle[2] **1** †twiddle (the fingers etc). **2** cheat, deceive *NE*.

tweel[1], **twill** *noun* **1** twill, a diagonally-ribbed cloth. **2** *ploughing* the angle at which the coulter is set in the beam, which determines the lie of the furrow. *verb* weave as in *noun* 1.

†**tweeling** cloth, usually linen, woven thus.

tweel[2] *exclamation* indeed!

tweelie *see* **tulyie**

tween between.

tween hands between times, meantime. **tween heid** *ploughing* the part of the reins joining the heads of two horses in a team.

tweest *see* **twist**

tweeter twitter.

tweetle whistle, warble, sing.

tweezlick *see* **twist**

twel, twelt, twelve, twelvesie *see* **twal**

twenty, twinty, twonty, twunty, toontie 1
twenty. **2** †twentieth.

twice, twise *now Shetland Orkney,* **twic(e)t**
twice.

  twiser *in the game of* **buttons** a button
valued at two shots.

  the twice(t) for a second time.

twig[1] jerk, tug, twitch.

twig[2] a quick or sidelong glance; a
glimpse *NE*.

twill *see* **tweel**[1]

twilt quilt.

twin, twine 1 divide, separate, part *now
Shetland.* **2** part company, go one's
separate way *now Shetland.* **3** part with,
give up *now Shetland Orkney Caithness.* **4** take (something) from, deprive
(a person) of (something). **5** take a
lamb from a weak ewe and give it to a
strong one to suckle with her own.

twine *noun* string.

  verb **1** †join, unite in marriage. **2** twist;
twist the body, wriggle, writhe.

  twiner the person or machine
employed to twist spun yarn into a
thicker thread *S*.

twinter, quinter *SW, S* a two-year old
farm animal, especially a thrice-shorn
ewe.

twinty *see* **twenty**

twise, twiser *see* **twice**

twist, tweest *now Orkney NE* **1** a twist; (a)
thread; an act of twisting. **2** a small
amount (of food or drink).

  twister, tweezlick *NE* an instrument
used to twist straw or rush ropes.

twit chirp, twitter.

twit *see* **white**[2]

twitter[1] (cause to) quiver or tremble.

twitter[2] a thin part of unevenly spun yarn.

two *see* **twa**

twol *see* **twal**

twonty *see* **twenty**

two-penny *see* **tippeny**

twosie, twosome *see* **twa**

twull *see* **twal**

twunty *see* **twenty**

tyach [tee**ach**], **tach** exclamation of
impatience, contempt or bad temper.

tyangs *see* **tangs**

tyarr [tee**arr**] fight, be likely to quarrel.

tyauve [tee**awve**] *verb, past tense* **tew,**
†**tyeuve** [tee**oo**(**ve**)] **1** knead, work
(dough). **2** pull or knock about, treat
roughly *NE*. **3** fatigue, wear out. **4**
struggle physically, tumble or toss
about. **5** *also* **chauve** strive, struggle
(frequently with little result), live or
work hard, exert oneself *NE*. **6** walk
heavily or with difficulty through snow
etc *NE*.

  noun, also **chauve** labouring, exertion,
a hard struggle; a laborious walk *NE:*
"Ye ken the tyauve it is to work a ferm."

tyce move about slowly and easily; walk
cautiously *NE*.

tydy *see* **tidy**

tye yes, indeed, certainly *NE*.

tyeuch *see* **teuch**

tyeuve *see* **tyauve**

tyke *see* **tike**[1], **tike**[2]

tyking *see* **tike**[2]

tylor *see* **tailor**

tympany a gable-shaped raised middle
part of the front of a house.

tyne, tine *verb, past tense, past participle
also* **tint 1** lose, suffer the loss, destruction or disappearance of, mislay; cause
the loss of. **2** fail to get, miss, be
deprived of, lose *now NE*. **3** lose or
miss (one's way), stray from (the right
road), get lost; lose (one's footing),
miss (a step). **4** lose by letting fall; *knitting* drop (a stitch) *NE*. **5** get rid of,
abandon. **6** forget, be unaware of. **7**
spend in vain, waste (time, effort etc).
8 draw away from, leave behind *NE*. **9**
of things lose value, fade away; *of people or animals* die *now Shetland NE*.

  between (the) tyning and (the) winning

in a critical state, hovering between success and failure. **tint** lost; bewildered.

tyoch *see* **teuch**

type[1] *NE:* **typin** toilsome. **typit** worn out by hard work.

type[2] a low conical hill *SW*.

type *see* **teep**

tyran *see* **tirran**

Tysday, Tiseday, †**Teysday** Tuesday.

tyse *see* **tice**

U

ucha *see* **uhuh**

udder, ether, uther, edder *NE* an udder.
udderlocks locks of wool growing beside a ewe's udder.
verb **udderlock** pluck the wool from a ewe's udder to let lambs suck easily.

ug, oug *verb* **1** be sickened; feel repulsion. **2** disgust, sicken; annoy, upset, exasperate *now Shetland NE*.
noun NE **1** a dislike; a feeling of sickness, *often* **take an ug at** take a dislike to. **2** an object of disgust; a person with disgusting manners.
uggin disgusting, horrible; objectionable; annoying. **uggit** upset, annoyed; disgusted; fed up. **ug(g)some** disgusting, repulsive, horrible.

ugly, oogly *adjective* ugly.
noun a protective shade attached to the front of a woman's bonnet; a protective bonnet on a high cane frame, worn by women field-workers.

uhuh, ucha expression of agreement or attentiveness.

uilie *see* **oil**

ultimus haeres *law* last heir, a title applied to the Crown when succeeding to the property of someone who has died without a will or any known heir.

ultroneous *law, of a witness* one who gives evidence spontaneously without being formally cited; *of evidence* given voluntarily.

ulyie *see* **oil**

umberella an umbrella.

umman *see* **woman**

umost, eemost *NE* uppermost, highest.

†**umquhile** [umwhile] *mainly of people* former, late; *especially law* deceased.

un-, on-, one-, oon-, wan- un-, not, without.

unable: unable for unfit for, incapable of; having no appetite for (food).

unalike different.

unbekent 1 unknown, strange, unfamiliar (to). **2** unobserved, unnoticed.

unbeknowins unnoticed, secretly, unobtrusively.

unbonnie ugly, *eg "that's no unbonny"* that's pretty.

unbowsome [-ow- as in 'cow'] stiff; unable to bend or stoop.

unbraw plain, unattractive.

unca, uncan *see* **unco**

uncannie, oncanny *N,* **ooncanny** *N* **1** *of things* awkward, not easy to manage. **2** *especially of a blow or fall* hard, violent, severe. **3** dangerous, unreliable, insecure, treacherous, threatening; *of things* unlucky, tempting fate. **4** *of people* mischievous, malicious; not safe to meddle with, because thought to have connections with witchcraft, the devil etc. **5** *especially of things* mysterious, ominous, eerie.

uncassen 1 *of clothes* not faded or worn *NE.* **2** *of* **peats** not cut *Shetland NE.*

unce an ounce.

unchancy 1 unlucky; ill-omened, ill-fated. **2** dangerous, threatening, treacherous, not to be meddled with.

unco, unca, uncan *Shetland,* **unkin** *Shetland Orkney adjective* **1** unknown, unfamiliar, strange. **2** so much altered as to be scarcely recognizable *now NE.* **3** *of countries or lands* foreign *now Shetland.* **4** unusual; odd, strange, peculiar. **5** remarkable, extraordinary, great, awful. **6** reserved, shy *now Shetland.*
adverb very, extremely.
noun **uncos 1** strange or unusual things, rarities, novelties; news, gossip. **2** †strangers, foreigners.
uncoly very much. **unconess** strangeness, peculiarity, eccentricity.
†**unco body** a stranger, outsider, new-

comer. **unco folk** strangers. **the unco guid** the self-righteously moral or religious. **unco like** *adjective* **1** = unco. **2** *also* **unco leukin** having a strange or wild appearance; looking out of sorts, miserable.

unction auction.

undeemous, ondeemous extraordinary; immense, incalculable.

under, unner, onder, oon(d)er *Shetland N* under.

under night during the night, by night. **understane** the lower millstone; the bedstone. **underwater** water below the surface of the ground; water that has accumulated in the foundations of a house.

undocht, ondocht a feeble, weak or ineffective person.

une, oven, †**oon,** †**oen** an oven.

oon cake a thick bun made from oatmeal and yeast, baked in the oven. **une pot** a large shallow pan used as an oven by being set among the glowing embers of a fire.

unerstan(d), onerstan(d), oon(d)erstan(d), winnerstan *NE verb, past tense also* **unersteed** *NE* understand.

unfarrant unattractive, unpleasant; not refined.

†**unfeary, onfeirie** inactive, weak, unsteady on one's feet.

unfeel unpleasant, dirty, filthy; rough; uncomfortable *S*.

unfierdy overgrown, unwieldy, not in proper trim.

unfordersome, unfurthersome slow, hindering.

unfreely heavy, unwieldy.

unfriend, unfreend one who is not a friend, an enemy.

nunfurthersome *see* **unfordersome**

†**unhanty** clumsy, big and fat.

unheartsome cheerless, dismal.

unhearty listless, depressed; in poor condition; rather uncomfortable *now Shetland*.

unhonest dishonest.

united: United Free (Church) the church formed by the union in 1900 of the majority of the members of the **Free Church of Scotland** (*see* **free**) with the United Presbyterian Church, the majority of whose members later (1929) joined the **Church of Scotland** (*see* **church**).

universal *law, of an heir* taking over the total rights, obligations etc of his predecessor, usually **universal successor.**

unken, oonken †not to know, fail to recognize.

unkenning unknowing, ignorant. **onkent 1** *also* **unkent by** unknown, unfamiliar, strange (to). **2** *also* **unkent to** unnoticed, unobserved (by) *N*.

unkin *see* **unco**

unleeze disentangle.

unless, onless *conjunction* unless. *preposition* except, but (for).

unlucky, *often* **foul unlucky** slatternly, slovenly *NE*.

unmainnerfu rude, bad mannered.

unner *see* **under**

unresty unrestful, ill at ease *now Caithness*.

unricht, onricht not right, unjust; dishonest, improper.

unscaumit not burned or scorched, unscathed *Shetland NE*.

†**unscrapit** rude, insulting.

†**unsonsie 1** unlucky; unfortunate. **2** *of a blow etc* severe, causing death or injury. **3** unpleasant, treacherous, troublesome, mischievous. **4** plain, unattractive; slovenly, untidy.

†**unspoken** *of something used in folk-medicine* not spoken over, gathered or handled in silence.

untellin impossible to tell, beyond words.

until, ontil 1 until. **2** †to, unto, as far as, towards. **3** into *now NE*.

untowtherly [-ow- as in 'cow'], **untodderly** *adjective NE* **1** big and clumsy, badly-shaped. **2** slovenly, untidy in dress or appearance.

unweel, unwell not in good health, ill (suggesting a more seriousp illness than in English); sickly, ailing.

unwiselike indiscreet, unwise, foolish.

unwittins unwittingly, inadvertently.

up, oup, oop 1 up. **2** *of a river* in flood. **3** *of people* in a state of excitement or irritation *now NE*. **4** *also* **up in life, up in years** *of a child* growing up; *of an adult* advanced in years, elderly. **5** *of a chimney* on fire.

oopie stiffie, oopsie doopsie *encouraging a child to get to its feet* upsadaisy.

neither up nor doun 1 nowhere. **2** *especially of feelings etc* unaffected by events, the same as before. **up about** somewhere in or near. **up the country** in or from the upland or inner part of a district *now NE*. **up and doun** from every angle, in every aspect, thoroughly. **up or doun** one way or the other, here or there. **up the house** into the inner part of a house, from the door inwards. **up wi 1** as good as; equal to, fit for, capable of. **2** even with, quits with. **up wi't** *in songs* hurrah!, bravo!

upbiggit built up *NE*.

upbrak breaking up, *eg* of a gathering.

upbring *verb* bring up, rear.

noun training, education, maintenance during childhood.

upby up there, up the way, up at or to a place, especially somewhere thought of as being higher or better than where the speaker is, *eg* Heaven; upstairs.

upcast *verb* taunt, reproach, bring up against someone.

noun **1** a taunt, reproach, reason or occasion for criticism. **2** an upset, a state of being overturned. **3** *mining* a fault in a seam of coal which forces it upwards; *also* **up shaft** the shaft by which the ventilating current returns to the surface.

upcastin(g) a gathering of clouds, a cloud formation.

upcome 1 †outward appearance; promising aspect. **2** a comment, saying, turn of phrase *N*. **3** the final or decisive point, the result, outcome.

upcomin(g) 1 †an ascent, rise. **2** one's upbringing, development from childhood to adulthood.

upfeshin, upfessan upbringing, the rearing and training of young people *mainly NE*.

†**upgie, upgive** *verb, mainly law* give up, deliver up, resign.

uphaud, uphald, uphold *verb, past tense, past participle also* **upheeld** *NE* **1** uphold. **2** look after, maintain. **3** maintain in argument, guarantee. **4** raise, lift up.

noun **1** a person who upholds another, a support. **2** the support or maintenance of a person, estate etc; the upkeep of property.

upheeze lift up, raise; elate.

uplift [uplift] **1** collect, draw, take possession of (money, rents, etc). **2** dig up, harvest (potatoes and other root crops). **3** pick up, *eg* take on (passengers), collect (tickets, parcels).

uplifted elated, in high spirits, proud.

upmak 1 invention, composition, a made-up story, song, plan *Shetland NE*. **2** compensation, reparation *now Shetland Orkney*.

upmaking 1 the act of making up or preparing something, now especially the assembly of lines of type into pages for printing. **2** = **upmak** *noun* 1 *Shetland NE*.

upon, upo, apo(n) *Shetland* **1** upon, on. **2** about, concerning: *"think upon it"*. **3** *of time* during, on the occasion of *now Shetland Orkney NE*: *"sleep upon the day"*. **4** *of place or manner* in: *"meet one upon the street"*. **5** at *now Shetland NE*: *"I shook my neive apon him.* **6** (be married etc) to, with: *"my marriage upon my own cousin"*.

upper applied to the higher section of a divided estate, often in farm-names: *"Upperton"*.

uppie *in the game of hand-ball* a member of the team playing towards the upward goal, the **uppies** usually coming from the upper part of the town *Orkney S; compare* **doonie** (*under* **doon**).

uppitting, upputting 1 lodging, accommodation. **2** a business establishment, a domestic establishment or home; a (servant's) place or situation.

upple *mainly of rain or snow* stop falling, clear *N*.

upredd *verb* tidy, put in order.
noun a cleaning, tidying.
upreddin a scolding.

upset [up*set*] *noun* **1** *mining* a working place driven upwards following the course of the seam. **2** = **upset price** (*see adjective* 2).
adjective **1** set up, raised, erected. **2** *of a price at an auction* which will be acceptable to the seller; *latterly also of a price of property* below which bids will not be accepted: *"the upset price was £60,000 but the best bid was £75,000."*
upsetting *noun* arrogance. *adjective* haughty, presumptuous ambitious, giving oneself airs.

upsides: be upsides wi, be upsides doun wi be even with, have one's revenge on.

upslaag *Shetland*, **upslay** *NE*, **upsilly** *NE* a change in weather, especially from hard frost to milder conditions.

upstandin(g) *adjective, of wages* regular, fixed, basic.
noun, usually of foodstuffs substance, solidity *NE*. **be upstanding** stand up, rise to one's feet, *eg* ceremonially to drink a toast, for a prayer: *"Will you please be upstanding for the benediction".*

upstart *building* an upright or vertically set jamb- or reveal-stone in a door or window-case.

upsteer, upstir stir up, throw into turmoil; stimulate, encourage.

upstraucht straighten oneself up *NE*.

uptail: be uptail and awa leave in haste, flee at once.

uptak, uptake *verb* understand.
noun **1** the capacity for understanding, intelligence, *often* **gleg in the uptak, slow in the uptake. 2** dealings, involvement, relationship. **3** the lifting or gathering of a crop, especially a root-crop *Shetland NE*.

upthrou(gh), upthrow [rhymes with 'moo' or 'cow'] in the upper part of the country, in or from the uplands, in the Highlands, inland from the sea *Shetland Orkney Caithness N*.
adjective inland.

upwith upwards.

urban *law, of a lease etc* relating to a building, as opposed to land (whether in town or country); *compare* **rural.**

ure[1], **yower** [rhymes with 'pure'] an udder, usually of a cow or ewe *SW, S*.

ure[2] [rhymes with 'poor'] **1** a damp mist; fine rain, drizzle. **2** a haze, especially when lit by sunbeams.

ure[3] [rhymes with 'puir'], **eer** *NE* **1** †ore. **2** clay containing iron, barren iron-bearing soil, red gravelly earth *now Shetland.*

†**ure**[4] the monetary value of an ounce of silver.
urisland *Shetland Orkney*, **eyrisland** *Orkney*, **ure (of land)** *Shetland Orkney* a measure of land, originally assessed at the monetary value of an ounce of silver.

urlar [oorlar] *piping, in a* **pibroch**: the basic theme of the tune.

us, uz, wis, wiz *now Shetland*, **his, hiz, huz** *S*, **iz** *Shetland Caithness S*, **s, z 1** us. **2** we: *"us Edinburgh girls.."*. **3** me, *eg* "*I tell'd him a lee..he jist felled iz like a herrin".*
us anes, us yins we, us, those of our group etc.

use, yeese *N*, **eese** *N*, **us** *now Shetland*, **yuise** *noun, also* **yis(s) 1** use. **2** need, occasion, reason for or to.
verb, also **yaise 1** use. **2** *mainly* **used wi, eest wi** made familiar with, accustomed to. **3** be or become accustomed (to).

eesage usage *NE*. **useless** *adjective* **1** useless. **2** ill; unable, owing to illness or exhaustion *Shetland Orkney Caithness N. adverb, also* **ees(e)less** *NE* exceedingly, far too, *eg "he has put on useless many coals".*

†**usquebae, usquebaugh** [ooskibay] whisky.

usual, eeswal *NE* usual.

one's (auld) usual one's usual state of health, frame of mind; one's old self: *"he's in his usual".*

uts *exclamation* tut!

uther *see* **udder**

uver *see* **over**

uz *see* **us**

V

vacance, vagans S a holiday, vacation.

vage see **vaige**

vaig, vague, vyaug [vee**awg**] NE verb wander about idly, roam aimlessly; gad about.
noun 1 a tramp, vagrant, vagabond. 2 a rough-living person, a rascal, rogue; a coarse, disreputable, gossipy person. **vaiger** a gadabout. **vaigin(g)** roaming, vagrant, straying.

vaige now Shetland, **veage** now ECentral [**vay**-idge] 1 a voyage. 2 a journey; a trip, outing, expedition.
ill vage to ye bad luck to you now Shetland.

vaillie, vailye NE value.

vainish, wainish vanish.
wainisht shrunken-looking, painfully thin.

vainity vanity now Shetland Orkney.

vale see **veal**

vane call to a horse in harness to turn to the left.

vanquish, vinkish vanquish.
noun a sheep disease now SW.
vincust overcome; exhausted, tired out.

variorum 1 †a change, novelty; a constant variation. 2 a decoration (in furniture, handwriting etc), an ornament, trinket.

varra see **vera**

vary wander in the mind; show the first symptoms of delirium now S.

vassal law a person who holds **heritable** property in **feu** from a **superior.**

vast a large number, quantity or amount, a great deal.

vaudie proud, vain, showing off; highly excited; frisky, merry.

vauntie proud, boastful, vain; proud-looking, showy, pleased, highly excited.

vaut see **vowt**

veage see **vaige**

veal, vale now Shetland Orkney 1 a calf, especially one killed for food or reared for this purpose now Orkney. 2 veal.

veecious, vicious 1 vicious. 2 of weather very bad, severe.

veesion see **vision**

veesit visit now Orkney N.

veesy see **vizzy**

veet a vet Caithness NE.

veeve see **vieve**

veeze see **vise**

vendace, †vendiss a kind of char found in Britain only at Lochmaben, near Dumfries.

vennel a narrow alley or lane between buildings.

vent noun 1 the flue of a chimney; the duct used to let smoke out of a room. 2 the opening of a fireplace. 3 a chimney head or stack.
verb 1 of a chimney, room etc give out smoke, let smoke pass through or from it. 2 †of smoke, bad air etc find a way out, (have room to) pass away.

vera, varra, wery, verra very.

vergens ad inopiam law in the state preceding bankruptcy, approaching insolvency.

verilies verily, truly Orkney NE.

verity see **oath**

vermin a large quantity, swarm, crowd now Caithness NE.

vernish varnish now Orkney Angus.

verra see **vera**

version the translation of a passage of English prose into Latin, mainly as a school exercise; the translated passage.

†verter well, verter spring a medicinal spring.

vertie 1 †cautious, prudent. 2 energetic, active, up early and at work, early-rising now NE.

vertise warn *Shetland*.

veshel, vessel, weshel 1 a vessel. **2** the udder (of a cow etc).

vex a source of regret, sorrow or annoyance.

  be vexed for be sorry for (a person).

vice voice.

vicious *see* **veecious**

victual, vittal 1 victual, food. **2** (a crop of) corn, grain; peas, beans.

  victual stipend that part of a minister's **stipend** formerly paid in grain or the cash equivalent.

vieve, vive; veeve *now Shetland adjective* **1** *of pictures, images* lifelike, closely resembling the original. **2** bright, clear, vivid, distinct.

vincust, vinkish *see* **vanquish**

violent profits *law* penal damages due from a tenant when he refuses to leave premises after the end of his lease etc.

virl, virrel a ferrule, a band of metal round a rod etc to prevent splitting or fraying.

virr vigour, energy, force, impetuosity.

vise, veeze *mining* the line of fracture of a fault in a coal-seam.

visie *see* **vizzy**

vision, veesion, weeshan *NE* **1** a vision. **2** a puny, painfully thin person or animal, one who is wasting away; an unimportant characterless person.

vis major *law* a circumstance, *eg* a natural disaster, which cannot be reasonably expected or prevented, an act of God, which excludes responsibility for loss, damage or the non-performance of a contract.

vittal *see* **victual**

vive *see* **vieve**

vivers [rhymes with 'beavers'] food, provisions.

vizzy, veesy, †visie *verb* **1** †visit. **2** look at carefully, inspect, examine, squint at *now Shetland*. **3** take aim (with a gun etc), aim at (something) *now Shetland*. *noun* **1** a look, glimpse, survey *now Shetland*. **2** a view, prospect. **3** an aim *now Shetland*. **4** the sight on the barrel of a gun.

vogie 1 proud, vain; highly excited; *of things* imposing, showy. **2** merry, lighthearted, happy.

voluntar voluntary *mainly NE*.

voo 1 vow. **2** curse, swear *Orkney NE*.

vos(s) voice.

voust [-oo-], **voost** boast, brag.

vowt [-ow- as in 'cow'], **vaut** vault.

vrack *see* **wrack**[1]

vraith *see* **wreath**

vrang *see* **wrang**

vrat *see* **write**

vratch *see* **wratch**

vreet *see* **write**

vricht *see* **wricht**

vrutten *see* **write**

vyaug *see* **vaig**

vyow [veeow] a view *NE*.

W

wa[1], **waw, wall 1** a wall. **2 wa's** ruins.
  wall coal the middle section of coal in a seam. **wa drap** rainwater dripping from the eaves. **wa heid 1** the top of a wall; the space between this and the roof-beams, used for storage. **2 wa-heids** the horizon, skyline *mainly SW*.

wa[2], **waw, way** *adverb* away (*see also* **awa**).
  (gae) wa (wi ye) *expressing disbelief, impatience etc* go away.
  wa-cast something of little value. **wa-gang 1** departure, leave-taking *now NE*. **2** a lingering taste or flavour; an after-taste *now Shetland NE*. **3** an outflow of water, especially from a millwheel, the tail-race. **wa-gaun** *noun, also* †**wa-ganging 1** departure, going away. **2** the departure of a farmer from his tenancy, *eg* **wa-gaun crop** the last crop sown before leaving, **wa-going sale** the sale of the stock and possessions of someone leaving a farm, giving up a business etc. *adjective* departing, going away, *eg* **way-going tenant. wa-pit** *verb* put away *now Shetland*. **wa-takin** removal, carrying off.

wa *see* **waw**[2], **wey**[1]

waan *see* **wan**[3]

waar *see* **ware**[1], **ware**[2], **ware**[3]

wab, web, wob, wub 1 a web. **2** the fatty covering of the large intestine of animals.
  wobby covered with cobwebs *NE*.
  wab gless a magnifying glass for examining a web of cloth *Fife*.

wabbit, *also* **wabbit out** exhausted, weak, feeble.

wabble, wauble *verb* wobble; walk unsteadily, totter, waddle.
  noun wishy-washy, tasteless drink or liquid food.
  wabblie wishy-washy, thin.

wabster, wobster 1 a weaver. **2** a spider.

wachle *see* **wauchle**

wacht *see* **waucht, wecht**[1]

wad[1] [rhymes with 'sad'], **wed** *verb* **1** wager, bet. **2** wed, marry.
  noun **1** a pledge, something left as security. **2** a stake, bet. **3 wads** name for various games in which forfeits are demanded *now Shetland*.
  waddin a wedding. **waddin fowk** the wedding party.
  be in (a) wad be liable to a forfeit in a game.

wad[2] [rhymes with 'sad'] black lead, graphite; a mine of black lead; a lead pencil *now SW*.

wad[3] [rhymes with 'sad'] wadding, cotton wool.

wad *see* **will**[1]

wadder *see* **weather**

wade, wed *Shetland Orkney,* **wad, wide 1** wade, cross by wading. **2** *of the moon or sun* move through cloud or mist.
  noun wading; a distance covered by wading.

wadge wedge.

wadge *see* **wage**

wadna *see* **will**[1]

†**wadset** [-a- as in 'bad'] *verb* pledge (land or other heritable property) in security, mortgage.
  noun a mortgage of property, with a conditional right of redemption.
  wadsetter the creditor or holder of a **wadset.**

wae[1] woe.
  waesome sorrowful; causing sorrow.

wae[2] *exclamation* well!

wa'er *see* **water**

waff[1], **wauf** *verb* **1** wave, move to and fro, flap. **2** fan, set (air etc) in motion; blow, waft. **3** move.
  noun **1** a flapping, waving movement; a signal made by waving; a flag. **2** a

puff, blast (of air etc), a flurry (of snow). **3** a glimpse; a slight smell, illness etc.

waff[2], **waif, wauf** *noun* **1** a waif. **2** a worthless person.

adjective **1** *of animals* strayed, wandering ownerless. **2** †vagrant, homeless. **3** solitary, lonely. **4** good-for-nothing, like a tramp, scruffy. **5** feeble in body or mind; weak, shoddy, of little importance.

waffer a good-for-nothing. **waffie** *adjective* = **waff** *adjective* 4. *noun* = **waff** *noun* 2.

waffle [rhymes with 'baffle'], **wuffle 1** wave about, flap. **2** waver, hesitate. **3** stagger, totter. **4** crease, wrinkle; tangle.

noun a weak, silly person.

adjective **1** supple, flexible. **2** limp, weak, feeble, sluggish.

waffled, waffly 1 limp, feeble. **2** easily blown about, shaky *Orkney NE*.

waft, woft the weft, the woof or cross-threads of a web of cloth.

wag[1] *verb* **1** *of a leaf, plant etc* wave to and fro, shake in the wind. **2** shake; brandish (a weapon). **3** carry on, proceed. **4** beckon, signal to. **5** *often* **wag at, wag on** wave to (a person).

noun a signal made with the hand.

waggie, waggitie a pied wagtail.

wag-at-the-wa, waggity-wa a wall clock with an uncovered pendulum.

wag[2] name for the remains of iron-age houses in Caithness.

wage, wadge, wauge *noun* a wage.

verb **1** wage. **2** †pledge. **3** wager, bet. **4** use a tool etc, brandish or hurl (a weapon).

wager, wauger wager, bet.

waggle, waigle 1 waggle. **2** a marsh, bog, pool *N*.

waghorn a character in fable, the greatest of all liars; the Devil himself.

waif *see* **waff**[2]

waigle *see* **waggle**

waik, wake, wyke *NE* weak.

wain a waggon, a large open two- or four-wheeled cart *now Fife*.

wainish *see* **vainish**

wair *see* **ware**[1], **ware**[3], **ware**[4]

waird *see* **ward**

wairn *see* **warn**

wairsh *see* **wersh**

wait, wyte *NE* **1** wait. **2** await, wait for: *"she waits you at the altar"*. **3** lodge, live temporarily.

wait on 1 wait for, await. **2** attend to, look after (especially a sick or dying person) *now Caithness*. **3** remain in attendance, stay on. **4** be about to die. **wait or** wait until. **wait (the) table** wait at table, serve a meal.

wait(t)er *see* **water**

wak *see* **wauk**

wake *see* **waik, wauk**

waken *see* **wauken**

†**walawa, willyway** wellaway!, alas!

welcome welcome.

wald *see* **wield**

waldin-heat *see* **wall**

wale, wile, waul *noun* choice; scope for choice; the thing chosen as the best.

verb **1** choose, pick out. **2** arrange, separate into lots, sort.

waled (carefully) chosen, choice. **walin 1** choosing *NE*. **2** the pick, the best. **3** the leavings, refuse.

wale for choose carefully, look out for *Shetland NE*. **wile warst** the very worst *NE*. **wale yer feet, wile yer way** pick your way, step forward cautiously.

walgan [-a- as in 'bad'] **1** a leather woolsack, a bag *NE*. **2** a large clumsy person or thing.

walk, wauk *verb* **1** walk. **2** *eg of an overlarge shoe on the foot* move about.

noun **1** a walk. **2** a ceremonial procession. **3** a pasture for cattle. **4** a passageway in a cowshed.

walk *see* **waulk**

wall, well *noun* **1** a natural spring of water. **2** a well. **3** a drinking fountain. **4** a water stand-pump. **5** a cold-water tap at a sink.

verb weld.

wallie a small well *N*. **pee a wallie** urinate, often to coax a child. **wallin heat, waldin-heat, welland-heat 1** the degree of heat necessary for welding metals. **2** fever pitch, the heights of passion.

wall e(y)e a place in a bog from which a spring rises; a spring, a well. **wall grass, wall girse kail** watercress *now N*. **wall-wesher** a water-spider *SW, S*.

wall *see* **wa¹, waw²**

wallack *see* **walloch²**

wallan [rhymes with 'talon'] *of flowers* withered, drooping *NE*.

waller [rhymes with 'pallor'] toss or thrash about; heave.

wallicoat *see* **wyliecoat**

wallie, wally, waly *adjective* **1** fine, pleasant, beautiful. **2** big and strong, thriving, sturdy, plump. **3** made of porcelain, china, glazed.
noun **1** †an ornament, trinket, toy. **2** †**wallies** fine clothes, finery. **3** porcelain, glazed earthenware or tiling; a dish or ornament made of such. **4 wallies** broken pieces of china used as toys. **5 wallies** a set of false teeth.
wallie close a tiled **close²** (*noun* 4). **wallie dugs** ornamental porcelain dogs displayed in pairs on mantelpieces. **wally money** broken pieces of china used as toy money.

wallit *see* **wallow**

walloch¹ [-a- as in 'bad'] make violent heavy movements, especially in water or mud, move clumsily, flounder.

walloch², wallack [-a- as in 'bad'] *verb* cry, shriek, howl *NE*.
noun, now NE **1** a scream, howl, wail. **2** a lapwing.

wallop¹ [rhymes with 'gallop'] *verb* **1** gallop. **2** move clumsily and very quickly *now NE*. **3** struggle violently, thrash about, flounder. **4** *of the heart* throb, beat violently. **5** move to and fro, dangle, swing, flap.
noun **1** a violent jerky movement, a floundering *now Shetland NE*. **2** a leap, a movement in a lively dance. **3** a constant motion to and fro, a wagging (of the tongue) *Shetland NE*. **4** a strong beat of the heart or pulse, a throb. **5** a fluttering rag, ragged clothing *now NE*.
play wallop thrash about, tumble over. **wallop at** put all one's energies into.

wallop² [rhymes with 'gallop'], **wallopie, wallopieweet** a lapwing.

wallow [rhymes with 'mallow'] wither, fade, waste away.
wallit withered, faded.

wally *see* **wallie, waw²**

wallydrag, warridrag *NE*, **wallydraigle, warydraggel** [-a- as in 'bad'] **1** a good-for-nothing, a slut *now NE*. **2** an undersized person or animal. **3** the smallest, weakest or youngest bird in the nest.

walt [-a- as in 'bad'] welt.

waltams [-a- as in 'bad'], **wull-tams = nickie-tams.**

walter [-a- as in 'bad'] roll to and fro, toss about.

walth [-a- as in 'bad'] wealth.

waly [rhymes with 'Sally'] *cry of sorrow* oh dear!, alas!

waly *see* **wallie**

wamble *see* **wammle**

wame, wime 1 the belly, tummy. **2** the womb. **3** the heart, the mind.
wamie big-bellied.

wamfle *verb* flap, flutter.
adjective limp, weak, flexible *now NE*.

wammle, wamble, waumle, wummle *verb* **1** *of the stomach or its contents* stir uneasily, rumble queasily. **2** roll, wriggle; toss, twist and turn; turn over and over; tangle; wind, coil. **3** stagger. **4** sway, flap, dangle. **5** *of thoughts* creep into someone's mind, go round and round in someone's head.
noun **1** a churning of the stomach, a feeling of sickness. **2** a rolling or unsteady motion, a wriggle.
wammily tottery, weak, feeble.

wampish [-a- as in 'bad'] **1** move to and

fro, wave. **2** †wave, flourish.

wample [rhymes with 'ample'] **1** wriggle, writhe *SW*. **2** *of a stream* meander, flow gently.

wan[1] [rhymes with 'can'] one *mainly WCentral, SW*.

wan[2] [rhymes with 'can'] the direction of.., -wards: *"eastwan"; "gaein to Aberdeenwan"*.

wan[3], **waan, wane** hope, expectation; *latterly* liking *now Shetland Orkney Caithness*.

wan *see* **win**[1], **win**[2], **wind**[2].

wan- [rhymes with 'can'] *see* **un-**.

wance *see* **aince**

wan(d), whaun 1 a wand. **2** a slender flexible stick, *eg* a rod or stick used for punishment. **3** a young shoot of willow used in making baskets. **4** a fishing rod.

wander, wanner, waun(n)er 1 wander. **2** lose one's way, get lost. **3** lead astray, make (someone) lose his way. **4** confuse, bewilder.
   wandert lost; confused, bewildered.
   wandering folk beggars, gipsies, tramps.
   wander the road be a tramp, have no home.

wane *see* **wan**[3], **wean**

wanluck [-a- as in 'can'] bad luck, misfortune *now Shetland*.

wanner *see* **wander**

wannle [rhymes with 'flannel'] supple, agile; active *S*.

wanrest [-a- as in 'can'] unrest, a state of uneasiness or trouble *now Shetland*.
   wanrestfu, wanrestie restless, unsettled.

want [rhymes with 'pant'], **wint** *NE*, **wunt** *NE verb* **1** want. **2** lack the basic necessities of life: *"I've plenty o' siller and I dinna want"*. **3** lack, be without, be free from: *"the cup wants a handle"*. **4** be able to do or go without, be able to spare: *"we can't want the car the day"*. **5** wish to go or come (in, home etc): *"the dog wants out"*.
   noun **1** want. **2** a defect, a missing or faulty part of something.

wanter an unmarried man or woman, a widow(er) *now Orkney*. **wantin 1** not having, without. **2** mentally defective.
   dae wantin do without.
   hae a want be mentally defective.

wanthriven, wantriven *Shetland* [-a- as in 'can'] stunted, weakly *now Shetland*.

wanwordy [-a- as in 'can'] unworthy, worthless.

wanworth [-a- as in 'can'] *noun* **1** a very low price for an article, a bargain. **2** a worthless person or thing *now Shetland*.
   adjective †unworthy, worthless.

wap[1], **whap, waup** *verb* **1** throw violently, thrust, fling *now Shetland Orkney NE*. **2** flap, wave, move to and fro. **3** strike, thrash, hit *now Orkney*.
   noun **1** a blow, a thump *now Orkney NE*. **2** a sweeping or swinging movement, a flap, wave, shake *now Shetland NE*. **3** a puff or gust of wind *now Shetland NE*. **4** a disturbance, brawl, quarrel.
   wappin(g) large.

wap[2], **wop** *verb* **1** wrap, fold. **2** bind, tie, join, especially by splicing; whip with cord.
   noun a bundle of hay or straw.

wap *see* **wasp**

wappen a weapon.

wappenshaw 1 †a review of the men under arms in a particular district. **2 wapinschaw** a rifle-shooting competition.

waps *see* **wasp**

war *see* **be, waur**

warba [-a- as in 'bad'], **blade** waybread, greater plantain.

warback [-a- as in 'bad'] a warble-fly or gadfly, any of the flies of the family *Oestridae* which breed under the skin of cattle.

warble *see* **wurble**

ward [rhymes with 'card'], **waird** *noun* **1** ward. **2** †custody, imprisonment; jail. **3** a division of a county or (now) a **district** or **region**. **4** †an enclosed piece of land, usually for pasture. **5** †*law* the

oldest form of feudal land tenure, *ie*
by military service, with various rights
and obligations.
verb **1** ward. **2** †imprison, confine.

ward *see* **ware**³

wardle *see* **warld**

ware¹, **wair**, **waar**, **waur** *noun* a kind of
seaweed, often used as manure.
verb manure with seaweed.

ware², **waur**, **waar** *Shetland Orkney*
aware, conscious, cautious of *now
Shetland Orkney*: "*he was nae ware of
a trap till he fell in it*".

ware³, **wair**, **waur**, **waar** *Shetland Orkney
Caithness verb, past tense also* **ward 1**
spend (money etc). **2** spend, waste
(one's time, life, efforts etc); waste
(words).

ill wared wasted, out of place. **well
wared** well-spent, well deserved,
worthwhile. **weel wared on him** *etc* it
served him etc right.

ware⁴, **wair** †spring, springtime.

ware day the first day of spring.

ware *see* **be, wire**

wark [rhymes with 'bark'], **wirk, work,
werk, wurk** *noun* **1** work. **2** a building,
especially a public or large impressive
one. **3** a fuss; goings-on; trouble.
verb, past participle also **wrocht 1** work.
2 look after, herd (animals). **3** act as a
laxative on. **4** affect physically or mentally, especially for the worse; trouble,
annoy.

warklumes tools, implements, instruments *now Shetland*.

haud a wark about make a great fuss
over, make a song-and-dance about.
like a day's wark with great vigour, for
all one is worth. **wirk one's wark** do
(one's) work, do what one is employed
to do. **wirk wi** employ, use.

**warld, wardle, warle, world, wordle, worl
1** the world. **2 warlds** things in general,
one's circumstances: "*it's braw wardles
wi them that disna need tae wark*". **3**
worldly wealth, riches: "*Du's gaen ta
hae plenty o da warld*".

warldlike normal in appearance, like
everyone else. **warldlin** a worldling; a
mean, grasping person. **warldly 1**
worldly. **2** greedy.

warld's gear worldly goods. **warld's
wonder** *usually in a bad sense* a person
who surprises. †**warldis wrack** worldly
goods; the troubles and hardships of
life.

like the warld like everyone else, normal.

warlock [-a- as in 'car'] *noun* **1** the male
equivalent of a witch; a wizard,
magician. **2** contemptuous term for an
old, ugly or nasty man.
adjective bewitched, magical, supernatural; malevolent, mischievous.

warm [rhymes with 'farm'] beat, thrash,
hit.

warmer *of a person, used in admiration
or disapproval* an extreme example of
his or her kind, 'a right one'.

warn [rhymes with 'barn'], **wairn** *verb* **1**
warn. **2** summon. **3** *of a clock* make a
clicking or whirring noise before striking, *often* **warn (for) nine, ten** *etc*.

warning a premonition, an omen.

warnish [rhymes with 'varnish'], †**warnice
1** warn, caution, advise. **2** *of a clock* =
warn *verb* **3**.

warnisin warning. **warnishment** advice.

warp [rhymes with 'carp'], **werp, worp 1**
warp, arrange threads in a warp; twist.
2 weave; plait; knit, cast on (stitches).
3 interlace the cross or horizontal
ropes in the thatching of a cornstack.

warple 1 intertwine, twist, entangle;
confuse. **2** wrestle, tumble, wriggle. **3**
stagger, go in a zigzag course; struggle
through.

warran, warrant [-a- as in 'car'], **waurn** a
warrant.

warranty *usually referring to the sale of
livestock* a guarantee, assurance.

I'se warran I'll bet, I'll be bound.

warrandice [rhymes with 'miss'] *law* the
undertaking by a granter or seller to a
grantee or buyer of property thre-

atened with eviction through defect of title.

warridrag *see* **wallydrag;**

warrior 1 humorous or affectionate term for a lively, spirited person, often a child, *often a great warrior.* **2 the Warriors** nickname for various football teams, especially Stenhousemuir and occasionaly Third Lanark and Dumbarton.

warroch [-a- as in 'car'] a feeble, stunted, person or plant, a weakling.

warse [-a- as in 'car'], **worse** worse.

the worse of drink the worse for drink, having drunk too much alcohol.

warsh *see* **wersh**

warsle, wrastle, wrestle *verb* **1** wrestle. **2** pray earnestly. **3** manage to do something by great effort. **4** labour, try hard, exert oneself physically and mentally. **5** struggle, wriggle, sprawl about, as in an effort to rise or free oneself. **6** make one's way through life with much effort and difficulty, scrape along.
noun **1** a wrestling match, a physical tussle; a struggle, effort. **2** a mental or moral struggle, a fight against circumstances or hardship.

warslin struggling; energetic, hardworking.

warsle through scrape through, get by.

warydraggel *see* **wallydrag**

wase, wease, wazz *Caithness,* **wizzie** *Shetland,* **wassock** *now NE* **1** a bundle of straw, especially for thatching. **2** a circular band of straw worn to relieve the pressure when carrying heavy burdens on the head or used to protect the hands, *eg* when knocking the husks from the ears of barley. **3** a bundle of twigs etc placed against a cottage door as a windbreak or draught-excluder.

wash [rhymes with 'bash'], **wesh, wish** *verb, past tense also* **woosh, wuish, weesh** *now NE,* **washt.** *past participle also* **washen** *now NE,* **wuishen, weeshen, wishen, washt 1** wash. **2** *usually* **wash down, wash off** cut to a slope or bevel

now WCentral.
noun **1** a wash. **2** urine, especially when stale and used as a cleansing agent. **3** a bevelled edge or slope on a board, stone etc.

washer a person who scrubs and cleans fish after gutting, in preparation for curing *Shetland NE.* **washer-wife 1** a washer-woman, laundress. **2** a water-spider. **washing boyne, wash bine** *now WCentral* a (portable) wash-tub. **washing house** a wash-house. **wash board** skirting-board.

wash its face *of a commercial enterprise* pay its way, break even.

wasna *see* **be**

wasp [rhymes with 'clasp'], **waps, wap** [rhymes with 'top(s)'] **1** child's word for a wasp. **2 the Wasps** nickname for Alloa Athletic football team.

wasp bike a wasps' nest.

wassock *see* **wase**

wast [rhymes with 'fast'], **west** *adverb* west; away from the speaker or the person to whom one is speaking.
preposition above, along, across, over, to the west, on the west side of.
verb, of the wind change to the west.

wasten western *now Shetland.* **waster** lying towards the west, western. **wastert** westward. **wastle** westward, to the west. **wastlin** western, from or in the west, westerly. **wastlins** westward, to or in the west.

wast-by westward. **West Highland** *adjective* from the west Highlands. *noun* **1** a hardy breed of beef cattle. **2** a small white rough-haired breed of terrier. **wastland** coming from or situated in the west of Scotland, western; westerly.

wast awa, wast ower (bye) to or in the west.

wastcoat *see* **weskit**

waste *verb* **1** spoil by ill-usage or misuse. **2** spoil, pamper (a child, pet etc). *adjective* †*of buildings* ruined; empty.

waster 1 an idler, good-for-nothing. **2**

something on the wick of a candle causing it to gutter. **3** a person, animal or object of no further use, due to disease etc. **wasterful, wastrife** wasteful, extravagant. **wastry** *noun* **1** reckless extravagance; wastefulness. **2** †a waste of (food etc). *adjective* = **wasterful**.

wastel [rhymes with 'hassle'] a kind of bread, scone or cake baked with the finest flour; a large scone made of oatmeal and wholemeal flour *now NE*.

waster a fishing spear with several prongs.

wastle, wastlin *see* **wast**

wat [rhymes with 'cat'], **wite** *NE*, †**wate** *verb* wot, know *now NE*.

I wat (ye), weel I wat, weel a wat indeed, I must say, I can tell you: *"well I wat that's true"*.

wat *see* **weet**

watch [rhymes with 'catch']: **watch oneself** look after oneself, be on one's guard, watch out: *"watch yourself or the parkie'll catch you"*.

watchie a watchmaker *now NE*.

watch knowe a hill high enough to serve as a lookout station *S*.

wate *see* **wat**

water, watter, wait(t)er, wa'er 1 water. **2** a stream, a river, *latterly usually* a small one: *"Afton Water"*, *"Water of Leith"*. **3** a river valley, the area and its inhabitants bordering a river *now S*.

waterins a trough, pool in a stream etc where farm animals go to drink.

watering stone a stone horse-trough. **watery** *noun* **1** a pied wagtail *NE*. **2** a lavatory. **watery-nebbit** pale and sickly; starved looking; having a drip at the end of one's nose. **watery pox** chickenpox. **watery wagtail** a pied wagtail; a yellow wagtail.

water bailie 1 a water-bailiff employed to prevent poaching in rivers *N*. **2** †a magistrate of Leith and Edinburgh and of Glasgow who had local jurisdiction over maritime cases in the Forth and Clyde respectively. **3** one

of the water-bug family, especially the water-strider. **water blackbird, water bobbie** a dipper. **water brash** heartburn. **water broo, water brose** oatmeal mixed with boiling water. **water burn** a name for the phosphorescence seen on the sea *NE*. **water clearer** one of the small insects that skim over the surface of water and are said to clean it. **water craw** = **water blackbird**. **water dog** a water-rat; a water-vole. **water fit** the mouth of a river. **water-fur** a drainage furrow to carry off surface water. **water gate 1** = **water** *noun* 3 *S*. **2** a road and its branches which serve a valley *S*. **3** a fence or grating over a stream to keep animals or floating rubbish out of a mill-race. **watergaw** a rainbow which is not complete. **water heid** the source of a river, the upper end of a valley. **water hole** a hole or pit in which water collects, a well or pool. **water horse, water kelpie** *Celtic folklore* a mythical spirit in the form of a horse found in lakes and rivers. **water meggie** = **water blackbird**. **water mouth** the mouth of a river. **water pig** a container for water, a pitcher. **water pyot** = **water blackbird**. **water stowp** a wooden bucket. **water trip** an annual inspection of the waterworks, an occasion for a social outing for town councillors. **water water** river water *S*. **water wrack** weeds, leaves, sticks etc carried down by a river. †**water wraith** *folklore* a water spirit. **water yett** = **water gate** 3.

Water of Ayr stone a kind of stone found on the banks of the Ayr used for making whetstones and in polishing.

Waterloo *marbles* a soft, brittle, clay marble.

wather *see* **weather, wedder**

watter *see* **water**

wattle [rhymes with 'battle'] *noun* **1** †a supple stick or twig. **2 wattles** *thatching* the interwoven twigs on which the turf or thatch was laid; also originally used to form the walls of buildings.

wauble *see* **wabble**

wauch, waugh [-ch, -gh as -ch in 'loch'], **wauf 1** *of a taste or smell* unpleasant, stale *now NE*. **2** *of food, cooking etc* tasteless, not appealing; not nourishing. **3** unwell, faint, weary. **4** good-for-nothing, worthless.

wauchle, wachle, wochle *verb* **1** walk clumsily; stumble with fatigue etc. **2** plod on amid difficulties, struggle with a situation or task; last out (a period of time) in a weary, listless way.
noun **1** a struggle, effort. **2** a staggering awkward movement, a wobble.
wauchled perplexed, bewildered, muddle-headed.

waucht, wacht, †waught [-ch, -gh as -ch in 'loch'] *verb, sometimes* **waucht out, ower, up** drink deeply, gulp, drain.
noun **1** a swallow or gulp of a drink. **2** a deep breath of air.

wauf *see* **waff¹, waff², wauch**

wauge *see* **wage**

wauger *see* **wager**

waugh *see* **wauch**

waught *see* **waucht**

wauk, wake, †wak *verb* **1** wake. **2** be or stay awake, be sleepless or have wakened from sleep. **3** guard, watch over (places, livestock etc), especially during the night; stay up all night with, watch over (a sick person or corpse).
noun a wake, watching over a corpse.
waukrife 1 not ready or unable to sleep; able to do with little sleep; watchful. **2** easily awakened, lightly sleeping *now Orkney NE*.

wauk *see* **walk, waulk**

wauken, waken *verb* **1** waken, wake. **2** *law* revive (a legal process) in which no action has been taken for a year; *compare* **sleep**. **3** **wauken on** lose one's temper with (someone) *now Orkney N*.
waukened awake.
waukenin 1 wakening. **2** a severe scolding, a talking-to.

waul 1 *of the eyes* roll wildly. **2** roll the eyes, look at or on (someone) with wide rolling eyes in a stupid, surprised, or fierce way.

waul *see* **wale**

waulk, wauk, walk *verb* **1** full (cloth), make (cloth) thick and felted by soaking, beating and shrinking. **2** *also* **waukin** *of cloth* shrink as a result of being wetted.
waukit *of skin, wool etc* matted, hardened, roughened.
waulking song any suitably rhythmic Gaelic song formerly sung by a team of women engaged in **waulking** cloth in the Hebrides.

waumish faint and sick, dizzy.

waumle *see* **wammle**

waun(n)er *see* **wander**

waup *see* **wap¹**

waur, war *adjective, adverb* worse.
verb get the better of, overcome, outdo.
noun the worse.
waur-faured uglier *Orkney NE*.
come by the waur, win the waur come off worst, get the worst of something. **ten waurs** ten times worse *NE*. **(the) waur o(f)** (the) worse for.

waur *see* **ware¹, ware², ware³**

waurn *see* **warran**

wave: wave on attract the attention of (someone) by waving.
wavel 1 rock unsteadily, sway, stagger. **2** flutter, waver, wag.
waverin leaf waybread, the plant *now Shetland Orkney*.

waw¹ *verb of cats (and children)* mew pathetically, wail.
noun the sound made by a cat or child in distress.

waw², wall, wa a wave (of the sea).
wally *of the sea* stormy, wave-tossed.

waw *see* **wa¹, wa²**

wax cloth canvas cloth coated with wax used especially for floor and table coverings: oilcloth; linoleum.

way 1 a call to a horse to stop. **2** a call to a sheepdog to make a run round or move away from the sheep.

way *see* **wa¹, wey¹**

Waysiders nickname for Airdrieonians football team.

wazz *see* **wase**

wazzin *see* **wizzen**

we *see* **wi**

wean, wane (*Central* rhymes with 'rain', *N*, *ECentral* rhymes with 'Ian'] a child, especially a young one.

wear, weer, weir *verb, past tense also* **wure** *now Shetland,* **weared.** *past participle also* **wurn 1** wear. **2** go, proceed, usually slowly and cautiously.

wearin(g) *of clothes* for everyday use, especially outside working hours.

wear awa 1 leave quietly, slip away. **2** die, pass away. **wear doun (the brae)** grow old. **wear into** go slowly towards; approach (a time of the day etc). **wear on 1** = **wear into. 2** grow older. **wear ower 1** *of time* grow late. **2** *of people* grow older *Shetland NE.* **wear throu** do a piece of work bit by bit. **wear up** grow, advance in time, age or amount.

wear *see* **weir**[2]

weary *adjective* **1** †*of people* sad, miserable. **2** depressing. **3** annoying, troublesome.

verb become bored or listless.

wearifu troublesome, annoying; sad.

weary fa, †**weary on,** †**weary tak** damn! **weary for** long for.

wease *see* **wase**

weason *see* **wizzen**

weather, wather [rhymes with 'lather'], **wither** *now NE,* **wedder, wadder** *now Shetland,* **widder** *NE* **1** weather. **2** weather suitable for a particular purpose, favourable or seasonable weather *now NE: "I widna set my tatties yet, it's nae weather".*

weather gaw 1 a weather gall, a sign of bad weather to come, *eg* a broken rainbow. **2** a bright calm spell between two periods of bad weather thought to give warning of snow.

this weather just now, at the moment.

weave, wyve *NE verb, past tense also* **wuive** *S,* **weave** *NE. past participle also* **wuven,**

wivven *NE,* **weyvt** *now NE* **1** weave. **2** knit (usually stockings or socks) *now NE.*

weaver, wyver *NE* **1** a weaver. **2** a spider. **weaver-kneed 1** knock-kneed. **2** having sensitive or ticklish knees *WCentral.*

web *see* **wab**

wecht[1]**, weight, wacht** *NE noun* **1** weight. **2** physical force. **3 wechts** a pair of scales. **4** a large amount, a great number (of things).

verb **1** weight. **2** add weight to, increase the burden of, press down by weight.

wecht[2]**, weicht** a wooden hoop, with skin or canvas stretched over it, originally used for winnowing corn, now usually for carrying grain or potatoes.

wed *see* **wad**[1]**, wade, weed**

wedder, wather [rhymes with 'lather'] a wether.

wedder *see* **weather**

wede *see* **weed**[1]

wee *adjective* **1** small, tiny, little, *often* **wee wee, little wee, wee sma. 2** *football* used to describe the reserve team: *"wee Celtic".*

noun **a wee** a small measure, quantity or degree of some thing or of time, distance etc.

wee hauf a nip of spirits, a small whisky. **wee heavy** a type of strong beer, usually sold in small bottles of $\frac{1}{3}$ pint (approx. 0.2 litre). **wee house** an outside lavatory. **wee man 1** an odd-job man. **2** the Devil: *"in the name o the wee man!"* **the Wee Rangers** nickname for Berwick Rangers football team. **wee school** the infant department in a school. **wee thing** a small child. **wee yins** younger children.

wee *see* **wey**[2]

weeack *verb* chirp, whine, speak or sing in a thin squeaky voice *NE.*

noun a squeak, a screech.

weed[1] *verb, past tense, past participle also* **wed** *now NE,* **wede** weed.

wede awa(y) *literary* carry off, remove,

especially by death.

weed² **1** a (sudden) high fever. **2** a chill with trembling and chattering teeth. **3** *of farm animals* a feverish illness thought to have been caused by a chill; *of female animals* mastitis.

weedow *see* **widow**

weegle wiggle.

     wigglety-wagglety very unstable, tottery; unsteadily.

week a wick (of a candle etc).

week *see* **wick**¹

weel¹, **well** *adverb* **1** well. **2** very, quite, much.

     adjective **1** well. **2** healthy. **3** *of food* fully cooked, ready to eat.

     weel come 1 welcome. **2** *of people* of good family, of honourable parentage. **weel-daein** well-to-do, prosperous. **weel-faured 1** good looking. **2** decent, respectable. †**weel-hained 1** *of people* well preserved, in good shape. **2** used sparingly or economically, saved to good purpose.

     no weel unwell, in poor health. **weel a weel** very well, all right. **weel to be seen** having a good appearance, very presentable. **the weel warst** the very worst, the worst of the lot *now NE*.

weel², **weil** a deep pool; an eddy, a whirlpool.

weel *see* **wield**

weem 1 †*also in place-names* a cave. **2** an Iron Age underground storehouse, usually a curved slab-lined passageway.

weemen *see* **woman**

ween *see* **wind**¹

weeng *see* **wing**

weenth width *WCentral, SW*.

weer †doubt, uncertainty.

     (the) weers o in danger of, on the brink of, just about to *NE: "I wis jist on the weers o calling for help"*.

weer *see* **our, wear, wire**

weesh *see* **wash, wiss**¹

weeshan *see* **vision**

weeshen *see* **wash**

weeshie-washie *see* **wishy-washy**

weet, weit, wat [rhymes with 'cat'], **wet** *adjective* wet.

     noun **1** wet. **2** rain, drizzle, dew.

     verb, past tense also **wat, weetit.** *past participle also* **wat, wutten** *now NE* **1** wet. **2** celebrate with a drink, drink to the success of (a bargain etc).

     weetie wet, damp, rainy. **weetin** an alcoholic drink, a drinking party. **watshod 1** wet-shod. **2** *of the eyes* wet with tears.

     weet the bairn's heid toast the health of a newborn baby. **wat (a cup o) tea** make (a cup of) tea *WCentral*. **weet-my-fit** a corncrake.

weicht *see* **wecht**²

weigh *see* **wey**²

weight *see* **wecht**¹

weik *see* **wick**¹

weil *see* **weel**²

weir¹ war.

weir², **wear** [weer] *verb, past participle also* †**worn 1** guard, defend. **2** stand guard over, keep a watch on; *of a sheepdog* stand in front of (a group of sheep) to prevent them breaking loose *now S*. **3** **weir aff** keep off, ward off, hold at bay. **4** drive (animals or people) gradually in a desired direction, shepherd.

     noun a weir, a river dam.

weir *see* **wear, wire**

weird, wierd *noun* **1** fate, fortune, destiny. **2** †**weirds** the Fates, the three goddesses of destiny. **3** a prophecy, prediction; a mysterious saying. **4** someone with supernatural skill or knowledge.

     adjective **1** weird, strange, uncanny. **2** troublesome, mischievous, harmful.

     verb **1** ordain by fate; decree a particular fate or fortune to. **2** †prophesy (someone's fate); warn ominously.

     weirdless unfortunate; inept, incapable.

     weird wife a prophetess, fortune-teller.

weirdie the smallest or least thriving of a brood of animals, especially pigs or birds *ECentral*.

weise *see* **wise**

weit *see* **weet**

well *see* **wall, weel**[1]

welland-heat *see* **wall**

welter reel, stagger, stumble, flounder.

wench, winch *noun* a wench, *latterly often* a little girl.

verb court, go with someone of the opposite sex.

went, wint a quick or passing view, a short glimpse *NE*.

werk *see* **wark**

werp *see* **warp**

werrock a corn, bunion etc on the foot.

wersh, wairsh, †**warsh 1** *of food or drink* tasteless, insipid; cooked without salt; *of beer* flat. **2** bitter, harsh in taste, sour. **3** *of a piece of writing* dull, tame, uninspiring; *of life, feelings, activity* dull. **4** *of the stomach or appetite* not wanting food; faint from hunger, squeamish. **5** *of people* sickly, feeble, depressed. **6** *of weather* raw, cold and damp.

wery *see* **vera**

wes *see* **be**

wesh *see* **wash**

weshel *see* **veshel**

weskit, wastcoat, wystcoat *NE* a waistcoat.

west *see* **wast**

Western Isles *see* **isle**

wet *see* **weet**

wey[1]**, wye,** [rhymes with 'gey'], **way,** †**wa 1** a way. **2** one's circumstances, way of life, business.

weys -wise, in the manner specified: *"says he, affhand weys"*.

way-flude the outflow of water from a mill-wheel, the tail-race; a water channel *now NE*. **waygate 1** a passageway. **2** speed, progress; push, drive, energy. **a'wey** everywhere. **ae wey** one way. **all weys** in every way or respect. **by his wey o't** according to him, by his account. **come one's way(s)** come away or on one's way. **in a (dreedfu) way** in a state of great distress, worried and upset.

be in the way of have a habit of. **naewey** nowhere. **say ae wye** agree. **somewey 1** somehow. **2** somewhere. **some ither wey** somewhere else. **that wey** in that manner, so; in that respect. **the wey 1** *often* **the wey that** because of the way or manner in which, from the way (that). **2** because. **the wey at** the reason why. **the wey o** in the direction of. **wey o daein 1** a means of livelihood, a job. **2** *also* **wey-dain** a fuss; a disturbance, uproar; a celebration. **what wey 1** how. **2** why.

wey[2]**, weigh, wee, wye** *verb* weigh.

noun **1 weys** a (public) weighing-machine; a steelyard, beam and scales; the weights used with scales. **2** a measure of weight varying according to the district and the commodity.

weigh bauk the beam of a pair of scales; **wey bauks** the scales themselves. **wey butter, wey cheese** a game in which two people stand back to back with arms linked and lift one another alternately until one gives in. **wey wecht** the weights used with scales; **wey wechts** the scales themselves.

weyvt *see* **weave**

wha, whae *NE,* **fa, whee** who. †**wham** whom. **whase, whaus** whose.

wha but he the 'cock of the walk', a self-important person. **wha (i)s aucht?** who is the owner, parent etc of? **wha like(s)** whoever (it may be), no matter who.

whaap *see* **whaup**[1]

whaal, whaul, faal *NE* a whale.

whack, whauk *verb* whack.

noun **1** a whack. **2** a cut. **3** a great number, a large quantity.

get one's whacks be punished, get one's just deserts.

whae *see* **wha**

whair *see* **whar**

whaizle *see* **wheeze**

whammle *see* **whummle**

whalp, whaulp, whulp, folp *N, noun* **1** a whelp. **2** contemptuous term for a person.

verb whelp.

wham *noun* **1** a valley, a broad hollow among hills through which a stream runs. **2** a marshy hollow in a field etc.

wham *see* **wha**

whan, when, whun, fan *N* when.

whanever 1 whenever. **2** as soon as, at the very moment when.

whang, whing *now S,* **whank, fang** *N,* **thwang** *noun* **1** a thong. **2** a leather bootlace; any kind of shoe-tie. **3** a thong for whipping; a whiplash. **4** the penis. **5** a long stretch of rather narrow road: **the Lang Whang** the old Edinburgh to Lanark road. **6** a large thick slice of food, especially of cheese; a large amount or number, a chunk, large slice. **7** a rascal, nasty person *NE.* **8** a stroke, blow; a cut with a whip.

verb **1** cut, slice; slash, chop, snip. **2** beat, lash, whip; defeat.

whanker a large or impressive example.

whankie a sickle-blade mounted on a long handle, for cutting down thistles, twigs etc.

whing-hole an eyelet for a lace in a boot or shoe.

whap *see* **wap**[1]

whar, whair, whare, whaur, far *N* where.

whase *see* **wha**

what[1] [rhymes with 'cat'], **whit, whut, fat** *N,* **fit** *N* **1** what. **2** *exclamation* how!, how very!: *"what pretty it is!"* **3** why?, in what way?, how?: *"It cam open in my hand - what could I help it?"* **4** as much, as far or as hard as: *"she cried what she could cry".*

whatever in any case, however, under any circumstances.

but what that: *"I dinna think but what it'll be rain".* **what a** how many!, what a lot of!: *"what a houses".* **what .. at** why?: *"what's she roarin and greetin at?"* **what for 1** what kind of a? **2** why?, for what reason? **what for no** why not? **fat ither** what else?, of course. **what like 1** what sort of?, like what in appear-

ance, nature etc? **2 fat like** how are you? *NE.* **what o'clock is it?** a popular name for a dandelion as used by children as a clock. **fat time** *NE* when, whenever, as soon as. **what way 1** how?, in what manner? **2** why?, for what reason?

what[2] [rhymes with 'cat'] whet.

whatten, whitten, fat(t)en *N,* **whatna** [-a- as in 'cat'] **1** what kind of, what sort of. **2 whatten** what: *"I wish I had whatten books you wanted", "whatten queer folk!".* **3** which.

whattie *see* **wheet**[1]

whauk *see* **whack**

whaul *see* **whaal**

whaulp *see* **whalp**

whaun *see* **wan(d)**

whaup[1], **faup, faap** *N,* **whaap** *noun* a curlew.

verb whistle shrilly like a curlew.

whaup-nebbit having a long beaky nose.

†**whaup i(n) the nest** something, usually annoying or unpleasant, likely to make its presence felt, trouble brewing.

whaup[2] **1** the seed-pod of peas, beans etc, especially one before the peas etc have begun to develop or after they have been shelled. **2** *mainly* **lang (teem) whaup** a tall skinny person.

whaur *see* **whar**

whaus *see* **wha**

whauze, whazzle *see* **wheeze**

whee *see* **wha**

wheeber *verb* whistle.

noun **1** a whistle. **2** a tall, thin clumsy person *NE.* **3** a person with unpleasant manners *NE.*

wheech[1] [rhymes with 'dreich'], **wheek** *verb* **1** move through the air, dash with a whizzing sound. **2** sweep, snatch or whisk away. **3** beat, hit.

noun **1** a soft whizzing sound. **2** a blow which makes a whizzing sound; *especially* **wheechs** strokes with the **tawse** (*see* **taw**[1]), a belting at school. **3** a sudden sweeping movement, a whisk.

wheech[2] [rhymes with 'dreich'] a stink, bad smell.

wheef *see* **wheich, whiff**

wheefle whiffle, puff, blow.

wheegee a whim; humming and hawing.

wheegle, wheetle wheedle.

wheek squeak, whine, whistle; complain, whine.

wheek *see* **wheech**[1]

wheel 1 whirl round in dancing, swing (one's partner) round, pirouette, reel. **2** make a bid at an auction for the purpose of raising the price *NE*.

wheen 1 a wheen (o) a few, a small number, several. **2** *usually* **wheens** a separate number (of people etc), a group, some as opposed to others.
a bonnie wheen, a gey wheen a considerable amount.

wheenge *see* **whinge**

wheep 1 whistle; pipe shrilly like a bird, especially a lapwing. **2** make a shrill noise, squeak, buzz.
noun a sharp cry or whistle.
wheeple *verb* **1** *of a bird, the wind* whistle shrilly or with a long drawn-out note. **2** *of people* whistle, especially tunelessly *now NE*. **3** whistle (a tune). **4** whine, whimper. *noun* **1** the shrill call or whistle of a bird, especially a curlew. **2** a tuneless, unmusical whistling or playing on a whistle.

wheep *see* **whip**

wheeriorum a toy; a thingumajig.

wheerum something unimportant, a toy.

wheesh *see* **whisht, whush**

wheesht *see* **whisht**

wheet[1], **wheetie, whattie** [rhymes with 'fatty'] **1** a call to ducks. **2** *of birds* twitter, chirp. **3** *of people* whistle, warble, usually tunelessly.

wheet[2] a whit.

wheetie mean, stingy, shabby; underhand, shifty, evasive *NE*.

wheetie *see* **wheet**[1]

wheetle *see* **wheegle**

wheety-whattie *see* **whittie-whattie**

wheeze, whauze *NE*, **foze** *NE* wheeze.

wheezle, whazzle, fozle *NE*, **huzle** *S*, †**whaizle** *verb* wheeze, pant. *noun* **1** a wheeze. **2 the wheezles** asthma; bronchitis.

wheich, wheuch [-ch as in 'dreich'], **wheef** alcoholic drink, booze; whisky.

when *see* **whan**

wherry a kind of sailing barge with one sail, and a mast stepped forward.

whether, whither, whuther, fither *NE* whether.
whether-or-no uncertain, indecisive, dithering.

wheuch *see* **wheich**

whey, fey *N*, **fy** *NE* [rhymes with 'gey or 'my'] whey.
fy brose *now NE*, **whey brose** *now Orkney NE* **brose** made with whey instead of water.

whid[1] *noun* **1** *also* **fud** a squall, (sudden) gust of wind. **2** *eg of a hare* a quick silent movement.
verb **1** *of or like wind:* sweep in gusts *now Shetland Orkney*. **2** *often of a hare* move quickly and noiselessly; zigzag, scamper.

whid[2], **whud** *noun* a lie, exaggeration.
verb lie.

whidder, whither, whudder, whuther, fudder *NE*, **futher** *NE verb* **1** move violently, rush about; hum or whizz through the air, rage like the wind. **2** *of the wind* blow fiercely in gusts. **3** beat, hit; floor. **4** potter about, be busy doing nothing.
noun **1** a sudden or loud gust of wind; a whirlwind; a blowing, spurt of water etc *now Shetland*. **2** a rush, a flurry; a scurry.
whitherspale a small whizzing toy; something very light.

whiff, whuff, wheef *noun* **1** a whiff. **2** *of illness, mood etc* a slight attack, a touch.
verb **1** whiff. **2** drive or carry by blowing; blow out (a candle etc).
in a whiff in a jiffy.

whig[1] a name for various products resulting from the souring of milk, *eg* whey, buttermilk.

†**whig**² go quickly, move at an easy, steady pace, jog.

†**whig**³ nickname for a supporter of the National Covenant of 1638 and hence of Presbyterianism in the 17th century, later applied to the **Covenanters** (*see* **covenant**) of South-West Scotland who rebelled in the reigns of Charles II and James VII.

whiggamore a **Covenanter** (*see* **covenant**), originally one who took part in the Whiggamore Raid of 1648, a Presbyterian of the 17th century, a **whig**³.

whigmaleerie, figmaleerie 1 a fanciful decoration, ornament or contraption. **2** a whim, fanciful idea, fad.

while, file *N noun* a while.
conjunction **1** while. **2** until, up to the time that.
whilie, whil(e)ock a little while.
a while back some time ago, in the past.
a while's time some time, a period of time. **a while syne** a certain time ago, for some time past. **this while** (**back** *etc*) for some time past, for the past days, weeks etc.

whiles, files, fyllies *NE* sometimes, at times, occasionally.

whilk, filk *N* which.

whilly cheat, trick.

whillywha *verb* wheedle, coax (a person for something or a thing from a person).
noun **1** a flatterer, a person who deceives by wheedling. **2** flattery, wheedling.

whilock *see* **while**

whilom(s) sometimes, at times.

whimper, fumper *N* **1** whimper. **2** a rumour, a whisper.

whin¹, **whun, fun** *NE* **1** one of several hard rocks, *eg* basalt, flint; any hard stone used as road stone. **2** a piece of **whin**¹, a boulder, slab or stone.

whin², **whun, fun** *NE* gorse; **whins** a clump or area of gorse.

whin dyke a fence consisting of gorse bushes.
gie (someone) through the whins (cause a person to) come through an unpleasant or painful experience; punish (someone).

whing *see* **whang**

whinge, wheenge whine, whimper.

†**whinger** [rhymes with 'singer'] a short stabbing sword.

whink a sharp bark or yelp.

whinner, whunner *verb* whizz, whistle through the air; move quickly.
noun **1** a whizzing sound, the noise made by rapid movement; a crash, clatter; (the sound of) a heavy fall. **2** a ringing blow, a whack.

whip, wheep *NE*, **whup, fup** *NE* **1** a whip. **2** a blow with a whip; **whips** a whipping. **3** a sudden quick movement, a start, jerk, swirl, gust. **4** a crack, go at. **5** **whips** plenty, lots.
verb whip.
adverb with a quick or sudden movement, in a jiffy.
whipper-in a school attendance-officer.
whippie *noun* **1** contemptuous term for a girl, a hussy. **2** a rope of twisted straw. *adjective* quick or brisk, agile.
whipman a carter.
at a whip, in a whip at one stroke, suddenly.

whippitie-stourie, whuppity-stoorie 1 name for a kind of household fairy or **brownie** (*see* **broon**). **2** a light-footed nimble person.

whirl, whurl, furl *NE* **1** whirl. **2** wheel, trundle, cart; drive on.
whirly-gate, furlin yett a turnstile.

whirligig 1 a revolving chimney cowl. **2** a complicated ornament, design or diagram.

whirliwha a fanciful ornament or decoration.

whirr, †whurr 1 whirr. **2** commotion, rush *NE*. **3** a burr in speech *SW*.

†**whirry** carry off, drive away or out.

whisht, wisht, wheesht, wheesh, whush *verb*

1 be quiet!, shut up! **2** call for silence. **3** silence, quieten. **4** be quiet, remain silent.

noun, also **whishtie** the slightest sound, the least whisper; the faintest rumour or report: *"there is na a wheesht against him"*.

adjective quiet, silent, hushed.

haud yer wheesht, be quiet, keep silent, hold your tongue.

whisk, wisk *verb* **1** whisk. **2** †beat, whip (a person). **3** †*of the heart* flutter, beat too fast.

noun **1** a rapid sweeping movement; a sudden light stroke. **2** a blow, swipe. **3** a bunch, a tangled mass (of threads etc) *Shetland Orkney NE*.

wisker a bunch of short straws etc bound at one end to form a kind of handbrush or used as a sheath for knitting needles at a woman's waist *NE*.

whisky, whusky, fuskie *NE* an alcoholic drink distilled from malted barley (**malt whisky** (*see* **maut**)), or with the addition of unmalted grain spirit (usually maize) (**blended whisky**).

whissle *see* **wissel**

whistle, whustle, fussle *NE* **1** whistle. **2** cuff, hit, wallop *NE*.

whistler a large example of something. †**whistle-binkie** a person who attended a **penny wedding** (*see* **penny**) without paying and had no right to share in the entertainment; a mere spectator (who sometimes whistled for his own amusement).

whit *see* **what**¹

white¹, **fite** **1** white. **2** *of coins* silver. **3** *of arable land* fallow, unploughed; *of hill land* covered with coarse grass instead of heather, bracken or scrub.

whitie-broon, whited-broon of linen thread in which the brown colour of the flax has been lightened by washing but not bleaching.

white breid white wheat bread etc as opposed to oat or barley cakes. **white hare** an Alpine, Scottish mountain or blue hare, especially in its white winter coat. **white hoolet** a barn owl. **white iron** tin-plate, tinned iron. **white meal** oatmeal as distinct from barley meal. **white meat** the flesh of poultry or game. **white pudding** a kind of sausage stuffed with oatmeal, suet, salt, pepper and onions; *compare* **pudding**. **white siller** silver money, cash in silver.

white², **fite** *NE*, **twit** *Shetland Orkney* cut with a knife, pare, whittle.

white³ wheat *NE*.

white gowan *see* **gowan**

whither *see* **whether, whidder**

whitling a young sea trout.

whitrat, futrat, whitterick **1** a weasel, a stoat; a ferret. **2** a thin, small, sharp-featured, inquisitive person.

Whitsunday, Whussenday **1** Whitsunday. **2** a Scottish quarter day, either 15 or 28 May depending on the context.

whitten *see* **whatten**

whitter¹ (a drink of) alcohol.

whitter² *verb* **1** *of birds* twitter, warble, chirp. **2** *of persons* whisper, mutter. **3** flutter, scamper, patter; flicker, quiver. *noun* chatter.

whitterick a curlew.

whitterick *see* **whitrat**

whittie-whattie, wheety-whattie excuses, stories which hide the truth; indecision.

whittle¹, **whuttle, futtle** *N* *noun* **1** a knife. **2** a sickle, scythe. **3** a whetstone, especially one for sharpening scythes. *verb* whittle.

whittle², **futley** *NE*, **whittle beal(in)** a whitlow.

whole *see* **hale**¹

whommle *see* **whummle**

whud *see* **whid**²

whudder *see* **whidder**

whuff *see* **whiff**

whulp *see* **whalp**

whummle, whommle, whammle, fummle *NE*, **fommle** *NE*, †**whumble** *verb* **1** capsize, overturn. **2** turn (a container etc) upside down. **3** overthrow, throw into ruin or confusion. **4** empty (a container) or its contents. **5** cover or hide (something) with an upsidedown container. **6** cause to turn, turn inside out, stir or toss round and round. **7** roll, whirl; toss and turn, rock to and fro. **8** go head over heels, fall, or sprawl suddenly; move unsteadily, stumble. **9** knock down, push (over). **10** defeat; astonish *Fife*.

noun **1** a capsizing, upset. **2** a turning, a rocking, tossing. **3** a tumble, fall; a downfall, misfortune.

dish o whammle no food, nothing to eat or drink.

whun *see* **whan, whin**¹, **whin**²

whunner *see* **whinner**

whup *see* **whip**

whuppity-stoorie *see* **whippitie-stoorie**

whurl *see* **whirl**

whurr *see* **whirr**

whush, wheesh *noun* a whish, a rushing noise; a stir, commotion.

verb make a rushing sound.

wheesher anything large of its kind, a whopper.

whush *see* **whisht**

whusky *see* **whisky**

Whussenday *see* **Whitsunday**

whustle *see* **whistle**

whut *see* **what**¹

whuther *see* **whether, whidder**

whuttle *see* **whittle**¹

why for (no) why (not)?: *"Why for no couldn't you come yesterday?"*

wi, with, we **1** with. **2** by means of, by the action of: *"eaten with the mice"*. **3** by reason of, through: *"wi being ill he couldna come"*. **4** *referring to parents* by: *"a woman with whom he had four children"*. **5** by (bus, train etc). **6** *with 'not'* because of; on account of: *"they coudna fecht wi cauld"*.

dee wi die of. **gude nicht wi** good night to. **marry wi** marry, be married to. **be used wi** be used to. **wi his tale** according to him; so he says. **will dae wi me** can be done by me: *"that buik winna read*

wi me".

wice *see* **wise**

wicht¹, **wight** [-ch-, -gh- as -ch in 'dreich'] **1** *often with contempt or pity* a wight, a human being, person. **2** a supernatural being; one with supernatural powers.

wicht², **wight** [-ch-, -gh- as -ch in 'dreich'] courageous, bold; strong; stronglymade.

wick¹, **week, weik** **1** a corner of the mouth or the eye. **2** a cleft in the face of a hill: **Wicks o Baiglie** (on the edge of the Ochil Hills).

wick² a naughty child.

wick *see* **ouk**

wicked, wickit **1** wicked. **2** bad-tempered, ill-natured, viciously angry.

wicker *of the lip or eyelid* twitch, flicker.

wid *see* **will**¹

widd *see* **wuid**¹, **wuid**²

widder *see* **weather**

widdershins *see* **withershins**

widdie, woodie, wuddie **1** withy, willow. **2** a twig or wand of willow or other tough but flexible wood; several such intertwined to form a rope: (1) used *eg* for halters and harness; (2) †made into a container for carrying things over the shoulder. **2** the gallows rope.

widdiefu a gallowsbird, scoundrel; a rogue, scamp.

cheat the widdie *verb* escape hanging. *noun* a rogue.

widdle, wuddle *verb* **1** move slowly and unsteadily, stagger, waddle. **2** make slow progress, struggle on *now S*. *noun* a struggle.

widdy *see* **widow**

wide: wide to the wa *of a door* wide open *now Shetland Orkney NE*.

wide *see* **wade**

widna *see* **will**¹

widow, weedow, widdy **1** a widow. **2** *also* **widow man** a widower.

wield, wald *now Orkney*, **weel** *NE* **1** wield. **2** †direct, control (one's body, limbs etc).

wierd *see* **weird**

wife *noun, plural also* **wifes** a woman, now only a middle-aged or older woman.
wifie, wifock, wifockie *N* a wife; a little girl. †**wife-carl** a man who occupies himself with women's affairs.

wig a kind of small oblong currant bun.

wigglety-wagglety *see* **weegle**

wight *see* **wicht**[1], **wicht**[2]

wild, wile, will, wull, wuld *adjective* 1 wild. 2 strong-tasting.
adverb extremely, very.
will cat, wullcat a wild cat. **tummle the wullcat, tummle ower one's wullcat(s), tummle ower one's wilkies** tumble head over heels, somersault. **wild fire** 1 summer lightning, lightning without thunder. 2 *mining* fire-damp. 3 name of various wild flowers. **wild parrot** an inferior kind of soft coal. **wild rhubarb** butterbur.

wile 1 deceive by a wile. 2 get or bring by a wile (a person or animal to or from a place, or a thing from a person).
wylie clever, wise *now Shetland NE.*

wile *see* **wale, wild**

wilk *see* **wulk**

wilkies *see* **wild**

will[1], **wull** will. **wiltu, wilter** will you.
winna, wunna will not. **wad, wud, wid** would. **wadna, wudna, widna** would not.
twad it would *now NE Perth.* **wullint** willing.
it will be .. I think or expect it is .., it is approximately ..: *"Ye will be the same lad that was here yestreen?"; "It will be about forty miles from here".*

will[2], **wull** will, wish, intent.
†**willed,** †**willy** wilful, headstrong.
at one's ain will of one's own free will, as one wishes. **at all will** as much as one could wish for. **get one's will(s) o, take one's will(s) o** get one's way with, do what one likes with, have at one's disposal or mercy. **hae nae will o** take no pleasure in, have no liking for. **I hinna will that** I hope that .. not *NE: "I hinna wull that he maks a fule o*

himsel wi her". **what's your will** 1 said by (1) a shopkeeper to a customer; (2) †a servant in answering a summons. 2 pardon? *(when asking someone to repeat something).* **wi one's will** with one's agreement.

will[3], **wull** 1 going or gone astray, wandering *now Orkney NE.* 2 bewildered, at a loss. 3 *of a place* out of the way, desolate.
will-like having a dazed look *NE.* **wilsome, wulsome** *of a path etc* leading through wild country, confusing; *of a place* desolate, wild, dreary.
go will lose one's way *now Orkney NE.*

will *see* **wild**

willie willow.

Willie, Wullie: Willie Cossar, Wull o Cossar a long thick pin used especially for fastening shawls etc. **willie goo** *NE* 1 a herring gull. 2 a lost- or stupid-looking person. **willie wagtail** a pied wagtail. **Willie Wassle** a children's game *(similar to English* Tom Tiddler's Ground). **Willie Winkie** a nursery character supposed to send children to sleep, the sandman.

willie-waught [-gh- as -ch in 'loch'] a hearty swig, usually of ale etc.

willsome wilful.

willyart 1 *of animals* wild; *of people* awkward, shy; backward, dull. 2 bewildered; undisciplined. 3 wilful, obstinate; *of an animal* unmanageable.

willyway *see* **walawa**

wilsome *see* **will**[3]

wilter, wiltu *see* **will**[1]

wimble *see* **wummle**

wime *see* **wame**

wimple, wumple *noun* 1 a wimple, a (nun's) headdress. 2 *of a road or stream* a twist, turn, winding. 3 a tangle; a complication; a piece of trickery.
verb 1 enfold, entangle *NE.* 2 wriggle, writhe; whirl; curl. 3 *of a river etc* twist, turn, ripple. 4 †complicate; bewilder; tell a story in an involved deceitful way.

win[1], **won, wun** *verb, past tense also* **wan,** *past participle also* **wun 1** win. **2** beat, defeat, overpower *N*. **3** earn, gain by labour. **4** gather in (crops etc), harvest; *mining* extract (coal etc) by mining or quarrying; sink a pit or shaft to (a coal seam). **5** give, drive home (a blow etc) *S*. **6** make one's way; reach (with difficulty); be allowed to go. **7 win to do** *etc* succeed in doing etc, manage to do *now Shetland Orkney NE*.

winnie *marbles* a game in which the winner keeps his gains.

win abune overcome, recover from (an illness etc) *Shetland NE*. **win aff** get away, escape; 'get off'. **win afore** get ahead of. **win asleep** get to sleep. **win at** reach, get at or to. **win awa 1** leave; escape, be allowed or find it possible to go *Shetland Orkney N*. **2** die, especially after great suffering. **win by(e)** get past; avoid. **win farrer ben** find more favour with *Shetland Orkney Angus*. **win frae** be allowed to leave, escape from *now Shetland Orkney*. **win free** become free, escape, be released. **win in** get in. **win in about** get near or close to. **win in ahin** get the better of *NE*. **win in wi** find favour with. **win on** get on (horseback), mount. **win on for** be elected or appointed as *NE*. **win out** get out, escape. **win ower 1** (be allowed to). **2** recover from, overcome. **win redd o** escape from, get rid of. **win tae 1** arrive at. **2** come near or within reach. **3** †take a seat at table, begin eating. **4 win tae wi** overtake, make up on; be even with *NE*. **win to (the) fit** get to one's feet *Shetland Orkney*. **win tae the road** get a start. **win up 1** rise to one's feet, stand up. **2 win up tae** get as far as, catch up on, overtake *now NE*.

win[2], **wun** *verb, past tense* **wan,** *past participle* **won, win 1** *of hay, peats etc* dry and make or become ready for storage. **2** dry out, season (wood, cheese etc).

†**win**[3] dwell, live.

win *see* **wind**[1]

wincey a type of cloth with a woollen weft and a linen or cotton warp.

winch *see* **wench**

wind[1], **win** *NE*, **wund, wun** *now WCentral*, **ween** *NE noun* **1** wind. **2** breath, the air breathed. **3** †breath as used for speaking; talk, speech, what one has to say. **4** a boast, brag; a boaster *now Shetland*. *verb* **1** winnow *now Orkney*. **2** exaggerate, boast *NE*.

windy proud, conceited; boastful. **windy wallets** a boastful person *now S*. **wind-blawn** *of a horse* broken-winded. **win-casten** blown down by the wind. **oon-egg** a wind-egg, an egg laid without a shell *now Perth*. **wind-raw** a row or line into which mown hay or small piles of cut peats are set to dry. **wind-skew** a smoke-deflector in a chimney, a chimney cowl *now Orkney*.

brak the wind *of a medicine* relieve flatulence *Shetland Caithness NE*. **save one's wind to cool one's kail** keep quiet. **wind and watertight** *usually a house, especially in leases* secure against wind and rain or flood.

wind[2], **wund, wun** *NE verb, past tense also* **wan** *now NE* **1** wind, turn. **2** draw (coal) to the pithead by means of a winding-engine.

windle *weaving* a device for winding yarn or thread on to bobbins.

wind the (blue) clue wind a ball of worsted in a kiln at **Halloween** (*see* **hallow**[2]) in order to find out the name of one's future husband or wife.

wind *see* **wynd**[2], **wynt**

winda, windae *see* **window**

winder *see* **wunner**

windie *see* **window**

windle, winle, wunnle make up (straw or hay) into bundles.

windlin(g) a bundle of straw, usually as much as a man can carry in the crook of his arm *now Shetland Orkney N*.

windlestrae 1 a tall, thin, withered stalk of grass. **2** name given to various kinds of natural grass with long thin stalks.

3 a very small piece, a jot. **4** *contemptuous* a weapon, dagger. **5** *contemptuous* a thin or lanky person; a person who is weak in health or character.·

windle *see* **wind**[2]

windock *see* **winnock**

window, windie, winda, windae, wundae a window.

window-bole an opening in the outer wall of a house, the lower half often being unglazed, with wooden shutters. **window-brod, window-board** a window-shutter. **wunda-swalla** a house-martin.

window *see* **winnow**

wine cheap fortified red wine or sherry *mainly Glasgow*.

wine shop a public house which serves cheap wine *Glasgow*. **wine slide** a coaster for a wine bottle or decanter which can be slid along a table.

wing, weeng 1 a wing. **2** a detachable board which can be added to the side of a cart to increase its capacity.

wingle *now mainly Shetland verb* **1** walk unsteadily, stagger. **2** twist, wriggle; *of a stream etc* meander. **3** hang loosely, dangle; flap, wag.
noun a winding object, something which bends or twists.

wink: winkers the eyelids, eyelashes. **winkie 1** a lamp, light, especially an unsteady or flickering one. **2** a lighted buoy marking the end of a line of herring nets.

winle *see* **windle**

winna *see* **will**[1]

winner *see* **wunner**

winnerstand *see* **unerstan(d)**

winnie *see* **win**[1]

winnock, windock a window.

winnow, window *now Shetland Orkney* winnow.

winnowster a machine for winnowing corn; the fanning apparatus on a threshing machine *now NE*.

wint *see* **want, went, wont**

winter[1] the last load of grain to be brought to the stackyard in harvest *now NE*.

winterer a farm animal kept for fattening over winter. **winterin(g) 1** a winter pasture, winter keep for animals. **2** an animal which is kept over the winter *now N*. **weel-** *or* **ill-wintert** *of an animal* well- or ill-fed.

winter-dykes, winter green *WCentral* a clothes-horse. **winter town** the arable part of a farm as opposed to the summer pasture.

get winter, mak winter *etc* reach the end of the harvest. **he never died o winter yet** he survived, pulled through all difficulties.

winter[2] a rack which hangs on the bars of a fire-grate to support a kettle or pot; a trivet *now Perth*.

wintle, wuntle 1 †stagger, rock from side to side, roll about. **2 wintle ower** tumble, upset, go headlong.

wipe strike, beat, attack.

wir *see* **our**

wip(p) *see* **wup**

wird *see* **word**

wire, weir, weer *now NE*, **ware** *now Shetland* **1** wire. **2** a knitting needle.

wirk *see* **wark**

wirl 1 a small, stunted or deformed person, animal or plant *now Fife*. **2** *of a mischievous child* a young scamp.

wirm *see* **worm**

wirr, wurr growl, snarl *mainly NE*.

wirricow *see* **worricow**

wirt *brewing* wort.

wirry *see* **worry**

wirsit *see* **worset**

wirsum *see* **wursom**

wirt, wirth *see* **worth**[1]

wis *see* **be, us**

wise, wyss, weise, wice *adjective* **1** wise. **2** clever, knowing, well-informed. **3** sane, rational. **4** skilled in magic or witchcraft. *mainly* **wise wife, wise woman** a witch *now Orkney*.
verb **1** guide, direct, show (a person) to (a place etc). **2** *of a shepherd or his dog*

direct, lead (sheep). **3** coax, lead round by advice. **4** aim, shoot (a missile). **5** (cause to) move gradually in a certain direction. **6** make one's way, go; *of an object* work itself, slide in a certain direction.

wiselike 1 sensible, reasonable, prudent. **2** respectable, proper, decent. **3** of good appearance, handsome, pretty.

wise-lookin handsome, good-looking.

wise-spoken wise, sensible in speech.

no wise (eneuch) off one's head, insane.

wisgan [**wiz**gan] *contemptuous* a stunted, useless creature *NE*.

wish *see* **wash, wiss**[1]

wishen *see* **wash**

wisht *see* **whisht**

wishy-washy, weeshie-washie *adjective* wishy-washy.

noun **1** thin watery drink, *eg* weak tea. **2 wishy-washies** humming and hawing, excuses.

wisk *see* **whisk**

wisp, wusp *noun* **1** a wisp, a handful (of hay etc). **2** a bundle containing a definite quantity of fish originally tied up with a wisp of straw etc *NE*.

verb put warmed straw into (boots etc) as an insole in cold weather.

wiss[1]**, wish, wuss, wush, weesh 1** wish. **2** want, wish for: *"Do you wish any more?"*

wiss[2] show, direct *now Shetland*.

wissel, whissle 1 exchange, barter *now Caithness*. **2** †change (money); spend (money).

†**get the wissel of one's groat** be paid in one's own coin, get one's just deserts.

wit, wut *noun* **1** wit. **2** sanity, reason, one's senses. **3** intelligence, wisdom, common sense. **4** knowledge, information.

verb **1** wit. **2** †know as a fact. **3** become aware, realize, be conscious.

get wit learn, find out, become aware (of). **let wit** let (a person) know something, inform of. †**out o one's wit** out of one's senses.

witch, wutch 1 a witch. **2** *used of various animals, insects and objects associated with witches*, *eg* a moth (*now NE*), a tortoise-shell butterfly (*S*), a pole flounder, a dab; a red clay marble.

witches' paps *WCentral*, **witch(es')-thimbles** a foxglove.

wite *see* **wat, wyte**

with *see* **wi**

wither *see* **weather**

withershins, widdershins, witherlins *NE*, *often* **withershins about** in a direction opposite to the usual, the wrong way round; anti-clockwise, in a direction usually suggesting bad luck or disaster.

within: within itself *of a house* complete in itself, **self-contained** (*see* **sel**[1]).

witter[1] inform, guide, direct.

witter[2] **1** the barb of a fish-hook etc. **2** †**witters** the teeth.

†**be in someone's witters** start a quarrel with, fly at.

witter[3]**, wutter** *noun* a restless, impatient person.

verb **1** fret; grumble; keep muttering on about nothing. **2** struggle, earn one's living with difficulty.

wittin 1 the fact of knowing or being aware of something, knowledge. **2 wittins** information, intelligence, news.

wivven *see* **weave**

wiz *see* **us**

wiznan *see* **be**

wizzen, weason, wazzin *now Shetland Orkney Caithness* **1** the gullet. **2** the windpipe; the breath, life itself. **3** the throat as the source of the voice.

wizzie *see* **wase**

wizzy *child's word* **do a wizzy** urinate *Edinburgh*.

wob, wobby *see* **wab**

wobster *see* **wabster**

wochle *see* **wauchle**

wode *see* **wuid**[2]

woft *see* **waft**

woman, wumman, oman *NE*, **umman** *NE* *noun, plural* **weemen** a woman.

woman-body a woman. **woman-grown,**

woman-muckle grown to womanhood, adult.

womill see **wummle**

won *literary* live, stay habitually.

won see **win**¹, **win**²

wonder, wonner see **wunner**

wont, wunt, wint be in the habit of, be used to.

wood see **wuid**¹, **wuid**²

woodie see **widdie**

wook see **ouk**

wool see **oo**¹

woosh see **wash**

wop see **wap**²

word, wird 1 a word. **2** something said, a remark. **3** reputation, character. **4 words** prayers. **5** the power of speech; the sound of one's voice.

put up a word say a prayer.

wordle see **warld**

wordy see **worth**¹

work see **wark**

worl see **warld**

world see **warld**

worm, wirm 1 a worm. **2** *also* **worm i(n) the cheek** toothache.

†**worm web** a spider's web, a cobweb.

worn see **weir**²

worp see **warp**

worricow, wirricow 1 a hobgoblin, demon; a frightening- or repulsive-looking person. **2** †the Devil; an imp.

worry, wirry 1 worry. **2** strangle. **3** choke, suffocate. **4** gobble up.

eat the cow and worry on the tail fail because of one small thing; be fussy about small details.

worset, wirsit worsted.

worse see **warse**

worship family prayers.

worth¹, **wirth, wirt** *Shetland Orkney* **1** worth. **2** of use or service (for some purpose).

worthy, wordy worthy.

worth²: **gae (aa) worth** go to pot, become spoilt or useless, go to ruin.

woun, oun, oon [rhymes with 'moon'] wound.

woup see **wup**

wow [rhymes with 'cow'] a howl, cry, bark.

wowf [-ow- as in 'cow'] (slightly) mad; violently agitated or excited.

wowff [-ow- as in 'cow'] *noun* a low-pitched bark.

verb give a low bark.

adverb with a dull thudding noise.

wrack, wreck, wreak, vrack *NE*, **rack 1** wreck. **2** fresh- or salt-water weed, algae. **3** seaweed and flotsam washed up by the sea. **4** field weeds, vegetable rubbish; (the roots of) couch grass etc.

wrait see **write**

wran 1 *also* **wrannie** a wren. **2** term of endearment.

wranch, runch wrench.

wrang, wrong, vrang *adjective* **1** wrong. **2** *of a person, limb etc* crooked, deformed, out of joint. **3** (slightly) mad.

noun a wrong.

verb **1** wrong. **2** damage, hurt; spoil.

wrangous 1 wrongous. **2** *law* **wrongous** illegal, wrongful. **3** unjust; ill-gotten.

not come wrang (to) not come amiss (to), not be unwelcome (for). **gae wrang** *of food* go off. **rise aff one's wrang side** get up in a bad temper. **not say a wrang word** not use harsh, unjust or improper language. **wrang in the heid** = **wrang** *adjective* 3.

wrapper 1 a loose dressing-gown or bed-jacket. **2** a woman's household overall, a smock.

wrastle see **warsle**

wrat a wart.

wrat see **write**

wratch, vratch a wretch.

wreak see **wrack**

wreat see **write**

wreath, vraith *NE noun* **1** a wreath. **2** a bank or drift of snow.

verb **1** wreathe. **2** *of snow* accumulate into drifts; cover or bury *now SW*.

wreck see **wrack**

wreckling see **rickling**

wrest, wrist 1 wrest. **2** sprain or wrench.

wrest see **reest**[3]

wrestle see **warsle**

wreth wrath now Shetland.

wricht, wright, vricht NE [-ch, -gh-, as -ch in 'dreich'] noun **1** a wright, a craftsman. **2** a carpenter or joiner.
verb work as a carpenter or joiner NE.

wrist see **wrest**

writ 1 a writ. **2** writing, handwriting; a piece of writing. **3** a formal or legal document or writing, a deed (used more generally than in English where it is now usually restricted to written orders of a court).

write, wreat, vreet NE verb, past tense also **wrait, wrat, vrat** NE, **writ.** past participle also **vrutten** NE write.
noun **1** writing, as opposed to speech. **2** a written record of any transaction, especially of a legal or formal one. **3** handwriting, especially in ink; the art or style of writing.
writer a lawyer. **writer to the Signet (W.S.)** a member of a society of solicitors in Edinburgh (which originally had the exclusive privilege of preparing certain legal documents, eg **signet writs** (see **signet** and **writ**)).

wrocht see **wark**

wrong see **wrang**

wrunkle wrinkle.

W.S. see **write**

wub see **wab**

wud see **will**[1]

wud(d) see **wuid**[1], **wuid**[2]

wuddie see **widdie**

wuddle see **widdle**

wudna see **will**[1]

wuffle see **waffle**

wuid[1], **wood, widd, wud(d)** wood.
wuiden breeks, wuiden overcoat WCentral a coffin.
wood hyacinth an English bluebell, wild hyacinth.

wuid[2], **wood, wode, widd, wud(d) 1** mad. **2** fierce, violent, wild. **3** furiously angry. **4 wuid for** etc eager, desperately keen to.
in a wuiden dream with a sudden frantic motion or effort, like fury.
wuiddrim a dazed state, great mental confusion as in waking from a dream; a brainstorm.

wuish, wuishen see **wash**

wuive see **weave**

wuld see **wild**

wulk, wilk, wylk 1 a whelk. **2** the periwinkle mollusc and shell. **3** humorous the nose.
as fou as a wulk very drunk.

wull see **wild, will**[1], **will**[2], **will**[3]

wullcat see **wild**

Wullie see **Willie**

wullint see **will**[1]

Wull o Cossar see **Willie**

wull-tams see **waltams**

wulsome see **will**[3]

wumble see **wummle**

wumman see **woman**

wummle, wimble, womill, †wumble an auger, gimlet.
heat a wummle a game with a young child held on the knee.

wummle see **wammle**

wumple see **wimple**

wun see **win**[1], **win**[2], **wind**[1], **wind**[2]

wund see **wind**[1], **wind**[2]

wundae, wunda-swallow see **window**

wunna see **will**[1]

wunner, wonder, winder, wonner, winner NE **1** wonder. **2** contemptuous term for a person.
I widna wunner but what I shouldn't be surprised if.

wunnle see **windle**

wunt see **want, wont**

wuntle see **wintle**

wup, woup [woop], **wip(p)** verb **1** bind together by wrapping string, tape etc round and round a joint, splice, whip. **2** wind (a cord etc) round an object tightly. **3** tie, join, lash. **4** coil, become entangled or involved.
noun **1** a splice, tying or binding with coils of string etc. **2** a ring; an ear-ring.

wuppen *see* **open**

wur *see* **our**

wurble, †**warble** wriggle, crawl.

wure *see* **wear**

wurf a puny person, especially a child.

wurk *see* **war**

wurn *see* **wear**

wurr *see* **wirr**

wursom, **wirsum** pus, the discharge from a sore.

wus *see* **be**

wush *see* **wiss**

wusp *see* **wisp**

wuss juice (from vegetable substances) *now Shetland*.

wuss *see* **wiss**[1]

wut *see* **wit**

wutch *see* **witch**

wutten *see* **weet**

wutter *see* **witter**[3]

wuven *see* **weave**

wye *see* **wey**[1], **wey**[2]

wyke *see* **waik**

wyle, **wylie** an instrument for making straw ropes.

wylie *see* **wile**

wyliecoat, †**wallicoat** a warm garment worn between underclothes and outer garments, *eg* a (flannel) undercoat worn by men.

wylk *see* **wulk**

wynd[1], **wyne** [rhymes with 'line(d)'] a narrow (winding) street.

wynd[2], **wind** [rhymes with 'bind'] a call to a yoked animal to turn to the left *now SW*.

    wyndin, **wyndins** 1 a long, awkwardly-shaped or steep piece of land. 2 a division of a field for ploughing.

wynt [rhymes with 'pint'], †**wind**: (allow) to go bad or sour.

wyss *see* **wise**

wystcoat *see* **weskit**

wyte, **wite** *verb* blame, accuse.

    noun 1 blame, reproach, responsibility for some error or mischief. 2 **one's wyte** one's fault.

wyte *see* **wait**

wyve *see* **weave**

Y

ya *see* yea

yaavins *see* yawins

yabb talk without stopping *now Shetland Orkney N.*

yabble, yabber *now ECentral verb* 1 talk excitedly, chatter, gossip. 2 scold, complain. 3 *of animals, birds* chatter, bark etc excitedly *now Orkney NE.*
noun 1 a loud noise of voices. 2 a chatterbox *now NE.*

yable *see* able

yachis [-ch- as in 'dreich'] a thump, thud, grunt *NE.*

yack, ya(c)kie an Eskimo *now Shetland Orkney N.*

yad, yade *see* yaud[1]

yae *see* ae

yaes *see* ye

yaff, yauff *verb* 1 bark, yelp. 2 chatter on, talk cheekily. 3 scold, criticize.
noun a chatterbox, a cheeky person; a person of no importance.

yafu *see* awfu

yagiment [-g- as in 'get'] (a state of) excitement, agitation *NE.*

yaik *see* yawk

yain a call to a horse in harness to turn left.

yair, yare a fish-trap across a river or bay, often with a net *now SW.*

yaird[1], yard, †yeard 1 a yard. 2 a garden, now especially a cottage- or kitchen-garden. 3 *also* yird a churchyard. 4 †yards a school playground *Edinburgh.*
yaird dyke a garden wall.

yaird[2], yeard, yird *S* a yard, the measure; see p 360.

yairn yarn.
yarlins a yarn-reel for winding yarn into skeins *NE.*

yaise *see* use

yak *mainly gipsy* the eye *S.*

yak *see* yawk

yakie *see* yack

yald *see* yaul(d)

yaldie *see* yoldrin

yall, †yawl yell, howl *now Shetland N.*

yall *see* yea

yalla, yallochie, yallow *see* yella

yammer, yaumer, †yamour *verb* 1 howl, whine, whimper, complain. 2 make a loud noise, talk on and on (senselessly), keep insisting. 3 *of a bird or animal* utter repeated cries, chatter.
noun 1 wailing, whining, a cry, whimper *now Shetland.* 2 a great outcry, clamour, incessant talk.

yamp *see* yaup

†yamph bark, yap, yelp.

yank *verb* 1 pull sharply, jerk, twitch. 2 drive or force on energetically. 3 move quickly and vigorously.
noun 1 a sudden jerk or pull. 2 †a sudden severe blow, especially with the hand.
yanker a smart agile person.

yap[1], yaup, yawp *verb* 1 yap, bark. 2 cry shrilly, scream; whimper; chirp *now Shetland Caithness.* 3 chatter (on), nag, complain. 4 *of English speakers or Scots who copy them* speak in an affected way.
noun 1 a yap, a bark. 2 a yelping dog. 3 the call of a bird in distress *SW.* 4 talking without stopping, usually implying nagging. 5 a chatterbox; a windbag.

yap[2] child's word for an apple *Edinburgh.*

yap *see* yaup

yape *see* yaup

yard *see* yaird[1]

yare 1 ready, prepared. 2 eager, agile.

yare *see* yair

yark *see* yerk

yarlin *see* yoldrin

yarlins *see* yairn

yarp grumble *now Shetland*.

yarr corn-spurrey.

yat *Shetland,* †**yet** *verb, now Shetland* **1** †pour. **2** pour out. **3** gush. **4** found, cast (metal).

yetlin(g) 1 an article made of cast-iron, *eg* a (three-legged) pot or kettle. **2** cast-iron *now Shetland*.

yate *see* **yett**

yatter *verb* **1** nag, scold. **2** chatter, ramble on. **3** *of a person* gabble; *of an animal* yelp. **4** *of teeth* rattle, chatter, *eg* from fear.
noun **1** (continual) scolding, grumbling *now Orkney Angus*. **2** continuous chatter, talking on and on. **3** the confused noise of loud talk, unintelligible speech. **4** a person who talks on and on; a gossip.

yatterin, yattery fretful, complaining, scolding *now Shetland*.

yaucht *see* **aucht**³

yaud, yad, †**yade 1** an old mare or horse, especially a worn-out horse *now Shetland*. **2** contemptuous term for a woman.

yauff *see* **yaff**

yaul(d), yald active, alert, vigorous, healthy.

yaumer *see* **yammer**

yaup, yap, †**yape** *adjective* **1** †clever; shrewd; active. **2** †eager, ready. **3** *also* **yamp** *NE,* **yaupish** having a keen appetite, hungry.
verb be very hungry.
noun a fool, oaf, yokel.

yaup *see* **yap**¹

yaval *see* **awald**¹, **awald**²

yaw *see* **awe**²

yawins, ya(a)vins *N,* **yewns** awns, the beard or bristle of barley or oats.

yawk, ya(i)k ache.

yawl *see* **yall**

yawp *see* **yap**¹

ye, you, yow *now S pronoun, plural also* **yeez, yez, yiz, yaes, youz(e), yooz** you, ye; in dialect where **thou** survives, **ye** and **you** are used *eg* by an inferior to a superior, by a younger to an older person; *see* **thou**.

yea, ya *now Shetland Orkney adverb* **1** yes. **2** *used before a repeated verb* again, over and over *NE:* "he tried and yea tried".

yeltie, †**yall** you would, would you; be careful; that's enough, now.

†**yean** *of a ewe* give birth to (a lamb).

year, 'ear a year.
year aul(d) *noun* a yearling. *adjective* year-old.
monie a year and day for a very long time *NE*. **up in years** elderly.

yeard *see* **yaird**¹, **yaird**²

yearn *see* **yirn**¹, **yirn**²

†**yed** *in poetry* strife; struggle.

yeel *see* **Yule**

yeese *see* **use**

yeeze *see* **ye**

yeld, yield, yell, eild, eel 1 *of animals* barren, not having young because of age or accident. **2** *of cows etc* not giving milk because of age or being in calf. **3** *of things* of no use, unproductive, unprofitable.

yella, yellow, yallow, yalla yellow.
yallochie yellowish.
yella fin a young sea-trout. **yella fish, yella haddie, yella haddock** smoked (now also dyed) fish, especially haddock; *compare* **Finnan haddock**. **yella gum** *see* **gum**³. **yella lintie** the yellowhammer; *see also* **yite**¹.

†**yelloch** scream, shriek, yell.

†**yellyhooing** shouting and screaming, yelling.

yeltie *see* **yea**

yer *see* **yere, yerk**

yerb, yirb a herb.

yerd *see* **yird**

yere, yer, yir your.

yerk, yark, yirk *verb* **1** bind tightly, tie firmly together (*eg* shoeleather in shoemaking). **2** beat, whip, strike; break by striking; hammer; crack down (on), make a sharp sound by striking. **3** nag, find fault. **4** throb, ache, tingle. **5**

snatch, tug, wrench, pull; throw, toss, pitch; jerk, slam. **6** drive hard, put pressure on, stir to activity. **7** go at (a task), set to, exert oneself, press on *now Shetland NE.* **8** rattle off (a speech), strike up (a tune), do in a smart or lively way: *"he yerkit oot the tune".*

noun **1** a blow, a hard knock, a slap; the sound of a blow or collision. **2** a jerk, tug, twitch. **3** a throb of pain; an ache *NE.*

yerker anything very large of its kind. **come (a) yerk against** come against, collide with. **hae a yerk at** have a go at *Shetland NE.*

yerl *see* **earl**

yerm *see* **yirm**

yerp *see* **yirp**

yesk, esk *N,* **isk** *Caithness,* **yisk** *verb* hiccup, belch; vomit.

noun a hiccup, belch.

yestreen, the streen *now Orkney N,* **estreen** *now NE adverb* yesterday evening; last night; *latterly* yesterday.

noun yesterday evening.

yet, yit 1 yet. **2** up to now, at the present time, still: *"are ye at the school yet?"* **3** †a cheer or rallying cry hurrah for ..!, .. for ever! *eg: "Haddington yet!"*

yet *see* **yat**

†**yether** *noun* a severe blow; the mark left by such a blow or by tight binding, a weal, bruise.

verb **1** tie very firmly. **2** beat or lash severely, bruise with a cane *S.*

yetlin(g) *see* **yat**

yett, yate *noun* **1** a gate. **2** *on castles etc* a kind of door made of interlacing iron bars. **3** a natural pass between hills.

as daft as a yett in a windy day scatterbrained, crazy.

yeuk, yuke, youk, yook, yuck, yock *verb* **1** itch, feel ticklish or itchy. **2** be keen or eager; have a strong urge (to do something). **3** scratch.

noun itching, the itch; an itchiness.

yeukie 1 itching, itchy. **2** excitedly eager, impatiently waiting to do something. **3** shabby, rough, filthy. **4** *of work* rough and careless, badly finished.

gar someone claw where it's no yeukie *often in threats* (make someone) smart or regret what he has done. **his neck is yeukin** he is heading for the gallows.

yewns *see* **yawins**

yez *see* **ye**

yibble *see* **able**

yeld *see* **eild**

yield *see* **yeld**

yiff-yaff a small, unimportant, chattery person.

yill *see* **ale**

yim[1] a very small piece *mainly SW, S.*

yim[2] a thin film or coating on a surface *NE.*

yin *see* **ane**[1]

yince *see* **aince**

ying *see* **young**

yip *especially of a child* a cheeky imp.

yir *see* **yere**

yirb *see* **yerb**

yird, yirth, †**yerd** *noun* **1** earth. **2** *ploughing* the depth of a furrow; the angle at which the plough-sock is set to achieve this. **3** a heap of large boulders forming a den or small cave *SW.*

verb **1** bury. **2** press or cause to sink into the ground. **3** †drive (a hunted animal) to earth.

†**yirden** earthen; of the world. **yirdie tam** a mound of earth and weeds, a compost heap *NE.* **yirdit 1** buried. **2** bogged down *Shetland NE.*

yird drift drifting snow *now NE.* **yird fast** firmly fixed in the ground.

yird the cogie *children's game* a rhythmic chant and quick stamping (to warm the feet) *NE.*

yird *see* **yaird**[1], **yaird**[2]

yirk *see* **yerk**

yirlin *see* **yoldrin**

yirm, yerm *of an animal* whine, wail; *of a person* complain, whine, harp on *now S.*

yirn[1]**, yearn, earn** *verb* (cause to) solidify, set or curdle; *of milk* form curds with

rennet and heat *now Shetland Orkney N*.
yirned milk curds; junket. **yirnin 1**
setting, curdling. **2** rennet. **3** the stomach of an unweaned calf etc used in
making rennet. **4** the human stomach.

yirn², **yearn** *verb, of a dog* whine; whimper; *of a person* wail, whine, complain
now SW.

noun a complaint, whine *now SW*.

yirn *see* **earn**

yirp, yerp 1 *of a very young bird* chirp. **2**
of people harp on something, make a
fuss or complaint.

yirr snarl, growl *now Shetland*.

yirth *see* **yird**

yisk *see* **yesk**

yis(s) *see* **use**

yit *see* **ait, yet**

yite¹, yowt, yoit 1 *often* **yella yite** a yellowhammer. **2** a small person; contemptuous term for a person.

yite² play truant.

yitter chatter.

yivvery *see* **aiverie**

yiz *see* **ye**

yo *contradicting another's 'no'* but yes.

yoal *see* **yole**

yoam *see* **oam**

yochel [-ch- as in 'loch'] a yokel.

yock *see* **yeuk, yoke**

yod *as an oath* God *NE*.

yoit *see* **yite¹**

yoke, yock *noun* **1** a yoke, especially the
harness of a plough, cart etc; the main
swingle-tree of a plough. **2** a horse and
cart, horse and carriage attached in full
harness. **3** = **yokin 3, 4.**

verb **1** yoke. **2** marry, join in marriage.
3 start on some activity, set to, go
about something (vigorously); set (a
person) to do something, start (a person) to work. **4** deal with, have to do
with (a person or persons). **5** **yoke on,
yoke to** set on (a person), attack.

yokin 1 yoking (horses etc). **2** the starting of a spell of work, *often* **yokin time.**
3 the period during which a team of
horses or oxen is in harness at one

stretch, usually half a day's work; a
spell of work, a stint, shift. **4** a spell,
bout of some leisure activity, a stretch.
5 a fight, contest, scuffle; a rough handling, a severe telling off. **ill-yokit** ill-
matched in marriage.

yoldrin, yorlin, yirlin, yarlin, yaldie *NE,
also* **yella yoldrin** a yellowhammer.

yole, yoal, yoll, yowl a kind of small,
undecked, two-masted fishing boat
now Shetland Orkney N.

yolk, yowk 1 a yolk. **2** †a hard lump
within a softer rock etc. **3** a kind of
soft, good-burning coal.

yoll *see* **yole**

yoller speak loudly, excitedly, angrily or
confusedly, shout.

yon, yun *Shetland adjective, pronoun* that
(one), those over there, usually indicating a person or thing further away
than **that** *etc*.

adverb **1** over there, **yonder** *now Shetland N*. **2** to that place over there.

yon kind used to describe persons or
things in a poor state or persons who
are uncomfortably embarrassed *Shetland N: "Oh, dinna speak about that.
Ye mak me yon kind."* **yon time:** *it will
be yon time before they come* they won't
come for a long time.

yonder, yonner *adverb* in that place, over
there, indicating a person or thing at
some distance.

adjective that (over there), distant, *NE*.
yonder-abouts in that district, there or
thereabouts. **yonder awa, yondru** *Shetland Orkney* over there, in that place.

far frae a' yonder, nae (near) a' yonder
half-witted, not all there *NE*.

yont *adverb* **1** farther away or along,
beyond, aside. **2** yonder, over there, on
or to the other side.

preposition **1** beyond, on or to the other
side of. **2** along, further along, onwards
through or over.

adjective †far, distant.

yont by over **yonder**, across.

yook *see* **yeuk**

yooz *see* ye

yorlin *see* yoldrin

you *see* ye

youdith *see* youth

youf *see* yowf

youk *see* yeuk

young, †ying young; *in titles* prefixed to the name of a Highland chieftain or his estate to indicate his eldest son and heir.

younger younger; used after a person's name to distinguish him from an older person of the same name, often the title for an heir-apparent: *"Charles Hazlewood, younger of Hazlewood"; "Malcolm MacGregor of MacGregor, younger"*.

young folk a newly-married couple, irrespective of age. young laird the heir-apparent of a landowner below peerage rank. young man 1 the best man at a wedding *Orkney NE.* 2 an unmarried man *now Orkney.*

younker 1 a youngster, a young lad or girl, a youth. 2 a young bird, a nestling.

yout *see* yowt

youth: youthheid, youdith youth. youthie young, youthful, especially looking younger than one is.

youz(e) *see* ye

yow *see* ye

yowden 1 *past participle of 'yield'.* 2 *adjective* soft, limp; tired out.

yowdendrift [-ow- as in 'cow'] snow driven by the wind.

†yowder, yowther [-ow- as in 'cow'], ewder, euther 1 a very unpleasant smell of fumes from burning. 2 steam, smoke, vapour.

yowe [rhymes with 'cow'], ewe 1 a ewe. 2 *often* yowie a fir cone *NE.*

yowe hog a young female sheep.

yowe(s) trummle a cold spell in early summer, about the time of sheep-shearing.

yower *see* ure[1]

yowf, youf bark.

yowff [-ow- as in 'cow'] *noun* a sharp blow, a swipe, thump.

verb knock, strike, swipe.

yowk *see* yolk

yowl *see* yole

yowt, yout shout, roar, yell, cry.

yowt *see* yite[1]

yowther *see* yowder

yuck a stone, pebble.

yuck *see* yeuk

yuffie a lavatory, especially one on a tenement stair.

yuise *see* use

yuke *see* yeuk

Yule, yeel, eel *N* 1 Christmas; the day itself; the festive season associated with it, often beginning before Christmas day and (especially Shetland) continuing until after New Year. 2 the entertainment provided at Christmas, Christmas cheer *now Shetland.*

Yule feast a Christmas dinner *now Shetland.* Yule strae the supply of straw needed on a farm over Christmas and the New Year *NE.* Yule's yaud *insulting* a person ill-prepared for Yule, *eg* one who leaves work unfinished before Christmas or the New Year, or who has nothing new to wear for the festivities *latterly N.*

Auld Yule Christmas day (Old Style): *latterly* 7 January *Shetland NE.*

yun *see* yon

yunk *marbles* a stake marble.

Z

z, ӡ: z was sometimes used for Older Scots ӡ, which represented the sound [y]. In most cases the later spelling gave rise to new pronunciations with [z], *eg* in Mackenzie. In a small number of words the [z] sound was not adopted, *eg* capercailzie [-kailie], Dalziel [day-ell]. In some words y was substituted for ӡ, *eg* tailyie.

z *see* us

SCOTTISH CURRENCY, WEIGHTS AND MEASURES

Money

SCOTS	STERLING	DECIMAL
1 penny	1/12 penny	—
2 pennies = 1 bodle	1/6 penny	—
2 bodles = 1 plack	1/3 penny	—
3 bodles = 1 bawbee	1 halfpenny	—
2 bawbees = 1 shilling	1 penny	.42 penny
13 shillings 4 pence = 1 merk	1s 1½d.	5½ pence
20 shillings = 1 pound	1s 8d	8 pence

Weights and Measures

There was much confusion and diversity in early Scottish weights and measures and a succession of enactments from the 15th century failed to improve matters till in 1661 a commission was set up by Parliament which recommended the setting up of national standards, the exemplars of which were to be kept in the custody of certain burghs, the *ell* for lineal measure to be kept by Edinburgh, the *jug* for liquid capacity by Stirling, the *firlot* for dry measure by Linlithgow, and the *troy stone* for weight by Lanark. These recommendations in the main prevailed throughout Scotland, though there was some irregularity between commodities in dry measure; a further recommendation that *tron* weight should be entirely abolished was ignored and this measure fluctuated within fairly wide limits as between 22 and 28 ounces per pound. By Act of Parliament in 1824 uniformity of weights and measures was statutorily established and gradually this was conformed to although the names of the older measures like **firlot, forpet, lippie** were transferred to fractions of the Imperial hundred-weight and are still sometimes heard.

Weights

1. According to the standard of Lanark, for troy weight:

SCOTS	AVOIRDUPOIS	METRIC
1 drop	1.093 drams	1.921 grammes
16 drops = 1 ounce	1 oz. 1.5 drams	31 grammes
16 ounces = 1 pound	1 lb. 1 oz. 8 dr.	496 grammes
16 pounds = 1 stone	17 lbs. 8 oz.	7.936 kilogrammes

2. According to the standard of Edinburgh for **tron** weight:

SCOTS	AVOIRDUPOIS	METRIC
1 drop	1.378 drams	2.4404 grammes
16 drops = 1 ounce	1 oz. 6 drams	39.04 grammes
16 ounces = 1 pound	1 lb. 6 oz. 1 dram	624.74 grammes
16 pounds = 1 stone	1 stone 8 lbs. 1 oz.	9.996 kilogrammes

Capacity

Liquid measure according to the standard of Stirling. See **joug.**

SCOTS	IMPERIAL	METRIC
1 gill	.749 gill	.053 litres
4 gills = 1 mutchkin	2.996 gills	.212 litres
2 mutchkins = 1 chopin	1 pint 1.992 gills	.848 litres
2 chopins = 1 pint	2 pints 3.984 gills	1.696 litres
8 pints = 1 gallon	3 gallons .25 gills	13.638 litres
1 pint = 104.2034 Imp. cub. ins.	1 pint = 34.659 Imp. cub. ins.	1 litre = 61.027 cub. ins.

Dry measure according to the standard of Linlithgow.

1. For wheat, peas, beans, meal, etc.

SCOTS	IMPERIAL	METRIC
1 lippie (or forpet)	.499 gallons	2.268 litres
4 lippies = 1 peck	1.996 gallons	9.072 litres
4 pecks = 1 firlot	3 pecks 1.986 gallons	36.286 litres
4 firlots = 1 boll	3 bushels 3 pecks 1.944 galls.	145.145 litres
16 bolls = 1 chalder	7 quarters 7 bushels 3 pecks 1.07 galls	2322.324 litres
1 firlot = 2214.322 cub. ins.	1 gallon = 277.274 cub. ins.	1 litre = 61.027 cub. ins.

2. For barley, oats, malt.

1 lippie (or forpet)	.728 gallons	3.037 litres
4 lippies = 1 peck	1 peck .912 gallons	13.229 litres
4 pecks = 1 firlot	1 bushel 1 peck 1.650 gallons	52.916 litres
4 firlots = 1 boll	5 bushels 3 pecks .600 gallons	211.664 gallons
16 bolls = 1 chalder	11 quarters 5 bushels 1.615 gallons	3386.624 litres
1 firlot = 3230.305 cub. ins.		

Linear and Square Measures

According to the standard **ell** of Edinburgh.

Linear

1 inch	1.0016 inches	2.54 centimetres
8.88 inches = 1 Scots link	8.8942 inches	22.55 centimetres
12 inches = 1 foot	12.0192 inches	30.5287 centimetres
3½ feet = 1 ell	37.0598 inches (1 1/37 yards)	94.1318 centimetres
6 ells = 1 fall	6.1766 yards (1.123 poles)	5.6479 metres
4 falls = 1 chain	24.7064 yards (1.123 chains)	22.5916 metres
10 chains = 1 furlong	247.064 yards (1.123 furlongs)	225.916 metres
8 furlongs = 1 mile	1976.522 yards (1.123 miles)	1.8073 kilometres

Square

1 sq. inch	1.0256 sq. inch	6.4516 sq. centimetre
1 sq. ell	1.059 sq. yards	.8853 sq. metre
36 sq. ells = 1 sq. fall	38.125 sq. yards (1 pole 7.9 sq. yards)	31.87 sq. metres
40 falls = 1 sq. rood	1525 sq. yards (1 rood 10 poles 13 sq. yards)	12.7483 acres
4 roods = 1 sq. acre	6100 sq. yards (1.26 acres)	.5099 hectare

Yarn measure

1 cut = 300 yards
1 heere = 2 cuts or 600 yards
1 heid = 2 heeres or 1200 yards
1 hank or hesp = 3 heids or 3600 yards
1 spinle = 4 hanks or 14400 yards

The above applies to linen and handspun woollen yarn in the early 19th century. Earlier the measure was considerably shorter, and varied considerably with the kind of yarn spun.